LEARN TO READ LATIN

LEARN TO READ
LATIN

PART II

Andrew Keller
Colgate University and Collegiate School
Stephanie Russell
Collegiate School

Yale University Press   New Haven & London

The authors thank Dr. Hans-Friedrich Mueller of the University of Florida and Dr. John Miller of the University of Virginia for reviewing their manuscript.

Learn to Read Latin was first published as one volume in 2004.

PUBLISHER: Mary Jane Peluso
DEVELOPMENT EDITOR: Brie Kluytenaar
PRODUCTION CONTROLLER: Aldo R. Cupo
EDITORIAL ASSISTANT: Gretchen Rings
DESIGNER: James J. Johnson
MARKETING MANAGER: Timothy Shea
Set in E & F Scala type by Integrated Publishing Solutions.
Printed in the United States of America.

The Library of Congress has catalogued the original one-volume edition of the textbook as follows:

Library of Congress Cataloging-in-Publication Data
Keller, Andrew, 1960–
    Learn to read Latin / Andrew Keller, Stephanie Russell.
        p.   cm. — (Yale language series)
    Includes bibliographical references and indexes.
    ISBN 0-300-10084-1 — ISBN 0-300-10215-1 (pbk.)
        1. Latin language—Grammar. 2. Latin language—Grammar—Problems, exercises, etc.
    3. Latin language—Readers.   I. Russell, Stephanie, 1946– .   II. Title.   III. Series.
    PA2087.5.K45   2004
    478.2′421—dc21

                                                2003053828

Two-volume edition:
Part I, hardcover ISBN-13: 978-0-300-12092-9 ISBN-10 0-300-12092-3
Part I, paperback ISBN-13: 978-0-300-12094-3 ISBN-10: 0-300-12094-X
Part II, hardcover ISBN-13: 978-0-300-12093-6 ISBN-10: 0-300-12093-1
Part II, paperback ISBN-13: 978-0-300-12095-0 ISBN-10: 0-300-12095-8

A catalogue record for this book is available from the British Library.

10 9 8 7 6 5 4 3 2 1

CONTENTS

PART I

CHAPTER I

CHAPTER II

CHAPTER III

CHAPTER IV

CHAPTER V

CHAPTER VI

CHAPTER VII

CHAPTER VIII

PART II

CHAPTER XI

CHAPTER XII

CHAPTER XIII

CHAPTER XIV

CHAPTER XV

PREFACE TO PART II

Learn to Read Latin, Part II, contains the last seven chapters (63 sections) of the single-volume textbook *Learn to Read Latin,* which is also available from Yale University Press. Part II is meant to be used with the corresponding workbook, *Learn to Read Latin: Workbook,* Part II, which contains all drills for these chapters and sections. It is the companion volume to *Learn to Read Latin,* Part I. All back matter in the single-volume edition is included here. In addition, the English to Latin Vocabulary contained only in the workbook in the single-volume edition is included here.

* * *

ABBREVIATIONS

*	indicates that a form is hypothetical
< >	enclose an element added by editors
[ ]	used to indicate that, contrary to the tradition, an author is *not* the writer of a work
<	(derived) from
>	becomes
§	section
1-intr.	first conjugation intransitive verb
1-tr.	first conjugation transitive verb
abl.	ablative
acc.	accusative
act.	active
adj.	adjective
adv.	adverb
cf.	*confer,* compare
conj.	conjunction
dat.	dative
demonstr.	demonstrative
etc.	*et cētera,* and the remaining things
f.	feminine
fem.	feminine

frag.	fragment
fut.	future
gen.	genitive
IE	Indo-European
imper.	imperative
imperf.	imperfect
indef.	indefinite
indic.	indicative
interj.	interjection
interrog.	interrogative
intr.	intransitive
loc.	locative
m.	masculine
masc.	masculine
n.	neuter
neut.	neuter
nom.	nominative
pass.	passive
perf.	perfect
PIE	Proto-Indo-European
pl.	plural
pluperf.	pluperfect
prep.	preposition
pres.	present
pron.	pronoun
rel.	relative

sc.	*scīlicet,* namely
sēd inc.	*sēdēs incerta,* uncertain location
sing.	singular
subj.	subject

subjunc.	subjunctive
subst.	substantive
tr.	transitive
voc.	vocative
→	changes to

CHAPTER IX

Vocabulary

➤ **ex(s)ilium, ex(s)iliī** *n.* exile, banishment
➤ **modus, modī** *m.* measure; limit; rhythm, meter; manner, way
  ➤ **quō modō**, in what manner, how
  oculus, oculī *m.* eye

➤ **lēx, lēgis** *f.* law
➤ **lībertās, lībertātis** *f.* freedom
➤ **pāx, pācis** *f.* peace; favor

➤ **metus, metūs** *m.* fear, dread, anxiety

  spēs, speī *f.* hope

  quī, quae, quod (rel. pron.) who, which, that (§85)
  quī, quae, quod (interrog. adj.) what . . ., which . . . (§88)
  quis, quid (interrog. pron.) who, what (§87)

➤ **hortor** (1-tr.) urge, encourage, exhort (§84)
➤ **imperō** (1-intr.) give an order, order, command (+ dat.) (§84, §90)

➤ **moneō, monēre, monuī, monitus** warn; remind; advise (§84)
➤ **pāreō, pārēre, pāruī, pāritūrus** be obedient, obey (+ dat.) (§90)
➤ **placeō, placēre, placuī, placitum** be pleasing, please (+ dat.) (§90)

➤ **patior, patī, passus sum** experience, suffer, endure; permit, allow
➤ **pellō, pellere, pepulī, pulsus** push, drive (off)

➤ **quaerō, quaerere, quaesiī** or **quaesīvī, quaesītus** search for, seek, ask (§84)

➤ **caecus, -a, -um** blind; hidden, secret, dark

  gravis, grave heavy, deep; important, serious; severe
  levis, leve light; trivial; fickle

➤ **alius, alia, aliud** other, another (§89)
➤ **alter, altera, alterum** the other (of two) (§89)
➤ **īdem, eadem, idem** same
➤ **neuter, neutra, neutrum** neither (of two) (§89)
  nūllus, -a, -um not any, no (§89)
  sōlus, -a, -um alone, only (§89)
  tōtus, -a, -um whole (§89)
  ūllus, -a, -um any (§89)
  ūnus, -a, -um one; only (§89)
➤ **uter, utra, utrum** (interrog. adj.) which (of two) (§89)

➤ **iam** (adv.) now; by now, by then, already
  nē (conj.) *introduces negative Purpose clause,* in order that . . . not; *introduces negative Indirect Command,* that . . . not (§83, §84)
  ob (prep. + acc.) on account of, because of
➤ **quam ob rem** (rel. or interrog. adv.) on account of which thing; therefore; why
➤ **quārē** (rel. or interrog. adv.) because of which thing; therefore; why
➤ **tandem** (adv.) finally, at last; *in questions and commands,* pray, I ask you, then
  ut (conj.) *introduces Purpose clause,* in order that; *introduces Indirect Command,* that (§83, §84)

Vocabulary Notes

ex(s)ilium, ex(s)iliī *n.* may refer to the act of banishment or the place to which one is exiled. The **s** placed in parentheses in the vocabulary entry indicates that the word may be spelled either with or without an **s**.

modus, modī *m.* is derived from the PIE root ***med-**, "measure, take appropriate measures." It means "measure" in the sense of a "quantity" (of land, of grain). From this basic notion of "quantity" or "amount" arise several extended meanings, including "limit" (an amount that should not be exceeded) and more abstractly "moderation" or "restraint." In musical and poetic contexts, it may mean "rhythm," "meter," or even the "tone" of a voice or a song. Another very common meaning of **modus** is "mode," "way," or "manner."

Modum agrī fīliīs dedit.	He gave a *measure* of land (field) to his sons.
Modum īrae pōnet?	Will he place a *limit* to (his) anger?
Sine *modō* sē gerit.	He conducts himself without *moderation*.
Id eō *modō* fēcī.	I did it in this *way*.

The prepositional phrases **in . . . modum** and **ad . . . modum** (in the manner, according to the manner) frequently occur with a genitive or with an adjective modifying **modum**.

Rēgis *in/ad modum* dīxit.	She spoke *in/according to the manner* of a king.
In/Ad hunc modum dīxit.	She spoke *in/according to this manner*.

The **quō** in the phrase **quō modō** is an interrogative adjective. **Quō modō** is an Ablative of Manner.

lēx, lēgis *f.* means a particular law proposed (bill) or passed (statute). It may be used of a "regulation" laid down by a variety of authorities. It may also mean "law" as the collective legal authority of a state. **Lēx** appears in the idiom **lēgem ferre**, "to pass a law."

lībertās, lībertātis *f.* is an abstract noun formed by the addition of the suffix **-tās** to the stem of the adjective **līber**.

pāx, pācis *f.* initially meant a "pact" or "agreement," usually to avert or end hostilities. It then came to mean more broadly the opposite of **bellum**. It may also have the specialized meaning of "blessing" or "favor" granted by one or more of the gods. The ablative singular, with or without the preposition **in**, may be used as an Ablative of Time When.

metus, metūs *m.* is the more general term for "fear" or "dread," while **timor** tends to refer to a more immediate fear.

hortor, hortārī, hortātus sum is a transitive verb that may introduce an Indirect Command (see §84) or take a direct object only.

Caesar suōs hortātus est nē timērent.	Caesar urged his own men that they not fear.
Caesar suōs hortātus est.	Caesar encouraged his (own) men.

imperō, imperāre, imperāvī, imperātum is an intransitive verb that may take a Dative with an Intransitive Verb (see §90). It may also introduce an Indirect Command (see §84). ANY INTRANSITIVE VERB THAT MAY TAKE A DATIVE WITH AN INTRANSITIVE VERB WILL BE INDICATED IN THE VOCABULARY LIST BY THE ADDITION OF (+ dat.) AT THE END OF THE ENTRY. THIS INFORMATION MUST BE MEMORIZED ALONG WITH THE PRINCIPAL PARTS AND ENGLISH MEANINGS GIVEN.

Caesar suīs imperāvit nē fugerent.	Caesar commanded his own men that they not flee.

moneō, monēre, monuī, monitus may introduce an Indirect Command (see §84). Compounds of **moneō** do *not* exhibit vowel weakening. WHEN A COMPOUND OF **MONEŌ** APPEARS IN READINGS, ITS PRINCIPAL PARTS ARE NOT SUPPLIED, BUT THE PREFIX AND SIMPLE VERB ARE GIVEN.

pāreō, pārēre, pāruī, pāritūrus is an intransitive verb that may be used absolutely or may take a Dative with an Intransitive Verb (see §90). The fourth principal part, **pāritūrus** (about to obey), is a future active participle.

placeō, placēre, placuī, placitum is an intransitive verb that may be used absolutely or may take a Dative with an Intransitive Verb (see §90). **Placeō** may be used *impersonally* to mean "seem good." In public contexts it may mean "be resolved" (by the senate, etc.). When **placeō** is used impersonally, it often has a Subject Infinitive (see §27).

Mihi *placet* rūs īre.	To go to the country *is pleasing* to me.
	It is pleasing to me to go to the country.
Placuit populō bellum gerere.	*It seemed good* to the people to wage war.

The basic meaning of **patior, patī, passus sum** is "experience" a process or an action. It thus may mean "suffer" or "undergo" when the process or action is a difficult one. By extension **patior** may mean "permit" or "allow" a person or thing (accusative) to perform an action (Object Infinitive).

Multa mala *passus sum.*	*I have experienced (suffered)* many bad things.
Pompeium Rōmam redīre *patiar.*	*I shall permit* Pompey to return to Rome.

pellō, pellere, pepulī, pulsus has a reduplicated third principal part (cf. **dō**).

quaerō, quaerere, quaesiī or **quaesīvī, quaesītus** may introduce an Indirect Command (see §84). **Quaerō** has *two* third principal parts, either of which may be used to make any of the forms of the perfect active system. The person from whom something is sought is expressed by **ā, ab** + ablative (cf. **petō**).

> **Marcus *ā mē* quaesīvit nē frātrem ad bellum mitterem.**
> Marcus asked *from me* that I not send (his) brother to war.
> Marcus asked *me* not to send (his) brother to war.

caecus, -a, -um may have either an active sense—"blind" (i.e., not *seeing*)—or a passive one—"hidden," "secret," "dark" (i.e., not *being seen*). Many adjectives in Latin convey a variety of meanings based on an active and a passive idea in their root meaning.

The genitive singular form **alterīus** is regularly used for both **alius, alia, aliud** and **alter, altera, alterum**. **Alius, alia, aliud** and **alter, altera, alterum** are used in various expressions in which the adjectives are repeated and special translations are required. For example:

> ***Alia* aurum, *alia* sapientiam optat.**
> *One woman* desires gold, *another* wisdom.
> ***Alter* in agrō labōrat, *alter* in urbe.**
> *One man* (of two) works in the field, *the other* in the city.
> ***Aliī* cīvēs bellum gerere optant, *aliī* timōre fugere.**
> *Some citizens* desire to wage war, *others* to flee because of fear.

In these sentences forms of **alius** or **alter** are used in *parallel* constructions. The forms of these words in each sentence are the same gender, number, and case. Singular forms of **alius** arranged in parallel constructions should be translated "one . . . another . . . " Plural forms so arranged should be translated "some . . . other(s) . . . " Singular forms of **alter** should be translated "(the) one . . . the other . . . "

> ***Aliōs* servōs *aliō* in agrō vīdērunt.**
> They saw *some* slaves in *one* field, *other* slaves in *another* field.

In this sentence two forms of **alius** in different cases are used *in the same sentence*. When this occurs, the two forms have a *complementary* relation. A comparison is implied, and the first part of the comparison should be supplied in the English translation.

The adjective **īdem, eadem, idem** is formed by the addition of the suffix **-dem** to the demonstrative adjective **is, ea, id.** MEMORIZE THE FOLLOWING IRREGULAR DECLENSION.

	Singular			Plural		
	M.	F.	N.	M.	F.	N.
Nom.	īdem	eadem	idem	īdem/eīdem	eaedem	eadem
Gen.	eiusdem	eiusdem	eiusdem	eōrundem	eārundem	eōrundem
Dat.	eīdem	eīdem	eīdem	īsdem/eīsdem	īsdem/eīsdem	īsdem/eīsdem
Acc.	eundem	eandem	idem	eōsdem	eāsdem	eadem
Abl.	eōdem	eādem	eōdem	īsdem/eīsdem	īsdem/eīsdem	īsdem/eīsdem

The declension of **īdem, eadem, idem** follows the declension of **is, ea, id** with certain variations:

1. The masculine singular nominative **īdem** is formed by the addition of **-dem** to **is.** When the **-s-** is dropped, the **i-** is lengthened because of compensatory lengthening (cf. **auferō**).

2. In the neuter singular nominative and accusative, the final **-d** of **id** is dropped before the ending **-dem.**

3. In the masculine and feminine singular accusative and the masculine, feminine, and neuter plural genitive, the final **-m** changes to an **-n-** before **-dem.**

4. In the masculine plural nominative and the masculine, feminine, and neuter plural dative and ablative, disyllabic forms of **is, ea, id** (e.g., **iī, iīs**) usually exhibit contraction of the two i's (e.g., **īdem, īsdem**). Occasionally the uncontracted forms **iīdem** and **iīsdem** occur.

uter, utra, utrum is an interrogative adjective that means "which (of two)?" It assumes that there are only two possible answers to the question it poses. **Uter** is often used substantively.

In *utrō* oppidō vīvis?	In *which* town (of two [towns]) do you live?
Utrum vidēre optās?	*Which (man or thing)* (of two) do you desire to see?

neuter, neutra, neutrum is an adjective formed by the addition of the negative particle **nē-** to **uter**. It thus means "neither (of two)." A word that is neuter in gender is *neither* masculine *nor* feminine.

iam is an adverb that may indicate a variety of moments in time depending on the tense of the verb and the context in which it appears. It may mean "now" as opposed to any other moment in the passage of time. It may mark the completion of an action before the time indicated by the verb: "(by) now" with a present time verb, "(by) then" or "already" with a past time verb. When **iam** appears with a future tense, it often emphasizes the time immediately approaching and may be translated "at once," "presently."

Accipe *iam* haec dōna.	Receive *now* these gifts.
Hic *iam* mihi hostis est.	This man is *(by) now* an enemy to me.
Carmen *iam* perfēcerat.	*By then (already)* he had completed (his) poem.
Iam veniet meus amīcus.	My friend will come *presently (at once)*.

When **iam** is used with any negative expression it is often best translated "longer."

Nōn prō patriā *iam* pugnābō.	I shall *no longer (not any longer)* fight on behalf of (my) country.

The **quam** of the adverb **quam ob rem** may be either a relative adjective (see §86)—"on account of which thing," "therefore"—or an *interrogative* adjective (see §88), "on account of which thing," "why." **Quam ob rem** may be written as a single word (**quamobrem**).

The **quā** of the adverb **quārē** may be either a relative adjective (see §86)—"because of which thing," "therefore,"—or an interrogative adjective (see §88), "because of which thing," "why." **Quārē** was originally an Ablative of Cause. **Quārē** may be written as two words (**quā rē**).

tandem is an adverb that has a temporal meaning (finally, at last). With imperatives and questions it often expresses impatience or indignation (pray, I ask you, then).

Ad urbem *tandem* accessimus.	*Finally* we approached the city.
Cūr *tandem* hoc fēcistī?	Why, *pray*, did you do this thing?

	Derivatives	Cognates
alius	*ali*as; *ali*en; hid*algo*	*alter*;[1] *al*arm; *al*ligator; *else*; *al*legory
alter	*alter*; *alter*nate; sub*altern*	*alius*;[1] par*all*ax
modus	*mode*; *mod*ern; *mod*ify; *mo*ld; *mood*	*mete*; *med*ical; *med*itate
oculus	mon*ocle*; *eye*let	*op*tic; aut*opsy*; *op*hthalmologist
patior	*pass*ion; *pass*ive; *patient*; com*pass*ion	*fiend*
pellō	*pul*se; *push*; re*pel*; com*pel*	*polish*; an*vil*; *felt*
quī/quis	*qui*bble; *qui*ddity; *qui*p	*who*; *what*; *how*; *when*; *whither*; *where*

---

1. **alius** and **alter** are both derived from the PIE root **al-*. Thus, all cognates listed under **alius** are cognates also of **alter** (and vice versa). Both are listed because English words are derived from both Latin words.

§83. Purpose Clauses and the Sequence of Tenses

Sometimes the precise relation between the meanings of two sentences is implied but not expressed. For example:

I like him. He's nice.

Although it is likely that the second sentence (He's nice) is stating the reason or cause for the first sentence (I like him), this causal relation *is not expressed*. When independent clauses or sentences are *placed next to each other*, with neither being subordinated to the other, such an arrangement is called **parataxis** (< Greek *parataxis*, placing beside) or **coordination**. The principal feature of **paratactic** writing is the *absence of subordination*.

When the precise relation between the meanings of two independent sentences *is expressed*, a complex sentence is created with a main clause and a subordinate clause.[2] For example:

I like him *because he is nice.*

Such complex sentences are said to exhibit **hypotaxis** (< Greek *hypotaxis*, placing under) or **subordination**. Many types of subordinate clauses in Latin began as independent sentences in paratactic arrangement with other sentences. When one idea was subordinated to another, subordinating conjunctions were added, and two simple sentences arranged paratactically were joined to make one complex **hypotactic** sentence. For example:

Hunc eī librum dōnō. Rēs gestās Rōmānōrum intellegat.
I am giving him this book. Let him understand the history of the Romans.

The second of these two sentences, containing a Jussive subjunctive, appears to express the aim, intention, or *purpose* for the action of the first sentence. This relation was eventually expressed in a particular kind of subordinate clause called a **Purpose clause.**

Main Clause   Purpose Clause
Hunc eī librum dōnō *ut rēs gestās Rōmānōrum intellegat.*
I am giving him this book *in order that he may understand the history of the Romans.*

OBSERVATIONS
_____

1. The subordinate clause italicized in the Latin sentence above is a Purpose clause.

2. Purpose clauses in Latin are introduced by the conjunctions **ut** (in order that) or **nē** (in order that . . . not).

3. The subjunctive verb in a Purpose clause was in origin a Jussive subjunctive. Also, the action of the verb in a Purpose clause is only *aimed at* or *intended*. As always, *nonfactual ideas* are expressed in the subjunctive mood in Latin.

4. A Purpose clause is considered an **adverbial clause** because the clause *modifies the action of the main verb as a whole:* it indicates the purpose for which the subject performs the action of the main clause.

2. For a review of complex sentences and subordinate clauses see §48.

The verb in the main clause in the sentence above—**dōnō**, the **main verb**—is in the present tense, but sentences containing Purpose clauses may have main verbs in any tense. For example:

Hunc eī librum dōnāveram ut rēs gestās Rōmānōrum intellegeret.
I had given him this book *in order that he might understand the history of the Romans.*

The particular *tense* of the *subjunctive verb* in any Purpose clause—*and in most other subordinate clauses in Latin that require verbs in the subjunctive mood*—is determined by fixed rules called the **sequence of tenses**. These rules are represented by the following chart:

	Verb in Main Clause	*Verb in Subordinate Clause*
PRIMARY	**Indicative**[3] Present Future Perfect (present completed) Future Perfect	**Subjunctive** Present Perfect
SECONDARY	Imperfect Perfect (past simple) Pluperfect	Imperfect Pluperfect

Memorize this chart.

The tenses of the indicative in the box at the upper left all refer to *present or future time* and are called **primary tenses**. When any of these tenses appears as the verb in a main clause, the verb in a subordinate clause requiring the subjunctive mood *must be either the present or the perfect subjunctive,* as is represented by the box at the upper right. These tenses of the subjunctive *have no absolute time value of their own:* they have only **relative time**. The *present* subjunctive is used to represent an action that is *simultaneous* with the main verb or *subsequent* to the main verb. The *perfect* subjunctive is used to represent an action that is *prior* to the main verb. When a complex sentence includes a main verb in a primary tense and a subordinate verb in either the present or perfect subjunctive, the subordinate subjunctive verb is said to be following **primary sequence**.

The tenses of the indicative in the box at the lower left all refer to *past time* and are called **secondary tenses**. When any of these tenses appears as the verb in a main clause, the verb in a subordinate clause requiring the subjunctive mood *must be either the imperfect or the pluperfect subjunctive,* as is represented by the box at the lower right. These tenses of the subjunctive *have no absolute time value of their own:* they have only *relative time*. The *imperfect* subjunctive is used to represent an action that is *simultaneous* with the main verb or *subsequent* to the main verb. The *pluperfect* subjunctive is used to represent an action that is *prior* to the main verb. When a complex sentence includes a main verb in a secondary tense and a subordinate verb in either the imperfect or pluperfect subjunctive, the subordinate subjunctive verb is said to be following **secondary sequence**.

---

3. Sometimes the verb in the main clause is in the subjunctive mood. See p. 187.

1. The perfect indicative may be a *primary* tense or a *secondary* tense, depending on whether it expresses *present* time (with *completed* aspect) or *past* time (with *simple* aspect).

2. Almost all subordinate clauses that require subjunctive verbs follow the sequence of tenses.[4]

Since the verb in every Purpose clause represents an action that may occur at a time *subsequent to (after)* the verb in the main clause, the only possible tenses of the subjunctive that can be used for Purpose clauses are the *present subjunctive* in primary sequence and the *imperfect subjunctive* in secondary sequence.[5]

When a Purpose clause occurs in primary sequence and its verb is therefore in the *present* subjunctive, it should be translated: "in order that . . . *may*." When a Purpose clause occurs in secondary sequence and its verb is in the *imperfect* subjunctive, it should be translated: "in order that . . . *might*." For example:

Gladium capiō *ut pugnem*. (Primary Sequence)
I am taking up a sword *in order that I* **may** *fight*.
Gladium capiēbam *ut pugnārem*. (Secondary Sequence)
I was taking up a sword *in order that I* **might** *fight*.

The syntax of the verb **pugnem** is **present subjunctive, Purpose clause, primary sequence.** The syntax of the verb **pugnārem** is **imperfect subjunctive, Purpose clause, secondary sequence.**

Since the perfect indicative may be a primary tense *or* a secondary tense, *the tense of the subjunctive verb in the Purpose clause indicates* whether a main verb in the perfect tense is present time (with completed aspect) or past time (with simple aspect). For example:

Gladium *cēpī* ut *pugnem*. (primary sequence: perfect must be *present completed*)
I have taken up a sword in order that *I may fight*.
Gladium *cēpī* ut *pugnārem*. (secondary sequence: perfect must be *past simple*)
I took up a sword in order that *I might fight*.

Sometimes a verb in the subjunctive introduces a purpose clause (or other subordinate clause with a verb in the subjunctive). When a subjunctive verb expresses an action in *present* or *future time*, it introduces *primary sequence*. When a subjunctive verb expresses an action in *past time*, it introduces *secondary sequence*. For example:

Pres.   Primary
Subj.   Sequence

Sī hostis accēdat, arma *capiāmus* ut *pugnēmus*.
If an enemy should approach, we *would take up* arms in order that *we may fight*.

Pluperf.   Secondary
Subj.   Sequence

Sī hostis accessisset ut *pugnāret*, arma *cēpissēmus*.
If an enemy *had approached* in order that *he might fight*, we would have taken up arms.

---

4. Although conditional sentences are complex sentences containing main clauses (apodoses) and subordinate clauses (protases), the protases *do not follow the rules of sequence of tenses.*

5. The remaining subjunctive tenses that appear on the sequence of tenses chart (perfect and pluperfect) are used in many other subordinate clauses to represent actions that occurred *prior to* the main verb, but they are *not* used in Purpose clauses.

Summary of the Rules of Sequence of Tenses

1. IF THE VERB IN THE MAIN CLAUSE IS *PRIMARY,* THE SUBJUNCTIVE VERB IN A SUBORDINATE CLAUSE *MUST BE PRIMARY.* THE SUBJUNCTIVE VERB HAS *ONLY RELATIVE TIME.*

A *PRESENT* SUBJUNCTIVE REPRESENTS AN ACTION THAT IS *SIMULTANEOUS* WITH OR *SUBSEQUENT* TO THE MAIN VERB.

A *PERFECT* SUBJUNCTIVE REPRESENTS AN ACTION THAT IS *PRIOR* TO THE MAIN VERB.

2. IF THE VERB IN THE MAIN CLAUSE IS *SECONDARY,* THE SUBJUNCTIVE VERB IN A SUBORDINATE CLAUSE *MUST BE SECONDARY.* THE SUBJUNCTIVE VERB HAS *ONLY RELATIVE TIME.*

AN *IMPERFECT* SUBJUNCTIVE REPRESENTS AN ACTION THAT IS *SIMULTANEOUS* WITH OR *SUBSEQUENT* TO THE MAIN VERB.

A *PLUPERFECT* SUBJUNCTIVE REPRESENTS AN ACTION THAT IS *PRIOR* TO THE MAIN VERB.

☛ DRILL 83 MAY NOW BE DONE.

§84. Indirect Commands

A *direct* command may be expressed in Latin by the imperative mood or a Jussive subjunctive. For example:

> *Audīte* dicta rēgis! (Imperative)
> *Listen to (pl.) the words of the king!*
> *Nē audiātis* dicta illīus rēgis malī! (Jussive)
> *Do not (pl.) listen to the words of that evil king!*

In each of these sentences the command is expressed directly to a group in the second person plural.

When a command is *reported indirectly* as part of a complex sentence, the command is subordinated to a main verb, and the resulting subordinate clause is called an **Indirect Command**. The verb of an Indirect Command is in the subjunctive mood according to the rules of sequence. For example:

> **Petō *ut dicta rēgis audiātis.***
> I ask *that you (pl.) listen to the words of the king.*
> I ask *you (pl.) to listen to the words of the king.*
> **Petimus *nē dicta illīus rēgis malī audiātis.***
> We ask *that you (pl.) not listen to the words of that evil king.*
> We ask *you (pl.) not to listen to the words of that evil king.*
> **Ā dīs petīvī *nē meus fīlius interficerētur.***
> I asked from the gods *that my son not be killed.*

OBSERVATIONS

1. The subordinate clauses italicized in the sentences above are all Indirect Commands. Indirect Commands in Latin are introduced by the conjunctions **ut** (that) or **nē** (that . . . not).

2. The subjunctive verb in an Indirect Command was in origin a Jussive subjunctive. Also, the action of the verb in an Indirect Command is only *ordered*. As always, *nonfactual ideas* are expressed in the subjunctive mood in Latin.

3. Indirect Commands may be distinguished from Purpose clauses by the verbs that introduce them. Verbs that mean "beg," "ask," "advise," "urge," "command," "order," etc. regularly introduce Indirect Commands. Verbs in Chapters I–IX that introduce Indirect Commands are **hortor, imperō, moneō, petō,** and **quaerō. Iubeō,** which regularly takes an Object Infinitive (with a subject in the accusative), less frequently introduces Indirect Command. Other verbs that introduce Indirect Commands are identified in the vocabulary notes.

4. Since the verb in every Indirect Command represents an action that may occur at a time *subsequent to (after)* the verb in the main clause, the only possible tenses of the subjunctive that can be used in Indirect Commands are the *present subjunctive* in primary sequence and the *imperfect subjunctive* in secondary sequence.

5. An Indirect Command is regularly translated using the *English present subjunctive.*[6] There is *no difference* between the translation of an Indirect Command in primary sequence and the translation of one in secondary sequence. An Indirect Command may also be translated using an English infinitive, as in the second translations for the first two sentences above.

6. An Indirect Command is considered a **noun clause** because the clause *functions as the direct object (less frequently the subject) of the main verb*: it indicates *what* is asked for, begged, advised, ordered, etc. Contrast Purpose clauses, which are *adverbial* clauses.

☛ Drill 83–84 may now be done.

§85. The Relative Pronoun *quī, quae, quod* and the Relative Clause

A **relative pronoun** introduces a subordinate clause that qualifies an **antecedent**, a word that "goes before" (< **antecēdō**, go before) the relative pronoun. For example:

> People ***who*** *live in glass houses* shouldn't throw stones.
> The evil ***that*** *men do* lives after them.

In these English sentences "who" and "that" are examples of relative pronouns. Each *refers to* the word that goes before it.[7] "People" is the *antecedent* of "who," and "evil" is the *antecedent* of "that."[8] The italicized portion of each sentence (*including* the relative pronoun) is called a **relative clause.** Each relative clause has a verb of its own (in addition to the verb in the main clause). A relative clause is an **adjectival clause.**

---

6. The English present subjunctive is the infinitive form of the verb with the word "to" omitted (e.g., "work," "complete," "do," etc.). For example: "I advised the dog that he not *cross* the street when there was heavy traffic."

7. The word "relative" is derived from the fourth principal part of the verb **referō, referre, rettulī, relātus** "bring back, refer": a relative pronoun "refers" to its antecedent.

8. In addition to "who" and "that," other forms of English relative pronouns include "whom" (direct object, object of a preposition), "whose" (possessive), "which," and sometimes "what." For more on when to use "which" and "that" in translating Latin relative pronouns, see the *Note on Restrictive and Nonrestrictive Relative Clauses,* p. 191.

The relative pronoun in Latin has singular and plural forms in all three genders.
MEMORIZE THE DECLENSION OF THE RELATIVE PRONOUN *ACROSS THE SINGULAR AND THEN ACROSS THE PLURAL.*

	Singular			*Plural*		
	M.	F.	N.	M.	F.	N.
Nom.	quī	quae	quod	quī	quae	quae
Gen.	cuius	cuius	cuius	quōrum	quārum	quōrum
Dat.	cui	cui	cui	quibus	quibus	quibus
Acc.	quem	quam	quod	quōs	quās	quae
Abl.	quō	quā	quō	quibus	quibus	quibus

OBSERVATIONS

1. The relative pronoun does *not* have vocative forms.

2. The **-i-** of **cuius** in the genitive singular is consonantal and is pronounced like English **y**. Thus **cu-ius** *(cu-yus)* is disyllabic. The **-ui** of **cui** in the dative singular is a diphthong and is pronounced like English **wi**. Thus **cui** (kwi) is monosyllabic.

3. When a form of the relative pronoun functions as an Ablative of Accompaniment, the preposition **cum** may be attached directly to the pronoun. Thus **quōcum** (with whom) and **quibuscum** (with whom). The neuter forms are rarely used as Ablatives of Accompaniment.

MEMORIZE THE FOLLOWING RULE: THE RELATIVE PRONOUN AGREES WITH ITS ANTECEDENT IN GENDER AND NUMBER. ITS *CASE,* HOWEVER, IS DETERMINED BY ITS SYNTAX WITHIN THE RELATIVE CLAUSE. For example:

> Carmina *quae nunc legō* ā Catullō scrīpta sunt.
> The poems *that (d.o.) now I am reading* by Catullus were written.
> The poems *that I am now reading* were written by Catullus.
> Librum *quī est in manibus tuīs* legere optō.
> The book (d.o.) *that is in your hands* to read I desire.
> I desire to read the book *that is in your hands.*
> Ager *in quō meus frāter labōrābat* ab hostibus captus est.
> The field *in which my brother was working* by the enemies was captured.
> The field *in which my brother was working* was captured by the enemies.

In the first sentence, the relative pronoun (**quae**) introduces a relative clause (**quae nunc legō**) that describes its antecedent (**carmina**). **Quae** is *neuter* and *plural* in order to agree with **carmina**, its antecedent. It is *accusative,* however, because it is the direct object of **legō**, the verb in the relative clause. In the second sentence, **quī** is *masculine* and *singular* to agree with **librum**, its antecedent. It is *nominative,* however, because it is the subject of **est**, the verb in the relative clause. In the third sentence, **quō** is *masculine* and *singular* to agree with **ager**, its antecedent. It is *ablative,* however, because its syntax in the relative clause is Ablative of Place Where.

OBSERVATIONS

1. The relative pronoun usually comes first in its clause *unless* it is the object of a preposition.

2. The relative pronoun is often placed immediately after its antecedent.

3. The verb of the relative clause is often placed at the *end* of the relative clause (e.g., **quae . . . legō, in quō . . . labōrābat**).

A Note on Restrictive and Nonrestrictive Relative Clauses

In both Latin and English there are two different kinds of relative clauses. A **restrictive** relative clause contains information about the antecedent that is *essential* to the meaning of the sentence. In English such a clause *is not set off in commas,* and an antecedent that is not a person is referred to in English by the relative pronoun "that." A **nonrestrictive** relative clause contains information about the antecedent that is *not essential* to the meaning of the sentence. In English such a clause *is always set off in commas,* and an antecedent that is not a person is referred to in English by the relative pronoun "which." For example:

> Restrictive Relative Clauses
> Men *who are without weapons* will not fight.
> I lost the book *that you lent me.*

In each of these sentences the relative clause *restricts* the meaning of the antecedent in a way that is essential for the sense of the sentence. The men who "will not fight" are not men in general, but "men who are without weapons." The book that "I lost" is not any book, but "the book that you lent me." Note that such restrictive relative clauses are *not set off in commas.* "That" is used when the antecedent is not a person.

> Nonrestrictive Relative Clauses
> Horace, *who was a close friend of Vergil,* lived in the country.
> You would enjoy this book, *which was written by my sister.*

In each of these sentences the relative clause contains additional but *nonessential* information about the antecedent. Note that such *nonrestrictive* clauses are *always set off in commas.* "Which" is used when the antecedent is not a person.

In Latin there are *no different pronouns* used to distinguish restrictive and nonrestrictive clauses. The two types may be distinguished *by punctuation only.*[9]

☛ DRILL 85 MAY NOW BE DONE.

§86. Special Features of the Relative Pronoun

The Indefinite or Generic Antecedent

An indefinite or generic antecedent is often *omitted* in Latin, but an antecedent should be supplied in English. Words such as "he," "she," "it," "a thing," "that thing," "they," "those," "those things," "a man," "people," etc. may be used. The gender and number of the relative pronoun indicate what word(s) should be supplied. For example:

---

9. In modern Latin texts different conventions in punctuation make even punctuation an unreliable method of distinguishing between restrictive and nonrestrictive clauses.

Quī nihil timent bellum cupiunt. (relative pron. = masc. pl.)
(They/Those/Those men/Men/People) *who* nothing (d.o.) fear war (d.o.) desire.
People *who* fear nothing desire war.
Catilīna, *quod* **saepe dīxī, novās rēs cōgitat.** (relative pron. = neut. sing.)
Catiline, (a thing) *that* (d.o.) I have often said, revolution (d.o.) is pondering.
Catiline, a thing *that* I have often said, is pondering revolution.

OBSERVATION

In the second sentence the antecedent for **quod** is *either* the entire main clause (Catiline is pondering revolution) *or* an ellipsed neuter pronoun such as **id,** "a thing," which itself is in apposition to the main clause.

While certain kinds of antecedents may be omitted in Latin, the relative pronoun itself can *never* be omitted, although it is often omitted in English. For example:

English: I have the book you were desiring. (relative pronoun omitted)
Latin: **Librum** *quem* **optābās habeō.** (relative pronoun introduces relative clause)
I have the book *that* you were desiring.

The Connective Relative

When a relative pronoun *begins a sentence* in Latin, its antecedent may be generic and implied, but it may also be *a specific word or an entire idea expressed in the preceding sentence.* A relative pronoun whose antecedent is to be found in a preceding sentence is called a **connective** relative pronoun.

The connective relative pronoun gives greater cohesion to the ideas being presented and makes the closest possible connection between sentences. Since standard English usage does not allow a relative pronoun at the beginning of a new sentence, a demonstrative pronoun or adjective may be used in translation. For example:

Crassus Rōmam vēnit. *Quem* **quoniam timeō, ex urbe discēdam.**
Crassus to Rome has come. *Whom* since I fear, from the city I shall depart.
Crassus has come to Rome. [*And*] since I fear *this man*, I shall depart from the city.
Hostēs accēdēbant cīvēsque arma capiēbant. *Quae* **mē terruērunt.**
The enemies were approaching, and the citizens arms (d.o.) were taking up. *Which things* me (d.o.) terrified.
The enemies were approaching, and the citizens were taking up arms. [*And*] *these things* terrified me.

OBSERVATIONS

1. Because a connective relative joins two sentences, the conjunction "and" may be added to the English translation, and a demonstrative pronoun or adjective may be used to translate the relative pronoun. In the first sentence **quem** is the equivalent of **et hunc.** In the second sentence **quae** is the equivalent of **et haec.**

2. The antecedent of **quem** in the second sentence of the first example is **Crassus,** with which it agrees in gender and number (masculine and singular). The antecedent of **quae** in the second sentence of the second example is not a specific word, but is the *actions* in the first sentence, with which it agrees in gender and number (neuter and plural).

3. **Quem** is Accusative, Direct Object of **timeō,** the verb in the causal clause introduced by **quoniam.** A connective relative *always* appears first in its clause even if, as here, the clause has an introductory conjunction.

Placement of the Antecedent in and After the Relative Clause

Although a relative clause usually follows its antecedent, sometimes a relative clause *precedes* its antecedent. When this occurs, the antecedent is often simply a demonstrative pronoun that appears immediately after the relative clause.[10] The antecedent also may be *drawn inside* the relative clause and then *restated* in the main clause as a pronoun. For example:

> ***Quōs** multum laudābās, **eōs** in bellum mīsī.*
> *Whom (pl.) you were praising a lot, them (those men) (d.o.) into war I sent.*
> I sent into war *those men whom* you were praising a lot.
> ***Quam urbem** hostēs cēpērunt, **hanc** līberāre dēbētis.*
> *Which city (d.o.) the enemies have captured, this (one) (d.o.) to free you (pl.) ought.*
> You (pl.) ought to free *this city that* the enemies have captured.

OBSERVATIONS

1. In the second sentence the antecedent **urbem** has been drawn inside the relative clause, and the relative word **quam** is virtually an *adjective* modifying **urbem**. It may be called a **relative adjective**.

2. The second translation, in which **urbem** has been placed in the main clause, is to be preferred.

☞ DRILL 86 MAY NOW BE DONE.

§87. The Interrogative Pronoun *quis, quid*

A pronoun used *to ask a question* is called an **interrogative pronoun**. In the questions "Who are you?" and "What are you doing?" the words "who" and "what" are examples of interrogative pronouns in English. Most of the forms of the interrogative pronoun in Latin are identical with the forms of the relative pronoun.

MEMORIZE THE DECLENSION OF THE INTERROGATIVE PRONOUN *ACROSS THE SINGULAR AND THEN ACROSS THE PLURAL.*

	Singular				*Plural*		
	M./F.		N.		M.	F.	N.
Nom.	**quis**	who?	**quid**	what?	quī	quae	quae
Gen.	**cuius**	whose? of whom?	**cuius**	of what?	quōrum	quārum	quōrum
Dat.	**cui**	to/for whom?	**cui**	to/for what?	quibus	quibus	quibus
Acc.	**quem**	whom?	**quid**	what (d.o.)?	quōs	quās	quae
Abl.	**quō**	from whom?	**quō**	from what?	quibus	quibus	quibus
		(etc.)		(etc.)			

OBSERVATIONS

1. In the singular there is one set of forms for *both masculine and feminine*. All forms are identical with those of the relative pronoun *except* the masculine/feminine nominative form (**quis**) and the neuter nominative and accusative form (**quid**).

2. In the plural there are different forms for all three genders, and *all* the forms are identical with those of the relative pronoun. The English translations of the plural forms are identical with those of the singular except for the addition of notes about number and gender. For example:

---

10. The demonstrative pronoun "points back" to the relative pronoun and the relative clause.

quis	who?	**quī**	who (masc. pl.)?
quid	what? (*or* what thing?)	**quae**	what (pl.)? (*or* what things?)

3. When a form of the interrogative pronoun functions as an Ablative of Accompaniment, the preposition **cum** is occasionally attached directly to the pronoun. Thus **quōcum** (with whom?) and **quibuscum** (with whom [pl.]?).

4. In Latin, as in English, an interrogative pronoun is placed first in a question, unless it is the object of a preposition. For example:

Quis illud dīxit?	*Who* said that thing?
Ā quō amāris?	*By whom* are you loved?
Quid tē terret?	*What* is frightening you?
Quae dīxit rēx?	*What things* did the king say?

5. The interrogative enclitic **-ne** is *not* added to an interrogative pronoun since the pronoun itself indicates a question.

§88. The Interrogative Adjective *quī, quae, quod*

In the questions "What book are you reading?" and "Which poems were written by Horace?" the words "what" and "which" are examples of interrogative adjectives in English because each modifies an *expressed noun* that directly follows. An interrogative pronoun, by contrast, stands alone. For example:

What man was chosen consul? ("what" modifies "man" and is an interrogative *adjective*)
What are you doing? ("what" stands alone and is an interrogative *pronoun*)

In Latin, the interrogative adjective *is identical in all its forms, singular and plural, with the relative pronoun.* For example:

Quem virum amās?	*Which man* do you love?
In quibus oppidīs vīxistī?	*In which towns* have you lived?
Quod animal in agrō erat?	*What animal* was in the field?
Cum quā fēminā ambulābat?	*With what woman* was he walking?

OBSERVATIONS

1. The interrogative adjective may be translated either "what" or "which."

2. The interrogative enclitic **-ne** is *not* added to an interrogative adjective since the adjective itself indicates a question.

☞ DRILL 87–88 MAY NOW BE DONE.

§89. Nine Irregular Adjectives

There are nine first-second-declension adjectives that have slight irregularities. These adjectives are:

alius, alia, aliud other, another	**tōtus, -a, -um** whole
alter, altera, alterum the other (of two)	**ūllus, -a, -um** any
neuter, neutra, neutrum neither (of two)	**ūnus, -a, -um** one; only
nūllus, -a, -um not any, no	**uter, utra, utrum** which (of two)
sōlus, -a, -um alone, only	

The declension of these adjectives differs from ordinary first-second-declension adjectives in the *genitive* and *dative singular only*. For example:

Nom.	tōtus	tōta	tōtum
Gen.	tōt*īus*	tōt*īus*	tōt*īus*
Dat.	tōt*ī*	tōt*ī*	tōt*ī*
Acc.	tōtum	tōtam	tōtum
Abl.	tōtō	tōtā	tōtō

OBSERVATIONS

1. The genitive and dative singular endings used for these adjectives are identical with those used for the intensive adjective **ipse, ipsa, ipsum** and the demonstrative pronouns/adjectives **iste, ista, istud** and **ille, illa, illud**. Because of this similarity and because these adjectives are often used substantively, they are sometimes called **pronominal adjectives**.

2. **Alius, alia, aliud** also differs from ordinary first-second-declension adjectives in its *neuter singular nominative and accusative form* (**aliud**). (Cf. **istud, illud**.)

3. The genitive singular form **alterīus** is regularly used for both **alius** and **alter**.

§90. Dative with an Intransitive Verb

Certain intransitive verbs regularly appear with a Dative of Reference indicating the person or thing affected by the action of the verb. Such a dative is called the **Dative with an Intransitive Verb**. For example:

> **Mea sententia *Antōniō* placet. (placeō, placēre, placuī, placitum** be pleasing, please)
> My opinion is pleasing to *Antony*.
> My opinion pleases *Antony*.
> ***Rēgī* nostrō pāreātur. (pāreō, pārēre, pāruī, pāritūrus** be obedient, obey)
> Let there be an obeying to our *king*.
> Let our *king* be obeyed.

The syntax of each italicized word (**Antōniō, rēgī**) is **Dative with an Intransitive Verb**.

OBSERVATIONS

1. Verbs that take a Dative with an Intransitive Verb are so indicated in the vocabulary list by the addition of "(+ dat.)" at the end of their entries. Although these verbs are *intransitive* in *Latin*, they may often be translated less literally by *transitive* English verbs. For example, in the second translation of the first sentence, "Antony" is the direct object of the English verb "pleases."

2. Verbs that take a Dative with an Intransitive Verb may occur in the passive voice *in an impersonal use only*. In such a construction, it is often convenient to translate the Dative with an Intransitive Verb as the personal subject of an English verb in the passive voice. For example, in the second translation of the second sentence, "king" is the subject of the passive voice English verb "let . . . be obeyed."

Short Readings

1. The first line of Ennius's epic poem

    Mūsae, quae pedibus magnum pulsātis Olympum . . . (ENNIUS, *ANNĀLĒS* I.1)

    Mūsa, Mūsae *f.* Muse
    Olympus, Olympī *m.* (Mount) Olympus
    pēs, pedis *m.* foot
    pulsō (1-tr.) strike, beat

2. A fragment from the poetry of Ennius

    quī vincit nōn est victor nisi victus fatētur. (ENNIUS, *SĒD. INC.* FRAG. 513)

    victor, victōris *m.* conqueror, victor

3. Eunomia asks her brother a pressing question.

    dīc mihi, quaesō, quis ea est quam vīs* dūcere† uxōrem? (PLAUTUS, *AULULĀRIA* 170)

    ***volō, velle, voluī,** —— be willing, want, wish; **vīs** = *2nd sing. pres. act. indic.*
    †dūcō, *here,* bring home
    quaesō, *quaesere, ——, —— seek, pray for; *1st sing. pres. act. indic.,* I ask you, please
    uxor, uxōris *f.* wife

4. Hegio is ordered by an ecstatic and near-mad Ergasilus to fetch a sacrificial animal.

    Heg. Cūr? *Erg.* Ut sacrificēs.

    H. Cui deōrum? *E.* Mī hercle, nam ego nunc tibi sum summus Iuppiter,

    īdem ego sum Salūs, Fortūna, Lūx, Laetitia, Gaudium. (PLAUTUS, *CAPTĪVĪ* 862–64)

    gaudium, gaudiī *n.* joy   **mī = mihi**
    laetitia, laetitiae *f.* happiness   **sacruficō (= sacrificō)** (1-intr.) perform a sacrifice
    lūx, lūcis *f.* light   **summus, -a, -um** highest

5. A woman's fate is reported with heavy irony.

    placēre occēpit graviter postquam ēmortuast. (CAECILIUS STATIUS, *PALLIĀTAE* FRAG. 163)

    ēmorior (ē- + morior) die
    occipiō (ob- + capiō) take up, begin

6. Cato's view of love

    aliud est, Philippe, amor, longē aliud est cupīdō. accessit īlicō alter ubi alter recessit.

    alter bonus, alter malus. (CATO, *ŌRĀTIŌNĒS* FRAG. 71)

    cupīdō, cupīdinis *f.* desire
    īlicō (adv.) at once; at that moment
    longē (adv.) far
    Philippus, Philippī *m.* Philip
    recēdō (re- + cēdō) withdraw, recede

7. Cicero notes the relation between the value of things and the degree to which they are desired.

etenim quī modus est in hīs rēbus cupiditātis, īdem est aestimātiōnis; difficile est fīnem facere pretiō nisi libīdinī fēceris. (CICERO, *IN VERREM II* 4.14)

aestimātiō, aestimātiōnis *f.* value
cupiditās, cupiditātis *f.* desire
fīnis, fīnis, -ium *m.* end, limit
libīdō, libīdinis *f.* desire
pretium, pretiī *n.* price, value

8. A character discusses the consequence of the agnostic and atheistic beliefs of certain Greek philosophers.

hōrum enim sententiae omnium nōn modo* superstitiōnem tollunt, in quā inest timor inānis deōrum, sed etiam religiōnem, quae deōrum cultū piō continētur.

(CICERO, *DĒ NĀTŪRĀ DEŌRUM* I.117)

*nōn modo = nōn sōlum
contineō (con- + teneō), continēre, continuī, contentus hold in, enclose; *in pass.*, be dependent upon
cultus, cultūs *m.* cultivation; worship
inānis, ināne empty, hollow; illusory
īnsum (in- + sum), inesse, īnfuī, —— be in; be present, be contained

religiō, religiōnis *f.* religious constraint *or* fear; superstition; sanctity; religious practice
superstitiō, superstitiōnis *f.* (irrational) religious awe, superstition
tollō, tollere, sustulī, sublātus lift, raise; take away, remove

9. Laelius considers the plight of the tyrant who, though wealthy, loves no one and is loved by no one.

Haec enim est tyrannōrum vīta nīmīrum, in quā nūlla fidēs, nūlla cāritās, nūlla stabilis benivolentiae potest esse fidūcia, omnia semper suspecta atque sollicita, nūllus locus amīcitiae. (CICERO, *DĒ AMĪCITIĀ* 52–53)

benivolentia, benivolentiae *f.* goodwill, friendliness
cāritās, cāritātis *f.* affection
fidūcia, fidūciae *f.* confidence, trust, reliance
nīmīrum (adv.) without doubt, presumably
sollicitus, -a, -um disturbed, troubled

stabilis, stabile (standing) firm, constant
suspectus, -a, -um viewed with suspicion, suspect
tyrannus, tyrannī *m.* monarch; absolute ruler; tyrant

10. Laelius makes this observation about Fortune.

nōn enim sōlum ipsa Fortūna caeca est, sed eōs etiam plērumque efficit caecōs, quōs conplexa est. (CICERO, *DĒ AMĪCITIĀ* 54)

conplector (= complector), conplectī, conplexus sum embrace
efficiō (ex- + faciō) make, render
plērumque (adv.) on most occasions; to a great extent

11. Cicero speaks about areas of excellence.

    itaque sē aliī ad philosophiam, aliī ad iūs cīvīle, aliī ad ēloquentiam applicant, ip-

    sārumque virtūtum in aliā alius māvult excellere. (CICERO, *DĒ OFFICIIS* I.115–16)

applicō (1-tr.) bring into contact; lead; apply
cīvīlis, cīvīle of *or* connected with citizens, civil
ēloquentia, ēloquentiae *f.* eloquence; rhetoric
excellō, excellere, ——, —— be superior, be
    conspicuous, excel

itaque (conj.) and so, accordingly
mālō, mālle, māluī, —— prefer; **māvult =** *3rd*
    sing. pres. act. indic.
philosophia, philosophiae *f.* philosophy

12. Cicero contrasts Rome with other societies.

    aliae nātiōnēs servitūtem patī possunt, populī Rōmānī est propria lībertās.

    (CICERO, *PHILIPPICS VI* 7)

nātiō, nātiōnis *f.* nation
proprius, -a, -um one's own; peculiar (to), characteristic (of) (+ gen.)

13. Cicero asks a rhetorical question about Caesar's being allowed to run for consul *in absentia.*

    cūr imperium illī aut cūr illō modō prōrogātum est? (CICERO, *AD ATTICUM* VII.3.4)

prōrogō (1-tr.) extend, prolong

14. The poet summarizes his doctrine of the eternal regeneration of atoms.

    sīc alid* ex aliō numquam dēsistet orīrī

    vītaque mancipiō nūllī datur, omnibus ūsū. (LUCRETIUS, *DĒ RĒRUM NĀTŪRĀ* III.

    970–71)

*alid = aliud
dēsistō, dēsistere, dēstitī, —— cease
mancipium, mancipiī *n.* ownership
orior, orīrī, ortus sum rise, arise
ūsus, ūsūs *m.* use; enjoyment

15. A shepherd laments his inability to make money from selling his animals.

    nōn umquam gravis aere domum mihi dextra redībat. (VERGIL, *ECLOGUES* I.35)

aes, aeris *n.* copper, bronze; coin, money
dexter, dextra, dextrum right; *as fem. subst.* (*sc.* **manus**), right hand

16. Aeneas speaks to his comrades as Troy falls.

    ūna salūs victīs nūllam spērāre salūtem. (VERGIL, *AENEID* II.354)

spērō (1-tr.) hope (for)

17. King Latinus agrees to an alliance with the Trojans and their leader, Aeneas.

    pars mihi pācis erit dextram tetigisse* tyrannī. (VERGIL, *AENEID* VII.266)

*tetigisse, *perfect active infinitive,* to have touched
dexter, dextra, dextrum right; *as fem. subst.* (*sc.* **manus**), right hand
tangō, tangere, tetigī, tāctus touch
tyrannus, tyrannī *m.* monarch; absolute ruler; tyrant

18. Which is better, city or country?

> Rōmae rūs optās; absentem rūsticus urbem
>
> tollis ad astra levis. . . . (HORACE, *SERMŌNĒS* II.7.28–29)

absēns, absentis not present, absent
astrum, astrī *n.* star; *in pl.,* the heavens, sky
rūsticus, -a, -um of *or* belonging to the country *or* a farm, rustic
tollō, tollere, sustulī, sublātus lift, raise

19. One advantage of being in love

> omne in amōre malum, sī patiāre, leve est. (PROPERTIUS II.5.16)

20. The poet responds when a friend asks him why he is so vulnerable to his beloved's cruelty.

> . . . "quārē" nōn habet ūllus amor. (PROPERTIUS II.22A.14)

21. A shrewd observation on protesting too much

> quī nimium multīs "nōn amo"* dīcit amat. (OVID, *REMEDIA AMŌRIS* 648)

*The **-ō** of **amō** here scans *short.*
nimium (adv.) too much, excessively

22. Part of the poet's description of the creation of animals out of soil, rock, and water after the great flood

> . . . et eōdem in corpore saepe
>
> altera pars vīvit, rudis est pars altera tellūs. (OVID, *METAMORPHŌSĒS* I.428–29)

rudis, rude unformed, rough, raw
tellūs, tellūris *f.* earth, land

23. A couplet about the human condition

> tendimus hūc omnēs, mētam properāmus ad ūnam,
>
> omnia sub lēgēs Mors vocat ātra suās. (*EPICĒDĪON DRŪSĪ* 359–60)

āter, ātra, ātrum black, dark
hūc (adv.) to this place, hither
mēta, mētae *f.* goalpost; end, limit
properō (1-intr.) hasten, rush
tendō, tendere, tetendī, tentus or **tēnsus** stretch out, extend; proceed

24. A faithful old dog responds to his master after he is scolded for losing his prey.

> quod fuimus laudā sī iam damnās quod sumus.
>
> (PHAEDRUS, *FĀBULAE AESŌPĪAE* V.10.9)

damnō (1-tr.) condemn

25. A remark of an orator taking part in a debate

> quod servāre tibi difficile est avō dōnā. (SENECA THE ELDER, *CONTRŌVERSIAE* IX.5.1)

avus, avī *m.* grandfather
servō (1-tr.) preserve, save

26. The chorus puzzles over why the gods do not seem concerned with human justice.

   rēs hūmānās ordine nūllō

   Fortūna regit sparsitque manū

   mūnera caecā . . . (SENECA THE YOUNGER, PHAEDRA 978–80)

hūmānus, -a, -um human
mūnus, mūneris *n.* present, gift
ordō, ordinis *m.* order
spargō, spargere, sparsī, sparsus scatter, distribute

27. The philosopher cites a remark of Aristotle about the poetic mind.

   nūllum magnum ingenium sine mixtūrā dēmentiae fuit. (SENECA THE YOUNGER,
   DIALOGĪ IX.17.10)

dēmentia, dēmentiae *f.* madness, insanity
mixtūra, mixtūrae *f.* mixture; admixture

28. Quintilian cites an example of a rhetorical figure employing reversal.

   nōn ut edam vīvō, sed ut vīvam edō. (QUINTILIAN, *ĪNSTITŪTIŌ ŌRĀTŌRIA* IX.3.85)

edō, ēsse, ēdī, ēsus (irregular 3rd conj. verb) eat

29. The poet suggests an example of madness.

   Hostem cum* fugeret, sē Fannius ipse perēmit.

      hic, rogo, nōn furor est: nē moriāre morī? (MARTIAL II.80)

*****cum**, *here* (conj. + subjunc.), when
Fannius, Fanniī *m.* Fannius
furor, furōris *m.* madness
perimō, perimere, perēmī, perēmptus destroy
rogō (1-tr.) ask; the final **-ō** of **rogō** here scans *short*.

30. The poet explains something to an acquaintance named Pontilianus.

   cūr nōn mitto* meōs tibi, Pontiliāne, libellōs?

      nē mihi tū mittās, Pontiliāne, tuōs. (MARTIAL VII.3)

*The **-ō** of **mittō** here scans *short*.
libellus, libellī *m.* (little) book
Pontiliānus, Pontiliānī *m.* Pontilianus, an acquaintance of the poet

31. The poet addresses a friend or lover.

   Difficilis facilis, iūcundus acerbus es īdem:

      nec tēcum possum vīvere nec sine tē. (MARTIAL XII.46)

iūcundus, -a, -um pleasing, delightful, agreeable

32. An example of Cato the Elder's rhetoric when he expresses indignation at the beating of
    Roman citizens

   quis hanc contumēliam, quis hoc imperium, quis hanc servitūtem ferre potest?

   (AULUS GELLIUS, *NOCTĒS ATTICAE* X.3.17)

contumēlia, contumēliae *f.* abuse

Longer Readings

1. Cicero, *Dīvinātiō in Caecilium* 19

Cicero attacks Verres, who had been proconsul in Sicily.

Sicilia tōta sī ūnā vōce loquerētur, hoc dīceret: "Quod aurī, quod argentī, quod ornā-
mentōrum in meīs urbibus, sēdibus, dēlūbrīs fuit, quod in ūnā quāque* rē beneficiō
senātūs populīque Rōmānī iūris habuī, id mihi tū, C. Verrēs, ēripuistī atque abs-
tulistī . . . "

quāque = *fem. sing. abl. of indef. adj.*, each
argentum, argentī *n.* silver
beneficium, beneficiī *n.* service, kindness; favor,
  benefit
C. Verrēs, C. Verris *m.* C. Verres, proconsul of
  Sicily, prosecuted by Cicero in 70 B.C.E.
dēlūbrum, dēlūbrī *n.* temple, shrine

ēripiō, ēripere, ēripuī, ēreptus tear away, snatch
  away
loquor, loquī, locūtus sum speak
ornāmentum, ornāmentī *n.* adornment, embellishment
sēdēs, sēdis, -ium *f.* seat; home, abode
Sicilia, Siciliae *f.* Sicily

The *Dīvinātiō in Caecilium* was delivered in 70 B.C.E. A **dīvinātiō** was a legal inquiry held to determine who should
conduct the prosecution of a case. Cicero successfully argued that he—and not Q. Caecilius, a corrupt alternative—
should try the case against C. Verres, a Roman nobleman charged with severe misgovernment of the province of
Sicily. The case pitted Cicero against the leading lawyer of the day, Hortensius, and Cicero's victory established him
as the foremost orator in Rome. Verres was forced into exile.

2. Cicero, *Dē Fīnibus* IV.34

Cicero compares wisdom to an artist.

ut Phīdiās potest ā prīmō īnstituere signum idque perficere, potest ab aliō inchoātum
accipere et absolvere, huic est sapientia similis; nōn enim ipsa genuit hominem, sed
accēpit ā nātūrā inchoātum.

absolvō, absolvere, absolvī, absolūtus finish,
  complete
gignō, gignere, genuī, genitus create, beget (of a
  father)
inchoō (1-tr.) start, begin
īnstituō, īnstituere, īnstituī, īnstitūtus set up,
  establish; set to work (on), start (on)

Phīdiās, Phīdiae *m.* Phidias, fifth-century Athenian sculptor, designer of Parthenon sculpture
prīmum, prīmī *n.* first part, beginning
signum, signī *n.* sign, signal; statue, figure
similis, simile similar (+ dat.)

In the *Dē Fīnibus Bonōrum et Malōrum* (*Concerning the Ends of Goods and Evils*) Cicero surveys the doctrines of three
prominent schools of philosophical thought of his day: Epicurean, Stoic, and Old Academic, the school of thought
associated with the philosopher Antiochus. The *Dē Fīnibus* is considered Cicero's most technical philosophical work.

3. Lucretius, *Dē Rērum Nātūrā* II.75–79

The poet describes the never-ending life and change of the physical world.

... sīc rērum summa novātur

semper, et inter sē mortālēs mūtua vīvunt.

augēscunt aliae gentēs, aliae minuuntur,

inque brevī spatiō mūtantur saecla animantum

et quasi cursōrēs vītāī* lampada trādunt.

*vītāī = vītae
animāns, animantis, -ium *m.* or *f.* or *n.* living
    creature; **animantum = animantium**
**augēscō, augēscere, auxī, —— ** increase, grow
brevis, breve short, brief
cursor, cursōris *m.* runner
gēns, gentis, -ium *f.* nation, people; clan, family
lampas, lampadis *f.* torch; **lampada** = *acc. sing.*
minuō, minuere, minuī, minūtus make smaller,
    reduce, diminish

mortālis, mortāle mortal
mūtō (1-tr.) change
mūtua (adv.) through successive changes, recip-
    rocally, with mutual interaction
novō (1-tr.) make new, renew
quasi (adv.) as (if), as (it were)
saec(u)lum, saec(u)lī *n.* age, generation
spatium, spatiī *n.* course, track; lap; space,
    interval
summa, summae *f.* sum, whole, total, totality

Virtually nothing is known about the life of **Tītus Lucrētius Cārus** (98?–55? B.C.E.), but his didactic epic poem *Dē Rērum Nātūrā* (*Concerning the Nature of Things*) is one of the masterpieces of Latin literature. Lucretius explains the Greek philosopher Epicurus's atomic theory of the universe in order to dispel the fear of death and so to free mankind from religion and superstition. His style owes much to his predecessor Ennius and is thus more archaic than that of his contemporary Catullus. Lucretius's command of meter and poetic diction exerted considerable in-fluence on Vergil's poetic development, and several lines of Lucretius's poem appear in slightly altered form in Vergil's works.

4. Catullus XCII

The poet and his beloved Lesbia have something in common.

Lesbia mī dīcit semper male nec tacet umquam

    dē mē: Lesbia mē dispeream nisi amat.

quō signō? quia sunt totidem mea: dēprecor illam

    assiduē, vērum dispeream nisi amō.

assiduē (adv.) continually, constantly
dēprecor (1-tr.) ward off by prayer; deprecate,
    abuse
dispereō (dis- + pereō), disperīre, disperiī, ——
    perish
mī = mihi

quia (conj.) because
signum, signī *n.* sign, signal
taceō, tacēre, tacuī, tacitūrus be silent, keep
    silent
totidem (indeclinable numerical adj.) just as
    many; just the same

Gaius Valerius Catullus (84?–54? B.C.E.) was born at Verona, but as a young man he came to live in Rome, where he became associated with several other young poets. These **poētae novī** were very much influenced by the Greek lyric poets and Hellenistic poets. Reacting against long epic and didactic models in earlier Latin poetry, the **neoterics** (< Greek *neōteros*, newer) chose to write shorter, personal lyrics, of which the 116 poems of Catullus are the best sur-viving examples. By coining new words and by giving new meanings to existing words Catullus created a new po-etic diction for Latin. His vocabulary added liveliness, humor, and even obscenity to the language. Many later Latin poets, including Vergil and Horace, were significantly influenced by Catullan diction and style.

5. Caesar, *Dē Bellō Gallicō* I.1

Caesar begins his commentary on the Gallic war.

Gallia est omnis dīvīsa in partēs trēs; quārum ūnam incolunt Belgae, aliam Aquītānī, tertiam quī ipsōrum linguā Celtae, nostrā Gallī appellantur. Hī omnēs linguā, īnstitūtīs, lēgibus inter sē differunt.

appellō (1-tr.) name, call
Aquītānī, Aquītānōrum *m. pl.* (the) Aquitani
Belgae, Belgārum *m. pl.* (the) Belgae
Celtae, Celtārum *m. pl.* (the) Celts
dīvidō, dīvidere, dīvīsī, dīvīsus separate, divide
Gallī, Gallōrum *m. pl.* (the) Gauls

Gallia, Galliae *f.* Gaul
incolō, incolere, incoluī, —— inhabit
īnstitūtum, īnstitūtī *n.* custom, institution
lingua, linguae *f.* tongue; language
tertius, -a, -um third
trēs, tria (numerical adj.) three; **trēs** = *fem. pl. acc.*

Gaius Iūlius Caesar (100–44 B.C.E.) was born at Rome and began his political career in the 60s. After entering into an alliance with the two most powerful people in Rome—the wealthy M. Licinius Crassus and the general Pompey—Caesar became consul for the first time in 59. After his consulship Caesar was chosen to govern the province Gaul (modern France and northern Italy). At the time Rome controlled only the southernmost portion of Gaul. Over the next several years Caesar conquered the remainder of it. Caesar then sought to return to Rome as consul in 49, but Pompey, his supporters, and others at Rome—fearing Caesar's increasing power—blocked his candidacy. As a result, Caesar invaded Italy and set off the civil war that lasted until 45 in various parts of the Roman Empire. On 15 March 44, after it had become clear that he had decided not to resign his dictatorship (a legal, temporary office in Rome), Caesar was assassinated.

The *Commentāriī dē Bellō Gallicō* (Commentaries About the Gallic War) were probably written during the campaigns in Gaul. They provide both an account of those campaigns and a description of the customs of the peoples Caesar encountered in Gaul and Britain. Written in seven books, the *Commentāriī* are a third-person account in a plain, lucid, and orderly style with a notable absence of florid rhetoric. When Quintilian surveys the orators of the late Republic, he rates Caesar second only to Cicero himself. Both Cicero and Quintilian praise Caesar's purity of vocabulary and clarity of thought as a speaker—qualities also apparent in his writings.

6. Vergil, *Aeneid* II.65–74

Aeneas, in Carthage, narrates the downfall of Troy. In this passage he begins his account of the deception of Sinon, whose false tale ensures that the Trojan horse is brought into the city.

accipe nunc Danaum īnsidiās et crīmine ab ūnō   65

disce omnīs.*

namque ut cōnspectū in mediō turbātus, inermis

cōnstitit atque oculīs Phrygia agmina circumspexit,

"heu, quae nunc tellūs," inquit, "quae mē aequora possunt

accipere? aut quid iam miserō mihi dēnique restat,   70

cui neque apud Danaōs usquam locus, et super ipsī

Dardanidae īnfēnsī poenās cum sanguine poscunt?"

quō gemitū conversī animī compressus et† omnis

impetus.

*A few lines of the *Aeneid* remained unfinished at the time of Vergil's death.

†**et** in poetry is frequently placed in the position of **-que**.

aequor, aequoris *n.* level surface; sea

agmen, agminis *n.* (battle-)line; throng

apud (prep. + acc.) at, near; in the presence of, among

circumspiciō, circumspicere, circumspexī, circumspectus look around (at)

comprimō, comprimere, compressī, compressus crush; subdue, suppress

cōnspectus, cōnspectūs *m.* sight, view

cōnstō, cōnstāre, cōnstitī, cōnstātūrus stand still

convertō, convertere, convertī, conversus turn upside down, reverse; change; win over

crīmen, crīminis *n.* charge, accusation; crime

Danaī, Danaōrum *m. pl.* Danaans, Greeks; **Danaum** = *gen. pl.*

Dardanidēs, Dardanidae *m.* descendant of Dardanus (founder of Troy), Trojan

dēnique (adv.) finally, at last; in short, to sum up

discō, discere, didicī, —— learn

gemitus, gemitūs *m.* groan(ing), moan(ing)

impetus, impetūs *m.* attack, assault; (violent) impulse *or* urge

inermis, inerme unarmed

īnfēnsus, -a, -um hostile, threatening

inquam (defective verb) say; **inquit** = *3rd sing. pres. act. indic.*

medius, -a, -um middle (of)

Phrygius, -a, -um of *or* belonging to Phrygia (the region in which Troy was situated), Phrygian, Trojan

poscō, poscere, poposcī, —— demand

restō, restāre, restitī, —— remain, be left

sanguis, sanguinis *m.* blood

super (adv.) in addition

tellūs, tellūris *f.* earth, land

turbō (1-tr.) stir up, confuse, throw into confusion

usquam (adv.) anywhere

7. Vergil, *Aeneid* IV.651–58

Before committing suicide, Dido mounts her funeral pyre and addresses relics of her love affair with Aeneas.

dulcēs exuviae, dum fāta deusque sinēbat,

accipite hanc animam mēque hīs exsolvite cūrīs.

vīxī et quem dederat cursum Fortūna perēgī,

et nunc magna meī sub terrās ībit imāgō.

urbem praeclāram statuī, mea moenia vīdī,   655

ulta virum poenās inimīcō ā frātre recēpī,

fēlīx, heu nimium fēlīx, sī lītora tantum

numquam Dardaniae tetigissent nostra carīnae.

carīna, carīnae *f.* keel; ship
cursus, cursūs *m.* course
Dardanius, -a, -um Dardanian, Trojan
dulcis, dulce sweet
dum (conj. + indic.) while, as long as
exsolvō, exsolvere, exsolvī, exsolūtus set free, release
exuviae, exuviārum *f. pl.* (stripped) armor; mementos
imāgō, imāginis *f.* image, likeness
lītus, lītoris *n.* shore, beach

nimium (adv.) too much, excessively
peragō (per- + agō), peragere, perēgī, perāctus thoroughly do; accomplish, complete
praeclārus, -a, -um very famous
recipiō (re- + capiō) take back, receive
sinō, sinere, siī or sīvī, situs allow, permit
statuō, statuere, statuī, statūtus cause to stand, set up, establish
tangō, tangere, tetigī, tāctus touch; reach
tantum (adv.) only
ulcīscor, ulcīscī, ultus sum avenge

8. Horace, *Epistulae* I.11.25–30

The poet reflects on the restless discontent of men.

. . . nam sī ratiō et prūdentia cūrās,   25

nōn locus effūsī lātē maris arbiter aufert,

caelum nōn animum mūtant quī trāns mare currunt.

strēnua nōs exercet inertia: nāvibus atque

quadrīgīs petimus bene vīvere. quod petis, hīc est,

est Ulubrīs, animus sī tē nōn dēficit aequus.   30

aequus, -a, -um level, even; calm, tranquil
arbiter, arbitrī *m.* spectator, onlooker; *here,* commanding a view (of)
currō, currere, cucurrī, cursum run, rush
dēficiō (dē- + faciō) let down, fail
effundō, effundere, effūdī, effūsus pour out; spread out
exerceō, exercēre, exercuī, exercitus keep busy, occupy; train, exercise
hīc (adv.) here
inertia, inertiae *f.* inactivity, laziness

lātē (adv.) widely, far and wide
mūtō (1-tr.) change
nāvis, nāvis, -ium *f.* ship
prūdentia, prūdentiae *f.* good sense, judgment, prudence
quadrīga, quadrīgae *f.* (four-horse) chariot
ratiō, ratiōnis *f.* account, reason; reasoning
strēnuus, -a, -um active, vigorous, energetic
trāns (prep. + acc.) across
Ulubrae, Ulubrārum *f. pl.* Ulubrae, a small town in Latium

Written some time after 20 B.C.E., the *Epistulae* (*Letters*) are poems in dactylic hexameter in a conversational style. Much of our information about Horace's own life is derived from these *Epistulae*.

9. Propertius I.11.23–26

The poet concludes a poem with an address to his beloved Cynthia.

> tū mihi sōla domus, tū, Cynthia, sōla parentēs,
>
>> omnia tū nostrae tempora laetitiae.
>
> seu trīstis veniam seu contrā laetus amīcīs,   25
>
>> quicquid erō, dīcam "Cynthia causa fuit."

contrā (adv.) in opposition, in turn
laetitia, laetitiae *f.* happiness
parēns, parentis, -ium *m.* or *f.* parent
quicquid = *neut. sing. nom. of indef. rel. pron.,*
   whatever

seu (conj.) or if, whether; **seu . . . seu . . .**
   whether . . . or (if) . . .
trīstis, trīste sad, gloomy, melancholy, grim

10. Propertius II.8.1–6

The poet reflects on his emotional state now that he has lost his love.

> Ēripitur nōbīs iam prīdem cāra puella:
>
>> et tū mē lacrimās fundere, amīce, vetās?
>
> nūllae sunt inimīcitiae nisi amōris acerbae:
>
>> ipsum mē iugulā, lēnior hostis erō.
>
> possum ego in alterius* positam spectāre lacertō?   5
>
>> nec mea dīcētur,† quae modo dicta meast?†

*The **-i-** of **alterīus** here scans *short.*
†**dīcō,** *here,* call
ēripiō, ēripere, ēripuī, ēreptus tear away, snatch
   away
fundō, fundere, fūdī, fūsus pour out, shed
iugulō (1-tr.) kill (by cutting the throat), slaughter
lacertus, lacertī *m.* (upper) arm
lacrima, lacrimae *f.* tear

lēnior, lēnius (comparative adj.) weaker, gentler;
   lēnior = *masc. sing. nom.*
modo (adv.) only, now; just now
prīdem (adv.) formerly, previously; **iam prīdem,**
   long since, for a long time now
spectō (1-tr.) look (at), observe
vetō, vetāre, vetuī, vetitus forbid

11. Ovid, *Metamorphōsēs* I.5–9

Ovid describes the beginning of the universe.

> ante mare et terrās et quod tegit omnia caelum   5
>
> ūnus erat tōtō nātūrae vultus in orbe,
>
> quem dīxēre* Chaos: rudis indīgestaque mōlēs
>
> nec quicquam nisi pondus iners congestaque eōdem†
>
> nōn bene iūnctārum discordia sēmina rērum.

***dīcō,** *here,* call
†**eōdem,** *here* (adv.) to the same place
Chaos, *Chaī *n.* Chaos
congerō (**con-** + **gerō**) gather together, collect
discors, discordis discordant, unlike
indīgestus, -a, -um unarranged, without order,
   confused
iners, inertis inactive, idle, inert
iungō, iungere, iūnxī, iūnctus join

mōlēs, mōlis, -ium *f.* mass, weight, burden
orbis, orbis, -ium *m.* ring, circle; world
pondus, ponderis *n.* weight
quicquam = *neut. sing. nom. of indef. pron.,*
   anything
rudis, rude unformed, rough, raw
sēmen, sēminis *n.* seed
tegō, tegere, tēxī, tēctus cover
vultus, vultūs *m.* expression, countenance; face

12. Seneca the Younger, *Agamemnōn* 79–86

The chorus states what it believes inevitably happens to royal houses.

iūra pudorque

et coniugiī sacrāta fidēs   80

fugiunt aulās; sequitur trīstis

sanguinolentā Bellōna manū

quaeque superbōs ūrit Erīnys,

nimiās semper comitāta domōs,

quās in plānum quaelibet hōra   85

tulit ex altō.

aula, **aulae** *f.* royal hall, palace
Bellōna, **Bellōnae** *f.* Bellona, goddess of war
comitor (1-tr.) accompany, attend
coniugium, **coniugiī** *n.* marriage
Erīnys, **Erīnyos (= Erīnyis)** *f.* Erinys, a Fury
hōra, **hōrae** *f.* hour
nimius, **-a**, **-um** excessive, too great
plānum, **plānī** *n.* flat *or* level ground
pudor, **pudōris** *m.* shame, decency, modesty

quaelibet = *fem. sing. nom. of indef. adj.,*
  any . . . it pleases
sacrātus, **-a**, **-um** hallowed, sacred
sanguinolentus, **-a**, **-um** covered with blood;
  greedy for blood
superbus, **-a**, **-um** proud; haughty
trīstis, **trīste** sad, gloomy, melancholy, grim
ūrō, **ūrere**, **ussī**, **ustus** burn, scorch, inflame,
  consume

Based in part on Aeschylus's *Agamemnon*, Seneca's play of the same name tells the tale of Agamemnon's home-coming from Troy and his subsequent murder by his wife, Clytaemnestra, and his cousin, her lover, Aegisthus.

13. Seneca the Younger, *Agamemnōn* 698–709

> Cassandra, the daughter of Priam, explains to the chorus why she has nothing left to fear.

> Fortūna vīrēs ipsa cōnsūmpsit suās.

> quae patria restat, quis* pater, quae iam soror?

> bibēre tumulī sanguinem atque ārae meum.†   700

> quid illa fēlīx turba frāternī gregis?

> exhausta nempe: rēgiā miserī senēs

> vacuā relictī, totque per thalamōs vident

> praeter Lacaenam cēterās viduās nurūs.

> tot illa rēgum māter et regimen Phrygum,   705

> fēcunda in†† ignēs Hecuba fātōrum novās

> experta lēgēs induit vultūs ferōs:

> circā ruīnās rabida latrāvit suās,

> Troiae superstes, Hectorī, Priamō, sibi.

*quis, *here, interrog. pron. used adjectivally*
†meum = meōrum
††in, *here,* toward
bibō, bibere, bibī, —— drink
cēterus, -a, -um rest (of), remaining part (of), (the) other
circā (prep. + acc.) around, near
cōnsūmō, cōnsūmere, cōnsūmpsī, cōnsūmptus expend, use up
exhauriō, exhaurīre, exhausī, exhaustus drain dry
fēcundus, -a, -um fertile, productive, fruitful
ferus, -a, -um wild, uncultivated; fierce, ferocious
frāternus, -a, -um brotherly, fraternal
grex, gregis *m.* flock, herd
Hectōr, Hectoris *m.* Hector, son of Priam
Hecuba, Hecubae *f.* Hecuba, wife of Priam
ignis, ignis, -ium *m.* fire
induō, induere, induī, indūtus put on, clothe; assume, adopt
Lacaena, Laecaenae *f.* Laconian woman; Helen
latrō (1-intr.) bark, bay

nempe (adv.) without doubt, to be sure
nurus, nurūs *f.* daughter-in-law
Phryx, Phrygis Phrygian, Trojan
praeter (prep. + acc.) beyond, except; besides
rabidus, -a, -um raging, rabid, mad
rēgia, rēgiae *f.* royal residence, palace
regimen, regiminis *n.* control, management; controller, manager
restō, restāre, restitī, —— remain, be left
ruīna, ruīnae *f.* downfall, ruin
sanguis, sanguinis *m.* blood
senex, senis old; *as masc. subst.,* old man
superstes, superstitis surviving (+ dat.)
thalamus, thalamī *m. in sing. or pl.,* inner room, wedding chamber; marriage
tot (indeclinable adj.) so many
tumulus, tumulī *m.* burial mound, grave
turba, turbae *f.* crowd, throng
vacuus, -a, -um empty
viduus, -a, -um widowed
vultus, vultūs *m.* expression, countenance; face

14. Tacitus, *Annālēs* I.1

The historian summarizes concisely modes of Roman rule from the city's beginnings down to Augustus.

Urbem Rōmam ā prīncipiō rēgēs habuēre; lībertātem et cōnsulātum L. Brūtus īnstituit. dictātūrae ad tempus* sūmēbantur; neque decemvirālis potestās ultrā biennium, neque tribūnōrum mīlitum cōnsulāre iūs diū valuit. nōn Cinnae, nōn Sullae longa dominātiō: et Pompeī Crassīque potentia citō in Caesarem, Lepidī atque Antōniī arma in Augustum cessēre, quī cūncta discordiīs cīvīlibus fessa nōmine prīncipis sub imperium accēpit.

*ad tempus, for the occasion, in emergencies
biennium, benniī *n.* biennium, two years
L. Brūtus, L. Brūtī *m.* L. (Junius) Brutus, legendary founder of the Roman republic
Cinna, Cinnae *m.* (L. Cornelius) Cinna (Roman dictator 87–84 b.c.e.), enemy of Sulla
citō (adv.) quickly
cīvīlis, cīvīle of *or* connected with citizens, civil
cōnsulāre iūs, cōnsulāris iūris *n.* consular right *or* power (sometimes granted to military tribunes)
cūnctus, -a, -um all
decemvirālis, decemvirāle pertaining to the *decemvirī*, a commission of ten magistrates
dictātūra, dictātūrae *f.* dictatorship, an emergency office with unlimited powers
discordia, discordiae *f.* discord, dissension, conflict
diū (adv.) for a long time
dominātiō, dominātiōnis *f.* absolute rule, dominion

fessus, -a, -um weary, exhausted, worn out
īnstituō, īnstituere, īnstituī, īnstitūtus set up, establish
Lepidus, Lepidī *m.* (M. Aemilius) Lepidus, member of second triumvirate with Antony and Octavian
nōmen, nōminis *n.* name
potentia, potentiae *f.* (illegitimate) power, influence
potestās, potestātis *f.* (legitimate) power
prīnceps, prīncipis first, foremost, chief; *as subst.,* leading man, *princeps,* the name chosen by Augustus as his title
prīncipium, prīncipiī *n.* beginning
sūmō, sūmere, sūmpsī, sūmptus take up, seize; take on, assume
tribūnus, tribūnī *m.* tribune, military commander
ultrā (prep. + acc.) beyond

The *Annālēs* appear to have comprised eighteen books, of which only eight survive completely and four others in part. Their subject is the history of Rome from the death of Augustus to the death of Nero (14–68 c.e.) The *Annālēs* is generally considered Tacitus's most mature work. The first six books in particular are marked by Tacitus's love of compression and his pronounced *avoidance* of Ciceronian balance. In these books the complexity of Tacitus's thought is combined with his commanding use of the Latin language's natural tendency toward economy. The resulting narrative is vivid, surprising, and inimitable.

§91. Numbers in Latin

Cardinal numbers are adjectives that answer the question "how many?" They are the numbers used in counting. Most but not all cardinal numbers in Latin are indeclinable. **Ordinal numbers** are adjectives that answer the question "which one in a series?" *All* ordinal numbers in Latin are first-second-declension adjectives. Most ordinal numbers are derived from the corresponding cardinal numbers.

Arabic Numeral	Roman Numeral	Cardinal Number	Ordinal Number
1	I	**ūnus, -a, -um** one	**prīmus, -a, -um** first
2	II	**duo, duae, duo** two	**secundus, -a, -um** second
3	III	**trēs, tria** three	**tertius, -a, -um** third
4	IIII or IV	**quattuor** four	**quartus, -a, -um** fourth
5	V	**quīnque** five	**quintus, -a, -um** fifth
6	VI	**sex** six	**sextus, -a, -um** sixth
7	VII	**septem** seven	**septimus, -a, -um** seventh
8	VIII	**octō** eight	**octāvus, -a, -um** eighth
9	VIIII or IX	**novem** nine	**nōnus, -a, -um** ninth
10	X	**decem** ten	**decimus, -a, -um** tenth
11	XI	**ūndecim** eleven	**ūndecimus, -a, -um** eleventh
12	XII	**duodecim** twelve	**duodecimus, -a, -um** twelfth
13	XIII	**tredecim** thirteen	**tertius decimus, -a, -um** thirteenth
14	XIIII or XIV	**quattuordecim** fourteen	**quartus decimus, -a, -um** fourteenth
15	XV	**quīndecim** fifteen	**quintus decimus, -a, -um** fifteenth
16	XVI	**sēdecim** sixteen	**sextus decimus, -a, -um** sixteenth
17	XVII	**septendecim** seventeen	**septimus decimus, -a, -um** seventeenth
18	XVIII	**duodēvīgintī** eighteen	**duodēvīcēsimus, -a, -um** eighteenth
19	XVIIII or XIX	**ūndēvīgintī** nineteen	**ūndēvīcēsimus, -a, -um** nineteenth
20	XX	**vīgintī** twenty	**vīcēsimus, -a, -um** twentieth
21[1]	XXI	**vīgintī ūnus, -a, -um** or **ūnus et vīgintī** twenty-one	**vīcēsimus prīmus, -a, -um** or **ūnus et vīcēsimus, -a, -um** twenty-first
22	XXII	**vīgintī duo** or **duo et vīgintī** twenty-two	**vīcēsimus, -a, -um alter, altera, alterum** or **alter, altera, alterum et vīcēsimus, -a, -um** twenty-second

1. In the numbers from 21 to 29, for example, the numbers up to 27 are made by *adding to twenty* the necessary numbers from 1 to 7. The numbers 28–29 are made by *subtracting from thirty* the numbers 2 and 1. Such a system is followed in every unit of ten numbers.

Arabic Numeral	Roman Numeral	Cardinal Number	Ordinal Number
23	XXIII	**vīgintī trēs** or **trēs et vīgintī** twenty-three	**vīcesimus tertius, -a, -um** or **tertius et vīcēsimus, -a, -um** twenty-third
28	XXVIII	**duodētrīgintā** twenty-eight	**duodētrīcēsimus, -a, -um** twenty-eighth
29	XXVIIII or XXIX	**ūndētrīgintā** twenty-nine	**ūndētrīcēsimus, -a, -um** twenty-ninth
30	XXX	**trīgintā** thirty	**trīcēsimus, -a, -um** thirtieth
40	XXXX or XL	**quadrāgintā** forty	**quadrāgēsimus, -a, -um** fortieth
50	L	**quīnquāgintā** fifty	**quīnquāgēsimus, -a, -um** fiftieth
60	LX	**sexāgintā** sixty	**sexāgēsimus, -a, -um** sixtieth
70	LXX	**septuāgintā** seventy	**septuāgēsimus, -a, -um** seventieth
80	LXXX	**octōgintā** eighty	**octōgēsimus, -a, -um** eightieth
90	LXXXX or XC	**nōnāgintā** ninety	**nōnāgēsimus, -a, -um** ninetieth
100	C	**centum** hundred	**centēsimus, -a, -um** hundredth
200	CC	**ducentī, -ae, -a**	**ducentēsimus, -a, -um**
300	CCC	**trecentī, -ae, -a**	**trecentēsimus, -a, -um**
400	CCCC	**quadringentī, -ae, -a**	**quadringentēsimus, -a, -um**
500	D	**quīngentī, -ae, -a**	**quīngentēsimus, -a, -um**
600	DC	**sēscentī, -ae, -a**	**sēscentēsimus, -a, -um**
700	DCC	**septingentī, -ae, -a**	**septingentēsimus, -a, -um**
800	DCCC	**octingentī, -ae, -a**	**octingentēsimus, -a, -um**
900	DCCCC	**nōngentī, -ae, -a**	**nōngentēsimus, -a, -um**
1000	M	**mīlle; mīlia, mīlium**	**mīllēsimus, -a, -um**

duo, duae, duo has an irregular declension. **trēs, tria** is declined regularly as a third-declension adjective *(plural forms only)*. The stem is **tr-**.

	Plural				*Plural*	
	M.	F.	N.		M./F.	N.
Nom.	**duo**	**duae**	**duo**	Nom.	**trēs**	**tria**
Gen.	**duōrum**	**duārum**	**duōrum**	Gen.	**trium**	**trium**
Dat.	**duōbus**	**duābus**	**duōbus**	Dat.	**tribus**	**tribus**
Acc.	**duo**	**duae**	**duo**	Acc.	**trēs**	**tria**
Abl.	**duōbus**	**duābus**	**duōbus**	Abl.	**tribus**	**tribus**

MEMORIZE THE CARDINAL NUMBERS 1 TO 10 (INCLUDING THE DECLENSIONS OF **DUO, DUAE, DUO** AND **TRĒS, TRIA**), 100, AND 1000. MEMORIZE THE ORDINAL NUMBERS THAT CORRESPOND TO 1 TO 10. REFER TO THIS SECTION WHENEVER CARDINAL OR ORDINAL NUMBERS APPEAR IN READINGS.

The cardinal numbers 200 to 900 are all declined (plural forms only) as first-second-declension adjectives. **Mīlle** is indeclinable in the singular, but **mīlia, mīlium** is declined regularly as a neuter plural substantive of a third-declension adjective. The stem is **mīl-**. The Romans frequently measured distance in "thousands of paces" or "miles." For example:

mīlle passuum	one thousand of paces, one mile (**passus, passūs** *m.* pace)
decem mīlia passuum	ten thousands of paces, ten miles

OBSERVATION

In the expressions above **passuum** is Partitive Genitive.

CHAPTER X

Vocabulary

➤ **lēgātus, lēgātī** *m.* legate, envoy; lieutenant

➤ **nātus, nātī** *m.* son

➤ **dux, ducis** *m.* or *f.* leader

➤ **fīnis, fīnis, -ium** *m.* or *f.* end, limit, boundary; *in pl.,* territory

➤ **genus, generis** *n.* descent, origin; race, stock; kind, sort

➤ **labor, labōris** *m.* work; effort, hardship

➤ **mōs, mōris** *m.* custom, practice; *in pl. (sometimes),* character

➤ **nēmō, nēminis** *m.* or *f.* no one

➤ **opus, operis** *n.* work; need
  ➤ **opus est** (idiom) there is need of (+ abl. or nom.)

➤ **ōrātiō, ōrātiōnis** *f.* oration, speech
    ōrātiōnem habēre (idiom) to make a speech
    ōrātor, ōrātōris *m.* speaker

➤ **pectus, pectoris** *n.* chest, breast; heart

➤ **cāsus, cāsūs** *m.* fall; occurrence; chance, misfortune

➤ **quīdam, quaedam, quiddam** (indef. pron.) (a) certain person, (a) certain thing

➤ **quīdam, quaedam, quoddam** (indef. adj.) (a) certain

➤ **oppugnō** (1-tr.) attack
    servō (1-tr.) save, preserve

➤ **stō, stāre, stetī, statum** stand; stand fast, endure

  dēleō, dēlēre, dēlēvī, dēlētus destroy

➤ **cadō, cadere, cecidī, cāsum** fall, sink; die

➤ **nāscor, nāscī, nātus sum** be born

➤ **nōscō, nōscere, nōvī, nōtus** come to know, learn, recognize; *in perfect,* know
  ➤ **cognōscō, cognōscere, cognōvī, cognitus** come to know, learn, recognize; *in perfect,* know

➤ **proficīscor, proficīscī, profectus sum** set out, set forth

➤ **ūtor, ūtī, ūsus sum** use; experience, enjoy (+ abl.)

➤ **perferō, perferre, pertulī, perlātus** suffer, endure; report

➤ **referō, referre, rettulī, relātus** bring back; report

➤ **aequus, -a, -um** level, even; equitable, just; calm, tranquil
  ➤ **inīquus, -a, -um** uneven; inequitable, unjust

➤ **honestus, -a, -um** honorable, respectable

➤ **medius, -a, -um** middle (of); *as subst.,* midst

➤ **apud** (prep. + acc.) at, near; at the house of, in the presence of, among

➤ **contrā** (adv.) face to face; in opposition; in turn
      (prep. + acc.) facing; against, contrary to

➤ **magnopere** (adv.) greatly
   quīn (conj.) *introduces Relative Clause of Characteristic,* who/that . . . not (§93)
   quō (rel. adv.) to where, whither (§92)
➤ **satis** or **sat** (indeclinable n. subst.) enough (adv.) enough, sufficiently
   ubi (rel. adv.) where (§92)
   unde (rel. adv.) from where, whence (§92)

Vocabulary Notes

lēgātus, lēgātī *m.* may refer to a "legate" or "envoy" involved in matters of diplomacy. It may also be used to identify an assistant to an army commander or provincial governor (lieutenant, legate).

nātus, nātī *m.* means "a male having been born" and is a substantive of the perfect passive participle of **nāscor.** Less common is the feminine substantive **nāta, nātae** *f.,* "daughter."

dux, ducis *m.* or *f.* may mean a "leader" in the sense of a "guide," but it is commonly used for a political or military "leader."

The gender of **fīnis, fīnis, -ium** is regularly masculine, but in early Latin and in poetry the *singular only* is sometimes treated as feminine. In the plural, **fīnis** may refer to the "boundary" of a territory or country and, by extension, the "territory" that is enclosed by boundaries.

genus, generis *n.* is derived from the PIE root ***genE-** (give birth, bear). **Genus** may refer to an individual's "origin" or "birth." It may refer more broadly to a "race" or "class" of people or things that arise from a single origin (human race, race of the gods, Greek stock). When used of abstract things, it often means "sort" or "kind," the abstract class to which someone or something belongs.

labor, labōris *m.* means the abstract concept of "work" or "the act of working" (exertion). **Labor** may also mean the "effort" or "hardship" required to accomplish something.

mōs, mōris *m.* means "custom," an established practice as opposed to an enacted law. The plural **mōrēs** may mean "customs," but it may also refer to the collective habits of an individual and thus may be translated "character."

nēmō, nēminis *m.* or *f.* occurs in the singular only. Although the genitive and ablative singular forms occasionally appear, usually the genitive and ablative singular forms of **nūllus** (**nūllīus, nūllō,** or **nūllā**) replace the forms of **nēmō** (**nēminis, nēmine**). **Nēmō** is formed by the addition of the negative particle **nē-** to the noun **homō.**

opus, operis *n.* may mean something that needs to be done (work [to do], need) or something that has been accomplished ([piece of] work, product, achievement). **Opus** may convey the sense of how much is required to accomplish something (effort), and it is often used for the products of artistic endeavor (poetic work).

Hoc *opus* perficere nōn poterit.	He will not be able to complete this *work.*
Clāra sunt *opera* poētārum.	The *works (achievements)* of the poets are famous.

The idiom **opus est** most often takes an ablative to express *the thing needed.* This ablative is translated with the English preposition "of." It is also common for a Dative of Reference to occur with this idiom.

Mihi opus est *magnā dīligentiā.*	There is need *to me of great diligence.*
	I need great diligence.

Less frequently, the thing needed is the Nominative, Subject, and **opus** functions as a Predicate Nominative. A Nominative, Subject occurs most often when the subject is a *neuter pronoun.*

Hoc mihi opus est.	*This thing* is a need to me.
	There is need to me *of this thing.*
	I need this thing.

Rarely **opus est** takes a genitive of the thing needed.

ōrātiō, ōrātiōnis *f.* may mean the abstract notion of "speaking," the power of "speech," or a particular "speech" or "oration."

When **pectus, pectoris** *n.* appears in the plural, it may refer to the heart or soul of a single person and may be translated in the singular.

cāsus, cāsūs *m.* is an abstract noun formed by the addition of the suffix **-tus** to a stem of the verb **cadō.** The **-t-** of the suffix assimilated to the **-s-** of the stem **cās-** and was then lost. In addition to its basic meaning of "fall," **cāsus** refers to the "occurrence" of an event, usually by chance (accident), which may be positive (fortune) or negative (misfortune). It may also refer to the "situation" that is the result of an occurrence or series of occurrences.

quīdam, quaedam, quiddam is an *indefinite pronoun* formed by the addition of the suffix **-dam** to the relative pronoun **quī, quae, quod**. An **indefinite pronoun** is a pronoun that does *not* define or specify the person or thing for which it stands. MEMORIZE THE FOLLOWING IRREGULAR DECLENSION.

	Singular			Plural		
	M.	F.	N.	M.	F.	N.
Nom.	quīdam	quaedam	quiddam	quīdam	quaedam	quaedam
Gen.	cuiusdam	cuiusdam	cuiusdam	quōrundam	quārundam	quōrundam
Dat.	cuidam	cuidam	cuidam	quibusdam	quibusdam	quibusdam
Acc.	quendam	quandam	quiddam	quōsdam	quāsdam	quaedam
Abl.	quōdam	quādam	quōdam	quibusdam	quibusdam	quibusdam

The declension of **quīdam** follows the declension of **quī, quae, quod** with certain variations:

1. The neuter singular nominative and accusative are formed by the addition of **-dam** to **quid**.
2. In the masculine and feminine singular accusative and the masculine, feminine, and neuter plural genitive, the final **-m** changes to an **-n-** before **-dam**.

quīdam, quaedam, quoddam is an *indefinite adjective* formed by the addition of the suffix **-dam** to the relative pronoun **quī, quae, quod**. An **indefinite adjective** is an adjective that does *not* define or specify the person or thing it modifies. The declension of **quīdam, quaedam, quoddam** is identical with that of **quīdam, quaedam, quiddam** *except* in the neuter singular nominative and accusative (cf. **quoddam** with **quiddam**).

Quīdam Rōmam vēnit.	A *certain* man came to Rome. (indefinite pronoun)
Poēta *quīdam* Rōmam vēnit.	A *certain* poet came to Rome. (indefinite adjective)

oppugnō, oppugnāre, oppugnāvī, oppugnātus is a compound verb formed by the addition of the prefix **ob-** to **pugnō**. (For the prefix **ob-** see Appendix P.) *Unlike* **pugnō**, **oppugnō** is a *transitive* verb.

Incolae oppidum oppugnant.	The inhabitants are attacking the town.

stō, stāre, stetī, statum is an irregular intransitive first-conjugation verb. The third principal part exhibits reduplication, and the fourth principal part has a *short* **-a-**. In addition to its basic meaning of "stand," **stō** may also mean "remain standing," "endure," or "last."

cadō, cadere, cecidī, cāsum is an intransitive verb. The third principal part, **cecidī**, exhibits reduplication. In addition to its basic meaning of "fall" or "sink," **cadō** may also mean "cease" (when the subject is winds, noise, etc.). It may also have the extended meaning of "die" or "perish."

nāscor, nāscī, nātus sum is an intransitive deponent verb. Compounds of **nāscor** do *not* exhibit vowel weakening. WHEN A COMPOUND OF **NĀSCOR** APPEARS IN READINGS, ITS PRINCIPAL PARTS ARE NOT SUPPLIED, BUT THE PREFIX AND SIMPLE VERB ARE GIVEN.

nōscō, nōscere, nōvī, nōtus is derived from the PIE root *gneO-* (know). It is an *inchoative* (< **incohō**, start) or *inceptive* (< **incipiō**, begin) verb. An **inchoative** verb indicates that an action is *beginning to occur*. All verbs whose first and second principal parts end in **-scō** and **-scere** are in origin inchoative verbs. The basic meaning of **nōscō** is "begin to know" and thus "learn." The *perfect* indicative of many inchoative verbs is often equivalent to an English *present* tense since the perfect tense indicates the *completion* of the action of the verb. **Nōvī** means "I have learned" and thus "I know." The *pluperfect* forms may be translated as if they were *imperfect*, and the *future perfect* forms as if they were *future*. On occasion, the perfect tense may be translated "have learned" or "learned," but the meaning "know" is more common. When **nōscō** in the perfect tenses takes an infinitive, it means "know how."

Nātūram hominum *nōscere* optō.	I desire *to learn* the nature of human beings.
Lēgēs huius urbis *nōvistī*?	*Do you know [= Have you learned]* the laws of this city?
***Nōverāsne* lēgēs huius urbis?**	*Did you know (progressive/repeated [=Had you learned])* the laws of this city?

The present forms of **nōscō** may mean "recognize" or "become acquainted with" a person. The perfect forms may mean "be aware of" or "be acquainted with" a person or an object of study.

> **Cicerōnem nōn *nōvī*.**   *I do* not *know* [am not *acquainted with*] Cicero.

cognōscō, cognōscere, cognōvī, cognitus is a compound verb formed by the addition of the prefix **com-** to **nōscō**. (For the prefix **com-** see Appendix P.) It exhibits irregular vowel weakening in the fourth principal part. **Cognōscō** is a strengthened form of **nōscō** with all the same meanings.

proficīscor, proficīscī, profectus sum is an *intransitive* third-conjugation deponent verb. In origin an inchoative verb, **proficīscor** means "set out" or "set forth" on a journey or from a certain starting point.

ūtor, ūtī, ūsus sum is an intransitive verb that takes an *ablative* of the thing used or experienced. The ablative is translated as a direct object in English. Compounds of **ūtor** do *not* exhibit vowel weakening. WHEN A COMPOUND OF **ŪTOR** APPEARS IN READINGS, ITS PRINCIPAL PARTS ARE NOT SUPPLIED, BUT THE PREFIX AND SIMPLE VERB ARE GIVEN.

> **Tuō cōnsiliō ūtar.**   I shall use *your advice.*
> **Utinam *bonā* nunc *fortūnā* ūterēmur.**   If only we were experiencing *good fortune* now.

perferō, perferre, pertulī, perlātus is a compound verb formed by the addition of the prefix **per-** to **ferō**. (For the prefix **per-** see Appendix P.) **Perferō** regularly means "endure" or "suffer" (hardships, troubles), but it may also mean "report" or "express."

referō, referre, rettulī, relātus is a compound verb formed by the addition of the prefix **re-** to **ferō**. (For the prefix **re-** see Appendix P.) Although **referō** may mean "carry back," it most commonly means "report."

From the basic physical meaning of **aequus, -a, -um** (level or even) come its more expanded senses of "fair" or "just" (level in a legal or political context) and "calm" or "tranquil" (i.e., level-headed). **Inīquus, -a, -um** is a compound adjective formed by the addition of the prefix **in-**[2] (not) to **aequus**. (For **in-**[2] see Appendix P.)

honestus, -a, -um is an adjective derived from the noun **honor, honōris** m. "(political) office"; "honor," "repute." In the strictest sense **honestus** describes a person who is "honorable" or "respectable" because he has held a public office. **honestus** has a more extended sense of being "morally honorable" *or* "respectable."

medius, -a, -um expresses the notion of the "middle of" a place by *modifying that place*. It usually appears *before* the noun it modifies. As a substantive, **medius** is often translated "midst."

> **Mīlitēs *in mediā urbe* ā rēge positī sunt.**
> Soldiers were placed *in the middle of the city* by the king.
> **Postquam populō dīxit, *ē mediō* discessit.**
> After he spoke to the people, he departed *(out) from* (their) *midst.*

apud is a preposition that takes the accusative. It may mean "at" or "near" (places), "at the house of," "in the presence of," "among," or "with" (individuals, groups), and "in (the writings of)" (authors, books). Context helps to determine the appropriate translation.

> **Virī *apud* Carthāginem manēbant.**   The men were remaining *near* Carthage.
> **Cicerō *apud* frātrem manet.**   Cicero is staying *at the house of/with* (his) brother.
> **Haec *apud* Rōmānōs sunt iūra.**   These are the laws *among* the Romans.
> **Haec verba *apud* Cicerōnem lēgī.**   I have read the following words *in (the writings of)* Cicero.

contrā may be an adverb or a preposition that takes the accusative. With verbs expressing standing, seeing, looking, and the like, the adverb usually means "face to face" or "opposite." With verbs of motion, **contrā** may mean "against." **contrā** may also be used to connect a second thought or opinion that balances or opposes a preceding one (in turn, on the other hand).

> **Mē *contrā* videt.**
> He sees me *face to face.*
> **Caesaris ille erat amīcus; tū *contrā* Pompeī.**
> That man was a friend of Caesar; you *in turn* [were a friend] of Pompey.

The preposition **contrā** has meanings analogous to the meanings of the adverb.

| Domum *contrā* templum pōnit. | He places (his) house *opposite* the temple. |
| Auxilia *contrā* hostem mittimus. | We are sending auxiliary troops *against* the enemy. |

The adverb **magnopere** is in origin the Ablative of Manner **magnō opere**, and it is sometimes written as two words.

satis may be an indeclinable neuter substantive, which is often followed by a Partitive Genitive, or an adverb. The shortened form **sat** is more common in poetry.

Satis agricolae est ager bonus.	A good field is *enough* for the farmer. (subst.)
Satisne pecūniae tibi est?	Do you have *enough* (of) money? (subst. + Partitive Gen.)
Satisne labōrābās?	Were you working *enough*? (adverb)

	Derivatives	**Cognates**
cadō	*cad*aver; *cad*ence; cas*cade*; *case*; chance; ac*cid*ent; oc*cas*ion; de*cid*uous	
fīnis	de*fine*; *fin*al; fine; finish	
genus	*genu*ine; *gen*der; *gen*re; en*gine*; *germ*; *gen*ital; mali*gn*	kind; *king*; *gen*ocide; *gene*
mōs	*mor*al; *mor*ose; mores	*mood*
nōscō	*not*ice; *not*orious; *not*ify	know; can; ken; dia*gn*osis; *n*oble
cognōscō	*cogn*ition; re*cogn*ition	
satis	*sat*isfy; *sat*urate; *sat*ire	sad
ūtor	use; *ut*ility; *ut*ensil	

§92. Relative Clauses of Purpose

Purpose clauses are regularly introduced by the conjunctions **ut** (in order that) or **nē** (in order that . . . not) (see §83). When a Purpose clause is instead introduced by a relative pronoun or adverb, it is called a **Relative Clause of Purpose**. For example:

> **Rēgīna mīlitēs in prōvinciam mittet *quī incolās terreant.***
> The queen soldiers (d.o.) into the province will send *who the inhabitants (d.o.)*
> *   may frighten.*
> The queen will send soldiers into the province *who may frighten the inhabitants.*
> The queen will send soldiers into the province *in order that they may frighten the*
> *   inhabitants.*

OBSERVATIONS

1. A relative pronoun regularly replaces **ut** in introducing a Purpose clause *only when there is a clear antecedent, usually not the subject,* in the main clause.

2. When a main clause contains a verb that involves motion (**eō, mittō, veniō,** etc.), a Relative Clause of Purpose often follows.

3. In the sentence above the relative pronoun **quī** makes the closest possible connection in Latin between the subordinate clause and the main clause by referring directly to its antecedent **mīlitēs.** The third English translation (in order that they may . . .) is to be preferred, however, because it most clearly indicates the idea of purpose that the clause expresses.

4. In the sentence above the syntax of **terreant** is **present subjunctive, Relative Clause of Purpose, primary sequence.**

Certain relative adverbs (**ubi,** where; **unde,** whence, from where; **quō,** whither, to where) may also introduce Relative Clauses of Purpose. For example:

> **Rōmam vēneram *ubi* auxilium ab amīcīs *peterem.***
> To Rome I had come *where* aid (d.o.) from friends *I might seek.*
> I had come to Rome *where I might seek* aid from friends.
> I had come to Rome *in order that there I might seek* aid from friends.
> **Eāmus *quō* laetī *sīmus.***   Let us go *whither (to where) we may be* happy.
>   Let us go *(to a place) where we may be* happy.
>   Let us go *where we may be* happy.

OBSERVATIONS

1. In the first sentence **Rōmam** is the antecedent for the relative adverb **ubi.** The third English translation (in order that there . . . might . . .) is to be preferred. The addition of the English adverb "there" preserves the close connection between the main clause and the subordinate clause that the relative adverb in Latin achieves. The words "in order that . . . might" clearly indicate the idea of purpose that the clause expresses.

2. The syntax of **peterem** in the first sentence is **imperfect subjunctive, Relative Clause of Purpose, secondary sequence.**

3. In the second sentence the antecedent for the relative adverb **quō** is *implied* (to a place) but *is not expressed.*

§93. Relative Clauses of Characteristic

When the verb in a relative clause is in the indicative mood, the relative clause helps make clear *what specific person or thing* is indicated by the antecedent. For example:

Virum quī rem pūblicam petit nōn laudāmus.
The (specific) man (d.o.) who the republic (d.o.) is (actually) attacking we do not praise.
We do not praise the man who is attacking the republic.

When the verb in a relative clause is in the *subjunctive* rather than the indicative mood, the relative clause may supply information about *what sort of person or thing* is indicated by the antecedent. Such a clause is called a **Relative Clause of Characteristic.**[1] For example:

> **Virum *quī rem pūblicam petat* nōn laudāmus.**
> A man (d.o.) *who the republic (d.o.) (would) attack* we do not praise.
> We do not praise a man *who would attack the republic.*
> We do not praise *the sort of* man *who attacks the republic.*
> **Virum *quī rem pūblicam petīverit* nōn laudāmus.**
> The (sort of) man (d.o.) *who the republic (d.o.) attacked* we do not praise.
> We do not praise *the sort of* man *who attacked the republic.*

OBSERVATIONS

1. The subjunctive mood in Relative Clauses of Characteristic developed from the Potential subjunctive, and it both *generalizes about* and *characterizes* an indefinite antecedent.

2. The *tenses* of the subjunctive verbs in Relative Clauses of Characteristic *follow the rules of sequence.* The syntax of **petat** in the first sentence is **present subjunctive, Relative Clause of Characteristic, primary sequence, time subsequent to the main verb.** The syntax of **petīverit** in the second sentence is **perfect subjunctive, Relative Clause of Characteristic, primary sequence, time prior to the main verb.**

3. Unlike Purpose clauses and Indirect Commands, Relative Clauses of Characteristic may use both the *perfect* subjunctive (in primary sequence) and the *pluperfect* subjunctive (in secondary sequence) because the action of a Relative Clause of Characteristic may occur prior to the main verb. Thus in the second sentence above **petīverit** is used to indicate time *prior* to the main verb and is translated accordingly.

4. When translating a Relative Clause of Characteristic, the formula "the sort of _____ who/that . . . (subjunctive verb translated as indicative)" is to be preferred. When the subjunctive verb is either *present* or *imperfect*, the alternate formula "a/an _____ who/that . . . would (subjunctive verb translated as potential)" may also be used.

Certain formulaic phrases with *indefinite antecedents* regularly introduce Relative Clauses of Characteristic. MEMORIZE THE FOLLOWING PHRASES:

Quis est quī . . .	Who is there (of the sort) who . . . (would)
Quid est quod . . .	What is there (of the sort) that . . . (would)
Nēmō est quī . . .	There is no one (of the sort) who . . . (would)
	(**nēmō, nēminis** *m.* no one)
Nihil est quod . . .	There is nothing (of the sort) that . . . (would)
Sunt quī . . .	There are people (of the sort) who . . . (would)
Sōlus est quī . . .	He is the only one (of the sort) who . . . (would)

1. The Relative Clause of Characteristic is also known as the **Generic Relative Clause.**

In addition to various unspecified or indefinite antecedents, *any* person or thing may serve as the antecedent for a Relative Clause of Characteristic. For example:

> **Cicerō erat quī vītam prō rē pūblicā daret.**
> Cicero was (a man) who would give (his) life for the republic.
> **Librum habeō quem amēs.**
> A book (d.o.) I have that you would love.
> I have a book that you would love.
> I have the sort of book that you love.

When the main clause contains an expressed or implied negation, the conjunction **quīn** (without its being the case that) may replace a relative pronoun in introducing a Relative Clause of Characteristic. A relative pronoun and the English adverb "not" should be added to the translation of such a clause. For example:

> **Nēmō est *quīn* prō patriā pugnet.**
> There is no one *who* would *not* fight for (his) homeland.
> **Sōla erat *quīn* haec intellegeret.**
> She was the only one *of the sort who* did *not* understand these things.

☛ Drill 92–93 may now be done.

§94. Introduction to Participles

A participle (< **particeps**, sharing in) has been defined as a *verbal adjective* with the properties of *tense* and *voice,* and one participle, the perfect passive participle, has already been learned.[2] There are a total of four participles in Latin: *present active, perfect passive, future active,* and *future passive.*[3] The following chart presents all the participles and their basic translations:

	Active	Passive
Present	Present Stem + **-ns, -ntis** (for 3rd i-stem- and 4th-conjugation verbs, change the stem vowel to **-ie-**) **vocāns, vocantis** **movēns, moventis** **regēns, regentis** "_____ing" **capiēns, capientis** **audiēns, audientis**	——
Perfect	——	4th Principal Part **vocātus, -a, -um** **mōtus, -a, -um** **rēctus, -a, -um** "(having been) **captus, -a, -um** _____ed" **audītus, -a, -um**
Future	drop the **-us, -a, -um** from 4th Principal Part and add **-ūrus, -a, -um** **vocātūrus, -a, -um** "about to **mōtūrus, -a, -um** _____" **rēctūrus, -a, -um** **captūrus, -a, -um** "going to **audītūrus, -a, -um** _____"	Present Stem + **-ndus, -a, -um** (for 3rd i-stem- and 4th-conjugation verbs, change the stem vowel to **-ie-**) **vocandus, -a, -um** "having to be **movendus, -a, -um** _____ed" **regendus, -a, -um** **capiendus, -a, -um** "deserving to be **audiendus, -a, -um** _____ed"

OBSERVATIONS

1. A present active participle is a third-declension adjective with one nominative singular form for the masculine, feminine, and neuter (cf. **ingēns, ingentis**). Its stem is found by dropping the ending **-is** from the genitive singular form (see §74). *Unlike* other third-declension adjectives, the present active participle has **-ī** or **-e** as its *masculine/feminine singular ablative* ending. When the participle functions as an adjective and modifies an expressed noun, the ablative singular ending is usually **-ī**. When the participle functions as a substantive, the ablative singular ending is usually **-e**. For example:

dē virō regentī	about the ruling man (adjective)
dē regente	about the ruling man/ruler (substantive)

2. See §§50–51, in particular the *Note on the Perfect Passive Participle.*

3. The Latin verb has neither a present passive nor a perfect active participle.

2. A short vowel *lengthens* before the nominative singular ending of the present active participle (**-ns**) (e.g., **regēns** < **rege-** + **ns**). However, a long vowel *shortens* before the **-nt-** at the end of the stem (e.g., **vocant-** < **vocā-** + **-nt-**).

3. The perfect passive participle of intransitive verbs (e.g., **veniō**) may occur only in the impersonal passive construction with a neuter singular ending (e.g., **ventum est**) (see §59).

4. The fourth principal parts of certain intransitive verbs that lack perfect passive participles are future active participles (e.g., **fugitūrus**, about to/going to flee).

5. A long vowel *shortens* before the **-nd-** at the end of the *stem* of the future passive participle (e.g., **vocand-** < **vocā-** + **-nd-**).

6. The future passive participle conveys a sense of obligation or necessity. For example:

oppidum capiendum	the town having to be captured (nom./acc.)
verba audienda	words deserving to be heard (nom./acc.)

Participles of Irregular Verbs

Sum has *only* a future active participle (the fourth principal part), **futūrus, -a, -um,** "about to/going to be." **possum** has *no* participles.

The present active participle of **eō** is irregular: **iēns, euntis** (stem = **eunt-**). The future passive participle of **eō** is also irregular: **eundum**. It is used in the impersonal passive construction only. MEMORIZE THESE IRREGULAR PARTICIPLES. **Eō** forms its future active participle *regularly*: **itūrus, -a, -um.**

The irregular third-conjugation verb **ferō** forms its present active participle *regularly*: **ferēns, ferentis.**

The verb **morior** has an *irregular* future active participle: **moritūrus, -a, -um.** MEMORIZE THIS IRREGULAR PARTICIPLE.

Participles of Deponent and Semideponent Verbs

The participles of deponent and semideponent verbs follow all the same rules of formation that apply to nondeponent verbs. However, deponent and semideponent verbs have the following participles:

Present active participles that are *active* in both *form* and *meaning*
Perfect passive participles that are *passive* in *form* but *active* in *meaning*
Future active participles that are *active* in both *form* and *meaning*
Future passive participles that are *passive* in both *form* and *meaning*

The following chart provides an example of the forms and basic translations of the participles of deponent verbs.

	Active	Passive
Present	patiēns "enduring"	——
Perfect	——	passus, -a, -um "having endured"
Future	passūrus, -a, -um "about to/going to endure"	patiendus, -a, -um "having to be/deserving to be endured"

§95. Synopsis VI: Indicative, Subjunctive, Participles, Infinitives, and Imperative

When one generates a synopsis that includes the participle, the participle follows the subjunctive and precedes the infinitive and imperative. Here is a model synopsis of **sentiō** in the third-person singular feminine:

Principal Parts:		**sentiō, sentīre, sēnsī, sēnsus**		
Person, Number, and Gender:		**3rd sing. f.**		
	Active	Translation	Passive	Translation
Indicative				
Present	**sentit**	she perceives	**sentītur**	she is (being) perceived
Imperfect	**sentiēbat**	she was perceiving	**sentiēbātur**	she was being perceived
Future	**sentiet**	she will perceive	**sentiētur**	she will be perceived
Perfect	**sēnsit**	1. she perceived 2. she has perceived	**sēnsa est**	1. she was perceived 2. she has been perceived
Pluperfect	**sēnserat**	she had perceived	**sēnsa erat**	she had been perceived
Future Perfect	**sēnserit**	she will have perceived	**sēnsa erit**	she will have been perceived
Subjunctive				
Present	**sentiat**		**sentiātur**	
Imperfect	**sentīret**		**sentīrētur**	
Perfect	**sēnserit**		**sēnsa sit**	
Pluperfect	**sēnsisset**		**sēnsa esset**	
Participle				
Present	**sentiēns**	perceiving	———	
Perfect	———		**sēnsus, -a, -um**	(having been) perceived
Future	**sēnsūrus, -a, -um**	about to perceive	**sentiendus, -a, -um**	having to be perceived
Infinitive				
Present	**sentīre**	to perceive	**sentīrī**	to be perceived
Imperative				
Singular	**sentī**	perceive	**sentīre**	be perceived
Plural	**sentīte**	perceive	**sentīminī**	be perceived

OBSERVATIONS

1. This synopsis reviews the indicative, subjunctive, and imperative moods, the participle, and the infinitive. When new verbal forms are introduced, the synopsis form will expand accordingly.

2. In a synopsis basic English translations should be given for indicative, participle, infinitive, and imperative forms.

3. Since participles are not *finite* forms, always give the *full nominative singular* no matter what person, number, and gender have been chosen for the indicative and subjunctive forms.

4. Imperatives appear in the second-person singular and plural only. Always give the second-person singular and plural imperative forms no matter what person, number, and gender have been chosen for the indicative and subjunctive forms.

☛ DRILL 94–95 MAY NOW BE DONE.

§96. Notes on the Participle: Relative Time; Attributive and Circumstantial Uses

The three tenses of the participle—present, perfect, future—*have no absolute time values of their own*; rather, they have only *relative time*:

> A *present* participle indicates an action that is *simultaneous* with the main verb.
> A *perfect* participle indicates an action that is *prior* to the main verb.
> A *future* participle indicates an action that is *subsequent* to the main verb.

For example:

> **Hominēs in agrīs *labōrantēs* vīdī.** (present active participle)
> The men (d.o.) in the fields *working* I saw.
> I saw the men *working* in the fields.
> **Mihi dē mīlitibus *captīs* dīcit.** (perfect passive participle)
> To me about the (having been) *captured* soldiers he speaks.
> He speaks to me about the *captured* soldiers.
> **Rēx *discessūrus* arma cēpit.** (future active participle)
> The king *about to depart* took up arms.

OBSERVATIONS

1. In the first sentence the present active participle **labōrantēs** indicates an action occurring *at the same time* as the main verb, **vīdī**.

2. In the second sentence the perfect passive participle **captīs** indicates an action that occurred *before* the main verb, **dīcit**.

3. In the third sentence the future active participle **discessūrus** indicates an action that is to occur *after* the main verb, **cēpit**.

4. Since a participle is a verbal adjective, it usually follows the noun it modifies. Often a participle is separated from its noun by several words in order to enclose a phrase that is *syntactically connected* to the participle. For example, **labōrantēs** is separated from **hominēs** to enclose the prepositional phrase **in agrīs**.

As in the sentences above, a participle may be used simply to indicate that the noun it modifies has the *attribute* or *quality* described by the participle. Such a use of the participle is called **attributive**. The basic translations supplied for the four Latin participles (_____ing, [having been] _____ed, about to _____, and having to be _____ed) are usually used for translating attributive participles. It is sometimes convenient to translate an attributive participle with a relative clause in English. For example, the last sentence above may be translated "The king *who was about to depart* took up arms." In such a translation care must be taken to show the relative time of the participle to the main verb.

A participle may also be used to describe the *circumstances* under which the action of the main clause occurs. This use of the participle is called **circumstantial**. Often the circumstances described by such a participle may be more specifically **temporal**, **causal**, **concessive**, or **conditional**. A phrase containing a circumstantial participle is often best translated into English as a subordinate clause introduced by a subordinating conjunction. For example:

> **Marcus ad forum iēns** interfectus est.
> *Marcus going to the forum* was killed.
> *While/When Marcus was going to the forum*, he was killed. (temporal)
> *Because Marcus was going to the forum*, . . . (causal)
> *Although Marcus was going to the forum*, . . . (concessive)
>
> **Marcus ad forum iēns** interficiātur.
> *Marcus going to the forum* would be killed.
> *If Marcus should go to the forum*, he would be killed. (conditional)
>
> **Caesar suōs hortātus** discessit.
> *Caesar his own (men) (d.o.) having encouraged* departed.
> *When Caesar had encouraged his own men*, he departed. (temporal)
> *After Caesar encouraged his own men*, . . . (temporal)
>
> **Rēx moritūrus** servōs līberāvit.
> *The king about to die* freed (his) slaves.
> *When the king was about to die*, he freed (his) slaves. (temporal)
> *Because the king was about to die*, . . . (causal)
> *Although the king was about to die*, . . . (concessive)
>
> **Mīles timōre carēns** nōn tamen pugnat.
> *Although the soldier is without fear*, nevertheless he is not fighting. (concessive)

OBSERVATIONS

1. A circumstantial participle may be translated using the basic translation of the participle, but often the full meaning of the participial phrase requires that it be translated as a subordinate clause. When a circumstantial participle is translated as part of a subordinate clause, the participle is translated as a *finite verb*. In such a translation care must be taken to show the relative time of the participle to the main verb.

2. A circumstantial participle with *conditional* force always functions as the *protasis* of a conditional sentence. The main verb is the verb of the *apodosis*, and it provides the only indication of what type of conditional sentence is represented. In the second sentence above, the main verb **interficiātur** (present subjunctive) indicates that the conditional sentence is a Future Less Vivid, and the participle **iēns** is translated accordingly (If . . . should go).

3. The appropriate force of a circumstantial participle (temporal, causal, concessive, or conditional) can usually be determined by *context only*. A circumstantial participle with *concessive* force may be indicated by the presence of the adverb **tamen** (nevertheless) at or near the beginning of the main clause. When **tamen** appears in the main clause, the participle is translated as part of a concessive subordinate clause beginning with the conjunction "although." A circumstantial participle with *conditional* force is often indicated by the presence of a main verb in the *subjunctive*, as in the second sentence above.

☞ DRILL 96 MAY NOW BE DONE.

§97. Ablative Absolute

A noun in the ablative case that is *accompanied by a circumstantial participle* and *unconnected in syntax* with the rest of the sentence is called an **Ablative Absolute** (< ab-**solūtus**, having been freed from). For example:

> ***Mīlitibus discēdentibus**, omnēs cīvēs ob timōrem fugiēbant.*
> *(With) the soldiers departing,* all the citizens on account of fear were fleeing.
> *When the soldiers were departing, . . .*
> *Because the soldiers were departing, . . .*
> *Although the soldiers were departing, . . .*
> ***Carmine perfectō**, Horātius ab Augustō laudātus est.*
> *(With) the poem having been completed,* Horace by Augustus was praised.
> *When the poem had been completed,* Horace was praised by Augustus.
> *Because the poem had been completed, . . .*

OBSERVATIONS

1. An Ablative Absolute functions as a subordinate clause and is part of a complex sentence. Like all participles, the participle in an Ablative Absolute shows time relative to the main verb. In translations of Ablatives Absolute care must be taken to show the relative time of the participle.

2. An Ablative Absolute is often best translated with a temporal, causal, concessive, or conditional clause.

3. The present active and the perfect passive participles appear most often in Ablatives Absolute.

4. An Ablative Absolute often appears first in a sentence, and several Ablatives Absolute may appear together. The Ablative Absolute allows for the compression of several actions or events into one complex sentence.

Sometimes two nouns (or a noun and an adjective) in the ablative case may form an Ablative Absolute. For example:

> ***Rōmulō rēge**, fēlīx erat urbs.*
> *(With) Romulus (being) king,* the city was fortunate.
> *When Romulus was king, . . .*
> ***Dīs inimīcīs**, Aenēās ad Italiam accēdere nōn poterat.*
> *(With) the gods (being) hostile,* Aeneas was not able to approach Italy.
> *Because the gods were hostile, . . .*

OBSERVATION

Since the verb **sum** lacks a present active participle, no participle appears in this type of Ablative Absolute, but the English present participle "being" is supplied as a copulative verb when translating an Ablative Absolute of this type. If the Ablative Absolute is translated as a subordinate clause, a finite form of **sum** is supplied, and care must be taken to show relative time.

☛ DRILL 97 MAY NOW BE DONE.

§98. Active and Passive Periphrastics

A finite, compound verb form that comprises a form of the *future active participle* and a form of **sum** is called an **active periphrastic** (< Greek *periphrazō*, speak around). For example:

Rōmā *discessūrī sumus.*	*We are going to depart* from Rome.
Rōmā *discessūrī erāmus.*	*We were going to depart* from Rome.
Rōmā *discessūrī erimus.*	*We shall be about to depart* from Rome.

OBSERVATIONS

1. An active periphrastic indicates a *future* or *intended* action (the future active participle) viewed from another point in time (the form of **sum**). The tense and mood of the active periphrastic are identical with the tense and mood of the form of **sum**. For example, **discessūrī sumus** is first person plural masculine *present indicative* of the active periphrastic. An active periphrastic may occur in *any* of the six tenses of the indicative or the four tenses of the subjunctive.

2. The gender and number of the subject determine the ending of the future active participle in an active periphrastic.

3. An active periphrastic is best translated *word by word,* beginning with the form of **sum**.

4. As in the compound forms of the perfect passive system, the form of **sum** may appear before or after the participle in the active periphrastic. For example, **captūrus est** and **est captūrus** are equally correct.

A finite, compound verb form that comprises a form of the *future passive participle* and a form of **sum** is called a **passive periphrastic**. For example:

Cīvēs *regendī sunt.*	The citizens *are having to be ruled.*
	The citizens *must be ruled.*
	The citizens *have to be ruled.*
Cīvēs *regendī erant.*	The citizens *were having to be ruled.*
	The citizens *had to be ruled.*
Cīvēs *regendī erunt.*	The citizens *will be having to be ruled.*
	The citizens *will have to be ruled.*

OBSERVATIONS

1. A passive periphrastic indicates an action that is viewed as *obligatory* (the future passive participle) at a certain point in time (the form of **sum**). The tense and mood of the passive periphrastic are identical with the tense and mood of the form of **sum**. For example, **regendī erant** is third person plural masculine *imperfect indicative* of the passive periphrastic. A passive periphrastic may occur in *any* of the six tenses of the indicative or the four tenses of the subjunctive.

2. The gender and number of the subject determine the ending of the future passive participle in a passive periphrastic.

3. Although passive periphrastics may be translated word by word, the alternate translations given above (must, have to, had to, will have to) are to be preferred. Note that "must" can be used *only* for the present indicative of the passive periphrastic.

4. As in the compound forms of the perfect passive system, the form of **sum** may appear before or after the participle in the passive periphrastic. For example, **capiendus est** and **est capiendus** are equally correct.

An active or passive periphrastic may appear wherever any finite verb form may be used. For example:

> **Mīles, sī hostem capiat, *laudandus sit*.**
> The soldier, if the enemy (d.o.) he should capture, *would be having to be praised*.
> If the soldier should capture the enemy, *he would have to be praised*.

§99. Dative of Agent with the Passive Periphrastic

A noun in the dative case is usually used with a passive periphrastic to express the *agent* or *person by whom* the action of the verb must be done. Such a dative is called the **Dative of Agent with the passive periphrastic.** For example:

> **Carmen *mihi* scrībendum est.**   A poem *by me* must be written.
>   A poem must be written *by me*.

The syntax of the italicized word (**mihi**) is **Dative of Agent with the passive periphrastic.**

OBSERVATIONS

1. The Dative of Agent with the passive periphrastic is regularly used *instead of* an Ablative of Personal Agent when the verb is a passive periphrastic.[4]

2. Occasionally the Ablative of Personal Agent may be used with the passive periphrastic for the sake of clarity. For example:

> **Carmen tibi ā mē scrībendum est.**   A poem must be written for you *by me*.

In this sentence the Ablative of Personal Agent (**ā mē**) is used to avoid the confusion that might arise if there were two datives in the same sentence.

☞ DRILL 98–99 MAY NOW BE DONE.

§100. Genitive of Description

When a noun in the genitive case *modified by an adjective* is used to *describe* another noun, it is called the **Genitive of Description.** For example:

> **Rōmulus, vir magnae *dīligentiae*, multa perfēcit.**
> Romulus, a man of great *diligence*, accomplished many things.

The syntax of the italicized word (**dīligentiae**) is **Genitive of Description.**

---

4. The Dative of Agent may be derived from the Dative of the Possessor. Thus, **Carmen mihi scrībendum est** may be understood to mean "I have a poem having to be written." Therefore, "A poem must be written *by me*."

§101. Ablative of Description

When a noun in the ablative case *modified by an adjective* is used to *describe* another noun, it is called the **Ablative of Description**. For example:

> **Sōlus cum multīs hostibus pugnābat. Erat enim magnā *virtūte*.**
> He alone with many enemies was fighting. For he was of (with) great *courage*.
> He alone was fighting with many enemies. For he was of great *courage*.

The syntax of the italicized word (**virtūte**) is **Ablative of Description**.

OBSERVATION

Like Latin, English attaches some descriptions with "of" and some with "with." Compare, for example, the phrases "men of great courage" and "men with blue eyes." English and Latin usages do not always coincide; therefore, idiomatic English may require "of" (rather than with) in the translation of an Ablative of Description.

The noun-adjective phrases that make up Genitives or Ablatives of Description function *adjectivally* in that they *define* or *limit* another noun. The Genitive of Description is thus an extension of the basic function of the genitive case. The Ablative of Description derives from that case's associative function since an Ablative of Description is an *accompanying* feature of the noun it describes. Although some kinds of descriptions are limited to the genitive (size, number) and some to the ablative (qualities of the body), in many expressions the Genitive and Ablative of Description appear to have converged in use and meaning during the classical period.

§102. Ablative of Origin

When the ablative case, with or without the preposition **ē/ex** or **dē**, reports *parentage* or *ancestry*, it is called the **Ablative of Origin**. For example:

> **Aenēās (ē) deā nātus est.**   Aeneas *from a goddess* was born.
> (**nāscor, nāscī, nātus sum** be born)   Aeneas was born *from a goddess*.

The syntax of the italicized word (**deā**) is **Ablative of Origin**. The Ablative of Origin is a particular variety of the Ablative of Separation (see §54).

☛ DRILL 99–102 MAY NOW BE DONE.

Short Readings

1. A proverbial utterance

   dictum sapientī sat est. (PLAUTUS, *PERSA* 729; TERENCE, *PHORMIŌ* 541)

   sapiēns, sapientis sensible, wise

2. An exchange of pleasantries between two characters

   Callicles. Ehō tū, tua uxor, quid* agit? *Megaronides.* Immortālis est:

   vīvit victūraque est. (PLAUTUS, *TRINUMMUS* 55–56)

   ***quid**, *here*, how
   ehō (interj.) *used to attract attention*, hey
   immortālis, immortāle immortal
   uxor, uxōris *f.* wife

3. A fragment from Ennius cited by Cicero for its brevity and truth

   mōribus antīquīs rēs stat Rōmāna virīsque. (ENNIUS, *ANNĀLĒS* V.156)

4. An alliterative line from Ennius

   ōrātor sine pāce redit rēgīque refert rem. (ENNIUS, *ANNĀLĒS* VI.202)

5. The speaker of the prologue of the play generalizes about originality.

   nūllumst iam dictum quod nōn sit dictum prius. (TERENCE, *EUNUCHUS* 41)

   prius (adv.) earlier, before

6. A fragment from the comic poet Lucilius about the relation between work and reward

   hunc labōrem sūmās laudem quī tibi ac frūctum ferat. (LUCILIUS, *SATURAE* FRAG. 620)

   frūctus, frūctūs *m.* profit, benefit, advantage
   laus, laudis *f.* praise
   sūmō, sūmere, sūmpsī, sūmptus take up, seize; take on

7. The character Thyestes speaks in a fragment of a Greek tragedy.

   vigilandum est semper; multae īnsidiae sunt bonīs. (ACCIUS, *TRAGOEDIAE* FRAG. 214)

   vigilō (1-intr.) stay awake; be watchful, remain vigilant

8. In arguing that Pompey be given special command in the East, Cicero makes a transition to the next part of his argument.

   quoniam dē genere bellī dīxī, nunc dē magnitūdine pauca dīcam. (CICERO, *PRŌ LĒGE*

   MANILIĀ 20)

   magnitūdō, magnitūdinis *f.* size, magnitude

9. Cicero asks Catiline a rhetorical question.

> quid est enim, Catilīna, quod tē iam in hāc urbe dēlectāre possit, in quā nēmō est,
>
> extrā istam coniūrātiōnem perditōrum hominum, quī tē nōn metuat, nēmō quī nōn
>
> ōderit? (CICERO, *IN CATILĪNAM I* 13)

coniūrātiō, coniūrātiōnis *f.* conspiracy
dēlectō (1-tr.) delight, please, charm
extrā (prep. + acc.) outside
metuō, metuere, metuī, —— fear, dread
perditus, -a, -um lost, desperate, degenerate

10. Cicero addresses Catiline directly.

> ēgredere ex urbe, Catilīna. lībera rem pūblicam metū; in exsilium, sī hanc vōcem
>
> exspectās, proficīscere. (CICERO, *IN CATILĪNAM I* 20)

ēgredior, ēgredī, ēgressus sum go out, depart
ex(s)pectō (1-tr.) wait for, await, expect

11. Cicero begins the conclusion of the defense of his client Caelius.

> cōnservāte igitur reī pūblicae, iūdicēs, cīvem bonārum artium, bonārum partium,
>
> bonōrum virōrum. (CICERO, *PRŌ CAELIŌ* 77)

cōnservō (con- + servō) (1-tr.) keep from danger, save, preserve
igitur (postpositive conj.) therefore
iūdex, iūdicis *m.* juror, judge

12. Cicero reflects on a difference between the state and mankind.

> itaque nūllus interitus est reī pūblicae nātūrālis ut hominis, in quō mors nōn
>
> modo* necessāria est, vērum etiam optanda persaepe. (CICERO, *DĒ RĒ PŪBLICĀ*
>
> III.34, FRAG. 2)

*nōn modo = nōn sōlum
interitus, interitūs *m.* death, demise
itaque (conj.) and so, accordingly

nātūrālis, nātūrāle natural
necessārius, -a, -um necessary
persaepe (adv.) very often

13. A definition of law

> lēx est ratiō summa īnsita in nātūrā, quae iubet ea quae facienda sunt, prohibetque
>
> contrāria. (CICERO, *DĒ LĒGIBUS* I.18)

contrārius, -a, -um opposite, contrary
īnsitus, -a, -um inborn
prohibeō (prō- + habeō), prohibēre, prohibuī, prohibitus prevent; prohibit, forbid
ratiō, ratiōnis *f.* account, reason; rationale
summus, -a, -um highest

14. Cicero comments on the fate of the venerable Cato in the contemporary world.

Catōnem vērō quis nostrōrum ōratōrum, quī quidem nunc sunt, legit? aut quis

nōvit omnīnō? at quem virum,* dī bonī! mittō† cīvem aut senātōrem aut im-

perātōrem: ōrātōrem enim hōc locō quaerimus.‡ (Cicero, *Brūtus* 65)

*quem virum, *Accusative of Exclamation,* what   at (conj.) but
   a man!   imperātor, imperātōris *m.* commander, general
†mittō, *here,* send away, dismiss   senātor, senātōris *m.* senator
‡quaerō, *here,* inquire into, examine, consider

15. While pleading in court before Caesar on behalf of a Roman ally, Cicero praises Caesar for
   his temperate behavior in the wake of his victory over Pompey.

quae semper in cīvīlī victōriā sēnsimus, ea tē victōre nōn vīdimus. sōlus, inquam,

es, C. Caesar, cuius in victōriā ceciderit nēmō nisi armātus. (Cicero, *Prō Rēge*

Dēiotarō 32)

armātus, armātī *m.* armed man, soldier
cīvīlis, cīvīle of *or* connected with citizens, civil; resulting from civil war
inquam (defective verb) say; **inquam** = *1st sing. pres. act. indic.*
victor, victōris *m.* conqueror, victor
victōria, victōriae *f.* victory

16. Laelius describes a great friendship with Scipio.

equidem ex omnibus rēbus, quās mihi aut fortūna aut nātūra tribuit, nihil habeō,

quod cum amīcitiā Scīpiōnis possim comparāre. (Cicero, *Dē Amīcitiā* 103)

comparō (1-tr.) prepare, get together; compare
Scīpiō, Scīpiōnis *m.* (P.) Scipio (Africanus Aemilianus) (consul 147, 134)
tribuō, tribuere, tribuī, tribūtus grant, bestow, assign

17. Cicero expresses his opinion on the only legitimate purpose for war.

quārē suscipienda quidem bella sunt ob eam causam, ut sine iniūriā in pāce

vīvātur. (Cicero, *Dē Officiīs* I.35)

iniūria, iniūriae *f.* injustice, injury
suscipiō (sub- + capiō) undertake, venture upon

18. Cicero notes that only one group of Romans was captured at the Battle of Cannae.

octō hominum millia tenēbat Hannibal, nōn quōs in aciē cēpisset, aut quī perīculō

mortis diffūgissent, sed quī relictī* in castrīs fuissent* ā Paulō et ā Varrōne

cōnsulibus. (Cicero, *Dē Officiīs* III.114)

*relictī . . . fuissent = relictī . . . essent   millia = mīlia
castra, castrōrum *n. pl.* (military) encampment,   Paulus, Paulī *m.* (L. Aemilius) Paulus (consul
   camp   216), leader at the battle of Cannae
diffugiō (dis- + fugiō) run away, flee in several   Varrō, Varrōnis *m.* (C. Terentius) Varro (consul
   directions, scatter   216), leader at the battle of Cannae

19. Cicero compares Marc Antony to Rome's ancient enemy Hannibal.

> oppugnat* D. Brūtum, imperātōrem, cōnsulem dēsignātum, cīvem nōn sibi, sed nōbīs et reī pūblicae nātum. ergō Hannibal hostis, cīvis Antōnius? quid ille fēcit hostīliter quod hic nōn aut fēcerit aut faciat aut mōliātur et cōgitet?

(CICERO, *PHILIPPICS V* 24–25)

*oppugnat, subject is Antony
D. Brūtus, D. Brūtī *m.* D. Brutus, brother of M. Brutus
dēsignātus, -a, -um elect, appointed (but not yet installed)

ergō (adv.) therefore
hostīliter (adv.) in the manner of an enemy
imperātor, imperātōris *m.* commander, general
mōlior, mōlīrī, mōlītus sum strive to bring about, plan

20. In May 49 B.C.E., after the outbreak of the civil war, Cicero writes despairingly to his friend Ser. Sulpicius Rufus about the state of Rome.

> vidēs . . . urbem sine lēgibus, sine iūdiciīs, sine iūre, sine fidē relictam dīreptiōnī et incendiīs. itaque mihi venīre in mentem nihil potest nōn modo quod spērem sed vix iam quod audeam optāre. (CICERO, *AD FAMILIĀRĒS* IV.1.2)

dīreptiō, dīreptiōnis *f.* plundering, pillage
incendium, incendiī *n.* fire
itaque (conj.) and so, accordingly
iūdicium, iūdiciī *n.* judgment, opinion; trial

nōn modo = nōn sōlum
spērō (1-tr.) hope (for)
vix (adv.) scarcely, hardly

21. Cicero begins a letter to his friend Atticus in an inauspicious fashion.

> erat autem nihil novī quod aut scrīberem aut ex tē quaererem.

(CICERO, *AD ATTICUM* XV.1.1)

22. In a letter written in early 54 B.C.E. Cicero comments on the quality of Lucretius's poetry.

> Lucrētī poēmata, ut scrībis, ita sunt, multīs lūminibus ingenī, multae tamen artis.

(CICERO, *AD QUINTUM FRĀTREM* II.10.3)

Lucrētius, Lucrētiī *m.* Lucretius (94?–55? B.C.E.), author of the poem *Dē Rērum Nātūrā*
lūmen, lūminis *n.* light; illumination; ray of light
poēma, poēmatis *n.* poem; *in pl.,* poetry

23. Caesar describes what the Romans did after the Germans' formation repelled their assault.

> repertī sunt complūrēs nostrī quī in phalangem īnsilīrent et scūta manibus re- vellerent et dēsuper vulnerārent. (CAESAR, *DĒ BELLŌ GALLICŌ* I.52)

complūrēs, complūra or complūria several, very many
dēsuper (adv.) from above
īnsiliō, īnsilīre, īnsiluī, —— jump (on), leap (on)
phalanx, phalangis *f.* phalanx, a close formation of troops

reperiō, reperīre, repperī, repertus find, discover
revellō, revellere, revellī, revulsus tear, tear away
scūtum, scūtī *n.* shield
vulnerō (1-tr.) wound

24. The deaths of brave centurions change the course of an apparently hopeless battle.

    mīlitum pars hōrum* virtūte submōtīs hostibus praeter spem incolumis in castra

    pervēnit, pars ā barbarīs circumventa periit. (Caesar, *Dē Bellō Gallicō* VI.40)

*hōrum refers to the dead centurions.
barbarus, barbarī *m.* foreigner; barbarian
castra, castrōrum *n. pl.* (military) encampment,
  camp
circumveniō (circum- + veniō) surround
incolumis, incolume unharmed, safe

pereō (per- + eō), perīre, periī, peritūrus pass
  away, be destroyed; perish, die
perveniō (per- + veniō) come through, arrive
praeter (prep. + acc.) beyond
submoveō (sub- + moveō) move from an
  occupied position, drive off

25. Caesar describes his disposition of troops.

    C. Fabium lēgātum cum legiōnibus duābus castrīs praesidiō relinquit.*

    (Caesar, *Dē Bellō Gallicō* VII.40)

*relinquit, subject is Caesar
castra, castrōrum *n. pl.* (military) encampment, camp
C. Fabius, C. Fabiī *m.* C. Fabius
legiō, legiōnis *f.* legion
praesidium, praesidiī *n.* guard, garrison

26. In his monograph on the conspiracy of Catiline, the historian introduces Catiline.

    L. Catilīna, nōbilī genere nātus, fuit magnā vī et animī et corporis, sed ingeniō

    malō prāvōque. (Sallust, *Bellum Catilīnae* 5)

nōbilis, nōbile noble
prāvus, -a, -um twisted, corrupt, perverse

27. The historian describes the reaction to Cato's speech advocating harsh punishment of the
    Catilinarian conspirators.

    postquam Catō adsēdit, cōnsulāres omnēs itemque senātūs magna pars senten-

    tiam eius laudant, virtūtem animī ad caelum ferunt, aliī aliōs increpantēs timidōs

    vocant. Catō clārus atque magnus habētur. (Sallust, *Bellum Catilīnae* 53)

adsīdō, adsīdere, adsēdī, —— sit down, take one's seat
cōnsulāris, cōnsulāris, -ium *m.* ex-consul
increpō, increpāre, increpuī, increpitus make a noise, roar; reproach, upbraid
item (adv.) similarly, in turn, likewise
timidus, -a, -um fearful, cowardly

28. A Roman proverb

    Amōrī fīnem tempus, nōn animus facit. (Publilius Syrus, *Sententiae* A42)

29. The severed head of Orpheus still calls for his wife in the underworld.

> . . . Eurydicēn vōx ipsa et frīgida lingua
>
> ā miseram Eurydicēn! animā fugiente vocābat;
>
> Eurydicēn tōtō referēbant flūmine rīpae. (VERGIL, *GEORGICS* IV.525–27)

ā (interj.) ah!
Eurydicē, Eurydicēs *f.* Eurydice, wife of Orpheus;
   Eurydicēn = *acc. sing.*
flūmen, flūminis *n.* river, stream

frīgidus, -a, -um cold, icy
lingua, linguae *f.* tongue
rīpa, rīpae *f.* (river) bank

30. As Troy falls, the ghost of Hector speaks to Aeneas in a dream.

> "heu, fuge, nāte deā, tēque hīs," ait, "ēripe flammīs." (VERGIL, *AENEID* II.289)

aiō (defective verb) say; **ait** = *3rd sing. pres. act. indic.*
ēripiō, ēripere, ēripuī, ēreptus tear away, snatch away
flamma, flammae *f.* flame

31. As the battle turns, Turnus encourages himself.

> audentīs Fortūna iuvat. . . . (VERGIL, *AENEID* X.284)

iuvō, iuvāre, iūvī, iūtus help, assist, aid

32. The poet comments on Turnus's exultation in victory.

> nescia mēns hominum fātī sortisque futūrae
>
> et servāre modum rēbus sublāta secundīs! (VERGIL, *AENEID* X.501–2)

nescius, -a, -um not knowing, unaware (+ gen.); not knowing how (+inf.)
secundus, -a, -um favorable
sors, sortis, -ium *f.* lot, portion; destiny
tollō, tollere, sustulī, sublātus lift, raise; take away, carry off

33. Aeneas addresses his son Ascanius.

> disce, puer, virtūtem ex mē vērumque labōrem,
>
> fortūnam ex aliīs. . . . (VERGIL, *AENEID* XII.435–36)

discō, discere, didicī, —— learn

34. The poet addresses his patron Maecenas.

> . . . magnum hoc ego dūcō,
>
> quod* placuī tibi, quī turpī sēcernis honestum
>
> nōn patre praeclārō, sed vītā et pectore pūrō. (HORACE, *SERMŌNĒS* I.6.62–64)

***quod,** *here* (conj.) the fact that
praeclārus, -a, -um very famous
pūrus, -a, -um pure
sēcernō, sēcernere, sēcrēvī, sēcrētus separate, distinguish
turpis, turpe foul, ugly; base, shameful

35. The poet warns the would-be writer.

> tū nihil invītā dīcēs faciēsve Minervā. (Horace, *Ars Poētica* 385)

invītus, -a, -um unwilling
-ve (enclitic conj.) or

36. The poet comments on the nature of love.

> errat quī fīnem vēsānī quaerit amōris:
>
> > vērus amor nūllum nōvit* habēre modum. (Propertius II.15.29–30)

***nōvit**, *here,* knows how (+ inf.)
vēsānus, -a, -um frenzied, mad, insane

37. The poet summarizes his view of one part of human nature.

> singula nē referam, nīl nōn mortāle tenēmus
>
> > pectoris exceptīs ingeniīque bonīs. (Ovid, *Trīstia* III.7.43–44)

excipiō (ex- + capiō) take out; exclude
mortālis, mortāle mortal
singulī, -ae, -a individual, single, one at a time

38. The historian describes the distribution of responsibilities by the senate after an embassy to the Latin tribe of the Aequi fails.

> Rōmam ut rediēre lēgātī, senātus iussit alterum cōnsulem contrā Gracchum in Al-
>
> gidum exercitum dūcere, alterī populātiōnem fīnium Aequōrum prōvinciam*
>
> dedit. (Livy, *Ab Urbe Conditā* III.25.9)

***prōvincia,** *here,* special assignment *or* task
Aequī, Aequōrum *m. pl.* (the) Aequi, an ancient people of Latium
Algidus, Algidī *m.* Algidus, a mountain in Latium
Gracchus, Gracchī *m.* Gracchus
populātiō, populātiōnis *f.* plundering

39. The historian summarizes the situation on the Roman side after the disastrous defeat at Cannae.

> ad Cannās fugientem cōnsulem vix quīnquāgintā secūtī sunt, alterīus morientis
>
> prope tōtus exercitus fuit. (Livy, *Ab Urbe Conditā* XXII.50.3)

Cannae, Cannārum *f. pl.* Cannae, a village in southeast Italy, site of Hannibal's greatest victory
prope (adv.) nearly, almost
vix (adv.) scarcely, hardly

40. The historian's pithy description of Sulla

    . . . cōnsulātum iniērunt Q. Pompeius et L. Cornēlius Sulla, vir quī neque ad*

    fīnem victōriae satis laudārī neque post victōriam abundē vituperārī potest.

    (VELLEIUS PATERCULUS, *HISTORIA RŌMĀNA* II.17)

***ad**, *here,* up to, until
abundē (adv.) amply, fully
ineō (**in-** + **eō**), **inīre, iniī** or **inīvī, initus** enter
victōria, victōriae *f.* victory
vituperō (1-tr.) find fault with, criticize

41. The poet raises the question of how to judge whether Pompey or Caesar more justly went
to war.

    victrīx causa deīs placuit, sed victa Catōnī. (LUCAN, *BELLUM CĪVĪLE* I.128)

deīs = dīs
victrīx, victrīcis victorious

42. The poet offers a comment on loyalty.

    . . . stat nūlla diū mortālibus usquam,

    Fortūnā titubante, fidēs. . . . (SILIUS ITALICUS, *PŪNICA* XI.3–4)

diū (adv.) for a long time
mortālis, mortāle mortal
titubō (1-intr.) totter, stagger, falter
usquam (adv.) anywhere

43. The historian offers an explanation of the emperor Domitian's hatred of the general
Agricola.

    proprium hūmānī ingeniī est ōdisse quem laeseris. (TACITUS, *DĒ VĪTĀ AGRICOLAE* 42)

hūmānus, -a, -um human
laedō, laedere, laesī, laesus injure, harm
proprius, -a, -um one's own; peculiar (to), characteristic (of) (+ gen.)

44. The biographer reports what participants in a mock sea battle said to Claudius before
commencing.

    havē imperātor, moritūrī tē salūtant! (SUETONIUS, *VĪTA CLAUDIĪ* 21)

havē greetings! hail!
imperātor, imperātōris *m.* commander, general
salūtō (1-tr.) greet, hail, salute

Longer Readings

1. Plautus, *Mīles Glōriōsus* 33–35

    In an aside to the audience the parasite Artotrogus explains why he is forced to cater to the ego of Pyrgopolynices, no matter how distasteful.

    Artotrogus. venter creat omnīs hāsce aerumnās: auribus

    peraudienda sunt* nē dentēs dentiant,

    et adsentandumst quidquid hic mentībitur.

    ---

    * **peraudienda sunt**, subject is the boasts of
      Pyrgopolynices
    adsentor (1-intr.) agree, assent
    aerumna, aerumnae *f.* task, trouble, affliction
    auris, auris, -ium *f.* ear
    creō (1-tr.) create, conceive
    dēns, dentis, -ium *m.* tooth
    dentiō, dentīre, ——, —— cut teeth; grow longer

    hāsce = intensive form of **hās**
    mentior, mentīrī, mentītus sum lie, state falsely;
      mentībitur = *3rd sing. fut. act. indic.*
    peraudiō (per- + **audiō**) listen to (to the end)
    quidquid = *neut. sing. acc. of indef. rel. pron.,*
      whatever
    venter, ventris *m.* belly, stomach

    Tītus Maccius Plautus (ca. 255–184 B.C.E.) was born in north-central Italy. He is the most well-known and successful of Roman comic writers, and twenty of his plays survive. Plautus is renowned for his explosive comic sensibility and verbal creativity, and his plays are an important source of information about living, spoken Latin. Ellipsis, parataxis, colloquialisms, and unusual syntax and word choice abound in Plautus's plays, which are for the most part romantic comedies inhabited by stock characters.

    The *Mīles Glōriōsus* (Braggart Soldier) is considered one of Plautus's finest comedies. Its plot centers on a clever slave (Palaestrio) helping his young master secure the girl of his dreams, but the play also features a host of other memorable characters, including the swaggering, self-important, lying soldier, Pyrgopolynices (Great Tower-Taker), and a clever sycophant, Artotrogus (Bread-Eater).

2. Plautus, *Mīles Glōriōsus* 42–46

    Artotrogus has brought out a make-believe record book of Pyrgopolynices' make-believe victories. Pyrgopolynices asks to be reminded of his military greatness.

    Pyrgopolynices. ecquid meministī? *Artotrogus.* meminī centum in Ciliciā

    et quīnquāgintā, centum in Scytholatrōniā,

    trīgintā Sardōs, sexāgintā Macedones—

    sunt hominēs quōs tū occīdistī ūnō diē.   45

    Pyrgo. Quanta istaec hominum summast? *Arto.* septem mīlia.

    Cilicia, Ciliciae *f.* Cilicia, a country in eastern
      Asia Minor
    ecquid = *neut. sing. acc. of indef. pron.,* anything
    istaec = archaic form of **ista**
    Macedones, Macedonum *m. pl.* Macedonians
    occīdō, occīdere, occīdī, occīsus kill, slaughter

    quantus, -a, -um how much, how great
    Sardī, Sardōrum *m. pl.* Sardinians
    ***Scytholatrōnia,** ***Scytholatrōniae** *f.* Scythian-
      Thief-Land
    summa, summae *f.* sum, total

3. Ennius, *Annālēs* VIII.248–51

The poet describes what happens when news of battle is proclaimed.

pellitur ē mediō sapientia, vī geritur rēs;

spernitur ōrātor bonus, horridus mīles amātur;

haud doctīs dictīs certantēs, sed maledictīs

miscent inter sēsē inimīcitiās agitantēs.

agitō (1-tr.) stir up, set in motion
certō (1-intr.) struggle, contend, strive
doctus, -a, -um learned, erudite
haud (adv.) not at all, by no means
horridus, -a, -um rough, wild; horrible

maledictum, maledictī *n.* insult, taunt
misceō, miscēre, miscuī, mixtus mix, stir up, produce
spernō, spernere, sprēvī, sprētus scorn, reject

4. Cicero, *In Catilīnam II* 1

The opening of Cicero's second speech against Catiline

Tandem aliquandō, Quirītēs, L. Catilīnam, furentem audāciā, scelus anhelantem, pestem patriae nefāriē mōlientem, vōbīs atque huic urbī ferrō flammāque minitantem ex urbe vel ēiēcimus vel ēmīsimus vel ipsum ēgredientem verbīs prōsecūtī sumus. abiit, excessit, ēvāsit, ērūpit. nūlla iam perniciēs ā mōnstrō illō atque prōdigiō moenibus ipsīs intrā moenia comparābitur. atque hunc quidem ūnum huius bellī domesticī ducem sine contrōversiā vīcimus. nōn enim iam inter latera nostra sīca illa versābitur, nōn in campō, nōn in forō, nōn in cūriā, nōn dēnique intrā domesticōs parietēs pertimēscēmus. locō ille mōtus est, cum* est ex urbe dēpulsus. palam iam cum hoste, nūllō impediente, bellum iūstum gerēmus. sine dubiō perdidimus hominem magnificēque vīcimus, cum* illum ex occultīs īnsidiīs in apertum latrōcinium coniēcimus.

*cum, *here* (conj.) when
aliquandō (adv.) sometimes, occasionally; at (long) last (often coupled with tandem to express finality)
anhelō (1-tr.) breathe out
apertus, -a, -um open
audācia, audāciae *f.* boldness; recklessness
campus, campī *m.* plain; *here, sc.* Martius, plain of Mars
comparō (1-tr.) prepare, get together; devise
coniciō, conicere, coniēcī, coniectus throw (together), cast, bring
contrōversia, contrōversiae *f.* dispute, controversy
cūria, cūriae *f.* (the) Curia, (the) senate house
dēnique (adv.) finally, at last
dēpellō (dē- + pellō), dēpellere, dēpulī, dēpulsus drive away
domesticus, -a, -um *of or* belonging to the house; personal, domestic
dubium, dubiī *n.* doubt
ēgredior, ēgredī, ēgressus sum go out, depart
ēiciō, ēicere, ēiēcī, ēiectus throw out
ēmittō (ē- + mittō) send out
ērumpō, ērumpere, ērūpī, ēruptus break out, burst forth
ēvādō, ēvādere, ēvāsī, ēvāsus go out, escape
excēdō (ex- + cēdō) go out, depart
flamma, flammae *f.* flame

furō, furere, ——, —— be crazy; rage, rave
impediō, impedīre, impedīvī or impediī, impedītus obstruct, hinder, impede
intrā (prep. + acc.) within
iūstus, -a, -um just, fair, right
latrōcinium, latrōciniī *n.* robbery; criminality
latus, lateris *n.* side, flank
magnificē (adv.) splendidly, excellently
minitor (1-intr.) threaten (+ dat.)
mōlior, mōlīrī, mōlītus sum plan
mōnstrum, mōnstrī *n.* omen, portent; monster
nefāriē (adv.) unspeakably, wickedly
occultus, -a, -um hidden, secret
palam (adv.) openly, publicly
pariēs, parietis *m.* wall (of a house)
perdō (per- + dō) lose; destroy
perniciēs, perniciēī *f.* destruction, ruin, disaster
pertimēscō, pertimēscere, pertimuī, —— become very afraid, take fright
pestis, pestis, -ium *f.* plague, destruction, ruin
prōdigium, prōdigiī *n.* unnatural event, prodigy; creature, monstrosity
prōsequor (prō- + sequor) accompany, escort
Quirītēs, Quirītium *m. pl.* Quirites, the name for Roman citizens in their public capacity
scelus, sceleris *n.* wicked deed, crime; villainy
sīca, sīcae *f.* dagger
vel (conj.) or; vel . . . vel . . . either . . . or . . .
versō (1-tr.) twist

The *Ōrātiō Secunda in Catilīnam* was delivered on 9 November 63 B.C.E., one day after the first speech and immediately after Catiline's departure from the city. This second speech was delivered before the people.

5. Cicero, *Dē Lēgibus* III.1

An exchange between Marcus (Tullius Cicero) and Atticus at the beginning of the third book of Cicero's *Dē Lēgibus*, in which he will discuss the magistrates.

Marcus. Sequar igitur, ut īnstituī, dīvīnum illum virum . . .

Atticus. Platōnem vidēlicet dīcis.

M. Istum ipsum, Attice.

A. Tū vērō eum nec nimis valdē umquam nec nimis saepe laudāveris; nam hoc mihi etiam nostrī illī, quī nēminem nisi suum laudārī volunt, concēdunt . . .

M. Bene hercle faciunt.

Atticus, Atticī *m.* (T. Pomponius) Atticus, friend of Cicero
concēdō (con- + cēdō) (tr.) concede, grant
igitur (postpositive conj.) therefore
īnstituō, īnstituere, īnstituī, īnstitūtus set up, establish; set to work (on), start

nimis (adv.) too
Platō, Platōnis *m.* Plato
vidēlicet (adv.) plainly, of course
volō, velle, voluī, —— be willing, want, wish;
    volunt = *3rd pl. pres. act. indic.*

The *Dē Lēgibus* may not have been published in Cicero's lifetime. Written in the last years of Cicero's life, the *Dē Lēgibus* is a philosophical dialogue between Cicero, his brother Quintus, and his friend Atticus. Only three books of the *Dē Lēgibus* have survived (with fragments of two others). The dialogue is inspired by Plato's dialogues (in particular the *Phaedrus* and the *Laws*), and the topics discussed are the nature of law and the best regime.

6. Cicero, *Paradoxa Stōicōrum* 5.36

A passage from Cicero's description of the truly free man

an ille mihi līber, cui mulier imperat, cui lēgēs impōnit, praescrībit, iubet, vetat quod vidētur?* quī nihil imperantī negāre potest, nihil recūsāre audet? poscit, dandum est; vocat, veniendum est; ēicit, abeundum; minātur, extimēscendum.

***vidētur,** *here,* seems best
an (conj.) *introduces an indignant or surprised question expecting a negative answer,* can it really be that
ēiciō, ēicere, ēiēcī, ēiectus throw out
extimēscō, extimēscere, extimuī, —— take fright, be scared
impōnō (in- + pōnō) place, impose (acc.) upon (dat.)

minor (1-intr.) threaten
mulier, mulieris *f.* woman
negō (1-tr.) deny, refuse
poscō, poscere, poposcī, —— demand
praescrībō (prae- + scrībō) prescribe
recūsō (1-tr.) refuse, reject, oppose
vetō, vetāre, vetuī, vetitus forbid

7. Cicero, *Tusculānae Disputātiōnēs* II.65

   A reflection on the causes of human responses to perilous situations

   saepe enim multī quī aut propter victōriae cupiditātem aut propter glōriae aut etiam
   ut iūs suum et lībertātem tenērent volnera excēpērunt fortiter et tulērunt, īdem
   omissā contentiōne dolōrem morbī ferre nōn possunt; neque enim illum, quem
   facile tulerant, ratiōne aut sapientiā tulerant, sed studiō potius et glōriā.

   contentiō, contentiōnis *f.* tension; effort; rivalry,
     competition
   cupiditās, cupiditātis *f.* desire
   dolor, dolōris *m.* grief, sorrow, pain
   excipiō (ex- + capiō) take out; receive, absorb,
     sustain

   morbus, morbī *m.* disease, illness
   omittō (ob- + mittō) discontinue, leave off
   potius (adv.) rather
   ratiō, ratiōnis *f.* account, reason; reasoning
   victōria, victōriae *f.* victory
   volnus (= vulnus), volneris *n.* wound

8. Cicero, *Dē Nātūrā Deōrum* II.140

   In speaking of the wonders of the human body and nature's miraculous contribution to it,
   the character Balbus, recalling Aristotle, attributes to a god one particular human attribute
   and tells how it sets humans apart from other animals.

   quī* prīmum† eōs humō excitātōs celsōs et ērectōs cōnstituit, ut deōrum cogni-
   tiōnem caelum intuentēs capere possent. sunt enim ex terrā hominēs nōn ut incolae
   atque habitātōrēs sed quasi spectātōrēs superārum rērum atque caelestium, quārum
   spectāculum ad nūllum aliud genus animantium pertinet.

   ***quī**, *connecting relative whose antecedent is an un-*
     specified god or divine force
   †**prīmum**, *here* (adv.) first; for the first time
   animāns, animantis, -ium *m.* or *f.* or *n.* living
     creature
   caelestis, caeleste heavenly, divine
   celsus, -a, -um lofty, tall; upright, erect
   cognitiō, cognitiōnis *f.* acquaintance, knowledge
   cōnstituō, cōnstituere, cōnstituī, cōnstitūtus set
     up, establish
   ērēctus, -a, -um upright, erect

   excitō (1-tr.) cause to move, stir up; raise
   habitātor, habitātōris *m.* inhabitant, occupier
   humus, humī *f.* earth, ground
   intueor, intuērī, intuitus sum look upon, gaze at;
     reflect upon, consider
   pertineō (per- + teneō), pertinēre, pertinuī, per-
     tentus extend, pertain
   quasi (adv.) as (if), as (it were)
   spectāculum, spectāculī *n.* sight, spectacle
   spectātor, spectātōris *m.* witness, spectator
   superus, -a, -um upper, above

   The *Dē Nātūrā Deōrum* is a philosophical work in three books. Each book discusses the approach to divine things of
   a different school of philosophy: Epicurean, Stoic, and Academic.

9. Cicero, *Dē Senectūte* 37

Cicero describes App. Claudius Caecus—consul, censor, builder of the Via Appia—near the end of his life.

quattuor rōbustōs fīliōs, quīnque fīliās, tantam domum, tantās clientēlās Appius regēbat et caecus et senex; intentum enim animum tamquam arcum habēbat nec languēscēns succumbēbat senectūtī; tenēbat nōn modo* auctōritātem, sed etiam imperium in† suōs, metuēbant servī, verēbantur līberī, cārum omnēs habēbant; vigēbat in illā domō mōs patrius, disciplīna.

*nōn modo = nōn sōlum
†in, *here,* over
arcus, arcūs *m.* bow (for shooting arrows)
auctōritās, auctōritātis *f.* authority, influence, prestige
clientēla, clientēlae *f.* client's relation to patron; *in pl.,* clients, dependents (individuals, cities, or provinces)
disciplīna, disciplīnae *f.* training; orderly conduct
intentus, -a, -um stretched; attentive, intent
languēscō, languēscere, languī, —— grow feeble, decline
metuō, metuere, metuī, —— fear, dread

patrius, -a, -um of *or* belonging to a father, paternal; ancestral
rōbustus, -a, -um (physically) strong; mature
senectūs, senectūtis *f.* old age
senex, senis old
succumbō, succumbere, succubuī, succubitum give in, yield (+ dat.)
tamquam (conj.) as it were, as if
tantus, -a, -um so great
vereor, verērī, veritus sum respect, be in awe of, dread
vigeō, vigēre, viguī, —— be vigorous, thrive, flourish

10. Lucretius, *Dē Rērum Nātūrā* I.1–9

The poet begins his poem with an address to Venus.

> Aeneadum genetrīx, hominum dīvomque* voluptās,
> alma Venus, caelī subter lābentia signa
> quae mare nāvigerum, quae terrās frūgiferentīs
> concelebrās, per tē quoniam genus omne animantum
> concipitur vīsitque exortum lūmina sōlis: 5
> tē, dea, tē fugiunt ventī, tē nūbila caelī
> adventumque tuum, tibi suāvīs daedala tellūs
> summittit flōrēs, tibi rīdent aequora pontī
> plācātumque nitet diffūsō lūmine caelum.

*dīvom = dīvum = dīvōrum
adventus, adventūs *m.* arrival
Aeneadēs, Aeneadum *m. pl.* descendants of Aeneas; descendants of Aeneas's companions; Romans
aequor, aequoris *n.* level surface; sea, water
almus, -a, -um nourishing; gracious, kindly
animāns, animantis, -ium *m.* or *f.* or *n.* living creature; **animantum = animantium**
concelebrō (1-tr.) visit frequently; fill
concipiō (**con-** + **capiō**) conceive, produce
daedalus, -a, -um skillful, dexterous, artful
diffundō, diffundere, diffūdī, diffūsus spread widely, extend, diffuse
exorior, exorīrī, exortus sum rise out, emerge, appear
flōs, flōris *m.* flower, blossom
frūgiferēns, frūgiferentis fruit-bearing
genetrīx, genetrīcis *f.* mother, creator

lābor, lābī, lāpsus sum slip, glide
lūmen, lūminis *n.* light
nāviger, nāvigera, nāvigerum ship-bearing, navigable
niteō, nitēre, nituī, —— be radiant, shine
nūbila, nūbilōrum *n. pl.* clouds
plācō (1-tr.) make calm, soothe, placate
pontus, pontī *m.* sea
rīdeō, rīdēre, rīsī, rīsus smile, laugh
signum, signī *n.* sign, signal; constellation
sōl, sōlis *m.* sun
suāvis, suāve sweet(-smelling), fragrant
subter (prep. + acc.) under, beneath
summittō (**sub-** + **mittō**) send up (from below), put forth
tellūs, tellūris *f.* earth, land
ventus, ventī *m.* wind
vīsō, vīsere, vīsī, vīsus go to see, visit; view
voluptās, voluptātis *f.* pleasure, joy

11. Lucretius, *Dē Rērum Nātūrā* V.783–85

The poet describes an early state of the world.

> prīncipiō genus herbārum viridemque nitōrem
> terra dedit circum collīs campōsque per omnīs,
> flōrida fulsērunt viridantī prāta colōre . . .

campus, campī *m.* plain
circum (prep. + acc.) around
collis, collis, -ium *m.* hill
color, colōris *m.* color
fulgeō, fulgēre, fulsī, —— shine, gleam
flōridus, -a, -um abounding in flowers, producing flowers

herba, herbae *f.* small plant, herb, grass
nitor, nitōris *m.* brightness, splendor, brilliance
prātum, prātī *n.* meadow
prīncipium, prīncipiī *n.* beginning
viridis, viride green, verdant, covered in vegetation
viridō (1-intr.) be green

12. Catullus XLVI (hendecasyllable; see §112)

A spring poem

Iam vēr ēgelidōs refert tepōrēs,
iam caelī furor aequinoctiālis
iūcundīs Zephyrī silēscit aurīs.
linquantur Phrygiī, Catulle, campī
Nīcaeaeque ager ūber aestuōsae: 5
ad clārās Asiae volēmus urbēs.
iam mēns praetrepidāns avet vagārī,
iam laetī studiō pedēs vigēscunt.
ō dulcēs comitum valēte coetūs,
longē quōs simul ā domō profectōs   10
dīversae variē viae reportant.

aequinoctiālis, aequinoctiāle equinoctial, of the
   equinox
aestuōsus, -a, -um full of heat, burning, very hot
Asia, Asiae f. Asia, a Roman province (modern
   Asia Minor)
aura, aurae f. breeze
aveō, avēre, ——, —— be eager
campus, campī m. plain
coetus, coetūs m. gathering
comes, comitis m. or f. companion, comrade
dīversus, -a, -um different
dulcis, dulce sweet
ēgelidus, -a, -um tepid, lukewarm, mild
furor, furōris m. madness
iūcundus, -a, -um pleasing, delightful, agreeable
linquō, linquere, līquī, lictus leave (behind)
longē (adv.) far, a long way
Nīcaea, Nīcaeae f. Nicaea, a city in Bithynia (a
   Roman province on the coast of Asia Minor)

pēs, pedis m. foot
Phrygius, -a, -um of or belonging to Phrygia (the
   region around Troy), Phrygian, Trojan
praetrepidō (1-intr.) tremble in anticipation
reportō (1-tr.) carry back
silēscō, silēscere, ——, —— become still, fall
   silent, grow calm
simul (adv.) at the same time
tepor, tepōris m. in sing. or pl., warmth, mildness
ūber, ūberis rich, fertile
vagor (1-intr.) wander
variē (adv.) variously, differently
vēr, vēris n. spring
vigēscō, vigēscere, ——, —— come alive, be vigorous
volō (1-intr.) fly
Zephyrus, Zephyrī m. Zephyr, the west wind

13. Caesar, *Dē Bellō Gallicō* I.24–25

In the midst of hostilities with the Helvetians, Caesar is compelled to turn his troops away to seek supplies. The Helvetians follow and harass Caesar's men from behind.

postquam id* animadvertit, cōpiās suās Caesar in proximum collem subdūcit† equi-
tātumque quī sustinēret hostium impetum mīsit. ipse interim in colle mediō trip-
licem aciem īnstrūxit legiōnum quattuor veterānārum; in summō iugō duās le-
giōnēs quās in Galliā citeriōre proximē cōnscrīpserat, et omnia auxilia collocārī, ac
tōtum montem hominibus complērī, et intereā sarcinās in ūnum locum cōnferrī, et
eum ab iīs quī in superiōre aciē cōnstiterant, mūnīrī iussit. Helvētiī, cum omnibus
suīs carrīs secūtī, impedīmenta in ūnum locum contulērunt; ipsī cōnfertissimā aciē,
reiectō nostrō equitātū, phalange factā, sub prīmam nostram aciem successērunt.

Caesar prīmum‡ suō, deinde omnium ex cōnspectū remōtīs equīs, ut aequātō
omnium perīculō spem fugae tolleret, cohortātus suōs proelium commīsit. Mīlitēs
ē locō superiōre pīlīs missīs facile hostium phalangem perfrēgērunt. Eā disiectā,
gladiīs dēstrictīs in eōs impetum fēcērunt.

*id = the pursuit of the Helvetians
†subdūcit, historical use of present tense; translate as perfect
‡prīmum, *here* (adv.) first
aequō (1-tr.) make equal
animadvertō, animadvertere, animadvertī,
   animadversus turn one's attention to, notice
carrus, carrī *m.* cart, wagon
cohortor (1-tr.) exhort, encourage
collis, collis, -ium *m.* hill
collocō (1-tr.) place, position, arrange
committō (con- + mittō) join, engage in
compleō, complēre, complēvī, complētus fill
   completely, cover
cōnferō (con- + ferō) collect, gather together
cōnfertissimus, -a, -um very crowded, very dense,
   very packed close together
cōnscrībō (con- + scrībō) enlist, enroll
cōnsistō, cōnsistere, cōnstitī, —— take one's position, make a stand, halt
cōnspectus, cōnspectūs *m.* (range of) sight, view
deinde (adv.) thereupon, then, next
dēstringō, dēstringere, dēstrīnxī, dēstrictus draw
disiciō, disicere, disiēcī, disiectus break, rout,
   disperse
equitātus, equitātūs *m.* cavalry
equus, equī *m.* horse
Gallia citerior, Galliae citeriōris *f.* Nearer *or*
   Cisalpine Gaul (on the Italian side of the Alps)
Helvētiī, Helvētiōrum *m. pl.* (the) Helvetians
impedīmentum, impedīmentī *n.* hindrance;
   in pl., baggage
impetus, impetūs *m.* attack, assault

īnstruō, īnstruere, īnstrūxī, īnstrūctus arrange,
   draw up
intereā (adv.) meanwhile
interim (adv.) meanwhile
iugum, iugī *n.* yoke; (mountain) ridge
legiō, legiōnis *f.* legion
mōns, montis, -ium *m.* mountain
mūniō, mūnīre, mūnīvī or mūniī, mūnītus
   fortify
perfringō, perfringere, perfrēgī, perfrāctus break
   through
phalanx, phalangis *f.* phalanx, a close formation
   of troops
pīlum, pīlī *n.* spear, javelin
proximē (superlative adv.) most recently
proximus, -a, -um nearest
reiciō, reicere, reiēcī, reiectus throw back, drive
   back
removeō (re- + moveō) move back, remove
sarcina, sarcinae *f.* pack, bundle; *in pl.,* luggage,
   baggage
subdūcō (sub- + dūcō) lead up (from below),
   draw up
succēdō (sub- + cēdō) approach (from below)
summus, -a, -um highest; top (of)
superior, superius (comparative adj.) upper,
   higher; superiōre = *masc./fem. sing. abl.*
sustineō (sub- + teneō), sustinēre, sustinuī, ——
   withstand
tollō, tollere, sustulī, sublātus lift, raise; take
   away
triplex, triplicis threefold; triple
veterānus, -a, -um veteran, composed of veterans

14. Sallust, *Bellum Catilīnae* 6

The historian begins a brief survey of Roman history.

urbem Rōmam, sīcutī ego accēpī, condidēre atque habuēre initiō Troiānī, quī Aenēā
duce profugī sēdibus incertīs vagābantur, cumque hīs Aborīginēs, genus hominum
agreste, sine lēgibus, sine imperiō, līberum atque solūtum.

Aborīginēs, Aborīginum *m. pl.* (the) Aborigines,
a tribe in Italy from whom the Romans
descended
agrestis, agreste of *or* living in the fields, rustic;
uncivilized
condō, condere, condidī, conditus found, build
initium, initiī *n.* beginning

profugus, -a, -um fugitive, fleeing; *as subst.*, exile;
refugee
sēdēs, sēdis, -ium *f.* seat; home, abode
sīcutī (conj.) just as
solūtus, -a, -um unrestricted, free; unconnected
Troiānus, -a, -um Trojan
vagor (1-intr.) wander

15. Sallust, *Bellum Iugurthae* 2

The historian reflects on the dual nature of man.

nam utī genus hominum conpositum ex corpore et animā est, ita rēs cūnctae stu-
diaque omnia nostra, corporis alia, alia animī nātūram secuntur.* igitur praeclāra
faciēs,† magnae dīvitiae, ad hoc‡ vīs corporis et alia omnia huiusce modī brevī dīlā-
buntur; at ingenī ēgregia facinora, sīcutī anima, inmortālia sunt. postrēmō corporis
et fortūnae bonōrum, ut initium, sīc fīnis est, omniaque orta occidunt et aucta senēs-
cunt; animus incorruptus, aeternus, rēctor hūmānī generis agit atque habet cūncta
neque ipse habētur.

***secuntur = sequuntur**
†**faciēs, faciēī** *f.* face; appearance
‡**ad hoc** (added) to this
aeternus, -a, -um eternal, everlasting
at (conj.) but
augeō, augēre, auxī, auctus grow, increase
brevis, breve short, brief; **brevī**, *sc.* **tempore**
conpōnō (con- + pōnō) (= compōnō) put together, compose
cūnctus, -a, -um all
dīlābor, dīlābī, dīlāpsus sum slip away, disappear
dīvitiae, dīvitiārum *f. pl.* wealth, riches
ēgregius, -a, -um outstanding, extraordinary
facinus, facinoris *n.* deed
huiusce = intensive form of **huius**

hūmānus, -a, -um human
igitur (conj.) therefore *(usually postpositive)*
incorruptus, -a, -um uncorrupted, pure
initium, initiī *n.* beginning
inmortālis (= immortālis), inmortāle immortal
occidō (ob- + cadō), occidere, occidī, occāsūrus
fall; perish, die
orior, orīrī, ortus sum rise, arise
postrēmō (adv.) finally
praeclārus, -a, -um very famous; radiant, beautiful
rēctor, rēctōris *m.* director, ruler, master
senēscō, senēscere, senuī, —— grow old, grow
weak, decline
sīcutī (conj.) just as
utī = ut

The *Bellum Iugurthae* (War of Jugurtha) is the second of Sallust's surviving historical monographs. It recounts the
war between Rome and Jugurtha, king of Numidia (in North Africa), which lasted from 111 to 105 B.C.E. Sallust's
focus is the corruption of the Roman aristocracy, which allowed Jugurtha to maintain power by bribing those sent
to wage war against him.

16. Vergil, *Eclogues* IV.4–7

The poet describes the beginning of a new age.

ultima Cūmaeī vēnit iam carminis aetās;

magnus ab integrō saeclōrum nāscitur ordō.

iam redit et Virgō, redeunt Sāturnia rēgna,

iam nova prōgeniēs caelō dēmittitur altō.

aetās, aetātis *f.* age, time of life; era
Cūmaeus, -a, -um of *or* belonging to Cumae; of *or* belonging to the Sibyl of Cumae
dēmittō (dē- + mittō) send down
integer, integra, integrum whole; fresh; **ab integrō,** afresh, anew
ordō, ordinis *m.* order; series, sequence
prōgeniēs, *prōgeniēī *f.* offspring, progeny

rēgnum, rēgnī *n.* kingdom, realm
saec(u)lum, saec(u)lī *n.* age, generation
Sāturnius, -a, -um of Saturn, king of the Titans and father of Jupiter and Juno; **Sāturnia rēgna,** (golden) age of Saturn
ultimus, -a, -um farthest, most remote; last, final
Virgō, Virginis *f.* (the) Virgin (Astraea), goddess of Justice

Vergil's first work, the *Eclogues* (< Greek *Eklogai,* Selections) or *Bucolics* (< Greek *Boukolika,* [Poems] of Oxherds), is a collection of ten pastoral poems written between 42 and 39 B.C.E. and published shortly thereafter. The poetry of the *Eclogues* demonstrates Vergil's knowledge of Greek Hellenistic poetry (particularly the work of Theocritus) and his ability to translate this genre into a Roman context. The poems are marked by rustic settings, shepherd-poets engaged in love affairs, poetic contests, and an apparent escapist atmosphere. Closer examination of these poems reveals a sociopolitical element absent from Vergil's Greek models. When first published, the *Eclogues* won Vergil wide praise in Rome's literary circle, and Vergil soon came under the patronage of Maecenas, a wealthy patron of the arts and perhaps Octavian's closest friend.

17. Vergil, *Georgics* I.505–14

The peace-loving poet describes the effects of civil war. These lines conclude the first book of the Georgics.

> . . . tot bella per orbem,   505
> tam multae scelerum faciēs,* nōn ūllus arātrō
> dignus honōs, squālent abductīs arva colōnīs,
> et curvae rigidum falcēs cōnflantur in ēnsem.
> hinc movet Euphrātēs, illinc Germānia bellum;
> vīcīnae ruptīs inter sē lēgibus urbēs   510
> arma ferunt; saevit tōtō Mars impius orbe,
> ut cum† carceribus sēsē effūdēre quadrīgae,
> addunt in spatia, et frūstrā retinācula tendēns
> fertur equīs aurīga neque audit‡ currus habēnās.

faciēs, faciēī f. face; appearance, sight

†cum, *here* (conj. + perf. indic.) whenever;
  cum . . . effūdēre whenever . . . pour forth

‡audiō, *here,* heed

abdūcō (ab- + dūcō) lead away, take away, carry off

addō (ad- + dō) add; increase speed

arātrum, arātrī *n.* plough

arvum, arvī *n.* (ploughed) field

aurīga, aurīgae *f.* charioteer, driver

carcer, carceris *m.* prison; barrier (at the beginning of a racecourse)

colōnus, colōnī *m.* farmer

cōnflō (1-tr.) forge

currus, currūs *m.* chariot

curvus, -a, -um curved

dignus, -a, -um worthy (of) (+ abl.)

effundō, effundere, effūdī, effūsus pour out, pour forth; send forth; **effūdēre** *translate as present*

ēnsis, ēnsis *m.* sword

equus, equī *m.* horse

Euphrātēs, Euphrātī or Euphrātae *m.* (the river) Euphrates

falx, falcis *f.* scythe, sickle

frūstrā (adv.) in vain

Germānia, Germāniae *f.* Germany

habēna, habēnae *f.* rein

hinc (adv.) from *or* on this side

honōs, honōris *m.* office; honor, respect

illinc (adv.) from *or* on that side

orbis, orbis, -ium *m.* ring, circle; world

quadrīga, quadrīgae *f.* (four-horse) chariot

retināculum, retināculī *n.* rope, rein

rigidus, -a, -um rigid, stiff; erect; inflexible

rumpō, rumpere, rūpī, ruptus split, burst, break

saeviō, saevīre, saeviī, saevītum behave savagely, rage

scelus, sceleris *n.* wicked deed, crime

spatium, spatiī *n.* course, track; lap; **in spatia** lap by lap

squāleō, squālēre, squāluī, —— be dirty; lie barren (from neglect)

tam (adv.) so

tendō, tendere, tetendī, tentus or tēnsus stretch out, extend

tot (indeclinable adj.) so many

vīcīnus, -a, -um neighboring

Because of the success of the *Eclogues,* Vergil joined the poets Horace and Propertius in receiving the patronage of Maecenas, a close personal friend of Octavian. Vergil's next work was completed ca. 29 B.C.E. The *Georgics* (< Greek *Geōrgica,* [Poems] About Farming) is a didactic poem in four books on the art of farming. In addition to offering practical advice for farmers, the *Georgics* describes and praises the simplicity and purity of rustic life, and Vergil paints a picture of Italian country life and virtue that stands in stark contrast to the turmoil of actual life in the city Rome.

18. Vergil, *Georgics* II.490–99

In his praise of the life of the farmer the poet makes reference to the Roman poet Lucretius, the Greek philosopher Epicurus, and, more generally, to any follower of the Epicurean school of philosophy.

fēlīx quī potuit rērum cognōscere causās   490

atque metūs omnīs et inexōrābile fātum

subiēcit pedibus strepitumque Acherontis avārī;

fortūnātus et ille deōs quī nōvit agrestīs

Pānaque Silvānumque senem Nymphāsque sorōrēs.

illum nōn populī fascēs, nōn purpura rēgum   495

flexit et īnfīdōs agitāns discordia frātrēs,

aut coniūrātō dēscendēns Dācus ab Histrō,

nōn rēs Rōmānae peritūraque rēgna; neque ille

aut doluit miserāns inopem aut invīdit habentī.

Acherōn, Acherontis *m.* Acheron, a river of the underworld

agitō (1-tr.) stir up, set in motion; vex, harass

agrestis, agreste of *or* living in the fields, rustic

avārus, -a, -um greedy, rapacious

coniūrō (1-intr.) join in a plot, form a conspiracy; **coniūrātō** = *perf. pass. part. used with active meaning*

Dācus, Dācī *m.* Dacian, inhabitant of Dacia, a province north of the Danube (modern Romania and Hungary)

dēscendō, dēscendere, dēscendī, dēscēnsus go down, descend

discordia, discordiae *f.* discord, dissension, conflict

doleō, dolēre, doluī, —— suffer, grieve, feel pain

fascēs, fascium *m. pl.* the *fasces*, bundle of rods with an axe, symbol of power

flectō, flectere, flexī, flexus bend

fortūnātus, -a, -um fortunate

Hister, Histrī *m.* (the) Hister, the lower Danube (river)

inexōrābilis, inexōrābile inexorable, relentless

īnfīdus, -a, -um faithless, treacherous

inops, inopis poor, in want

invideō (**in-** + **videō**) envy (+dat.)

miseror (1-tr.) pity

Nympha, Nymphae *f.* Nymph, a semidivine female spirit of nature

Pān, Pānos *m.* Pan, an Arcadian pastoral god; **Pāna** = *acc. sing.*

pereō (**per-** + **eō**), **perīre, periī, peritūrus** pass away, be destroyed; perish, die

pēs, pedis *m.* foot

purpura, purpurae *f.* purple-dyed cloth; purple color

rēgnum, rēgnī *n.* kingdom, realm

senex, senis old

Silvānus, Silvānī *m.* Silvanus, a Roman god of the forest

strepitus, strepitūs *m.* noise; roar

subiciō, subicere, subiēcī, subiectus place (acc.) below (dat.)

19. Vergil, *Georgics* III.242–44

The poet speaks of a common impulse in all living creatures.

omne adeō genus in terrīs hominumque ferārumque*

et genus aequoreum, pecudēs pictaeque volucrēs,

in furiās ignemque ruunt: amor omnibus īdem.

*ferārumque elides into the next line.

adeō (adv.) to that point; to such an extent; indeed, in fact

aequoreus, -a, -um of the sea, marine

fera, ferae *f.* wild animal, beast

furiae, furiārum *f. pl.* madness, mad desire,
   frenzy

ignis, ignis, -ium *m.* fire; rage, passion

pecus, pecudis *f.* (herd) animal

pictus, -a, -um painted, colored

ruō, ruere, ruī, rutūrus rush

volucris, volucris, -ium *f.* bird

20. Vergil, *Aeneid* I.1–4

The first four lines of Vergil's epic poem

Arma virumque canō, Troiae quī prīmus ab ōrīs

Ītaliam fātō profugus Lāvīnaque vēnit

lītora, multum ille et terrīs iactātus et altō

vī superum, saevae memorem Iūnōnis ob īram.

iactō (1-tr.) throw, toss; harass, torment

Lāvīnus, -a, -um of Lavinium, a town in Italy;
   Lavinian

lītus, lītoris *n.* shore, beach

memor, memoris mindful, remembering

ōra, ōrae *f.* shore, coast

profugus, -a, -um fugitive, fleeing; *as subst.*, exile;
   refugee

saevus, -a, -um cruel, savage

superī, superōrum *m. pl.* gods above; superum
   = superōrum

21. Vergil, *Aeneid* X.466–72

Jupiter speaks consoling words to his son Hercules, who is distressed at the imminent death of Pallas.

tum genitor nātum dictīs adfātur amīcīs:

"stat sua* cuique† diēs, breve et inreparābile tempus

omnibus est vītae; sed fāmam extendere factīs,

hoc virtūtis opus. Troiae sub moenibus altīs

tot gnātī cecidēre deum, quīn‡ occidit ūnā   470

Sarpēdōn, mea prōgeniēs. etiam sua§ Turnum

fāta vocant mētāsque datī pervēnit ad aevī."

*sua refers to cuique, his/her own.
†cuique = *masc./fem./neut. sing. dat. of indef. pron.*, each man, each person, each thing
‡quīn, *here*, (conj.) really, verily; nay, in fact
§sua refers to Turnum, his own.
adfor (1-tr.) address
aevum, aevī *n.* age, lifetime; life
brevis, breve short, brief
extendō, extendere, extendī, extentus stretch out, extend
genitor, genitōris *m.* father
gnātī = nātī

inreparābilis, inreparābile irretrievable
mēta, mētae *f.* goal post; end, limit
occidō (ob- + cadō), occidere, occidī, occāsūrus fall; perish, die
perveniō (per- + veniō) arrive at (+ ad + acc.)
prōgeniēs, *prōgeniēī *f.* offspring, progeny
Sarpēdōn, Sarpēdonis *m.* Sarpedon, Lycian king and Trojan ally, son of Zeus
tot (indeclinable adj.) so many
tum (adv.) then, at that time
ūnā (adv.) together, at the same time

22. Vergil, *Aeneid* XII.92–102

Fierce Turnus takes up a spear with which he hopes to kill Aeneas and speaks to it.

exim quae mediīs ingentī adnīxa columnae

aedibus astābat validam vī corripit hastam,

Actoris Auruncī spolium, quassatque trementem

vōciferāns: "nunc, ō numquam frūstrāta vocātūs   95

hasta meōs, nunc tempus adest; tē maximus Actor,

tē Turnī nunc dextra gerit; dā sternere corpus

lōrīcamque manū validā lacerāre revulsam

sēmivirī Phrygis et foedāre in pulvere crīnīs

vibrātōs calidō ferrō murrāque madentīs."   100

hīs agitur furiīs, tōtōque ardentis ab ōre

scintillae absistunt, oculīs micat ācribus ignis . . .

absistō, absistere, abstitī, —— move apart; burst forth

Actor, Actoris *m.* Actor, the man who used to own the spear

adnītor, adnītī, adnīxus sum lean against (+ dat.)

adsum (ad- + sum), adesse, adfuī, adfutūrus be present

aedēs, aedis, -ium *f.* sanctuary, shrine; *in pl.,* house, abode

ardeō, ardēre, arsī, arsūrus burn, be on fire; rage

astō (ad- + stō), astāre, astitī, —— stand (near)

Auruncus, -a, -um of Aurunca, a town in Campania, Auruncan

calidus, -a, -um hot

columna, columnae *f.* column

corripiō, corripere, corripuī, correptus snatch up

crīnis, crīnis, -ium *m.* hair

dexter, dextra, dextrum right; *as fem. subst. (sc.* **manus**), right hand

exim (adv.) then, next, thereafter

foedō (1-tr.) befoul, defile

frūstror (1-tr.) deceive, disappoint

furiae, furiārum *f. pl.* madness, mad desire, frenzy

hasta, hastae *f.* spear

ignis, ignis, -ium *m.* fire

lacerō (1-tr.) tear to pieces, rend, mutilate

lōrīca, lōrīcae *f.* corselet, cuirass, breastplate

madeō, madēre, ——, —— be wet, drip

maximus, -a, -um biggest, greatest, very great

micō (1-tr.) dart, flicker, flash

murra, murrae *f.* myrrh, an aromatic gum

ōs, ōris *n.* mouth; face

Phryx, Phrygis Phrygian, Trojan

pulvis, pulveris *m.* dust

quassō (1-tr.) shake, wave, brandish

revellō, revellere, revulsī, revulsus pull away, tear off

scintilla, scintillae *f.* spark

sēmivir, sēmivirī *m.* or *adj.* half-man; semimasculine

spolium, spoliī *n.* booty, spoil

sternō, sternere, strāvī, strātus strew; lay low, slay, kill

tremō, tremere, tremuī, —— tremble, quiver, quake

vibrō (1-tr.) give a wavy appearance, crimp, curl

vocātus, vocātūs *m.* summons, call

vōciferor (1-intr.) shout, yell, cry out

23. Horace, *Carmina* I.23 (Asclepiadean; see §112)

The poet addresses a timid girl.

Vītās innuleō mē similis, Chloē,
quaerentī pavidam montibus āviīs
　　mātrem nōn sine vānō
　　　　aurārum et silvae metū.

nam seu mōbilibus vēris inhorruit　　　　　　　　　　5
adventus foliīs seu viridēs rubum
　　dīmōvēre lacertae,
　　　　et corde et genibus tremit.

atquī nōn ego tē tigris ut aspera
Gaetūlusve leō frangere persequor:　　　　　　　　　10
　　tandem dēsine mātrem
　　　　tempestīva sequī virō.

adventus, adventūs *m.* arrival
asper, aspera, asperum harsh, fierce, pitiless
atquī (conj.) but, and yet
aura, aurae *f.* breeze
āvius, -a, -um pathless, trackless
Chloē, Chloēs Chloe, addressee of the poem
cor, cordis *n.* heart
dēsinō, dēsinere, dēsiī or dēsīvī, dēsitum stop,
　　cease (+ inf.)
dīmoveō (dis- + moveō) separate; set in motion
folium, foliī *n.* leaf
frangō, frangere, frēgī, frāctus break, shatter,
　　crush
Gaetūlus, -a, -um Gaetulian, Moroccan
genū, genūs *n.* knee
inhorreō, inhorrēre, inhorruī, —— bristle, quiver,
　　shudder
(h)innuleus, (h)innuleī *m.* young deer, fawn
lacerta, lacertae *f.* lizard
leō, leōnis *m.* lion

mōbilis, mōbile movable; moving, shifting
mōns, montis, -ium *m.* mountain
pavidus, -a, -um trembling, frightened
persequor (per- + sequor) follow earnestly, pursue
rubus, rubī *m.* bramble, blackberry bush
seu (conj.) or if, whether; seu . . . seu . . .
　　whether . . . or (if) . . .
silva, silvae *f.* forest; *for purposes of scansion,* silvae
　　= siluae
similis, simile similar (+ dat.)
tempestīvus, -a, -um timely, ripe, ready
tigris, tigris, -ium *m.* or *f.* tiger
tremō, tremere, tremuī, —— tremble, quiver,
　　quake
vānus, -a, -um empty, illusory; groundless, false
-ve (enclitic conj.) or
vēr, vēris *n.* spring
viridis, viride green, verdant
vītō (1-tr.) avoid

Horace's *Carmina* (usually referred to as Odes) comprise three books (eighty-eight poems) of lyric poetry published in 23 B.C.E. and a fourth book (fifteen poems), written considerably later, perhaps at the request of Augustus himself. These poems, written in the Greek lyric meters of Sappho, Alcaeus, Archilochus, and others, take as their themes all aspects of poetry, life, and death, but they do so in a delightfully enigmatic fashion. The hallmark of a Horatian ode is meticulous word choice and word placement that impart to the poem many levels of meaning.

24. Ovid, *Amōrēs* III.9.37–42

The poet reflects with bitterness on the early death of fellow elegiac poet Tibullus (55?–19? B.C.E.).

vīve pius—moriēre; pius cole sacra—colentem

    mors gravis ā templīs in cava busta trahet;

carminibus cōnfīde bonīs—iacet, ecce, Tibullus:

    vix manet ē tōtō parva quod urna capit!   40

tēne, sacer vātēs, flammae rapuēre rogālēs

    pectoribus pāscī nec timuēre tuīs?

bustum, bustī *n.* funeral pyre; grave mound, tomb

cavus, -a, -um hollow

colō, colere, coluī, cultus cultivate, tend; worship

cōnfīdō, cōnfīdere, cōnfīsus sum put trust in, have confidence in (+ dat.)

flamma, flammae *f.* flame

iaceō, iacēre, iacuī, —— lie, rest; lie dead

pāscor, pāscī, pāstus sum feed upon (+ abl.)

rapiō, rapere, rapuī, raptus tear away, carry off; consume

rogālis, rogāle of *or* belonging to a funeral pyre

sacer, sacra, sacrum sacred

Tibullus, Tibullī *m.* Tibullus

trahō, trahere, trāxī, tractus draw, drag

urna, urnae *f.* urn

vātēs, vātis, -ium *m.* or *f.* prophet; bard, poet

vix (adv.) scarcely, hardly

25. Ovid, *Ars Amātōria* I.113–24

The poet describes the legendary Roman rape of the Sabine women, which takes place in the middle of a public entertainment to which the Sabines have been invited.

in mediō plausū (plausūs tunc arte carēbant)

    rēx populō praedae signa petīta dedit.

prōtinus exiliunt, animum clāmōre fatentēs,   115

    virginibus cupidās iniciuntque manūs.

ut fugiunt aquilās, timidissima turba, columbae,

    ut fugit invīsōs agna novella lupōs:

sīc illae timuēre virōs sine mōre* ruentēs;

    cōnstitit in nūllā quī fuit ante color.   120

nam timor ūnus erat, faciēs nōn ūna timōris:

    pars laniat crīnēs, pars sine mente sedet;

altera maesta silet, frūstrā vocat altera mātrem:

    haec queritur, stupet haec; haec manet, illa fugit . . .

*sine mōre, *here,* lawlessly, wildly
agna, agnae *f.* ewe, lamb
aquila, aquilae *f.* eagle
clāmor, clāmōris *m.* shout, shouting
color, colōris *m.* color
columba, columbae *f.* dove
cōnsistō, cōnsistere, cōnstitī, —— make a stand, halt; remain
crīnis, crīnis, -ium *m.* hair
ex(s)iliō, ex(s)ilīre, ex(s)iluī, —— spring forth, jump out
faciēs, faciēī *f.* face; appearance
frūstrā (adv.) in vain
iniciō, inicere, iniēcī, iniectus throw (acc.) on (dat.), lay (acc.) on (dat.)
invīsus, -a, -um hateful, odious
laniō (1-tr.) tear, mutilate
lupus, lupī *m.* wolf

maestus, -a, -um sad, mournful, gloomy, grim
novellus, -a, -um young, tender
plausus, plausūs *m.* clapping, applause
praeda, praedae *f.* booty, plunder; prey
prōtinus (adv.) immediately, straightway
queror, querī, questus sum complain, protest; lament
ruō, ruere, ruī, rutūrus rush
sedeō, sedēre, sēdī, sessūrus sit, be seated
signum, signī *n.* sign, signal
sileō, silēre, siluī, —— be silent
stupeō, stupēre, stupuī, —— be stunned, be speechless
timidissimus, -a, -um very fearful, very afraid, very timid
tunc (adv.) then, at that time
turba, turbae *f.* crowd
virgō, virginis *f.* maiden, virgin

The *Ars Amātōria* (Art of Love) is a collection of three books of elegiac poems that are both erotic and didactic in subject matter and style. The poet offers detailed advice to men (books I and II) and to women (book III) on how to seduce and hold love partners. With a mixture of irony and genuine enthusiasm Ovid's counsel favors fun and pleasure over fidelity and morality. This work of the poet may have aroused the displeasure of Augustus and may have led to Ovid's exile.

26. Augustus, *Rēs Gestae Dīvī Augustī*, Proem, 1–2

The preface and opening words of Augustus's autobiographical report to the Roman people

Rērum gestārum dīvī Augustī, quibus orbem terrārum imperiō populī Rōmānī subiēcit, et impēnsārum quās in* rem pūblicam populumque Rōmānum fēcit, incīsārum in duābus ahēneīs pīlīs, quae sunt Rōmae positae, exemplar subiectum.

Annōs undēvīgintī nātus exercitum prīvātō cōnsiliō et prīvātā impēnsā comparāvī, per quem rem pūblicam ā dominātiōne factiōnis oppressam in lībertātem vindicāvī. eō nōmine senātus dēcrētīs honōrificīs in ordinem suum mē adlēgit, C. Pānsā et A. Hirtiō cōnsulibus, cōnsulārem locum sententiae dīcendae† tribuēns, et imperium mihi dedit.

*in, *here, for*

†dīcendae, *fem. sing. gen. of a gerundive;*
  sententiae dīcendae, of speaking (my) opinion

adlegō (ad- + legō), adlegere, adlēgī, adlēctus elect, admit

a(h)ēneus, -a, -um (made of) bronze

comparō (1-tr.) prepare, get together; raise

cōnsulāris, cōnsulāre of *or* belonging to a consul, consular; of consular rank

dēcrētum, dēcrētī *n.* decision, order, decree

dominātiō, dominātiōnis *f.* absolute power, dominion; despotism

exemplar, exemplāris, -ium *n.* copy

factiō, factiōnis *f.* faction, partisanship

A. Hirtius, A. Hirtiī *m.* A. Hirtius (consul 43)

honōrificus, -a, -um conferring honor, honorific

impēnsa, impēnsae *f.* expense

incīdō, incīdere, incīdī, incīsus cut into, inscribe onto

nōmen, nōminis *n.* name; reason, purpose

opprimō, opprimere, oppressī, oppressus press down; suppress

orbis, orbis, -ium *m.* ring, circle; orbis terrārum, circle of lands, world

ordō, ordinis *m.* order, rank, class, body

C. Pānsa, C. Pānsae *m.* C. (Vibius) Pansa (consul 43)

pīla, pīlae *f.* column; squared pillar

prīvātus, -a, -um private

subiciō, subicere, subiēcī, subiectus place below; make (acc.) subject to (dat.)

tribuō, tribuere, tribuī, tribūtus grant, bestow, assign

vindicō (1-tr.) lay claim to; in lībertātem vindicāre, to claim as free, to free, to liberate

The *Rēs Gestae Dīvī Augustī* is one of three documents that Augustus left with the Vestal Virgins shortly before his death in 14 c.e. This first-person description of Augustus's accomplishments is written in an unadorned and clear style. After Augustus's death, and by his order, the *Rēs Gestae* were inscribed on two pillars placed in front of his mausoleum in Rome and also on numerous copies throughout the Empire (often with an accompanying Greek translation). The best surviving copy comes from Ankara in Turkey and includes the initial paragraph presented above.

27. Velleius Paterculus, *Historia Rōmāna* II.18.1–3

The historian describes a Roman enemy in the East in 88 B.C.E.

Per ea tempora Mithridātēs, Ponticus rēx, vir neque silendus neque dīcendus sine cūrā, bellō ācerrimus, virtūte eximius, aliquandō fortūnā, semper animō maximus, cōnsiliīs dux, mīles manū,* odiō in Rōmānōs Hannibal, occupātā Asiā necātīsque in eā omnibus cīvibus Rōmānīs quōs quidem eādem diē atque hōrā redditīs cīvitātibus litterīs ingentī cum pollicitātiōne praemiōrum interimī iusserat, quō tempore neque fortitūdine adversus Mithridātem neque fidē in† Rōmānōs quisquam Rhodiīs pār fuit—hōrum fidem Mytilēnaeōrum perfidia illūmināvit, quī M'. Aquilium aliōsque Mithridātī vīnctōs trādidērunt, quibus lībertās in ūnīus Theophanis grātiam posteā ā Pompeiō restitūta est—cum‡ terribilis Italiae quoque vidērētur imminēre, sorte obvēnit Sullae Asia prōvincia.

*__manus__, *here*, deed, action
†__in__, *here*, toward
‡__cum__, *here* (conj. + subjunc.) (under the circumstances) when
__ācerrimus, -a, -um__ most *or* very fierce
__adversus__ (prep. + acc.) in opposition to, against, in the face of
__aliquandō__ (adv.) sometimes, occasionally
__M'. Aquilius, M'. Aquiliī__ *m.* M'. Aquilius
__Asia, Asiae__ *f.* Asia, a Roman province (modern Asia Minor)
__eximius, -a, -um__ outstanding, remarkable
__fortitūdō, fortitūdinis__ *f.* bravery, fortitude
__grātia, grātiae__ *f.* favor, kindness; __in grātiam__, for the purpose of pleasing (+ gen.)
__hōra, hōrae__ *f.* hour
__illūminō__ (1-tr.) illuminate, reveal
__immineō, imminēre,__ ——, —— hang over, threaten (+ dat.)
__interimō, interimere, interēmī, interēmptus__ kill, do away with
__litterae, litterārum__ *f. pl.* letter, epistle
__maximus, -a, -um__ biggest, greatest, very great
__Mithridātēs, Mithridātis__ *m.* Mithridates (the Great), king of Pontus, defeated by Sulla, Lucullus, and Pompey
__Mytilēnaeī, Mytilēnaeōrum__ *m. pl.* Mytileneans, citizens of Mytilene, a city on the island Lesbos off the coast of Asia Minor

__necō__ (1-tr.) put to death, kill
__obveniō__ (ob- + veniō) be assigned to (+ dat.)
__occupō__ (1-tr.) seize; occupy
__pār, paris__ equal
__perfidia, perfidiae__ *f.* faithlessness, treachery
__pollicitātiō, pollicitātiōnis__ *f.* promise
__Ponticus, -a, -um__ of *or* belonging to the region adjoining the Black Sea (Pontus), of Pontus
__posteā__ (adv.) after, afterward
__praemium, praemiī__ *n.* reward, prize
__quisquam__ = *masc./fem. nom. sing. of indef. pron.,* anyone
__reddō__ (red- + dō) give back, return; hand over, deliver
__restituō, restituere, restituī, restitūtus__ set up again, restore
__Rhodiī, Rhodiōrum__ *m. pl.* Rhodians, inhabitants of the island Rhodes off the coast of Asia Minor
__sileō, silēre, siluī,__ —— be silent; pass over in silence
__sors, sortis, -ium__ *f.* lot, portion; lottery
__terribilis, terribile__ terrifying, frightening
__Theophanēs, Theophanis__ *m.* Theophanis, Greek historian from Mytilene, friend of Pompey
__vinciō, vincīre, vīnxī, vīnctus__ bind, join, fetter

__Velleius Paterculus__ was born in southern Italy and served under the future emperor Tiberius as commander of the cavalry in Germany. After his rise to the rank of praetor in 14 C.E., almost nothing is known of his life. The only known work of Velleius Paterculus is the *Historiae Rōmānae*, published in 30 C.E. in two books. The first book, the surviving text of which contains gaps, gives a cursory account of Roman history from Romulus to the fall of Carthage. The second book treats more contemporary history and includes a consistently positive portrait of Tiberius. Notable in the style of Velleius are a certain awkwardness and a pronounced lack of clarity in his long periodic sentences.

28. Seneca the Younger, *Agamemnōn* 507–11

Eurybates describes the effect of a storm on the Greek sailors and their Trojan captives as they return from Troy.

Nīl ratiō et ūsus audet: ars cessit malīs;

tenet horror artūs, omnis officiō stupet

nāvita relictō, rēmus effugit manūs.

in vōta miserōs ultimus cōgit timor   510

eademque superōs Trōes et Danaī rogant.

artus, artūs *m.* joint (of the body), limb
cōgō (cō- + agō), cōgere, coēgī, coāctus drive together, force, compel
Danaī, Danaōrum *m. pl.* Danaans, Greeks
effugiō (ex- + fugiō) flee from, escape, slip from
horror, horrōris *m.* bristling, stiffening; trembling, dread
nāvita = nauta
officium, officiī *n.* obligation; duty, task
ratiō, ratiōnis *f.* account, reason; reasoning

rēmus, rēmī *m.* oar
rogō (1-tr.) ask (someone, acc.) for (something, acc.)
stupeō, stupēre, stupuī, —— be stunned, be speechless
superī, superōrum *m. pl.* gods above
Trōs, Trōis *m.* Trojan (man); **Trōes** = *nom. pl.*
ultimus, -a, -um farthest, most remote; last, final
ūsus, ūsūs *m.* use, experience
vōtum, vōtī *n.* vow, prayer

29. Juvenal, *Saturae* X.283–88

After recovering from a fever that might have killed him, Pompeius Magnus was killed and beheaded in Egypt, to where he had fled during the civil wars with Caesar. The poet reflects on this end in comparison to the deaths of other Roman leaders.

prōvida Pompeiō dederat Campānia febrēs

optandās, sed multae urbēs et pūblica vōta

vīcērunt; igitur fortūna ipsīus et urbis   285

servātum victō caput abstulit. hōc cruciātū

Lentulus, hāc poenā caruit ceciditque Cethēgus

integer, et iacuit Catilīna cadāvere tōtō.

cadāver, cadāveris *n.* corpse
Campānia, Campāniae *f.* Campania, a province in southern Italy south of Latium
caput, capitis *n.* head
Cethēgus, Cethēgī *m.* Cethegus, one of the leaders in the Catilinarian conspiracy
cruciātus, cruciātūs *m.* torture, torment
febris, febris, -ium *f. in sing. or pl.* an attack of fever, fever

iaceō, iacēre, iacuī, —— lie, rest; lie dead
igitur (postpositive conj.) therefore; then
integer, integra, integrum whole
Lentulus, Lentulī *m.* Lentulus, one of the leaders in the Catilinarian conspiracy
prōvidus, -a, -um having foreknowledge, provident
vōtum, vōtī *n.* vow, prayer

Decimus Iūnius Iuvenālis was born in southern Latium in the middle of the first century c.e. Juvenal began to write poetry some time after the death of Domitian in 96 and continued to do so for the next thirty years. He lived until at least 127.

The *Saturae* (Satires) are sixteen satirical poems written in the dactylic hexameter, which have been divided into five books. The poet caricatures and attacks various manifestations of what he views as the corruption of Roman society. Rhetoric, hypocrisy, the atmosphere surrounding the emperor, women, and human frailty in general are among the subjects scathingly attacked by the poet. Although Juvenal's subject matter is often crude, his poetry is highly developed and often colored by the language of epic and of tragedy.

Continuous Readings

1. Vergil, *Aeneid* II.479–90

While recounting the fall of Troy, Aeneas describes how Pyrrhus (= Neoptolemus), son of Achilles, breaks into the palace of Priam and slaughters the last members of the royal line.

ipse* inter prīmōs correptā dūra bipennī

līmina perrumpit postīsque ā cardine vellit   480

aerātōs; iamque excīsā trabe firma cavāvit

rōbora et ingentem lātō dedit ōre fenestram.

appāret domus intus et ātria longa patēscunt;

appārent Priamī et veterum penetrālia rēgum,

armātōsque vident stantīs in līmine prīmō.   485

at domus interior gemitū miserōque tumultū

miscētur, penitusque cavae plangōribus aedēs

fēmineīs ululant; ferit aurea sīdera clāmor.

tum pavidae tēctīs mātrēs ingentibus errant

amplexaeque tenent postīs atque ōscula fīgunt.   490

***ipse** refers to Pyrrhus (= Neoptolemus).

aedēs, aedis, -ium *f.* sanctuary, shrine; *in pl.*, house, abode

aerātus, -a, -um made of bronze

amplector, amplectī, amplexus sum embrace; clasp (for protection)

appāreō, appārēre, appāruī, appāritus be visible, be clear; appear, become evident

armō (1-tr.) equip (with arms), arm

at (conj.) but

ātrium, ātriī *n.* atrium, the main room of a Roman house

aureus, -a, -um golden

bipennis, bipennis *f.* two-edged axe, **bipennī** = *abl. sing.*

cardō, cardinis *m.* pivot; hinge

cavō (1-tr.) hollow out; cut through

cavus, -a, -um hollow

clāmor, clāmōris *m.* shout, shouting; noise

corripiō, corripere, corripuī, correptus snatch up

excīdō, excīdere, excīdī, excīsus cut down, cut out

fēmineus, -a, -um of *or* belonging to a woman, feminine

fenestra, fenestrae *f.* window; hole, breach

feriō, ferīre, ——, —— strike, hit

fīgō, fīgere, fīxī, fīxus fix, affix; plant

firmus, -a, -um strong, sturdy

gemitus, gemitūs *m.* groan(ing), moan(ing)

interior, interius (comparative adj.) inner; **interior** = *fem. sing. nom.*

intus (adv.) within, inside

lātus, -a, -um broad, wide

līmen, līminis *n.* entrance, doorway, threshold

longus, -a, -um long

misceō, miscēre, miscuī, mixtus mix, stir up; throw into confusion

ōs, ōris *n.* mouth; face; aperture, opening

ōsculum, ōsculī *n.* kiss

patēscō, patēscere, patuī, —— become visible, be disclosed

pavidus, -a, -um trembling, frightened

penetrāle, penetrālis, -ium *n.* inner part, inmost recess; inner shrine

penitus (adv.) (from) within, deeply

perrumpō, perrumpere, perrūpī, perruptus break *or* burst through

plangor, plangōris *m.* beating (of the breast in grief); lamentation

postis, postis, -ium *m.* doorpost, jamb

rōbur, rōboris *n.* oak tree; timber

sīdus, sīderis *n.* star; constellation

tēctum, tēctī *n.* roof; house, dwelling

trabs, trabis *f.* tree trunk; beam

tum (adv.) then, at that time

tumultus, tumultūs *m.* commotion, uproar

ululō (1-intr.) howl (in grief or as part of a religious ritual), wail

vellō, vellere, vellī or **vulsī, vulsus** pull (up), tear (from)

vetus, veteris old, ancient; **veterum** = *gen. pl.*

2. Ovid, *Metamorphōsēs* I.452–62

The poet recounts the tale of Apollo and Daphne.

prīmus amor Phoebī Daphnē Pēnēia, quem nōn

fors ignāra dedit, sed saeva Cupīdinis īra.

Dēlius hunc nūper victā serpente superbus

vīderat adductō flectentem cornua nervō   455

"quid" que "tibī,* lascīve puer, cum fortibus armīs?"

dīxerat: "ista decent umerōs gestāmina nostrōs,

quī† dare certa ferae, dare vulnera possumus hostī,

quī modo pestiferō tot iūgera ventre prementem

strāvimus innumerīs tumidum Pythōna sagittīs.   460

tū face nescio quōs‡ estō contentus amōrēs

inrītāre tuā, nec laudēs adsere§ nostrās!"

---

*The final **-i** of **tibi** here scans *long*.

†**quī**, antecedent is **nōs** implied in **nostrōs**

‡**nescio quōs** = *masc. pl. acc. of indef. adj.,* I-don't-know-what, some . . . or other; the **-ō** of **nesciō** here scans *short*.

§**nec . . . adsere** = *negative imperative*

addūcō (**ad-** + **dūcō**) lead toward; draw back, bend

adserō, adserere, adseruī, adsertus grasp, claim as one's own

contentus, -a, -um content, satisfied

cornū, cornūs *n.* horn; *in sing. or pl.,* bow; **cornua** = *acc. pl.*

Daphnē, Daphnēs *f.* Daphne, a nymph, daughter of the river Peneus; **Daphnēs** = *gen. sing.*

deceō, decēre, ——, —— fit, befit; add grace to, adorn, become

Dēlius, -a, -um of Delos, Delian; *as masc. subst.,* Delian Apollo

estō = *2nd sing. fut. act. imper., used in formal language or general precepts for orders,* (you will) be

fax, facis *f.* firebrand, torch

fera, ferae *f.* wild animal, beast

flectō, flectere, flexī, flexus bend

fors, fortis, -ium *f.* chance, luck

gestāmen, gestāminis *n.* something worn *or* carried; ornament, weapon

ignārus, -a, -um not knowing, ignorant

innumerus, -a, -um innumerable, countless

inrītō (= **irrītō**) (1-tr.) provoke, stimulate

iūgerum, iūgerī *n.* iugerum, measure of land (= $\frac{2}{3}$ acre); acre

lascīvus, -a, -um playful, naughty, free from restraint

laus, laudis *f.* praise

modo (adv.) only, now; just now

nervus, nervī *m.* sinew; (bow-)string

nūper (adv.) recently

Pēnēius, -a, -um of Peneus (a river god)

pestifer, pestifera, pestiferum disease-carrying, deadly

Phoebus, Phoebī *m.* Phoebus (Apollo)

premō, premere, pressī, pressus press (down), burden; afflict

Pythōn, Pythōnis *m.* Python; **Pythōna** = *acc. sing.*

saevus, -a, -um cruel, savage

sagitta, sagittae *f.* arrow

serpēns, serpentis, -ium *f.* snake, serpent

sternō, sternere, strāvī, strātus strew; lay low, slay, kill

superbus, -a, -um proud; haughty

tot (indeclinable adj.) so many

tumidus, -a, -um swollen

umerus, umerī *m.* shoulder

venter, ventris *m.* belly, stomach

vulnus, vulneris *n.* wound

§103. Rhetorical Terms

Writers of Latin prose and poetry regularly employed many modes of expression that are called **rhetorical devices**. Rhetoric, the principal subject studied in Roman education, may be defined as the art of persuasion in speech or in writing. *How* Roman speakers or writers expressed something was virtually inseparable from *what* they said or wrote. Indeed, the chosen style of any writer is in large part reflected in his distinctive use of the devices of rhetoric. LEARN THE FOLLOWING BASIC RHETORICAL TERMS AND THEIR DEFINITIONS. BE PREPARED TO IDENTIFY THEM IN THE READINGS.

Tricolon	(< Greek *trikōlos,* "three-limbed") three-part structure comprising three words, phrases, or clauses
Anaphora	(< Greek *anaphora,* "rising; repetition") repetition of the same word or words at the beginning of successive phrases or clauses
Asyndeton	(< Greek *asyndetos,* "unconnected") absence of connectives between phrases or clauses
Ellipsis	(< Greek *elleipsis,* "ellipse, omission") omission of one or more grammatical elements that may be supplied from context
Antithesis	(< Greek *antithesis,* "opposition") opposition or contrast of two ideas
Chiasmus	(< Greek *chiasmus,* "placing crosswise") arrangement of pairs, the second element of which is in inverted order (ABBA)
Hyperbaton	(< Greek *hyperbatos,* "going beyond") separation of two words that normally belong together
Hendiadys	(< Greek *hen dia duoin,* "one through two") one idea expressed through two nouns connected by "and" when a closer relation is suggested
Alliteration	repetition of the same sound at the beginning of successive words
Assonance	(< **assonō**, "sound in accompaniment") repetition of identical or similar sounds in words

Examples

quis hanc contumēliam, quis hoc imperium, quis hanc servitūtem ferre potest?
(Cato, quoted in Aulus Gellius, *Noctēs Atticae* X.3.17)

      (tricolon, anaphora, asyndeton, ellipsis)

Who is able to endure *this abuse, who this authority, who this slavery?*

haec enim est tyrannōrum vīta nīmīrum, in quā *nūlla fidēs, nūlla cāritās, nūlla* stabilis benivolentiae potest esse *fidūcia* . . . (Cicero, *Dē Amīcitiā* 52–53)

      (tricolon, anaphora, asyndeton, hyperbaton)

This is without doubt the life of tyrants, in which *no faith, no affection, no trust* of constant goodwill is able to exist.

ergō *Hannibal hostis, cīvis Antōnius?* (Cicero, *Philippics* V 24)

      (chiasmus, antithesis, asyndeton, ellipsis)

Therefore *(is) Hannibal an enemy, (but) Antony a citizen?*

omnēs enim in cōnsulis iūre et imperiō dēbent esse *prōvinciae*. (Cicero, *Philippics IV* 9)
    (hyperbaton)

For *all the provinces* ought to be in the right and power of the consul.

neque enim illum, quem facile tulerant, ratiōne aut sapientiā tulerant, sed *studiō*
potius *et glōriā*. (Cicero, *Tusculānae Disputātiōnēs* II.65)
    (hendiadys)

Nor indeed that (pain), which they had easily endured, had they endured because of reason or wisdom, but rather because of *a zeal for glory*.

tēne, sacer vātēs, flammae *r*apuēre *r*ogālēs

    *p*ectoribus *p*āscī nec *t*imuēre *t*uīs? (Ovid, *Amōrēs* III.9.41–42)
    (alliteration)

Sacred poet, have the flames of the funeral pyre consumed you
    and have they not feared to feed on your chest?

. . . hau*d doctīs dictīs* certan*tēs, se*d male*dictīs* . . . (Ennius, *Annālēs* VIII.250)
    (assonance)

contending not at all by learned words, but by insults . . .

OBSERVATIONS

1. Several rhetorical devices may be combined in the same sentence. In the first example the tricolon gains speed through the use of anaphora and asyndeton. The repeated element **quis** emphasizes the structure of the tricolon and allows the succeeding elements to be highlighted (**contumēliam, imperium, servitūtem**).

2. Although the limbs of a tricolon are often of uniform length, the third limb (**nūlla . . . fidūcia**) is often expanded, as in the second example.

3. Hyperbaton (**nūlla . . . fidūcia, omnēs . . . prōvinciae**) adds liveliness or surprise to the words that have been separated.

4. The hendiadys **studiō . . . et glōriā** (because of zeal . . . and glory) expresses one idea: because of a zeal for glory.

When one studies a particular writer's use of rhetoric, it is convenient to refer to the unit known as the **period** (< Greek *periodos*, "a going around") or periodic sentence. A **periodic sentence** is a complex sentence arranged in such a way that meaning is not fully grasped until the end. The most important elements of the main clause are often placed at the beginning and the end, enclosing several subordinate structures. Additional elements and subordinate clauses are arranged within the whole for maximum cohesion and clarity. For example:

Helvētiī cum omnibus suīs carrīs secūtī impedīmenta in ūnum locum *contulērunt; ipsī* cōnfertissimā aciē, reiectō nostrō equitātū, phalange factā, sub prīmam nostram aciem *successērunt*.

The Helvetians, having followed with all their wagons, *brought together* (their) baggage into one place; *they themselves,* with the battle line being very dense, with our cavalry having been driven back, with a phalanx having been made, *approached* up to our first battle line.

The periodic structure of this sentence may be represented as follows:

> *Helvētiī*
> > cum omnibus suīs carrīs secūtī
> impedīmenta in ūnum locum *contulērunt*;
> *ipsī*
> > cōnfertissimā aciē,
> > reiectō nostrō equitātū,
> > phalange factā,
> sub prīmam nostram aciem *successērunt*.

CHAPTER XI

Vocabulary

➤ **audācia, audāciae** *f.* boldness; recklessness, audacity

➤ **campus, campī** *m.* (flat) plain
➤ **castra, castrōrum** *n. pl.* (military) camp
mūrus, mūrī *m.* wall
➤ **paulum, *paulī**[1] *n.* small amount, a little
➤ **signum, signī** *n.* sign, signal; standard
➤ **tēlum, tēlī** *n.* spear; weapon

➤ **ignis, ignis, -ium** *m.* fire
➤ **imperātor, imperātōris** *m.* commander,
general
➤ **legiō, legiōnis** *f.* legion
➤ **lūx, lūcis** *f.* light, daylight
➤ **prīmā lūce** (idiom) at daybreak
➤ **maiōrēs, maiōrum** *m. pl.* ancestors

➤ **sēnsus, sēnsūs** *m.* perception, feeling;
sense

arbitror (1-tr.) judge, consider, think
putō (1-tr.) think, suppose

➤ **soleō, solēre, solitus sum** be accustomed

➤ **crēdō, crēdere, crēdidī, crēditus** trust, believe (+ dat.)
➤ **iaciō, iacere, iēcī, iactus** throw; utter; lay,
establish
➤ **ēiciō, ēicere, ēiēcī, ēiectus** throw out,
expel

➤ **loquor, loquī, locūtus sum** speak

➤ **inveniō, invenīre, invēnī, inventus** find,
discover
➤ **sciō, scīre, scīvī** or **sciī, scītus** know
➤ **nesciō, nescīre, nescīvī** or **nesciī ,
nescītus** not know

➤ **pereō, perīre, periī, peritūrus** pass away,
be destroyed; perish, die

longus, -a, -um long; far; long-standing;
far-reaching
➤ **summus, -a, -um** highest; top (of); last,
final

brevis, breve short, brief
humilis, humile humble
sapiēns, sapientis wise
➤ **similis, simile** similar (+ gen. *or* dat.)
➤ **dissimilis, dissimile** dissimilar, unlike,
different (+ gen. *or* dat.)

➤ **diū** (adv.) for a long time
fore = **futūrus, -a, -um esse** (§104)
➤ **igitur** (postpositive conj.) therefore
longē (adv.) a long way, far; by far
➤ **parum** (indeclinable subst.) too little, not
enough
(adv.) too little, inadequately
prīmum (adv.) first; for the first time
quam prīmum, as soon as possible
quam (adv.) as, how; (conj.) than (§111)

---

1. The asterisk before the genitive singular form of **paulum** indicates that the form does not occur in the Latin
that survives.

Chapter XI

Vocabulary Notes

audācia, audāciae *f.* is an abstract noun formed by the addition of the suffix **-ia** to the stem of an adjective meaning "bold" or "audacious." **Audācia** may have a positive sense (boldness, confidence), but more often has a negative sense of excessive boldness (recklessness or audacity).

    campus, campī *m.* is a flat expanse of land or "plain." The **Campus Martius** (< **Martius, -a, -um,** of *or* belonging to Mars) was the plain just outside the sacred boundary of Rome, in which the Roman troops trained, Roman armies mustered before entering the city in triumph, and Roman citizens gathered in assembly in order to elect consuls and other high magistrates. The noun **campus** without an accompanying adjective may refer to the *Campus Martius.*

    Although **castra, castrōrum** *n. pl.* is plural in form, it has a singular meaning (military encampment). **castra** appears in two common idioms: **castra pōnere,** "to pitch *or* make camp" and **castra movēre,** "to break camp."

    paulum, *paulī *n.* appears in the nominative, accusative, and ablative singular only. It often functions as an Ablative of Degree of Difference (see §111). It is also commonly found with a Partitive Genitive.

Paulō ante discesserant.	They had departed earlier *by a little* (a little earlier).
Paulum eī erat *pecūniae.*	There was a little *of money* to him.
	He had a little *(of) money.*

signum, signī *n.* may mean any sort of "mark" or "sign." It may also mean "signal" or, in military contexts, a "standard" or identifying flag carried by each legion.

    tēlum, tēlī *n.* originally referred only to a throwing weapon (spear, javelin, dart), but its use was soon extended to include other weapons. It may also refer to the "shaft" of a throwing weapon as opposed to the point.

    The ablative singular of **ignis, ignis, -ium** *m.* is usually **ignī** (by analogy with *neuter* third-declension i-stem nouns). In poetry and in post-Augustan Latin, the regular form **igne** also occurs.

    imperātor, imperātōris *m.* is formed by the addition of the suffix **-tor** to the present stem of the verb **imperō.** An **imperātor** is one who gives orders, and it is most often used of a military "commander" or "general." It is also an honorific title granted to a victorious commander either by his troops or by the senate.

    legiō, legiōnis *f.* was the largest unit of the Roman army. Its size ranged at various periods of the Roman Republic and Empire from 4,200 to 6,000 men.

    lūx, lūcis *f.* may mean "light" generally or "daylight." It may also mean "light" more metaphorically (mental illumination, light [of hope], etc.). **Prīmā lūce,** literally "at first light," is an Ablative of Time When.

    maiōrēs, maiōrum *m. pl.* is a substantive of the comparative adjective **maior, maius** (see §110).

    sēnsus, sēnsūs *m.* is an abstract noun formed by the addition of the suffix **-tus** to a stem of the verb **sentiō.** The **-t-** of the suffix assimilated to the **-s-** of the stem **sēns-** and was then lost.

    soleō, solēre, solitus sum is an intransitive semideponent verb. It regularly takes a Complementary Infinitive.

Bonus sine īrā dīcere *solet.*	A good man *is accustomed* to speak(ing) without anger.

crēdō, crēdere, crēdidī, crēditus may be transitive *or* intransitive. When transitive, it often takes a neuter pronoun as a direct object. When **crēdō** is intransitive, it may take a Dative with an Intransitive Verb. In the *passive,* **crēdō** may have a personal subject. **Crēdō** may also introduce an Indirect Statement.

Tē amō, crēde *mihi.*	I love you, believe *me.* (Dative with an Intransitive Verb)
Crēdunt *id* quod vident.	They believe *that thing* that they see. (d.o.)
Crēditur captus esse.	He is believed to have been captured. (passive voice, personal subject)
Crēdisne mē tē amāre?	Do you believe that I love you? (Indirect Statement)

    The first letter of the verb **iaciō, iacere, iēcī, iactus** is a *consonantal* **i** and is thus pronounced like English **y.** **Iaciō** may mean "throw" or "cast" in a literal sense (rocks, javelins, lightning bolts) or a metaphorical one (injury, abuse, ridicule, remarks, kisses). It may also mean "lay" or "establish" (foundations, walls, ramparts).

    ēiciō, ēicere, ēiēcī, ēiectus is a compound verb formed by the addition of the prefix **ē-** to **iaciō.** It exhibits regular vowel weakening in the first, second, and fourth principal parts. (For the prefix **ē-** see Appendix P.) In the first two principal parts (and all forms made from them), the first **-i-** is pronounced as a consonantal **-i-** followed by the vocalic **-i-,** as if they were spelled **ēiiciō, *ēiicere.* In the third principal part (**ēiēcī**), the root vowel exhibits ablaut and changes to **-ē-.** The **-i-** in the third and fourth principal parts is consonantal. THE PRINCIPAL PARTS OF *ALL* COMPOUNDS OF **IACIŌ** FOLLOW THE PATTERN OF THE PRINCIPAL PARTS OF **ĒICIŌ.** WHEN

A COMPOUND OF **IACIŌ** APPEARS IN READINGS, ITS PRINCIPAL PARTS ARE NOT SUPPLIED, BUT THE PREFIX AND SIMPLE VERB ARE GIVEN. When **ēiciō** takes a reflexive pronoun as a direct object, the combination may mean "rush forth."

Compounds of **loquor, loquī, locūtus sum** do *not* exhibit vowel weakening. WHEN A COMPOUND OF **LOQUOR** APPEARS IN READINGS, ITS PRINCIPAL PARTS ARE NOT SUPPLIED, BUT THE PREFIX AND SIMPLE VERB ARE GIVEN.

inveniō, invenīre, invēnī, inventus is a compound verb formed by the addition of **in-** to **veniō** and does *not* exhibit vowel weakening. (For the prefix **in-**[1] see Appendix P.) Unlike **veniō, inveniō** is a transitive verb.

sciō, scīre, scīvī or **sciī, scītus** means "know" in the broadest sense of the word. In particular, **sciō** means "know" facts. **Sciō** has *two* third principal parts, either of which may be used to make any of the forms of the perfect active system. When **sciō** takes an infinitive, it means "know how."

Poēta causās rērum *scit.*	The poet *knows* the causes of things.
Caesar vincere *scīvit.*	Caesar *knew how* to conquer.

The present active imperative forms of **sciō** almost never appear in the Latin that survives, but this verb uses instead the future active imperative forms **scītō** (singular) and **scītōte** (plural) with present meanings. MEMORIZE THESE FORMS.

nesciō, nescīre, nescīvī or **nesciī, nescītus** is a compound verb formed by the addition of the negative prefix **ne-** to **sciō**. **Nesciō** has *two* third principal parts, either of which may be used to make any of the forms of the perfect active system. When **nesciō** takes an infinitive, it means "not know how."

pereō, perīre, periī, peritūrus is a compound verb formed by the addition of the prefix **per-** to the irregular verb **eō**. (For the prefix **per-** see Appendix P.) **Pereō** conjugates exactly as **eō** *except* that it has only *one* third principal part. **Pereō** may be used synonymously for **morior** and be translated "perish" or "die." When its subject is not human, **pereō** may mean "pass away" or "be destroyed." It is also used metaphorically to mean "die" or "pine away" for love. The first person singular present active subjunctive may be used as an Optative, future wish capable of fulfillment, to assert something strongly. The first person (singular and plural) perfect active indicative—and occasionally other forms—may be used hyperbolically to express panic (I am/We are destroyed/lost/done for).

Multī mīlitum *periērunt.*	Many of the soldiers *died.*
Magnae urbēs cum moenibus *pereunt.*	Great cities with their (city) walls *pass away.*
***Peream** nisi ista mē movent verba.*	*May I die* if those words do not move me.
Ingeniō meō *periī!*	*I am lost* because of my own talent!

When **summus, -a, -um** expresses the notion of the "top of" a place by *modifying that place,* it usually appears *before* the noun it modifies.

similis, simile and **dissimilis, dissimile** may take either a genitive or a dative expressing that which something is "similar" or "dissimilar" *to.*

***Patris** similis est hic fīlius.*	This son is similar *to (his) father.*
Quid *illī* simile *bellō* fuit?	What was similar *to that war?*

The temporal adverb **diū** often appears in the phrase **iam diū**, "for a long time now." When this phrase occurs with a verb in the present tense, the present tense reports an action that has been going on for some time and is still going on. This use of the present tense requires a special English translation.

Hoc iam diū dīcō.	I have been saying this thing for a long time now.
Hoc iam diū scīmus.	We have known this thing for a long time now.

In classical Latin, **igitur** is most frequently a postpositive conjunction. (In the historians Sallust and Tacitus, however, **igitur** is nearly always placed first.) **Igitur** is used to join a sentence with a preceding one to indicate the consequence or inference of a preceding idea or series of ideas. Occasionally it is used to indicate the resumption of an idea after a digression (well then).

Like **satis**, **parum** may be an indeclinable neuter substantive or an adverb. While **satis** means "enough," **parum** describes what falls short of enough (too little).

Chapter XI

	Derivatives	**Cognates**
audācia	*audac*ity	
brevis	brief; ab*brev*iate	***brach*ium**; *merry*; *pretzel*
campus	campus	
crēdō	*credo*; *credit*; *cred*ible; mis*cre*ant	heart; dis*cord*; *cour*age; *card*iac
iaciō	in*ject*; ad*jec*tive; *jet*	ca*thet*er
ignis	*ign*ite; *ign*eous	
longus	*long*itude; lunge; *long*evity; pur*loin*	long; *linger*; be*long*; *Lent*
loquor	*loqu*acious; circum*locut*ion; soli*loqu*y	
lūx	*Luci*fer; *luc*ulent	*light*
mūrus	*mur*al	
parum		*poor*; *filly*; *puer*
putō	com*put*e	
sciō	*sci*ence; pre*sci*ent	*shy*ster; *sch*ism; re*scind*; *shed*
signum	*sign*; *sign*al; seal	
similis	*simil*ar; as*simi*late; re*semb*le	*simplex*; *simple*; same; *single*; *sandhi*; seem

§104. Infinitives

In addition to the present active infinitive (the second principal part) and present passive infinitive (see §31), there are three other infinitives in regular use in Latin: the perfect active infinitive, perfect passive infinitive, and future active infinitive. The following chart presents these infinitives and their basic translations:

	Active	Passive
Present	2nd Prin. Part vocāre movēre regere "to _____" capere audīre	Change final **-e** of 2nd Prin. Part to **-ī** (In 3rd conj., change final **-ere** to **-ī**) vocārī movērī regī "to be _____ed" capī audīrī
Perfect	Perfect Active Stem from 3rd Prin. Part + **-isse** vocāvisse mōvisse rēxisse "to have cēpisse _____ed" audīvisse	Perfect Passive Participle + **esse** vocātus, -a, -um esse mōtus, -a, -um esse rēctus, -a, -um esse "to have been captus, -a, -um esse _____ed" audītus, -a, -um esse

Future	Future Active Participle + **esse**
	vocātūrus,
	   -a, -um esse
	mōtūrus,
	   -a, -um esse "to be
	rēctūrus, about to/
	   -a, -um esse going to
	captūrus, _____"
	   -a, -um esse
	audītūrus,
	   -a, -um esse
		Rare

OBSERVATIONS

1. The perfect active infinitive of **īre** may be either **īvisse** or **īsse** (< i- + -isse).

2. Deponent verbs have three infinitives: present passive (second principal part), perfect passive, and future active. All have active meanings. For example: **cōnārī**, "to attempt," **cōnātus, -a, -um esse**, "to have attempted," and **cōnātūrus, -a, -um esse**, "to be going to attempt."

3. Semideponent verbs have three infinitives: present active (second principal part), perfect passive, and future active. All have active meanings. For example: **audēre**, "to dare," **ausus, -a, -um esse**, "to have dared," and **ausūrus, -a, -um esse**, "to be going to dare."

4. A future passive infinitive exists in Latin, but it is rarely used. For its formation see §142, n. 4.

5. The future active infinitive of sum (**futūrus, -a, -um esse**) has an alternate form: **fore**. MEMORIZE THIS IRREGULAR INFINITIVE FORM.

Periphrastic Infinitives

The active and passive periphrastics also have infinitive forms. For example:

Active Periphrastic Infinitives		
Present	**rēctūrus, -a, -um esse**	to be about to rule
Perfect	**rēctūrus, -a, -um fuisse**	to have been about to rule

Passive Periphrastic Infinitives		
Present	**regendus, -a, -um esse**	to be having to be ruled
Perfect	**regendus, -a, -um fuisse**	to have been having to be ruled

OBSERVATION

The present infinitive of the active periphrastic is also used as the future active infinitive of the verb. Thus, for example, **rēctūrus, -a, -um esse** may be identified as the present infinitive of the active periphrastic of **regō** or the future active infinitive of **regō**.

§105. Synopsis VII: Complete

When one generates a synopsis that includes the infinitive, the infinitive follows the participle and precedes the imperative. Here is a model synopsis of **agō** in the third person plural neuter:

	Active	Translation	Passive	Translation
Principal Parts:	**agō, agere, ēgī, āctus**			
Person, Number, and Gender:	**3rd pl. n.**			
Indicative				
Present	**agunt**	they are driving	**aguntur**	they are (being) driven
Imperfect	**agēbant**	they were driving	**agēbantur**	they were being driven
Future	**agent**	they will drive	**agentur**	they will be driven
Perfect	**ēgērunt/ ēgēre**	1. they drove 2. they have driven	**ācta sunt**	1. they (n.) were driven 2. they (n.) have been driven
Pluperfect	**ēgerant**	they had driven	**ācta erant**	they (n.) had been driven
Future Perfect	**ēgerint**	they will have driven	**ācta erunt**	they (n.) will have been driven
Subjunctive				
Present	**agant**		**agantur**	
Imperfect	**agerent**		**agerentur**	
Perfect	**ēgerint**		**ācta sint**	
Pluperfect	**ēgissent**		**ācta essent**	
Participle				
Present	**agēns**	driving	—	
Perfect	—		**āctus, -a, -um**	(having been) driven
Future	**āctūrus, -a, -um**	about to drive	**agendus, -a, -um**	having to be driven
Infinitive				
Present	**agere**	to drive	**agī**	to be driven
Perfect	**ēgisse**	to have driven	**āctus, -a, -um esse**	to have been driven
Future	**āctūrus, -a, -um esse**	to be going to drive	RARE	
Imperative				
Singular	**age**	drive	**agere**	be driven
Plural	**agite**	drive	**agiminī**	be driven

OBSERVATIONS

1. This complete synopsis reviews the indicative, subjunctive, and imperative moods, the participle and the infinitive.

2. In a synopsis basic English translations should be given for *all* forms *except* the subjunctive.

3. Since participles and infinitives are not *finite* forms, always give participles (including those in compound infinitives) in the *full nominative singular* form no matter what person, number, and gender have been chosen for the indicative and subjunctive forms.

4. Imperatives appear in the second person singular and plural only. Always give the second person singular and plural imperative forms no matter what person, number, and gender have been chosen for the indicative and subjunctive forms.

☛ DRILL 104–105 MAY NOW BE DONE.

§106. Indirect Statement and the Subject Accusative

In both English and Latin what someone says may be reported in a *direct quotation*. For example:

> He says, "I understand well the poems of Vergil."
> **Dīcit, "Carmina Vergilī bene intellegō."**

Speech, thoughts, and perceptions may also be reported *indirectly*. In English, no comma and no quotation marks are used, the conjunction "that" is usually added, and changes in pronouns and verb tenses regularly occur. For example:

> He says *that he understands well the poems of Vergil.*
> (Original statement: I understand well the poems of Vergil.)
> We thought *that he understood well the poems of Vergil.*
> (Original thought: He understands well the poems of Vergil.)

Each italicized phrase is a subordinate clause, part of a complex sentence, the main clause of which is the introductory phrase (He says, We thought). Such subordinate clauses are rendered in Latin by a construction called **Indirect Statement**. An Indirect Statement in Latin:

1. *is introduced by* a **verb of perception**
2. *lacks* a subordinating conjunction equivalent to the English "that"[2]
3. has a *subject* in the *accusative* case (called a **Subject Accusative of an Indirect Statement**)[3]
4. has a *verb* in the *infinitive*[3]

OBSERVATION

A verb of perception is a verb of speaking, thinking, knowing, perceiving, and the like. In addition, certain phrases with related meanings—"There is a rumor," "There was a story," etc.—may also introduce Indirect Statement.

THE TENSE AND VOICE OF THE INFINITIVE IN INDIRECT STATEMENT CORRESPOND AS CLOSELY AS POSSIBLE TO THE TENSE AND VOICE OF THE VERB IN THE DIRECT STATEMENT, THOUGHT, OR PERCEPTION THAT IS BEING REPORTED INDIRECTLY. In addition, the in-

---

2. It is possible in colloquial English to omit the subordinating conjunction "that." For example: "We thought he understood well the poems of Vergil."

3. Cf. the English "I know *him to be* honorable" (= I know that he is honorable).

finitive in an Indirect Statement shows time relative to the verb of perception that introduces it.

A *present* infinitive represents an action that is *simultaneous* with the main verb.

A *perfect* infinitive represents an action that is *prior* to the main verb.

A *future* infinitive represents an action that is *subsequent* to the main verb.[4]

For example:

Carmina Vergilī bene *intellegit*.		*He understands* well the poems of Vergil.
Cōgitō	*eum* **carmina Vergilī**	*I think that he understands . . .*
Cōgitābam	**bene *intellegere*.**	*I was thinking that he understood . . .*
Cōgitābō		*I shall think that he understands . . .*
Carmina Vergilī bene *intellēxit*.		*He understood* well the poems of Vergil.
Cōgitō	*eum* **carmina Vergilī**	*I think that he understood . . .*
Cōgitābam	**bene *intellēxisse*.**	*I was thinking that he had understood . . .*
Cōgitābō		*I shall think that he understood . . .*
Carmina Vergilī bene *intelleget*.		*He will understand* well the poems of Vergil.
Cōgitō	*eum* **carmina Vergilī**	*I think that he will understand . . .*
Cōgitābam	**bene *intellēctūrum***	*I was thinking that he would understand . . .*
Cōgitābō	**esse.**	*I shall think that he will understand . . .*

OBSERVATIONS

1. A Subject Accusative is usually the first word of an Indirect Statement in Latin. THE WORD "THAT" SHOULD BE ADDED AT THE BEGINNING OF AN ENGLISH TRANSLATION OF AN INDIRECT STATEMENT, AND THE INFINITIVE SHOULD BE TRANSLATED AS A FINITE VERB.

2. In each Indirect Statement the syntax of **eum** is **Subject Accusative of an Indirect Statement**.

3. The infinitives **intellegere**, **intellēxisse**, and **intellēctūrum esse** are, respectively, present active, perfect active, and future active. Each is translated into English by a *finite verb* that shows *time relative to the main verb*. CARE MUST BE TAKEN TO INDICATE THE RELATIVE TIME TO THE MAIN VERB OF THE INFINITIVE IN AN INDIRECT STATEMENT.

4. Any participle that is part of an infinitive in Indirect Statement agrees with the Subject Accusative in *gender, number, and case*. For example, the future active participle **intellēctūrum** (part of the future active infinitive) is *masculine singular accusative* to agree with **eum**.

5. An Indirect Statement is a noun clause. It most often functions as the direct object of the verb of perception that introduces it.

When the infinitive in an Indirect Statement is a linking verb such as **sum**, it is often accompanied by a **Predicate Accusative** or a **Predicate Adjective in the Accusative case**. For example:

Cōgitāsne nostram rēgīnam esse *fēminam* magnae sapientiae?
Do you think that our queen is *a woman* of great wisdom?
Cōgitāsne nostram rēgīnam esse *fēlīcem*?
Do you think that our queen is *fortunate*?

4. Cf. the relative time of participles, §96.

The syntax of **fēminam** is **Predicate Accusative**, and the syntax of **fēlīcem** is **Predicate Adjective in the Accusative case**.

The **esse** of infinitives that are compound forms may be omitted.[5] For example:

> **Dīcit sē quattuor diēbus ad prōvinciam *profectūram*.** (future active infinitive)
> She says that she within four days to the province *will set forth*.
> She says that she *will set forth* to the province within four days.

In the English sentence "It is said that Marcus will lead the troops into battle," the verb of perception "It is said" is used impersonally. In classical Latin this impersonal use of a verb of perception in the passive voice is avoided in the present system, and the subject of the Indirect Statement becomes the subject of the verb of perception. This is called the **personal construction** of an Indirect Statement. For example:

> **Marcus dīcitur cōpiās in proelium ductūrus esse.**
> Marcus is said the troops (d.o.) into battle to be going to lead.
> Marcus is said to be going to lead the troops into battle.

OBSERVATIONS

1. In the personal construction the subject of the verb of perception in the passive voice is *nominative*, the English word "that" is *not* added, and the infinitive is translated with its basic meaning (see §104). If the infinitive is a compound form, as in the sentence above, the participle agrees in gender, number, and case with the nominative subject of the sentence.

2. If the verb of perception is a compound form in the perfect passive system, it may be used impersonally with the entire Indirect Statement functioning as the impersonal subject. For example:

> **Dictum est Marcum cōpiās in proelium ductūrum esse.**
> It was said that Marcus the troops (d.o.) into battle would lead.
> That Marcus would lead the troops into battle was said.
> It was said that Marcus would lead the troops into battle.

☛ DRILL 106 MAY NOW BE DONE.

§107. A Note on the Subject Accusative

A Subject Accusative may appear as the subject of an infinitive in constructions other than Indirect Statement. For example:

> **Optō *mē* esse bonum.**   I desire *myself* to be good.
> **Satis est *mē* servitūte līberārī.**   Enough (it) is *for me* from slavery to be freed.
>   It is enough *for me* to be freed from slavery.
>   It is enough *that I* be freed from slavery.

OBSERVATIONS

1. In the first sentence the syntax of **esse** is **Object Infinitive**, and the syntax of **mē** is **Subject Accusative**. (**Optō** is *not* a verb of perception.)

---

5. Cf. the omission of the forms of **sum** in compound forms of the perfect passive system (§51).

2. In the second sentence, the syntax of **līberārī** is **Subject Infinitive**, and the syntax of **mē** is **Subject Accusative**. It is often convenient to translate such noun clauses with the English words "for . . . to . . . " *or* "that . . . (English present subjunctive) . . . "

§108. Subordinate Clauses in Indirect Statement

When a complex sentence is subordinated in Indirect Statement, the main clause appears with a *Subject Accusative* and *verb in the infinitive*. The *subordinate clause* appears with a verb in the subjunctive according to the rules of sequence.[6] Compare the same sentence presented first as a direct quotation and then in Indirect Statement:

> **Dux dīcit/dīcēbat, "Mīles quī fūgit poenās dabit."**
> The leader says/was saying, "The soldier who fled will pay the penalty."
> **Dux dīcit mīlitem quī *fūgerit* poenās datūrum esse.**
> The leader says that the soldier who *fled* will pay the penalty.
> **Dux dīcēbat mīlitem quī *fūgisset* poenās datūrum esse.**
> The leader was saying that the soldier who had fled would pay the penalty.

OBSERVATIONS
___

1. The perfect indicative verb (**fūgit**) in the relative clause of the direct quotation appears as a perfect subjunctive in primary sequence and a pluperfect subjunctive in secondary sequence when the direct quotation is reported indirectly. These tenses reflect the fact that the action of the verb in the relative clause in the direct quotation happened *prior* to the time of the main verb (**dīcit/dīcēbat**).

2. The syntax, for example, of **fūgisset** in the third sentence is **pluperfect subjunctive, Relative Clause Subordinated in Indirect Statement, secondary sequence, time prior to the main verb.**

Although there is no special English translation for the subjunctive verb in a subordinate clause in Indirect Statement, the subjunctive mood indicates that the subordinate clause is to be understood as *part of the original statement or perception* being reported indirectly.

By contrast, the *indicative* mood appears in a subordinate clause in indirect statement when the subordinate clause: 1. is an addition of the writer or speaker of the sentence or 2. contains information vouched for by the writer or speaker. For example:

> **Cicerō sēnsit rem pūblicam, quam magnopere amābat, servandam esse.**
> Cicero perceived that the republic, which he greatly loved, had to be saved.

OBSERVATION
___

In this sentence the person reporting Cicero's feeling that the republic had to be saved indicates by the use of the indicative mood (**amābat**) in the relative clause either 1. that the entire subordinate clause is *not* part of what Cicero felt, but is rather an addition of the writer or speaker, *or* 2. that the writer vouches for Cicero's love of the republic.

☛ DRILL 108 MAY NOW BE DONE.

___

6. When certain types of conditional sentences are subordinated in Indirect Statement, they are treated differently from other complex sentences. The rules for the subordination of conditional sentences are not presented in this book.

§109. Comparison of Adjectives and Adverbs

In both English and Latin, adjectives and adverbs may appear in *three degrees*. For example:

Positive	*Comparative*	*Superlative*
tall	taller; rather tall	tallest; very tall
quickly	more quickly; rather quickly	most quickly, very quickly

Comparative Degree of Adjectives

All regular first-second- and third-declension adjectives in Latin form the comparative degree in the same way. The comparative degree of every adjective in Latin is a *third*-declension adjective with *two* forms in the nominative singular. The endings -ior (m./f.), -ius (n.) are added to the stem of the positive degree of the adjective. For example:

Positive degree	**pulcher, pulchra, pulchrum**
Stem for forming the comparative	**pulchr-**
Comparative degree	**pulchrior, pulchrius**
Stem of the comparative adjective	**pulchriōr-**

For example, the comparative degree of the adjective **pulcher, pulchra, pulchrum** is declined as follows:

	Singular		*Plural*	
	M./F.	N.	M./F.	N.
Nom./Voc.	pulchrior	pulchrius	pulchriōrēs	pulchriōra
Gen.	**pulchriōr**is	**pulchriōr**is	pulchriōrum	pulchriōrum
Dat.	pulchriōrī	pulchriōrī	pulchriōribus	pulchriōribus
Acc.	pulchriōrem	pulchrius	pulchriōrēs/pulchriōrīs	pulchriōra
Abl.	pulchriōre/ pulchriōrī	pulchriōre/ pulchriōrī	pulchriōribus	pulchriōribus

OBSERVATIONS

1. The stem of adjectives in the comparative degree is obtained by dropping the ending of the genitive singular. For example: genitive singular = **pulchriōris**; stem = **pulchriōr-**.

2. The declension of the comparative degree of adjectives uses *some but not all i-stem features* of third-declension adjectives:

   a. the ablative singular ending may be either -e or -ī.
   b. the neuter plural nominative/vocative and accusative is -a (*not* -ia).
   c. the genitive plural ending is -um (*not* -ium).
   d. the masculine/feminine plural accusative ending may be either -ēs or -īs

3. The comparative degree of an adjective has a variety of translations: _____-er," "more _____," "quite _____," "rather _____," "too _____."

4. Since participles are verbal adjectives, some participles appear in the comparative degree. For example: **amantior, amantius**, "more loving"; **optātior, optātius**, "more (having been) desired."

Comparative Degree of Adverbs

To form the *comparative degree* of an *adverb* in Latin, add the ending **-ius** to a stem found by dropping the ending of the positive degree. For example:

Positive degree	**pulchrē, fortiter**
Stem for forming the comparative	**pulchr-, fort-**
Comparative degree	**pulchrius, fortius**

OBSERVATIONS

1. All regular adverbs formed from first-second- and third-declension adjectives form the comparative degree in the same way.

2. The comparative degree of every adverb is identical with the neuter accusative singular form of the comparative adjective.

3. The comparative degree of an adverb has a variety of translations: "more _____-ly," "quite _____-ly," "rather _____-ly," "too _____-ly."

Superlative Degree of Adjectives

To form the superlative degree of an adjective in Latin, add **-issimus, -a, -um** to the stem of the adjective in the positive degree. If the masculine singular nominative form of the positive degree ends in **-r**, add **-rimus, -a, -um** to that form. For example:

Positive degree	**fortis, forte**	Stem: **fort-**
Superlative degree	**fortissimus, -a, -um**	
Positive degree	**pulcher, pulchra, pulchrum**	masc. sing. nom. = **pulcher**
Superlative degree	**pulcherrimus, -a, -um**	

Five adjectives in Latin form the superlative degree by adding **-limus, -a, -um** to the stem.[7] These adjectives are:

facilis, facile	easy
difficilis, difficile	difficult
similis, simile	similar
dissimilis, dissimile	dissimilar
humilis, humile	humble

For example:

Positive degree	**humilis, humile**	Stem: **humil-**
Superlative degree	**humillimus, -a, -um**	

OBSERVATIONS

1. The superlative degree of an adjective has a variety of translations: " _____-est," "most _____," "very _____."

2. Since participles are verbal adjectives, some participles appear in the superlative degree. For example: **amantissimus, -a, -um**, "most loving," **amātissimus, -a, -um**, "most loved."

---

7. A sixth adjective, **gracilis, gracile**, "slender, fine, graceful," also forms its superlative degree by the addition of **-limus**, but the superlative degree of this adjective is extremely rare.

Superlative Degree of Adverbs

To form the *superlative degree* of an *adverb* in Latin, add the ending **-ē** to the stem of the superlative degree of the adjective. For example:

Superlative degree of the adjective	**fortissimus, -a, -um**
Stem of the superlative adjective	**fortissim-**
Superlative degree of the adverb	**fortissimē**

OBSERVATION

The superlative degree of an adverb is translated "most _____-ly," "very _____-ly."

When one generates the comparative and superlative forms of an adjective or adverb from the positive form, one is said to **compare** that adjective or adverb. For example:

Positive	Comparative	Superlative
Adjective		
honestus, -a, -um	**honestior, honestius**	**honestissimus, -a, -um**
honorable	more honorable, etc.	most honorable, etc.
pulcher, pulchra, pulchrum	**pulchrior, pulchrius**	**pulcherrimus, -a, -um**
beautiful	more beautiful, etc.	most beautiful, etc.
fortis, forte	**fortior, fortius**	**fortissimus, -a, -um**
brave	braver, rather brave, etc.	bravest, most brave, etc.
Adverb		
honestē	**honestius**	**honestissimē**
honorably	more honorably, etc.	most honorably, etc.
pulchrē	**pulchrius**	**pulcherrimē**
beautifully	more beautifully, etc.	most beautifully, etc.
fortiter	**fortius**	**fortissimē**
bravely	more bravely, etc.	most bravely, etc.

☛ DRILL 109 MAY NOW BE DONE.

§110. Irregular Comparison of Adjectives and Adverbs

Certain adjectives and adverbs in Latin have *irregular forms* in the comparative and superlative degrees. MEMORIZE THE FOLLOWING IRREGULAR FORMS:

ADJECTIVES

Positive	Comparative	Superlative
bonus, -a, -um	**melior, melius**	**optimus, -a, -um**
good	better	best
malus, -a, -um	**peior, peius**[8]	**pessimus, -a, -um**
bad	worse	worst
magnus, -a, -um	**maior, maius**[8]	**maximus, -a, -um**
great	greater	greatest
parvus, -a, -um	**minor, minus**	**minimus, -a, -um**
small	smaller	smallest
multus, -a, -um	**plūs/plūrēs, plūra**	**plūrimus, -a, -um**
much, many	more	most
————	**prior, prius**	**prīmus, -a, -um**
	earlier	first

OBSERVATIONS

1. The declensions of all irregular comparative adjectives follow the pattern of **pulchrior, pulchrius**.

2. The comparative degree of the adjective **multus, -a, -um** has regular comparative adjective forms in the *plural*, but the *singular* exists *only as a neuter substantive*, "(the amount) more," which is usually followed by a Partitive Genitive. For example, **plūrēs amīcī** (more friends [subj.]; **plūrēs** is masculine plural nominative to agree with **amīcī**), but **plūs pecūniae** ([the amount] more of money; **plūs** = neuter substantive, singular nominative or accusative, followed by **pecūniae**, Partitive Genitive).

3. The masculine singular comparative forms of **magnus** and **parvus** are used to identify a father and son with the same name. For example: **Dionȳsius Maior**, "Dionysius the Elder," **Dionȳsius Minor**, "Dionysius the Younger."

ADVERBS

Positive	Comparative	Superlative
bene well	**melius** better	**optimē** best
male badly	**peius**[9] worse	**pessimē** worst
magnopere greatly	**magis** more greatly	**maximē** most greatly; especially
parum too little	**minus** less	**minimē** least; not at all
multum much	**plūs** more	**plūrimum** most
	prius before, sooner	**prīmum** first
————		
saepe often	**saepius** more often	**saepissimē** most often
diū for a long time	**diūtius** longer	**diūtissimē** longest

OBSERVATION

In the comparative degree several irregular adverbs are identical with the neuter singular accusative of the corresponding comparative adjectives: **melius, peius, minus,** and **prius**.

☛ DRILL 110 MAY NOW BE DONE.

8. **Peior, peius** and **maior, maius** are pronounced as if they were spelled *peiior, *peiius and *maiior, *maiius. In each word the first **-i-** combines with the preceding vowel to create a diphthong, **-ei-** or **-ai-**, the latter of which is pronounced exactly the same as **-ae-**. In each case the second **-i-** is *consonantal* and is thus pronounced like English **-y-**.

9. **Peius** is pronounced as if it were spelled *peiius. The first **-i-** combines with the preceding vowel to create a diphthong, **-ei-**. The second **-i-** is *consonantal* and is thus pronounced like English **-y-**.

§111. Constructions with the Comparative and Superlative Degrees

The comparative degree of adjectives and adverbs is regularly used to *make comparisons* between two persons or things. For example:

> *Altior* est fīlius *quam* pater (est).
> *Taller* is the son *than* (his) father (is).
> The son is *taller than* (his) father.
> **Omnēs sentiunt hunc hominem *pulchrius* cecinisse *quam* illum.**
> All men feel that this man *more beautifully* sang *than* that (man).
> All men feel that this man sang *more beautifully than* that (man).

OBSERVATIONS

1. The Latin word that corresponds to the English conjunction "than" is **quam**.

2. When comparisons are made with **quam**, the elements being compared *must be in the same case.*

When someone or something is compared to what is viewed as the *absolute standard* of a particular quality, the **Ablative of Comparison** is used instead of **quam** and the same case. For example:

> **Patria mihi *vītā* meā est cārior.**
> The homeland is dearer to me *than my life.* (Life is viewed as the absolute standard of dearness.)
> **Quis est nostrō *rēge* peior?**
> Who is worse *than our king*? (Our king is viewed as the absolute standard of badness.)

The syntax of each italicized word (**vītā**, **rēge**) is **Ablative of Comparison**.

OBSERVATION

The Ablative of Comparison arose from the original separative or "from" function of the ablative case (e.g., From [the standpoint of] my life the country is dearer).

A noun or, more commonly, a neuter singular substantive in the ablative case is used to indicate *the degree* or *amount* by which persons or things being compared differ. Such an ablative is called the **Ablative of Degree of Difference**. For example:

Multō altior est fīlius quam pater.	*By much* taller is the son than (his) father.
	The son is *much* taller than (his) father.
Multīs ante *diēbus* Rōmā discessit.	Earlier *by many days* from Rome he departed.
	He departed from Rome many *days* earlier.

The syntax of each italicized word (**multō**, **diēbus**) is **Ablative of Degree of Difference**.

OBSERVATION

The Ablative of Degree of Difference is a variety of the Ablative of Means.

A Purpose clause that contains an adjective or adverb in the comparative degree is frequently introduced by **quō** instead of **ut**. Such a clause is a type of Relative Clause of Purpose (see §92). For example:

> **Clārā vōce dīcō** *quō* **melius audiās.**
> By means of a clear voice I speak *by which degree* better you may hear.
> I speak by means of a clear voice *in order that by this (degree)* you may hear better.

OBSERVATIONS

1. In this construction **quō** is neuter singular ablative of the relative pronoun, and its antecedent is the *entire idea expressed by the main clause*. The syntax of **quō** is Ablative of Degree of Difference (modifying the comparative adverb in the Purpose clause). That is, "I speak by means of a clear voice in order that, *by the degree to which I speak in that way, (by that degree)* you may hear *better*."

2. The second English translation given above (in order that . . . by this [degree] . . . may) is to be preferred. The English phrase "by this (degree)" preserves the close connection between the main clause and the subordinate clause that the relative pronoun in Latin achieves. The words "in order that . . . may" clearly indicate the idea of *purpose* that the clause expresses.

The Partitive Genitive (§34) and the Ablative of Degree of Difference may be found with adjectives and adverbs in the superlative degree. For example:

> **Fortissimus** *omnium* **es.**
> The bravest *of all people* you are. (**omnium** = Partitive Genitive)
> You are the bravest *of all people*.
> **Gladium** *multō* **optimum habeō.**
> A sword (d.o.) *by much* the best I have. (**multō** = Ablative of Degree of Difference)
> I have *by far* the best sword.

The adverb **quam**, "as," "how," may be added to an adjective or adverb in the superlative degree to express the *highest possible* degree. The resulting phrase is translated "as _____ as possible."

> *Quam* **clārissima** **est vōx eius.**   As *clear as possible* is her voice.
>   Her voice is *as clear as possible*.
> **Pugnāte** *quam* **ācerrimē.**   Fight (pl.) *as fiercely as possible*.

☞ DRILL 111 MAY NOW BE DONE.

Short Readings

1. The slave Toxilus explains why he is about to throw a party for all those who helped him overcome his enemy.

   improbus est homō quī beneficium scit accipere et reddere nescit.

   (PLAUTUS, *PERSA* 762)

   beneficium, beneficiī *n.* service, kindness; favor, benefit
   improbus, -a, -um wicked; shameless
   reddō (red- + dō) give back, return

2. The character Chremes responds to a suggestion that he mind his own business.

   homō sum: hūmānī nīl ā mē aliēnum putō. (TERENCE, *HEAUTON TIMOROUMENOS* 77)

   aliēnus, -a, -um belonging to another; alien; estranged
   hūmānus, -a, -um human

3. An example of a proposition based on a false cause

   amor fugiendus nōn est: nam ex eō vērissima nāscitur amīcitia.

   (*RHĒTORICA AD HERENNIUM* II.35)

4. Cicero sums up a description of a Sicilian house that was plundered by Verres.

   Domus erat nōn dominō magis ornāmentō quam cīvitātī. (CICERO, *IN VERREM II* 4.5)

   ornāmentum, ornāmentī *n.* adornment, embellishment

5. Cicero comments on why elections are so unpredictable.

   nihil est incertius vulgō, nihil obscūrius voluntāte hominum, nihil fallācius ratiōne

   tōtā comitiōrum. (CICERO, *PRŌ MURĒNĀ* 36)

   comitia, comitiōrum *n. pl.* (elective) assembly (of the Roman people)
   fallāx, fallācis deceptive, treacherous
   obscūrus, -a, -um dark, dim, obscure; uncertain

   ratiō, ratiōnis *f.* account, reason; reasoning; way, method
   voluntās, voluntātis *f.* will, intention; choice
   vulgus, vulgī *n.* common people, (the) multitude, crowd

6. Cicero tells Catiline clearly that the conspiracy is at an end.

   tenēris undique; lūce sunt clāriōra nōbīs tua cōnsilia. (CICERO, *IN CATILĪNAM I* 6)

   undique (adv.) from all sides, on all sides

7. After Cicero reassures the Senate that all classes of the Roman people will support strong action against Catiline, he summarizes the nature of the plebs.

   multō vērō maxima pars eōrum quī in tabernīs sunt, immō vērō*—id enim

   potius est dīcendum—genus hoc ūniversum amantissimum est ōtī.

   (CICERO, *IN CATILĪNAM IV* 17)

   *immō vērō, *introduces a remark that makes a preceding phrase or comment more precise,* rather, more precisely
   ōtium, ōtiī *n.* leisure

   potius (comparative adv.) rather
   taberna, tabernae *f.* shop
   ūniversus, -a, -um all together, entire, whole

8. In a speech delivered after Cicero's return from exile, the orator recalls those whom he missed most.

   quid dulcius hominum generī ab nātūrā datum est quam suī* cuique† līberī?‡ mihi

   vērō et propter indulgentiam meam et propter excellēns eōrum ingenium vīta sunt

   meā cāriōrēs. (Cicero, *Post Reditum Ad Populum* 2)

   *suī refers to cuique, his own.   dulcis, dulce sweet, pleasant
   †cuique = *masc. sing. dat. of indef. pron.*, each   excellēns, excellentis outstanding
     man   indulgentia, indulgentiae *f.* leniency, indulgence
   ‡līberī, *here*, children

9. After Cicero describes the many different areas of expertise required of an orator, he gives the following summary.

   quam ob rem nihil in hominum genere rārius perfectō* ōrātōre invenīrī potest.

   (Cicero, *Dē Ōrātōre* I.127)

   *perfectus, -a, -um complete, perfect
   rārus, -a, -um rare, uncommon

10. A Ciceronian closing

    haec, ut brevissimē dīcī potuērunt, ita ā mē dicta sunt. (Cicero, *Dē Ōrātōre* II.174)

11. Cicero resumes stating his main point after a short digression.

    dictum est igitur ab ērudītissimīs virīs nisi sapientem līberum esse nēminem.

    (Cicero, *Paradoxa Stōicōrum* 5.33)

    ērudītus, -a, -um learned, accomplished

12. In a rhetorical overstatement Cicero favorably compares Roman writers to their Greek predecessors.

    . . . sed meum semper iūdicium fuit omnia nostrōs aut invēnisse per sē sapientius

    quam Graecōs aut accepta ab illīs fēcisse meliōra . . .

    (Cicero, *Tusculānae Disputātiōnēs* I.1)

    Graecus, -a, -um Greek
    iūdicium, iūdiciī *n.* judgment, opinion

13. An opinion about the nature of death

    sunt quī discessum animī ā corpore putent esse mortem.

    (Cicero, *Tusculānae Disputātiōnēs* I.18)

    discessus, discessūs *m.* departure

14. A remark of Aristotle is recalled in a discussion of the relative longevity of mortal beings.

> apud Hypanim fluvium, quī ab Eurōpae parte in Pontum īnfluit, Aristotelēs
>
> ait bestiolās quāsdam nāscī quae ūnum diem vīvant.

(CICERO, *TUSCULĀNAE DISPUTĀTIŌNĒS* I.94)

aiō (defective verb) say; **ait** = *3rd sing. pres. act. indic.*
Aristotelēs, Aristotelis *m.* Aristotle
bestiola, bestiolae *f.* little creature
Eurōpa, Eurōpae *f.* Europe
fluvius, fluviī *m.* river, stream
Hypanis, Hypanis *m.* Hypanis, a river in Asia Minor; **Hypanim** = *acc. sing.*
īnfluō, īnfluere, īnfluxī, īnfluxus flow (into)
Pontus, Pontī *m.* Black Sea

15. Cicero suggests avoiding pretense.

> quodsī vultum tibi, sī incessum fingerēs, quō gravior vidērēre, nōn essēs tuī simi-
>
> lis; verba tū fingās et ea dīcās quae nōn sentiās? (CICERO, *DĒ DĪVINĀTIŌNE* II.77)

fingō, fingere, fīnxī, fictus form, fashion, make; imagine
incessus, incessūs *m.* walking, gait
quodsī (conj.) but if
vultus, vultūs *m.* expression, countenance; face

16. After Cicero recommends that extraordinary powers be granted to the young Octavian, the orator explains to the senate why he is sure that Caesar's adopted son will not repeat the mistakes of his father.

> nihil est illī* rē pūblicā cārius, nihil vestrā auctōritāte gravius, nihil bonōrum
>
> virōrum iūdiciō optātius, nihil vērā glōriā dulcius. (CICERO, *PHILIPPICS* V 50)

*illī refers to Octavian.
auctōritās, auctōritātis *f.* authority
dulcis, dulce sweet, pleasant
iūdicium, iūdiciī *n.* judgment, opinion

17. Cicero speaks affectionately of his best friend Atticus.

> . . . Pompōnium Atticum sīc amō ut alterum frātrem. nihil est illō mihi nec*
>
> cārius nec* iūcundius. (CICERO, *AD FAMILIĀRĒS* XIII.1.5)

*These redundant negatives strengthen the negative idea.
iūcundus, -a, -um pleasing, delightful, agreeable
Pompōnius Atticus, Pompōniī Atticī *m.* Pomponius Atticus

18. When Cicero finds his movements carefully monitored and controlled by Caesar's right-hand man, Antony, he complains to Atticus.

> quidnam mihi futūrum est aut quis mē nōn sōlum īnfēlīcior sed iam etiam
>
> turpior? (CICERO, *AD ATTICUM* X.12.1)

quisnam, quidnam (interrog. pron.) who, tell me; what, tell me
turpis, turpe foul, ugly; base, shameful

19. Caesar describes a moment of confusion in his camp as the enemy unexpectedly attacks.

   tōtīs trepidātur castrīs, atque alius ex aliō causam tumultūs quaerit.

   (CAESAR, *DĒ BELLŌ GALLICŌ* VI.37)

trepidō (1-intr.) tremble; panic
tumultus, tumultūs *m.* commotion, uproar

20. Caesar describes rumors flying through the camp.

   alius castra iam capta prōnuntiat, alius dēlētō exercitū atque imperātōre victōrēs

   barbarōs vēnisse contendit. (CAESAR, *DĒ BELLŌ GALLICŌ* VI.37)

barbarus, -a, -um foreign
contendō, contendere, contendī, contentus struggle; claim
prōnuntiō (1-tr.) proclaim, pronounce, declare
victor, victōris *m.* conqueror, victor

21. The historian describes the character of the early Romans.

   igitur domī mīlitiaeque bonī mōrēs colēbantur; concordia maxuma, minuma avāri-

   tia erat; iūs bonumque apud eōs nōn lēgibus magis quam nātūrā valēbat.

   (SALLUST, *BELLUM CATILĪNAE* 9)

avāritia, avāritiae *f.* greed, avarice
colō, colere, coluī, cultus cultivate
concordia, concordiae *f.* harmony

maxuma = maxima
mīlitia, mīlitiae *f.* military service; **mīlitiae** = *loc.*
minuma = minima

22. Catiline exhorts his troops before the final battle against Cicero's forces.

   semper in proeliō eīs maxumum est perīculum quī maxumē timent; audācia prō

   mūrō habētur. (SALLUST, *BELLUM CATILĪNAE* 58)

maxumum = maximum
maxumē = maximē

23. The biographer offers his opinion about the egotism of the Athenian politician and general
   Alcibiades.

   huic maximē putāmus malō fuisse nimiam opīniōnem ingeniī atque virtūtis.

   (CORNELIUS NEPOS, *VĪTA ALCIBIADIS* 7)

nimius, -a, -um excessive, too great
opīniō, opīniōnis *f.* opinion, judgment

24. The shepherd Mopsus shows deference to his friend Menalcas.

   tū maior: tibi mē est aequum pārēre . . . (VERGIL, *ECLOGUES* V.4)

25. After a storm has torn apart the Trojan fleet, Aeneas tries to revive the spirits of his
   companions.

   ō sociī, (neque enim ignārī sumus ante malōrum),

   ō passī graviōra, dabit deus hīs quoque fīnem. (VERGIL, *AENEID* I.198–99)

ignārus, -a, -um not knowing, ignorant, unaware

26. The Trojan Ilioneus, fearing that his friend and leader is dead, describes Aeneas to Dido.

> rēx erat Aenēās nōbīs, quō iūstior alter
>
> nec pietāte fuit nec bellō maior et armīs. (VERGIL, *AENEID* I.544–45)

iūstus, -a, -um just, fair, right
pietās, pietātis *f.* sense of duty, dutifulness, piety

27. The poet declares a new beginning for the war books that make up the second half of his epic.

> . . . maior rērum mihi nāscitur ordō,
>
> maius opus moveō. . . . (VERGIL, *AENEID* VII.44–45)

ordō, ordinis *m.* order, rank, class

28. The poet advises a friend to take nothing for granted.

> inter spem cūramque, timōrēs inter et īrās
>
> omnem crēde diem tibi dīlūxisse suprēmum:
>
> grāta superveniet quae nōn spērābitur hōra. (HORACE, *EPISTULAE* I.4.12–14)

dīlūcēscō, dīlūcēscere, dīlūxī, — become light, dawn
grātus, -a, -um grateful, pleased; charming, pleasing
hōra, hōrae *f.* hour

spērō (1-tr.) hope (for)
superveniō (super- + veniō) come down from above, arrive (unexpectedly)
suprēmus, -a, -um final, last

29. The elegist makes reference to Vergil's *Aeneid* as it is being written.

> cēdite, Rōmānī scrīptōrēs, cēdite, Graī!
>
> nescio quid* maius nāscitur Īliade. (PROPERTIUS II.34.65–66)

*nescio quid = *neut. sing. nom. of indef. pron.,* I-don't-know-what, something; the **-ō** of **nesciō** here scans *short.*
Graius, -a, -um Greek; **Graī** = *voc. pl.;* **Graī** scans as if it were spelled **Graiī
Īlias, Īliadis *f.* the *Iliad*
scrīptor, scrīptōris *m.* writer

30. Helen addresses Paris in an imaginary letter.

> apta magis Venerī quam sunt tua corpora* Martī.
>
> bella gerant fortēs, tū, Pari, semper amā! (OVID, *HĒRŌIDES* XVII.253–54)

*corpus, *here, in pl.,* (physical) bearing, physique
aptus, -a, -um suitable, fit
Paris, Paridis *m.* Paris, son of Priam; **Pari** = *voc. sing.*

31. The poet gives advice on concealing a particular physical flaw.

> sī brevis es, sedeās nē stāns videāre sedēre. (OVID, *ARS AMĀTŌRIA* III.263)

sedeō, sedēre, sēdī, sessūrus sit, be seated

32. When Hannibal hesitates to follow up his victory at Cannae by pressing his advantage, his lieutenant Maharbal criticizes him. The historian comments on the benefit to Rome.

"nōn omnia nīmīrum eīdem dī dedēre. vincere scīs, Hannibal, victōriā ūtī nescīs."

mora eius diēī satis crēditur salūtī fuisse urbī atque imperiō.

(LIVY, *AB URBE CONDITĀ* XXII.51.4)

nīmīrum (adv.) without doubt, evidently
victōria, victōriae *f.* victory

33. After a murderous plot is foiled in the Sicilian town of Syracuse, the public's emotions rage back and forth concerning what to do with the conspirators. The historian characterizes the crowd.

ea nātūra multitūdinis est: aut servit humiliter aut superbē dominātur; lībertātem,

quae media est, nec struere modicē nec habēre sciunt.

(LIVY, *AB URBE CONDITĀ* XXIV.25.8)

dominor (1-intr.) be a master
modicē (adv.) moderately, temperately
multitūdō, multitūdinis *f.* multitude

serviō, servīre, servīvī or **serviī, servītum** be a slave
struō, struere, strūxī, strūctus construct, devise
superbē (adv.) proudly; haughtily, arrogantly

34. The historian describes the valor of C. Popilius Sabellus in a battle against the Histri, a people living along the lower Danube river.

is pede sauciō relictus longē plūrimōs hostium occīdit.

(LIVY, *AB URBE CONDITĀ* XLI.4.6)

occīdō, occīdere, occīdī, occīsus kill
pēs, pedis *m.* foot
saucius, -a, -um wounded

35. An utterance of a jurist in a rhetorical exercise

quaedam iūra nōn scrīpta, sed omnibus scrīptīs certiōra sunt.

(SENECA THE ELDER, *CONTRŌVERSIAE* I.1.14)

36. The philosopher quotes the opinion of the Greek philosopher Epicurus about the nature of poverty and comments upon it.

"honesta," inquit, "rēs est laeta paupertās." Illa vērō nōn est paupertās sī laeta est;

nōn quī parum habet sed quī plūs cupit pauper est.

(SENECA THE YOUNGER, *EPISTULAE MŌRĀLĒS* II.6)

inquam (defective verb) say; **inquit** = *3rd sing. pres. act. indic.*
pauper, pauperis poor
paupertās, paupertātis *f.* poverty

37. Phaedra explains her silence.

cūrae levēs locuntur,* ingentēs stupent. (SENECA THE YOUNGER, *PHAEDRA* 607)

*locuntur = loquuntur
stupeō, stupēre, stupuī, —— be stunned (into silence)

38. Age and wisdom are not necessarily linked.

saepe grandis nātū senex nūllum aliud habet argumentum quō sē probet diū

vīxisse praeter aetātem. (SENECA THE YOUNGER, DIALOGĪ IX.3.8)

aetās, aetātis *f.* age, time of life   **praeter** (prep. + acc.) beyond, except
argumentum, argumentī *n.* proof   **probō** (1-tr.) prove, demonstrate
grandis, grande great   **senex, senis** old
nātus, nātūs *m.* birth; age

39. Pompey the Great rushes to arms without fear.

aut nihil est sēnsūs animīs ā morte relictum

aut mors ipsa nihil. . . . (LUCAN, *BELLUM CĪVĪLE* III.39)

40. The writer expresses a preference for depth over breadth.

. . . multā magis quam multōrum lēctiōne formanda mēns et dūcendus* color.

(QUINTILIAN, *ĪNSTITŪTIŌ ŌRĀTŌRIA* X.1.59)

***dūcō,** *here,* fashion, mold, produce
color, colōris *m.* color; (rhetorical) tone
formō (1-tr.) mold, fashion, shape, form
lēctiō, lēctiōnis *f.* reading

41. Pliny identifies two worthy human endeavors.

equidem beātōs putō quibus deōrum mūnere datum est aut facere scrībenda aut

scrībere legenda. (PLINY THE YOUNGER, *EPISTULAE* VI.16.3)

beātus, -a, -um blessed, happy, fortunate
mūnus, mūneris *n.* present, gift; favor

42. Aulus Gellius recalls the opinion of an ancient poet.

alius quīdam veterum poētārum, cuius nōmen mihi nunc memoriae nōn est,

vēritātem temporis fīliam esse dīxit. (AULUS GELLIUS, *NOCTĒS ATTICAE* XII.11)

memoria, memoriae *f.* memory
nōmen, nōminis *n.* name
vēritās, vēritātis *f.* truth
vetus, veteris old; **veterum** = *gen. pl.*

Longer Readings

1. Plautus, *Captīvī* 461–63

   The hungry parasite Ergasilus laments his fate.

   miser homō est, quī ipse sibi quod edit quaerit et id aegrē invenit,

   sed ille est miserior, quī et aegrē quaerit et nihil invenit;

   ille miserrimust, quī cum* ēsse cupit, tum quod edit nōn habet.

   *cum, *here* (conj.) when
   aegrē (adv.) scarcely, with difficulty
   edō, ēsse, ēdī, ēsus (irregular 3rd conjugation verb) eat; **edit** = *3rd sing. pres. act. subj.*
   tum (adv.) then, at that time

   The *Captīvī* (Captives) involves a war, two lost sons, and several cases of switched identity.

2. Plautus, *Casīna* 3–6

   An excerpt from a prologue spoken by an actor to the audience

   sī vērum dīxī, signum clārum date mihi

   ut vōs mī esse aequōs iam inde ā prīncipiō sciam.

   quī ūtuntur vīnō vetere sapientīs putō   5

   et quī libenter veterēs spectant fābulās.

   fābula, fābulae *f.* story, tale; play, drama   **prīncipium, prīncipiī** *n.* beginning
   inde (adv.) from there   **spectō** (1-tr.) look (at), observe
   libenter (adv.) gladly   **vetus, veteris** old
   mī = **mihi**   **vīnum, vīnī** *n.* wine

   The *Casīna,* produced after 186 B.C.E., revolves around a father's and son's pursuit of the same woman, Casina, who has lived in the father's house since she was found as a baby.

3. Plautus, *Boeōtia* frag.1–9

A fragment from a lost play of Plautus, in which a parasite makes a lament

ut* illum dī perdant, prīmus quī hōrās repperit

quīque adeō prīmus statuit hīc sōlārium;

quī mihi comminuit miserō articulātim diem.

nam ūnum mē puerō venter erat sōlārium,

multō omnium istōrum optimum et vērissimum.   5

ubi is tē monēbat, ēssēs, nisi cum† nīl erat;

nunc etiam quod est nōn ēstur nisi sōlī libet.

itaque adeō iam opplētum oppidum est sōlāriīs:

maior pars populī āridī reptant fame.

***ut** = utinam
†**cum**, *here* (conj.) when
adeō (adv.) to that point; to such an extent; in addition to that, moreover
āridus, -a, -um dry; parched, shriveled
articulātim (adv.) limb by limb, limb from limb
comminuō, comminuere, comminuī, comminūtus break into pieces, shatter
edō, ēsse, ēdī, ēsus (irregular 3rd conjugation verb) eat; **ēssēs** = *2nd sing. imperf. act. subjunc., iterative subjunc.,* "you used to eat"; **ēstur** = *3rd sing. pres. pass. indic.*
famēs, famis *f.* hunger, starvation
hīc (adv.) here

hōra, hōrae *f.* hour
itaque (conj.) and so, accordingly
libet, libēre, libuit or **libitum est** (impersonal verb) it is pleasing
oppleō, opplēre, opplēvī, opplētus fill completely, fill up
perdō (per- + dō) lose; destroy, kill
reperiō, reperīre, repperī, repertus find, discover
reptō (1-intr.) crawl about, creep along
sōlārium, sōlāriī *n.* sundial
sōl, sōlis *m.* Sun
statuō, statuere, statuī, statūtus cause to stand, set up, erect, station
venter, ventris *m.* belly, stomach

4. Cicero, *Prō Murēnā* 30

Cicero compares two skills of great importance in Roman life.

duae sint artēs igitur quae possint locāre hominēs in amplissimō gradū dignitātis,

ūna imperātōris, altera ōrātōris bonī. ab hōc enim pācis ornāmenta retinentur, ab illō

bellī perīcula repelluntur. cēterae tamen virtūtēs ipsae per sē multum valent, iūstitia,

fidēs, pudor, temperantia; quibus tē, Servī, excellere omnēs intellegunt.

amplus, -a, -um great, distinguished
cēterus, -a, -um rest (of), remaining part (of), (the) other
dignitās, dignitātis *f.* dignity, rank, status
excellō, excellere, ——, —— be superior, be conspicuous, excel
gradus, gradūs *m.* step, pace; tier, rank
iūstitia, iūstitiae *f.* justice, fairness, equity
locō (1-tr.) place
ornāmentum, ornāmentī *n.* adornment, embellishment

pudor, pudōris *m.* shame, decency, modesty
repellō (re- + pellō), repellere, reppulī, repulsus push back, repel
retineō (re- + teneō), retinēre, retinuī, retentus keep hold of, retain, grasp
Servius, Serviī *m.* Servius (Sulpicius Rufus), the prosecutor in the case
temperantia, temperantiae *f.* self-control, moderation

The *Prō Murēnā* is Cicero's speech in defense of L. Licinius Murena (consul 62 B.C.E.), who was charged with corruption after his victory in the consular elections in 63. The trial took place at the time of the exposure of the Catilinarian conspiracy. The prosecution was supported by, among others, Cato the Younger, the staunch moral and political conservative.

5. Cicero, *In Catilīnam I* 27

In his speech attacking Catiline, Cicero uses the rhetorical device of *prosopopoeia,* a sustained speech in character with words and gestures appropriate to the assumed identity.

etenim sī mēcum patria, quae mihi vītā meā multō est cārior, sī cūncta Italia, sī omnis rēs pūblica loquātur: "M. Tullī, quid agis? tūne eum quem esse hostem comperistī, quem ducem bellī futūrum vidēs, quem exspectārī imperātōrem in castrīs hostium sentīs, auctōrem sceleris, prīncipem coniūrātiōnis, ēvocātōrem servōrum et cīvium perditōrum, exīre patiēre, ut abs tē nōn ēmissus ex urbe, sed immissus in urbem esse videātur?"

abs = ab
auctor, auctōris *m.* source, author
comperiō, comperīre, comperī, compertus find out, learn
coniūrātiō, coniūrātiōnis *f.* conspiracy
cūnctus, -a, -um all
ēmittō (ē- + mittō) send out
ēvocātor, ēvocātōris *m.* summoner

exeō (ex- + eō), exīre, exiī or exīvī, exitum go out
ex(s)pectō (1-tr.) wait for, await, expect
immittō (in- + mittō) send in, send against
perditus, -a, -um lost, degenerate, desperate
prīnceps, prīncipis first, foremost, chief; *as subst.,* leading man
scelus, sceleris *n.* wicked deed, crime; villainy

6. Cicero, *Dē Ōrātōre* II.178

Cicero explains why it is important for an orator to appeal to an audience's emotions.

plūra enim multō hominēs iūdicant odiō aut amōre aut cupiditāte aut īrācundiā aut dolōre aut aliquā permōtiōne mentis quam vēritāte aut praescrīptō aut iūris normā aliquā aut iūdicī formulā aut lēgibus.

aliquā = *fem. sing. abl. of indef. adj.,* some, any
cupiditās, cupiditātis *f.* desire
dolor, dolōris *m.* grief, sorrow, pain
formula, formulae *f.* formula, rule, standard
īrācundia, īrācundiae *f.* hot temper, anger
iūdicium, iūdiciī *n.* judgment, opinion; legal proceeding

iūdicō (1-tr.) form an opinion, judge, determine
norma, normae *f.* standard
permōtiō, permōtiōnis *f.* strong emotion
praescrīptum, praescrīptī *n.* rule, precept
vēritās, vēritātis *f.* truth

The *Dē Ōrātōre* is a dialogue written shortly after Cicero's forced retirement from public life in 55 B.C.E. The dialogue is set in 91, and the chief speakers are the orators L. Licinius Crassus and M. Antonius (the grandfather of Marc Antony). The date places the dialogue immediately before the beginning of the war between Rome and her Italian allies or *sociī.* This Social War marks the beginning of a series of internal conflicts in the Roman Republic. All the characters in this fictional dialogue are historical, and many of them were to die within a few years of the dramatic date of the dialogue. In the first of the three books of the *Dē Ōrātōre,* the speakers discuss the importance of a liberal education for an orator. The remaining books are devoted to a closer analysis of the various parts of oratory.

7. Cicero, *Ōrātor* 226–27

Cicero summarizes the advantage to the orator of proper prose rhythm.

et quoniam plūra dē numerōsā ōrātiōne dīximus quam quisquam ante nōs, nunc dē eius generis ūtilitāte dīcēmus. nihil enim est aliud, Brūte, quod quidem tū minimē omnium ignōrās, pulchrē et ōrātōriē dīcere nisi optumīs sententiīs verbīsque lēctissimīs dīcere: et nec sententia ūlla est, quae frūctum ōrātōrī ferat, nisi aptē exposita atque absolūtē, nec verbōrum lūmen appāret nisi dīligenter collocātōrum. et hōrum utrumque* numerus illūstrat, numerus etiam—saepe enim hoc testandum est— nōn modo† nōn poēticē vīnctus vērum etiam fugiēns illum eīque omnium dissimillimus.

*utrumque = *neut. sing. acc. of indef. pron.* each (of two)

†nōn modo = nōn sōlum

absolūtē (adv.) completely, perfectly

appāreō, appārēre, appāruī, appāritus be visible, be clear; appear, become evident

aptē (adv.) properly, fittingly

Brūtus, Brūtī *m.* (M. Junius) Brutus, the addressee of the *Ōrātor*

collocō (1-tr.) place, position, arrange

dīligenter (adv.) diligently

expōnō (ex- + pōnō) explain; display

frūctus, frūctūs *m.* profit, benefit, advantage

ignōrō (1-tr.) be unaware of, fail to recognize

illūstrō (1-tr.) illuminate, make clear

lūmen, lūminis *n.* light; illumination; enlightenment

numerōsus, -a, -um harmonious, rhythmical

numerus, numerī *m.* number; rhythm, cadence

optumīs = optimīs

ōrātōriē (adv.) in the manner of an orator, oratorically

poēticē (adv.) poetically

quisquam = *masc./fem. sing. nom. of indef. pron.,* anyone

testor (1-tr.) testify to, affirm solemnly

ūtilitās, ūtilitātis *f.* use, advantage

vinciō, vincīre, vīnxī, vīnctus bind, join

The *Ōrātor* is the last of Cicero's treatises on oratory. Written in 46 B.C.E., it is addressed to M. Brutus and supposedly responds to Brutus's request that Cicero describe the "best form and, as it were, figure of speaking." In the *Ōrātor* Cicero devotes considerable space to his own views on the history and importance of prose rhythm (**numerus**) in Greek and Roman oratory.

8. Catullus I (hendecasyllable; see §112)

The dedicatory poem of Catullus's published **libellus**

Cui dōnō lepidum novum libellum
āridā modo pūmice expolītum?
Cornēlī, tibi; namque tū solēbās
meās esse aliquid putāre nūgās
iam tum, cum* ausus es ūnus Ītalōrum   5
omne aevum tribus explicāre cartīs
doctīs, Iuppiter, et labōriōsīs.
quārē habē tibi quidquid hoc libellī
quālecumque; quod, <ō>† patrōna virgō,
plūs ūnō maneat perenne saeclō.   10

***cum,** *here* (conj.) when
†Pointed brackets mark an element added by scholars.
aevum, aevī *n.* age, lifetime; period of time, generation
aliquid = *neut. sing. acc. of indef. pron.,* something
āridus, -a, -um dry
c(h)arta, c(h)artae *f.* leaf (of papyrus); book
Cornēlius, Cornēlī *m.* Cornelius (Nepos), addressee of the poem, writer of history and biography
doctus, -a, -um learned, erudite
explicō (1-tr.) unfold, reveal, explain
expoliō, expolīre, expolīvī, expolītus smooth, polish, finish
Ītalī, Ītalōrum *m. pl.* Italians

labōriōsus, -a, -um full of labor, elaborate
lepidus, -a, -um pleasant, charming, elegant
libellus, libellī *m.* (little) book
modo (adv.) only, now; just now
nūgae, nūgārum *f. pl.* trifles, nuggets; nonsense
patrōna, patrōnae *f.* patroness, protectress
perennis, perenne everlasting, perpetual, perennial
pūmex, pūmicis *f.* pumice stone
quālecumque = *neut. sing. nom. of indef. rel. adj.,* of whatever sort
quidquid = *neut. sing. nom. of indef. rel. pron.,* whatever
saec(u)lum, saec(u)lī *n.* age, generation
tum (adv.) then, at that time
virgō, virginis *f.* maiden, virgin

9. Catullus XIII (hendecasyllable; see §112)

The poet issues an unusual invitation.

Cēnābis bene, mī Fabulle, apud mē
paucīs, sī tibi dī favent, diēbus,
sī tēcum attuleris bonam atque magnam
cēnam, nōn sine candidā puellā
et vīnō et sale et omnibus cachinnīs.   5
haec sī, inquam, attuleris, venuste noster,
cēnābis bene: nam tuī Catullī
plēnus sacculus est arānearum.
sed contrā accipiēs merōs amōrēs
seu quid* suāvius ēlegantiusve est: 10
nam unguentum dabo,† quod meae puellae
dōnārunt Venerēs Cupīdinēsque;
quod tū cum‡ olfaciēs, deōs rogābis,
tōtum ut tē faciant, Fabulle, nāsum.

*quid, *here, neut. sing. nom. of indef. pron.,* anything
†The **-ō** of **dabō** here scans *short.*
‡cum, *here* (conj. + indic.) when
afferō (ad- + ferō), afferre, attulī, allātus bring toward, bring along
arānea, arāneae *f.* spider; cobweb
cachinnus, cachinnī *m.* loud laugh
candidus, -a, -um white, clear, bright, radiant
cēna, cēnae *f.* dinner
cēnō (1-intr.) dine
dōnārunt = dōnāvērunt
ēlegāns, ēlegantis select, tasteful, elegant
Fabullus, Fabullī *m.* Fabullus
faveō, favēre, fāvī, fautum be favorable, favor (+ dat.)

inquam (defective verb) say; **inquam** = *1st sing. pres. act. indic.*
merus, -a, -um pure, unmixed
nāsus, nāsī *m.* nose
olfaciō, olfacere, olfēcī, olfactus smell
plēnus, -a, -um full
rogō (1-tr.) ask
sacculus, sacculī *m.* (little) bag, wallet
sal, salis *n.* salt; wit
seu (conj.) or if
suāvis, suāve sweet, pleasant; fragrant
unguentum, unguentī *n.* ointment; perfume
-ve (enclitic conj.) or
venustus, -a, -um charming, pleasing
vīnum, vīnī *n.* wine

10. Sallust, *Bellum Iugurthae* 14

Adherbal addresses the Roman senate about his cousin Jugurtha's cruel treatment of captives.

captī ab Iugurthā pars in crucem āctī, pars bestiīs obiectī sunt, paucī, quibus relicta
est anima, clausī in tenebrīs cum maerōre et lūctū morte graviōrem vītam exigunt.

bestia, bestiae *f.* beast, animal
claudō, claudere, clausī, clausus close, shut; confine, enclose
crux, crucis *f.* wooden frame, cross
exigō (ex- + agō), exigere, exēgī, exāctus drive out; spend, pass
Iugurtha, Iugurthae *m.* Jugurtha, king of Numidia

lūctus, lūctūs *m.* mourning
maeror, maerōris *m.* grief, sorrow, mourning
obiciō (ob- + iaciō) throw in front of, throw to (+ dat.)
tenebrae, tenebrārum *f. pl.* darkness, shadows

11. Vergil, *Aeneid* II.40–56

As the Trojans debate whether to bring the Greeks' gift of a horse into the city, their priest Laocoön utters a vain warning.

prīmus ibi ante omnīs magnā comitante catervā   40

Lāocoōn ardēns summā dēcurrit ab arce,

et procul "ō miserī, quae tanta īnsānia, cīvēs?

crēditis āvectōs hostīs? aut ūlla putātis

dōna carēre dolīs Danaum? sīc nōtus Ulīxēs?

aut hōc inclūsī lignō occultantur Achīvī,   45

aut haec in nostrōs fabricāta est māchina mūrōs,

īnspectūra* domōs ventūraque* dēsuper urbī,

aut aliquis latet error; equō nē crēdite,† Teucrī,

quidquid id est, timeō Danaōs et dōna ferentīs."

---

*īnspectūra, ventūra, *fut. act. participles expressing purpose,* in order to . . .

†nē crēdite = negative imper.

Achīvī, Achīvōrum *m. pl.* Achaeans, Greeks

aliquis = *masc. nom. sing. of indef. pron. used as an adjective,* some

ardeō, ardēre, arsī, arsūrus burn, be on fire; rage

arx, arcis *f.* tower, citadel

āvehō, āvehere, āvexī, āvectus convey away; *in passive,* go away, depart

caterva, catervae *f.* throng, crowd, troop

comitor (1-tr.) accompany, attend

Danaī, Danaōrum *m. pl.* Danaans, Greeks; **Danaum = Danaōrum**

dēcurrō, dēcurrere, dē(cu)currī, dēcursum run down, hurry down

dēsuper (adv.) from above

dolus, dolī *m.* deceit, trick; cunning

equus, equī *m.* horse

error, errōris *m.* mistake; deceit

fabricō (1-tr.) fashion, construct, devise

ibi (adv.) there; then

inclūdō, inclūdere, inclūsī, inclūsus enclose

īnsānia, īnsāniae *f.* madness, insanity

īnspiciō, īnspicere, īnspexī, īnspectus examine, inspect, observe

Lāocoōn, Lāocoöntis *m.* Laocoön

lateō, latēre, latuī, —— (intr.) hide, lie hidden, be concealed

lignum, lignī *n.* wood

māchina, māchinae *f.* mechanism; structure

occultō (1-tr.) hide, conceal

procul (adv.) at a distance, from a distance

quidquid = *neut. sing. nom. of indef. rel. pron.,* whatever

tantus, -a, -um so great

Teucrī, Teucrōrum *m. pl.* descendants of Teucer, Teucrians, Trojans

Ulīxēs, Ulīxis *m.* Ulysses (Odysseus)

sīc fātus validīs ingentem vīribus hastam   50

in latus inque ferī curvam compāgibus alvum

contorsit. stetit illa tremēns, uterōque recussō

īnsonuēre cavae gemitumque dedēre cavernae.

et, sī fāta deum, sī mēns nōn laeva fuisset,

impulerat* ferrō Argolicās foedāre latebrās,   55

Troiaque nunc stāret, Priamīque arx alta, manērēs.

*impulerat, pluperf. indic. used for vividness in apodosis of Mixed Contrary-to-Fact conditional sentence; subj. is "he" (Laocoön)

Argolicus, -a, -um of Argos, Argive; Greek

alvus, alvī *f.* belly

arx, arcis *f.* tower, citadel

caverna, cavernae *f.* cavern, cavity, hollow

cavus, -a, -um hollow

compāgēs, compāgis *f.* joint, seam; fastening

contorqueō, contorquēre, contorsī, contortus twist; hurl

curvus, -a, -um curved

ferus, ferī *m.* wild beast

foedō (1-tr.) befoul, defile; wound savagely, mangle; *sc.* **nōs** as subj. of **foedāre**

for (1-tr.) speak, utter

gemitus, gemitūs *m.* groan(ing), moan(ing)

hasta, hastae *f.* spear

impellō (in- + pellō), impellere, impulī, impulsus push on; drive, compel

īnsonō, īnsonāre, īnsonuī, —— make a loud noise, resound

laevus, -a, -um left; unfavorable, adverse; dull

latebra, latebrae *f.* hiding place, lair, recess

latus, lateris *n.* side, flank

recutiō, recutere, recussī, recussus strike (back), shake

tremō, tremere, tremuī, —— tremble, quiver, shake

uterus, uterī *m.* belly, womb

12. Vergil, *Aeneid* III.374–80

Helenus the seer begins his response to Aeneas, who has asked for advice on how to proceed to Italy.

Nāte deā (nam tē maiōribus īre per altum

auspiciīs manifesta fidēs; sīc fāta deum rēx   375

sortītur volvitque vicēs, is vertitur ordō)

pauca tibi ē multīs, quō tūtior hospita lūstrēs

aequora et Ausoniō possīs cōnsīdere portū,

expediam dictīs; prohibent nam cētera Parcae

scīre Helenum fārīque vetat Sāturnia Iūnō . . .   380

aequor, aequoris *n.* level surface; sea, water
Ausonius, -a, -um of Ausonia, Ausonian, Italian
auspicium, auspiciī *n.* augury, omen
cēterus, -a, -um rest (of), remaining part (of),
  (the) other
cōnsīdō, cōnsīdere, cōnsēdī, —— sit; settle,
  make one's home
expediō, expedīre, expedīvī, expedītus unravel,
  explain
for (1-tr.) speak, utter
Helenus, Helenī *m.* Helenus, son of Priam and
  seer
hospitus, -a, -um hospitable
lūstrō (1-tr.) roam through, traverse; survey,
  look upon
manifestus, -a, -um revealed by clear signs, plain,
  obvious

ordō, ordinis *m.* order; series, sequence
Parcae, Parcārum *f. pl.* Parcae, goddesses of fate
portus, portūs *m.* harbor; refuge, haven
**prohibeō (prō- + habeō), prohibēre, prohibuī,
  prohibitus** prevent; prohibit, forbid
Sāturnius, -a, -um of Saturn, king of the Titans
  and father of Juno; Saturnian
sortior, sortīrī, sortītus sum assign by lot,
  determine
tūtus, -a, -um safe
vertō, vertere, vertī, versus turn; spin
vetō, vetāre, vetuī, vetitus forbid
——, vicis *f.* turning, turn; succession; situation,
  lot
volvō, volvere, volvī, volūtus turn, turn over, roll;
  unroll; bring round

13. Vergil, *Aeneid* XII.653–57

The wounded Rutulian Saces implores Turnus to enter the battle.

Turne, in tē suprēma salūs, miserēre tuōrum.

fulminat Aenēās armīs summāsque minātur

dēiectūrum* arcēs Italum excidiōque datūrum,*   655

iamque facēs ad tēcta volant. in† tē ōra Latīnī,

in† tē oculōs referunt;‡ . . .

***dēiectūrum, datūrum,** subject is **sē**
†**in,** *here,* toward
‡**referō,** *here,* direct
arx, arcis *f.* tower, citadel
dēiciō (dē- + iaciō) throw down, topple,
  overthrow
excidium, excidiī *n.* (military) destruction
fax, facis *f.* firebrand, torch
fulminō (1-intr.) strike (like lightning), flash
  fiercely

Italī, Italōrum *m. pl.* Italians; **Italum = Italōrum**
Latīnī, Latīnōrum *m. pl.* (the) Latins, the peoples
  of Latium
minor (1-intr.) threaten
misereor, miserērī, miseritus sum pity, take pity
  on (+ gen.)
ōs, ōris *n.* mouth; face
suprēmus, -a, -um final, last
tēctum, tēctī *n.* roof; house
volō (1-intr.) fly

14. Horace, *Carmina* I.5 (Asclepiadean; see §112)

The poet addresses an old and dangerous flame.

> Quis* multā gracilis tē puer in rosā
> perfūsus liquidīs urget odōribus
>   grātō, Pyrrha, sub antrō?
>   cui flāvam religās comam
>
> simplex munditiīs? heu quotiēns fidem   5
> mūtātōsque deōs flēbit et aspera
>   nigrīs aequora ventīs
>   ēmīrābitur īnsolēns,
>
> quī nunc tē fruitur crēdulus aureā,
> quī semper vacuam, semper amābilem   10
>   spērat, nescius aurae
>   fallācis. miserī, quibus
>
> intemptāta nitēs: mē tabulā sacer
> vōtīvā pariēs indicat ūvida
>   suspendisse potentī   15
>   vestīmenta maris deō.

*__quis__, *here, interrog. pron. used adjectivally,* what, which

aequor, aequoris *n.* level surface; sea, water

amābilis, amābile lovable

antrum, antrī *n.* cave, cavern, grotto

asper, aspera, asperum harsh, fierce, pitiless; severe

aura, aurae *f.* breeze

aureus, -a, -um golden

coma, comae *f.* hair

crēdulus, -a, -um trusting, credulous

ēmīror (1-tr.) (thoroughly) admire, marvel at, be astonished at

fallāx, fallācis deceptive, treacherous

flāvus, -a, -um golden-yellow, flaxen, blond

fleō, flēre, flēvī, flētus weep (for)

fruor, fruī, frūctus sum enjoy, delight in (+ abl.)

gracilis, gracile slender, thin, fine

grātus, -a, -um grateful, pleased; charming, pleasing

indicō (1-tr.) declare, indicate

īnsolēns, īnsolentis unaccustomed, unfamiliar

intemptātus, -a, -um untried

liquidus, -a, -um liquid, clear

munditia, munditiae *f.* elegance, neatness

mūtō (1-tr.) change

nescius, -a, -um not knowing, unaware (+ gen.)

niger, nigra, nigrum dark, black

niteō, nitēre, nituī, —— be radiant, shine

odor, odōris *m.* odor, scent

pariēs, parietis *m.* wall (of a building)

perfundō, perfundere, perfūdī, perfūsus pour over, spray, drench

potēns, potentis powerful, having power over (+ gen.)

Pyrrha, Pyrrhae *f.* Pyrrha, addressee of the poem

quotiēns (adv.) how many times

religō (1-tr.) bind back, bind up; unbind

rosa, rosae *f.* rose

sacer, sacra, sacrum sacred

simplex, simplicis simple, plain

spērō (1-tr.) hope (for)

suspendō, suspendere, suspendī, suspēnsus hang, suspend, hang up

tabula, tabulae *f.* plank, tablet; plaque, picture

urgeō, urgēre, ursī, —— weigh down; press hard; urge, pursue

ūvidus, -a, -um moist, wet, damp

vacuus, -a, -um empty; idle; free, available; carefree, disengaged

ventus, ventī *m.* wind

vestīmentum, vestīmentī *n.* garment, clothing

vōtīvus, -a, -um votive, offered in fulfillment of a vow

15. Horace, *Carmina* II.9 (Alcaic strophe; see §112)

The poet advises a lugubrious friend, Valgius.

> Nōn semper imbrēs nūbibus hispidōs
> mānant in agrōs aut mare Caspium
>   vexant inaequālēs procellae
>   ūsque nec Armeniīs in ōrīs,
>
> amīce Valgī, stat glaciēs iners   5
> mēnsīs per omnīs aut Aquilōnibus
>   querquēta Gargānī labōrant
>   et foliīs viduantur ornī:
>
> tū semper urgēs flēbilibus modīs
> Mystēn adēmptum nec tibi vesperō   10
>   surgente dēcēdunt amōrēs
>   nec rapidum fugiente sōlem.

adimō, adimere, adēmī, adēmptus remove, take away

Aquilō, Aquilōnis *m.* Aquilo, the north wind

Armenius, -a, -um Armenian

Caspius, -a, -um Caspian

dēcēdō (dē- + cēdō) go down, depart

flēbilis, flēbile plaintive; tearful

folium, foliī *n.* leaf

Gargānus, Gargānī *m.* Garganus, a mountain in Horace's home district of Apulia

glaciēs, glaciēī *f.* ice

hispidus, -a, -um hairy; rough, bristly

imber, imbris, -ium *m.* rain, shower

inaequālis, inaequāle uneven, unlike; that roughens the sea

iners, inertis inactive, idle, inert

mānō (1-intr.) trickle, drip, stream, flow

mēnsis, mēnsis, -ium *m.* month

Mystēs, Mystae *m.* Mystes; **Mystēn** = *acc. sing.*

nūbēs, nūbis, -ium *f.* cloud

ōra, ōrae *f.* shore

ornus, ornī *f.* ash tree

procella, procellae *f.* blast (of wind), windstorm

querquētum, querquētī *n.* oak forest, oak grove

rapidus, -a, -um tearing away, consuming; rushing, rapid

sōl, sōlis *m.* sun

surgō, surgere, surrēxī, surrēctus rise, rise up

urgeō, urgēre, ursī, —— weigh down; press hard

ūsque (adv.) continuously

Valgius, Valgiī *m.* (C.) Valgius (Rufus), an Augustan elegiac poet and addressee of the poem

vesper, vesperī *m.* Vesper, the evening star; evening

vexō (1-tr.) trouble, disturb, harass

viduō (1-intr.) deprive of (+ abl.)

at nōn ter aevō fūnctus amābilem
plōrāvit omnīs Antilochum senex
    annōs nec inpūbem parentēs   15
        Trōilon aut Phrygiae sorōrēs

flēvēre semper. dēsine mollium
tandem querellārum et potius nova
    cantēmus Augustī tropaea
        Caesaris et rigidum Niphātēn,   20

Mēdumque flūmen gentibus additum
victīs minōrēs volvere verticēs
    intrāque praescrīptum Gelōnōs
        exiguīs equitāre campīs.

addō (ad- + dō) add

aevum, aevī *n.* age, lifetime; period of time, generation

amābilis, amābile lovable

Antilochus, Antilochī *m.* Antilochus, son of Nestor, slain by Memnon

at (conj.) but

Augustus, Augustī *m.* Augustus

cantō (1-tr.) sing (of)

dēsinō, dēsinere, dēsiī or **dēsīvī, dēsitum** stop, cease; cease (from) (+ gen.)

equitō (1-intr.) ride (on horseback)

exiguus, -a, -um small, slight, brief

fleō, flēre, flēvī, flētus weep (for)

flūmen, flūminis *n.* river, stream

fungor, fungī, fūnctus sum perform, execute; complete (+ abl.)

Gelōnī, Gelōnōrum *m. pl.* the Geloni, a nomadic tribe of Scythians who often made raids on horseback into Roman territory

gēns, gentis, -ium *f.* nation, people; clan, family

inpūbēs, inpūbis underage, youthful, beardless

intrā (prep. + acc.) within

Mēdus, -a, -um of *or* belonging to the Medes, Median, Persian; **Mēdum flūmen** = the Euphrates, by which dwelled the Parthians

mollis, molle gentle, mild, soft

Niphātēs, Niphātae *m.* the Niphates, a mountain range in Armenia; **Niphātēn** = *acc. sing.*

parēns, parentis, -ium *m.* or *f.* parent

Phrygius, -a, -um of *or* belonging to Phrygia (the region around Troy), Phrygian, Trojan

plōrō (1-tr.) weep for, mourn

potius (adv.) rather

praescrīptum, praescrīptī *n.* boundary line, limit

querella, querellae *f.* complaint, lament

rigidus, -a, -um rigid, stiff; inflexible; frozen

senex, senis old; *as masc. subst.,* old man

ter (adv.) three times, thrice

Trōilus, Trōilī *m.* Troilus, youngest son of Priam and Hecuba, killed by Achilles; **Trōilon** = *acc. sing.*

tropaeum, tropaeī *n.* trophy; victory

vertex, verticis *m.* swirling water, whirlpool, eddy

volvō, volvere, volvī, volūtus turn, turn over, roll

16. Horace, *Ars Poëtica* 323–26

The poet compares Greeks and Romans.

Graīs ingenium, Graīs dedit ōre rotundō

Mūsa loquī, praeter laudem nūllīus avārīs.

Rōmānī puerī longīs ratiōnibus assem   325

discunt in partīs centum dīdūcere . . .

as, assis, -ium *m. as* (a small denomination of
   Roman money)
avārus, -a, -um greedy, rapacious; hungry (for)
   (+ gen.)
dīdūcō (dis- + dūcō) divide, split
discō, discere, didicī, —— learn (how) (+ inf.)
Graius, -a, -um Greek; **Graīs** = *dat. pl.;*
   Graīs scans as if it were spelled ***Graiīs.**

laus, laudis *f.* praise
Mūsa, Mūsae *f.* Muse
ōs, ōris *n.* mouth
praeter (prep. + acc.) beyond, except
ratiō, ratiōnis *f.* account, reason; calculation
rotundus, -a, -um rounded

The *Ars Poëtica* is one of Horace's *Epistulae,* a collection of long hexameter didactic poems on a variety of subjects.
The poet of the *Ars Poëtica* offers observations and guidance on poetry generally and drama in particular. This playful, imaginative, and insightful 476-line poem speaks with authority on both style and content, but its overall structure and prescription for poetry are elusive.

17. Ovid, *Ars Amātōria* I.61–66

The poet reassures a whole variety of future lovers.

seu caperis prīmīs et adhūc crēscentibus annīs,

   ante oculōs veniet vēra puella tuōs:

sīve cupis iuvenem, iuvenēs tibi mīlle placēbunt.

   cōgēris vōtī nescius esse tuī:

seu tē forte* iuvat sēra et sapientior aetās,   65

   hoc quoque, crēde mihī,† plēnius agmen erit.

*fors, fortis, -ium *f.* chance, luck
†The final **-i** of **mihi** here scans *long.*
adhūc (adv.) up to the present time; still
aetās, aetātis *f.* age, time of life
agmen, agminis *n.* (battle) line; throng; train
cōgō (cō- + agō), cōgere, coēgī, coāctus drive together, force, compel
crēscō, crēscere, crēvī, crētus grow, increase
iuvenis, iuvenis *m.* or *f.* young man, young
   woman

iuvō, iuvāre, iūvī, iūtus help, assist, aid; give
   pleasure, delight
nescius, -a, -um not knowing, unaware (+ gen.)
plēnus, -a -um full
sērus, -a, -um late; advanced
sīve or **seu** (conj.) or if; **sīve (seu)** . . . **sīve**
   (seu) . . . whether . . . or if . . .
vōtum, vōtī *n.* vow, prayer; desire

18. Ovid, *Metamorphōsēs* VII.17–23

After the Colchian king Aeetes explains the impossible labors that Jason and the Argonauts must perform in order to win the Golden Fleece, the king's daughter Medea scolds herself for the feelings aroused in her by the handsome stranger Jason.

excute virgineō conceptās pectore flammās,

sī potes, īnfēlīx! sī possem, sānior essem!

sed trahit invītam nova vīs, aliudque cupīdō,

mēns aliud suādet: videō meliōra probōque,   20

dēteriōra sequor! quid* in† hospite, rēgia virgō,

ūreris et thalamōs aliēnī concipis orbis?

haec quoque terra potest quod amēs dare...

*quid, *here* (adv.), why
†in, *here,* in the case of
aliēnus, -a, -um belonging to another; alien,
   strange; foreign
concipiō (con- + capiō) conceive, produce;
   imagine
cupīdō, cupīdinis *f.* desire
dēterior, dēterius worse
excutiō, excutere, excussī, excussus throw out,
   shake off, drive away
flamma, flammae *f.* flame
hospes, hospitis *m.* guest, visitor, stranger; host
invītus, -a, -um unwilling
orbis, orbis, -ium *m.* ring, circle; world, region

probō (1-tr.) approve of
rēgius, -a, -um royal
sānus, -a, -um healthy, sane
suādeō, suādēre, suāsī, suāsus recommend,
   urge, advise
thalamus, thalamī *m. in sing. or pl.* inner room,
   wedding chamber; marriage
trahō, trahere, trāxī, tractus draw, drag
ūrō, ūrere, ussī, ustus burn, scorch, inflame,
   consume
virgineus, -a, -um of *or* belonging to a maiden,
   maidenly
virgō, virginis *f.* maiden, virgin

19. Ovid, *Trīstia* II.421–30

After defending his poetic license by reference to Greek writers, the poet turns to Roman writers for support as well.

> nēve peregrīnīs tantum dēfendar ab armīs,
>
>   et Rōmānus habet multa iocōsa liber.
>
> utque suō Martem cecinit gravis Ennius ōre—
>
>   Ennius ingeniō maximus, arte rudis—
>
> explicat ut causās rapidī Lucrētius ignis,   425
>
>   cāsūrumque triplex vāticinātur opus,*
>
> sīc sua† lascīvō cantāta est saepe Catullō‡
>
>   fēmina, cui falsum Lesbia nōmen erat;
>
> nec contentus eā, multōs vulgāvit amōrēs,
>
>   in quibus ipse suum fassus adulterium est.   430

*cāsūrum ... triplex ... opus refers to Lucretius's prediction about the future of the universe, which he divides into the sea, land, and sky.

†sua, refers to **Catullō**, his own

‡**Catullō**, Dative of Agent

adulterium, adulteriī *n.* adultery

cantō (1-tr.) sing (of)

contentus, -a, -um content, satisfied; contained

dēfendō, dēfendere, dēfendī, dēfēnsus protect, defend

Ennius, Enniī *m.* Ennius

explicō (1-tr.) unfold, reveal, explain

iocōsus, -a, -um full of jokes; laughable, funny

lascīvus, -a, -um playful, naughty, free from restraint

Lucrētius, Lucrētiī *m.* Lucretius

nēve (conj.) = nē + -ve (enclitic conj.) or

nōmen, nōminis *n.* name

ōs, ōris *n.* mouth; voice; eloquence

peregrīnus, -a, -um foreign

rapidus, -a, -um tearing away, consuming; rushing, rapid

rudis, rude unformed, rough; crude, unrefined, unfinished

tantum (adv.) only

triplex, triplicis threefold; tripartite

vāticinor (1-tr.) warn of, predict, prophesy

vulgō (1-tr.) make (something) public; make famous

The *Trīstia* is one of two works composed by Ovid after he was forced to leave Rome by Augustus in 8 C.E. In five books of elegiac verse the poet interweaves appeals to Augustus for his recall with accounts of life and weather in an uncivilized land far from Rome.

20. Livy, *Ab Urbe Conditā* V.49.6

After the long, painful siege of Rome by the Gauls that nearly ends in surrender, the Romans, led by the dictator Camillus, rout the Gauls first in Rome and then outside it. The historian describes the second battle.

ibi caedēs omnia obtinuit; castra capiuntur et nē nuntius quidem clādis relictus. dictātor reciperātā ex hostibus patriā triumphāns in urbem redit, interque iocōs mīlitārēs quōs inconditōs iaciunt, Rōmulus ac parēns patriae conditorque alter urbis haud vānīs laudibus appellābātur.

appellō (1-tr.) name, call
caedēs, caedis, -ium *f.* slaughter
clādēs, clādis *f.* slaughter, destruction
conditor, conditōris *m.* founder
dictātor, dictātōris *m.* dictator, an emergency officer with unlimited powers
haud (adv.) not at all, by no means
ibi (adv.) there; then
inconditus, -a, -um unpolished, rough, crude
iocus, iocī *m.* joke, jest

laus, laudis *f.* praise
mīlitāris, mīlitāre military
nuntius, nuntiī *m.* messenger
obtineō (ob- + teneō), obtinēre, obtinuī, obtentus persist in; extend over, have a hold on
parēns, parentis, -ium *m.* or *f.* parent
reciperō (1-tr.) get back, recover, regain
triumphō (1-intr.) celebrate a triumph, triumph
vānus, -a, -um empty, illusory; groundless, false

21. Livy, *Ab Urbe Conditā* XXII.49.10

Aemilius Paulus responds to Cn. Lentulus's request that he, Paulus, save himself and leave the ravaged battlefield.

"abī, nuntiā pūblicē patribus: urbem Rōmānam mūniant ac priusquam victor hostis adveniat praesidiīs firment; prīvātim Q. Fabiō L. Aemilium praeceptōrum eius memorem et vīxisse adhūc et morī. mē in hāc strāge mīlitum meōrum patere exspīrāre, nē aut reus iterum ē cōnsulātū sim <aut>* accūsātor collēgae exsistam ut aliēnō crīmine innocentiam meam prōtegam." haec eōs agentēs† prius turba fugientium cīvium, deinde hostēs oppressēre.

*Pointed brackets mark an element added by scholars.

†**agō**, *here*, speak about, discuss

accūsātor, accūsātōris *m.* accuser, prosecutor

adhūc (adv.) up to this time

adveniō (**ad-** + **veniō**) arrive; **adveniat**, *subjunc. expressing anticipation,* can arrive

L. Aemilius, L. Aemiliī *m.* L. Aemilius (Paulus) (consul 216 B.C.E.), one of the Roman leaders at the disastrous battle of Cannae

aliēnus, -a, -um belonging to another; done by another

collēga, collēgae *m.* colleague (in office)

crīmen, crīminis *n.* charge, accusation; crime

deinde (adv.) then, thereupon; next

ex(s)istō, ex(s)istere, ex(s)titī, —— stand out, appear; prove to be

ex(s)pīrō (1-intr.) breathe out, expire; die

Q. Fabius, Q. Fabiī *m.* Q. Fabius (Maximus) (consul 233, 228, 215, 214, 209 B.C.E.; censor 230, dictator 217), one of the heroes of the second Punic war

firmō (1-tr.) strengthen

innocentia, innocentiae *f.* innocence

iterum (adv.) again, a second time

memor, memoris mindful, remembering (+ gen.)

mūniō, mūnīre, mūnīvī or **mūniī, mūnītus** fortify

nuntiō (1-tr.) announce, report

opprimō, opprimere, oppressī, oppressus press down; suppress; overwhelm, crush

praeceptum, praeceptī *n.* (piece of) advice, instruction

praesidium, praesidiī *n.* guard, garrison

priusquam (conj. + indic. *or* subjunc.) before

prīvātim (adv.) in private, privately

prōtegō, prōtegere, prōtēxī, prōtēctus protect, defend

reus, reī *m.* defendant; *when Paulus was first consul in 219, he was accused of embezzlement*

strāgēs, strāgis *f.* destruction, slaughter

turba, turbae *f.* crowd

victor, victōris *m.* conqueror, victor

22. Livy, *Ab Urbe Conditā* XXX.30.18

In 202 B.C.E. a besieged Hannibal attempted to negotiate terms of peace with his respected Roman counterpart, the great Roman general Scipio Africanus. Scipio rejected Hannibal's pleas and then decisively defeated the Carthaginians in the last battle of the second Punic war. The following passage is a portion of Hannibal's speech to Scipio, as reported by the historian. Hannibal tries to convince Scipio to avoid a pitched battle.

maximae cuique* fortūnae minimē crēdendum est. in bonīs tuīs rēbus, nostrīs

dubiīs, tibi ampla ac speciōsa dantī est pāx, nōbīs petentibus magis necessāria quam

honesta. melior tūtiorque est certa pāx quam spērāta victōria; haec in tuā, illa in

deōrum manū est. nē tot annōrum fēlīcitātem in† ūnīus hōrae dederis† discrīmen.

*cuique = *fem. sing. dat. of indef. adj.,* each
†dare . . . in . . . to consign . . . to . . .
amplus, -a, -um great, distinguished
discrīmen, discrīminis *n.* dividing line, difference; decision; critical point
dubius, -a, -um uncertain, doubtful
fēlīcitās, fēlīcitātis *f.* good fortune, luck; prosperity

hōra, hōrae *f.* hour
necessārius, -a, -um necessary
speciōsus, -a, -um attractive, splendid
spērō (1-tr.) hope (for), expect
tot (indeclinable adj.) so many
tūtus, -a, -um safe
victōria, victōriae *f.* victory

23. Seneca the Younger, *Dialogī* IV.31.4

The philosopher advises Novatus on what kind of behavior he may expect from human beings.

quid enim mīrum est malōs mala facinora ēdere? quid novī est sī inimīcus nocet, amīcus offendit, fīlius lābitur, servus peccat? turpissimam aiēbat Fabius imperātōrī excūsātiōnem esse "nōn putāvī." ego turpissimam hominī putō. omnia putā, expectā: etiam in bonīs mōribus aliquid existet asperius. fert* hūmāna nātūra īnsidiōsōs animōs, fert ingrātōs, fert cupidōs, fert impiōs. cum† dē ūnīus mōribus iūdicābis, dē pūblicīs cōgitā. ubi maximē gaudēbis, maximē metuēs; ubi tranquilla tibi omnia videntur, ibi nocitūra nōn dēsunt sed quiēscunt. semper futūrum aliquid quod tē offendat exīstimā.

*fer**ō**, *here,* produce
†**cum**, *here* (conj.) when
aiō (defective verb) say; **aiēbat** = *3rd sing. imperf. act. indic.*
aliquid = *neut. sing. nom. or acc. of indef. pron.,* something
asper, aspera, asperum harsh, fierce, pitiless; severe
dēsum (dē- + sum), dēesse, dēfuī, dēfutūrus be absent, be lacking
ēdō (ē- + dō) emit; produce, perform; commit
ex(s)istō, ex(s)istere, ex(s)titī, —— stand out, appear
exīstimō (1-tr.) reckon, suppose, think
ex(s)pectō (1-tr.) wait for, await, expect
Fabius, Fabiī *m.* (Q.) Fabius (Maximus), hero of the second Punic war
facinus, facinoris *n.* deed; crime
gaudeō, gaudēre, gāvīsus sum rejoice (in), be glad, be pleased

hūmānus, -a, -um human
ibi (adv.) there; then
ingrātus, -a, -um ungrateful; unpleasant, displeasing
īnsidiōsus, -a, -um treacherous, deceitful
iūdicō (1-tr.) form an opinion, judge, determine
lābor, lābī, lāpsus sum slip, glide; fall, fall into error
metuō, metuere, metuī, —— fear, dread
mīrus, -a, -um marvelous, astonishing
noceō, nocēre, nocuī, nocitūrus be harmful, do harm
offendō, offendere, offendī, offēnsus trouble, upset, give offense to, annoy
peccō (1-intr.) make a mistake; do wrong
quiēscō, quiēscere, quiēvī, quiētum be asleep, be dormant, lie quiet
tranquillus, -a, -um calm, quiet, still
turpis, turpe foul, ugly; base, shameful

In twelve books together given the title *Dialogī* (Dialogues), although they are not written in dialogue form, Seneca discusses a number of moral and philosophical ideas. For the most part each book is addressed to a different person and treats a single question. Three books of the *Dialogī* (III–V) discuss fully the question of how anger may be restrained. Taken together they are often entitled *Dē Īrā*.

24. Florus, *Epitoma Bellōrum Omnium* I.31

Florus summarizes the opinions of two famous Romans about how best to deal with Carthage after that city had rearmed itself for the first time in fifty years (ca. 152 B.C.E.).

Catō inexpiābilī odiō dēlendam esse Carthāginem, et cum* dē aliō cōnsulerētur, prōnuntiābat, Scīpiō Nāsīca servandam, nē metū ablātō aemulae luxuriārī fēlīcitās urbis inciperet; medium senātus ēlēgit ut urbs tantum locō movērētur.† nihil enim speciōsius vidēbātur quam esse Carthāginem quae nōn timērētur.

***cum**, *here* (conj. + subjunc.), (under the circumstances) when

†**ut . . . movērētur** is a substantive clause explaining **medium**; translate "that . . . be moved."

aemulus, -a, -um emulous, rival; **aemulus**, sc. **urbis**

cōnsulō, cōnsulere, cōnsuluī, cōnsultus take counsel, consult, consider

ēligō (ē- + legō), ēligere, ēlēgī, ēlēctus select, choose

fēlīcitās, fēlīcitātis *f.* good fortune, luck; prosperity

incipiō (in- + capiō) take on, begin

inexpiābilis, inexpiābile implacable

luxurior (1-tr.) revel, luxuriate, become intoxicated

prōnuntiō (1-tr.) proclaim, pronounce, declare

Scīpiō Nāsīca, Scīpiōnis Nāsīcae *m.* (P. Cornelius) Scipio Nasica (consul 162 B.C.E., censor 159), political opponent of Cato the Elder

speciōsus, -a, -um attractive, splendid

tantum (adv.) only

Nothing certain is known about the writer Florus—not even his first name. One of the works that is attributed to a writer named Florus is entitled *Epitoma dē Titō Līviō Bellōrum Omnium Annōrum DCC* (An Abridgement from Titus Livius of All the Wars of Seven Hundred Years). The work is a concise summary and reconstruction of the history of Roman military encounters and the rise of the Roman people to prominence in the Mediterranean. Although the title suggests that the author is summarizing the historian Livy, Florus's *Epitoma* makes reference to that historian among many other historians and writers. Internal evidence, as well as the association of the Florus of the *Epitoma* with other writers of the same name, suggests that the work was written in the second century C.E.

Continuous Readings

1. Cicero, *In Catilīnam I* 11

Having revealed Catiline's dangerous plans, Cicero boasts of his own survival.

magna dīs immortālibus habenda est atque huic ipsī Iovī Statōrī, antīquissimō custōdī huius urbis, grātia, quod* hanc tam taetram, tam horribilem tamque īnfestam reī pūblicae pestem totiēns iam effūgimus. nōn est saepius in† ūnō homine summa salūs perīclitanda reī pūblicae. quam diū‡ mihi cōnsulī dēsignātō, Catilīna, īnsidiātus es, nōn pūblicō mē praesidiō, sed prīvātā dīligentiā dēfendī. cum§ proximīs comitiīs cōnsulāribus mē cōnsulem in campō et competītōrēs tuōs interficere voluistī, com-pressī cōnātūs tuōs nefāriōs amīcōrum praesidiō et cōpiīs nūllō tumultū pūblicē concitātō; dēnique, quotiēnscumque mē petīstī, per mē tibi obstitī, quamquam vidē-bam perniciem meam cum magnā calamitāte reī pūblicae esse coniūnctam.

*quod, *here* (conj.), because
†in, *here,* in the case of
‡quam diū, *here,* as long as
§cum, *here,* (conj. + indic.), when
calamitās, calamitātis *f.* disaster, misfortune, injury
comitia cōnsulāria, comitiōrum cōnsulārium *n. pl.* election of consuls
competītor, competītōris *m.* competitor, rival
comprimō, comprimere, compressī, compressus crush; subdue, suppress
cōnātus, cōnātūs *m.* attempt
concitō (1-tr.) stir up, rouse
coniungō, coniungere, coniūnxī, coniūnctus join together
custōs, custōdis *m.* or *f.* guardian, protector, sentry
dēfendō, dēfendere, dēfendī, dēfēnsus protect, defend
dēnique (adv.) finally, at last
dēsignātus, -a, -um elect, appointed (but not yet installed)
effugiō (ex- + fugiō) flee from, escape

grātia, grātiae *f.* favor, kindness; gratitude, thanks
horribilis, horribile terrifying, dreadful
immortālis, immortāle immortal
īnfestus, -a, -um hostile, harmful
īnsidior (1-intr.) lie in wait for; plot against (+ dat.)
nefārius, -a, -um unspeakable, wicked
obstō (ob- + stō), obstāre, obstitī, obstātum stand in the way; hinder, block (+ dat.)
perīclitor (1-tr.) put in peril, endanger
perniciēs, perniciēī *f.* destruction, ruin, disaster
pestis, pestis, -ium *f.* plague, destruction, ruin
praesidium, praesidiī *n.* guard, garrison
prīvātus, -a, -um private
proximus, -a, -um nearest; most recent, last
quotiēnscumque (conj.) however often, as often as
Stator, Statōris *m.* (the) Stayer *or* Protector
taeter, taetra, taetrum repulsive, foul
tam (adv.) so
totiēns (adv.) so many times
tumultus, tumultūs *m.* commotion, uproar
volō, velle, voluī, —— be willing, want, wish

Cicero's first speech, *In Catilīnam I,* was delivered before the members of the senate (including Catiline himself) in 63 B.C.E. Having learned that Catiline had recruited an army and was planning the murders of all the leading men of the state, the consul Cicero sought to inform the senate and win their approval for action against the conspirators. Despite some strong support, even among the senators, Catiline and his forces were ultimately defeated, and Cati-line was killed in a battle north of Rome.

2. Sallust, *Bellum Catilīnae* 1

> Sallust begins his account of the Catilinarian conspiracy with a broad discussion of the
> human condition.

Omnīs hominēs quī sēsē student praestāre cēterīs animālibus summā ope nītī decet

nē vītam silentiō trānseant, velutī pecora quae nātūra prōna atque ventrī oboedientia

fīnxit. sed nostra omnis vīs in animō et corpore sita est: animī imperiō, corporis servi-

tiō magis ūtimur; alterum nōbīs cum dīs, alterum cum bēluīs commūne est. quō

mihi rēctius vidētur ingenī quam vīrium opibus glōriam quaerere, et, quoniam vīta

ipsa quā fruimur brevis est, memoriam nostrī quam maxumē longam* efficere; nam

dīvitiārum et formae glōria fluxa atque fragilis est, virtūs clāra aeternaque habētur.

*quam maxumē longam = quam longissimam
aeternus, -a, -um eternal, everlasting
bēlua, bēluae *f.* wild beast
cēterus, -a, -um rest (of), remaining part (of),
  (the) other
commūnis, commūne common, shared; held in
  common
decet, decēre, decuit, —— (impersonal verb) it is
  becoming, it is proper (+ acc. + inf.)
dīvitiae, dīvitiārum *f. pl.* wealth, riches
efficiō (ex- + faciō) bring about
fingō, fingere, fīnxī, fictus form, fashion, make;
  imagine
fluxus, -a, -um flowing, loose; weak, fleeting,
  perishable
forma, formae *f.* shape, form; beauty
fragilis, fragile easily broken, frail
fruor, fruī, frūctus sum enjoy, delight in (+ abl.)
maxumē = maximē
memoria, memoriae *f.* memory, remembrance
nītor, nītī, nīxus or nīsus sum rest upon, rely on
  (+ abl.); make an effort, strive

oboediēns, oboedientis obedient, compliant,
  subject
ops, opis *f.* power, ability, might, effort; *in pl.*,
  power, resources, wealth
pecus, pecoris *n.* (herd) animal, livestock; *in pl.*,
  farm animals
praestō, praestāre, praestitī, praestitum stand
  before, be superior, excel (+ dat.)
prōnus, -a, -um leaning *or* bending forward
rēctus, -a, -um straight; right, correct
servitium, servitiī *n.* slavery
silentium, silentiī *n.* silence; silentiō, *Ablative of
  Manner*, in silence
situs, -a, -um placed, set, situated
studeō, studēre, studuī, —— be eager, desire
trānseō (trāns- + eō), trānsīre, trānsiī or trānsīvī,
  trānsitus go across, pass through
velutī (conj.) even as, just as
venter, ventris *m.* belly, stomach

3. Vergil, *Aeneid* II.491–505

īnstat vī patriā* Pyrrhus; nec claustra nec ipsī

custōdēs sufferre valent; labat ariete crēbrō

iānua, et ēmōtī prōcumbunt cardine postēs.

fit via vī; rumpunt aditūs prīmōsque trucīdant

immissī Danaī et lātē loca mīlite complent.   495

nōn sīc, aggeribus ruptīs cum† spūmeus amnis

exiit oppositāsque ēvīcit gurgite mōlēs,

fertur in arva furēns cumulō campōsque per omnīs

cum stabulīs armenta trahit. vīdī ipse furentem

caede Neoptolemum geminōsque in līmine Atrīdās,   500

vīdī Hecubam centumque nurūs Priamumque per ārās

sanguine foedantem quōs ipse sacrāverat ignīs.

***patrius, -a, -um,** of *or* belonging to a father, paternal; ancestral

†**cum,** *here* (conj. + perf. indic.), whenever; translate **exiit** and **ēvīcit** as pres. indic.

aditus, aditūs *m.* approach, entrance, doorway

agger, aggeris *m.* mound; bank (of a river)

amnis, amnis, -ium *m.* stream, torrent

ariēs, arietis *m.* (battering) ram; the **-i-** of **ariete** is here consonantal for purposes of scansion

armentum, armentī *n.* herd; bull, head of cattle; *in pl.,* cattle

arvum, arvī *n.* (ploughed) field

Atrīdēs, Atrīdae *m.* son of Atreus (either Agamemnon or Menelaus)

caedēs, caedis, -ium *f.* slaughter

cardō, cardinis *m.* pivot; hinge

claustrum, claustrī *n.* bolt, bar

compleō, complēre, complēvī, complētus fill completely

crēber, crēbra, crēbrum frequent, repeated

cumulus, cumulī *m.* heap, pile; mass, wave

custōs, custōdis *m.* or *f.* guard(ian), protector, sentry

Danaī, Danaōrum *m. pl.* Danaans, Greeks

ēmoveō (ē- + moveō) remove, dislodge

ēvincō (ē- + vincō) defeat utterly, overcome

exeō (ex- + eō), exīre, exiī or **exīvī, exitum** go out

fīō, fierī, factus sum be made; **fit** = *3rd sing. pres. act. indic.*

foedō (1-tr.) befoul, defile

furō, furere, ——, —— be crazy; rage, rave

geminus, -a, -um twin-born, twin

gurges, gurgitis *m.* swirling water, eddy, whirlpool

Hecuba, Hecubae *f.* Hecuba, wife of Priam

iānua, iānuae *f.* door

immittō (in- + mittō) send in, send against

īnstō (in- + stō), īnstāre, īnstitī, īnstātūrus press (hostilely), press on

labō, labāre, labāvī, —— be shaky, totter, give way

lātē (adv.) widely, far and wide

līmen, līminis *n.* entrance, doorway, threshold

mōlēs, mōlis, -ium *f.* mass; dam

Neoptolemus, Neoptolemī *m.* Neoptolemus, son of Achilles (= Pyrrhus)

nurus, nurūs *f.* daughter-in-law

oppōnō (ob- + pōnō) place in the way, place against

postis, postis, -ium *m.* doorpost, jamb

prōcumbō, prōcumbere, prōcubuī, prōcubitum bend forward; fall down, crash

Pyrrhus, Pyrrhī *m.* Pyrrhus, son of Achilles (= Neoptolemus)

rumpō, rumpere, rūpī, ruptus split, burst, break

sacrō (1-tr.) make sacred, consecrate

sanguis, sanguinis *m.* blood

spūmeus, -a, -um foamy, frothy

stabulum, stabulī *n.* stable, shed, stall

sufferō (sub- + ferō), sufferre, sustulī, sublātus endure, withstand

trahō, trahere, trāxī, tractus draw, drag

trucīdō (1-tr.) slaughter, butcher

quīnquāgintā illī thalamī, spēs tanta nepōtum,

barbaricō postēs aurō spoliīsque superbī

prōcubuēre; tenent Danaī quā* dēficit ignis.   505

*quā, *here* (adv.), where
barbaricus, -a, -um barbarian
Danaī, Danaōrum *m. pl.* Danaans, Greeks
dēficiō (**dē-** + **faciō**) let down, fail
nepōs, nepōtis *m.* grandson
postis, postis, -ium *m.* doorpost, jamb

prōcumbō, prōcumbere, prōcubuī, prōcubitum
  bend forward; fall down, crash
spolium, spoliī *n.* booty, spoil
superbus, -a, -um proud; haughty
tantus, -a, -um so great
thalamus, thalamī *m. in sing. or pl.* inner room,
  wedding chamber; marriage

4. Ovid, *Metamorphōsēs* I.463–77

> fīlius huic Veneris "fīgat tuus omnia, Phoebe,
>
> tē meus arcus," ait: "quantōque animālia cēdunt
>
> cūncta deō, tantō minor est tua glōria nostrā."   465
>
> dīxit et ēlīsō percussīs āere pennīs
>
> inpiger umbrōsā Parnāsī cōnstitit arce
>
> ēque sagittiferā prōmpsit duo tēla pharetrā
>
> dīversōrum operum: fugat hoc, facit illud amōrem.
>
> quod facit, aurātum est et cuspide fulget acūtā: 470
>
> quod fugat, obtūsum est et habet sub harundine plumbum.
>
> hoc deus in nymphā Pēnēide fīxit, at illō
>
> laesit Apollineās trāiecta per ossa medullās.
>
> prōtinus alter amat, fugit altera nōmen amantis
>
> silvārum latebrīs captīvārumque ferārum   475
>
> exuviīs gaudēns innuptaeque aemula Phoebēs.
>
> vitta coërcēbat positōs sine lēge capillōs.

acūtus, -a, -um sharp, pointed

aemulus, -a, -um emulous, rivaling (+ gen.)

āēr, āeris *m.* air

aiō (defective verb) say; **ait** = *3rd sing. pres. act. indic.*

Apollineus, -a, -um of *or* belonging to Apollo

arcus, arcūs *m.* bow (for shooting arrows)

arx, arcis *f.* tower, citadel; height, peak

at (conj.) but

aurātus, -a, -um made of gold, golden

capillus, capillī *m. in sing. or pl.* hair

captīvus, -a, -um captive, captured (in hunting or fishing)

coërceō, coërcēre, coërcuī, coërcitus restrain, keep back

cōnsistō, cōnsistere, cōnstitī, —— make a stand, halt

cūnctus, -a, -um all

cuspis, cuspidis *f.* sharp point, tip

dīversus, -a, -um different

ēlīdō, ēlīdere, ēlīsī, ēlīsus break thoroughly, batter, cut

exuviae, exuviārum *f. pl.* (stripped) armor; skin(s)

fera, ferae *f.* wild animal, beast

fīgō, fīgere, fīxī, fīxus fix, pierce

fugō (1-tr.) cause to flee, put to flight

fulgeō, fulgēre, fulsī, —— shine, gleam

gaudeō, gaudēre, gāvīsus sum rejoice (in), be glad, be pleased

harundō, harundinis *f.* reed; (arrow) shaft

innuptus, -a, -um unmarried, maiden

inpiger, inpigra, inpigrum not slow, energetic, brisk

laedō, laedere, laesī, laesus injure, harm, wound

latebra, latebrae *f.* hiding place, lair, recess

medulla, medullae *f.* marrow; *in pl.*, vitals, innards

nōmen, nōminis *n.* name

nympha, nymphae *f.* nymph, a semidivine spirit

obtūsus, -a, -um blunt, dull

os, ossis *n.* bone

Parnāsus, Parnāsī *m.* Parnassus, a mountain in Greece

Pēnēis, Pēnēidos descended from the river god Peneus; **Pēnēide** = *abl. sing.*

penna, pennae *f.* wing

percutiō, percutere, percussī, percussus strike, beat; **percussīs . . . pennīs**, by the beating of wings

pharetra, pharetrae *f.* quiver

Phoebē, Phoebēs *f.* Phoebe (Diana); **Phoebēs** = *gen. sing.*

Phoebus, Phoebī *m.* Phoebus (Apollo)

plumbum, plumbī *n.* lead

prōmō, prōmere, prōmpsī, prōmptus bring forth, draw

prōtinus (adv.) immediately, straightway

quantus, -a, -um how much

sagittifer, sagittifera, sagittiferum arrow-bearing

silva, silvae *f.* forest

tantus, -a, -um so much

trāiciō (trāns- + iaciō) pierce, transfix

umbrōsus, -a, -um shady

vitta, vittae *f.* headband

§112. About Meter II

The Roman poets learned from Greek models the dactylic hexameter, the meter of epic, and the elegiac couplet, the meter of love poetry (see §82). Some also chose to imitate meters of such Greek lyric poets as Archilochus, Sappho, and Alcaeus.[1]

Lyric poetry (originally so called because it was recited with the accompaniment of music played on a lyre) most often found its subject matter in the events and concerns of personal, private life: friendship, humor, love, wine, mortality. Both Catullus and Horace brought lyric meters into Latin poetry, but in his four books of *Odes*, Horace demonstrated mastery of a far greater variety of these meters.

Since *all* Latin poetry is quantitative, the basic rules for scanning lyric meters (for determining long and short syllables and marking elisions) are the same as those used for scanning dactylic hexameters and elegiac couplets. Some lyric poems use dactylic lines or sequences of dactylic feet, but many lyric meters have lines that are *not* divided into feet.

Certain lyric units may be learned and identified, but one generally learns the metrical scheme for each complete lyric line. Some lyric poems have only one metrical scheme that is repeated in every line (**stichic verse**), some have two metrical schemes in alternation (**couplets**), and others have four lines that repeat (**strophic** or **stanzaic verse**).

Stichic verse is indicated when each line begins at the left-hand margin. (For example, dactylic hexameter is stichic verse.) Each *indented* line indicates a metrically different line.

Common Terms and Metrical Units of Latin Lyric Poetry

acephalous (< Greek *akephalos,* headless) missing the first element
metron (< Greek *metron,* measure) the smallest metrical unit allowed in a given scheme

dimeter consisting of two metra
trimeter consisting of three metra
tetrameter consisting of four metra
pentameter consisting of five metra
hexameter consisting of six metra
> NOTE: FOR DACTYLS *ONE* DACTYLIC FOOT = *ONE* METRON
>
> FOR IAMBS, TROCHEES, AND ANAPESTS *TWO* FEET = *ONE* METRON

iamb ‿ –
iambic metron x – ‿ –
bacchiac ‿ – –
dactyl – ‿ ‿

---

1. Other Roman poets wrote tragedies and imitated the meters found in Greek tragic poetry. The Roman adaptations of these meters are not presented in this book.

spondee – –
adonic – ‿ ‿ – x
hemiepes – ‿ ‿ – ‿ ‿ x
anapest ‿ ‿ –
trochee – ‿
trochaic metron – ‿ – x
cretic – ‿ –
choriamb – ‿ ‿ –
glyconic x x – ‿ ‿ – ‿ x
hipponactean x x – ‿ ‿ – ‿ ‿ – x
pherecratean x x – ‿ ‿ – x

Hendecasyllable

Many of the short poems of Catullus employ a repeating eleven-syllable line with this scheme:

   x x – ‿ ‿ – ‿ – ‿ – x

   –   – – ‿ ‿ – ‿ – ‿ – –
   Iam vēr ēgelĭdōs refert tepōrēs

   –   – – ‿ ‿ –   ‿   – ‿ – ‿
   iam caelī furor aequinoctiālis

OBSERVATIONS

1. The first two syllables and the last syllable are anceps (see §82).

2. The hendecasyllabic line is basically *iambic* in rhythm. An **iamb** is a metrical unit composed of one short syllable followed by one long syllable (‿ –). The unit – ‿ ‿ –, called a **choriamb**, is characteristic of this meter and several other lyric meters. Meters constructed around the choriamb are called **Aeolic** meters.

3. A word usually ends after the fifth or sixth syllable, and this word end may be considered the line's caesural pause.

Choliambic (Limping Iambic)

Several of Catullus's short poems employ a repeating iambic line with this scheme:

   x – ‿ – | x – ‿ – | x – – x

   ‿   – –   ‿ –   – ‿   – – ‿
   Miser Catul/le, dēsinās / ineptīre

   ‿   – –   ‿   – – ‿   –   – –
   et quod vidēs / perīsse per/ditum dūcās.

OBSERVATIONS

1. The sequence x – ‿ – is called an **iambic metron** (< Greek *metron*, measure) and is composed of two iambs (‿ – ‿ –), although the first syllable is *anceps*. When scanning, one regularly marks off each iambic metron.

2. Because a long is substituted for a short in the second iamb of the last metron of the line, this meter is said to "limp" or slow down.

3. A word usually ends after the fifth syllable, and this word end may be considered the line's caesural pause.

Sapphic Strophe

Two of Catullus's and many of Horace's poems employ a stanzaic form possibly created by the Greek poet Sappho and bearing her name:

$- \smile - \text{x} - \,\|\, \smile \smile - \smile - \text{x}$ (cretic and acephalous hipponactean)

$- \smile - \text{x} - \,\|\, \smile \smile - \smile - \text{x}$

$- \smile - \text{x} - \,\|\, \smile \smile - \smile - \text{x}$

$\quad\quad - \smile \smile - \text{x}$ (adonic)

$- \quad \smile \quad - \quad - \quad - \,\|\, \smile \quad \smile \quad - \quad \smile \quad - \quad \smile$
Integer vītae $\|$ **scelerisque pūrus**

$- \quad \smile \quad - \quad - \quad - \,\|\, \smile \quad \smile \quad - \quad \smile \quad - \quad -$
nōn eget Mauris $\|$ **iaculis neque arcū**

$- \quad \smile \quad - \quad - \quad - \,\|\, \smile \quad \smile \quad - \quad \smile \quad - \quad -$
nec venēnātīs $\|$ **gravidā sagittīs**

$\quad\quad - \quad \smile \quad \smile \quad - \quad -$
Fusce, pharetrā . . .

OBSERVATIONS

1. The first three lines of the Sapphic strophe have the same metrical scheme, a line composed of two lyric units, the **cretic** ($- \smile -$) and the **hipponactean** (x x $- \smile \smile - \smile - $ x). Because the hipponactean is *missing the first element,* it is called "headless" or **acephalous**. Note that the choriamb ($- \smile \smile -$) is present in the hipponactean. There is a regular caesura after the fifth syllable.

2. The last line of the Sapphic strophe resembles the last two feet of a dactylic hexameter line. This short line is called an **adonic**.

Asclepiadean Meters

Lyric meters that feature a unit known as a **glyconic** (x x $- \smile \smile - \smile$ x) are called **Asclepiadean** meters after an Alexandrian love poet, Asclepiades, who lived in the third century B.C.E. Horace employs several Asclepiadean meters, some of which are presented below.

One Asclepiadean meter employs a repeating glyconic line in which the choriamb within the glyconic is doubled:

x x $- \smile \smile - \,\|\, - \smile \smile -$ x

$- \quad - \quad - \quad \smile \quad \smile \quad - \quad \quad - \quad \smile \quad \smile \quad - \quad \smile\smile$
Exēgī monumentum aere perennius

$- \quad - \quad - \quad \smile \quad \smile \quad - \,\|\, \smile \quad \smile \quad \smile \quad - \quad \smile\smile$
rēgālīque sitū $\|$ **pȳramidum altius**

Another Asclepiadean meter employs a repeating glyconic line in which the choriamb within the glyconic is tripled:

x x – ◡ ◡ – ‖ – ◡ ◡ – ‖ – ◡ ◡ – ◡ x

Tū nē quaesierīs ‖ scīre nefās ‖ quem mihi, quem tibi

fīnem dī dederint, ‖ Leuconoē, ‖ nec Babylōniōs

A third Asclepiadean meter employs a glyconic line alternating with a glyconic line in which the choriamb within the glyconic is doubled:

x x – ◡ ◡ – ◡ x
  x x – ◡ ◡ – ‖ – ◡ ◡ – ◡ x

Dōnec grātus eram tibi

  nec quīsquam potior bracchia candidae

A stanzaic meter features the glyconic and variations:

x x – ◡ ◡ – ‖ – ◡ ◡ – ◡ x   (glyconic with doubled choriamb)

x x – ◡ ◡ – ‖ – ◡ ◡ – ◡ x

  x x – ◡ ◡ – x   (pherecratean)

    x x – ◡ ◡ – ◡ x   (glyconic)

Quis multā gracilis ‖ tē puer in rosā

perfūsus liquidīs ‖ urget odōribus

  grātō, Pyrrha, sub antrō?

    cuī flāvam religās comam

Archilochian Meter

Horace borrowed several meters from the Greek poet Archilochus. One of them employs a couplet form, the first line of which is dactylic hexameter, the second line of which is a hemiepes.

– ◡◡ | – ◡◡ | – ◡◡ | – ◡◡ | – ◡ ◡ | – x

  – ◡ ◡ | – ◡ ◡ | x

Diffū|gēre ni|vēs, ‖ rede|unt iam |grāmina |campīs

  arbori|busque co|mae

Alcaic Strophe

Horace's most intricate metrical form was borrowed from the Greek poet Alcaeus:

$$\text{x} - \smile - \,\big|\, \text{x} \,\big\|\, - \smile \smile - \smile \text{ x}\qquad\text{(iambic metron and acephalous glyconic)}$$

$$\text{x} - \smile - \,\big|\, \text{x} \,\big\|\, - \smile \smile - \smile \text{ x}$$

$$\text{x} - \smile - \,\big|\, \text{x} - \smile - \,\big|\, -\qquad\text{(iambic dimeter and one syllable)}$$

$$- \smile \smile - \smile \smile - \,\big|\, \smile \smile - \text{ x}\qquad\text{(hemiepes and bacchiac)}$$

Nōn semper im/brēs // nūbibus hispidōs

mānant in a/grōs // aut mare Caspium

vexant inae/quālēs procel/lae

ūsque nec Armeniīs in ōrīs

CHAPTER XII

Vocabulary

➤ **grātia, grātiae** *f.* favor, kindness; gratitude, thanks

➤ **littera, litterae** *f.* letter (of the alphabet);
in pl., letter, epistle
memoria, memoriae *f.* memory

➤ **dubium, dubiī** *n.* doubt, hesitation (§116)

➤ **gēns, gentis, -ium** *f.* nation, people; clan,
family
fors, fortis, -ium *f.* chance, luck
mōns, montis, -ium *m.* mountain

➤ **rūmor, rūmōris** *m.* rumor

➤ **fās** (indeclinable noun) *n.* (what is
divinely) right; (what is) permitted
➤ **nefās** (indeclinable noun) *n.* (what is
divinely) forbidden; sacrilege

➤ **dubitō** (1-tr.) hesitate; doubt (§116)
➤ **ōrō** (1-tr.) pray (for), beg (for)
➤ **rogō** (1-tr.) ask (for)
➤ **spērō** (1-tr.) hope (for)

➤ **cōnficiō, cōnficere, cōnfēcī, cōnfectus**
accomplish, complete
➤ **oblīvīscor, oblīvīscī, oblītus sum** forget
(+ gen.)

➤ **praeficiō, praeficere, praefēcī, praefectus**
put in charge (of)

➤ **īnferō, īnferre, intulī, illātus** carry (into);
inflict (on)
➤ **praeferō, praeferre, praetulī, praelātus**
prefer
➤ **praesum, praeesse, praefuī, praefutūrus**
be in charge (of), be in command (of)
➤ **volō, velle, voluī, ——** be willing, want,
wish (§118)
➤ **mālō, mālle, māluī, ——** want more,
prefer (§118)
➤ **nōlō, nōlle, nōluī, ——** be unwilling,
not want, not wish (§118)

➤ **dignus, -a, -um** worthy (of) (+ abl.)
➤ **indignus, -a, -um** unworthy (of) (+ abl.)
➤ **dubius, -a, -um** doubtful (§116)

an (conj.) *introduces an alternative question,* or (§113); *introduces an Indirect Question,* whether (§115)
➤ **cum** (conj.) when; since; although (§117)
➤ **modo** (adv.) only, just; now, just now
necne (conj.) *in Indirect Question,* or not
(§115)

nōnne (interrog. particle) *introduces a direct question expecting the answer "yes"* (§113)

num (interrog. particle) *introduces a direct question expecting the answer "no"* (§113); *introduces an Indirect Question, whether* (§115)

➤ **praeter** (prep. + acc.) beyond; except

quīn (conj.) *introduces Doubting clause, that* (§116)

quō (interrog. adv.) to where, whither

➤ **tum** or **tunc** (adv.) then, at that time

unde (interrog. adv.) from where, whence

utrum (interrog. particle) *introduces the first question of a double direct question or Indirect Question* (§113, §115)

utrum . . . an . . .	whether . . .
-ne . . . an . . .	or . . .
—— **. . . an . . .**	(§113, §115)

Vocabulary Notes

grātia, **grātiae** *f.* may mean the "favor" or "kindness" that one shows to another or the "gratitude" one feels in return for a favor or kindness. Both the singular and the plural may be used in a variety of idioms: **grātiās agere**, "to give thanks"; **grātiam** or **grātiās habēre**, "to feel grateful"; **grātiam** or **grātiās referre**, "to render thanks," "to return a favor."

In the singular **littera**, **litterae** *f.* refers to a "letter" of the alphabet. In the plural it most often means a single "epistle" or "letter." An adjective of quantity or number may be added to indicate more than one letter.

Fīliō *litterās* mīsī.	I sent *a letter* to (my) son.
Fīliō *multās litterās* mīsī.	I sent *many letters* to (my) son.

The plural of **littera** may also mean, more abstractly, "(humane) letters," "literature."

dubium, **dubiī** *n.* is a substantive of the adjective **dubius, -a, -um**. It regularly appears with an Indirect Question or a Doubting clause (see §116).

gēns, **gentis**, **-ium** *f.* may refer to a collective "people" or "nation." Among Roman citizens, a **gēns** was a group of families (clan) that shared the same **nōmen** (name) (see §16). **Gēns** may also refer to an individual family. In the plural, **gentēs** may mean "nations of the world" or "the human race" as a whole.

rūmor, **rūmōris** *m.* may mean "rumor" or "gossip," or it may refer more generally to "noise" made by many voices. The phrase **rūmor est** introduces an Indirect Statement (see §106).

Rūmor est Caesarem venīre.	There is a rumor that Caesar is coming.

fās is an indeclinable neuter noun. Its strict meaning is what is "right" according to divine law, as opposed to **iūs**, which indicates "right" according to human law. It may also be used of "(what is) permitted" or "(what is) lawful" in a more general sense. It commonly occurs in parenthetical remarks, such as **sī fās (est)** (if it is right). It is also often used as a predicate noun.

Fās est hoc facere.	To do this thing is *right*.

nefās is an indeclinable neuter noun formed by the addition of the negative prefix **ne-** to **fās**. Thus its strict meaning is what is an "offense" according to divine law (sacrilege).

When the verb **dubitō**, **dubitāre**, **dubitāvī**, **dubitātus** means "hesitate," it is often followed by a Complementary Infinitive. When it means "doubt," it regularly introduces an Indirect Question or a Doubting clause (see §116).

ōrō, **ōrāre**, **ōrāvī**, **ōrātus** takes a **double accusative**; that is, it may have *two* Accusative, Direct Objects, the *person begged* or *prayed to* and *the thing begged* or *prayed for*. It may also introduce an Indirect Command.

Cīvēs *deōs pācem* ōrant.	The citizens pray *to the gods for peace*.
Mīlitēs ōrēmus *nē discēdant*.	Let us beg *the soldiers that they not depart*.

rogō, **rogāre**, **rogāvī**, **rogātus** may introduce an Indirect Question (see §115) or an Indirect Command. It may take an Accusative, Direct Object expressing the *person asked* or *the thing asked for*. Like **ōrō**, **rogō** may take a double accusative.

Mīlitēs *auxilium* rogēmus.	Let us ask *the soldiers for aid*.

spērō, spērāre, spērāvī, spērātus is a *denominative* verb formed from the noun **spēs**. **Spērō** may be followed by an Accusative, Direct Object, or it may introduce an Indirect Statement.

cōnficiō, cōnficere, cōnfēcī, cōnfectus is a compound verb formed by the addition of the prefix **con-** to **faciō**. (For the prefix **con-** see Appendix P.) It may mean "accomplish" or "complete" (tasks, duties, written works, periods of time). It is a synonym of **perficiō**. **Cōnficiō** may also mean "wear out" or "kill."

oblīvīscor, oblīvīscī, oblītus sum may introduce an Indirect Statement. It often takes a Genitive with Verbs of Remembering and Forgetting (Objective Genitive) (cf. **meminī**). **Oblīvīscor** may also take an Accusative, Direct Object, particularly when the object is a neuter pronoun. When it takes an Object Infinitive, **oblīvīscor** may mean "forget" *or* "forget how."

Numquam oblīvīscar *illīus noctis.*	I shall never forget *that night.* (Objective Genitive)
Omnia oblīvīscēbar.	I was forgetting *all things.* (Accusative, Direct Object)
Miser poëta *scrībere* oblītus est.	The wretched poet forgot how *to write.* (Object Infinitive)

praeficiō, praeficere, praefēcī, praefectus is a compound verb formed by the addition of the prefix **prae-** to **faciō**. (For the prefix **prae-** see Appendix P.) **Praeficiō** is a transitive verb and also takes a Dative with a Compound Verb (see §120).

Senātus Caesarem *cōpiīs* in Italiā praeficiet.	
The senate will put Caesar *in charge of the troops* in Italy.	

īnferō, īnferre, intulī, illātus is a compound verb formed by the addition of the prefix **in-**[1] to **ferō**. (For the prefix **in-**[1] see Appendix P.) **Īnferō** is a transitive verb and also takes a Dative with a Compound Verb (see §120). It may mean "carry in" or "inflict" (war, injury, disgrace).

Bellum *incolīs* intulimus.	We inflicted war *on the inhabitants.*

praeferō, praeferre, praetulī, praelātus is a compound verb formed by the addition of the prefix **prae-** to **ferō**. (For the prefix **prae-** see Appendix P.) **Praeferō** is a transitive verb and also takes a Dative with a Compound Verb (see §120).

Mortemne *servitūtī* praefers?	Do you prefer death *to slavery?*

praesum, praeesse, praefuī, praefutūrus is a compound verb formed by the addition of the prefix **prae-** to **sum**. (For the prefix **prae-** see Appendix P.) **Praesum** is an intransitive verb that takes a Dative with a Compound Verb (see §120).

Cōpiīs praeerat.	He was in command *of the troops.*

volō, velle, voluī, —— is an irregular verb. For its forms see §118. **Volō** may be transitive (want, wish) or may be used absolutely (be willing). While **optō, cupiō,** and **volō** all express desire, **volō** suggests a stronger sense of will or purpose on the part of the subject and may thus mean "intend" or "be about to." **Volō** appears in two common idioms: **bene velle,** "to wish well," and **male velle,** "to wish ill." Both are followed by a Dative of Reference.

Quid facere *vīs?*	What do you *intend* to do?
Is tibi nōn *bene vult.*	He does not *wish well* for you.

mālō, mālle, māluī, —— is an irregular compound verb formed by the addition of the comparative adverb **magis** to **volō**. For its forms and the constructions that accompany it, see §118.

nōlō, nōlle, nōluī, —— is an irregular compound verb formed by the addition of the adverb **nōn** to **volō**. For its forms see §118. It has meanings that are parallel to **volō** (not want, not wish, be unwilling), and it may mean "refuse."

Mīlitēs iussī īre *nōluērunt.*	Although the soldiers had been ordered, *they refused* to go.

dignus, -a, -um is an adjective that takes an Ablative of Respect to indicate that which someone is worthy of. Such an Ablative of Respect is regularly translated with the English preposition "of." **Dignus** may also be used absolutely (deserving, worthwhile).

Hoc opus *vestrā cūrā dignum* est.	This work is *worthy of your (pl.) concern.*
Dignum est multa scīre.	To know many things is *worthwhile.*

indignus, -a, -um is an adjective that takes an Ablative of Respect to indicate that which someone is *un*worthy of. Such an Ablative of Respect is regularly translated with the English preposition "of."

dubius, -a, -um regularly appears with an Indirect Question or a Doubting clause (see §116).

The conjunction **cum** was developed from an old accusative form of the relative pronoun **quī, quae, quod**, and the archaic form **quom** is common in Roman writers prior to Cicero. This conjunction is *not* linguistically related to the preposition that is spelled identically. For its use see §117.

modo is an adverb that was in origin the ablative singular of **modus**, but note that the final **-o** is short. **Modo** is often used to strengthen an imperative. It may be used as a temporal adverb (now, just now) and may appear in place of **sōlum** in the expression **nōn modo . . . sed/vērum etiam . . .**

Tū *modo* omnia ad mē scrībe.	You *just* write all things to me.

The preposition **praeter** takes the accusative case. It may mean "beyond" or "exceeding," or it may mean "except" or "other than."

tum (adv.) and **tunc** (adv.) are synonymous. **tunc** is formed by the addition of the emphatic suffix **-ce** to **tum**. In early Latin **tunc** was more emphatic than **tum**. By the Augustan period this emphasis was less pronounced. **Tum** may be used *correlatively* with **cum** with a variety of emphases. The correlatives **cum . . . tum . . .** may be translated "when . . . then/at the same time . . .," "both . . . and (especially) . . .," or "not only . . . but also . . . "

> *Cum* illud faciēbat, *tum* discēdēbam.
> *When* he was doing that thing, *then/at the same time* I was departing.
> Cōnsilium *cum* patriae *tum* sibi inimīcum capiēbat.
> He was forming a plan hostile *both* to his country *and (especially)* to himself.
> Dīcere vīsa est *cum* honestam sententiam, *tum* vēram.
> She seemed to speak *not only* an honorable opinion, *but also* a true (one).

	Derivatives	**Cognates**
dignus	*dign*ity; in*dign*ant; dis*dain*; *dainty*	*dec*ent; *doc*tor; *dog*ma
gēns	*gen*tle; *gen*tile	*kin*; *king*; *gen*der; *gen*ealogy; *gene*
memoria	*memor*able	*mourn*
mōns	*moun*tain; a*moun*t	*mou*th; im*min*ent; *men*ace
oblīvīscor	*obliv*ious; *oubli*ette	*slime*; *slip*
rogō	inter*rog*ate; ab*rog*ate	**regō**; *rich*; *reckless*
volō	*vol*untary; *velle*ity; *vol*ition; male*vol*ence	*vol*uptuous; *will*; *wealth*; well

§113. Direct Questions

A **direct question** is a question written or uttered directly. In Latin a direct question may be introduced by the enclitic **-ne** attached to the first word of the question or by nothing at all. For example:

Lēgistīne illud carmen?	Did you read that poem?
Illud carmen lēgistī?	Did you read that poem?

Direct questions may also be introduced by the interrogative particles **nōnne** and **num**. **Nōnne** introduces a question to which the expected answer is *yes*. **Num** introduces a question to which the expected answer is *no*. For example:

Nōnne illud carmen lēgistī?	You read that poem, didn't you? (Yes)
Num illud carmen lēgistī?	You didn't read that poem, did you? (No)

OBSERVATIONS

1. **Nōnne** is formed from the combination of **nōn** and **-ne**. In translating Latin direct questions introduced by **nōnne**, a phrase such as "didn't you?" is added to make clear that the expected answer is *yes*.

2. In translating Latin direct questions introduced by **num**, a negative adverb *and* a phrase such as "did you?" are added to make clear that the expected answer is *no*.

Direct questions may also be introduced by a variety of interrogative pronouns, adjectives, and adverbs. The following is a list of all the words presented in Chapters I–XII that may introduce questions.

quis, quid	who, what
quī, quae, quod	what _____, which
cūr	
quam ob rem	why
quārē	
ubi	when
ubi	where
unde	from where, whence
quō	to where, whither
quō modō	in what way, how
uter, utra, utrum	which one (of two)

A question such as "Will you come to Rome or will you stay in the country?" is called a **double direct question**. A double direct question in Latin may be introduced by the interrogative particle **utrum**, by **-ne**, or by nothing at all. The conjunction **an** (or) introduces the second question. For example:

> *Utrum* Rōmam veniēs *an* rūrī manēbis?
>
> Rōmam*ne* veniēs *an* rūrī manēbis?
>
> Rōmam veniēs *an* rūrī manēbis?
>
> To Rome will you come *or* in the country will you stay?
>
> Will you come to Rome *or* will you stay in the country?
>
> *Utrum* Rōmam veniēs *an* nōn?
>
> Will you come to Rome *or* (will you) not (come to Rome)?

OBSERVATIONS

1. There are no differences in meaning among the first three double direct questions. Double direct questions introduced by **utrum** or **-ne** are more common in classical Latin than those introduced by nothing at all.

2. **Utrum** is in origin the neuter singular accusative of the interrogative adjective **uter**, **utra**, **utrum** used adverbially (whether). In double direct questions it may introduce the first question, but it should not be translated.

3. The ellipsis of certain words from one or both questions is a regular feature of double direct questions. Although in the last sentence only **nōn** appears after **an**, the rest of the second question may easily be supplied from the first question.

4. Additional alternate questions may be added to double direct questions using the conjunction **an**.

§114. Deliberative Subjunctive

A verb in the *present* subjunctive in a direct question may be used to indicate that the subject is *deliberating about or weighing courses of action for the present or the future*. A verb in the *imperfect* subjunctive in a direct question may be used to indicate that the subject is *deliberating about an action in the past*. The adverb **nōn** is used for negation. This *independent* use of the subjunctive is called **Deliberative** (< **dēlīberō**, "weigh"). For example:

Quid nunc *agam*?	What *should I do* now?
	What *am I to do* now?
Quid illō tempore *agerem*?	What *should I have done* at that time?
	What *was I to do* at that time?
Nōn *venīrem* Rōmam?	*Should I not have come* to Rome?
	Was I not to have come to Rome?

OBSERVATIONS

1. The Deliberative subjunctive is a variety of the Hortatory subjunctive. Unlike the Hortatory subjunctive, which expresses the will of the subject, the Deliberative subjunctive *asks* about the will of the person addressed. The Deliberative subjunctive most commonly occurs in the first person.

2. The English words "am/are/is . . . to" or "should" are regularly used to translate the Deliberative subjunctive in present or future time.

3. The English words "was/were . . . to" or "should have" are regularly used to translate the Deliberative subjunctive in past time.

4. The syntax of, for example, **agerem** is **imperfect subjunctive, Deliberative, past time**.

5. Sometimes an independent subjunctive appearing in a question is *Potential* rather than *Deliberative*. For example:

> **Quis rem pūblicam perīre *cupiat*?**   Who *would desire* the republic to perish?

☛ DRILL 113–114 MAY NOW BE DONE.

§115. Indirect Questions

When a question is *reported indirectly* as part of a complex sentence, the question is subordinated to a main verb, and the resulting subordinate clause is called an **Indirect Question**. For example:

> What do those poets think about the nature of the gods? (Direct Question)
> I do not know *what those poets think about the nature of the gods.* (Indirect Question)

When a direct question is reported indirectly in English, the subject and the verb of the direct question may have to be changed (for example, "do . . . think" becomes "think"). In Latin, *the verb of the indirect question is in the subjunctive mood according to the rules of sequence.* For example:

> **Nesciō quid illī poētae dē nātūrā deōrum *cōgitent*.**
> I do not know what those poets about the nature of the gods *think.*
> I do not know what those poets *think* about the nature of the gods.
> **Nesciō quid illī poētae dē nātūrā deōrum *cōgitāverint*.**
> I do not know what those poets *thought* about the nature of the gods.
> **Nesciō quid dē nātūrā deōrum *dictūrus sīs*.**
> I do not know what *you will* (are going to) *say* about the nature of the gods.

OBSERVATIONS
_____

1. An Indirect Question is a *noun* clause. It functions as either the direct object or (less frequently) the subject of the verb that introduces it.

2. Many Indirect Questions in early Latin appear with their verbs in the indicative. The use of the subjunctive mood in Indirect Questions may have its origin in Deliberative subjunctives that were then made indirect. Regardless of the origin, the use of the subjunctive mood in Indirect Questions reflects the view of the subjunctive as simply the mood appropriate for certain subordinate clauses.

3. Future time in Indirect Questions is frequently indicated by the active periphrastic.

4. The syntax of, for example, **cōgitāverint** is **perfect subjunctive, Indirect Question, primary sequence, prior time**.

5. Most often the subjunctive verb in an Indirect Question should be translated into English as if it were indicative. The tense of the translation is determined by the relative time of the subjunctive to the main verb.

An Indirect Question may be introduced by any of the interrogative words used to introduce direct questions. When an original direct question has no interrogative word or is introduced by the enclitic **-ne**, the indirect form may be introduced by the interrogative particle **num** or **an**, "whether." For example:

Rōmam īre optat?	Is she desiring to go to Rome?
Quaesīvērunt *num* **Rōmam īre optāret.**	They asked *whether* she was desiring to go to Rome.

Double Indirect Questions may be introduced by **utrum**, **-ne**, or by nothing at all. The conjunction **an** (or) introduces the second question. Double Indirect Questions use the negative conjunction **necne**, "or not," instead of **an nōn** (as in double direct questions). For example:

Utrum Rōmam īre optat an rūrī manēre?
Is she desiring to go to Rome or to remain in the country?
Quaesiī *utrum* **Rōmam īre optāret** *an* **rūrī manēre.**
I asked *whether* she was desiring to go to Rome *or* to stay in the country.

Utrum Rōmam īre optat an nōn?
Is she desiring to go to Rome or not?
Quaesiī *utrum* **Rōmam īre optāret** *necne.*
I asked *whether* she was desiring to go to Rome *or not.*

OBSERVATIONS

1. Double Indirect Questions introduced by **utrum** or **-ne** are more common in classical Latin than those introduced by nothing at all.

2. In double Indirect Questions, the English word "whether" is used to translate **utrum** or **-ne**. "Whether" must be *added* to the English translation when the beginning of a double Indirect Question is not indicated in Latin.

Occasionally the verb in the subjunctive mood in an Indirect Question represents an *original* independent use of the subjunctive. For example:

Nesciō *quid faciam.*	I do not know *what I should do.*

OBSERVATIONS

1. In this sentence, although **faciam** could represent a direct question with a verb in the indicative mood (**quid faciō?** What am I doing?), the translation indicates that the original question had a verb in the subjunctive mood (**quid faciam?** What should I do? [Deliberative subjunctive]).

2. The Deliberative subjunctive is the most common kind of independent subjunctive to appear in an Indirect Question. Occasionally a Potential subjunctive may also appear in an Indirect Question.

§116. Doubting Clauses

When an Indirect Question introduced by **num**, **an** (whether), or another interrogative word is preceded by a *verb or other expression of doubting*, the Indirect Question is sometimes called a **Doubting clause**. For example:

> **Omnēs dubitābant *num* Cicerō locūtūrus esset. (dubitō [1-tr] doubt)**
> All men were doubting *whether* Cicero was going to speak.
> **Dubium est *an* nostrī vincant. (dubium, dubiī *n.* doubt)**
> There is a doubt *whether* our men are conquering.

When the expression of doubting is *negated,* or when *negation is implied,* the Doubting clause is introduced by the conjunction **quīn** (that). For example:

> **Nōn dubitāvī *quīn* Cicerō locūtūrus esset.**
> I did not doubt *that* Cicero was going to speak.
> **Nūllum dubium est *quīn* nostrī vincant.**
> There is no doubt *that* our men are conquering.
> **Quis dubitet *quīn* nostrī vincant?**
> Who would doubt *that* our men are conquering?

OBSERVATIONS

1. Because they are essentially Indirect Questions, Doubting clauses have their verbs in the subjunctive according to the rules of sequence.

2. In the third sentence negation is implied because the answer to this rhetorical question would be "no one."

☛ DRILL 115–116 MAY NOW BE DONE.

§117. Subordinate Clauses II: The Conjunction *cum*

The *subordinating conjunction* **cum** has a variety of meanings. The verb in a **cum** clause may be in the indicative or the subjunctive mood, depending on what particular type of clause **cum** introduces.

Type of Clause	Mood of Verb	Translation of **cum**
Temporal	Indicative	"(at the time) when"[1]
Circumstantial	Indicative (present or future time)	"(under the circumstances) when"
	Subjunctive (past time)	
Causal	Subjunctive	"since/because"
Concessive	Subjunctive	"although"

1. When **cum** is followed by a *perfect* indicative and the verb in the main clause is *present* indicative, **cum** should be translated "whenever," and the perfect indicative should be translated as a *present.* When **cum** is followed by the *pluperfect* indicative and the verb in the main clause is *imperfect* indicative, **cum** should be translated "whenever," and the *pluperfect* indicative should be translated as an *imperfect.*

Like other subordinate clauses, **cum** clauses may *precede or follow* main clauses. When the subjunctive mood is used for the verb in a **cum** clause, the rules of sequence are followed. For example:

Temporal
Mīlitēs ad campum accessērunt *cum signum datum est.*
The soldiers toward the plain approached *(at the time) when the signal was given.*
The soldiers approached the plain *when the signal was given.*
Cum mīlitēs in campō vīdī, **magnopere timeō.**
Whenever soldiers (d.o.) on the plain I see, greatly I am afraid.
Whenever I see soldiers on the plain, I am greatly afraid.
Cum mīlitēs in campō vīderam, **magnopere timēbam.**
Whenever I saw (repeatedly) soldiers on the plain, I used to be greatly afraid.
Circumstantial
Caesar, *cum loquerētur,* **ab inimīcīs interfectus est.**
Caesar, *(under the circumstances) when he was speaking,* by (his) enemies was killed.
When Caesar was speaking, he was killed by (his) enemies.
Causal
Pugnāre nōn possum *cum gladiō caream.*
To fight I am not able *because a sword I am lacking.*
I am not able to fight *because I am lacking a sword.*
Concessive
Cicerō, *cum in oppidō parvō nātus esset,* **Rōmae tamen vīvēbat.**
Cicero, *although in a small town he had been born,* in Rome nevertheless he used to live.
Although Cicero had been born in a small town, nevertheless he used to live in Rome.

OBSERVATIONS

1. The use of the subjunctive mood in circumstantial, causal, and concessive **cum** clauses reflects the view of the subjunctive as simply the mood appropriate for certain subordinate clauses.

2. A **cum** clause followed by a verb in the subjunctive mood may introduce a circumstantial, causal, or concessive clause. Context helps to determine which sense is appropriate. For example, in the last sentence above the presence of **tamen** in the main clause indicates that the preceding subordinate clause is *concessive*.

3. The subjunctive verb in a **cum** clause should be translated into English as if it were indicative. The tense of the translation is determined by the relative time of the subjunctive to the main verb.

☞ DRILL 117 MAY NOW BE DONE.

§118. The Irregular Verbs *volō, nōlō,* and *mālō*

The irregular verbs **volō**, **velle**, **voluī**, ——, "be willing, want, wish"; **nōlō**, **nōlle**, **nōluī**, ——, "be unwilling, not want, not wish"; and **mālō**, **mālle**, **māluī**, ——, "want more, prefer" have *active forms only.* They have a number of irregular forms in the present system. All the forms of the perfect active system are regular. MEMORIZE THE FOLLOWING IRREGULAR CONJUGATIONS AND FORMS:

	Present Active Indicative			Present Active Subjunctive		
Singular						
1	volō	nōlō	mālō	velim	nōlim	mālim
2	vīs	nōn vīs	māvīs	velīs	nōlīs	mālīs
3	vult	nōn vult	māvult	velit	nōlit	mālit
Plural						
1	volumus	nōlumus	mālumus	velīmus	nōlīmus	mālīmus
2	vultis	nōn vultis	māvultis	velītis	nōlītis	mālītis
3	volunt	nōlunt	mālunt	velint	nōlint	mālint

Present Active Infinitive: **velle**   Present Active Participle: **volēns, volentis**
                              nōlle   **nōlēns, nōlentis**
                              mālle

Present Active Imperative: **nōlī** (singular); **nōlīte** (plural)

OBSERVATIONS

1. There are two common, older forms of **vult** and **vultis**: **volt** and **voltis**. The forms given above replaced these older forms during the first century B.C.E., but the older forms occur frequently in many classical authors, including Cicero. BE PREPARED TO RECOGNIZE THESE ARCHAIC FORMS.

2. **Nōlō** was formed by the addition of **nōn** to **volō**. In the present active indicative conjugation of **nōlō**, three forms (the second and third person singular and the second person plural) are simply **nōn** and the corresponding form of **volō**.

3. **Mālō** was formed by the addition of **magis** to **volō**, and it therefore may take structures that regularly accompany the comparative degree. For example:

> **Sapiēns amīcitiam omnibus rēbus mālit.** (Ablative of Comparison)
> A wise man friendship (d.o.) than all things would want more.
> A wise man would want friendship more than all things.
> **Nostrī pugnāre quam fugere māluērunt.** (Comparison with **quam**)
> Our men to fight than to flee preferred.
> Our men preferred to fight rather than to flee.

4. In the imperfect and future active indicative, **volō**, **nōlō**, and **mālō** are conjugated as if they were regular third-conjugation verbs with the stems **vole-**, **nōle-**, and **māle-**, respectively. The first person singular future active indicative forms of **nōlō** (*nōlam) and **mālō** (*mālam) do not occur in the Latin literature that survives.

5. The present active subjunctive of **volō**, **nōlō**, and **mālō** may be compared to the present active subjunctive of **sum** (**sim, sīs, sit**, etc.). The imperfect active subjunctive is formed *regularly* from the *irregular* present active infinitives **velle**, **nōlle**, and **mālle**.

6. **Mālō** does not have a present active participle.

7. **Volō** and **mālō** do *not* have imperative forms. For the use of the imperative forms of **nōlō** (**nōlī** and **nōlīte**) see §119.

§119. Negative Commands with *nōlī* or *nōlīte* and an Infinitive

Nōlī and **nōlīte** are used *with infinitives to express negative commands*. For example:

Nōlī, amīce, mē *ōdisse.*	*Be unwilling*, friend, me (d.o.) *to hate.*
	Do not hate me, friend.
Nōlīte ex prōvinciā *discēdere.*	*Be unwilling (pl.)* from the province *to depart.*
	Do not (pl.) depart from the province.

1. Although a Jussive subjunctive may be used to express a negative command, **nōlī** or **nōlīte** is a more common way of expressing this idea in classical Latin prose.

2. The second translations given above are to be preferred.

☛ DRILL 118–119 MAY NOW BE DONE.

§120. Dative with a Compound Verb

Many compound verbs, which have been formed by the addition of certain prepositions as prefixes to simple verbs, regularly appear with a dative that is connected in sense with the meaning of the preposition. Such a dative is called the **Dative with a Compound Verb**. For example:

> **Ille *cōpiīs* praeest.** (praesum [prae- + sum] be in charge [of])
> That man *(with reference) to the troops* is in charge.
> That man is in charge *of the troops.*
> **Iste *patriae* bellum īnferet.** (īnferō [in- + ferō] carry [in], inflict [on])
> That (contemptible) man *(with reference) to the country* war (d.o.) will inflict.
> That contemptible man will inflict war *on the country.*

The syntax of each italicized word (**cōpiīs, patriae**) is **Dative with a Compound Verb.**

OBSERVATIONS

1. When a preposition is compounded with a transitive verb, the resulting compound verb may take *both* an Accusative, Direct Object *and* a Dative with a Compound Verb.

2. A Dative with a Compound Verb replaces a prepositional phrase that has an equivalent meaning. For example, the idea expressed by the dative **patriae** in the second sentence above might also have been conveyed by **in patriam**, "against the country." Many compound verbs that take a Dative with a Compound Verb are also found with corresponding prepositional phrases.

3. When prefixes related to the following prepositions are used to form compound verbs, the resulting compound verbs *may* take a Dative with a Compound Verb:

ad	ob (prep. + acc.) in front of[2]
ante	post
circum (prep. + acc.) around	prae (prep. + abl.) in front of, before
cum	sub
in	super (prep. + acc. *or* abl.) above
inter	

4. A Dative with a Compound Verb is seldom translated with the English prepositions "to" or "for." The second English translations of the two sentences above are to be preferred because they best represent the meanings of the compounds that result from the addition of the prepositions to the simple verbs.

---

2. Although the preposition **ob** regularly means "on account of," "because of," its original meaning was spatial (in front of, in the way of).

Short Readings

1. A frustrated wife responds to her husband.

   vēra dīcō, sed nēquīquam, quoniam nōn vīs crēdere. (PLAUTUS, AMPHITRUŌ 835)

   nēquīquam (adv.) to no avail, in vain

2. A truism from Plautus

   tum dēnique hominēs nostra intellegimus bona,

   quom, quae in potestāte habuimus, ea āmīsimus. (PLAUTUS, CAPTĪVĪ 142–43)

   āmittō (ā- + **mittō**) send away; lose
   dēnique (adv.) finally, at last
   potestās, potestātis *f.* (legitimate) power; possession
   quom = cum

3. A comic character states his dilemma.

   nunc ego inter sacrum saxumque stō, nec quid faciam sciō. (PLAUTUS, CAPTĪVĪ 617)

   sacrum, sacrī *n.* sacred place
   saxum, saxī *n.* rock, stone

4. The slave Tranio responds understandingly to an obnoxious remark of his friend Grumio.

   quasi invidēre mī hōc vidēre, Grumiō,

   quia mihi bene est et tibi male est; dignissumumst. (PLAUTUS, MOSTELLĀRIA 51–52)

   dignissumumst = dignissimumst
   Grumiō, *Grumiōnis *m.* Grumio
   invideō (in- + **videō**) envy, be jealous of
   mī = mihi
   quasi (adv.) as (if), as (it were)
   quia (conj.) because

5. A slave answers a question about his future.

   ūnum hoc sciō: quod fors feret, ferēmus aequō animō. (TERENCE, PHORMIŌ 138)

6. A definition of a rhetorical term

   frequentātiō est, cum rēs tōta causā dispersae cōguntur in ūnum locum quō gravior

   aut ācrior aut crīminōsior ōrātiō sit. (RHĒTORICA AD HERENNIUM IV.52)

   cōgō (cō- + **agō**), **cōgere, coēgī, coāctus** drive together; bring together, collect
   crīminōsus, -a, -um accusatory, damning
   dispergō, dispergere, dispersī, dispersus spread about, scatter, disperse
   frequentātiō, frequentātiōnis *f.* concentration; assembling

7. Cicero gives this as an example of a rhetorical statement that is obviously false.

   nēmō est quīn pecūniam quam sapientiam mālit. (CICERO, DĒ INVENTIŌNE I.80)

8. The orator exhorts Catiline directly.

> mūtā iam istam mentem, mihi crēde, oblīvīscere caedis atque incendiōrum.

(CICERO, *In Catilīnam I* 6)

caedēs, caedis, -ium *f.* slaughter
incendium, incendiī *n.* fire; arson
mūtō (1-tr.) change

9. The orator utters some dramatic rhetorical questions.

> ō dī immortālēs! ubinam gentium sumus? in quā urbe vīvimus? quam rem pūbli-cam habēmus? (CICERO, *In Catilīnam I* 9)

immortālis, immortāle immortal
ubinam (interrog. adv.) where ever, where indeed

10. After yet another attack on Catiline, Cicero asks a rhetorical question.

> sed cūr iam diū dē ūnō hoste loquimur et dē eō hoste quī iam fatētur sē esse hostem,
> et quem, quia, quod semper voluī, mūrus interest, nōn timeō; dē hīs quī dissimu-
> lant, quī Rōmae remanent, quī nōbīscum sunt nihil dīcimus?

(CICERO, *In Catilīnam II* 17)

dissimulō (1-tr.) conceal, pretend
intersum (inter- + sum), interesse, interfuī, —— be between
quia (conj. + indic.) because
remaneō (re- + maneō) remain

11. While speaking about fellow citizens who have joined Catiline's conspiracy, Cicero sums up his patriotic feelings.

> . . . iam nōn possum oblīvīscī meam hanc esse patriam, mē hōrum esse cōnsulem,
> mihi aut cum hīs vivendum aut prō hīs esse moriendum.

(CICERO, *In Catilīnam II* 27)

12. Cicero recounts what a leading man said about Cicero's exile.

> . . . L. Cotta dīxit id quod dignissimum rē pūblicā fuit, nihil dē mē āctum esse
> iūre, nihil mōre maiōrum, nihil lēgibus; . . . (CICERO, *Prō Sestiō* 73)

L. Cotta, L. Cottae *m.* L. (Aurelius) Cotta (consul 65 B.C.E.)

13. Cicero discusses the competing loyalties affecting many Romans.

ego mehercule et illī* et omnibus mūnicipibus duās esse cēnseō patriās, ūnam nātūrae, alteram cīvitātis: ut ille Catō, quom esset Tusculī nātus, in populī Rōmānī cīvitātem susceptus est, ita, quom ortū Tusculānus esset, cīvitāte Rōmānus, habuit alteram locī patriam, alteram iūris; . . . (CICERO, *DĒ LĒGIBUS* II.5)

*illī refers to Cato.
cēnseō, cēnsēre, cēnsuī, cēnsus hold as one's
   opinion, think
mūniceps, mūnicipis *m.* citizen *or* native of a
   mūnicipium, a self-governing community in
   Italy

ortus, ortūs *m.* origin, birth, ancestry
quom = **cum**
suscipiō (sub- + capiō) receive, adopt
Tusculānus, -a, -um Tusculan
Tusculum, Tusculī *n.* Tusculum, a town in
   Latium

14. Cicero explains why he attaches such importance to officeholders.

ut enim magistrātibus lēgēs, sīc populō praesunt magistrātūs vērēque dīcī potest
magistrātum lēgem esse loquentem, lēgem autem mūtum magistrātum.

(CICERO, *DĒ LĒGIBUS* III.2)

magistrātus, magistrātūs *m.* officeholder, magistrate
mūtus, -a, -um mute, incapable of speaking; silent

15. Cicero gives his opinion about the destiny of the Roman people.

populum Rōmānum servīre fās nōn est, quem dī immortālēs omnibus gentibus
imperāre voluērunt. (CICERO, *PHILIPPICS VI* 19)

immortālis, immortāle immortal
serviō, servīre, servīvī or **serviī, servītūrus** be a slave; serve

16. An excerpt from Cicero's translation of Plato's *Timaeus*

deus autem et ortū et virtūte antīquiōrem genuit animum eumque ut dominum
atque imperantem oboedientī praefēcit corporī . . . (CICERO, *TIMAEUS* 21)

gignō, gignere, genuī, genitus create, beget (of a father)
oboediēns, oboedientis obedient, compliant, subject
ortus, ortūs *m.* rising; origin, ancestry

17. Cicero explains to his friend Atticus why he is determined to erect a shrine in honor of his
    recently deceased daughter, Tullia.

sed iam quasi vōtō quōdam et prōmissō mē tenērī putō, longumque illud tempus
cum nōn erō magis mē movet quam hoc exiguum, quod mihi tamen nimium
longum vidētur. (CICERO, *AD ATTICUM* XII.18.1)

exiguus, -a, -um small, slight, brief
nimium (adv.) too much, excessively
prōmissum, prōmissī *n.* promise
quasi (adv.) as (if), as (it were)
vōtum, vōtī *n.* vow, prayer

18. Cicero describes the effects of receiving his friend Atticus's letters.

tamen adlevor cum loquor tēcum absēns, multō etiam magis cum tuās litterās

legō. (CICERO, *AD ATTICUM* XII.39.2)

absēns, absentis not present, absent
adlevō (1-tr.) lift up, raise; comfort, console

19. Caesar finds a convenient point in his narrative to begin a digression.

quoniam ad hunc locum perventum est, nōn aliēnum esse vidētur dē Galliae Ger-

māniaeque mōribus et quō differant hae nātiōnēs inter sēsē prōpōnere.

(CAESAR, *DĒ BELLŌ GALLICŌ* VI.11)

aliēnus, -a, -um belonging to another; alien,
strange; out of place
Gallia, Galliae *f.* Gaul
Germānia, Germāniae *f.* Germany

nātiō, nātiōnis *f.* nation
perveniō (per- + veniō) arrive at (+ ad + acc.)
prōpōnō (prō- + pōnō) put forward; state

20. Roman veterans, cornered and faced with difficult odds, refuse to panic.

itaque inter sē cohortātī duce C. Trebōniō equite Rōmānō, quī iīs erat praepositus,

per mediōs hostēs perrumpunt incolumēsque ad ūnum omnēs in castra perveni-

unt. (CAESAR, *DĒ BELLŌ GALLICŌ* VI.40)

cohortor (1-tr.) exhort, encourage
eques, equitis *m.* horseman, cavalryman
incolumis, incolume unharmed, safe
itaque (conj.) and so, accordingly
perrumpō, perrumpere, perrūpī, perruptus burst
through

perveniō (per- + veniō) arrive at; get through (to)
praepōnō (prae- + pōnō) put in front (of), put in
charge (of)
C. Trebōnius, C. Trebōniī *m.* C. Trebonius

21. Caesar recalls the endurance of his men when faced with starvation.

nūlla tamen ex iīs vōx est audīta populī Rōmānī maiestāte et superiōribus victōriīs

indigna. (CAESAR, *DĒ BELLŌ GALLICŌ* VII.17)

maiestās, maiestātis *f.* dignity, majesty
superior, superius upper, higher; earlier, previous
victōria, victōriae *f.* victory

22. Caesar explains why a certain Varus may have believed a false report.

. . . nam quae volumus, ea crēdimus libenter, et quae sentīmus ipsī, reliquōs sen-

tīre spērāmus . . . (CAESAR, *DĒ BELLŌ CĪVĪLĪ* II.27)

libenter (adv.) gladly, willingly
reliquus, -a, -um remaining, rest (of)

23. Catiline speaks of the strong bond between him and his fellow conspirators.

idem velle atque idem nōlle, ea dēmum firma amīcitia est.

(SALLUST, *BELLUM CATILĪNAE* 20)

dēmum (adv.) precisely, only
firmus, -a, -um strong, durable, steadfast

24. An observation about Cicero's closest friend, T. Pomponius Atticus

honōrēs nōn petiit, cum eī patērent propter vel grātiam vel dignitātem.

(Cornelius Nepos, *Vīta Atticī* 6)

dignitās, **dignitātis** *f.* dignity, rank, status
honor, **honōris** *m.* public *or* political office
pateō, **patēre**, **patuī**, —— lie open
vel (adv.) or; **vel** . . . **vel** . . . either . . . or . . .

25. A Roman proverb

Malus bonum ubi sē simulat tunc est pessimus. (Publilius Syrus, *Sententiae* M9)

simulō (1-tr.) pretend, simulate

26. A Roman proverb

Male facere quī vult numquam nōn causam invenit.

(Publilius Syrus, *Sententiae* M28)

27. A Roman proverb

Peccāre paucī nōlunt, nūllī nesciunt. (Publilius Syrus, *Sententiae* P35)

peccō (1-intr.) make a mistake; do wrong

28. A Roman proverb

Stultum facit Fortūna quem vult perdere. (Publilius Syrus, *Sententiae* S29)

perdō (**per-** + **dō**) lose; destroy
stultus, **-a**, **-um** stupid, foolish

29. The shepherd Tityrus describes the signs of evening's approach.

et iam summa procul vīllārum culmina fūmant

maiōrēsque cadunt altīs dē montibus umbrae. (Vergil, *Eclogues* I.83)

culmen, **culminis** *n.* summit, roof
fūmō, **fūmāre**, **fūmāvī**, —— emit smoke, smoke
procul (adv.) at a distance
vīlla, **vīllae** *f.* country house, farmhouse

30. Charon objects to ferrying Aeneas to the underworld.

corpora vīva nefās Stygiā vectāre carīnā. (Vergil, *Aeneid* VI.391)

carīna, **carīnae** *f.* keel; ship
Stygius, **-a**, **-um** of *or* belonging to the river Styx, Stygian
vectō (1-tr.) carry, convey
vīvus, **-a**, **-um** living

31. Horace describes the influence of Greek culture on the Romans.

> Graecia capta ferum victōrem cēpit et artīs
>
> intulit agrestī Latiō . . . (Horace, *Epistulae* II.1.156–57)

agrestis, agreste of *or* living in the fields, rustic; uncivilized
ferus, -a, -um wild, uncultivated; fierce, ferocious
Latium, Latiī *n.* Latium, an area in central Italy
victor, victōris *m.* conqueror, victor

32. The poet explains his poetic mission.

> mē Venus artificem tenerō praefēcit amōrī . . . (Ovid, *Ars Amātōria* I.7)

artifex, artificis skilled, artistic
tener, tenera, tenerum tender, soft, delicate, young

33. Juno reflects on her rivalry with Bacchus.

> ipse* docet quid agam (fās est ab hoste docērī) . . . (Ovid, *Metamorphōsēs* IV.428)

*ipse refers to Bacchus.
doceō, docēre, docuī, doctus teach

34. The philosopher gives his opinion about how the performance of good deeds is repaid by good men.

> aequissima vōx est et iūs gentium prae sē ferēns: "redde quod dēbēs."
>
> (Seneca the Younger, *Dē Beneficiīs* III.14.3)

prae (prep. + abl.) in front of, before; **prae sē ferre**, to exhibit in one's demeanor, display; declare
reddō (red- + dō) give back, return

35. A quotation from the Greek philosopher Hekaton

> sī vīs amārī, amā. (Seneca the Younger, *Epistulae Morālēs* IX.6.6)

36. Clytaemnestra describes her emotional state.

> . . . flūctibus variīs agor,
>
> ut cum hinc profundum ventus, hinc aestus rapit,
>
> incerta dubitat unda cui cēdat malō. (Seneca the Younger, *Agamemnōn* 138–40)

aestus, aestūs *m.* heat; surge, swell
flūctus, flūctūs *m.* wave, billow
hinc (adv.) from this place, from here;
   hinc . . . hinc . . . from *or* on this side . . .
   from *or* on that side . . .
profundum, profundī *n.* (the) deep, depths, deep
   sea, ocean

rapiō, rapere, rapuī, raptus tear away, carry off
unda, undae *f.* wave
varius, -a, -um varied; changeable; conflicting
ventus, ventī *m.* wind

37. A comparison of the workings of reason and anger

> ratiō id iūdicāre vult quod aequum est: īra id aequum vidērī vult quod iūdicāvit.

(SENECA THE YOUNGER, *DIALOGĪ* III.18.1)

iūdicō (1-tr.) judge, determine
ratiō, ratiōnis *f.* account, reason

38. Quintilian assesses the Roman elegists.

> elegīā quoque Graecōs prōvocāmus, cuius mihi tersus atque ēlegāns maximē vidē-tur auctor Tibullus. sunt quī Propertium mālint. Ovidius utrōque* lascīvior, sīcut dūrior Gallus. (QUINTILIAN, *ĪNSTITŪTIŌ ŌRĀTŌRIA* X.1.93)

*utrōque = *masc. sing. abl. of indef. adj.,* each
auctor, auctōris *m.* source; author
ēlegāns, ēlegantis refined, cultivated; graceful; apt (in choosing words)
elegīa, elegīae *f.* elegiac poetry, elegy
Gallus, Gallī *m.* (C. Cornelius) Gallus, elegiac poet (69?–26 B.C.E.)
Graecī, Graecōrum *m.* (the) Greeks

lascīvus, -a, -um playful, naughty, free from re-straint
prōvocō (prō- + vocō) (1-tr.) challenge, rival
sīcut (conj.) just as
tersus, -a, -um polished, refined, neat
Tibullus, Tibullī *m.* (Albius) Tibullus, elegiac poet (55?–19 B.C.E.)

39. A piece of Quintilian's wit

> . . . quī stultīs vidērī ērudītī volunt stultī ērudītīs videntur. (QUINTILIAN, *ĪNSTITŪTIŌ ŌRĀTŌRIA* X.7.21)

ērudītus, -a, -um learned, accomplished
stultus, -a, -um stupid, foolish

40. The satirist derides life in Rome.

> quid Rōmae faciam? mentīrī nescio;* . . . (JUVENAL, *SATURAE* III.41)

*The final **-ō** of **nesciō** here scans *short.*
mentior, mentīrī, mentītus sum tell a falsehood, lie

41. The satirist advocates telling the truth in court.

> summum crēde nefās animam praeferre pudōrī . . . (JUVENAL, *SATURAE* VIII.83)

pudor, pudōris *m.* shame, decency, modesty

42. What should men ask from the gods?

> ōrandum est ut sit mēns sāna in corpore sānō. (JUVENAL, *SATURAE* X.356)

sānus, -a, -um healthy, sane

43. After a catalogue of men's crimes the satirist appends a tart remark.

> hūmānī generis mōrēs tibi nōsse volentī
> sufficit ūna domus;* . . . (JUVENAL, *SATURAE* XIII.159–60)

*domus, *here,* courthouse
hūmānus, -a, -um human
nōsse = nōvisse
sufficiō (sub- + faciō) be sufficient, be adequate

44. The historian comments on the superstitious responses of Roman soldiers to a strange drought.

    quod in pāce fors seu nātūra, tunc fātum et īra deī vocābātur. (TACITUS, *HISTORIAE* IV.26)

seu (conj.) or if; or

45. Gellius comments on the importance of usage to common speech.

    sed nīmīrum cōnsuētūdō vīcit, quae cum omnium domina rērum, tum maximē verbōrum est. (AULUS GELLIUS, *NOCTĒS ATTICAE* XII.13.16)

cōnsuētūdō, cōnsuētūdinis *f.* custom, usage
domina, dominae *f.* mistress, ruler
nīmīrum (adv.) without doubt, of course

Longer Readings

1. Naevius, *alia carmina epica* frag. 64.1-4

The epitaph of the early Roman poet Naevius

Inmortālēs mortālēs sī foret fās flēre,

flērent dīvae Camēnae Naevium poētam.

itaque postquam est Orchī trāditus thēsaurō,

oblītī sunt Rōmae loquier linguā Latīnā.

Camēna, Camēnae *f.* Camena, any one of the Italic divinities connected with springs and waters and identified with the (Greek) Muses
fleō, flēre, flēvī, flētus weep (for)
foret = **esset**
inmortālis (= **immortālis**), **inmortāle** immortal
itaque (conj.) and so, accordingly
Latīnus, -a, -um of *or* belonging to Latium (an area in central Italy), Latin

lingua, linguae *f.* tongue; language
loquier = **loquī**
mortālis, mortāle mortal
Naevius, Naeviī *m.* Naevius
Orchus (= **Orcus**), **Orchī** *m.* Orcus, god of the underworld (= Dis)
thēsaurus, thēsaurī *m.* treasure-chamber, vault; storehouse

Gnaeus Naevius (270–201 B.C.E.) wrote tragedies, comedies, and an epic poem about the first war with Carthage entitled *Bellum Pūnicum,* approximately eighty lines of which survive. Naevius wrote in the accentual Saturnian rhythm native to Italy rather than in the quantitative dactylic hexameter adapted from Greek models by later Latin epic poets.

2. Cicero, *In Verrem II* 2.162

Cicero paints a dramatic portrait of one of Verres' victims, who was barbarously and illegally punished.

caedēbātur virgīs in mediō forō Messānae cīvis Rōmānus, iūdicēs, cum intereā nūllus gemitus, nūlla vōx alia illīus miserī inter dolōrem crepitumque plāgārum audiēbātur nisi haec: "Cīvis Rōmānus sum." hāc sē commemorātiōne cīvitātis omnia verbera dēpulsūrum cruciātumque ā corpore dēiectūrum arbitrābātur; is nōn modo hoc nōn perfēcit, ut virgārum vim dēprecārētur,* sed cum implōrāret saepius ūsurpāretque nōmen cīvitātis, crux—crux, inquam—īnfēlīcī et aerumnōsō, quī numquam istam pestem vīderat, comparābātur.

*ut . . . **dēprecārētur** is a substantive clause explaining **hoc**; translate "that . . . he ward off by prayer."

aerumnōsus, -a, -um wretched, suffering

caedō, caedere, cecīdī, caesus beat, strike

commemorātiō, commemorātiōnis *f.* memory; reminder

comparō (1-tr.) prepare, get together; set up

crepitus, crepitūs *m.* sharp sound, crashing, cracking

cruciātus, cruciātūs *m.* torture, torment

crux, crucis *f.* wooden frame, cross

dēiciō (dē- + iaciō) throw down, topple over; avert, divert

dēpellō (dē- + pellō), dēpellere, dēpulī, dēpulsus drive away

dēprecor (1-tr.) ward off by prayer

dolor, dolōris *m.* grief, sorrow, pain

gemitus, gemitūs *m.* groan(ing), moan(ing)

implōrō (1-tr.) ask for; implore, appeal to

inquam (defective verb) say; **inquam** = *1st sing. pres. act. indic.*

intereā (adv.) meanwhile

iūdex, iūdicis *m.* juror, judge

Messāna, Messānae *f.* Messana, a town in Italy

nōmen, nōminis *n.* name

pestis, pestis, -ium *f.* plague, destruction, ruin

plāga, plāgae *f.* blow, stroke

ūsurpō (1-tr.) take possession of; utter *or* invoke (repeatedly)

verbera, verberum *n. pl.* instrument for flogging, switch; blows, floggings, lashes

virga, virgae *f.* twig, shoot; rod, stick

In 70 B.C.E. Cicero had his first great legal success with his prosecution of C. Verres, who was found guilty of governing Sicily badly and corruptly. Cicero had been quaestor in Sicily some years earlier, and **clientēs** (dependents) acquired at the time asked Cicero to take the case. Cicero's preparation was so thorough and the evidence against Verres so damning that Cicero had delivered only the first of several speeches (*Āctiō Prīma in Verrem*, First Action Against Verres) when Verres admitted defeat. Cicero later published his remaining argument, the *Āctiō Secunda in Verrem*, which is divided into five books. The refined style of these speeches is evidence of the great rhetorical skill that Cicero had already achieved by the age of thirty-six.

3. Cicero, *Prō Archiā* 19

Cicero concludes his account of the special position and value of poets.

sit igitur, iūdicēs, sānctum apud vōs, hūmānissimōs hominēs, hoc poētae nōmen
quod nūlla umquam barbaria violāvit. saxa atque sōlitūdinēs vōcī respondent, bestiae
saepe immānēs cantū flectuntur atque cōnsistunt; nōs īnstitūtī rēbus optimīs nōn
poētārum vōce moveāmur?

barbaria, barbariae *f.* foreign or barbarian world;
  barbarity, barbarousness
bestia, bestiae *f.* beast, animal, creature
cantus, cantūs *m.* singing, song
cōnsistō, cōnsistere, cōnstitī, —— halt, stop,
  stand (still)
flectō, flectere, flexī, flexus bend; soften, influence
hūmānus, -a, -um human; humane, cultured
immānis, immāne savage, brutal; tremendous,
  immense

īnstituō, īnstituere, īnstituī, īnstitūtus set up,
  establish; train, instruct
iūdex, iūdicis *m.* judge, juror
nōmen, nōminis *n.* name
sānctus, -a, -um inviolate, blameless
saxum, saxī *n.* rock, stone
sōlitūdō, sōlitūdinis *f.* solitude, wasteland,
  uninhabited country
violō (1-tr.) treat without respect, dishonor,
  outrage, violate

4. Cicero, *Dē Ōrātōre* II.24

L. Licinius Crassus, a famous orator of his day, speaks to his friend Catulus in defense of relaxation. He recalls an earlier conversation with the orator and lawyer Scaevola.

itaque illud ego, quod in causā Curiānā Scaevolae dīxī, nōn dīxī secus ac sentiēbam:
nam "sī," inquam, "Scaevola, nūllum erit testāmentum rēctē factum, nisi quod tū
scrīpseris, omnēs ad tē cīvēs cum tabulīs veniēmus, omnium testāmenta tū scrībēs
ūnus. quid igitur?" inquam. "quandō agēs negōtium pūblicum? quandō amīcōrum?
quandō tuum? quandō dēnique nihil agēs?" tum illud addidī: "mihi enim līber esse
nōn vidētur, quī nōn aliquandō nihil agit." in quā permaneō, Catule, sententiā mēque,
cum hūc vēnī, hoc ipsum, nihil agere et plānē cessāre, dēlectat.

addō (ad- + dō) add
aliquandō (adv.) sometimes, occasionally
Catulus, Catulī *m.* (Q. Lutatius) Catulus (consul
  102 B.C.E.)
cessō (1-intr.) stop, desist; do nothing, rest
Curiānus, -a, -um of *or* belonging to Curius
dēlectō (1-tr.) delight, please, charm
dēnique (adv.) finally, at last; in short, to sum up
hūc (adv.) to this place, hither
inquam (defective verb) say; **inquam** = *1st sing.
  pres. act. indic.*
itaque (conj.) and so, accordingly
negōtium, negōtiī *n.* business

permaneō (per- + maneō) remain; persist (in),
  remain steady
plānē (adv.) plainly, clearly; utterly, absolutely
quandō (interrog. adv.) when
rēctē (adv.) rightly, correctly
Scaevola, Scaevolae *m.* (Q. Mucius) Scaevola
  (consul 117 B.C.E.)
secus (adv.) otherwise, differently; **secus ac,**
  other(wise) than
tabula, tabulae *f.* (writing) tablet; *in pl.,* docu-
  ment, deed, record
testāmentum, testāmentī *n.* will, testament

5. Cicero, *Paradoxa Stōicōrum* 5.34

Cicero reflects on the qualities of a truly free person.

quis igitur vīvit ut volt nisi quī rēctē vīvit? quī gaudet officiō, cui vīvendī* via cōn-
sīderāta atque prōvīsa est, quī nē lēgibus quidem propter metum pāret, sed eās sequitur et colit, quia id salūtāre esse maximē iūdicat, quī nihil dīcit, nihil facit, nihil
cōgitat dēnique nisi libenter ac līberē, cuius omnia cōnsilia rēsque omnēs, quās gerit,
ab ipsō proficīscuntur eōdemque† referuntur, nec est ūlla rēs quae plūs apud eum
polleat quam ipsīus voluntās atque iūdicium; cui quidem etiam, quae vim habēre
maximam dīcitur, Fortūna ipsa cēdit, sī, ut sapiēns poēta dīxit, "suīs‡ ea cuique§ fin-
gitur mōribus."

*vīvendī = *gen. sing. of verbal noun*, of living
†eōdem, *here* (adv.), to the same place
‡suīs refers to cuique, his/her own.
§cuique = *masc. or fem. sing. dat. of indef. pron.*, for
each person
colō, colere, coluī, cultus cultivate, tend, cherish
cōnsīderō (1-tr.) examine, contemplate
dēnique (adv.) finally, at last
fingō, fingere, fīnxī, fictus form, fashion, make
gaudeō, gaudēre, gāvīsus sum rejoice (in),
be glad, be pleased

iūdicium, iūdiciī *n.* judgment
iūdicō (1-tr.) judge, determine
libenter (adv.) willingly, with pleasure
officium, officiī *n.* obligation; duty, service
polleō, pollēre, ——, —— exert power, have
importance
prōvideō (prō- + videō) foresee; provide for
rēctē (adv.) rightly, correctly
salūtāris, salūtāre that promotes health, salutary
voluntās, voluntātis *f.* will, choice

6. Catullus XLV (hendecasyllable)

The poet paints a picture of mutual love.

Acmēn Septimius, suōs amōrēs,
tenēns in gremiō "mea" inquit "Acmē,
nī tē perditē amō atque amāre porrō
omnēs sum assiduē parātus annōs,
quantum quī pote plūrimum perīre,   5
sōlus in Libyā Indiāque tostā
caesiō veniam obvius leōnī."
hoc ut dīxit, Amor sinistrā ut ante
dextrā sternuit approbātiōnem.
at Acmē leviter caput reflectēns   10
et dulcis puerī ēbriōs ocellōs
illō purpureō ōre suāviāta,
"sīc," inquit "mea vīta, Septimille,
huic ūnī dominō ūsque serviāmus,
ut multō mihi maior ācriorque   15
ignis mollibus ardet in medullīs."
hoc ut dīxit, Amor sinistrā ut ante
dextrā sternuit approbātiōnem.

Acmē, Acmēs f. Acme; Acmēn = acc. sing.
approbātiō, approbātiōnis f. approval
ardeō, ardēre, arsī, arsūrus burn, be on fire (with passion)
assiduē (adv.) continually, constantly
at (conj.) but
caesius, -a, -um (of eyes only) cutting, sharp; cat-eyed, gray-eyed
caput, capitis n. head
dexter, dextra, dextrum right; as fem. subst., right side
dulcis, dulce sweet; pleasant
ēbrius, -a, -um drunk, intoxicated
gremium, gremiī n. bosom, lap
India, Indiae f. India, the Far East
inquam (defective verb) say; inquit = 3rd sing. pres. act. indic.
leō, leōnis m. lion
Libya, Libyae f. Libya, a province in north Africa
medulla, medullae f. marrow; in pl., vitals, innards
mollis, molle gentle, mild, soft
nī = nisi

obvius, -a, -um in the way, so as to meet, face to face with (+ dat.)
ocellus, ocellī m. (little) eye
ōs, ōris n. mouth
parō (1-tr.) prepare
perditē (adv.) ruinously, recklessly, desperately
porrō (adv.) forward; hereafter; in turn, furthermore
pote (indeclinable adj.) having the power, able; quī pote = is quī potest
purpureus, -a, -um dark red, crimson, purple
quantum (adv.) as much as
reflectō, reflectere, reflexī, reflexus bend back
Septimillus, Septimillī m. (little) Septimius
Septimius, Septimiī m. Septimius
serviō, servīre, servīvī or serviī, servītūrus be a slave; serve (+ dat.)
sinister, sinistra, sinistrum left; as fem. subst., left side
sternuō, sternuere, sternuī, ——— sneeze
suāvior (1-tr.) kiss
torreō, torrēre, torruī, tostus parch, roast, scorch, burn
ūsque (adv.) continuously

nunc ab auspiciō bonō profectī

mūtuīs animīs amant amantur: 20

ūnam Septimius misellus Acmēn

māvult quam Syriās Britanniāsque;

ūnō in Septimiō fidēlis Acmē

facit dēliciās libīdinēsque.

quis ūllōs hominēs beātiōrēs   25

vīdit, quis Venerem auspicātiōrem?

Acmē, Acmēs *f.* Acme; **Acmēn** = *acc. sing.*
auspicātus, -a, -um favorable, auspicious
auspicium, auspiciī *n.* augury, omen, divine sign
beātus, -a, -um happy, blessed, fortunate
Britannia, Britanniae *f.* Britain
dēliciae, dēliciārum *f. pl.* delight

fidēlis, fidēle faithful
libīdō, libīdinis *f.* desire, pleasure, passion, lust
misellus, -a, -um poor (little), wretched, pitiable
mūtuus, -a, -um shared, reciprocal, mutual
Septimius, Septimiī *m.* Septimius
Syria, Syriae *f.* Syria

7. Catullus LXIX

Why does Rufus repel women?

Nōlī admīrārī quārē tibi fēmina nūlla,

    Rūfe, velit tenerum supposuisse femur,

nōn sī illam rārae labefactēs mūnere vestis

    aut perlūcidulī dēliciīs lapidis.

laedit tē quaedam mala fābula, quā tibi fertur   5

    valle sub ālārum trux habitāre caper.

hunc metuunt omnēs; neque mīrum: nam mala valdē est

    bestia, nec quīcum bella* puella cubet.

quārē aut crūdēlem nāsōrum interfice pestem,

    aut admīrārī dēsine cūr fugiunt.   10

*****bellus, -a, -m** pretty, charming, lovely
admīror (1-tr.) be astonished (at), wonder (at)
āla, ālae *f.* wing; *here,* armpit
bestia, bestiae *f.* beast, animal, creature
caper, caprī *m.* billy goat
crūdēlis, crūdēle cruel
cubō, cubāre, cubuī, cubitum lie down, sleep
dēliciae, dēliciārum *f. pl.* delight
dēsinō, dēsinere, dēsiī or **dēsīvī, dēsitum** stop, cease (+ inf.)
fābula, fābulae *f.* story, tale
femur, femoris *n.* thigh
habitō (1-intr.) live
labefactō (1-tr.) cause to totter, weaken
laedō, laedere, laesī, laesus injure, harm
lapis, lapidis *m.* stone

**metuō, metuere, metuī, —— ** fear, dread
mīrus, -a, -um marvelous, astonishing
mūnus, mūneris *n.* present, gift
nāsus, nāsī *m.* nose
perlūcidulus, -a, -um transparent, translucent
pestis, pestis, -ium *f.* plague, destruction, ruin
quīcum = **quācum**
rārus, -a, -um loose-knit; exquisite, rare
Rūfus, Rūfī *m.* Rufus, the addressee of the poem
suppōnō (sub- + pōnō) put under; join
tener, tenera, tenerum tender, soft, delicate, young
trux, trucis wild, rough, fierce, ferocious
vallēs, vallis, -ium *f.* valley, vale
vestis, vestis, -ium *f.* clothing, garment

8. Catullus LXXII

The poet explains to Lesbia his conflicting feelings.

Dīcēbās quondam sōlum tē nōsse Catullum,

 Lesbia, nec prae mē velle tenēre Iovem.

dīlēxī tum tē nōn tantum ut vulgus amīcam,

 sed pater ut nātōs dīligit et generōs.

nunc tē cognōvī: quārē etsī impēnsius ūror,   5

 multō mī tamen es vīlior et levior.

"quī* potis est?" inquis. quod† amantem iniūria tālis

 cōgit amāre magis, sed bene velle minus.

*q; **quī**, *here* (adv.), how
†**quod**, *here* (conj.), because
amīca, amīcae *f.* (female) friend; mistress, courtesan
cōgō (cō- + agō), **cōgere, coēgī, coāctus** drive together; force, compel
dīligō, dīligere, dīlēxī, dīlēctus value, esteem, love
gener, generī *m.* son-in-law
impēnsus, -a, -um heavy; costly
iniūria, iniūriae *f.* injury, injustice
inquam (defective verb) say; **inquis** = *2nd sing. pres. act. indic.*

mī = mihi
nōsse = nōvisse
potis (indeclinable adj.) having the power, able; possible
prae (prep. + abl.) in front of, before
quondam (adv.) at one time, once, formerly
tālis, tāle such, of such a sort
tantum (adv.) so much; only
ūrō, ūrere, ussī, ustus burn, scorch, inflame, consume; sting
vīlis, vīle worthless, cheap
vulgus, vulgī *n.* common people, (the) multitude, crowd

9. Caesar, *Dē Bellō Gallicō* IV.15

Caesar describes the end of a battle against a German tribe.

Germānī, post tergum clāmōre audītō, cum suōs interficī vidērent, armīs abiectīs signīsque mīlitāribus relictīs, sē ex castrīs ēiēcērunt, et cum ad cōnfluentem Mosae et Rhēnī pervēnissent, relicuā fugā dēspērātā, magnō numerō interfectō, relicuī sē in flūmen praecipitāvērunt atque ibi timōre, lassitūdine, vī flūminis oppressī periērunt. nostrī ad ūnum omnēs incolumēs, perpaucīs vulnerātīs ex tantī bellī timōre, cum hostium numerus capitum quadrīngentōrum trīgintā mīlium fuisset, sē in castra recēpērunt.

abiciō (ab- + iaciō) throw away
caput, capitis *n.* head
clāmor, clāmōris *m.* shout, shouting
cōnfluēns, cōnfluentis, -ium *m.* meeting place (of rivers), confluence
dēspērō (1-tr.) give up as hopeless, despair of
flūmen, flūminis *n.* river, stream
Germānī, Germānōrum *m. pl.* (the) Germans
ibi (adv.) there
incolumis, incolume unharmed, safe
lassitūdō, lassitūdinis *f.* weariness, fatigue
mīlitāris, mīlitāre military
Mosa, Mosae *f.* (the) Meuse, a river in northern Gaul

numerus, numerī *m.* number
opprimō, opprimere, oppressī, oppressus press down; suppress, overwhelm, crush
perpaucī, perpaucae, perpauca very few
perveniō (per- + veniō) arrive at (+ ad + acc.)
praecipitō (1-tr.) throw *or* hurl headlong
recipiō (re- + capiō) take back; sē recipere, to withdraw
relicuus, -a, -um remaining, rest (of)
Rhēnus, Rhēnī *m.* (the) Rhine, a river in northeastern Gaul
tantus, -a, -um so great
tergum, tergī *n.* back
vulnerō (1-tr.) wound

10. Caesar, *Dē Bellō Gallicō* IV.25

From their ships anchored a short distance away in sufficiently deep water, Caesar's men attempt to come ashore in Britain. Frightened by the Celts on shore and by the deep water, they hesitate.

quod* ubi Caesar animadvertit, nāvēs longās, quārum et speciēs erat barbarīs inūsitātior et mōtus ad† ūsum expedītior, paulum removērī ab onerāriīs nāvibus et remīs incitārī et ad‡ latus apertum hostium cōnstituī atque inde fundīs, sagittīs, tormentīs hostēs prōpellī ac submovērī iussit. quae rēs magnō ūsuī nostrīs fuit. nam et nāvium figūrā et rēmōrum mōtū et inūsitātō genere tormentōrum permōtī barbarī cōnstitērunt ac paulum modo pedem rettulērunt. at nostrīs mīlitibus cūnctantibus maximē propter altitūdinem maris, quī decimae legiōnis aquilam ferēbat, obtestātus deōs ut ea rēs legiōnī fēlīciter ēvenīret, "dēsilīte," inquit, "commīlitōnēs, nisi vultis aquilam hostibus prōdere; ego certē meum reī pūblicae atque imperātōrī officium praestiterō." hoc cum vōce magnā dīxisset, sē ex nāvī prōiēcit atque in hostēs aquilam ferre coepit. tum nostrī cohortātī inter sē nē tantum dēdecus admitterētur, ūniversī ex nāvī dēsiluērunt.

*quod refers to the hesitation of Caesar's men.
†ad, *here,* for (the purpose of)
‡ad, *here,* at, near
admittō (ad- + mittō) allow, permit
altitūdō, altitūdinis *f.* height; depth
animadvertō, animadvertere, animadvertī, animadversus turn (one's) attention to, notice
apertus, -a, -um open; exposed
aquila, aquilae *f.* eagle; standard (of a legion)
at (conj.) but
barbarus, barbarī, *m.* foreigner
——, ——, coepī, coeptus (defective verb) began, have begun
cohortor (co- + hortor) exhort, encourage; speak encouragingly
commīlitō, commīlitōnis *m.* fellow soldier
cōnsistō, cōnsistere, cōnstitī, —— stop, stand still, halt
cōnstituō, cōnstituere, cōnstituī, cōnstitūtus set up, establish; draw up, station
cūnctor (1-intr.) delay, hesitate
dēdecus, dēdecoris *n.* disgrace, dishonor
dēsiliō, dēsilīre, dēsiluī, dēsultus jump *or* leap down
ēveniō (ē- + veniō) come out, turn out
expedītus, -a, -um unimpeded, light-armed, free
figūra, figūrae *f.* shape
funda, fundae *f.* sling

incitō (1-tr.) rouse, excite
inde (adv.) from there, thence
inquam (defective verb) say; inquit = *3rd sing. pres. act. indic.*
inūsitātus, -a, -um unusual, extraordinary
latus, lateris *n.* side, flank
nāvis, nāvis, -ium *f.* ship; nāvī = *abl. sing.*
obtestor (1-tr.) call to witness; swear by; beseech, implore
officium, officiī *n.* obligation; duty
onerārius, -a, -um for transport, cargo-
paulum (adv.) a little
permoveō (per- + moveō) disturb; frighten
pēs, pēdis *m.* foot; pedem referre, to retreat
praestō, praestāre, praestitī, praestitus perform, carry out
prōdō (prō- + dō) hand over
prōiciō (prō- + iaciō) hurl forward *or* forth
prōpellō (prō- + pellō), prōpellere, prōpulī, prōpulsus push forward; repel
removeō (re- + moveō) remove; move back
remus, remī *m.* oar
sagitta, sagittae *f.* arrow
submoveō (sub- + moveō) dislodge, ward off
tantus, -a, -um so much, so great
tormentum, tormentī *n.* engine of war, missile-shooting machine, catapult
ūniversus, -a, -um all together
ūsus, ūsūs *m.* use; benefit, advantage

11. Sallust, *Bellum Iugurthae* 110

Bocchus, the king of Mauretania (in northern Africa) and the former ally of Jugurtha in his war against the Romans, speaks to Sulla, a lieutenant of the Roman general Marius. Bocchus informs Sulla about his own future plans.

cēterum dē rē pūblicā vostrā, quoius cūrātor hūc missus es, paucīs* accipe. bellum

ego populō Rōmānō neque fēcī neque factum umquam voluī; at fīnīs meōs advor-

sum armātōs armīs tūtātus sum. id omittō, quandō vōbīs ita placet. gerite quod voltis

cum Iugurthā bellum.

*paucīs, *sc.* verbīs
advorsum (= adversum) (prep. + acc.) in opposition to, against, in the face of
armātus, armātī *m.* armed man, soldier
at (conj.) but
cēterum (adv.) moreover; however that may be,
  but
cūrātor, cūrātōris *m.* curator; guardian
hūc (adv.) to this place, hither

Iugurtha, Iugurthae *m.* Jugurtha, a Numidian
  king
omittō (ob- + mittō) disregard, pass over; discontinue, leave off
quandō (conj.) since, as
quoius = cuius
tūtor (1-tr.) protect, guard
vostrā = vestrā

12. Vergil, *Eclogues* IX.32–36

A young shepherd makes a modest boast.

        . . . et mē fēcēre poētam

Pīerides, sunt et mihi carmina, mē quoque dīcunt

vātem pāstōrēs; sed nōn ego crēdulus illīs.

nam neque adhūc Variō videor nec dīcere Cinnā   35

digna, sed argūtōs inter strepere ānser olōrēs.

adhūc (adv.) up to the present time
ānser, ānseris *m.* goose
argūtus, -a, -um sharp; clear-voiced; melodious,
  tuneful
Cinna, Cinnae *m.* (Helvius) Cinna, poet and
  friend of Catullus
crēdulus, -a, -um trusting (in) (+ dat.)
olor, olōris *m.* swan

pāstor, pāstōris *m.* herdsman, shepherd
Pīeris, Pīeridos *f.* daughter of Pierus, Muse;
  Pīerides = *nom. pl.*
strepō, strepere, strepuī, strepitum make a loud
  noise, screech
Varius, Variī *m.* (L.) Varius (Rufus), poet and
  friend of Horace and Vergil
vātēs, vātis, -ium *m.* or *f.* prophet; bard, poet

13. Vergil, *Aeneid* VI.847–53

In the underworld Aeneas learns of the Roman mission from the soul of his father, Anchises.

excūdent aliī spīrantia mollius aera

(crēdō equidem), vīvōs dūcent dē marmore vultūs,

ōrābunt* causās melius, caelīque meātūs

dēscrībent radiō et surgentia sīdera dīcent: 850

tū regere imperiō populōs, Rōmāne, mementō

(hae tibi erunt artēs), pācīque impōnere mōrem,

parcere subiectīs et dēbellāre superbōs.

*ōrō, *here,* plead
aes, aeris *n.* copper, bronze
dēbellō (1-tr.) fight (someone) to the finish, subdue
dēscrībō (dē- + scrībō) draw, mark out
excūdō, excūdere, excūdī, excūsus hammer out, forge, fashion
impōnō (in- + pōnō) place on, impose on
marmor, marmoris *n.* marble
meātus, meātūs *m.* movement, progress
mollis, molle gentle, mild, soft

parcō, parcere, pepercī, parsūrus be merciful, be sparing (+ dat.)
radius, radiī *m.* ray; rod; compass
sīdus, sīderis *n.* star
spīrō (1-intr.) breathe; live
subiectus, -a, -um subordinate, subject
superbus, -a, -um proud; haughty
surgō, surgere, surrēxī, surrēctus rise
vīvus, -a, -um living
vultus, vultūs *m.* expression, countenance; face

14. Vergil, *Aeneid* XII.657–71

As Aeneas and the Trojans make a strong attack, a comrade of Turnus describes the perilous situation.

"... mussat rēx ipse Latīnus

quōs generōs vocet aut quae sēsē ad foedera flectat.

praetereā rēgīna, tuī fīdissima, dextrā

occidit ipsa suā lūcemque exterrita fūgit.   660

sōlī prō portīs Messāpus et ācer Atīnās

sustentant aciēs. circum hōs utrimque phalangēs

stant dēnsae strictīsque seges mucrōnibus horret

ferrea; tū currum dēsertō in grāmine versās."

Atīnās (nom. only) Atinas, an Italian warrior
circum (prep. + acc.) around
currus, currūs *m.* chariot
dēnsus, -a, -um thick, dense; crowded together
dēserō, dēserere, dēseruī, dēsertus forsake, abandon, desert
dexter, dextra, dextrum right; *as fem. subst.* (*sc.* manus), right hand
exterreō (ex- + terreō) scare, terrify
ferreus, -a, -um made of iron
fīdus, -a, -um faithful, loyal, devoted; trusting
flectō, flectere, flexī, flexus bend
foedus, foederis *n.* agreement, treaty, pact
gener, generī *m.* son-in-law
grāmen, grāminis *n.* grass; pasture
horreō, horrēre, horruī, —— stand up, bristle; tremble, shudder
Latīnus, Latīnī *m.* Latinus, king of Latium

Messāpus, Messāpī *m.* Messapus, an Italian leader and ally of Latinus and Turnus
mucrō, mucrōnis *m.* point (of a sword); sword
mussō (1-intr.) mutter (in uncertainty)
occidō (ob- + cadō), occidere, occidī, occāsūrus fall; perish, die
phalanx, phalangis *f.* phalanx, a close formation of troops
porta, portae *f.* gate
praetereā (adv.) besides, furthermore, in addition
seges, segetis *f.* field *or* crop of standing corn
stringō, stringere, strīnxī, strictus bare, unsheathe
sustentō (1-tr.) support, uphold, sustain
utrimque (adv.) on both sides
versō (1-tr.) twist, keep turning around

obstipuit variā cōnfūsus imāgine rērum 665

Turnus et obtūtū tacitō stetit; aestuat ingēns

ūnō in corde pudor mixtōque īnsānia lūctū

et furiīs agitātus amor et cōnscia virtūs.

ut prīmum discussae umbrae et lūx reddita mentī,

ardentīs oculōrum orbīs ad moenia torsit 670

turbidus ēque rotīs magnam respexit ad urbem.

aestuō (1-intr.) burn, blaze, seethe
agitō (1-tr.) stir up, set in motion; vex, harass
ardeō, ardēre, arsī, arsūrus burn, be on fire
cōnfundō, cōnfundere, cōnfūdī, cōnfūsus pour together; confuse, trouble
cōnscius, -a, -um conscious, aware
cor, cordis *n.* heart
discutiō, discutere, discussī, discussus shatter; scatter, disperse, break up
furiae, furiārum *f. pl.* madness, mad desire, frenzy
imāgō, imāginis *n.* image, likeness; appearance
īnsānia, īnsāniae *f.* madness, insanity
lūctus, lūctūs *m.* mourning
misceō, miscēre, miscuī, mixtus mix, stir up, produce

obstipēscō, obstipēscere, obstipuī, ——
be dumbstruck, be stunned, be dazed
obtūtus, obtūtūs *m.* gaze, stare
orbis, orbis, -ium *m.* ring, circle, orb
pudor, pudōris *m.* shame, decency, modesty
reddō (red- + dō) give back, return; restore
respiciō, respicere, respexī, respectus look back (at)
rota, rotae *f.* wheel; *in pl.,* chariot
tacitus, -a, -um silent
torqueō, torquēre, torsī, tortus twist, turn
turbidus, -a, -um agitated, wild, frantic
varius, -a, -um varied; changeable; conflicting

15. Horace, *Carmina* I.11 (Asclepiadean)

Leuconoë longs to know the future.

Tū nē quaesierīs, scīre nefās, quem mihi, quem tibi
fīnem dī dederint, Leuconoē, nec Babylōniōs
temptāris numerōs. ut* melius, quidquid erit, patī.
seu plūrīs hiemēs seu tribuit Iuppiter ultimam,
quae nunc oppositīs dēbilitat pūmicibus mare   5
Tyrrhēnum: sapiās, vīna liquēs, et spatiō brevī
spem longam resecēs. dum loquimur, fūgerit invida
aetās: carpe diem quam minimum† crēdula posterō.

*ut, *here* (adv.) how
†minimum = minimē
aetās, aetātis *f.* age, time
Babylōnius, -a, -um of Babylonia, Babylonian
carpō, carpere, carpsī, carptus pluck, gather;
  seize; criticize, carp at
crēdulus, -a, -um trusting (in) (+ dat.)
dēbilitō (1-tr.) weaken
dum (conj. + indic.) while
hiem(p)s, hiemis *f.* winter; storm
invidus, -a, -um envious, bearing ill-will
Leuconoē, Leuconoēs *f.* Leuconoë, addressee of
  the poem
liquō (1-tr.) make liquid; strain, purify
numerus, numerī *m.* number; numerical symbol
oppōnō (ob- + pōnō) place in the way, expose
posterus, -a, -um next, following
pūmex, pūmicis *f.* pumice stone, volcanic rock
quidquid = *neut. sing. nom. of indef. rel. pron.,*
  whatever

resecō, resecāre, ——, resectum cut short,
  restrain, cut back
sapiō, sapere, sapiī or sapīvī, —— be intelligent,
  show good sense
seu (conj.) or if; seu . . . seu . . . whether . . .
  or if . . .
spatium, spatiī *n.* course, track; space, (interval
  of) time
temptō (1-tr.) test, try; make (experimental) use
  of; temptāris = temptāveris
tribuō, tribuere, tribuī, tribūtus grant, bestow,
  assign
Tyrrhēnus, -a, -um Tyrrhenian, Tuscan,
  Etruscan; mare Tyrrhēnum, Tyrrhenian Sea,
  the sea along the west coast of Italy
ultimus, -a, -um farthest, most remote; last, final
vīnum, vīnī *n.* wine

16. Horace, *Carmina* IV.7 (Archilochean)

Spring brings thoughts of death for mortals.

Diffūgēre nivēs, redeunt iam grāmina campīs
   arboribusque comae;
mūtat terra vicēs, et dēcrēscentia rīpās
   flūmina praetereunt.
Grātia* cum nymphīs geminīsque sorōribus audet   5
   dūcere nūda chorōs.
inmortālia nē spērēs, monet annus et almum
   quae rapit hōra diem.
frīgora mītēscunt Zephyrīs, vēr prōterit aestās,
   interitūra, simul   10
pōmifer autumnus frūgēs effūderit, et mox
   brūma recurrit iners.
damna tamen celerēs reparant caelestia lūnae:
   nōs ubi dēcidimus
quō pater Aenēās, quō dīves Tullus et Ancus,   15
   pulvis et umbra sumus.

*Grātia, *here,* a Grace, goddess of charm and
  beauty, attendant of Venus

aestās, aestātis *f.* summer

almus, -a, -um nourishing; gracious, kindly

Ancus, Ancī *m.* Ancus (Martius), fourth of the
  legendary kings of Rome

arbor, arboris *f.* tree

autumnus, autumnī *m.* autumn, fall

brūma, brūmae *f.* winter

caelestis, caeleste heavenly, celestial

celer, celeris, celere swift, fast

chorus, chorī *m.* dance, chorus, troop of dancers

coma, comae *f., in sing. or pl.,* hair

damnum, damnī *n.* loss; waning

dēcidō (dē- + cadō), dēcidere, dēcidī, —— fall down

dēcrēscō, dēcrēscere, dēcrēvī, dēcrētus diminish,
  decrease

diffugiō (dis- + fugiō) scatter

dīves, dīvitis rich, wealthy

effundō, effundere, effūdī, effūsus pour out;
  send forth

flūmen, flūminis *n.* river, stream

frīgus, frīgoris *n.* cold; *in pl.,* cold weather

frūx, frūgis *f.* fruit

geminus, -a, -um twin-born, twin

grāmen, grāminis *n.* grass; pasture

hōra, hōrae *f.* hour

iners, inertis inactive, idle, inert; motionless

inmortālis (= immortālis), inmortāle immortal

intereō (inter- + eō), interīre, interiī, interitūrus
  perish, be destroyed, disappear

lūna, lūnae *f.* moon

mītēscō, mītēscere, ——, —— grow mild,
  become gentle

mūtō (1-tr.) change

nix, nivis *f.* snow

nūdus, -a, -um naked, nude

nympha, nymphae *f.* nymph, a semidivine spirit

pōmifer, pōmifera, pōmiferum fruit-bearing

praetereō (praeter- + eō), praeterīre, praeteriī
  or **praeterīvī, praeteritus** go by, pass by;
  pass over

prōterō, prōterere, prōtrīvī, prōtrītus tread under
  foot, tramp down

pulvis, pulveris *m.* dust

rapiō, rapere, rapuī, raptus tear away, carry off;
  consume

recurrō, recurrere, recurrī, recursum run *or*
  hurry back

reparō (1-tr.) recover, restore, repair

rīpa, rīpae *f.* (river) bank

simul (conj.) at the same time as, as soon as

Tullus, Tullī *m.* Tullus (Hostilius), third of the
  legendary kings of Rome

vēr, vēris *n.* spring

——, **vicis** *f.* turning, turn; succession,
  alternation

Zephyrus, Zephyrī *m.* Zephyr, the west wind

quis scit an adiciant* hodiernae crāstina summae†

    tempora dī superī?

cūncta manūs avidās fugient hērēdis, amīcō‡

    quae dederis animō.   20

cum semel occideris et dē tē splendida Mīnōs

    fēcerit arbitria,

nōn, Torquāte, genus, nōn tē fācundia, nōn tē

    restituet pietās.

īnfernīs neque enim tenebrīs Diāna§ pudīcum   25

    līberat Hippolytum

nec Lēthaea valet Thēseus abrumpere cārō

    vincula Pīrithoō.

***adiciant** scans as *adiiciant with the first **-i-** being consonantal

†**summa, summae** *f.* sum, whole, total

‡**amīcus**, *here*, (your) own

§The **-i-** of **Diāna** here scans *long*.

abrumpō, abrumpere, abrūpī, abruptus break off, sever

adiciō (ad- + iaciō) add to

arbitrium, arbitriī *n.* judgment

avidus, -a, -um desirous, eager, greedy

crāstinus, -a, -um of tomorrow

cūnctus, -a, -um all

fācundia, fācundiae *f.* eloquence

hērēs, hērēdis *m.* or *f.* heir; heiress

Hippolytus, Hippolytī *m.* Hippolytus, son of Theseus

hodiernus, -a, -um of today

īnfernus, -a, -um lower, infernal

Lēthaeus, -a, -um of Lethe, the river of forgetfulness in the underworld

Mīnōs, Mīnōis *m.* Minos, judge (with Aeacus and Rhadamanthys) in the underworld

occidō (ob- + cadō), occidere, occidī, occāsūrus fall, perish, die

pietās, pietātis *f.* sense of duty, dutifulness, piety

Pīrithoüs, Pīrithoī *m.* Pirithoüs, friend of Theseus

pudīcus, -a, -um chaste, pure, honorable

restituō, restituere, restituī, restitūtus set up again, restore, revive

semel (adv.) once; once and for all

splendidus, -a, -um brilliant, glittering; magnificent

superus, -a, -um upper; **dī superī, deōrum superōrum** *m. pl.* gods above

tenebrae, tenebrārum *f. pl.* darkness, shadows

Thēseus, Thēseī *m.* Theseus, hero from Athenian myth and close friend of Pirithoüs

Torquātus, Torquātī *m.* Torquatus, addressee of the poem

vinculum, vinculī *n.* bond, chain

17. Horace, *Ars Poētica* 361–65

The poet compares poetry to painting.

ut pictūra poēsis: erit quae, sī propius stēs,

tē capiat magis, et quaedam, sī longius abstēs;

haec amat obscūrum, volet haec sub lūce vidērī,

iūdicis argūtum quae nōn formīdat acūmen;

haec placuit semel, haec deciēns repetīta placēbit.   365

abstō (ab- + stō), abstāre, ——, —— stand away, stand at a distance

acūmen, acūminis *n.* sharpness; mental acuteness, judgment

argūtus, -a, -um sharp; shrewd, clever

deciē(n)s (adv.) ten times

formīdō (1-tr.) fear, dread

iūdex, iūdicis *m.* juror, judge

obscūrus, -a, -um dark, dim, obscure

pictūra, pictūrae *f.* picture, painting

poēsis, poēsis *f.* poetry; poem

propius (adv.) nearer, more closely

repetō (re- + petō) seek again; return to

semel (adv.) once, one time

18. Ovid, *Metamorphōsēs* V.190–94

Just as the hero Perseus resolves to use the Gorgon's head to rout his enemies, one of them, Nileus—who falsely claims to be descended from the river Nile—begins to taunt Perseus.

"adspice" ait "Perseu, nostrae prīmordia gentis: 190

magna ferēs tacitās sōlācia mortis ad umbrās,

ā tantō cecidisse* virō;" pars ultima vōcis

in mediō suppressa sonō est, adapertaque velle

ōra loquī crēdās, nec sunt ea pervia verbīs.

*cecidisse, supply **tē** as subject accusative

adaperiō, adaperīre, adaperīvī, adapertus open wide

adspiciō (= aspiciō), adspicere, adspexī, adspectus look toward, look at; behold

aiō (defective verb) say; **ait** = *3rd sing. pres. act. indic.*

ōs, ōris *n. in sing. or pl.* mouth

Perseus, Perseī *m.* Perseus, son of Zeus and Danae, who killed the Gorgon and rescued Andromeda; **Perseu** = *voc. sing.*

pervius, -a, -um that makes a passage for, passable

prīmordia, *prīmordiōrum *n. pl.* beginnings, origin; source

sōlācium, sōlāciī *n.* comfort, solace, relief

sonus, sonī *m.* sound, noise; utterance

supprimō, supprimere, suppressī, suppressus press down, crush; check, block

tacitus, -a, -um silent

tantus, -a, -um so great

ultimus, -a, -um farthest, most remote; last, final

19. Livy, *Ab Urbe Conditā* XXII.50.6

> After the disastrous battle of Cannae, the remaining Roman soldiers were divided into two camps. In the smaller camp, the tribune urges his men to action.

P. Semprōnius Tuditānus tribūnus mīlitum "capī ergō māvoltis," inquit, "ab avāris-
simō et crūdēlissimō hoste aestimārīque capita vestra et exquīrī pretia ab interro-
gantibus Rōmānus cīvis sīs an Latīnus socius, ut ex tuā contumēliā et miseriā alterī
honōs quaerātur? nōn tū,* sī quidem L. Aemilī cōnsulis, quī sē bene morī quam
turpiter vīvere māluit, et tot fortissimōrum virōrum quī circā eum cumulātī iacent
cīvēs estis. sed antequam opprimit lūx maiōraque hostium agmina obsaepiunt iter,
per hōs, quī inordinātī atque incompositī obstrepunt portīs, ērumpāmus. ferrō
atque audāciā via fit quamvīs per cōnfertōs hostēs . . . "

*nōn tū, *sc.* capī mālēs; tū refers to each individual soldier in the group being addressed.
L. Aemilius, L. Aemiliī *m.* L. Aemilius (Paulus)
  (consul 216 B.C.E.), one of the Roman leaders
  at the disastrous battle of Cannae
aestimō (1-tr.) price, value, assess
agmen, agminis *n.* (battle) line; throng
antequam (conj.) before
avārus, -a, -um greedy, rapacious
caput, capitis *n.* head
circā (prep. + acc.) around, near
cōnfertus, -a, -um crowded, dense, packed close
  together
contumēlia, contumēliae *f.* abuse
crūdēlis, crūdēle cruel
cumulō (1-tr.) pile up, heap
ergō (adv.) therefore
ērumpō, ērumpere, ērūpī, ēruptus break out,
  burst forth
exquīrō (ex- + quaerō), exquīrere, exquīsīvī,
  exquīsītus ask (about), inquire
fīō, fierī, factus sum, be made; fit = *3rd sing. pres.
  act. indic.*
honōs, honōris *m.* office; honor, respect
iaceō, iacēre, iacuī, —— lie, rest; lie dead
incompositus, -a, -um not in proper formation,
  disorganized

inordinātus, -a, -um not regularly arranged,
  disordered
inquam (defective verb) say; inquit = *3rd sing.
  pres. act. indic.*
interrogō (1-tr.) ask, examine, interrogate
iter, itineris *n.* passage; road, route
Latīnus, -a, -um of *or* belonging to Latium,
  an area in central Italy; Latin
miseria, miseriae *f.* misery
obsaepiō, obsaepīre, obsaepsī, obsaeptus block,
  obstruct, shut off
obstrepō, obstrepere, obstrepuī, obstrepitum
  make a loud noise in front of (+ dat.)
opprimō, opprimere, oppressī, oppressus press
  down; suppress, overwhelm
porta, portae *f.* gate
pretium, pretiī *n.* price
quamvīs (adv.) even though
P. Semprōnius Tuditānus, P. Semprōniī
  Tuditānī *m.* P. Sempronius Tuditanus (consul
  204 B.C.E.), a military tribune at the battle of
  Cannae
tot (indeclinable adj.) so many
tribūnus, tribūnī *m.* tribune, military
  commander
turpiter (adv.) foully; basely, shamefully

20. Seneca the Younger, *Epistulae Mōrālēs* CVII.8

The philosopher muses on man's response to the ever-changing nature of things.

hanc rērum condiciōnem mūtāre nōn possumus; illud possumus, magnum sūmere animum et virō bonō dignum, quō fortiter fortuīta patiāmur et nātūrae cōnsentiā-mus. nātūra autem hoc, quod vidēs, rēgnum mūtātiōnibus temperat; turbantur maria cum quiēvērunt; flant in vicem ventī; noctem diēs sequitur; pars caelī cōn-surgit, pars mergitur. contrāriīs rērum aeternitās cōnstat.

aeternitās, aeternitātis *f.* eternity
condiciō, condiciōnis *f.* contract, agreement; condition
cōnsentiō (con-. + sentiō) be in harmony (with); assent (to)
cōnstō, cōnstāre, cōnstitī, cōnstātūrus stand still; be composed (of); depend (upon), consist (in) (+ abl.)
cōnsurgō, cōnsurgere, cōnsurrexī, cōnsurrēctus stand up, rise
contrārius, -a, -um opposite, contrary
flō (1-intr.) blow
fortuītus, -a, -um determined by chance, acciden-tal, fortuitous
mergō, mergere, mersī, mersus plunge, dip; *in pass.,* sink (below the horizon), go down

mūtātiō, mūtātiōnis *f.* change, alteration
mūtō (1-tr.) change
quiēscō, quiēscere, quiēvī, quiētus fall asleep; be at rest; subside
rēgnum, rēgnī *n.* kingdom, realm
sūmō, sūmere, sūmpsī, sūmptus take up, seize; take on, assume
temperō (1-tr.) restrain; moderate, temper
turbō (1-tr.) stir up, confuse, throw into confusion
ventus, ventī *m.* wind
——, **vicis** *f.* turn; succession; **in vicem**, in turn; against one another

Seneca's *Epistulae Mōrālēs* (*Letters Concerned with Ethics*) is a collection of 124 letters in which he attempts to answer questions concerning moral conduct and moral improvement. Written in a plain style, the *Epistulae* often end with pointed, epigrammatic **sententiae**.

21. Seneca the Younger, *Epistulae Mōrālēs* CVII.11–12

The philosopher concludes a letter to his friend Lucilius, in which he encourages Lucilius to learn to accept life's unpredictability. The first line of the passage is a translation of a line from the Greek philosopher Cleanthes.

dūcunt volentem fāta, nōlentem trahunt.

sīc vīvāmus, sīc loquāmur; parātōs nōs inveniat atque inpigrōs fātum. hic est mag-nus animus quī sē eī trādidit; at contrā ille pusillus et dēgener quī obluctātur et dē ordine mundī male exīstimat et ēmendāre māvult deōs quam sē. Valē.

at (conj.) but
dēgener, dēgeneris lowborn; degenerate, ignoble
ēmendō (1-tr.) correct, reform
exīstimō (1-tr.) reckon, suppose, think
inpiger (= impiger), inpigra, inpigrum active, energetic

mundus, mundī *m.* universe, world
obluctor (1-intr.) struggle, resist
ordō, ordinis *m.* order
parō (1-tr.) prepare, make ready
pusillus, -a, -um very small, petty, mean
trahō, trahere, trāxī, tractus draw, drag; pull

22. Seneca the Younger, *Agamemnōn* 466–76

> Eurybates describes the beginning of a storm that overwhelms the Greek fleet as it returns from Troy.

nox prīma caelum sparserat stellīs, iacent

dēserta ventō vēla. tum murmur grave,

maiōra minitāns, collibus summīs cadit

tractūque longō lītus ac petrae gemunt;

agitāta ventīs unda ventūrīs tumet   470

cum subitō lūna conditur, stellae latent;

nec ūna nox est: dēnsa tenebrās obruit

calīgō et omnī lūce subductā fretum

caelumque miscet. undique incumbunt simul

rapiuntque pelagus īnfimō ēversum solō   475

adversus Eurō Zephyrus et Boreae Notus.

adversus, -a, -um turned toward; opposite, hostile, adverse (+ dat.)

agitō (1-tr.) stir up, set in motion; vex, harass

Boreās, Boreae *m.* Boreas, the north wind

calīgō, calīginis *f.* dimness; fog, mist; darkness

collis, collis, -ium *m.* hill

condō, condere, condidī, conditus found, build; conceal; bury

dēnsus, -a, -um thick, dense

dēserō, dēserere, dēseruī, dēsertus forsake, abandon, desert

Eurus, Eurī *m.* Eurus, the east wind

ēvertō, ēvertere, ēvertī, ēversus turn upside down, churn up

fretum, fretī *n.* strait; sea, (the) deep

gemō, gemere, gemuī, gemitum groan, moan

iaceō, iacēre, iacuī, —— lie, rest, lie still

incumbō, incumbere, incubuī, —— fall (on), throw oneself (on), bear down (on)

īnfimus, -a, -um lowest, bottom (of), depths (of)

lateō, latēre, latuī, —— (intr.) hide, lie hidden, be concealed

lītus, lītoris *n.* shore, beach

lūna, lūnae *f.* moon

minitor (1-tr.) threaten

misceō, miscēre, miscuī, mixtus mix, stir up

murmur, murmuris *n.* rumble, roar

Notus, Notī *m.* Notus, the south wind

obruō, obruere, obruī, obrutus cover up, overwhelm

pelagus, pelagī *n.* (deep) sea

petra, petrae *f.* rock, boulder

rapiō, rapere, rapuī, raptus tear away, carry off; consume

simul (adv.) at the same time; together

solum, solī *n.* soil; base, foundation

spargō, spargere, sparsī, sparsus scatter, sprinkle

stella, stellae *f.* star

subdūcō (sub- + dūcō) lead up (from below); remove, take away

subitō (adv.) suddenly

tenebrae, tenebrārum *f. pl.* darkness, shadows

tractus, tractūs *m.* dragging; trail; extent, expanse

tumeō, tumēre, tumuī, —— swell

unda, undae *f.* wave, water

undique (adv.) from all sides, on all sides

ventus, ventī *m.* wind

Zephyrus, Zephyrī *m.* Zephyrus, the west wind

Continuous Readings

1. Cicero, *In Catilīnam I* 12–13

nunc iam* apertē rem pūblicam ūniversam petis, templa deōrum immortālium, tēcta urbis, vītam omnium cīvium, Italiam tōtam ad exitium et vāstitātem vocās. quā rē, quoniam id quod est prīmum, et quod huius imperī disciplīnaeque maiōrum proprium est, facere nōndum audeō, faciam id quod est ad† sevēritātem lēnius, ad† commūnem salūtem ūtilius. nam sī tē interficī iusserō, residēbit in rē pūblicā reliqua coniūrātōrum manus; sīn tū, quod tē iam dūdum hortor, exieris, exhauriētur ex urbe tuōrum comitum magna et perniciōsa sentīna reī pūblicae. quid est, Catilīna? num dubitās id mē imperante facere quod iam tuā sponte faciēbās? exīre ex urbe iubet cōnsul hostem. interrogās mē num in exsilium? nōn iubeō, sed sī mē cōnsulis, suādeō.

*nunc iam, now at last
†ad, *here,* with regard to, with a view to
apertē (adv.) openly
comes, comitis *m.* or *f.* companion, comrade
commūnis, commūne common
coniūrātor, coniūrātōris *m.* conspirator
cōnsulō, cōnsulere, cōnsuluī, cōnsultus take counsel, consult
disciplīna, disciplīnae *f.* training
dūdum (adv.) some time ago, before; iam dūdum, for a long time now, long since
exhauriō, exhaurīre, exhausī, exhaustus drain dry
exeō (ex- + eō), exīre, exiī or exīvī, exitum go out, depart
exitium, exitiī *n.* destruction, ruin
immortālis, immortāle immortal
interrogō (inter- + rogō) (1-tr.) ask, examine, interrogate
lēnis, lēne mild, gentle

nōndum (adv.) not yet
perniciōsus, -a, -um destructive, ruinous
proprius, -a, -um one's own; peculiar (to), characteristic (of) (+ gen.)
reliquus, -a, -um remaining, rest (of)
resideō, residēre, resēdī, —— be left, remain
sentīna, sentīnae *f.* bilgewater; cesspool; dregs, scum
sevēritās, sevēritātis *f.* gravity, seriousness, severity
sīn (conj.) but if
*spōns, *spontis *f.* (one's own) will
suādeō, suādēre, suāsī, suāsus recommend, urge, advise
tēctum, tēctī *n.* roof; house
ūniversus, -a, -um all together, entire, whole
ūtilis, ūtile useful
vāstitās, vāstitātis *f.* devastation

2. Sallust, *Bellum Catilīnae* 1–2

sed diū magnum inter mortālīs certāmen fuit vīne corporis an virtūte animī rēs mīlitāris magis prōcēderet. nam et priusquam incipiās, cōnsultō et, ubi cōnsulueris,*
mātūre factō opus est. ita utrumque** per sē indigēns; alterum alterīus auxiliō eget.

2. Igitur initiō rēgēs—nam in terrīs nōmen imperī id prīmum fuit—dīvorsī pars
ingenium, aliī corpus exercēbant: etiam tum vīta hominum sine cupiditāte agitābātur; sua† quoique satis placēbant. posteā vērō quam in Asiā Cȳrus, in Graeciā Lace-
daemoniī et Athēniēnsēs coepēre urbīs atque nātiōnēs subigere, lubīdinem domi-
nandī‡ causam bellī habēre, maxumam glōriam in maxumō imperiō putāre, tum
dēmum perīculō atque negōtiīs conpertum est in bellō plūrumum ingenium posse.
quod sī§ rēgum atque imperātōrum animī virtūs in pāce ita ut in bellō valēret, aequā-
bilius atque cōnstantius sēsē rēs hūmānae habērent,¶ neque aliud aliō# ferrī neque
mūtārī ac miscērī omnia cernerēs. nam imperium facile iīs artibus

*cōnsulueris, perfect subjunctive with an ideal-
ized second person; translate as indicative
**utrumque = *neut. sing. nom. of indef. pron.*,
each thing (of two)
†sua refers to quoique, his/her own things.
‡dominandī = *neut. sing. gen. of verbal noun of*
dominor (1-intr.) of being master, of ruling
§quod sī (conj.) but if
¶aequābilius . . . sēsē habērent . . . would be
more equable . . .
#aliō, *here* (adv.), to another place
aequābilis, aequābile consistent, equable
agitō (1-tr.) stir up, set in motion; spend, pass
Asia, Asiae *f.* Asia (modern Asia Minor)
Athēniēnsis, Athēniēnse Athenian; *as subst.*,
(an) Athenian
cernō, cernere, crēvī, crētus distinguish, determine, perceive
certāmen, certāminis *n.* competition; dispute,
quarrel
——, ——, coepī, coeptus (defective verb) began,
have begun
conperiō (= comperiō), conperīre, conperī,
conpertus find out, learn
cōnstāns, cōnstantis firm, steady, invariable,
constant
cōnsulō, cōnsulere, cōnsuluī, cōnsultus take
counsel, consult, consider, plan
cōnsultum, cōnsultī *n.* resolution, plan
cupiditās, cupiditātis *f.* desire
Cȳrus, Cȳrī *m.* Cyrus, a Persian king
dēmum (adv.) at length, at last; precisely, only;
tum dēmum, only then
dīvorsus (= dīversus), -a, -um opposite, separate,
different

egeō, egēre, eguī, —— lack, want, need (+ abl.)
exerceō, exercēre, exercuī, exercitus keep busy,
occupy; train, exercise
hūmānus, -a, -um human
incipiō (in- + capiō) take on, begin; incipiās,
subjunc. expressing anticipation, you can
begin
indigēns, indigentis needy, not self-sufficient
initium, initiī *n.* beginning
Lacedaemonius, -a, -um Lacedaemonian,
Spartan; *as subst.,* (a) Spartan
lubīdō (= libīdō), lubīdinis *f.* desire, pleasure,
passion, lust
mātūre (adv.) quickly, in good time
maxumam = maximam
maxumō = maximō
mīlitāris, mīlitāre military
misceō, miscēre, miscuī, mixtus mix, stir up
mortālīs, mortāle mortal
mūtō (1-tr.) change
nātiō, nātiōnis *f.* nation
negōtium, negōtiī *n.* business, (business)
activity
nōmen, nōminis *n.* name
plūrumum = plūrimum
posteā . . . quam = postquam
priusquam (conj. + subjunc.) before
prōcēdō (prō- + cēdō) go forward, progress,
succeed
quoique = *masc./fem. sing. dat. of indef. pron.,*
each *or* every man *or* woman
subigō (sub- + agō), subigere, subēgī, subāctus
drive under, force; subdue, conquer

retinētur, quibus initiō partum est. vērum ubi prō labōre dēsidia, prō continentiā et aequitāte lubīdō atque superbia invāsēre, fortūna simul cum mōribus inmūtātur. ita imperium semper ad optumum quemque* ā minus bonō trānsfertur. Quae hominēs arant, nāvigant, aedificant, virtūtī omnia pārent. sed multī mortālēs, dēditī ventrī atque somnō, indoctī incultīque vītam sīcutī peregrīnantēs trānsiēre; quibus profectō contrā nātūram corpus voluptātī, anima onerī fuit. eōrum ego vītam mortemque iuxtā aestumō, quoniam dē utrāque† silētur. vērum enim vērō‡ is dēmum mihi vīvere atque fruī animā vidētur, quī aliquō negōtiō intentus praeclārī facinoris aut artis bonae fāmam quaerit. sed in magnā cōpiā rērum aliud aliī nātūra iter ostendit.

*quemque = *masc. sing. acc. of indef. pron.,* each man

†utrāque = *fem. sing. abl. of indef. pron.,* each (of two)

‡vērum enim vērō but at the same time

aedificō (1-tr.) build

aequitās, aequitātis *f.* evenness, calmness; equity, fairness

aestumō (= aestimō) (1-tr.) estimate, value, reckon

aliquō = *neut. sing. abl. of indef. adj.,* some, any

arō (1-tr.) plough, till, cultivate

continentia, continentiae *f.* restraint, temperance, moderation

dēdō (dē- + dō) give up, surrender, deliver; dedicate

dēmum (adv.) at length, at last; precisely, only

dēsidia, dēsidiae *f.* idleness, inactivity, sloth

facinus, facinoris *n.* deed; crime

fruor, fruī, frūctus sum enjoy, delight in (+ abl.)

incultus, -a, -um uncouth, rough, uncultivated

indoctus, -a, -um not learned, ignorant

initium, initiī *n.* beginning

inmūtō (= immūtō) (1-tr.) alter, change

intentus, -a, -um stretched, attentive, intent, occupied

invādō, invādere, invāsī, invāsus enter (hostilely), invade, attack

iter, itineris *n.* passage; road, route

iuxtā (adv.) near, nearby; in like manner, equally

lubīdō (= libīdō), lubīdinis *f.* desire, pleasure, passion, lust

mortālis, mortāle mortal

nāvigō (1-tr.) sail

negōtium, negōtiī *n.* business

onus, oneris *n.* load, burden; trouble, difficulty

optumum = optimum

ostendō, ostendere, ostendī, ostentus or ostēnsus present, show; offer

pariō, parere, peperī, partus give birth to, bear (of a mother); create

peregrīnor (1-intr.) dwell abroad; be an alien; travel abroad

praeclārus, -a, -um very famous

profectō (adv.) in fact, actually; indeed, assuredly

retineō (re- + teneō), retinēre, retinuī, retentus keep hold of, retain, grasp

sīcutī (conj.) just as

sileō, silēre, siluī, —— be silent; pass over in silence

simul (adv.) at the same time

somnus, somnī *m.* sleep

superbia, superbiae *f.* pride; arrogance, haughtiness

trānseō (trāns- + eō), trānsīre, trānsiī or trānsīvī, trānsitus go across, pass through

trānsferō (trāns- + ferō), trānsferre, trānstulī, trānslātus carry across, shift

venter, ventris *m.* belly, stomach

voluptās, voluptātis *f.* pleasure, joy

3. Vergil, *Aeneid* II.506–17

> forsitan et Priamī fuerint quae fāta requīrās.
>
> urbis utī captae cāsum convulsaque vīdit
>
> līmina tēctōrum et medium in penetrālibus hostem,
>
> arma diū senior dēsuēta trementibus aevō
>
> circumdat nēquīquam umerīs et inūtile ferrum   510
>
> cingitur, ac dēnsōs fertur moritūrus in hostīs.
>
> aedibus in mediīs nūdōque sub aetheris axe
>
> ingēns āra fuit iuxtāque veterrima laurus
>
> incumbēns ārae atque umbrā complexa Penātīs.
>
> hīc Hecuba et nātae nēquīquam altāria circum,*   515
>
> praecipitēs ātrā ceu tempestāte columbae,
>
> condēnsae et dīvum† amplexae simulācra sedēbant.

*altāria circum = circum altāria by anastrophe, the reversal in order of a preposition and its object

†dīvum = dīvōrum

aedēs, aedis, -ium *f.* sanctuary, shrine; *in pl.,* house, abode

aethēr, aetheris *m.* ether, the upper region of the sky, heaven

aevum, aevī *n.* age, lifetime

altāria, altārium *n. pl.* (high) altar (for sacrifice)

amplector, amplectī, amplexus sum embrace; clasp (for protection)

āter, ātra, ātrum black, dark

axis, axis *m.* axis

ceu (conj.) (in the same way) as, like

cingō, cingere, cīnxī, cīnctus gird, equip, put on; **cingitur,** translate with active meaning

circum (prep. + acc.) around

circumdō (circum- + dō) place (something) around, put (something) on

columba, columbae *f.* dove

complector, complectī, complexus sum embrace; encircle, enclose

condēnsus, -a, -um close together, tightly packed

convellō, convellere, convellī, convulsus pull up (violently), tear up, wrench

dēnsus, -a, -um thick, dense; crowded together, closely packed

dēsuētus, -a, -um unfamiliar (from lack of use)

forsitan (adv.) perhaps

Hecuba, Hecubae *f.* Hecuba, wife of Priam

hīc (adv.) here

incumbō, incumbere, incubuī, —— fall (on), throw oneself (on); lean (on)

inūtilis, inūtile unfit for use; useless

iuxtā (adv.) near, nearby; in like manner, equally

laurus, laurī *f.* laurel tree

līmen, līminis *n.* entrance, doorway, threshold

nāta, nātae *f.* daughter

nēquīquam (adv.) to no avail

nūdus, -a, -um naked, nude; bare, deserted

Penātēs, Penātium *m. pl.* Penates, guardian deities of a household or country

penetrāle, penetrālis, -ium *n.* inner part, inmost recess

praeceps, praecipitis rushing forward, headlong

requīrō (re- + quaerō), requīrere, requīsiī or **requīsīvī, requīsītus** seek again; ask *or* inquire about

sedeō, sedēre, sēdī, sessūrus sit, be seated

senex, senis old

simulācrum, simulācrī *n.* image, statue

tēctum, tēctī *n.* roof; house

tempestās, tempestātis *f.* storm

tremō, tremere, tremuī, —— tremble, quiver, quake

umerus, umerī *m.* shoulder

utī = ut

vetus, veteris old, ancient; **veterrima** = *fem. sing. nom. of superlative adj.*

4. Ovid, *Metamorphōsēs* I.478–89

multī illam petiēre, illa āversāta petentēs

inpatiēns expersque virī nemora āvia lūstrat

nec quid Hymēn, quid Amor, quid sint cōnūbia cūrat.   480

saepe pater dīxit: "generum mihi, fīlia, dēbēs,"

saepe pater dīxit: "dēbēs mihi, nāta, nepōtēs";

illa velut crīmen taedās exōsa iugālēs

pulchra verēcundō suffūderat ōra rubōre

inque patris blandīs haerēns cervīce lacertīs   485

"dā mihi perpetuā, genitor cārissime," dīxit

"virginitāte fruī! dedit hoc pater ante Diānae."

ille quidem obsequitur, sed tē decor iste quod optās

esse vetat, vōtōque tuō tua forma repugnat.

āversor (1-tr.) turn away from; reject
āvius, -a, -um pathless, trackless
blandus, -a, -um charming, ingratiating, seductive
cervīx, cervīcis *f.* neck
cōnūbium, cōnūbiī *n. in sing. or pl.* marriage, marriage rites
crīmen, crīminis *n.* charge, accusation; crime
cūrō (1-tr.) watch over; care
decor, decōris *m.* good looks, beauty, grace
exōsus, -a, -um hating, detesting (+ acc.)
expers, expertis having no part, lacking experience
forma, formae *f.* shape, form; beauty
fruor, fruī, frūctus sum enjoy, delight in (+ abl.)
gener, generī *m.* son-in-law
genitor, genitōris *m.* father
haereō, haerēre, haesī, haesūrus cling, stick
Hymēn (nom. only) Hymen, god of marriage; marriage
inpatiēns, inpatientis not enduring, intolerant

iugālis, iugāle of *or* belonging to marriage, matrimonial, nuptial
lacertus, lacertī *m.* (upper) arm
lūstrō (1-tr.) move through, roam
nemus, nemoris *n.* wood, forest
nepōs, nepōtis *m. or f.* grandchild
obsequor (ob- + sequor) comply (with), submit
ōs, ōris *n. in sing. or pl.* mouth; face
perpetuus, -a, -um continual, without interruption; perpetual, everlasting
repugnō (1-intr.) fight against, resist (+ dat.)
rubor, rubōris *m.* redness; blush
suffundō, suffundere, suffūdī, suffūsus cover, fill, suffuse
taeda, taedae *f.* torch
velut (conj.) even as, just as
verēcundus, -a, -um modest, restrained
vetō, vetāre, vetuī, vetitus forbid
virginitās, virginitātis *f.* virginity; celibate life
vōtum, vōtī *n.* vow, prayer

§121. Unassimilated Forms, Archaic Spellings, and Syncopation

Unassimilated Forms and Archaic Spellings

Although classical Latin writers established strict rules of spelling and morphology for Latin words, many works that have survived indicate that these writers also allowed certain exceptions to the rules. Writers of both prose and poetry sometimes sought special effects of style by including certain words with **archaic spellings**. These forms had existed in the Latin of an earlier time, but they had gradually fallen out of use and been replaced by later spellings. In epic poetry these archaisms were felt to contribute to an appropriately august and elevated diction. In the works of the historian Sallust archaisms represented a deliberate rebellion against the Ciceronian standard and became a hallmark of his unique style. Even Cicero made use of such forms when their archaic feeling contributed to a desired stylistic effect.

One common type of archaism is the *unassimilated form* of a compound word.[1] An **unassimilated form** is a form in which the ordinary assimilation of two consonants does not occur or is not written.[2] For example:

adcēdō = accēdō	inpius = impius

Other archaic spellings give evidence of how the pronunciation of *vowels* changed as Latin developed.

maxumus = maximus (-u- > -i-)	antīquos = antīquus (-os > -us)
vostra = vestra (-o- > -e-)	suom = suum (-om > -um)

BE PREPARED TO RECOGNIZE UNASSIMILATED FORMS AND OTHER ARCHAIC SPELLINGS. IN ADDITION, LEARN TO RECOGNIZE THE FOLLOWING FORMS:

quoius = cuius	ollī = illī (dative singular)
quoi = cui	-āī = -ae (genitive singular)
quom = cum (conjunction)[3]	

Syncopation of Forms in the Perfect Active System

Forms of the perfect active system of first- and second-conjugation verbs may be shortened by removing *the -v- and the following vowel from the regular forms*. This shortening is sometimes called **syncopation** (< Greek *synkopē*, "cutting short"), and forms that have been shortened are called **syncopated forms**. For example:

---

1. For an explanation of assimilation see the vocabulary notes of Chapter V.

2. With few exceptions, the earliest surviving copies of ancient works were written at least eight hundred years after they were originally produced. Therefore, while the existence of both unassimilated and assimilated forms suggests that words continued to be pronounced in *both* ways, nothing can be said with complete certainty.

3. Cf. the vocabulary note on the conjunction **cum**, p. 322.

amāstī (< amā[vi]stī)	**optārim** (< optā[ve]rim)
dēlērunt (< dēlē[vē]runt)	
cōgitāram (< cōgitā[ve]ram)	**imperāssēmus** (< imperā[vi]ssēmus)
laudārō (< laudā[ve]rō)	**dēlēsse** (< dēlē[vi]sse)

OBSERVATION

Any form of the perfect active system may be syncopated *except* the *first person singular, third person singular*, and the *first person plural perfect active indicative*. Third person plural perfect active indicative forms made with the ending **-ēre** *also* cannot be syncopated.

Verbs of the third and fourth conjugations may also appear in shortened forms in the perfect active system, but these shortened forms do not always result from syncopation. For example:

audīstī (< audī[vi]stī)	**audieris** (= audīveris)
audīssem (< audī[vi]ssem)	**audiit** (= audīvit)
audīsse (< audī[vi]sse)	**audieram** (= audīveram)
nōrās (< nō[ve]rās)	**audierit** (= audīverit)
nōrint (< nō[ve]rint)	

OBSERVATION

Some shortened perfect active system forms of the third and fourth conjugations are generally believed to be the result of syncopation (e.g., **audīstī, audīssem, audīsse, nōrās, nōrint**). Others are thought to be formed from alternate (and earlier) third principal parts (e.g., **audieris** < **audiī**). In such cases the short **-i-** that appears is part of the perfect active stem (e.g., **audi-** < **audiī**).[4]

BE PREPARED TO RECOGNIZE THESE SHORTENED AND SYNCOPATED FORMS.

---

4. In third-conjugation verbs, the familiar third principal parts with a **-v-** are thought to have developed *by analogy* with the principal parts of other verbs. (Cf., for example, **petiī** *or* **petīvī**; **quaesiī** *or* **quaesīvī**). By the classical period forms derived from either principal part are common.

CHAPTER XIII

Vocabulary

➤ **nihilum, nihilī** or ***nīlum, nīlī** *n.* nothing
➤ **pretium, pretiī** *n.* price, value

➤ **honor, honōris** *m.* honor, respect; (political) office
➤ **lūmen, lūminis** *n.* light, radiance; *in pl.,* eyes
➤ **scelus, sceleris** *n.* wicked deed, crime; villainy
   vulnus, vulneris *n.* wound

➤ **aestimō** (1-tr.) estimate, value
➤ **ex(s)pectō** (1-tr.) wait (for), await, expect
➤ **moror** (1-tr.) hinder, delay, wait
➤ **mūtō** (1-tr.) change; take in exchange, give in exchange

   emō, emere, ēmī, ēmptus buy
➤ **faciō, facere, fēcī, factus** reckon (§128)
   gradior, gradī, gressus sum proceed, walk, step
   ➤ **ēgredior, ēgredī, ēgressus sum** go *or* come out
➤ **incipiō, incipere, incēpī, inceptus** take on, begin
➤ **perdō, perdere, perdidī, perditus** destroy; lose
   vendō, vendere, vendidī, venditus sell

➤ **——, ——, coepī, coeptus** (defective verb) began, have begun
   fīō, fierī, factus sum become, happen; be made, be done (§125)

➤ **cēterus, -a, -um** rest (of), remaining part (of), (the) other

➤ **grātus, -a, -um** charming, pleasing; grateful, pleased
   ➤ **ingrātus, -a, -um** unpleasant, displeasing; ungrateful, displeased
   saevus, -a, -um cruel, savage
   tantus, -a, -um so much, so great (§124)
   quantus, -a, -um how much, how great; as much, as great (§124)

   tālis, tāle such, of such a sort (§124)
   quālis, quāle what sort of; of which sort, as (§124)

   tot (indeclinable adj.) so many (§124)
   quot (indeclinable adj.) how many; as many (§124)

➤ **ad** (prep. + acc.) for the purpose of (§122)
   antequam (conj.) before (§123)
➤ **causā** (+ *preceding* gen.) for the purpose of, for the sake of (§122)
   dōnec (conj.) while, as long as; until (§123)
   dum (conj.) while, as long as; until; provided that (§123)
➤ **dummodo** (conj.) provided that (§123)
➤ **grātiā** (+ *preceding* gen.) for the purpose of, for the sake of (§122)
   modo (conj.) provided that (§123)
   priusquam (conj.) before (§123)
   quia (conj.) because (§123)
   quod (conj.) because (§123)
   tam (adv.) so (§124)

Vocabulary Notes

*nīlum, nīlī *n.* is a contracted form of **nihilum, nihilī** *n.* Both words are commonly used as Genitives of Indefinite Value (see §128), Ablatives of Price (see §129), and Ablatives of Degree of Difference (see §111).

pretium, pretiī *n.* is often used as a Genitive of Indefinite Value (see §128) or an Ablative of Price (see §129).

honor, honōris *m.* may indicate the general notion of "respect" or "honor" or a more concrete mark of respect given to someone. It commonly refers to a political "office." The archaic nominative singular form **honōs** remains common throughout the classical period.

lūmen, lūminis *n.* is formed by the addition of the suffix **-men** to a stem of the verb **lūceō, lūcēre, lūxī,** —— (shine, emit light). In addition to the meaning "light" or "radiance" **lūmen** is often used metaphorically to mean the "light" of life or the "enlightenment" of literature, the arts, etc. It is also used in the plural, particularly in poetry, to mean "eyes," either because the eye is an opening that admits light or from the idea that glancing at something casts light upon the object.

scelus, sceleris *n.* is used to refer to a specific "wicked deed" or "crime," or it may refer more generally to the abstract idea of "villainy" or "wickedness."

aestimō, aestimāre, aestimāvī, aestimātus often appears with either a Genitive of Indefinite Value (see §128) or an Ablative of Price (see §129).

ex(s)pectō, ex(s)pectāre, ex(s)pectāvī, ex(s)pectātus is a transitive verb that may be used absolutely with the meaning "wait." It may also be followed by a temporal clause introduced by **dum** or **dōnec** (see §123). The **s** placed in parentheses in the vocabulary entry indicates that the word may be spelled either with or without an **s**.

moror, morārī, morātus sum may be used transitively (hinder, delay) or intransitively (delay, wait). It may also be followed by a temporal clause introduced by **dum** or **dōnec** (see §123).

mūtō, mūtāre, mūtāvī, mūtātus may mean "take in exchange" or "give in exchange" with an Ablative of Price (see §129). When it is used absolutely, **mūtō** means "change" in the sense of "undergo a change" or "become different."

Quis servitūtem lībertāte mūtet?	Who would take slavery in exchange for freedom?
Quis lībertātem servitūte mūtet?	Who would give freedom in exchange for slavery?

When the verb **faciō** is used with a Genitive of Indefinite Value (see §128), it is best translated as "reckon."

ēgredior, ēgredī, ēgressus sum is a compound verb formed by the addition of the prefix **ē-** to **gradior**. (For the prefix **ē-** see Appendix P.) THE PRINCIPAL PARTS OF *ALL* COMPOUNDS OF **GRADIOR** FOLLOW THE PATTERN OF THE PRINCIPAL PARTS OF **ĒGREDIOR**. WHEN A COMPOUND OF **GRADIOR** APPEARS IN READINGS, ITS PRINCIPAL PARTS ARE NOT SUPPLIED, BUT THE PREFIX AND SIMPLE VERB ARE GIVEN.

incipiō, incipere, incēpī, inceptus is a compound verb formed by the addition of the prefix **in-**[1] to **capiō**. (For the prefix **in-**[1] see Appendix P.) **Incipiō** is a transitive verb that most frequently appears with an Object Infinitive. In classical Latin the perfect active and perfect passive forms of **incipiō** are very rare. The forms of the defective verb ——, ——, **coepī, coeptus** are used instead. However, the perfect passive participle **inceptus, -a, -um** is commonly used, as is the noun derived from it: **inceptum, inceptī** *n.*, "beginning," "undertaking."

perdō, perdere, perdidī, perditus is a compound verb formed by the addition of the prefix **per-** to **dō**. (For the prefix **per-** see Appendix P.) **Perdō** may mean "destroy" or "cause ruin to" (people, things) or "lose" (people, troops, citizenship, beauty). It may also mean "waste" (resources, opportunities). The perfect passive participle **perditus, -a, -um** is frequently used as an adjective meaning "(morally) lost," "ruined," or "depraved." The adverb **perditē** means "recklessly," "desperately," or "ruinously."

——, ——, **coepī, coeptus** is a defective verb. It has forms in the perfect active and perfect passive systems only. In classical Latin forms of **coepī** are regularly used instead of the perfect active and passive forms of **incipiō**.

cēterus, -a, -um is often used substantively to refer to the remaining part of a group or thing. The neuter singular (**cēterum**) of **cēterus, -a, -um** may be used as an Adverbial Accusative (see §126) to mean "for the rest," "moreover," or "in addition." In the historians it commonly has some adversative force (however that may be, but).

grātus, -a, -um and the compound adjective **ingrātus, -a, -um** (< **in-**[2] + **grātus, -a, -um**) have both active and passive senses. (For the prefix **in-**[2] see Appendix P.) The meanings given for these words in the vocabulary list reflect first their active senses and then their passive ones.

The preposition **ad** is regularly used with gerunds and gerundives to mean "for (the purpose of)" (see §122), but it may also have this sense with nouns or pronouns standing alone, particularly demonstratives.

Dux multa ad hoc fēcerat.	The leader had done many things *for this purpose.*

The words **causā** and **grātiā** are Ablatives of Cause used as prepositions that take the *genitive* case. The word in the genitive case *precedes* either **causā** or **grātiā**. These words most commonly appear with gerunds or gerundives (see §122), but they may also appear with nouns standing alone, particularly abstract nouns.

dummodo is a conjunction formed by the addition of the adverb **modo** to the conjunction **dum** and may be written as one or two words (**dummodo** or **dum modo**). It may introduce a Proviso clause (see §123), and, because of this combination, **modo** *alone* may also introduce a Proviso clause.

	Derivatives	Cognates
cēterus	etc. (et cetera)	*he, him, her, it*
gradior	di*gress*, pro*gress*, con*gress*	*grade*; de*gree*
grātus	*grace*; *grateful*; *gratify*; *gratis*; in*grate*; a*gree*; con*gratulate*	bard(?)
mūtō	*mutate*; com*mute*; per*mutation*	im*mune*; *mistake*
pretium	praise; price; precious	inter*pret*
vulnus	*vulnerable*	*Valhalla*; *Valkyrie*

§122. Gerunds and Gerundives

In English there are two verbal nouns, the infinitive (to _____) and the **gerund** (_____ing). For example:

> I like *to read*. (infinitive functioning as d.o. of the verb "like")
> *Reading* is enjoyable. (gerund functioning as subject of the verb "is")
> I exercise my mind by *reading*. (gerund functioning as object of the preposition "by")

In Latin there are the same two verbal nouns, the *infinitive* and the *gerund*. There is in addition a verbal adjective, the **gerundive**, which has no exact counterpart in English. The features of the gerund and the gerundive are listed and compared below.

GERUND (Verbal *Noun*)	GERUNDIVE (Verbal *Adjective*)
1. is a **neuter singular** noun appearing in the genitive, dative, accusative, and ablative cases. (The nominative is supplied by the *Subject Infinitive*.)	1. is **never a substantive** but *must* agree with a noun in gender, number, and case.
2. is formed with the present stem + **-ndī, -ndō, -ndum, -ndō** (*3rd i-stem- and 4th-conjugation verbs change Stem Vowel to* **-ie-**): [Nom. **vidēre** to see/seeing] Gen. **videndī** of seeing Dat. **videndō** to/for seeing Acc. **videndum** seeing (d.o.) Abl. **videndō** by (etc.) seeing	2. is identical in all forms with the *future passive participle* (e.g., **amandus, -a, -um, audiendus, -a, -um**).
3. represents the uncompleted action of a verb that *usually* has no direct object; *sometimes* appears with neuter pronouns, neuter plural substantives, and other direct objects.	3. represents the uncompleted action of a transitive verb onto a direct object, which it modifies in gender, number, and case.
4. can have any noun syntax (Objective Genitive, Ablative of Means, etc.) and is translated accordingly by the English gerund: **cupidus regendī** desirous of ruling (Objective Gen.)	4. is lacking in English and so must be changed into a *gerund with a direct object* when translating into English: **dōnīs mittendīs** by sending gifts (*not* by gifts to be sent)
5. is used to express *purpose* in the *genitive* with **causā** or **grātiā** (placed after) and in the *accusative* with **ad**: **videndī causā** for the sake of seeing **ad videndum** for the purpose of seeing	5. is used to express *purpose* in the *genitive* with **causā** or **grātiā** (placed after) and in the *accusative* with **ad**: **rēgis videndī causā** for the sake of seeing the king **ad rēgem videndum** for the purpose of seeing the king

The following sentences illustrate the uses of the gerund and the gerundive.

> **Mihi est amor *scrībendī*.** (gerund, Objective Gen.)
> I have a love *of writing*.
> **Mihi est amor *carminum scrībendōrum*.** (gerundive, modifies **carminum**,
> I have a love of *writing poems*.   Objective Gen.)

OBSERVATIONS

1. When a gerund would take a direct object, the gerundive construction is usually preferred, as in the second sentence.

2. The Latin gerundive, an *adjective* modifying a noun, is translated into English as a gerund, a verbal *noun*, with a direct object.

> **Arma cēpit *ad pugnandum*.** (gerund expressing purpose with **ad**, for the purpose of)
> He took up arms *for the purpose of fighting*.
> **Rōmam vēnī *ad mātrem videndam*.** (gerundive expressing purpose with **ad**)
> I came to Rome *for the purpose of seeing (my) mother*.
> **Rōmam vēnī multa *videndī causā*.** (gerund expressing purpose with **causā**, for the
>   sake of)
> I came to Rome *for the sake of seeing* many things.

OBSERVATION

In the third sentence a *gerund with a neuter plural substantive as direct object* is preferred to the gerundive construction to avoid ambiguity:

> **multōrum videndōrum causā**   "for the sake of seeing many *things*"
>   *or* "for the sake of seeing many *men*"

Occasionally the gerundive construction is used to express purpose in the accusative case *without* ad. For example:

> **Caesar Quintō lēgātō *sociōs dūcendōs* trādidit.**
> Caesar to Quintus (his) lieutenant *the allies to be led* handed over.
> Caesar handed over to (his) lieutenant Quintus *the allies to be led*.
> Caesar handed over *the allies* to (his) lieutenant Quintus *for leading*.

OBSERVATION

In such a construction the gerundive still expresses purpose, but it must be translated differently: "to be _____ed" *or* "for _____ing."

☛ DRILL 122 MAY NOW BE DONE.

§123. Subordinate Clauses III

Certain subordinating conjunctions are followed by verbs *sometimes in the indicative and sometimes in the subjunctive* with a difference in meaning.[1] When any of these conjunctions is followed by an indicative verb, the action of the verb is represented by the writer or speaker as actual or factual. When the same conjunction is followed by a subjunctive verb, the verbal action is represented as alleged, apparent, or anticipated—that is, *nonfactual*.

Conjunction	With Indicative	With Subjunctive
dum/dōnec	"while/as long as/until" (action accomplished)	"until . . . should" (action anticipated)
antequam/ priusquam	"before" (action accomplished)	"before . . . can/could" (action anticipated)
quod/quia	"because" (cause represented as true)	"allegedly *or* apparently because"

Subordinate Clauses with Verbs in the Indicative Mood

Dum/Dōnec mē amābās, fēlīx eram.
While (As long as) me (d.o.) *you were loving,* happy I was.
As long as you were loving me, I was happy.
In illō locō manēbant dum/dōnec verba Cicerōnis audīvērunt.
In that place they were remaining *until* the words (d.o.) of Cicero *they heard.*
They were remaining in that place *until they heard* the words of Cicero.
Discessimus ē forō antequam/priusquam Cicerō ōrātiōnem cōnfēcit.
We departed from the forum *before* Cicero (his) speech (d.o.) *completed.*
We departed from the forum *before* Cicero *completed* his speech.
Caesar suōs laudābit quod/quia fortiter pugnāvērunt.
Caesar his own men (d.o.) will praise *because* bravely *they fought.*
Caesar will praise his own men *because they fought* bravely.

OBSERVATIONS

1. In the first three sentences the actions in the subordinate clauses are presented as actually having occurred: you *did* use to love me, they *did* hear Cicero's words, and Cicero *did* complete his speech.

2. In the last sentence the reason given for Caesar's praise of his men *is vouched for* (by the writer of the sentence) as the *true* reason: his men *did* fight bravely, *and this is why* Caesar will praise them.

Dum haec ā mīlitibus geruntur, lēgātī ab hostibus vēnērunt.
While these things by the soldiers *were being managed,* legates from the enemies came.
While these things *were being managed* by the soldiers, legates came from the enemies.

---

1. For subordinating conjunctions followed by verbs in the indicative mood, see §48. For **cum** clauses see §117.

When the verb in the main clause is a past tense, the *present indicative*, the so-called "historical present," is regularly used with the conjunction **dum**, "while." This special use of the present indicative should be translated as an imperfect indicative.

Subordinate Clauses with Verbs in the Subjunctive Mood

When verbs in such subordinate clauses appear in the *subjunctive* mood, the writers or speakers represent the verbal actions as *nonfactual*.

> **In illō locō manēbānt** *dum/dōnec* **verba Cicerōnis** *audīrent*.
> They were remaining in that place *until they should hear* the words of Cicero.
> **Discessimus ē forō** *antequam/priusquam* **Cicerō ōrātiōnem** *cōnficeret*.
> We departed from the forum *before* Cicero *could complete* (his) speech.
> **Caesar suōs laudābit** *quod/quia* **fortiter** *pugnāverint*.
> Caesar will praise his own men *apparently because they fought* bravely.

OBSERVATIONS

1. The tenses of the subjunctive verbs in these subordinate clauses follow the rules of sequence.

2. In the first two sentences the actions of the verbs in the subordinate clauses are presented as merely *anticipated* and *not* as having actually occurred. In a temporal clause expressing anticipation with **dum** or **dōnec**, the English word "should" is used to translate a subjunctive verb in either primary or secondary sequence. In a temporal clause expressing anticipation with **antequam** or **priusquam**, the English word "can" is used to translate a subjunctive verb in primary sequence, and "could" is used to translate a subjunctive verb in secondary sequence.

3. In the last sentence the reason given *is not vouched for* but is merely surmised by the writer or speaker *or* alleged by someone else. In such a causal clause, the English adverb "apparently" or "allegedly" is added to the translation.

4. The syntax, for example, of **audīrent** in the first sentence is **imperfect subjunctive, secondary sequence, temporal clause expressing anticipation, subsequent time**. The syntax of **pugnāverint** in the third sentence is **perfect subjunctive, primary sequence, clause of apparent or alleged cause, prior time**.

Sometimes **antequam** and **priusquam** are *divided*. For example:

> **Multa** *ante/prius* **experiēris** *quam* **tuum inimīcum** *vincās*.
> Many things (d.o.) *sooner* you will try *than* your enemy (d.o.) *you can overcome*.
> *Sooner* will you try many things *than you can overcome* your enemy.
> You will try many things *before you can overcome* your enemy.

OBSERVATIONS

1. The conjunctions **antequam** and **priusquam** are made of the comparative adverbs **ante** and **prius** (sooner) and the conjunction **quam** (than). When **antequam** or **priusquam** is divided, each element *may* be translated separately, but the last translation given above, in which the conjunction is translated "before" where the **quam** appears, is to be preferred.

2. **antequam** and **priusquam** may be split when followed by either the indicative or subjunctive mood.

Proviso Clauses

The conjunction **dum**, sometimes strengthened by the adverb **modo**, "only," may introduce a subordinate clause stating a *provision under which* the event of the main clause can occur. Such a clause is called a **Proviso clause**. *Modo alone* may also introduce such a clause. The verb in a Proviso clause is always in the *subjunctive* mood. The particle **nē** is used for negation. For example:

> **Magnō mē metū līberābis *dum modo inter mē atque tē mūrus sit.***
> From great fear me (d.o.) you will free *provided that between me and you a wall be.*
> You will free me from great fear *provided that a wall be between me and you.*
> **Iūlia poētās canentēs audiat *dum verbum nē dīcat.***
> Let Julia poets (d.o.) singing listen to *provided that a word (d.o.) she not say.*
> Let Julia listen to the poets singing *provided that she not say a word.*

OBSERVATIONS

1. Subjunctive verbs in Proviso clauses follow the rules of sequence. The syntax, for example, of **sit** in the first sentence is **present subjunctive, primary sequence, Proviso clause**.

2. A Proviso clause is regularly translated with an English present subjunctive (e.g., "be" and "say" in the sentences above).[2]

☛ DRILL 123 MAY NOW BE DONE.

§124. Correlatives

Certain Latin adverbs and adjectives appear in two closely related forms.

Demonstrative	*Exclamatory/Interrogative/Relative*
tam (adv.) so	**quam** (adv.) how; as
tālis, tāle such, of such a sort	**quālis, quāle** what sort of; of which sort, as
tantus, -a, -um so much, so great	**quantus, -a, -um** how much, how great; as much, as great
tot (indeclinable adj.) so many	**quot** (indeclinable adj.) how many; as many

The words in the column on the left are demonstrative because they *point out* a certain degree, amount, or quality, often in the answer to a question. The words in the column on the right function in three distinct ways. They may be used to make exclamations (exclamatory), to ask questions (interrogative), and to correlate with corresponding demonstrative words (relative). The following sentences illustrate these various functions.

Quam altus est!	*How* tall he is! (exclamatory)
Quam altus est?	*How* tall is he? (interrogative)
Tam altus est.	He is *so* tall (i.e., this tall). (demonstrative)
Tam altus est *quam* pater.	He is *so* tall *as* (his) father. (demonstrative/relative)

2. The English present subjunctive is the infinitive form of the verb with the word "to" omitted (e.g., "work," "complete," "do," etc.).

1. The only difference in Latin between the exclamatory and interrogative sentences is the punctuation.

2. In the last sentence **quam** is *correlative* with **tam**. A **correlative** is an adjective, adverb, or pronoun that *corresponds with* a parallel adjective, adverb, or pronoun in the same sentence. In this sentence **tam**, a *demonstrative* adverb, and **quam**, a *relative* adverb, are correlatives, and the whole complex sentence is a **correlative sentence**. **Quam** introduces a *relative clause* in which certain grammatical elements are omitted. With no ellipsis the last example above would be written as follows:

Tam altus est quam *altus est* pater.   He is so tall as tall (his) father is.

3. When **quam** is correlative with **tam**, an idiomatic English translation uses "as" to translate *both* **quam** and **tam**: He is *as* tall *as* (his) father.

> *Quantam* pecūniam habuit!   *How much* money he had! (exclamatory)
> *Quantam* pecūniam habuit?   *How much* money did he have? (interrogative)
> *Tantam* pecūniam habuit.
> He had *so much* money (i.e., this much money). (demonstrative)
> *Tantam* pecūniam habuit *quanta* erat satis.
> He had *so much* money as *(much)* was enough. (demonstrative/relative)
> He had *as much* money *as* was enough.

In correlative sentences such as the last sentence, the relative adjective must agree in *gender* and *number* with its antecedent, but its *case* is determined by its syntax *within* the relative clause. Thus, **quanta** is *feminine* and *singular* to agree with **pecūniam**, but it is *nominative* because it is the subject (*sc.* **pecūnia**) of **erat**.

With adjectives or adverbs in the comparative degree,[3] a correlative sentence may appear, usually with the relative clause preceding the main clause. For example:

> *Quō* maius est perīculum, *eō* magis timēmus.
> *By* (the degree to) *which* greater is the danger, *by this* (degree) more greatly we fear.
> *The* greater the danger is, *the* more greatly we fear.
> *Quantō* fortius pugnābis, *tantō* plūs glōriae capiēs.
> *By how much* more bravely you will fight, *by so much* more of glory you will win.
> *The* more bravely you will fight, *the* more (of) glory you will win.

1. In the first example above **quō**, a *relative* pronoun, and **eō**, a *demonstrative* pronoun, are correlatives. The demonstrative **eō** is commonly used in this construction, but occasionally **hōc** appears instead.

2. The syntax of each italicized word (**quō**, **eō**, **quantō**, **tantō**) in the sentences above is Ablative of Degree of Difference.

3. The second translations given above are to be preferred.

Correlatives in correlative sentences are often best translated idiomatically. Here is a list of the correlatives included in this chapter and their respective idiomatic translations:

---

3. This construction also appears (less frequently) with superlative adjectives or adverbs.

tam . . . quam . . .	as . . . as . . .
tālis . . . quālis . . .	such . . . as . . . *or* of such a sort . . . as . . .
tantus . . . quantus . . .	as great . . . as . . . *or* as much . . . as . . .
tot . . . quot . . .	as many . . . as . . .
quō . . . eō (hōc) . . .	the (more) . . . the (more) . . .

☛DRILL 124 MAY NOW BE DONE.

§125. The Irregular Verb *fīō*

Fīō, fierī, factus sum "become, happen; be made, be done" is an irregular verb. The present system of **fīō** has *active forms with passive meanings,* and these forms supply the passive of the present system of **faciō**. The perfect system of **fīō** is supplied by the perfect passive system of **faciō**. MEMORIZE THE FOLLOWING IRREGULAR CONJUGATIONS:

	INDICATIVE			SUBJUNCTIVE	
	Present	*Imperfect*	*Future*	*Present*	*Imperfect*
Sing.					
1	**fīō**	**fīēbam**	**fīam**	**fīam**	**fierem**
2	**fīs**	**fīēbās**	**fīēs**	**fīās**	**fierēs**
3	**fit**	**fīēbat**	**fīet**	**fīat**	**fieret**
Pl.					
1	**fīmus**	**fīēbāmus**	**fīēmus**	**fīāmus**	**fierēmus**
2	**fītis**	**fīēbātis**	**fīētis**	**fīātis**	**fierētis**
3	**fīunt**	**fīēbant**	**fient**	**fīant**	**fierent**
Imperative:	Sing.	**fī**	Pl.	**fīte**	

OBSERVATIONS

1. The present, imperfect, and future indicative and present subjunctive conjugations of **fīō** are all formed with the stem **fī-**. By contrast, the present infinitive and imperfect subjunctive have a *short* **-i-**. The imperfect subjunctive is formed with an imaginary present active infinitive form (**fiere*), the final **-e** of which is lengthened to form the stem (**fierē-**).

2. The imperative forms **fī** and **fīte** are exceedingly rare in the Latin literature that survives.

3. **Fīō** has no participles.

4. When **fīō** means "become" or "be made," it may be accompanied by a Predicate Nominative or Predicate Adjective in the Nominative case. For example:

***Rēx* fīat.**	Let him become/Let him be made *king.* (predicate nom.)
***Misera* puella fīet.**	The girl will become *miserable.* (predicate adj.)

☛ DRILL 125 MAY NOW BE DONE.

§126. Adverbial Accusative

When a noun, pronoun, or adjective in the accusative case is used adverbially to express the *extent* to which the action of a verb is performed, it is called an **Adverbial Accusative**. For example:

> *Nihil* hās litterās intellegimus.
> *To the extent (of) nothing* this letter (d.o.) we understand.
> *Not at all* do we understand this letter.
> *Tantum* mē nōn amās *quantum* tē amō.
> *For so great an extent* me (d.o.) you do not love *as great an extent* you (d.o.) I love.
> You do not love me *as much as* I love you.

The syntax of each italicized word (**nihil, tantum, quantum**) is **Adverbial Accusative**.

Several nouns, pronouns, and adjectives in the singular accusative form are commonly used as Adverbial Accusatives. MEMORIZE THESE COMMON ADVERBIAL ACCUSATIVES:

> **magnam partem** "for a great part"
> **maximam partem** "for the greatest part," "for the most part"
> **multum** "much," "a lot"
> **nihil** "not at all"
> **plūrimum** "very much"
> **quantum** "how much," "as much"
> **quid** "to what extent," "why"
> **sōlum** "only"
> **tantum** "so much," "only (so much)"

OBSERVATIONS

1. When a substantive adjective is used as an Adverbial Accusative, it is always neuter singular.

2. In PIE and in early Latin the accusative case originally expressed an idea of *extent* that *limited* the action of the verb. The Adverbial Accusative is developed from this original idea of the accusative (cf. the Accusative of Duration of Time).

§127. Accusative of Exclamation

When a noun in the accusative case is used to express an exclamation, it is called an **Accusative of Exclamation**. Such an accusative is often accompanied by an exclamatory adjective or adverb or by an interjection. For example:

> **Quem *virum*!**   What a man!
> ***Mē* miserum!**   Miserable me!

The syntax of each italicized word (**virum, mē**) is **Accusative of Exclamation**.

OBSERVATION

The Accusative of Exclamation developed from the Accusative, Direct Object. It is understood as the direct object of an unexpressed thought or perception (e.g., What a man [I am thinking of]!).

§128. Genitive of Indefinite Value

With verbs of *considering*, *reckoning*, and *valuing*, certain words in the genitive case may express the *approximate worth or value* of something. This use of the genitive case is called the **Genitive of Indefinite Value**. For example:

> **Tuum cōnsilium *magnī (pretiī)* habeō. (pretium, pretiī** *n.* price, value)
> Your advice (d.o.) *of great (value)* I consider.
> I consider your advice *of great value.*
> **Quis pecūniam *plūris* quam amōrem faciat? (faciō,** reckon)
> Who money (d.o.) *of more (value)* than love would reckon?
> Who would reckon money *of more value* than love?

The syntax of each italicized word (**magnī**, **plūris**) is **Genitive of Indefinite Value.**

OBSERVATIONS

1. Each adjective in the sentences above is neuter singular genitive, either functioning as a substantive or modifying a usually unexpressed neuter singular noun meaning "value," **pretiī**. The Genitive of Indefinite Value is closely related to the Genitive of Description (see §100).

2. Although the Latin word for "value" may be unexpressed, such a word should be added to the English translation of the Genitive of Indefinite Value.

3. Certain nouns appear as Genitives of Indefinite Value to express ideas of *worthlessness*. For example:

> **Eum *nihilī* dūcō.** I consider him of *no value.* (**nihilum, nihilī** *n.* nothing)

§129. Ablative of Price

With verbs of *buying*, *selling*, *valuing*, and *exchanging*, certain words in the ablative case may express *the price at which* something is bought or sold. This use of the ablative case is called the **Ablative of Price**. For example:

> **Ista fēmina virī vītam *aurō* vendidit. (vendō, vendere, vendidī, venditus** sell)
> That contemptible woman of (her) husband the life (d.o.) *for gold* sold.
> That contemptible woman sold the life of her husband *for gold.*
> ***Magnō (pretiō)* ab omnibus virtūs aestimātur. (aestimō** [1-tr.] estimate, value)
> *At a great (price)* by all (people) excellence is valued.
> Excellence is valued *at a great price* by all people.

The syntax of each italicized word (**aurō**, **magnō**) is **Ablative of Price**.

OBSERVATIONS

1. The Ablative of Price was originally used instead of the Genitive of Indefinite Value to express the *exact amount of money* for which something was bought or sold. Its uses were later extended to less precise ideas of cost or value.

2. Although the Ablative of Price is essentially an Ablative of Means, it is often better translated with the English prepositions "for" or "at (the price of)."

3. A wide variety of words may be conceived as the price or cost of something (e.g., **vītā**, **patriā**). An adjective (e.g., **magnō**, **parvō**) used as an Ablative of Price either functions as a substantive or modifies a usually unexpressed neuter singular noun meaning "price," **pretiō**. However, four adjectives always appear in the Genitive of Indefinite Value rather than the expected Ablative of Price: **tantī**, **quantī**, **plūris**, and **minōris**.

☞ Drill 126–129 may now be done.

Short Readings

1. A fragment from the tragic poet Naevius

> . . . ego semper plūris fēcī
>
> potiōremque habuī lībertātem multō quam pecūniam.

(NAEVIUS, *PALLIĀTAE* FRAG. 9–10)

potior, potius more powerful; more desirable, more precious

2. Amphitruo and his slave Sosia enter the stage, and Amphitruo accuses Sosia of lying.

> *Amphitruō.* Age ī tū secundum. *Sōsia.* Sequor, subsequor tē.
>
> *Amph.* Scelestissimum tē arbitror. *Sōs.* Nam quam ob rem?
>
> *Amph.* Quia id quod neque est neque fuit neque futūrum est
>
> mihi praedicās. (PLAUTUS, *AMPHITRUŌ* 551–54)

praedicō (1-tr.) proclaim, declare
scelestus, -a, -um wicked
secundum (adv.) following, behind
subsequor (**sub-** + **sequor**) follow close behind

3. A slave recalls a Greek proverb.

> . . . quem dī dīligunt
>
> adulēscēns moritur, dum valet, sentit, sapit. (PLAUTUS, *BACCHIDĒS* 816–17)

adulēscēns, adulēscentis young, youthful
dīligō, dīligere, dīlēxī, dīlēctus value, esteem, love
sapiō, sapere, sapiī or **sapīvī, ——** be intelligent, show good sense

4. Mistaken for his twin brother, Menaechmus is reviled by his brother's parasite, Peniculus.

> *Menaechmus.* Quis hic est, quī adversus it mihī?* *Pēniculus.* Quid ais, homō
>
> levior quam plūma, pessime et nēquissime,
>
> flāgitium hominis, subdole ac minimī pretī? (PLAUTUS, *MENAECHMĪ* 487–89)

*The final **-i** of **mihi** here scans *long*.
adversus (adv.) opposite, **adversus īre**, to go to meet (+ dat.)
aiō (defective verb) say; **ais** = *2nd sing. pres. act. indic.*

flāgitium, flāgitiī *n.* shame, outrage, disgrace
nēquissimus, -a, -um most worthless, worst
plūma, plūmae *f.* feather
subdolus, -a, -um deceitful, treacherous, sly

5. In explaining why he will not boast of his victories, Stratophanes, a soldier and buffoon, speaks about the trustworthiness of different kinds of witnesses.

> plūris est oculātus testis ūnus quam aurītī decem;
>
> quī audiunt audīta dīcunt, quī vident plānē sciunt. (PLAUTUS, *TRUCULENTUS* 489–90)

aurītus, -a, -um having ears
oculātus, -a, -um having eyes
plānē (adv.) plainly, clearly; obviously
testis, testis, -ium *m.* witness

6. The character Geta despairs.

    hoccin saeclum! ō scelera, ō genera sacrilega, ō hominem inpium!

    (TERENCE, *ADELPHOE* 304)

hoccin = hocne; **-ne**, *here,* indicates an indignant statement
sacrilegus, -a, -um temple-robbing; sacrilegious
saec(u)lum, saec(u)lī *n.* age, generation

7. Chaerea concludes an account of a conversation with the long-winded Archimedes.

    dum haec dīcit, abiit hōra. (TERENCE, *EUNUCHUS* 341)

hōra, hōrae *f.* hour

8. A fragment from the satirist Lucilius

    ō cūrās hominum! ō quantum est in rēbus ināne! (LUCILIUS, *SATURAE* FRAG. 9)

ināne, inānis, -ium *n.* empty space, void

9. Cicero comments on Athens and its great lawgiver, Solon.

    prūdentissima cīvitās Athēniēnsium, dum ea rērum potīta est, fuisse trāditur; eius

    porrō cīvitātis sapientissimum Solōnem dīcunt fuisse, eum quī lēgēs quibus hodiē

    quoque ūtuntur scrīpserit. (CICERO, *PRŌ S. ROSCIŌ AMERĪNŌ* 70)

Athēniēnsis, Athēniēnse Athenian
hodiē (adv.) today
porrō (adv.) forward; hereafter; in turn, furthermore
potior, potīrī, potītus sum be master (of), control
(+ gen.)

prūdēns, prūdentis showing foresight, prudent,
sagacious
Solō(n), Solōnis *m.* Solon, sixth-century B.C.E.
lawgiver

10. Cicero describes his reception when he arrived in Sicily to collect evidence against Verres.

    nēminī meus adventus labōrī aut sūmptuī neque* pūblicē neque* prīvātim fuit:

    vim in inquīrendō tantam habuī quantam mihi lēx dabat, nōn quantam habēre

    poteram istōrum studiō quōs iste† vexārat. (CICERO, *IN VERREM II* 1.16)

*These redundant negatives strengthen
the negative idea.
†**iste** refers to Verres.
adventus, adventūs *m.* arrival
inquīrō (in- + quaerō), inquīrere, inquīsiī or
inquīsīvī, inquīsītus inquire into, investigate

prīvātim (adv.) in private, privately
sūmptus, sūmptūs *m.* expense, cost
vexō (1-tr.) trouble, disturb, harass

11. Cicero attacks Verres for one of his many illegal acts.

    ēripis hērēditātem quae vēnerat ā propinquō, vēnerat testāmentō, vēnerat lēgibus;

    quae bona is quī testāmentum fēcerat huic Hēracliō, aliquantō antequam est mor-

    tuus, omnia ūtenda ac possidenda trādiderat . . . (CICERO, *IN VERREM II* 2.46)

aliquantum, aliquantī *n.* a little, a small amount
ēripiō, ēripere, ēripuī, ēreptus tear away, snatch
away
Hēraclīus, Hēraclīī *m.* Heraclius
hērēditās, hērēditātis *f.* inheritance

possideō, possidēre, possēdī, possessus occupy;
take control of, possess
propinquus, -a, -um near, close; *as subst.,* relative
testāmentum, testāmentī *n.* will

12. Cicero expresses his willingness to endure unpopularity now that Catiline has left the city.

est mihi tantī, Quirītēs, huius invidiae falsae atque inīquae tempestātem subīre, dum modo ā vōbīs huius horribilis bellī ac nefāriī perīculum dēpellātur. dīcātur sānē ēiectus esse ā mē, dum modo eat in exsilium. sed mihi crēdite, nōn est itūrus. (CICERO, *IN CATILĪNAM II* 15)

dēpellō (dē- + pellō), dēpellere, dēpulī, dēpulsus drive away
horribilis, horribile terrifying, dreadful
nefārius, -a, -um unspeakable, wicked
Quirītēs, Quirītium *m. pl.* Quirites, the name for Roman citizens in their public capacity

sānē (adv.) by all means
subeō (sub- + eō), subīre, subiī or **subīvī, subitūrus** undergo, endure
tempestās, tempestātis *f.* storm

13. After his return from exile Cicero describes the debt he owes to Pompey the Great.

huic ego hominī, Quirītēs, tantum dēbeō quantum hominem hominī dēbēre vix fās est. (CICERO, *POST REDITUM AD POPULUM* 17)

Quirītēs, Quirītium *m. pl.* Quirites, the name for Roman citizens in their public capacity
vix (adv.) scarcely, hardly

14. Cicero asks a rhetorical question.

quid est ōrātōrī tam necessārium quam vōx?* (CICERO, *DĒ ŌRĀTŌRE* I.251)

*****vōx,** *here,* quality *or* tone of voice
necessārius, -a, -um necessary

15. A character in Cicero's dialogue about law explains the importance of **imperium**.

nihil porrō tam aptum est ad iūs condiciōnemque nātūrae—quod quom dīcō, lēgem ā mē dīcī intellegī volō—quam imperium, sine quō nec domus ūlla nec cīvitās nec gēns nec hominum ūniversum genus stāre, nec rērum nātūra omnis nec ipse mundus potest. (CICERO, *DĒ LĒGIBUS* III.2)

aptus, -a, -um suitable, fit
condiciō, condiciōnis *f.* contract; condition, situation
mundus, mundī *m.* universe, world
porrō (adv.) forward; hereafter; in turn, furthermore
ūniversus, -a, -um entire, (taken as a) whole

16. Pleading before Caesar on behalf of one of Pompey's followers, Cicero appeals to Caesar's merciful side.

nihil est tam populāre quam bonitās, nūlla dē virtūtibus tuīs plūrimīs nec* admīrābilior nec* grātior misericordiā est. hominēs enim ad deōs nūllā rē propius accēdunt quam salūtem hominibus dandō. (CICERO, *PRŌ LIGĀRIŌ* 37–38)

*These redundant negatives strengthen the negative idea.
admīrābilis, admīrābile astonishing; admirable, wonderful
bonitās, bonitātis *f.* (moral) goodness; kindness, generosity

misericordia, misericordiae *f.* pity
populāris, populāre of the **populus**; popular, admired
propius (adv.) nearer

17. Cicero explains the importance of knowing Latin.

    nōn enim tam praeclārum est scīre Latīnē quam turpe nescīre, neque tam* id

    mihi ōrātōris bonī quam* cīvis Rōmānī proprium vidētur. (CICERO, BRŪTUS 140)

    ***tam . . . quam . . .** *here,* so much . . . as . . .
    Latīnē (adv.) (in) Latin
    praeclārus, -a, -um very famous; excellent, outstanding.
    proprius, -a, -um one's own; peculiar (to), characteristic (+ gen.)
    turpis, turpe foul, ugly; base, shameful

18. One of the participants in a discussion about the soul's immortality makes his extreme position clear.

    errāre mehercule mālō cum Platōne, quem tū quantī faciās sciō et quem ex tuō ōre

    admīror, quam cum istīs* vēra sentīre. (CICERO, TUSCULĀNAE DISPUTĀTIŌNĒS I.39)

    ***istīs** refers to philosophers who disagree with Plato and deny the immortality of the soul.
    admīror (1-tr.) be astonished (at), wonder (at)
    ōs, ōris *n.* mouth
    Platō(n), Platōnis *m.* Plato

19. Cicero's translation of Simonides' epitaph for the Spartan dead at Thermopylae

    Dīc, hospes, Spartae nōs tē hīc vīdisse iacentēs,

        dum sānctīs patriae lēgibus obsequimur.

        (CICERO, TUSCULĀNAE DISPUTĀTIŌNĒS I.101)

    hīc (adv.) here
    hospes, hospitis *m.* guest, visitor, stranger
    iaceō, iacēre, iacuī, —— lie, rest; lie dead

    obsequor (ob- + sequor) comply with, submit to
    sānctus, -a, -um inviolate, blameless
    Sparta, Spartae *f.* Sparta

20. After one character states that even wise men are affected by passionate emotions, another character indicates his disagreement with the following surprising statement.

    Nē* ista glōriōsa sapientia nōn magnō aestimanda est, sī quidem nōn multum differt ab īnsāniā. (CICERO, TUSCULĀNAE DISPUTĀTIŌNĒS III.8)

    ***nē**, *here* (particle) *always followed by a demonstrative,* truly, assuredly
    glōriōsus, -a, -um boastful; glorious, illustrious
    īnsānia, īnsāniae *f.* madness, insanity

21. A suggestion worthy of Plato

    dēmus igitur nōs huic* excolendōs patiāmurque nōs sānārī.

        (CICERO, TUSCULĀNAE DISPUTĀTIŌNĒS IV.38)

    ***huic** refers to philosophy.
    excolō, excolere, excoluī, excultus cultivate, develop, improve
    sānō (1-tr.) heal, cure

22. A famous anecdote about the Athenian statesman Themistocles

> noctū ambulābat in pūblicō* Themistoclēs, quod somnum capere nōn posset, quaerentibusque respondēbat Miltiadis tropaeīs sē ē somnō suscitārī.

(Cicero, *Tusculānae Disputātiōnēs* IV.44)

*in pūblicō, in (a) public (place)
Miltiadēs, Miltiadis *m.* Miltiades, an Athenian commander at Marathon
noctū = **nocte**
somnus, somnī *m.* sleep

suscitō (1-tr.) cause to rise, rouse
Themistoclēs, Themistoclis *m.* Themistocles
tropaeum, tropaeī *n.* trophy (set up to mark the defeat of an enemy)

23. Meditating on how often philosophers have easily endured exile from their homelands, a character suggests a reevaluation of the importance of the state.

> quantī vērō ista cīvitās aestimanda est, ex quā bonī sapientēsque pelluntur?

(Cicero, *Tusculānae Disputātiōnēs* V.109)

24. The character Cotta utters a wish while speaking against the tenets of Epicureanism.

> utinam tam facile vēra invenīre possem quam falsa convincere!

(Cicero, *Dē Nātūrā Deōrum* I.91)

convincō (**con-** + **vincō**) overcome; prove wrong, refute

25. The character Balbus closes his presentation of the Stoic view of the gods.

> mala enim et impia cōnsuētūdō est contrā deōs disputandī, sīve ex animō id fit sīve simulātē. (Cicero, *Dē Nātūrā Deōrum* II.168)

cōnsuētūdō, cōnsuētūdinis *f.* practice, custom, habit
disputō (**dis-** + **putō**) (1-tr.) argue one's case, debate
simulātē (adv.) in pretence
sīve (conj.) or if, whether; **sīve . . . sīve . . .** whether . . . or (if) . . .

26. Although Cicero has been sleeping more since retiring from politics, he claims that his own dreams have remained pretty much the same.

> . . . nec tam multum dormiēns ūllō somniō sum admonitus, tantīs praesertim dē rēbus, nec mihi magis umquam videor quam cum aut in forō magistrātūs aut in cūriā senātum videō, somniāre. (Cicero, *Dē Dīvinātiōne* II.142)

admoneō (**ad-** + **moneō**) remind, advise
cūria, cūriae *f.* (the) Curia, (the) senate house
dormiō, dormīre, dormīvī or **dormiī, dormītum** sleep, be asleep
magistrātus, magistrātūs *m.* office holder, magistrate

praesertim (adv.) especially, above all
somniō (1-intr.) dream
somnium, somniī *n.* dream

27. Cicero adduces a famous Roman family as an example of how real glory endures.

> Tiberius enim Gracchus, P. f.,* tam diū laudābitur dum memoria rērum
> Rōmānārum manēbit . . . (CICERO, *DĒ OFFICIĪS* II.43)

*P. f. = Publiī fīlius

28. Cicero claims that Caesar often cited two lines of a Greek tragedy, which Cicero here translates.

> nam sī violandum est iūs, rēgnandī grātiā
>
> violandum est; aliīs rēbus pietātem colās. (CICERO, *DĒ OFFICIĪS* III.12)

colō, colere, coluī, cultus cultivate
pietās, pietātis *f.* sense of duty, dutifulness, piety
rēgnō (1-tr.) rule as king, reign
violō (1-tr.) violate, transgress against

29. Cicero pays his friend Atticus a compliment.

> Rōmae enim videor esse cum tuās litterās legō et, ut fit in tantīs rēbus, modo hoc
> modo illud audīre. (CICERO, *AD ATTICUM* II.15.1)

30. Cicero writes to Brutus about his opinion of the consuls for 43 B.C.E. and the young Octavian Caesar.

> quālis tibi saepe scrīpsī cōnsulēs, tālēs exstitērunt. Caesaris vērō puerī mīrifica in-
> dolēs virtūtis. utinam tam facile eum flōrentem et honōribus et grātiā regere ac
> tenēre possīmus quam facile adhūc tenuimus! (CICERO, *AD BRŪTUM* 9.1)

adhūc (adv.) up to the present time
ex(s)istō, ex(s)istere, ex(s)titī, —— stand out, appear; prove to be
flōreō, flōrēre, flōruī, —— blossom; prosper; be at the height of one's power
indolēs, indolis *f.* innate quality, nature; (natural) tendency (for) (+ gen.)
mīrificus, -a, -um causing wonder, amazing

31. While writing his autobiography, Cicero contemplates insulting two consuls, A. Gabinius and L. Calpurnius Piso Caesoninus, both of whom supported Clodius's prosecution of Cicero, which led to the latter's exile.

> itaque mīrificum embolium cōgitō* in secundum librum meōrum temporum in-
> clūdere dīcentem Apollinem in conciliō deōrum quālis reditus duōrum im-
> perātōrum futūrus esset, quōrum alter exercitum perdidisset, alter vendidisset.
>
> (CICERO, *AD QUINTUM FRĀTREM* III.1.24)

*cōgitō, *here,* have in mind, plan (+ inf.)
concilium, conciliī *n.* (popular) assembly, council
embolium, emboliī *n.* interlude; insertion
inclūdō, inclūdere, inclūsī, inclūsus enclose, include

itaque (conj.) and so, accordingly
mīrificus, -a, -um causing wonder, amazing
reditus, reditūs *m.* return

32. The poet laments man's irrational fear of death.

> ō miserās hominum mentēs, ō pectora caeca!
>
> quālibus in tenebrīs vītae quantīsque perīclīs
>
> dēgitur hoc aevī quodcumquest! . . . (Lucretius, *Dē Rērum Nātūrā* I.14–16)

aevum, aevī *n.* age, life(time)
dēgō (dē- + agō), dēgere, ——, —— spend, pass
perīclīs = perīculīs
quodcumque = *neut. sing. nom. of indef. rel. adj.,* whatever
tenebrae, tenebrārum *f. pl.* darkness, shadows

33. Imitation is the sincerest form of flattery. (hendecasyllable)

> Disertissime Rōmulī nepōtum,
>
> quot sunt quotque fuēre, Marce Tullī,
>
> quotque post aliīs erunt in annīs,
>
> grātiās tibi maximās Catullus
>
> agit pessimus omnium poēta,
>
> tantō pessimus omnium poēta,
>
> quantō tū optimus omnium patrōnus. (Catullus XLIX)

disertus, -a, -um well-spoken, eloquent
nepōs, nepōtis *m.* grandson; descendant
patrōnus, patrōnī *m.* patron; defender

34. The poet states a paradox.

> Ōdī et amō. quārē id faciam fortasse requīris.
>
>   nescio,* sed fierī sentiō et excrucior. (Catullus LXXXV)

*The final **-ō** of **nesciō** here scans *short.*
excruciō (1-tr.) torture
fortasse (adv.) perhaps
requīrō (re- + quaerō), requīrere, requīsiī or **requīsīvī, requīsītus** seek again, ask, inquire

35. The poet strives to express how much he loved Lesbia.

> Nūlla potest mulier tantum sē dīcere amātam
>
>   vērē, quantum ā mē Lesbia amāta mea est.
>
> nūlla fidēs ūllō fuit umquam foedere tanta,
>
>   quanta in amōre tuō ex parte reperta meā est. (Catullus LXXXVII)

foedus, foederis *n.* agreement, treaty, pact
mulier, mulieris *f.* woman
reperiō, reperīre, repperī, repertus find, discover

36. The soldiers of the enemy break ranks to the benefit of Caesar's men.

   ita sine ūllō perīculō tantam eōrum multitūdinem nostrī interfēcērunt quantum

   fuit diēī spatium, . . . (CAESAR, *Dē Bellō Gallicō* II.11)

multitūdō, multitūdinis *f.* multitude
spatium, spatiī *n.* course, track; space, interval

37. Caesar explains why he thinks certain Gallic tribes surrendered so quickly.

   nam ut ad bella suscipienda Gallōrum alacer ac prōmptus est animus, sīc mollis ac

   minimē resistēns ad calamitātēs ferendās mēns eōrum est.

   (CAESAR, *Dē Bellō Gallicō* III.19)

alacer, alacris, alacre quick, swift; keen, eager
calamitās, calamitātis *f.* disaster, misfortune,
   injury
Gallī, Gallōrum *m. pl.* (the) Gauls
mollis, molle gentle, soft, mild

prōmptus, -a, -um quick to respond, ready
resistō, resistere, restitī, —— halt; make a stand,
   resist
suscipiō (sub- + capiō) undertake, venture upon

38. In the territory of the Morini, Caesar—referring to himself in the third person—is about to launch an expedition to Britain.

   dum in hīs locīs Caesar nāvium parandārum causā morātur, ex magnā parte

   Morīnōrum ad eum lēgātī vēnērunt quī sē dē superiōris temporis cōnsiliō ex-

   cūsārent quod hominēs barbarī et nostrae cōnsuētūdinis imperītī bellum populō

   Rōmānō fēcissent, sēque ea quae imperāsset factūrōs pollicērentur. (CAESAR, *Dē*

   Bellō Gallicō IV.22)

barbarus, -a, -um foreign; barbarous, uncivilized
cōnsuētūdō, cōnsuētūdinis *f.* custom, usage
excūsō (1-tr.) excuse
imperītus, -a, -um inexperienced (in),
   unacquainted (with) (+ gen.)
Morīnī, Morīnōrum *m. pl.* (the) Morini, a Belgic
   tribe

nāvis, nāvis, -ium *f.* ship
parō (1-tr.) prepare, make ready; get, obtain
polliceor, pollicērī, pollicitus sum promise
superior, superius upper, higher; earlier

39. Several of Caesar's soldiers, against orders, leave their positions in the middle of a battle on land and sea and attempt to reach land on their own.

   pars eōrum studiō spectandī ferēbātur, pars etiam cupiditāte pugnandī.

   ([CAESAR], *Dē Bellō Alexandrīnō* 20)

cupiditās, cupiditātis *f.* desire
spectō (1-tr.) look at, observe

40. When he is recommending a harsh penalty against Catiline, Cato recalls an outstanding example of Roman austerity.

> apud maiōrēs nostrōs T. Manlius Torquātus bellō Gallicō fīlium suom, quod is
>
> contrā imperium in hostem pugnāverat, necārī iussit atque ille ēgregius
>
> adulēscēns inmoderātae fortitūdinis* morte poenās dedit.

(SALLUST, *BELLUM CATILĪNAE* 52)

*inmoderātae fortitūdinis, *genitive expresses the charge,* for (his) unrestrained bravery
adulēscēns, adulēscentis, -ium *m.* young man
ēgregius, -a, -um outstanding, extraordinary
fortitūdō, fortitūdinis *f.* bravery, fortitude

Gallicus, -a, -um Gallic
immoderātus, -a, -um unrestrained, immoderate
T. Manlius Torquātus, T. Manliī Torquātī *m.* T. Manlius Torquatus (dictator 353 B.C.E.)
necō (1-tr.) put to death, kill

41. The historian summarizes Cato's character.

> esse quam vidērī bonus mālēbat: ita, quō minus petēbat glōriam, eō magis illum
>
> adsequēbātur. (SALLUST, *BELLUM CATILĪNAE* 54)

assequor (ad- + sequor) go after, pursue

42. The historian compares Caesar and Cato.

> Caesar dandō, sublevandō, ignōscundō, Catō nihil largiundō glōriam adeptus est.
>
> in alterō miserīs perfugium erat, in alterō malīs perniciēs. illīus facilitās, huius
>
> cōnstantia laudābātur. (SALLUST, *BELLUM CATILĪNAE* 54)

adipīscor, adipīscī, adeptus sum reach, obtain, gain, get
cōnstantia, cōnstantiae *f.* firmness, steadfastness, resolution
facilitās, facilitātis *f.* facility, ease; indulgence
ignōscō (in- + nōscō), ignōscere, ignōvī, ignōtus forgive, pardon; ignōscundō = archaic form of ignōscendō

largior, largīrī, largītus sum give (generously), bestow; largiundō = archaic form of largiendō
perfugium, perfugiī *n.* place of refuge, shelter, sanctuary
perniciēs, perniciēī *f.* destruction, ruin, disaster
sublevō (1-tr.) raise; assist

43. A writer expresses indignation at a line in Cicero's poem about his consulship.

> tamen audet dīcere: "Ō fortūnātam nātam, mē cōnsule, Rōmam!" tē cōnsule
>
> fortūnātam, Cicerō? immō vērō īnfēlīcem et miseram . . .

([SALLUST], *IN M. TULLIUM CICERŌNEM* 5)

fortūnātus, -a, -um fortunate
immō vērō (adv.) no, even

44. A Roman proverb

> Beneficium accipere lībertātem est vendere. (PUBLILIUS SYRUS, *SENTENTIAE* B5)

beneficium, beneficiī *n.* service, kindness; favor, benefit

45. A Roman proverb

> Brevis ipsa vīta est, sed malīs fit longior. (Publilius Syrus, *Sententiae* B36)

46. After a refrain in a funeral song for the shepherd Daphnis, the poet gives evidence for the power of poetry.

> dūcite ab urbe domum, mea carmina, dūcite Daphnin.
>
> carmina vel caelō possunt dēdūcere lūnam,
>
> carminibus Circē sociōs mūtāvit Ulīxī, . . . (Vergil, *Eclogues* VIII.68–70)

Circē, Circēs *f.* Circe, a witch from Colchis who
   detained Odysseus and his men
Daphnis, Daphnidis *f.* Daphnis; **Daphnin** = *acc.
   sing.*

dēdūcō (dē- + dūcō) lead down; bring down
lūna, lūnae *f.* moon
Ulīxēs, Ulīxis or **Ulīxī** *m.* Ulysses (Odysseus)
vel (adv.) even

47. The poet concludes an enumeration of Aeneas's many trials.

> tantae mōlis erat Rōmānam condere gentem. (Vergil, *Aeneid* I.33)

condō, condere, condidī, conditus found
mōlēs, mōlis, -ium *f.* mass, weight, burden; enterprise, responsibility

48. Aeneas describes a grim scene in a wall painting he discovers in Carthage.

> ter circum Īliacōs raptāverat Hectora mūrōs
>
> exanimumque aurō corpus vendēbat Achillēs. (Vergil, *Aeneid* I.483–84)

Achillēs, Achillis *m.* Achilles
circum (prep. + acc.) around
exanimus, -a, -um lifeless
Hector, Hectoris *m.* Hector; **Hectora** = *acc. sing.*

Īliacus, -a, -um Ilian, Trojan
raptō (1-tr.) carry away by force; seize; drag
ter (adv.) three times

49. Angry Dido feels that further appeals to Aeneas will be useless.

> nam quid dissimulō aut quae mē ad maiōra reservō?
>
> num flētū ingemuit nostrō? num lūmina flexit?
>
> num lacrimās victus dedit aut miserātus amantem est? (Vergil, *Aeneid* IV.368–70)

dissimulō (1-tr.) conceal, pretend, dissemble
flectō, flectere, flexī, flexus bend, turn
flētus, flētūs *m.* weeping, tears
ingemō, ingemere, ingemuī, —— groan, lament

lacrima, lacrimae *f.* tear
miseror (1-tr.) pity
reservō (1-tr.) save, hold back

50. The poet comments on the lives of words.

> multa renāscentur quae iam cecidēre cadentque
>
> quae nunc sunt in honōre vocābula, sī volet ūsus,
>
> quem penes* arbitrium est et iūs et norma loquendī. (Horace, *Ars Poētica* 70–72)

*quem penes = penes quem by anastrophe, the
   reversal in order of a preposition and its object
arbitrium, arbitriī *n.* power of decision,
   determination; supervision, control
norma, normae *f.* standard

penes (prep. + acc.) in the power of
renāscor (re- + nāscor) be reborn; be revived
ūsus, ūsūs *m.* use; usage
vocābulum, vocābulī *n.* word; term

51. The poet has been away from Rome and away from Cynthia.

> nōn sum ego quī fueram: mūtat via longa puellās.
>
> > quantus in exiguō tempore fūgit amor!
>
> nunc prīmum longās sōlus cognōscere noctēs
>
> > cōgor et ipse meīs auribus esse gravis. (PROPERTIUS I.12.11–14)

auris, auris, -ium *f.* ear
cōgō (cō- + agō), cōgere, coēgī, coāctus drive together, force, compel
exiguus, -a, -um small, slight, brief

52. Addressing his beloved Cynthia, the poet links love and mortality.

> dum nōs fāta sinunt, oculōs satiēmus amōre:
>
> > nox tibi longa venit, nec reditūra diēs. (PROPERTIUS II.15.23–24)

satiō (1-tr.) sate, satisfy
sinō, sinere, siī or **sīvī, situm** allow, permit

53. The poet looks at the darker side of love.

> lītore quot conchae, tot sunt in amōre dolōrēs;
>
> > quae patimur, multō spīcula felle madent. (OVID, *ARS AMĀTŌRIA* II.519–20)

concha, conchae *f.* shellfish; seashell
dolor, dolōris *m.* grief, sorrow, pain
fel, fellis *n.* liver, (black) bile (the source of rage); venom; bitterness
lītus, lītoris *n.* shore, beach
madeō, madēre, ——, —— be wet, drip
spīculum, spīculī *n.* sharp point (of a weapon), arrow; sting

54. The poet in exile comments with emotion on the death of his parents.

> fēlīcēs ambō tempestīvēque sepultī,
>
> > ante diem poenae quod periēre meae!
>
> mē quoque fēlīcem, quod nōn vīventibus illīs
>
> > sum miser, et dē mē quod doluēre nihil! (OVID, *TRĪSTIA* IV.10.81–84)

ambō, ambae, ambō (*pl. adj. and pron.*) both; **ambō** = *masc. nom. pl.*
doleō, dolēre, doluī, —— suffer, grieve, feel pain
sepeliō, sepelīre, sepelīvī or **sepeliī, sepultus** bury
tempestīvē (adv.) opportunely, at the right time

55. A tribune of the people, A. Verginius, concludes a speech intended to warn the people about Caeso Quinctius, a champion of the patricians.

> exspectāte dum cōnsul aut dictātor fīat quem prīvātum vīribus et audāciā rēgnan-
>
> tem vidētis. (LIVY, *AB URBE CONDITĀ* III.11.13)

dictātor, dictātōris *m.* dictator, an emergency officer with unlimited powers
prīvātus, -a, -um private; *as subst.,* private citizen
rēgnō (1-tr.) rule; act in a kingly way, tyrannize

56. Clytaemnestra laments both the horrors of the house of Atreus and the beginning of the Trojan war.

    ō scelera semper sceleribus vincēns domus:

    cruōre ventōs ēmimus, bellum nece! (Seneca the Younger, *Agamemnōn* 169–70)

cruor, cruōris *m.* (fresh) blood, gore
nex, necis *f.* murder
ventus, ventī *m.* wind

57. While plotting revenge against his brother, Thyestes, Atreus speaks to himself.

    haec ipsa pollēns inclitī Pelopis domus

    ruat vel in mē, dummodo in frātrem ruat. (Seneca the Younger, *Thyestēs* 190–91)

inclitus, -a, -um famous, renowned
Pelops, Pelopis *m.* Pelops, son of Tantalus and father of Atreus and Thyestes
polleō, pollēre, ——, —— be powerful
ruō, ruere, ruī, rutūrus rush; fall (with violence)
vel (adv.) even

58. The poet remarks on the curious fate of one of his little books.

    Quem recitās meus est, ō Fīdentīne, libellus;

        sed male cum recitās, incipit esse tuus. (Martial I.38)

Fīdentīnus, Fīdentīnī *m.* Fidentinus, the addressee of the poem
libellus, libellī *m.* (little) book
recitō (1-tr.) read aloud (in public), recite

59. Unlike Romans of old, who were able to exercise the rights of free citizens all their lives, those of Pliny's generation have had this experience for a short time only.

    breve tempus (nam tantō brevius omne quantō fēlīcius tempus) quō libet scīre

    quid sīmus, libet exercēre quod scīmus. (Pliny the Younger, *Epistulae* VIII.14.10)

exerceō, exercēre, exercuī, exercitus keep busy; exercise, perform
libet, libēre, libuit or **libitum est** it is pleasing, there is a desire

60. Pliny suggests to the new emperor Trajan a means of evaluating the character of the senators.

    tālēsque nōs crēde, quālis fāma cuiusque est.

    (Pliny the Younger, *Panēgyricus* 62.9)

cuiusque = *masc. sing. gen. of indef. pron.,* each man

61. The historian describes the experience of repression under Domitian.

    memoriam quoque ipsam cum vōce perdidissēmus sī tam* in nostrā potestāte

    esset oblīvīscī quam* tacēre. (Tacitus, *Dē Vītā Agricolae* 2)

*****tam . . . quam . . .** *here,* as much . . . as . . .
potestās, potestātis *f.* (legitimate) power
taceō, tacēre, tacuī, tacitūrus be silent, keep silent

62. The historian quotes this tortured sentence from a letter written by Tiberius to the senate as proof of the emperor's inner torment.

> quid scrībam vōbīs, patrēs cōnscrīptī, aut quō modō scrībam, aut quid omnīnō nōn scrībam hōc tempore, dī mē deaeque peius perdant quam perīre mē cōtīdiē sentiō sī sciō. (TACITUS, *ANNĀLĒS* VI.6)

cōtīdiē (adv.) daily, every day

63. The historian comments on Tiberius's habit of consulting an astrologer.

> sed mihi haec ac tālia audientī in incertō iūdicium est fātōne rēs mortālium et necessitāte immūtābilī an forte volvantur. (TACITUS, *ANNĀLĒS* VI.22)

immūtābilis, immūtābile unchangeable, unalterable
iūdicium, iūdiciī *n.* judgment, opinion
mortālis, mortāle mortal
necessitās, necessitātis *f.* necessity
volvō, volvere, volvī, volūtus turn; determine

64. The historian reports one way Caesar found to keep up the population of the city.

> omnīsque medicīnam Rōmae professōs et līberālium artium doctōrēs, quō libentius et ipsī urbem incolerent et cēterī adpeterent, cīvitāte dōnāvit.
> (SUETONIUS, *VĪTA IŪLIĪ* 42)

adpetō (ad- + petō) strive after, seek; make for
doctor, doctōris *m.* teacher
incolō, incolere, incoluī, —— inhabit
libenter (adv.) gladly
līberālis, līberāle characteristic of a free man, liberal

medicīna, medicīnae *f.* medicine
profiteor, profitērī, professus sum profess; follow as a pursuit, practice

65. The historian quotes from a letter of Augustus to Tiberius.

> attenuātum tē esse continuātiōne labōrum cum audiō et legō, dī mē perdant nisi cohorrēscit corpus meum; tēque ōrō ut parcās tibi, . . . (SUETONIUS, *VĪTA TIBERIĪ* 21)

attenuō (1-tr.) make thin, impair, weaken
cohorrēscō, cohorrēscere, cohorruī, —— shudder, shiver
continuātiō, continuātiōnis *f.* continuance, prolongation
parcō, parcere, pepercī, parsūrus be merciful, be sparing (+ dat.)

66. According to the historian, these were Nero's last words.

> quālis artifex pereō! (SUETONIUS, *VĪTA NĒRŌNIS* 49)

artifex, artificis *m.* artist

67. A young man's epitaph

Decem et octō annōrum nātus vīxī ut potuī bene, grātus parentī atque amīcīs om-

nibus. iocēris, lūdās, hortor: hīc summa est sevēritās. (*CIL* VI.16169)

hīc (adv.) here, in this place
iocor (1-intr.) joke, jest
lūdō, lūdere, lūsī, lūsus play
parēns, parentis, -ium *m.* or *f.* parent
sevēritās, sevēritātis *f.* gravity, seriousness, severity

Longer Readings

1. Cicero, *Prō Archiā* 13

Cicero concludes his defense of the time he has spent on literary pursuits.

quā rē quis tandem mē reprehendat, aut quis mihi iūre suscēnseat, sī, quantum cēterīs ad suās rēs obeundās, quantum ad fēstōs diēs lūdōrum celebrandōs, quantum ad aliās voluptātēs et ad ipsam requiem animī et corporis concēditur temporum, quantum aliī tribuunt tempestīvīs convīviīs, quantum dēnique alveolō, quantum pilae, tantum mihi egomet ad haec studia recolenda sūmpserō?

alveolus, alveolī *m.* gaming board
celebrō (1-tr.) celebrate
concēdō (**con- + cēdō**) (tr.) concede, grant
convīvium, convīviī *n.* dinner party, banquet, feast
dēnique (adv.) finally, at last; in short, to sum up
egomet = intensive form of **ego**
fēstus, -a, -um festal; **fēstus diēs**, festival day, holiday
lūdus, lūdī *m.* game, play, sport; *in pl.,* (public) games
obeō (**ob- + eō**), **obīre, obiī** or **obīvī, obitus** go to meet; enter into, take on
pila, pilae *f.* ball
recolō, recolere, recoluī, recultus cultivate again; resume, practice again

reprehendō, reprehendere, reprehendī, reprehēnsus seize, catch; blame, censure
requiēs, requiētis *f.* rest, relaxation; **requiem** = *acc. sing.*
sūmō, sūmere, sūmpsī, sūmptus take up, seize; take (and use)
suscēnseō, suscēnsēre, suscēnsuī, —— be angry with (+ dat.)
tempestīvus, -a, -um timely, ripe, ready; **tempestīvum convīvium**, sumptuous *or* elaborate dinner party (that starts early)
tribuō, tribuere, tribuī, tribūtus grant, bestow, assign
voluptās, voluptātis *f.* pleasure, joy

2. Cicero, *Prō Archiā* 14

The study of literature stands in an important relation to public and political life.

nam nisi multōrum praeceptīs multīsque litterīs mihi ab adulēscentiā suāsissem nihil esse in vītā magnō opere* expetendum nisi laudem atque honestātem, in eā autem persequendā omnīs cruciātūs corporis, omnia perīcula mortis atque exsilī parvī esse dūcenda, numquam mē prō salūte vestrā in tot ac tantās dīmicātiōnēs atque in hōs prōflīgātōrum hominum cōtīdiānōs impetūs obiēcissem. sed plēnī omnēs sunt librī, plēnae sapientium vōcēs, plēna exemplōrum vetustās; quae iacērent in tenebrīs omnia, nisi litterārum lūmen accēderet.† quam multās nōbīs imāginēs nōn sōlum ad intuendum vērum etiam ad imitandum fortissimōrum virōrum expressās scrīptōrēs et Graecī et Latīnī relīquērunt! quās ego mihi semper in administrandā rē pūblicā prōpōnēns animum et mentem meam ipsā cōgitātiōne hominum excellentium cōnformābam.

*magnō opere = magnopere
†accēdō, *here,* be added
administrō (1-tr.) assist; manage, administer
adulēscentia, adulēscentiae *f.* youth, adolescence
cōgitātiō, cōgitātiōnis *f.* thinking, reflection, thought
cōnformō (1-tr.) shape, fashion
cōtīdiānus, -a, -um daily
cruciātus, cruciātūs *m.* torture, torment
dīmicātiō, dīmicātiōnis *f.* battle, fight, struggle
excellēns, excellentis outstanding
exemplum, exemplī *n.* example
expetō (ex- + petō) ask for, seek (after)
exprimō, exprimere, expressī, expressus squeeze out; stamp, portray, depict
Graecus, -a, -um Greek
honestās, honestātis *f.* honor, integrity
iaceō, iacēre, iacuī, —— lie, rest; lie dead
imāgō, imāginis *f.* image, likeness
imitor (1-tr.) practice, copy, imitate

impetus, impetūs *m.* attack, assault
intueor, intuērī, intuitus sum look upon, gaze at; reflect upon, consider
Latīnus, -a, -um Latin
laus, laudis *f.* praise
obiciō (ob- + iaciō) throw (in front of), throw (in the way of), interpose
persequor (per- + sequor) follow earnestly, pursue
plēnus, -a, -um full
praeceptum, praeceptī *n.* advice, instruction, precept
prōflīgātus, -a, -um dissolute, depraved
prōpōnō (prō- + pōnō) exhibit; keep (before one), bear in mind, hold up (as an example)
scrīptor, scrīptōris *m.* writer
suādeō, suādēre, suāsī, suāsum recommend, urge, advise; persuade (+ dat.)
tenebrae, tenebrārum *f. pl.* darkness, shadows
vetustās, vetustātis *f.* (old) age, antiquity

3. Cicero, *Prō Archiā* 18–19

Cicero muses on the divine endowment of all poets.

atque sīc ā summīs hominibus ērudītissimīsque accēpimus cēterārum rērum studia
ex doctrīnā et praeceptīs et arte cōnstāre, poētam nātūrā ipsā valēre et mentis vīribus
excitārī et quasi dīvīnō quōdam spīritū īnflārī. quā rē suō iūre noster ille Ennius sānc-
tōs appellat poētās, quod quasi deōrum aliquō dōnō atque mūnere commendātī nōbīs
esse videantur.

aliquō = *neut. sing. abl. of indef. adj.,* some, any
appellō (1-tr.) name, call
commendō (1-tr.) entrust
cōnstō (con- + **stō), cōnstāre, cōnstitī, cōnstātūrus** stand, be established; (+ **ex** + abl.)
  consist in, rest on, be composed of
doctrīna, doctrīnae *f.* teaching, instruction
Ennius, Enniī *m.* Ennius
ērudītus, -a, -um learned, accomplished

excitō (1-tr.) arouse
īnflō (1-tr.) blow on, inspire
mūnus, mūneris *n.* present, gift; tribute
praeceptum, praeceptī *n.* advice, instruction,
  precept
quasi (adv.) as if, as it were
sānctus, -a, -um sacred, holy
spīritus, spīritūs *m.* spirit

4. Cicero, *Post Reditum Ad Populum* 16

Cicero describes to the people the groundswell of support for him while he was in exile. He
singles out one man's aid in particular.

ita mē nūdum ā propinquīs, nūllā cognātiōne mūnītum, cōnsulēs, praetōrēs, tribūnī
plēbis, senātus, Italia cūncta semper ā vōbīs dēprecāta est, dēnique omnēs quī vestrīs
maximīs beneficiīs honōribusque sunt ornātī, prōductī ad vōs ab eōdem, nōn sōlum
ad mē cōnservandum vōs cohortātī sunt, sed etiam rērum meārum gestārum auc-
tōrēs, testēs, laudātōrēs fuērunt. quōrum prīnceps ad cohortandōs vōs et ad rogandōs
fuit Cn. Pompeius, vir omnium quī sunt, fuērunt, erunt, virtūte, sapientiā, glōriā
prīnceps: quī mihi ūnus ūnī prīvātō amīcō eadem omnia dedit quae ūniversae reī
pūblicae, salūtem, ōtium, dignitātem.

auctor, auctōris *m.* source, author
beneficium, beneficiī *n.* service, kindness; favor,
  benefit
cognātiō, cognātiōnis *f.* kinship
cohortor (co- + **hortor)** (1-tr.) exhort, encourage
cōnservō (con- + **servō)** (1-tr.) keep from danger,
  save, preserve
cūnctus, -a, -um all
dēnique (adv.) finally, at last; in short, to sum up
dēprecor (1-tr.) beg mercy for, intercede for
dignitās, dignitātis *f.* dignity, rank, status
laudātor, laudātōris *m.* praiser; character witness
mūniō, mūnīre, mūnīvī or **mūniī, mūnītus** fortify; defend, protect
nūdus, -a, -um naked, nude; bare; lacking the
  protection of (+ **ā** + abl.)

ornō (1-tr.) dress, adorn, decorate; show respect (to)
ōtium, ōtiī *n.* leisure
plēbs, plēbis *f.* (the) plebs, the general body of
  (nonpatrician) Roman citizens
praetor, praetōris *m.* praetor, a judicial official
  both in and outside of Rome
prīnceps, prīncipis first, foremost, chief; *as
  subst.,* leading man
prīvātus, -a, -um private
prōdūcō (prō- + **dūcō)** bring forth, present
propinquus, -a, -um near, close; *as subst.,* relative
testis, testis, -ium *m.* or *f.* witness
tribūnus, tribūnī *m.* tribune, military commander; (plebeian) magistrate
ūniversus, -a, -um all together, entire, whole

The *Post Reditum ad Populum* was delivered by Cicero after his return from exile in 57. Cicero gives thanks to the
people for their part in his recall, while at the same time recounting his role in important events of the past (notably,
of course, the suppression of the Catilinarian conspiracy).

5. Catullus VIII (choliambic)

The poet has a heart-to-heart talk with himself.

Miser Catulle, dēsinās ineptīre,
et quod vidēs perīsse perditum dūcās.
fulsēre quondam candidī tibī* sōlēs
cum ventitābās quō puella dūcēbat
amāta nōbīs† quantum amābitur nūlla.   5
ibi illa multa cum iocōsa fīēbant,
quae tū volēbās nec puella nōlēbat,
fulsēre vērē candidī tibī* sōlēs.
nunc iam‡ illa nōn volt: tū quoque inpotēns nōlī,
nec quae fugit sectāre, nec miser vīve,   10
sed obstinātā mente perfer, obdūrā.
valē, puella. iam Catullus obdūrat,
nec tē requīret nec rogābit invītam.
at tū dolēbis, cum rogāberis nūlla.
scelesta, vae tē, quae tibi manet vīta?   15
quis nunc tē adībit? cui vidēberis bella?
quem nunc amābis? cuius esse dīcēris?
quem bāsiābis? cui labella mordēbis?
at tū, Catulle, dēstinātus obdūrā.

*The final **-i** of **tibi** here scans *long*.
†**nōbīs**, Dative of Agent
‡**nunc iam**, *here*, now, at last
adeō (ad- + eō), adīre, adiī, aditum approach
at (conj.) but
bāsiō (1-tr.) kiss
bellus, -a, -um pretty, charming, lovely
candidus, -a, -um white, clear, bright, radiant
dēsinō, dēsinere, dēsiī or **dēsīvī, dēsitum** stop,
    cease (+ inf.)
dēstinō (1-tr.) determine, resolve
doleō, dolēre, doluī, —— suffer, grieve, feel pain
fulgeō, fulgēre, fulsī, —— shine, gleam
ibi (adv.) there; then
ineptiō, ineptīre, ——, —— be silly, play the fool
impotēns, impotentis powerless

invītus, -a, -um unwilling
iocōsus, -a, -um full of jokes; laughable, funny
labellum, labellī *n.* (little) lip
mordeō, mordēre, momordī, morsus bite, nibble
obdūrō (1-tr.) be hardened, hold out, persist, en-
    dure
obstinātus, -a, -um firmly set, determined, res-
    olute
quondam (adv.) at one time, once, formerly
requīrō (re- + quaerō), requīrere, requīsiī or **re-**
    quīsīvī, requīsītus seek again
scelestus, -a, -um criminal, wicked, accursed
sector (1-tr.) keep following, chase
sōl, sōlis *m.* sun
vae (interj.) alas! woe!
ventitō (1-intr.) come often, keep coming

6. Catullus LXXXIV

The poet comments on the pronunciation of a certain Arrius.

> "Chommoda" dīcēbat, sī quandō "commoda" vellet*
>> dīcere, et "īnsidiās" Arrius "hīnsidiās."
> et tum mīrificē spērābat sē esse locūtum,
>> cum quantum poterat dīxerat "hīnsidiās."
> crēdō, sīc māter, sīc līber avunculus eius,   5
>> sīc māternus avus dīxerat atque avia.
> hōc missō in Syriam requiērant omnibus aurēs:
>> audībant† eadem haec lēniter et leviter,
> nec sibi postillā metuēbant tālia verba,
>> cum subitō affertur‡ nuntius horribilis: 10
> Īoniōs flūctūs, postquam illūc Arrius īsset,
>> iam nōn Īoniōs esse sed Hīoniōs.

*__vellet__, _iterative subjunctive (indicating repeated action)_, used to want

†__audībant__ = __audiēbant__

‡__affertur__, historical use of present tense; translate as perfect

__afferō (ad- + ferō)__, __afferre__, __attulī__, __allātus__ bring toward, bring forth; report

__Arrius__, __Arriī__ _m._ Arrius

__auris__, __auris__, __-ium__ _f._ ear

__avia__, __aviae__ _f._ grandmother

__avunculus__, __avunculī__ _m._ (maternal) uncle

__avus__, __avī__ _m._ grandfather

__commodum__, __commodī__ _n._ convenience, advantage

__flūctus__, __flūctūs__ _m._ wave, billow

__horribilis__, __horribile__ horrible, terrible

__illūc__ (adv.) to that place, thither

__Ionius__, __-a__, __-um__ Ionian

__lēniter__ (adv.) gently, kindly

__māternus__, __-a__, __-um__ maternal

__metuō__, __metuere__, __metuī__, —— fear, dread

__mīrificē__ (adv.) wonderfully

__nuntius__, __nuntiī__ _m._ messenger; message

__postillā__ (adv.) afterward

__quandō__ (adv.) at any time, ever

__requiēscō__, __requiēscere__, __requiēvī__, __requiētum__ rest, find relief

__subitō__ (adv.) suddenly

__Syria__, __Syriae__ _f._ Syria

7. Caesar, *Dē Bellō Gallicō* I.1

Caesar begins his commentary on the Gallic war.

Gallia est omnis dīvīsa in partēs trēs; quārum ūnam incolunt Belgae, aliam Aquītānī, tertiam quī ipsōrum linguā Celtae, nostrā Gallī appellantur. Hī omnēs linguā, īnstitūtīs, lēgibus inter sē differunt. Gallōs ab Aquītānīs Garumna flūmen, ā Belgīs Matrona et Sēquana dīvidit. Hōrum omnium fortissimī sunt Belgae, proptereā quod ā cultū atque hūmānitāte prōvinciae longissimē absunt, minimēque ad eōs mercātōrēs saepe commeant atque ea, quae ad effēminandōs animōs pertinent, important; proximīque sunt Germānīs, quī trāns Rhēnum incolunt, quibuscum continenter bellum gerunt. Quā dē causā Helvētiī quoque reliquōs Gallōs virtūte praecēdunt, quod ferē cōtīdiānīs proeliīs cum Germānīs contendunt, cum aut suīs fīnibus eōs prohibent, aut ipsī in eōrum fīnibus bellum gerunt.

absum (ab- + sum), abesse, āfuī, āfutūrus be away from
appellō (1-tr.) name, call
Aquītānī, Aquītānōrum *m. pl.* (the) Aquitani
Belgae, Belgārum *m. pl.* (the) Belgae
Celtae, Celtārum *m. pl.* (the) Celts
commeō (1-intr.) go back and forth, travel
contendō, contendere, contendī, contentum struggle, strive
continenter (adv.) continuously
cōtīdiānus, -a, -um daily
cultus, cultūs *m.* cultivation; sophistication; luxury
dīvidō, dīvidere, dīvīsī, dīvīsus separate, divide
effēminō (1-tr.) emasculate, weaken
ferē (adv.) almost, nearly
flūmen, flūminis *n.* river, stream
Gallia, Galliae *f.* Gaul
Gallī, Gallōrum *m. pl.* (the) Gauls
Garumna, Garumnae *f.* (the) Garonne, a river in southwestern Gaul
Germānī, Germānōrum *m. pl.* (the) Germans
Helvētiī, Helvētiōrum *m. pl.* (the) Helvetii
hūmānitās, hūmānitātis *f.* (civilized) humanity; humaneness, kindness

importō (1-tr.) carry in, import
incolō, incolere, incoluī, —— inhabit; dwell, live
īnstitūtum, īnstitūtī *n.* custom, institution
lingua, linguae *f.* tongue; language
Matrona, Matronae *f.* (the) Marne, a river in north-central Gaul
mercātor, mercātōris *m.* trader, merchant
pertineō (per- + teneō), pertinēre, pertinuī, pertentus be aimed at, pertain; **pertinēre + ad + acc.**, to pertain to
praecēdō (prae- + cēdō) (tr.) excel, surpass
prohibeō (prō- + habeō), prohibēre, prohibuī, prohibitus prevent, keep off, exclude
proptereā (adv.) because of this; **proptereā quod**, because
proximus, -a, -um nearest
reliquus, -a, -um remaining, rest (of)
Rhēnus, Rhēnī *m.* (the) Rhine, a river in northeastern Gaul
Sēquana, Sēquanae *f.* (the) Seine, a river in northern Gaul
trāns (prep. + acc.) across

8. Vergil, *Aeneid* I.1-11

The proem of the *Aeneid*

Arma virumque canō, Troiae quī prīmus ab ōrīs
Ītaliam, fātō profugus, Lāvīnaque vēnit
lītora, multum ille et terrīs iactātus et altō
vī superum, saevae memorem Iūnōnis ob īram.
multa quoque et bellō passus, dum conderet urbem   5
īnferretque deōs Latiō; genus unde Latīnum
Albānīque patrēs atque altae moenia Rōmae.
Mūsa, mihī* causās memorā, quō nūmine laesō
quidve dolēns rēgīna deum tot volvere cāsūs
īnsignem pietāte virum, tot adīre labōrēs   10
impulerit. tantaene animīs caelestibus īrae?

*The final **-i** of **mihi** here scans *long*.

adeō (ad- + eō), adīre, adiī, aditum approach;
   encounter; undertake
Albānus, -a, -um Alban, of Alba Longa, a town in
   central Italy
caelestis, caeleste, heavenly, divine
condō, condere, condidī, conditus found
doleō, dolēre, doluī, —— suffer; grieve (over),
   feel pain (at)
iactō (1-tr.) throw, toss; harass, torment
impellō (in- + pellō), impellere, impulī, impulsus
   strike against, beat; impel, drive
īnsignis, īnsigne distinguished, remarkable
laedō, laedere, laesī, laesus injure, harm; offend
Latīnus, -a, -um Latin, of Latium, an area in
   central Italy
Latium, Latiī *n.* Latium, an area in central Italy
Lāvīnus, -a, -um Lavinian, of Lavinium, a town in
   central Italy

lītus, lītoris *n.* shore, beach
memor, memoris mindful, remembering
memorō (1-tr.) mention, recount, tell
Mūsa, Mūsae *f.* Muse
nūmen, nūminis *n.* divine power, divinity, divine
   spirit, numen
ōra, ōrae *f.* shore, coast
pietās, pietātis *f.* sense of duty, dutifulness,
   piety
profugus, -a, -um fugitive, fleeing; *as subst.*, exile;
   refugee
superī, superōrum *m. pl.* gods above; **superum**
   = **superōrum**
volvō, volvere, volvī, volūtus turn, turn over, roll;
   undergo
-ve (enclitic conj.) or

9. Vergil, *Aeneid* II.3–13

Addressing Dido, queen of Carthage, Aeneas begins his narrative of the fall of Troy.

īnfandum, rēgīna, iubēs renovāre dolōrem,

Troiānās ut* opēs et lāmentābile rēgnum

ēruerint Danaī, quaeque ipse miserrima vīdī   5

et quōrum pars magna fuī. quis tālia fandō

Myrmidonum Dolopumve aut dūrī mīles Ulīxī

temperet ā lacrimīs? et iam nox ūmida caelō

praecipitat suādentque cadentia sīdera somnōs.

sed sī tantus amor cāsūs cognōscere nostrōs   10

et breviter Troiae suprēmum audīre labōrem,

quamquam animus meminisse horret lūctūque refūgit,

incipiam. . . .

***ut**, *here* (interrog adv.), how
Danaī, Danaōrum *m. pl.* Danaans, Greeks
Dolopes, Dolopum *m. pl.* (the) Dolopes, a Greek
  people from Thessaly
dolor, dolōris *m.* grief, sorrow, pain
ēruō, ēruere, ēruī, ērutus uproot; destroy utterly
for (1-tr.) speak, utter
**horreō, horrēre, horruī, —— ** stand up, bristle;
  tremble, shudder
īnfandus, -a, -um unspeakable
lacrima, lacrimae *f.* tear
lāmentābilis, lāmentābile lamentable, arousing
  lamentation
lūctus, lūctūs *m.* mourning
Myrmidones, Mymidonum *m. pl.* (the) Myrmi-
  dons, a people of Thessaly, followers of
  Achilles
ops, opis *f.* power; *in pl.*, power, resources,
  wealth

praecipitō (1-tr.) throw *or* hurl headlong; *intr.*,
  fall headlong, plunge
refugiō (re- + fugiō), (turn and) flee, run away;
  recoil
rēgnum, rēgnī *n.* kingdom, realm
renovō (1-tr.) restore, renew, refresh, revive
sīdus, sīderis *n.* star
somnus, somnī *m.* sleep
suādeō, suādēre, suāsī, suāsus recommend,
  urge, advise
suprēmus, -a, -um final, last
temperō (1-tr.) restrain, hold back, refrain
Troiānus, -a, -um Trojan
Ulīxēs, Ulīxī *m.* Ulysses (Odysseus)
ūmidus, -a, -um wet, moist; rainy
-ve (enclitic conj.) or

10. Horace, *Carmina* I.22 (Sapphic strophe)

The poet has special protection from dangers.

Integer vītae scelerisque pūrus
nōn eget Maurīs iaculīs neque arcū
nec venēnātīs gravidā sagittīs,
    Fusce, pharetrā,

sīve per Syrtīs iter aestuōsās   5
sīve factūrus per inhospitālem
Caucasum vel quae loca fābulōsus
    lambit Hydaspēs.

namque mē silvā lupus in Sabīnā,
dum meam cantō Lalagēn et ultrā   10
terminum cūrīs vagor expedītīs,
    fūgit inermem,

aestuōsus, -a, -um full of heat, burning,
    very hot
arcus, arcūs *m.* bow
cantō (1-tr.) sing (of)
Caucasus, Caucasī *m.* (the) Caucasus mountains
egeō, egēre, eguī, —— lack, want, need (+ abl.)
expediō, expedīre, expedīvī or expediī, expedītus
    let loose, set free; fetch out, unpack
fābulōsus, -a, -um full of fables; celebrated in
    fable
Fuscus, Fuscī *m.* Fuscus, addressee of the poem
gravidus, -a, -um heavy, laden
Hydaspēs, Hydaspis *m.* (the) Hydaspes, a tribu-
    tary of the Indus River
iaculum, iaculī *n.* javelin
inermis, inerme unarmed, defenseless
inhospitālis, inhospitāle inhospitable
integer, integra, integrum untouched, whole;
    sound; blameless, virtuous
iter, itineris *n.* journey
Lalagē, f. Lalage; Lalagēn = *acc. sing.*

lambō, lambere, ——, —— lick, lap
lupus, lupī *m.* wolf
Maurus, -a, -um Moorish, Moroccan
pharetra, pharetrae *f.* quiver
pūrus, -a, -um clean, pure, unstained
Sabīnus, -a, -um Sabine (of a territory and people
    northeast of Rome)
sagitta, sagittae *f.* arrow
silva, silvae *f.* forest
sīve (conj.) or if; sīve . . . sīve . . . whether . . .
    or if . . .
Syrtis, Syrtis, -ium *f. in sing. or pl.*, Syrtis, the
    name of a sandbar on the coast between
    Carthage and Cyrene
terminus, terminī *m.* boundary line, boundary,
    limit
ultrā (prep. + acc.) beyond, past, over, across
vagor (1-intr.) wander
vel (conj.) or
venēnātus, -a, -um filled with poison, poisonous

quāle portentum neque mīlitāris
Dauniās lātīs alit aesculētīs
nec Iubae tellūs generat, leōnum   15
    ārida nūtrīx.

pōne mē pigrīs ubi nūlla campīs
arbor aestīvā recreātur aurā,
quod latus mundī nebulae malusque
    Iuppiter urget,   20

pōne sub currū nimium propinquī
sōlis, in terrā domibus negātā:
dulce rīdentem Lalagēn amābō,
    dulce loquentem.

aesculētum, aesculētī *n.* oak forest
aestīvus, -a, -um of summer
alō, alere, aluī, al(i)tus feed, nourish, support
arbor, arboris *f.* tree
āridus, -a, -um dry; parched
aura, aurae *f.* breeze
currus, currūs *m.* chariot
Dauniās *fem. sing. nom. of adj. used substantively,*
    Daunia, Apulia, a province of southeast Italy
dulce (adv.) sweetly, pleasantly
generō (1-tr.) beget, create, produce
Iuba, Iubae *m.* Juba, a Numidian king
Lalagē, Lalagēs *f.* Lalage; **Lalagēn** = *acc. sing.*
lātus, -a, -um broad, wide
latus, lateris *n.* side, flank
leō, leōnis *m.* lion

mīlitāris, mīlitāre military; warlike
mundus, mundī *m.* universe, world
nebula, nebulae *f.* mist, fog, cloud
negō (1-tr.) deny
nimium (adv.) too much, excessively
nūtrīx, nūtrīcis *f.* nurse
piger, pigra, pigrum sluggish, inactive;
    unfruitful
portentum, portentī *n.* sign, omen, portent
propinquus, -a, -um near, close
recreō (1-tr.) revive, refresh
rīdeō, rīdēre, rīsī, rīsus smile, laugh
sōl, sōlis *m.* sun
tellūs, tellūris *f.* earth, land
urgeō, urgēre, ursī, —— weigh down; press
    hard; threaten

11. Horace, *Ars Poētica* 136–55

The poet gives advice about poetic beginnings to the potential writer.

nec sīc incipiēs, ut scrīptor cyclicus ōlim:

"Fortūnam Priamī cantābō et nōbile bellum."

quid dignum tantō feret hic prōmissor hiātū?

parturient montēs, nāscētur rīdiculus mūs.

quantō rēctius hic, quī nīl mōlītur ineptē: 140

"Dīc mihi, Mūsa, virum, captae post tempora Troiae

quī mōrēs hominum multōrum vīdit et urbēs."

nōn fūmum ex fulgōre, sed ex fūmō dare* lūcem

cōgitat† ut speciōsa dehinc mīrācula prōmat,

Antiphatēn Scyllamque et cum Cyclōpe Charybdim;   145

nec reditum Diomēdis ab interitū Meleagrī

nec geminō bellum Troiānum ordītur ab ōvō:

semper ad ēventum festīnat et in mediās rēs

nōn secus ac nōtās‡ audītōrem rapit et quae

***dō**, *here,* bring forward, produce

†**cōgitō**, *here,* have in mind, plan (+ inf.)

‡**nōtus, -a, -um** well-known, famous, familiar

Antiphatēs, Antiphatae *m.* Antiphates, king of the Laestrygones, who tried to kill Odysseus

audītor, audītōris *m.* hearer, listener

cantō (1-tr.) sing (of)

Charybdis, Charybdis *m.* Charybdis, a whirlpool; **Charybdim** = *acc. sing.*

cyclicus, -a, -um of the epic cycle of poems, cyclic

Cyclōps, Cyclōpos or **Cyclōpis** *m.* (the) Cyclops (Polyphemus)

dehinc (adv.) after this, later, at a later stage

Diomēdēs, Diomēdis *m.* Diomedes, one of the Greek heroes at Troy

ēventus, ēventūs *m.* outcome, denouement

festīnō (1-intr.) hasten, proceed swiftly

fulgor, fulgōris *m.* brightness, radiance, splendor

fūmus, fūmī *m.* smoke, fumes

geminus, -a, -um twin-born, twin

hiātus, hiātūs *m.* gaping, (wide) opening, chasm

ineptē (adv.) improperly, inappropriately

interitus, interitūs *m.* death, demise

Meleager, Meleagrī *m.* Meleager, whose story is told by Phoenix in the *Iliad*

mīrāculum, mīrāculī *n.* amazing object, marvel, wonder

mōlior, mōlīrī, mōlītus sum plan, set in motion, begin

mūs, mūris *m.* mouse

Mūsa, Mūsae *f.* Muse

nōbilis, nōbile noble; remarkable; well known, famous

ōlim (adv.) once, formerly

ordior, ordīrī, orsus sum embark on, begin (to speak or write of)

ōvum, ōvī *n.* egg

parturiō, parturīre, parturīvī, —— be pregnant with, be in labor

Priamus, Priamī *m.* Priam, king of Troy

prōmissor, prōmissōris *m.* promiser, guarantor

prōmō, prōmere, prōmpsī, prōmptus bring forth, bring into view

rapiō, rapere, rapuī, raptus tear away, carry off; snatch up

rēctē rightly, correctly

reditus, reditūs *m.* return; homecoming

rīdiculus, -a, -um laughable, silly, ridiculous

scrīptor, scrīptōris *m.* writer

Scylla, Scyllae *f.* Scylla, a sea monster

secus (adv.) otherwise, differently; **nōn secus ac** not differently than, exactly as if

speciōsus, -a, -um attractive; spectacular, splendid

Troiānus, -a, -um Trojan

dēspērat tractāta nitēscere posse relinquit   150

atque ita mentītur, sīc vērīs falsa remiscet,

prīmō nē medium, mediō nē discrepet īmum.

tū, quid ego et populus mēcum dēsīderet audī,

sī plausōris egēs aulaea manentis et ūsque

sessūrī dōnec cantor "vōs plaudite" dīcat.   155

aulaeum, aulaeī *n.* curtain (of a theater)
cantor, cantōris *m.* singer (the person playing and singing the musical parts of a play)
dēsīderō (1-tr.) long for, desire
dēspērō (dē- + spērō) (1-tr.) despair (of)
discrepō, discrepāre, discrepuī or **discrepāvī,** ——— be out of harmony (with)
egeō, egēre, eguī, ——— be needy, lack, need (+ gen.)
īmus, -a, -um lowest, bottom (of); last, final
mentior, mentīrī, mentītus sum lie, tell a lie

nitēscō, nitēscere, ——, —— begin to shine, become bright
plaudō, plaudere, plausī, plausus clap the hands, applaud
plausor, plausōris *m.* one who applauds
remisceō, remiscēre, ——, **remixtus** mix
sedeō, sedēre, sēdī, sessūrus sit, be seated
tractō (1-tr.) keep on dragging; deal with, discuss, treat
ūsque (adv.) continuously

12. Propertius I.1–8

The poet describes how he came to be in love with Cynthia.

Cynthia prīma suīs miserum mē cēpit ocellīs,

    contāctum nūllīs ante cupīdinibus.

tum mihi cōnstantis dēiēcit lūmina fastūs

    et caput impositīs pressit Amor pedibus,

dōnec mē docuit castās ōdisse puellās   5

    improbus et nūllō vīvere cōnsiliō.

ei mihi, iam tōtō furor hic nōn dēficit annō,

    cum tamen adversōs cōgor habēre deōs.

adversus, -a, -um opposite, hostile, adverse
caput, capitis *n.* head
castus, -a, -um chaste
cōgō (cō- + agō), cōgere, coēgī, coāctus drive together, force, compel
cōnstāns, cōnstantis firm, constant
contingō, contingere, contigī, contāctus touch
cupīdō, cupīdinis *f.* desire
dēficiō (dē- + faciō) let down, fail; subside
dēiciō (dē- + iaciō) throw down, cast down

doceō, docēre, docuī, doctus teach
ei (interj.) alas!
fastus, fastūs *m.* pride, haughtiness, arrogance
furor, furōris *m.* madness; passion
impōnō (in- + pōnō) place *or* impose (on)
improbus, -a, -um wicked, shameless; relentless
ocellus, ocellī *m.* (little) eye
pēs, pedis *m.* foot
premō, premere, pressī, pressus press (hard); overpower

13. Propertius II.12

The poet ponders the artistic depiction of Love.

Quīcumque ille fuit, puerum quī pīnxit Amōrem,
    nōnne putās mīrās hunc habuisse manūs?
is prīmum vīdit sine sēnsū vīvere amantēs,
    et levibus cūrīs magna perīre bona.
īdem nōn frūstrā ventōsās addidit ālās,   5
    fēcit et* hūmānō corde volāre deum:
scīlicet alternā quoniam iactāmur in undā,
    nostraque nōn ūllīs permanet aura locīs.
et meritō hāmātīs manus est armāta sagittīs,
    et pharetra ex umerō Cnōsia utrōque† iacet: 10
ante ferit quoniam tūtī quam cernimus hostem,
    nec quisquam ex illō vulnere sānus abit.
in mē tēla manent, manet et puerīlis imāgō:
    sed certē pennās perdidit ille suās;
ēvolat heu nostrō quoniam dē pectore nusquam,   15
    assiduusque meō sanguine bella gerit.

*et in poetry is frequently placed in the position
  of -que.
†utrōque = *masc. sing. abl. of indef. adj.,* each
  (of two)
addō (ad- + dō) add
āla, ālae *f.* wing
alternus, -a, -um alternating
armō (1-tr.) equip (with arms), arm
assiduus, -a, -um continually present, busy;
  diligent, persistent
aura, aurae *f.* breeze
cernō, cernere, crēvī, crētus distinguish; perceive
Cnōsius, -a, -um of Cnossos, the ancient capital
  of Crete; Cretan
cor, cordis *n.* heart
ēvolō (1-intr.) fly out
feriō, ferīre, ——, —— strike, hit
frūstrā (adv.) in vain
hāmātus, -a, -um hooked, barbed
hūmānus, -a, -um human
iaceō, iacēre, iacuī, —— lie, rest; hang
iactō (1-tr.) throw, toss; harass, torment
imāgō, imāginis *f.* image, likeness
meritō (adv.) deservedly, with good reason

mīrus, -a, -um marvelous
nusquam (adv.) nowhere; on no occasion
penna, pennae *f.* wing
permaneō (per- + maneō) stay, remain; last long,
  endure
pharetra, pharetrae *f.* quiver
pingō, pingere, pīnxī, pictus paint, represent,
  depict
puerīlis, puerīle boyish, youthful
quīcumque = *masc. sing. nom. of indef. pron.,*
  whoever
quisquam = *masc./fem. sing. nom. of indef. pron.,*
  anyone
sagitta, sagittae *f.* arrow
sanguis, sanguinis *m.* blood
sānus, -a, -um healthy, sane
scīlicet (adv.) of course, no doubt, obviously
tūtus, -a, -um safe
umerus, umerī *m.* shoulder
unda, undae *f.* wave
ventōsus, -a, -um windy, full of wind; light,
  nimble
volō (1-intr.) fly

quid tibi iūcundumst siccīs habitāre medullīs?
sī pudor est, aliō* trāice tēla, puer!
intāctōs istō satius temptāre venēnō:
nōn ego, sed tenuis vāpulat umbra mea.
quam sī perdideris, quis erit quī tālia cantet,
(haec mea Mūsa levis glōria magna tuast),
quī caput et digitōs et lūmina nigra puellae
et canat ut† soleant molliter īre pedēs?

*aliō, *here* (adv.) to another place, elsewhere
†ut, *here* (interrog. adv.) how
cantō (1-tr.) sing (of)
caput, **capitis** *n.* head
digitus, **digitī** *m.* finger
habitō (1-intr.) dwell, live; stay, remain
intāctus, **-a**, **-um** untouched, uninjur
iūcundus, **-a**, **-um** pleasing, delig
medulla, **medullae** *f.* bone ma
innards
molliter (adv.) gently, s
Mūsa, **Mūsae** *f.* Mu
niger, **nigra**, **nig**

pēs

15. Ovid, *Metamorphōsēs* XIII.361–69

Odysseus boasts to Ajax, his rival for Achilles' armor, about the differences between them.

. . . tibi dextera bellō
ūtilis, ingenium est quod eget moderāmine nostrō;
tū vīrēs sine mente geris, mihi cūra futūrī;
tū pugnāre potes, pugnandī tempora mēcum
ēligit Atrīdēs; tū tantum corpore prōdes,
nōs animō; quantōque ratem quī temperat anteit[4]
rēmigis officium, quantō dux mīlite maior,
tantum ego tē superō. nec nōn* in corpore nostrō
pectora† sunt potiōra manū: vigor omnis in illīs.

*nec nōn, *here*, likewise
†pectora, *here*, intellectual faculties
anteeō (**ante-** + **eō**), **anteīre**, **anteiī** or **anteīvī**, —— go before; be better than, surpass
Atrīdēs, **Atrīdae** *m.* son of Atreus (either Agamemnon or Menelaus)
dexter, **dextra**, **dextrum** right; *as fem. subst.* (*sc.* **manus**) right hand; **dextera** = **dextra**
egeō, **egēre**, **eguī**, —— need, lack (+ abl.)
ēligō (**ē-** + **legō**), **ēligere**, **ēlēgī**, **ēlēctus** select, choose
moderāmen, **moderāminis** *n.* control, guidance
officium, **officiī** *n.* obligation; duty, task
potior, **potius** more powerful; more precious
prōsum (**prō-** + **sum**), **prōdesse**, **prōfuī**, **prōfutūrus** be helpful, be of use, be good (fo
prōdes = *2nd sing. pres. act. indic.*
ratis, **ratis**, **-ium** *f.* boat, ship
rēmex, **rēmigis** *m.* oarsman, rower
temperō (1-tr.) restrain, hold back, cont
ūtilis, **ūtile** useful
vigor, **vigōris** *m.* liveliness, activity, v

4. The short vowels **-e-** and **-i-** of **anteit**

365

13. Propertius II.12

The poet ponders the artistic depiction of Love.

Quīcumque ille fuit, puerum quī pīnxit Amōrem,
    nōnne putās mīrās hunc habuisse manūs?
is prīmum vīdit sine sēnsū vīvere amantēs,
    et levibus cūrīs magna perīre bona.
īdem nōn frūstrā ventōsās addidit ālās,   5
    fēcit et* hūmānō corde volāre deum:
scīlicet alternā quoniam iactāmur in undā,
    nostraque nōn ūllīs permanet aura locīs.
et meritō hāmātīs manus est armāta sagittīs,
    et pharetra ex umerō Cnōsia utrōque† iacet: 10
ante ferit quoniam tūtī quam cernimus hostem,
    nec quisquam ex illō vulnere sānus abit.
in mē tēla manent, manet et puerīlis imāgō:
    sed certē pennās perdidit ille suās;
ēvolat heu nostrō quoniam dē pectore nusquam,   15
    assiduusque meō sanguine bella gerit.

*et in poetry is frequently placed in the position of -que.

†utrōque = *masc. sing. abl. of indef. adj.,* each (of two)

addō (**ad-** + **dō**) add
āla, ālae *f.* wing
alternus, -a, -um alternating
armō (1-tr.) equip (with arms), arm
assiduus, -a, -um continually present, busy; diligent, persistent
aura, aurae *f.* breeze
cernō, cernere, crēvī, crētus distinguish; perceive
Cnōsius, -a, -um of Cnossos, the ancient capital of Crete; Cretan
cor, cordis *n.* heart
ēvolō (1-intr.) fly out
feriō, ferīre, ——, —— strike, hit
frūstrā (adv.) in vain
hāmātus, -a, -um hooked, barbed
hūmānus, -a, -um human
iaceō, iacēre, iacuī, —— lie, rest; hang
iactō (1-tr.) throw, toss; harass, torment
imāgō, imāginis *f.* image, likeness
meritō (adv.) deservedly, with good reason

mīrus, -a, -um marvelous
nusquam (adv.) nowhere; on no occasion
penna, pennae *f.* wing
permaneō (**per-** + **maneō**) stay, remain; last long, endure
pharetra, pharetrae *f.* quiver
pingō, pingere, pīnxī, pictus paint, represent, depict
puerīlis, puerīle boyish, youthful
quīcumque = *masc. sing. nom. of indef. pron.,* whoever
quisquam = *masc./fem. sing. nom. of indef. pron.,* anyone
sagitta, sagittae *f.* arrow
sanguis, sanguinis *m.* blood
sānus, -a, -um healthy, sane
scīlicet (adv.) of course, no doubt, obviously
tūtus, -a, -um safe
umerus, umerī *m.* shoulder
unda, undae *f.* wave
ventōsus, -a, -um windy, full of wind; light, nimble
volō (1-intr.) fly

quid tibi iūcundumst siccīs habitāre medullīs?

si pudor est, aliō* trāice tēla, puer!

intāctōs istō satius temptāre venēnō:

nōn ego, sed tenuis vāpulat umbra mea.   20

quam sī perdideris, quis erit quī tālia cantet,

(haec mea Mūsa levis glōria magna tuast),

quī caput et digitōs et lūmina nigra puellae

et canat ut† soleant molliter īre pedēs?

*aliō, *here* (adv.) to another place, elsewhere
†ut, *here* (interrog. adv.) how
cantō (1-tr.) sing (of)
caput, capitis *n.* head
digitus, digitī *m.* finger
habitō (1-intr.) dwell, live; stay, remain
intāctus, -a, -um untouched, uninjured; untried
iūcundus, -a, -um pleasing, delightful, agreeable
medulla, medullae *f.* bone marrow; *in pl.,* vitals,
    innards
molliter (adv.) gently, softly, mildly
Mūsa, Mūsae *f.* Muse
niger, nigra, nigrum dark, black

pēs, pedis *m.* foot
pudor, pudōris *m.* shame, decency, modesty
satius more satisfying, better; **satius** = *neut. sing.*
    nom.
siccus, -a, -um dry
temptō (1-tr.) touch; try, test; attack, assail
tenuis, tenue thin, meager, slight; poor, insig-
    nificant
trāiciō (**trāns-** + **iaciō**) pierce; shoot
vāpulō, vāpulāre, vāpulāvī, —— be beaten,
    be flogged
venēnum, venēnī *n.* poison

14. Propertius II.15.31–40

After a night of passion, the poet declares that he will love Cynthia come what may.

terra prius falsō partū dēlūdet arantīs,

   et citius nigrōs Sōl agitābit equōs,

flūminaque ad caput incipient revocāre liquōrēs,

   āridus et* siccō gurgite piscis erit,

quam possim nostrōs aliō† trānsferre dolōrēs: 35

   huius erō vīvus, mortuus huius erō.

quod‡ mihi sī‡ interdum tālīs concēdere noctēs

   illa velit, vītae longus et annus erit.

sī dabit et multās, fīam immortālis in illīs:

   nocte ūnā quīvīs vel deus esse potest.   40

*et in poetry is frequently placed in the position
   of -que.
†aliō, here (adv.) to another place, elsewhere
‡quod . . . sī but if
agitō (1-tr.) stir up, set in motion; drive
āridus, -a, -um dry; parched
arō (1-tr.) plough, till
caput, capitis n. head; source
citius (adv.) more quickly
concēdō (con- + cēdō) (tr.) concede, grant
dēlūdō, dēlūdere, dēlūsī, dēlūsus play false,
   mock, deceive
dolor, dolōris m. grief, sorrow, pain
equus, equī m. horse
flūmen, flūminis n. river, stream
gurges, gurgitis m. swirling water, eddy,
   whirlpool

immortālis, immortāle immortal
interdum (adv.) from time to time, occasionally
liquor, liquōris m. fluid, liquid; water
niger, nigra, nigrum dark, black
partus, partūs m. birth; offspring; crop
piscis, piscis, -ium m. fish
quīvīs = masc. sing. nom. of indef. pron., anyone
   you wish, anyone at all
revocō (1-tr.) call back
siccus, -a, -um dry
Sōl, Sōlis m. Sun
trānsferō (trāns- + ferō), trānsferre, trānstulī,
   trānslātus carry across, transfer
vel (adv.) even
vīvus, -a, -um living, alive

15. Ovid, *Metamorphōsēs* XIII.361–69

Odysseus boasts to Ajax, his rival for Achilles' armor, about the differences between them.

. . . tibi dextera bellō

ūtilis, ingenium est quod eget moderāmine nostrō;

tū vīrēs sine mente geris, mihi cūra futūrī;

tū pugnāre potes, pugnandī tempora mēcum

ēligit Atrīdēs; tū tantum corpore prōdes,   365

nōs animō; quantōque ratem quī temperat anteit[4]

rēmigis officium, quantō dux mīlite maior,

tantum ego tē superō. nec nōn* in corpore nostrō

pectora† sunt potiōra manū: vigor omnis in illīs.

*nec nōn, *here,* likewise
†pectora, *here,* intellectual faculties
anteeō (ante- + eō), anteīre, anteiī or anteīvī,
—— go before; be better than, surpass
Atrīdēs, Atrīdae *m.* son of Atreus (either
Agamemnon or Menelaus)
dexter, dextra, dextrum right; *as fem. subst.*
(*sc.* manus) right hand; dextera = dextra
egeō, egēre, eguī, —— need, lack (+ abl.)
ēligō (ē- + legō), ēligere, ēlēgī, ēlēctus select,
choose

moderāmen, moderāminis *n.* control, guidance
officium, officiī *n.* obligation; duty, task
potior, potius more powerful; more precious
prōsum (prō- + sum), prōdesse, prōfuī,
prōfutūrus be helpful, be of use, be good (for);
prōdes = *2nd sing. pres. act. indic.*
ratis, ratis, -ium *f.* boat, ship
rēmex, rēmigis *m.* oarsman, rower
temperō (1-tr.) restrain, hold back; control
ūtilis, ūtile useful
vigor, vigōris *m.* liveliness, activity, vigor

4. The short vowels -e- and -i- of **anteit** are pronounced as the diphthong -ei-.

16. Ovid, *Trīstia* III.7.45–52

The poet in exile predicts his own fate.

ēn ego, cum patriā caream vōbīsque* domōque,   45

    raptaque sint adimī quae potuēre mihi,

ingeniō tamen ipse meō comitorque fruorque:

    Caesar in† hoc potuit iūris habēre nihil.

quīlibet hanc saevō vītam mihi fīniat ēnse,

    mē tamen extīnctō fāma superstes erit,   50

dumque suīs victrīx septem dē montibus orbem

    prōspiciet domitum Martia Rōma, legar.

*vōbīs refers to all Ovid's friends and acquain-
   tances in Rome.

†in, *here*, over

adimō, adimere, adēmī, adēmptus remove, take
   away

comitō (1-tr.) accompany, attend

domō, domāre, domuī, domitus subdue, tame

ēn (interj.) behold! look!

ēnsis, ēnsis *m.* sword

ex(s)tinguō, ex(s)tinguere, ex(s)tīnxī,
   ex(s)tīnctus extinguish; annihilate, kill

fīniō, fīnīre, fīnīvī or **fīniī, fīnītus** define; end,
   finish

fruor, fruī, frūctus sum enjoy, delight in (+ abl.)

Martius, -a, -am of *or* belonging to Mars, Martial

orbis, orbis, -ium *m.* ring, circle; world

prōspiciō, prōspicere, prōspexī, prōspectus
   survey, watch over, look out over

quīlibet = *masc. sing. nom. of indef. pron.,*
   anyone (it pleases)

rapiō, rapere, rapuī, raptus tear away, carry off

superstes, superstitis remaining alive, surviving

victrīx, victrīcis *f.* conqueror, victor

17. Livy, *Ab Urbe Conditā* I.56.9

The last princes of the Tarquins went to Delphi, the seat of Apollo's oracle, in order to ask a question on behalf of their father. They took with them a lowly Roman, M. Brutus. The historian describes a surprising turn of events.

is* tum ab Tarquiniīs ductus Delphōs, lūdibrium vērius quam comes, aureum baculum inclūsum corneō cavātō ad id baculō tulisse dōnum Apollinī dīcitur, per ambāgēs effigiem ingeniī suī. quō postquam ventum est, perfectīs patris mandātīs cupīdō incessit animōs iuvenum scīscitandī ad quem eōrum rēgnum Rōmānum esset ventūrum. ex īnfimō specū vōcem redditam ferunt: imperium summum Rōmae habēbit quī vestrum prīmus, ō iuvenēs, ōsculum mātrī tulerit. Tarquiniī, ut Sextus, quī Rōmae relictus fuerat,† ignārus respōnsī‡ expersque imperiī esset, rem summā ope tacērī iubent;§ ipsī inter sē uter prior, cum Rōmam redīsset, mātrī ōsculum daret, sortī permittunt.§ Brūtus aliō¶ ratus spectāre Pȳthicam vōcem, velut sī prōlāpsus cecidisset, terram ōsculō contigit, scīlicet quod ea commūnis māter omnium mortālium esset.

*is refers to M. Brutus

†relictus fuerat = relictus erat

‡respōnsum, respōnsī *n.* answer, response

§iubent, permittunt, historical use of present tense; translate as perfect

¶aliō, *here* (adv.), elsewhere, to another place, in another direction

ambāgēs, ambāgum *f. pl.* roundabout path

aureus, -a, -um golden, made of gold

baculum, baculī *n.* staff, walking stick

Brūtus, Brūtī *m.* (M.) Brutus, legendary hero of early Rome

cavō (1-tr.) hollow out, make hollow

comes, comitis *m.* or *f.* companion, comrade

commūnis, commūne common, shared; held in common

contingō, contingere, contigī, contāctus touch

corneus, -a, -um made of cornel wood

cupīdō, cupīdinis *f.* desire

Delphī, Delphōrum *m. pl.* Delphi

effigiēs, effigiēī *f.* representation, statue; symbol

expers, expertis having no part (of)

ignārus, -a, -um not knowing, unaware

incēdō (in- + cēdō) (tr.) go in, enter; arise, come over

inclūdō, inclūdere, inclūsī, inclūsus enclose, seal

īnfimus, -a, -um lowest, deepest, lowest part (of), depths (of)

iuvenis, iuvenis *m.* young man

lūdibrium, lūdibriī *n.* plaything, toy; laughingstock

mandātum, mandātī *n.* order, instruction

mortālis, mortāle mortal

ops, opis *f.* power, ability, might, effort

ōsculum, ōsculī *n.* kiss

permittō (per- + mittō) entrust, commit

prōlābor, prōlābī, prōlāpsus sum slide *or* slip forward, slip down

Pȳthicus, -a, -um of Pytho (the oracle at Delphi), Pythian, Delphic

reor, rērī, ratus sum believe, think, imagine

reddō (red- + dō) give back, return

rēgnum, rēgnī *n.* kingdom, realm; kingship, rule

scīlicet (adv.) of course, no doubt, obviously

scīscitor (1-tr.) try to get to know by asking, inquire

Sextus, Sextī *m.* Sextus (Tarquinius), one of the sons of Tarquinius Superbus, last king of Rome

sors, sortis, -ium *f.* lot, portion; destiny

spectō (1-tr.) look (at), observe; face, point

specus, specūs *m.* cave, grotto, abyss, hollow

taceō, tacēre, tacuī, tacitūrus be silent, keep silent; leave unmentioned

Tarquinius, Tarquiniī *m.* Tarquinius, any male member of the Tarquin family

velut (conj.) even as, just as

18. Livy, *Ab Urbe Conditā* XXII.49.5

In 216 B.C.E. at Cannae in southern Italy, the Romans suffered one of their greatest military defeats in a battle against Hannibal and his Carthaginian army. In a single day most of the fifty thousand Romans who fought were killed. In the following passage Livy describes a meeting between L. Aemilius Paulus, one of the consuls in charge, and Cn. Lentulus, a military tribune. The final vestiges of the Roman army are being routed.

pepulērunt* tamen iam paucōs superantēs† et labōre ac volneribus fessōs. inde dissipātī omnēs sunt, equōsque ad fugam quī poterant repetēbant. Cn. Lentulus tribūnus mīlitum cum praetervehēns equō sedentem in saxō, cruōre opplētum, cōnsulem vīdisset, "L. Aemilī," inquit, "quem ūnum īnsontem culpae clādis hodiernae deī respicere dēbent, cape hunc equum, dum et tibi vīrium aliquid superest et comes ego tē tollere possum ac prōtegere. nē fūnestam hanc pugnam morte cōnsulis fēceris; etiam sine hōc lacrimārum satis lūctūsque est."

*pepulērunt, subject is the Carthaginians
†superō, *here,* survive; superantēs, *sc.* Rōmānōs
L. Aemilius, L. Aemiliī *m.* L. Aemilius (Paulus) (consul 216 B.C.E.), one of the Roman leaders at the disastrous battle of Cannae
aliquid = *neut. sing. nom. of indef. pron.,* something
clādēs, clādis, -ium *f.* slaughter, destruction
comes, comitis *m. or f.* companion, comrade
cruor, cruōris *m.* (fresh) blood, gore
culpa, culpae *f.* guilt, blame
dissipō (1-tr.) disperse, scatter
equus, equī *m.* horse
fessus, -a, -um weary, exhausted, worn out
fūnestus, -a, -um lamentable, grievous; polluted
hodiernus, -a, -um of this day, today's
inde (adv.) from there; thereupon, then
inquam (defective verb) say; inquit = *3rd sing. pres. act. indic.*
īnsōns, īnsontis innocent, not guilty
lacrima, lacrimae *f.* tear

Cn. Lentulus, Cn. Lentulī *m.* Cn. (Cornelius) Lentulus
lūctus, lūctūs *m.* mourning
oppleō, opplēre, opplēvī, opplētus fill completely, fill up; cover completely
praetervehō, praetervehere, praetervexī, praetervectus travel past, pass by
prōtegō, prōtegere, prōtēxī, prōtēctus cover, protect
pugna, pugnae *f.* fight, battle
repetō (re- + petō) seek again, get back
respiciō, respicere, respexī, respectus look back at; show concern for; regard
saxum, saxī *n.* rock, stone
sedeō, sedēre, sēdī, sessūrus sit, be seated
supersum (super- + sum), superesse, superfuī, —— remain, be left, survive
tollō, tollere, sustulī, sublātus lift, raise; take away, carry off
tribūnus, tribūnī *m.* tribune, military commander

19. Livy, *Ab Urbe Conditā* XXXVIII.23.1

In 278 B.C.E. many Gauls had migrated to Asia Minor. Livy reports the terror of the Gauls after the Romans break into their camp during the Macedonian wars in 189.

patentibus iam portīs, priusquam irrumperent victōrēs, fuga ē castrīs Gallōrum in omnēs partēs facta est. ruunt caecī per viās, per invia; nūlla praecipitia saxa, nūllae rūpēs obstant; nihil praeter hostem metuunt; itaque plērīque praecipitēs per vāstam altitūdinem prōlāpsī aut dēbilitātī exanimantur. cōnsul captīs castrīs dīreptiōne praedāque abstinet mīlitem; . . .

abstineō (abs- + teneō), abstinēre, abstinuī, abstentus hold back, restrain
altitūdō, altitūdinis *f.* height
dēbilitō (1-tr.) weaken
dīreptiō, dīreptiōnis *f.* plundering, pillaging
exanimō (1-tr.) deprive of life, kill
Gallī, Gallōrum *m. pl.* (the) Gauls
invius, -a, -um impassable; **invia,** *sc.* **loca**
irrumpō, irrumpere, irrūpī, irruptus break in, burst in
itaque (conj.) and so, accordingly
metuō, metuere, metuī, —— fear, dread
obstō (ob- + stō), obstāre, obstitī, obstātum stand in the way

pateō, patēre, patuī, —— lie open
plērīque, plēraeque, plēraque very many, most
porta, portae *f.* gate
praeceps, praecipitis precipitous, steep; rushing forward, headlong
praeda, praedae *f.* booty, plunder
prōlābor, prōlābī, prōlāpsus sum fall forward
ruō, ruere, ruī, rutūrus rush
rūpēs, rūpis, -ium *f.* cliff, crag
saxum, saxī *n.* rock, stone
vāstus, -a, -um immense, vast
victor, victōris *m.* conqueror, victor

20. Seneca the Younger, *Epistulae Mōrālēs* CVII.9

After stating that the law of nature is a continuous alternation of good and bad things, the philosopher suggests the proper human response.

ad hanc lēgem animus noster aptandus est; hanc sequātur. huic pāreat. et quae-cumque fīunt, dēbuisse fierī putet nec velit obiurgāre nātūram. optimum est patī quod ēmendāre nōn possīs, et deum, quō auctōre cūncta prōveniunt, sine mur-murātiōne comitārī; malus mīles est quī imperātōrem gemēns sequitur.

aptō (1-tr.) fit, adapt, attune
auctor, auctōris *m.* source, author
comitor (1-tr.) accompany, attend
cūnctus, -a, -um all
ēmendō (1-tr.) correct; remedy, cure
gemō, gemere, gemuī, gemitum groan, moan

murmurātiō, murmurātiōnis *f.* grumbling, muttering
obiurgō (1-tr.) find fault with, reprimand
prōveniō (prō- + veniō) come forth, emerge, arise
quaecumque = *neut. pl. nom. of indef. pron.,* whatever things

Continuous Readings

1. Cicero, *In Catilīnam* I 13–14

quid est enim, Catilīna, quod tē iam in hāc urbe dēlectāre possit? in quā nēmō est,
extrā istam coniūrātiōnem perditōrum hominum, quī tē nōn metuat, nēmō quī nōn
ōderit. quae nota domesticae turpitūdinis nōn inusta vītae tuae est? quod prīvātārum
rērum dēdecus nōn haeret in fāmā? quae libīdō ab oculīs, quod facinus ā manibus
umquam tuīs, quod flāgitium ā tōtō corpore āfuit? cui tū adulēscentulō quem cor-
ruptēlārum inlecebrīs inrētissēs nōn aut ad audāciam ferrum aut ad libīdinem facem
praetulistī?* quid vērō? nūper cum morte superiōris uxōris novīs nuptiīs locum va-
cuēfēcissēs, nōnne etiam aliō incrēdibilī scelere hoc scelus cumulāvistī? quod ego
praetermittō et facile patior silērī nē in hāc cīvitāte tantī facinoris immānitās aut
exstitisse aut nōn vindicāta esse videātur. praetermittō ruīnās fortūnārum tuārum
quās omnīs proximīs Īdibus tibi impendēre sentiēs: ad illa veniō quae nōn ad prīvā-
tam ignōminiam vitiōrum tuōrum, nōn ad domesticam tuam difficultātem ac turpi-
tūdinem, sed ad summam rem pūblicam atque ad omnium nostrum vītam salū-
temque pertinent.

*praeferō, *here,* means both offer (ferrum) and
carry in front (facem)

absum (ab- + sum), abesse, āfuī, āfutūrus be
absent, be distant

adulēscentulus, adulēscentulī *m.* (little) young
man

coniūrātiō, coniūrātiōnis *f.* conspiracy

corruptēla, corruptēlae *f.* corruption, seduction

cumulō (1-tr.) pile up, heap

dēdecus, dēdecoris *n.* shame, disgrace

dēlectō (1-tr.) delight, please, charm

difficultās, difficultātis *f.* difficulty

domesticus, -a, -um personal, domestic

exsistō, existere, exstitī, —— exist, arise, appear

extrā (prep. + acc.) outside

fax, facis *f.* firebrand, torch

facinus, facinoris *n.* deed; crime

flāgitium, flāgitiī *n.* shame, outrage, disgrace

haereō, haerēre, haesī, haesūrus cling, stick

Īdūs, Īduum *m. pl.* (the) Ides, fifteenth day of
March, May, July, and October; the thirteenth
of every other month

ignōminia, ignōminiae *f.* dishonor, disgrace

illecebra, illecebrae *f.* attraction, allurement

immānitās, immānitātis *f.* enormity

impendeō, impendēre, ——, —— hang over,
threaten (+ dat.)

incrēdibilis, incrēdibile unbelievable

inūrō, inūrere, inussī, inustus burn upon, brand
upon (+ dat.)

irrētiō, irrētīre, irrētīvī or irrētiī, irrētītus trap

libīdō, libīdinis *f.* desire, pleasure, passion, lust

metuō, metuere, metuī, —— fear, dread

nota, notae *f.* mark, sign

nūper (adv.) recently

nuptiae, nuptiārum *f. pl.* marriage, wedding

pertineō (per- + teneō), pertinēre, pertinuī,
pertentus be aimed at, pertain

praetermittō (praeter- + mittō) pass over, omit

prīvātus, -a, -um private

proximus, -a, -um nearest; most recent, last

ruīna, ruīnae *f.* downfall, ruin, destruction

sileō, silēre, siluī, —— be silent; pass over in
silence, leave unmentioned

superior, superius upper, higher; previous

turpitūdō, turpitūdinis *f.* ugliness; shamefulness,
baseness

uxor, uxōris *f.* wife

vacuēfaciō, vacuēfacere, vacuēfēcī, vacuēfactus
make empty

vindicō (1-tr.) avenge, punish

vitium, vitiī *n.* vice, fault

2. Sallust, *Bellum Catilīnae* 3

pulchrum est bene facere reī pūblicae, etiam bene dīcere haud absurdum est; vel pāce vel bellō clārum fierī licet; et quī fēcēre et quī facta aliōrum scrīpsēre, multī laudantur. ac mihi quidem, tametsī haudquāquam pār glōria sequitur scrīptōrem et auctōrem rērum, tamen in prīmīs* arduom vidētur rēs gestās scrībere: prīmum quod facta dictīs exaequanda sunt; dein quia plērīque quae dēlicta reprehenderis malevolentiā et invidiā dicta putant, ubi dē magnā virtūte atque glōriā bonōrum memorēs, quae sibi quisque† facilia factū‡ putat, aequō animō accipit, suprā ea velutī ficta prō falsīs dūcit. Sed ego adulēscentulus initiō, sīcutī plērīque, studiō ad rem pūblicam lātus sum, ibique mihi multa advorsa fuēre. nam prō pudōre, prō abstinentiā, prō virtūte audācia, largītiō, avāritia vigēbant. quae tametsī animus aspernābātur īnsolēns malārum artium, tamen inter tanta vitia inbēcilla aetās ambitiōne conrupta tenēbātur; ac mē, quom ab relicuōrum malīs mōribus dissentīrem, nihilō minus§ honōris cupīdō eadem quae cēterōs fāmā atque invidiā vexābat.

*in prīmīs, especially, above all; first
†quisque = *masc./fem. sing. nom. of indef. pron.,*
    each person
‡factū = *neut. sing. abl. of verbal noun of* faciō,
    in (respect to) the doing, to do
§nihilō minus or nihilōminus (adv.) no less, just
    as much
abstinentia, abstinentiae *f.* abstinence; self-
    restraint, integrity
absurdus, -a, -um discordant; inappropriate
adulēscentulus, adulēscentulī *m.* (little) young
    man
adversus, -a, -um opposite, hostile, adverse
aetās, aetātis *f.* age, time of life
ambitiō, ambitiōnis *f.* flattery, adulation; desire
    for power, ambition
arduus, -a, -um steep; difficult, arduous
aspernor (1-tr.) disdain, reject, despise
auctor, auctōris *m.* source, author, producer
avāritia, avāritiae *f.* greed, avarice
corrumpō, corrumpere, corrūpī, corruptus
    corrupt, bribe
cupīdō, cupīdinis *f.* desire
dein (adv.) thereupon, then, next
dēlictum, dēlictī *n.* offense, crime
dissentiō (**dis-** + **sentiō**) differ, disagree
exaequō (1-tr.) make equal, equal
fingō, fingere, fīnxī, fictus form, fashion, make;
    imagine
haud (adv.) not at all, by no means
haudquāquam (adv.) by no means whatever,
    not at all

ibi (adv.) there; then
inbēcillus, -a, -um weak, feeble
initium, initiī *n.* beginning
īnsolēns, īnsolentis unaccustomed, unfamiliar
    with (+ gen.)
largītiō, largītiōnis *f.* generosity, largess; bribery
licet, licēre, licuit or **licitum est** (impersonal verb)
    it is permitted
malevolentia, malevolentiae *f.* ill will, dislike,
    malevolence
memorō (1-tr.) mention, recount, tell; **memorēs**,
    Potential subjunctive with a generalized sec-
    ond person
pār, paris equal
plērīque, plēraeque, plēraque very many, most
pudor, pudōris *m.* shame, decency, modesty
relicuus, -a, -um remaining, rest (of)
reprehendō, reprehendere, reprehendī,
    reprehēnsus seize, catch; blame, censure;
    reprehenderis, Potential subjunctive with a
    generalized second person
scrīptor, scrīptōris *m.* writer
sīcutī (conj.) just as
suprā (prep. + acc.) over, above, beyond
tametsī (conj.) notwithstanding that, although
vel (conj.) or; **vel . . . vel . . .** either . . . or . . .
velutī (conj.) even as, just as
vexō (1-tr.) trouble, disturb, harass
vigeō, vigēre, viguī, —— be vigorous, thrive,
    flourish
vitium, vitiī *n.* fault, vice

3. Vergil, *Aeneid* II.518–32

ipsum autem sūmptīs Priamum iuvenālibus armīs

ut vīdit, "quae mēns tam dīra, miserrime coniūnx,

impulit hīs cingī tēlīs? aut quō ruis?" inquit.   520

"nōn tālī auxiliō nec dēfēnsōribus istīs

tempus eget; nōn, sī ipse meus nunc adforet Hectōr.

hūc tandem concēde; haec āra tuēbitur omnīs,

aut moriēre simul." sīc ōre effāta recēpit

ad sēsē et sacrā longaevum in sēde locāvit.   525

ecce autem ēlāpsus Pyrrhī dē caede Polītēs,

ūnus nātōrum Priamī, per tēla, per hostīs

porticibus longīs fugit et vacua ātria lūstrat

saucius. illum ardēns īnfestō vulnere Pyrrhus

īnsequitur, iam iamque* manū tenet et premit hastā.   530

ut tandem ante oculōs ēvāsit et ōra parentum,

concidit ac multō vītam cum sanguine fūdit.

---

*iam iamque now all but . . .

adforet = adesset

adsum (ad- + sum), adesse, adfuī, adfutūrus be present

ardeō, ardēre, arsī, arsūrus burn, be on fire

ātrium, ātriī *n.* atrium, the main room of a Roman house; *in sing. or pl.,* house, palace

caedēs, caedis, -ium *f.* slaughter

cingō, cingere, cīnxī, cīnctus gird, equip; **cingī,** to gird oneself

concēdō (con- + cēdō) concede, grant; withdraw

concidō (con- + cadō), concidere, concidī, —— fall down (in dying), fall dead

coniūnx, coniugis *m. or f.* spouse; husband; wife

dēfēnsor, dēfēnsōris *m.* defender, protector

dīrus, -a, -um dire, dreadful, frightful

*effor (1-tr.) utter, say

egeō, egēre, eguī, —— lack, want, need (+ abl.)

ēlābor, ēlābī, ēlāpsus sum slip out, steal away, escape

ēvādō, ēvādere, ēvāsī, ēvāsūrus go out; emerge

fundō, fundere, fūdī, fūsus pour out, pour forth, shed

hasta, hastae *f.* spear

Hectōr, Hectoris *m.* Hector, son of Priam

hūc (adv.) to this place, hither

impellō (in- + pellō), impellere, impulī, impulsus drive, impel

īnfestus, -a, -um hostile

inquam (defective verb) say; **inquit =** *3rd sing. pres. act. indic.*

īnsequor (in- + sequor) follow closely, pursue, chase

iuvenālis, iuvenāle youthful

locō (1-tr.) place

longaevus, -a, -um of great age, ancient

lūstrō (1-tr.) roam through, traverse

ōs, ōris *n. in sing. or pl.,* mouth; face

parēns, parentis, -ium *m. or f.* parent; **parentum = parentium**

Polītēs, Polītis *m.* Polites, a son of Priam

porticus, porticūs *m.* covered walk, colonnade

premō, premere, pressī, pressus press hard, overpower

Pyrrhus, Pyrrhī *m.* Pyrrhus, son of Achilles

recipiō (re- + capiō) take back, receive

ruō, ruere, ruī, rutūrus rush

sacer, sacra, sacrum sacred

sanguis, sanguinis *m.* blood

saucius, -a, -um wounded

sēdēs, sēdis, -ium *f.* seat

simul (adv.) at the same time

sūmō, sūmere, sūmpsī, sūmptus take up, seize; take on, assume

tueor, tuērī, tuitus or **tūtus sum** look at; protect

vacuus, -a, -um empty

4. Ovid, *Metamorphōsēs* I.490–503

> Phoebus amat vīsaeque cupit cōnūbia Daphnēs,   490
>
> quodque cupit, spērat, suaque illum ōrācula fallunt,
>
> utque levēs stipulae dēmptīs adolentur aristīs,
>
> ut facibus saepēs ardent, quās forte viātor
>
> vel nimis admōvit* vel iam sub lūce† relīquit,*
>
> sīc deus in flammās abiit, sīc pectore tōtō   495
>
> ūritur et sterilem spērandō nūtrit amōrem.
>
> spectat inornātōs collō pendēre capillōs
>
> et "quid sī cōmantur?" ait. videt igne micantēs
>
> sīderibus similēs oculōs, videt ōscula, quae nōn
>
> est vīdisse satis; laudat digitōsque manūsque   500
>
> bracchiaque et nūdōs mediā plūs parte lacertōs;
>
> sī qua‡ latent, meliōra putat. fugit ōcior aurā
>
> illa levī neque ad§ haec revocantis verba resistit:

*admōvit, relīquit, translate as present
†sub lūce near daylight, near dawn
‡qua = *neut. nom. pl. of indef. pron.,* any things
§ad, *here,* at
admoveō (ad- + moveō) move near
adoleō, adolēre, ——, adultus burn (ritually);
  destroy by fire, burn
aiō (defective verb) say; ait = *3rd sing. pres. act.
  indic.*
ardeō, ardēre, arsī, arsūrus burn, be on fire; rage
arista, aristae *f.* beard of barley *or* corn; ear *or*
  spike (of a plant)
aura, aurae *f.* breeze
bracchium, bracchiī *n.* (lower) arm
capillus, capillī *m. in sing. or pl.* hair
collum, collī *n.* neck
cōmō, cōmere, cōmpsī, cōmptus make beautiful,
  adorn; do (hair)
cōnūbium, cōnūbiī *n. in sing. or pl.* marriage,
  marriage rites
Daphnē, Daphnēs *f.* Daphne; Daphnēs = *gen.
  sing.*
dēmō, dēmere, dēmpsī, dēmptus remove, take
  way; cut off
digitus, digitī *m.* finger
fallō, fallere, fefellī, falsus deceive, trick; fail
fax, facis *f.* firebrand, torch

flamma, flammae *f.* flame
inornātus, -a, -um unadorned, plain
lacertus, lacertī *m.* (upper) arm
lateō, latēre, latuī, —— hide, lie hidden,
  be concealed
micō (1-tr.) dart, flicker, flash
nimis (adv.) excessively, too
nūdus, -a, -um naked, nude
nūtriō, nūtrīre, nūtrīvī or nūtriī, nūtrītus feed,
  nourish; encourage, foster
ōcior, ōcius more swift
ōrāculum, ōrāculī *n.* divine utterance, oracle
ōsculum, ōsculī *n.* kiss; *in pl.,* lips
pendeō, pendēre, pependī, —— hang,
  be suspended
Phoebus, Phoebī *m.* Phoebus (Apollo)
resistō, resistere, restitī, —— halt, stop
revocō (re- + vocō) (1-tr.) summon back, call back
saepēs, saepis *f.* (planted) hedge
sīdus, sīderis *n.* star
spectō (1-tr.) look at, observe
sterilis, sterile producing nothing; futile
stipula, stipulae *f.* stalk (of a plant)
ūrō, ūrere, ussī, ustus burn, scorch, inflame,
  consume
vel (conj.) or; vel . . . vel . . . either . . . or . . .
viātor, viātōris *m.* traveler

§130. Adverbs of Place

Vocabulary

eō (adv.) to that place, thither
eōdem (adv.) to the same place
hīc (adv.) here, in this place; at this time
hinc (adv.) from here, hence; henceforth
    hinc . . . hinc . . . on this side . . .
        on that side . . .
hūc (adv.) to here, hither
ibi (adv.) in that place, there; then,
    thereupon

illīc (adv.) there, in that place
illinc (adv.) from there, thence
    hinc . . . illinc . . . on this side . . .
        on that side . . .
illūc (adv.) to there, thither
inde (adv.) from that place, from there,
    thence; from that time, thereupon

Memorize these vocabulary words. Their meanings will not be given when they appear in the remainder of this book.

Certain common adverbs of place appear in these closely related forms:

Demonstrative	Interrogative/Relative
ibi there	
hīc here, in this place	**ubi** where
illīc there, in that place	
inde from there	
hinc from here, hence	**unde** from where, whence
illinc from there, thence	
eō to there	
eōdem to the same place	**quō** to where, whither
hūc to here, hither	
illūc to there, thither	

The adverbs in the column on the left are demonstrative because they point out a place *where, from where,* or *to where,* often in the answer to a question. The adverbs in the column on the right may be used either to ask questions (interrogative) or to correlate with corresponding demonstratives (relative) (cf. §124). For example:

Unde **vēnistī?**
Whence (From where) have you come? (interrogative)
Illinc **vēnī** *unde* **pater quoque vēnit.** (demonstrative/relative)
From there I have come *from where* my father also came.
I have come *from where* my father also came.
Ubi **mē stāre iubēbis,** *ibi* **manēbō.** (relative/demonstrative)
Where me to stand you will order *there* I shall remain.
I shall remain *where* you will order me to stand.

OBSERVATION

An idiomatic English translation of a sentence containing both a demonstrative and relative adverb of place often omits the translation of the demonstrative adverb, as in the second translation above.

Short Readings

1. A freed prisoner of war agrees to help his present and former masters.

> prō rotā mē ūtī licet:
> vel egō hūc vel illūc vortor quō imperābitis. (PLAUTUS, CAPTĪVĪ 369–70)

licet, licēre, licuit or **licitum est** it is permitted
rota, rotae *f.* wheel
vertō, vertere, vertī, versus turn

2. After revealing that Catiline's conspiracy is known to all, Cicero bids him depart.

> quae* cum ita sint, Catilīna, perge quō coepistī: ēgredere aliquandō ex urbe;
> patent portae: proficīscere. (CICERO, IN CATILĪNAM I 10)

*****quae,** *connective relative,* and . . . these things
aliquandō (adv.) at long last
pateō, patēre, patuī, —— lie open
pergō, pergere, perrēxī, perrēctus proceed
porta, portae *f.* gate

3. The poet addresses a collection of bad poetry that he is about to discard.

> vōs hinc intereā valēte abīte
> illūc, unde malum pedem attulistis. (CATULLUS XIV.21–22)

afferō (ad- + ferō), afferre, attulī, allātus bring, convey
intereā (adv.) meanwhile
pēs, pedis *m.* foot

4. After a detour to tend to ships damaged in a storm, Caesar resumes his pursuit of the Britons.

> ipse eōdem unde redierat proficīscitur.* (CAESAR, DĒ BELLŌ GALLICŌ V.11)

*****proficīscitur,** historical use of present tense; translate as perfect

CHAPTER XIV

Vocabulary

lūna, lūnae *f.* moon

➤ aetās, aetātis *f.* age; lifetime; time

➤ agmen, agminis *n.* line (of march),
column; army; multitude, throng
auctōritās, auctōritātis *f.* authority;
influence
nōmen, nōminis *n.* name
ōs, ōris *n. in sing. or pl.* mouth; face
sōl, sōlis *m.* sun

➤ aliquis, aliquid (indef. pron.) someone,
something; anyone, anything
➤ aliquī, aliqua, aliquod (indef. adj.)
some, any
➤ quis, quid (indef. pron.) someone, something; anyone, anything
➤ quī, qua, quod (indef. adj.) some, any
➤ quisquam, quicquam (indef. pron.) someone, something; anyone, anything
➤ quisque, quidque (quicque) (indef. pron.)
each *or* every man *or* woman, each *or*
every thing
➤ quīque, quaeque, quodque (indef. adj.)
each, every

spectō (1-tr.) look (at), observe

➤ accidō, accidere, accidī, —— happen
➤ efficiō, efficere, effēcī, effectus make;
bring about
metuō, metuere, metuī, —— fear, dread
➤ occidō, occidere, occidī, occāsūrus fall,
set; die
➤ premō, premere, pressī, pressus press
(hard); overpower; check

➤ opprimō, opprimere, oppressī,
oppressus press on; close; overwhelm,
oppress

➤ orior, orīrī, ortus sum rise, arise

➤ absum, abesse, āfuī, āfutūrus be absent,
be distant
➤ adsum, adesse, adfuī, adfutūrus be
present, be near
➤ cōnferō, cōnferre, contulī, collātus bring
together, collect; compare; direct;
confer (on)
➤ licet, licēre, licuit *or* licitum est it is
permitted (§135)
➤ oportet, oportēre, oportuit it is proper, it
is right (§135)

➤ cūnctus, -a, -um all
➤ reliquus, -a, -um remaining, rest (of)

absēns, absentis absent
➤ vetus, veteris old

➤ necesse (indecl. adj.) necessary (§135)

adeō (adv.) to such *or* so great an extent,
(so) very
haud (adv.) not at all, by no means
➤ quodsī (conj.) but if
➤ vel (conj.) or;
(adv.) even
vel . . . vel . . . either . . . or . . .
vix (adv.) scarcely, hardly

Vocabulary Notes

aetās, aetātis *f.* may mean "age" in the sense of the number of years one has lived or in the sense of the "age" or "period" in which one lives. It may also refer to: 1. the "lifetime" of a human being; 2. a particular "time of life" (old age, youth); or 3. "time."

agmen, agminis *n.* is a noun formed by the addition of the suffix **-men** to a stem of the verb **agō**, and its most general meaning is "a thing being driven." **Agmen** may be used of any "mass" of things (water, clouds, etc.) or of a "throng" or "body" of people moving or acting together. It may also carry a more specifically military sense, "(battle-)line" or "column" of troops, both on the march and drawn up for battle.

aliquis, aliquid is an indefinite pronoun formed by the addition of the indefinite prefix **ali-** to **quis, quid**. Its declension is identical with that of **quis, quid**. Its corresponding adjective is **aliquī, aliqua, aliquod**, whose declension is identical with that of **quī, quae, quod** *except* for the feminine singular nominative (**aliqua**). MEMORIZE THIS IRREGULAR FORM AS PART OF THE VOCABULARY ENTRY.

Aliquem in forō vīdī.	I saw *someone* in the forum. (indef. pron.)
Dōnō *aliquō* dōnāberis.	You will be presented with *some* gift. (indef. adj.)

The use of the indefinite pronoun **quis, quid** is *limited to subordinate clauses* in which this pronoun follows such conjunctions as **sī, nisi, num, nē, ut**, and **cum**. Its corresponding adjective is **quī, qua, quod**, whose declension is identical with that of **quī, quae, quod** *except* for the feminine singular nominative (**qua**) and the neuter plural nominative or accusative (**qua** or, less commonly, **quae**). MEMORIZE THESE IRREGULAR FORMS.

Sī *quis* mē vocet, veniam.	If *anyone* should call me, I would come. (indef. pron.)
Sī virum *quem* amās, dīc mihi.	If you love *any* man, tell me. (indef. adj.)

quisquam, quicquam is an indefinite pronoun formed by the addition of the indefinite suffix **-quam** to **quis, quid**. Its declension is identical with that of **quis, quid** *except* for the *assimilated* neuter singular nominative or accusative (**quicquam**). The unassimilated form **quidquam** appears rarely. The corresponding indefinite adjective for **quisquam, quicquam** is supplied by **ūllus, -a, -um**.

quisquam, quicquam is used primarily in sentences *containing or implying negation*.

Nōn *quicquam* tam miserum audīvī.	I have not heard *anything* so wretched. (indef. pron.)
Estne *quisquam* quī Catilīnae crēdat?	Is there *anyone* of the sort who trusts Catiline? (indef. pron.)

In the second sentence the use of **quisquam** implies that *no one* trusts Catiline.

quisque, quidque (quicque) is an indefinite pronoun formed by the addition of the indefinite suffix **-que** to **quis, quid**. Its declension is identical with that of **quis, quid** *except* for the alternate *assimilated* neuter singular nominative or accusative, **quicque**. Its corresponding adjective is **quīque, quaeque, quodque**, whose declension is identical with **quī, quae, quod**.

quisque is often used with and placed immediately after the third-person reflexive pronoun ——, **suī** or the reflexive-possessive adjective **suus, -a, -um**.

Sua cuique satis placēbant.	*His own things* were pleasing enough *to each man*.

When **quisque** appears in such sentences, the reflexive pronoun or reflexive-possessive adjective refers to the indefinite pronoun.

When **quisque** appears in the singular or plural with a superlative adjective, the resulting phrase may be translated into English with the plural and the English word "all."

optimus quisque	each best man *or* all the best men
antīquissima quaeque	all the oldest things

accidō, accidere, accidī, —— is a compound verb formed by the addition of the prefix **ad-** to **cadō**, and it exhibits regular vowel weakening. (For the prefix **ad-** see Appendix P.) **Accidō** is often used impersonally and may be accompanied by a Dative of Reference. For its use with Substantive Ut clauses see §133.

efficiō, efficere, effēcī, effectus is a compound verb formed by the addition of the prefix **ex-** to **faciō**. (For the prefix **ex-** see Appendix P.) For its use with Substantive Ut clauses see §133.

occidō, occidere, occidī, occāsūrus is a compound verb formed by the addition of the prefix **ob-** to **cadō**, and it exhibits regular vowel weakening. (For the prefix **ob-** see Appendix P.) While **occidō** may be used of any person or thing that falls, it is commonly used to mean "fall (into grief)," "be ruined," "die" (when the subject is a person), or "set" or "sink" (when the subject is a heavenly body). The present active participle of **occidō**—**occidēns, occidentis**, "setting"—may be used as a masculine substantive to refer to the "west" as a direction or as a part of the known world.

premō, premere, pressī, pressus is used in a wide variety of contexts and may be translated by a number of English equivalents. **Premō** may mean "press" in the sense of "exert pressure on" (inanimate objects, parts of the body). It may mean "press (hard)" in the sense of "propel," "drive," or "attack" (spears, people). It may also mean "overpower, overwhelm" (enemies, ships) or "overshadow," "cover" (often used of the sun or moon covered over by clouds or shadows). Finally, it may mean "check," "suppress," or "stop" (bodies of water, actions, voices).

opprimō, opprimere, oppressī, oppressus is a compound verb formed by the addition of the prefix **ob-** to **premō**, and it exhibits regular vowel weakening. (For the prefix **ob-** see Appendix P.) Its meanings and uses are similar to those of the simple verb **premō**. THE PRINCIPAL PARTS OF *ALL* COMPOUNDS OF **PREMŌ** FOLLOW THE PATTERN OF THE PRINCIPAL PARTS OF **OPPRIMŌ**. WHEN A COMPOUND OF **PREMŌ** APPEARS IN READINGS, ITS PRINCIPAL PARTS ARE NOT SUPPLIED, BUT THE PREFIX AND SIMPLE VERB ARE GIVEN.

orior, orīrī, ortus sum is a fourth-conjugation, intransitive deponent verb. It may be used of heavenly bodies and mean "rise," or it may mean more generally "arise" or "come into being." In the present indicative it is usually conjugated as a *third*-conjugation i-stem verb (e.g., **oritur**, *not* **orītur**). Orior has an irregular future active participle: **oritūrus, -a, -um** (cf. **moritūrus, -a, -um**). MEMORIZE THIS IRREGULAR FORM. The present active participle of orior—**oriēns, orientis**, "rising"—may be used as a masculine substantive to refer to the "east" as a direction or as a part of the known world. COMPOUND VERBS FORMED FROM **ORIOR** DO *NOT* EXHIBIT VOWEL WEAKENING.

absum, abesse, āfuī, āfutūrus is a compound verb formed by the addition of the prefix **ab-** to **sum**. (For the prefix **ab-** see Appendix P.)

adsum, adesse, adfuī, adfutūrus is a compound verb formed by the addition of the prefix **ad-** to **sum**. (For the prefix **ad-** see Appendix P.) **Adsum** often appears with a Dative with a Compound Verb. In legal contexts **adsum** may mean "be present as an advocate (for)." When the subject is a divinity, it may mean "be favorable (to)."

cōnferō, cōnferre, contulī, collātus is a compound verb formed by the addition of the prefix **con-** to **ferō**. (For the prefix **con-** see Appendix P.) The idiom **sē cōnferre** means "betake oneself," "go."

For the third person singular forms that appear in the principal parts of impersonal verbs, such as *licet*, *licēre*, *licuit* or *licitum est* and *oportet*, **oportēre**, *oportuit* see §135. Many impersonal verbs have alternate third principal parts formed as impersonal passives (see §59).

The verb **licet** indicates what is legal or permitted. The verb **oportet** indicates what is proper or necessary in accordance with one's duty. **necesse est** means "it is necessary" in the sense of "it is compulsory."

cūnctus, -a, -um is a synonym of **omnis, omne**, but contains more of an idea of "all (joined) together." **Cūnctus, -a, -um** is more commonly found in the plural.

The adjective **reliquus, -a, -um** is related to the verb **relinquō**. It often refers to the remaining portion of things or people left over after certain things or people have been mentioned. It may often be translated "rest of."

| Rēgīna *reliquam vītam* bene aget. | The queen will conduct *the rest of (her) life* well. |

vetus, veteris means "old" as opposed to "young," and "old" or "experienced" as opposed to "new." Less commonly, **vetus** is synonymous with **antīquus, -a, -um** and means "old" in the sense of "of an earlier *or* ancient time." The ablative singular form is *usually* **vetere**. Vetus has *no* i-stem features in the plural: its neuter nominative/accusative plural form is **vetera**, its genitive plural form is **veterum**, and its masculine/feminine accusative plural is **veterēs**. Vetus has an irregular superlative form: **veterrimus, -a, -um**. MEMORIZE THESE IRREGULAR FORMS.

The conjunction **quodsī** (sometimes written as two words, **quod sī**) is formed from the Adverbial Accusative of the relative pronoun **quod** (to the extent of which, as to which) and the conjunction **sī**. It nearly always has adversative force and is best translated "but if."

The conjunction **vel** is used to mark an indifferent choice and thus should be distinguished from **aut**, which indicates mutually exclusive propositions.

| *Vel* tēlō *vel* ferrō pugnābō. | I shall fight *either* with a spear *or* with a sword. |

	Derivatives	**Cognates**
accidō	accident	
aetās	*age*; *coetaneous*	*eternal*; *aught*; *ever*; aye; long*evity*; medi*eval*; *eon*
licet	il*licit*	
necesse	*necessary*	**cēdō**
nōmen	*nominate*; noun; *nomen*clature	pseud*onym*; *onoma*topoeia; patr*onym*ic; syn*onym*ous
occidō	occident; *occas*ion	
orior	orient; *origin*; ab*ort*	*hor*mone; are; *ear*nest
ōs	*or*al; *os*cillate; *os*tiary; *or*ifice	
premō	re*prim*and; *press*ure; *print*	
sōl	*sol*ar; *sol*arium; para*sol*; *sol*stice	*sun*; *south*
spectō	a*spect*; *spec*ulum; *spect*rum	*spy*; *es*pionage; tele*scope*; epi*s*copal
vetus	*veter*an; in*veter*ate; *veter*inary	*et*esian

§131. Result Clauses

In both English and Latin, the result of an action is reported in a subordinate clause called a **Result clause**. A result may be understood as an event *likely* to follow upon the action of the main verb *or* as an event *actually occurring* or *actually having occurred*. In English, a result clause is introduced by the conjunction "that." In Latin, Result clauses are introduced by the conjunction **ut** and have their verbs in the subjunctive according to the rules of sequence. For example:

> **Tam honestus est *ut eī crēdās*.** (likely result)
> So honorable is he (*with the result*) *that him you would trust.*
> He is so honorable (*with the result*) *that you would trust him.*
> **Ita dīxerat *ut sententiam intellegerem*.** (actual result)
> In such a way she had spoken *that (her) opinion (d.o.) I understood.*
> She had spoken in such a way *(with the result) that I understood her opinion.*

OBSERVATIONS

1. Result clauses began as independent sentences whose verbs were Potential subjunctives. For example:

> **Eī crēdās. Tam honestus est.**   You would trust him. He is so honorable.

Such a paratactic arrangement of two thoughts easily became one sentence: **Tam honestus est ut eī crēdās** (He is so honorable that you would trust him.). By the classical period, *both likely and actual* Result clauses had their verbs in the subjunctive mood, a reflection of the view of the subjunctive as simply the mood appropriate for certain subordinate clauses.

2. Result clauses are negated by **ut . . . nōn . . .**, **ut . . . nēmō . . .**, **ut . . . numquam . . .**, etc. They are *not* negated by **nē**.

3. The syntax of, for example, **intellegerem**, is **imperfect subjunctive, Result clause, secondary sequence**.

4. For a Result clause that reports a *likely* result, as in the first sentence above, the subjunctive verb is translated with the English word "would." For a Result clause that reports an *actual* result, as in the second sentence, the subjunctive verb is translated as if it were indicative. The tense of the translation is determined by the relative time of the subjunctive to the main verb.

Result clauses are usually *signaled* by an *adverb or adjective of degree* in the main clause. Such words include:

adeō (adv.) to such an extent	
ita	**tālis, tāle**
sīc	**tantus, -a, -um**
tam	**tot**

OBSERVATION

Occasionally a demonstrative such as **hic, iste, ille,** or **is** signals a Result clause and should be translated "such (a)."

When an actual result is reported in past time, a *perfect subjunctive that breaks the rules of sequence* may be used, perhaps to emphasize the actual completion of the action. For example:

> **Ita dīxerat *ut sententiam intellēxerim*.**
> She had spoken in such a way *that I actually understood her opinion.*

§132. Relative Clauses of Result

A blend of the idea of a Result clause with the idea of a Relative Clause of Characteristic (see §93) is called a **Relative Clause of Result**, in which *both* ideas are present. For example:

> **Quis est tam fortis *quī sine armīs pugnet?***
> Who is of so brave a sort *who without arms fights?*
> Who is so brave *that he would fight without arms?*
> **Nihil est tam difficile *quīn intellegī possit.***
> Nothing is of so difficult a sort *that to be understood it is not able.*
> Nothing is so difficult *that it is not able to be understood.*

OBSERVATIONS

1. In each sentence the word **tam** signals a Result clause, but the word **quī/quīn** instead of **ut** introduces a *Relative* Clause of Result. Each relative clause expresses an event that would *potentially or characteristically result* from the main clause.

2. In the second sentence, **quīn** is used to introduce a negative Relative Clause of Result. Compare this use of **quīn** to its use in Relative Clauses of Characteristic (§93).

3. The syntax of, for example, **pugnet**, is **present subjunctive, Relative Clause of Result, primary sequence**.

4. The second translations given above, in which the relative pronoun is replaced in English by "that . . . he/it . . . ," are to be preferred for clarity and simplicity. In addition, the English word "would" may be used in translating the subjunctive verb in a Relative Clause of Result, or the subjunctive verb may be translated as an indicative.

§133. Substantive *Ut* Clauses

A Result clause is an *adverbial clause* that modifies the action of the main verb as a whole (cf. Purpose clauses). Certain verbs and verb phrases appear with *noun clauses* called **Substantive Ut clauses**, which function as either subjects or direct objects (cf. Indirect Commands).[1] Some common expressions that introduce Substantive **Ut** clauses are:

accidit	"it happens . . ." (**accidō, accidere, accidī, —— happen**)
fit	"it happens . . ."
fierī potest	"it is able to happen . . .," "it is possible . . ."
efficere	"to bring it about . . ." (**efficiō, efficere, effēcī, effectus** bring about)
facere	"to bring it about . . .," "to see to it . . ."

OBSERVATION

The first three verbal expressions introduce **subject clauses**. The latter two introduce **object clauses**.

---

1. These noun clauses are sometimes known as **Substantive Clauses of Result.**

Substantive **Ut** clauses are negated by **ut . . . nōn**, **ut . . . nēmō**, etc. **Nē** *may* be used when a command or exhortation is being expressed. For example:

Accidit *ut* Caesar cōpiās per prōvinciam *dūceret*.
It happened *that* Caesar (his) troops (d.o.) through the province *was leading.*
It happened *that* Caesar *was leading* his troops through the province.
Efficiam *ut* cīvēs inter sē *nōn pugnent*.
I shall bring it about *that* the citizens among themselves *not fight.*
I shall bring it about *that* the citizens *not fight* among themselves.
Facite *nē* sociōs *relinquātis*, ō mīlitēs.
See to it *that* the allies (d.o.) *you not abandon,* o soldiers.
See to it *that you not abandon* the allies, o soldiers.

OBSERVATIONS

1. Substantive **Ut** clauses always have their verbs in the subjunctive according to the rules of sequence.

2. In the first sentence the clause **ut . . . dūceret** functions as the *subject* of the verb **accidit**. The entire subject clause is *what* "happened." The English pronoun "it" merely anticipates and refers to this subject clause.

3. In the second sentence the clause **ut . . . pugnent** functions as the *direct object* of the verb **efficiam**. The entire object clause is *what* "I shall bring about." The English pronoun "it" merely anticipates and refers to this object clause.

4. In the third sentence the Substantive **Ut** clause is introduced by **nē** because the equivalent of a negative Indirect Command is being expressed.

5. The syntax of, for example, **dūceret**, is **imperfect subjunctive, Substantive Ut clause, secondary sequence**.

☛ DRILL 131–133 MAY NOW BE DONE.

§134. *Fore ut* Construction

When a future passive verb is to be expressed in Indirect Statement, a periphrasis[2] is commonly used instead of the rare future passive infinitive.[3] This periphrasis employs the future active infinitive of the verb **sum (fore, futūrum esse)** and a Substantive **Ut** clause with a verb in the subjunctive according to the rules of sequence. The same construction is used when a future active verb that lacks a fourth principal part is expressed in Indirect Statement. For example:

Caesar dīcit *fore ut* bellum mox *cōnficiātur*.
Caesar says *that it will be that* the war *be completed* soon.
Caesar says *that* the war *will be completed* soon.
Spērābāmus *futūrum esse ut* Caesar bellum mox cōnficere *posset*.
We were hoping *that it would be that* Caesar the war (d.o.) soon to complete *be able.*
We were hoping *that* Caesar *would be able* to complete the war soon.

___

2. A **periphrasis** (< Greek *periphrazō,* speak around) is a roundabout way of saying something, a circumlocution (< **circumlocūtiō**, speaking around).

3. For the formation of the future passive infinitive see §142, n. 4.

1. The noun clause introduced by **ut** in each sentence functions as the *subject* of the infinitive **fore** or **futūrum esse** in Indirect Statement. The **-um** ending on **futūrum** is neuter singular accusative to agree with the subject clause. The English pronoun "it" merely anticipates and refers to this subject clause.

2. Substantive **Ut** clauses following **fore** and **futūrum esse** are negated by **ut . . . nōn, ut . . . nēmō,** etc.

3. The syntax of, for example, **posset** is **imperfect subjunctive, Substantive Ut clause in a fore ut construction, secondary sequence.**

4. The second translations given above are to be preferred because they combine the future tense expressed in the infinitives with the actions expressed in the subjunctive verbs. In primary sequence the word "will" and in secondary sequence the word "would" are used.

☛ DRILL 134 MAY NOW BE DONE.

§135. Impersonal Constructions I: *licet, necesse est,* and *oportet*

An **impersonal verb** is a verb that does not have a personal subject (cf. §59). Certain impersonal verbs that express ideas of *permission, necessity,* or *propriety* have forms in the third person singular, the infinitive, and (less commonly) the perfect passive participle. Three such verbs are:

> **licet, licēre, licuit** or **licitum est** it is allowed, it is permitted
> **necesse est** it is necessary
> **oportet, oportēre, oportuit** it is proper, it is right

OBSERVATIONS

1. The first and third principal parts of **licet** and **oportet** are given in the *third person singular* because impersonal verbs appear in that person and number *only.* **Licet** has an alternate third principal part, **licitum est,** formed as an impersonal passive.

2. **Necesse est** is actually a compound of the indeclinable neuter singular adjective **necesse** (functioning as a predicate adjective) and a form of the verb **sum.** The form of **sum** may be any third person singular form (**necesse erat, necesse sit,** etc.) or an infinitive (**necesse esse**).

These three impersonal verbs frequently appear with a Subject Infinitive (see §27), which may have an expressed Subject Accusative (see §107). For example:

> **Licet in urbe *manēre*.** (Subject Infinitive)
> It is permitted *to remain* in the city.
> **Necesse est *eōs* in urbe *manēre*.** (Subject Accusative, Subject Infinitive)
> It is necessary *for them to remain* in the city.
> It is necessary *that they remain* in the city.
> **Oportēbat *eōs* in urbe *manēre*.** (Subject Accusative, Subject Infinitive)
> It was proper *for them to remain* in the city.
> It was proper *that they remain* in the city.

OBSERVATIONS

1. In these sentences the syntax of **manēre** is Subject Infinitive. In the second and third sentences the syntax of **eōs** is Subject Accusative.

2. In each translation given above the English word "it" merely anticipates and refers to the Subject Infinitive. The first sentence, for example, may also be translated "To remain in the city is permitted."

Licet and **necesse est** may also appear with a Dative of Reference and a Subject Infinitive. For example:

Liceat *eīs* in urbe *manēre*.	Let it be permitted *for them to remain* in the city.
***Eīs* necesse erat in urbe *manēre*.**	It was necessary *for them to remain* in the city.

OBSERVATION

The Dative of Reference that may appear with **licet** or **necesse est** expresses the *person to whom* an action is permitted or *for whom* an action is necessary. When a Subject Accusative—rather than a Dative of Reference—appears with **licet** and **necesse est**, it expresses the *subject* of the infinitive.

Licet, **necesse est**, and **oportet** also frequently appear with a Jussive subjunctive in parataxis.[4] For example:

Iūs *valeat* necesse est.	*Let* right *be strong* it is necessary.
	It is necessary *that right be strong.*
Nōlī fugere: mēcum *moriāris* oportet.	Do not flee: with me *die* it is proper.
	Do not flee: it is proper *that you die* with me.

OBSERVATION

In these sentences two verbs stand paratactically with no subordination. The second English translations, which include the addition of the English conjunction "that" and make use of the English present subjunctive, are to be preferred for clarity.

☛ DRILL 135 MAY NOW BE DONE.

§136. Genitive of Characteristic

The Genitive of Possession is sometimes extended to express the person to whom a certain *characteristic* belongs. When this occurs, the genitive is called the **Genitive of Characteristic**.[5] For example:

***Sapientis* est pācem petere.**	*Of a wise person* it is peace (d.o.) to seek.
	To seek peace is *characteristic of a wise person.*

The syntax of the italicized word (**sapientis**) is **Genitive of Characteristic**.

OBSERVATIONS

1. A Genitive of Characteristic is often well translated with the addition of the word "characteristic" before the "of."

2. Subject Infinitives frequently appear in combination with Genitives of Characteristic.

3. Because the genitives of personal pronouns can be Partitive or Objective Genitive *only*, the possessive adjectives are often used to express an idea similar to the Genitive of Characteristic. For example:

Nōn est fugere meum.	To flee is not *my thing.*
	To flee is not *characteristic of me.*

4. Very rarely a Substantive **Ut** clause may appear as the subject of these impersonal verbs.

5. The Genitive of Characteristic is also known as the Predicate Genitive.

Short Readings

1. A fragment from the poet Naevius

   patī necesse est multa mortālēs mala. (Naevius, *Palliātae* frag. 106)

   mortālis, **mortāle** mortal

2. Pseudolus, a crafty slave, criticizes Ballio, a pimp who worships only money.

   deōs quidem, quōs maxumē aequom est metuere, eōs minimī facit.*

   (Plautus, *Pseudolus* 269)

   *facit, subject is Ballio

3. A fragment from the poet Ennius

   quem metuunt ōdērunt; quem quisque ōdit periisse expetit.

   (Ennius, *Tragoediae* frag. 348)

   expetō (**ex-** + **petō**) ask for; desire

4. The character Hegio utters a truism.

   quot hominēs tot sententiae: suos quoique mōs. (Terence, *Phormiō* 454)

5. Later writers often cite this fragment spoken by Atreus in a tragedy of the poet Accius. Suetonius reports that Caligula said it about his subjects.

   ōderint dum metuant. (Accius, *Tragoediae* frag. 204)

6. A fragment from the satirist

   hominī amīcō et familiārī nōn est mentīrī meum. (Lucilius, *Saturae* frag. 953)

   familiāris, **familiāre** of one's household; of one's family
   mentior, **mentīrī**, **mentītus sum** lie, tell a lie

7. The twenty-five-year-old Cicero explains why he believes he will win his case.

   nōn enim, quem ad modum* putātis, omnia sunt in ēloquentiā; est quaedam tamen

   ita perspicua vēritās ut eam īnfirmāre nūlla rēs possit. (Cicero, *Prō Quīnctiō* 80)

   *quem ad modum (rel. adv.) in what way, as
   ēloquentia, **ēloquentiae** *f.* eloquence; rhetoric
   īnfirmō (1-tr.) weaken; lessen; refute
   perspicuus, **-a**, **-um** clearly visible, plain, self-evident
   vēritās, **vēritātis** *f.* truth

8. Cicero reflects on why men turn to crime.

L. Cassius ille, quem populus Rōmānus vērissimum et sapientissimum iūdicem putābat, identidem in causīs quaerere solēbat cui bonō fuisset.* sīc vīta hominum est ut ad maleficium nēmō cōnētur sine spē atque ēmolumentō accēdere.

(CICERO, *PRŌ S. ROSCIŌ AMERĪNŌ* 84)

*fuisset, subject is any particular crime
L. Cassius, L. Cassiī *m.* L. Cassius
ēmolumentum, ēmolumentī *n.* benefit, advantage

identidem (adv.) again and again, repeatedly
iūdex, iūdicis *m.* juror, judge
maleficium, maleficiī *n.* misdeed, crime

9. Cicero reproaches Verres directly for having attempted to deprive an upstanding Roman citizen in Sicily of his rights.

homō āmentissime, quid putāstī? impetrātūrum tē? quantī is ā cīvibus suīs fieret, quantī auctōritās eius habērētur ignōrābās? (CICERO, *IN VERREM II* 4.19)

āmēns, āmentis demented, insane
ignōrō (1-tr.) be ignorant, be unaware (of)
impetrō (1-tr.) obtain; succeed

10. After describing another incident in which Verres degraded the local nobility of Sicily, Cicero asks Verres a rhetorical question.

quis tam fuit illō tempore ferreus, quis tam inhūmānus praeter ūnum tē, quī nōn illōrum aetāte, nōbilitāte, miseriā commovērētur? (CICERO, *IN VERREM II* 5.121)

commoveō (con- + moveō) move
ferreus, -a, -um made of iron; hard-hearted, unfeeling
inhūmānus, -a, -um inhumane
miseria, miseriae *f.* misery
nōbilitās, nōbilitātis *f.* renown, nobility, excellence

11. Addressing the Roman people, Cicero summarizes the effects of the *Lēx Gabīnia* (67 B.C.E.), which gave Pompey plenary powers to wipe out piracy in the Mediterranean sea.

itaque ūna lēx, ūnus vir, ūnus annus nōn modo vōs illā miseriā ac turpitūdine līberāvit sed etiam effēcit ut aliquandō vērē vidērēminī omnibus gentibus ac nātiōnibus terrā marīque imperāre. (CICERO, *DĒ LĒGE MĀNĪLIĀ* 56)

aliquandō (adv.) sometimes, occasionally; at long last
miseria, miseriae *f.* misery
nātiō, nātiōnis *f.* nation
turpitūdō, turpitūdinis *f.* ugliness; shamefulness, baseness

12. Cicero pays Q. Catulus a great compliment—before proceeding to disagree with him strongly.

etenim tālis est vir ut nūlla rēs tanta sit ac tam difficilis quam ille nōn et cōnsiliō regere et integritāte tuērī et virtūte cōnficere possit. (CICERO, *DĒ LĒGE MĀNĪLIĀ* 59)

integritās, integritātis *f.* moral uprightness, integrity
tueor, tuērī, tuitus or **tūtus sum** look at; protect, attend to

13. Cicero recalls an older, sterner morality.

> fuit, fuit ista quondam in hāc rē pūblicā virtūs ut virī fortēs ācriōribus suppliciīs
> cīvem perniciōsum quam acerbissimum hostem coërcērent.
>
> (CICERO, *IN CATILĪNAM I* 3)

coërceō, coërcēre, coërcuī, coërcitus restrain, check, suppress
perniciōsus, -a, -um destructive
quondam (adv.) at one time, once, formerly
supplicium, suppliciī *n.* punishment

14. Cicero characterizes Catiline derisively.

> neque enim is es, Catilīna, ut tē aut pudor umquam ā turpitūdine aut metus ā
>
> perīculō aut ratiō ā furōre revocārit. (CICERO, *IN CATILĪNAM I* 22)

furor, furōris *m.* madness
pudor, pudōris *m.* shame, decency, modesty
ratiō, ratiōnis *f.* account, reason; rationality
revocō (1-tr.) call back
turpitūdō, turpitūdinis *f.* ugliness; shamefulness, baseness

15. At the very time of the Catilinarian conspiracy, Cicero pleads directly to Cato, one of the most important men behind the accusation of election fraud against Murena.

> hīs tantīs in rēbus tantīsque in perīculīs est tuum, M. Catō, quī mihi nōn tibi, sed
> patriae nātus esse vidēris, vidēre quid agātur, retinēre adiūtōrem, dēfēnsōrem, so-
> cium in rē pūblicā, cōnsulem nōn cupidum, cōnsulem—quod maximē tempus hoc
> postulat—fortūnā cōnstitūtum ad amplexandum ōtium, scientiā ad bellum geren-
> dum, animō et ūsū ad quod velīs negōtium sustinendum. (CICERO, *PRŌ MURĒNĀ* 83)

adiūtor, adiūtōris *m.* helper, supporter
amplexor (1-tr.) embrace; value, esteem
cōnstituō, cōnstituere, cōnstituī, cōnstitūtus set up, establish; prepare
dēfēnsor, dēfēnsōris *m.* protector, defender
negōtium, negōtiī *n.* business
ōtium, ōtiī *n.* leisure; peace
postulō (1-tr.) demand
retineō (re- + teneō), retinēre, retinuī, retentus keep hold of, retain; uphold, preserve
scientia, scientiae *f.* knowledge
sustineō (sub- + teneō), sustinēre, sustinuī, —— withstand; support, sustain
ūsus, ūsūs *m.* use, experience

16. Cicero makes a clever observation to bolster his point about the importance of praise.

> trahimur omnēs studiō laudis, et optimus quisque maximē glōriā dūcitur. ipsī illī
> philosophī etiam in eīs libellīs quōs dē contemnendā glōriā scrībunt nōmen suum
> īnscrībunt . . . (CICERO, *PRŌ ARCHIĀ* 26)

contemnō, contemnere, contempsī, contemptus regard with contempt, scorn, disregard
īnscrībō (in- + scrībō) inscribe
laus, laudis *f.* praise
libellus, libellī *m.* (little) book
philosophus, philosophī *m.* philosopher
trahō, trahere, trāxī, tractus draw, drag

17. In the opening of his defense of Sestius, Cicero expresses to the jury his outrage at his opponents' strategy.

> . . . per vōs nōbīs, per optimōs virōs optimīs cīvibus perīculum īnferre cōnantur, et quōs lapidibus, quōs ferrō, quōs facibus, quōs vī, manū, cōpiīs dēlēre nōn potuērunt, hōs vestrā auctōritāte, vestrā religiōne, vestrīs sententiīs sē oppressūrōs arbitrantur. (Cicero, *Prō Sestiō* 2)

fax, facis *f.* firebrand, torch
lapis, lapidis *m.* stone
religiō, religiōnis *f.* religious constraint *or* fear; religious observance; sanctity, scruple

18. Cicero praises Milo's belief that life and freedom must be defended—even with arms.

> hoc* sentīre prūdentiae est, facere fortitūdinis; et sentīre vērō et facere perfectae† cumulātaeque virtūtis. (Cicero, *Prō Sestiō* 86)

*__hoc__, refers to Milo's belief
†**perfectus, -a, -um** perfect
cumulātus, -a, -um heaped up; vast, abundant
fortitūdō, fortitūdinis *f.* bravery, fortitude
prūdentia, prūdentiae *f.* good sense, judgment, prudence

19. Cicero distinguishes between what is proper and what is permitted.

> est enim aliquid quod nōn oporteat etiam sī licet; quicquid vērō nōn licet, certē nōn oportet. (Cicero, *Prō Balbō* 8)

quisquis, quidquid or **quicquid** (indef. rel. pron.) whoever, whatever

20. Marcus and Quintus conclude an exchange about the importance of law.

> *Marcus.* Lēge autem carēns cīvitās estne ob id ipsum habenda nūllō locō?
> *Quintus.* Dīcī aliter nōn potest.
> *Marcus.* Necesse est igitur lēgem habērī in rēbus optimīs.
> *Quintus.* Prorsus adsentior. (Cicero, *Dē Lēgibus* II.12)

adsentior, adsentīrī, adsēnsus sum agree
aliter (adv.) in another way, differently, otherwise
prorsus (adv.) thoroughly, in every respect, altogether

21. Cicero singles out Ser. Sulpicius Galba among a group of orators better at public speaking than at recording and refining their speeches in writing. He explains why this may be so.

> quem* fortasse vīs nōn ingenī sōlum sed etiam animī et nātūrālis quīdam dolor dīcentem incendēbat efficiēbatque ut et incitāta et gravis et vehemēns esset ōrātiō.
> (Cicero, *Brūtus* 93)

*__quem__, connective relative; antecedent is Galba
dolor, dolōris *m.* grief, sorrow, pain; indignation
fortasse (adv.) perhaps
incendō, incendere, incendī, incēnsus set on fire; inflame, provoke

incitātus, -a, -um rushing; excited, intense
nātūrālis, nātūrāle natural
vehemēns, vehementis energetic, vigorous, powerful

22. Cicero praises the power of rhetoric.

> sed nihil est tam incrēdibile quod nōn dīcendō fīat probābile, nihil tam horridum,
>
> tam incultum, quod nōn splendēscat ōrātiōne et tamquam excolātur.

(CICERO, *PARADOXA STŌICŌRUM* PREFACE 3)

excolō, excolere, excoluī, excultus cultivate, improve, develop, decorate
horridus, -a, -um rough; rude, uncouth
incrēdibilis, incrēdibile unbelievable
incultus, -a, -um not cultivated, unadorned, lacking in refinement

probābilis, probābile acceptable, plausible, credible
splendēscō, splendēscere, ——, —— become bright, begin to shine
tamquam (conj.) as it were, so to speak

23. Cicero defines some important moral terms.

> quicquid nōn oportet, scelus esse, quicquid nōn licet, nefās putāre dēbēmus.

(CICERO, *PARADOXA STŌICŌRUM* 3.25)

quisquis, quidquid or **quicquid** (indef. rel. pron.) whoever, whatever

24. An opinion about love

> tōtus vērō iste quī volgō appellātur amor—nec hercule inveniō quō nōmine aliō
>
> possit appellārī—tantae levitātis est ut nihil videam quod putem cōnferendum.

(CICERO, *TUSCULĀNAE DISPUTĀTIŌNĒS* IV.38)

appellō (1-tr.) name, call
levitās, levitātis *f.* lack of weight, lightness; unreliability, shallowness
volgō (adv.) publicly; commonly

25. What makes a man great?

> nēmō igitur vir magnus sine aliquō adflātū dīvīnō umquam fuit.

(CICERO, *DĒ NĀTŪRĀ DEŌRUM* II.167)

adflātus, adflātūs *m.* breath; inspiration

26. Having observed the nearly universal belief in the art of divination, Cicero's brother asks whether there will ever be an end to doubt on the subject.

> an* dum bestiae loquantur exspectāmus, hominum cōnsentiente auctōritāte
>
> contentī nōn sumus? (CICERO, *DĒ DĪVĪNĀTIŌNE* I.84)

*****an**, *here, introduces an indignant or surprised question expecting a negative answer,* can it really be that . . .
bestia, bestiae *f.* beast, animal
cōnsentiō (con- + sentiō) be in agreement, concur
contentus, -a, -um content, satisfied

27. The character Cato insists that the length of life is unimportant.

> breve enim tempus aetātis satis longum est ad bene honestēque vīvendum.

(CICERO, *DĒ SENECTŪTE* 70)

28. A reflection on the human soul

> atque etiam cum hominis nātūra morte dissolvitur, cēterārum rērum perspicuum est quō quaeque discēdat; abeunt enim illūc omnia unde orta sunt, animus autem sōlus nec cum adest nec cum discessit appāret. iam vērō vidētis nihil esse mortī tam simile quam somnum. (CICERO, DĒ SENECTŪTE 80)

appāreō, appārēre, appāruī, appāritus be visible, be clear; appear, become evident
dissolvō, dissolvere, dissolvī, dissolūtus undo, dissolve; set free
perspicuus, -a, -um clearly visible, plain, self-evident
somnus, somnī *m.* sleep

29. What value does Cicero place on farming?

> omnium autem rērum ex quibus aliquid adquīritur nihil est agrī cultūrā melius, nihil ūberius, nihil dulcius, nihil homine, nihil līberō dignius.
>
> (CICERO, DĒ OFFICIĪS I.151)

adquīrō (ad- + quaerō), adquīrere, adquīsiī or **adquīsīvī, adquīsītus** add to one's possessions, acquire
cultūra, cultūrae *f.* cultivation
dulcis, dulce sweet, pleasant
ūber, ūberis rich, fertile

30. A rhetorical question about the limits to profit seeking

> est ergō ūlla rēs tantī aut commodum ūllum tam expetendum ut virī bonī et splendōrem et nōmen āmittās? (CICERO, DĒ OFFICIĪS III.82)

āmittō (ā- + mittō) send away; lose, let go
commodum, commodī *n.* advantage, benefit
ergō (adv.) therefore
expetō (ex- + petō) ask for, seek; desire
splendor, splendōris *m.* brightness, radiance, glory

31. In the first of his *Philippics* Cicero declares his resolve to speak his mind no matter the danger.

> quid? dē reliquīs reī pūblicae malīs licetne dīcere? mihi vērō licet et semper licēbit dignitātem tuērī, mortem contemnere. potestās modo veniendī in hunc locum* sit, dīcendī perīculum nōn recūsō. (CICERO, PHILIPPICS I 14)

*hunc locum, *i.e.,* the senate house
contemnō, contemnere, contempsī, contemptus
    regard with contempt; pay no heed to,
    disregard

dignitās, dignitātis *f.* rank, status, dignity
potestās, potestātis *f.* (legitimate) power
recūsō (1-tr.) decline, reject, refuse to accept
tueor, tuērī, tuitus or **tūtus sum** look at; protect

32. Cicero speaks after a scheduled embassy to Antony has been canceled. In an imagined debate, Cicero explains why he approves of the decision to cancel it.

> cuiusvīs hominis est errāre; nūllīus nisi īnsipientis persevērāre in errōre; posteriōrēs
>
> enim cōgitātiōnēs, ut aiunt, sapientiōrēs solent esse. (CICERO, *PHILIPPICS XII* 5)

aiō (defective verb) say; **aiunt** = *3rd pl. pres. act. indic.*
cōgitātiō, cōgitātiōnis *f.* thought
error, errōris *m.* mistake, error
īnsipiēns, īnsipientis unwise, foolish

persevērō (1-intr.) persist, persevere
posterior, posterius later
quīvīs, quaevīs, quodvīs (indef. adj.) any . . . you wish, any . . . at all

33. In the context of thinking about pernicious citizens and civil war, Cicero poses a theoretical question.

> sed hoc prīmum videndum est, patrēs cōnscrīptī, cum omnibusne pāx esse possit
>
> an sit aliquod bellum inexpiābile, in quō pactiō pācis lēx sit servitūtis.
>
> (CICERO, *PHILIPPICS XIII* 2)

inexpiābilis, inexpiābile that cannot be atoned for, that cannot be appeased
pactiō, pactiōnis *f.* agreement, arrangement

34. Immediately after his recall from exile Cicero asks Atticus to come to Rome to visit and advise him. The orator expresses concern about his own future.

> tē exspectō et ōrō ut mātūrēs venīre eōque animō veniās ut mē tuō cōnsiliō egēre
>
> nōn sinās. alterīus vītae quoddam initium ordīmur. iam quīdam quī nōs* absentīs
>
> dēfendērunt incipiunt praesentibus occultē īrāscī, apertē invidēre.
>
> (CICERO, *AD ATTICUM* IV.1.8)

*****nōs** refers to Cicero.
apertē (adv.) openly
dēfendō, dēfendere, dēfendī, dēfēnsus defend
egeō, egēre, eguī, —— need, lack; be without (+ abl.)
initium, initiī *n.* beginning
invideō (in- + videō) envy; regard with ill will (+ dat.)

īrāscor, īrāscī, —— become angry (at) (+ dat.)
mātūrō (1-intr.) make haste, hurry (+ inf.)
occultē (adv.) secretly
ordior, ordīrī, orsus sum embark on, commence
praesēns, praesentis present
sinō, sinere, siī or **sīvī, situs** allow, permit

35. Cicero describes to Atticus his sense of alienation and despair once Pompey has fled to the East.

> alia rēs nunc tōta est, alia mēns mea. sōl, ut est in tuā quādam epistulā, excidisse
>
> mihi ē mundō vidētur. ut aegrōtō, dum anima est, spēs esse dīcitur, sīc ego, quoad
>
> Pompeius in Italiā fuit, spērāre nōn dēstitī. (CICERO, *AD ATTICUM* IX.10.3)

aegrōtus, -a, -um ill, sick
dēsistō, dēsistere, dēstitī, —— cease
epistula, epistulae *f.* letter

excidō (ex- + cadō), excidere, excidī, —— fall (out)
mundus, mundī *m.* world; sky
quoad (conj.) as long as, while

36. The beginning of a letter of Caesar to Cicero, quoted in a letter of Cicero to Atticus

rēctē augurāris dē mē (bene enim tibi* cognitus sum) nihil ā mē abesse longius crūdēlitāte. atque ego cum ex ipsā rē magnam capiō voluptātem tum meum factum probārī abs tē triumphō gaudiō. (CICERO, *AD ATTICUM* IX.16.1)

*tibi Dative of Agent
abs = ab
auguror (1-tr.) foretell, predict; surmise
crūdēlitās, crūdēlitātis *f.* cruelty
gaudium, gaudiī *n.* joy

probō (1-tr.) approve of
rēctē (adv.) rightly, correctly
triumphō (1-intr.) celebrate a triumph; (tr.) exult
  (+ Indirect Statement)
voluptās, voluptātis *f.* pleasure, joy

37. Cicero informs his friend M. Marcellus about the limits on speech and action in the present state of the republic.

at tibi ipsī dīcendum erit aliquid quod nōn sentiās aut faciendum quod nōn probēs.

prīmum temporī* cēdere, id est necessitātī pārēre, semper sapientis est habitum.

(CICERO, *AD FAMILIĀRĒS* IV.9.2)

*tempus, *here,* occasion, circumstance
at (conj.) but
necessitās, necessitātis *f.* necessity
probō (1-tr.) approve of

38. A witticism from Varro

postrēmō nēmō aegrōtus quicquam somniat tam īnfandum quod nōn aliquis* dīcat philosophus. (VARRO, *MENIPPEAE* FRAG. 122)

*aliquis, *here, indef. pron. used adjectivally,* some
aegrōtus, -a, -um sick, diseased
īnfandus, -a, -um unspeakable

philosophus, philosophī *m.* philosopher
postrēmō (adv.) finally
somniō (1-tr.) dream (of)

39. The poet begins a reflection on the purpose and power of philosophy.

Suāve marī magnō turbantibus aequora ventīs

ē terrā magnum alterius* spectāre labōrem;

nōn quia vexārī quemquamst iūcunda voluptās,

sed quibus ipse malīs careās quia cernere suāvest.

(LUCRETIUS, *DĒ RĒRUM NĀTŪRĀ* II.1–4)

*The -i- of alterīus here scans *short.*
aequor, aequoris *n.* level surface; sea, water
cernō, cernere, crēvī, crētus distinguish,
  determine; perceive, observe
iūcundus, -a, -um pleasing, delightful, agreeable
suāvis, suāve sweet, pleasant

turbō (1-tr.) stir up, confuse, throw into
  confusion
ventus, ventī *m.* wind
vexō (1-tr.) trouble, disturb, harass
voluptās, voluptātis *f.* pleasure, joy

40. The poet describes man's superstitious fear and its only medicine.

> nam vel utī puerī trepidant atque omnia caecīs
>
> in tenebrīs metuunt, sīc nōs in lūce timēmus
>
> interdum nihilō quae sunt metuenda magis quam
>
> quae puerī in tenebrīs pavitant finguntque futūra.
>
> hunc igitur terrōrem animī tenebrāsque necessest
>
> nōn radiī sōlis neque lūcida tēla diēī
>
> discutiant, sed nātūrae speciēs ratiōque. (Lucretius, Dē Rērum Nātūrā II.55–61)

discutiō, discutere, discussī, discussus shatter; dissipate, dispel
fingō, fingere, fīnxī, fictus form, fashion, make; imagine
interdum (adv.) from time to time, occasionally
lūcidus, -a, -um shining, bright, clear
pavitō (1-tr.) be in dread of, tremble at

radius, radiī m. ray (of light)
ratiō, ratiōnis f. account, reason; reasoning; rationale
tenebrae, tenebrārum f. pl. darkness, shadows
terror, terrōris m. (extreme) fear, terror
trepidō (1-intr.) tremble; panic
utī = ut

41. The poet describes how the earth, like all living things, is subject to decay and diminution of her powers.

> iamque adeō frācta est aetās effētaque tellūs
>
> vix animālia parva creat, quae cūncta creāvit
>
> saecla deditque ferārum ingentia corpora partū.
>
> (Lucretius, Dē Rērum Nātūrā II.1150–52)

creō (1-tr.) create
effētus, -a, -um worn out
fera, ferae f. wild animal
frangō, frangere, frēgī, frāctus break

partus, partūs m. birth
saec(u)lum, saec(u)lī n. age, generation
tellūs, tellūris f. earth

42. The poet reports an inner conflict.

> Hūc est mēns dēducta tuā mea, Lesbia, culpā,
>
> atque ita sē officiō perdidit ipsa suō,
>
> ut iam nec bene velle queat tibi, sī optima fīās,
>
> nec dēsistere amāre, omnia sī faciās. (Catullus LXXV)

culpa, culpae f. guilt, blame; fault
dēdūcō (dē- + dūcō) lead down; bring down
dēsistō, dēsistere, dēstitī, —— cease, stop
officium, officiī n. obligation; sense of duty
queō, quīre, quiī or quīvī, —— be able

43. The poet responds to his beloved's declaration.

> Iūcundum, mea vīta, mihi prōpōnis amōrem
>> hunc nostrum inter nōs perpetuumque fore.
> dī magnī, facite ut vērē prōmittere possit,
>> atque id sincērē dīcat et ex animō,
> ut liceat nōbīs tōtā perdūcere vītā
>> aeternum hoc sānctae foedus amīcitiae. (Catullus CIX)

aeternus, -a, -um eternal, everlasting
foedus, foederis *n.* agreement, treaty, pact
iūcundus, -a, -um pleasing, delightful, agreeable
perdūcō (per- + dūcō) extend, prolong
perpetuus, -a, -um continuous; everlasting

prōmittō (prō- + mittō) promise
prōpōnō (prō- + pōnō) put forward; declare
sānctus, -a, -um inviolate, blameless
sincērē (adv.) faithfully, truly

44. Having just described various geographical constraints (mountains, lakes, rivers), Caesar reports their effects on the actions and feelings of the Helvetians.

> hīs rēbus fīēbat ut et minus lātē vagārentur et minus facile fīnitimīs bellum īnferre
>
> possent; quā ex parte* hominēs bellandī cupidī magnō dolōre adficiēbantur.

(Caesar, *Dē Bellō Gallicō* I.2)

*qua ex parte** and on this account
adficiō (ad- + faciō) affect, stir, move strongly
bellō (1-intr.) wage war, fight
dolor, dolōris *m.* grief, sorrow, pain

fīnitimus, -a, -um neighboring, nearby; *as subst.*, neighbor
lātē (adv.) widely, far and wide
vagor (1-intr.) wander

45. Caesar explains his decision to cross the Rhine.

> Germānicō bellō cōnfectō, multīs dē causīs Caesar statuit sibi Rhēnum esse trānse-
>
> undum. quārum illa fuit iūstissima: quod cum vidēret Germānōs tam facile impellī
>
> ut in Galliam venīrent, suīs quoque rēbus eōs timēre voluit, cum intellegerent et
>
> posse et audēre populī Rōmānī exercitum Rhēnum trānsīre.

(Caesar, *Dē Bellō Gallicō* IV.16)

Gallia, Galliae *f.* Gaul
Germānī, Germānōrum *m. pl.* (the) Germans
Germānicus, -a, -um German
impellō (in- + pellō), impellere, impulī, impulsus push against; press upon; constrain, impel
iūstus, -a, -um just, fair, right

Rhēnus, Rhēnī *m.* (the) Rhine, a river in northeastern Gaul
statuō, statuere, statuī, statūtus cause to stand; decide
trānseō (trāns- + eō), trānsīre, trānsiī or **trānsīvī, trānsitus** go across, cross

46. Caesar comments on a confused moment caused by a surprise attack of Germans.

> nēmō est tam fortis quīn reī novitāte perturbētur. (Caesar, *Dē Bellō Gallicō* VI.39)

novitās, novitātis *f.* newness, novelty; unfamiliarity, unexpectedness
perturbō (1-tr.) throw into confusion, upset, confound

47. On the eve of civil war Caesar hears that the citizens of Massilia have closed their gates to
him and are siding with Pompey. He rushes to the city to negotiate with the Massilian
leaders.

ēvocat ad sē Caesar Massiliā xv prīmōs.* cum hīs agit† nē initium īnferendī bellī ā

Massiliēnsibus oriātur: dēbēre eōs Italiae tōtīus auctōritātem sequī potius quam

ūnīus hominis voluntātī obtemperāre. reliqua, quae ad eōrum sānandās mentēs per-

tinēre arbitrābātur, commemorat. (CAESAR, *DĒ BELLŌ CĪVĪLĪ* I.35)

*prīmus, *here used substantively,* chief
†agō, *here,* treat, negotiate
commemorō (1-tr.) make mention (of)
ēvocō (ē- + vocō) (1-tr.) call out, summon out
initium, initiī *n.* beginning
Massilia, Massiliae *f.* Massilia, a town in Gaul
Massiliēnsēs, Massiliēnsium *m. pl.* inhabitants
  of Massilia, Massilians

obtemperō (1-intr.) obey (+ dat.)
pertineō (per- + teneō), pertinēre, pertinuī,
  pertentus pertain; pertinēre + ad + acc.,
  to pertain to
potius (comparative adv.) rather
sānō (1-tr.) heal, make well
voluntās, voluntātis *f.* will

48. The historian explains why the consul Metellus proceeded cautiously through Numidia
despite no outward signs of resistance.

nam in Iugurthā tantus dolus tantaque perītia locōrum et mīlitiae erat ut absēns

an praesēns, pācem an bellum gerēns, perniciōsior esset in incertō habērētur.

(SALLUST, *BELLUM IUGURTHAE* 46)

dolus, dolī *m.* deceit, trick, cunning
Iugurtha, Iugurthae *m.* Jugurtha, king of
  Numidia
mīlitia, mīlitiae *f.* military service

perītia, perītiae *f.* knowledge (acquired through
  experience)
perniciōsus, -a, -um destructive, deadly
praesēns, praesentis present

49. The poet describes the lovesick Dido after the end of the banquet honoring Aeneas.

post ubi dīgressī, lūmenque obscūra vicissim

lūna premit suādentque cadentia sīdera somnōs,

sōla domō maeret vacuā strātīsque relictīs

incubat. illum absēns absentem auditque videtque . . . (VERGIL, *AENEID* IV.80–83)

dīgredior (dis- + gradior) go off, depart; separate;
  dīgressī, subject is Dido and Aeneas
incubō, incubāre, ——, incubitum lie on, recline
  on (+ dat.)
maereō, maerēre, ——, —— grieve, mourn
obscūrus, -a, -um dark, dim, obscure
sīdus, sīderis *n.* star

somnus, somnī *m.* sleep
strātum, strātī *n.* bedding; couch
suādeō, suādēre, suāsī, suāsus urge, advise;
  persuade
vacuus, -a, -um empty
vicissim (adv.) in turn

50. The poet sets a romantic scene.

Nox erat et caelō fulgēbat lūna serēnō

inter minōra sīdera . . . (HORACE, *EPODES* 15.1–2)

fulgeō, fulgēre, fulsī, —— gleam, shine
serēnus, -a, -um calm, serene
sīdus, sīderis *n.* star

51. The poet remarks on the advantages of delaying publication.

. . . dēlēre licēbit

quod nōn ēdideris, nescit vōx missa revertī. (Horace, *Ars Poētica* 389–90)

ēdō (**ē-** + **dō**) emit; produce; publish
revertor, revertī, reversus sum turn back; return

52. Cynthia is about to run off after a praetor from Illyria.

Tūne igitur dēmēns, nec tē mea cūra morātur?

an* tibi sum gelidā vīlior Illyriā?

et tibi iam tantī, quīcumquest, iste vidētur,

ut sine mē ventō quōlibet īre velīs? (Propertius I.8a.1–4)

***an**, *here, introduces an indignant or surprised*
question expecting a negative answer, can it
really be that . . .
dēmēns, dēmentis insane, (raving) mad
gelidus, -a, -um very cold, icy cold
Illyria, Illyriae *f.* Illyria, the territory of the
Illyrians east of the Adriatic Sea

quīcumque, quaecumque, quodcumque (indef.
rel. pron.) whoever, whatever
quīlibet, quaelibet, quodlibet (indef. adj.) any . . .
you wish, any . . . at all
ventus, ventī *m.* wind
vīlis, vīle worthless, cheap

53. Addressing Cynthia, the poet announces a momentous change.

Scrībant dē tē aliī vel sīs ignōta licēbit . . . (Propertius II.11.1)

ignōtus, -a, -um unknown

54. The poet states his theme.

Sī quis in hōc artem populō nōn nōvit amandī,

hoc legat et lēctō carmine doctus amet.

arte citae vēlōque ratēs rēmōque moventur,

arte levēs currūs, arte regendus amor. (Ovid, *Ars Amātōria* I.1–4)

citus, -a, -um quick, swift
currus, currūs *m.* chariot
doceō, docēre, docuī, doctus teach
ratis, ratis, -ium *f.* ship
rēmus, rēmī *m.* oar

55. Exiled to Tomis on the Black Sea, the poet comments on the locale and the native population.

> sīve locum spectō, locus est inamābilis, et quō
>> esse nihil tōtō trīstius orbe potest,
> sīve hominēs, vix sunt hominēs hōc nōmine dignī,
>> quamque lupī saevae plūs feritātis habent.
> nōn metuunt lēgēs, sed cēdit vīribus aequum,
>> victaque pugnācī iūra sub ēnse iacent. (OVID, *TRĪSTIA* V.7b.43–48)

ēnsis, ēnsis *m.* sword
feritās, feritātis *f.* wildness, fierceness; savagery, brutality
iaceō, iacēre, iacuī, —— lie
inamābilis, inamābile unlovable, disagreeable, unattractive

lupus, lupī *m.* wolf
orbis, orbis, -ium *m.* ring, circle; world
pugnāx, pugnācis fond of fighting, combative, warlike
sīve (conj.) or if; **sīve . . . sīve . . .** if . . . or if . . .
trīstis, trīste sad, gloomy, melancholy, grim

56. The poet describes the length of his banishment in epic terms.

> at mihi iam videor patriā procul esse tot annīs,*
>> Dardana quot Graiō Troia sub hoste fuit.
> stāre† putēs, adeō prōcēdunt tempora tardē . . . (OVID, *TRĪSTIA* V.10.3–5)

*****tot annīs,** *here,* for as many years
†**stō,** *here,* stand still
at (conj.) but
Dardanus, -a, -um Dardanian, Trojan

Graius, -a, -um Greek
prōcēdō (prō- + cēdō) go forward, progress
procul (adv.) at a distance, far
tardē (adv.) slowly

57. When the Romans are prevented by dusk from engaging the opposing army, an enemy taunts them from behind his battle line.

> "longiōre lūce ad id certāmen quod īnstat nōbīs opus est. crāstinō diē, oriente sōle redīte in aciem; erit cōpia pugnandī; nē timēte."* hīs vōcibus inrītātus mīles in† diem posterum in castra redūcitur,‡ longam venīre noctem ratus quae moram certāminī faceret. (LIVY, *AB URBE CONDITĀ* III.2.9)

*****nē timēte** = negative imperative
†**in,** *here,* until
‡**redūcitur** historical use of present tense; translate as perfect
certāmen, certāminis *n.* contest; fight, battle
crāstinus, -a, -um of tomorrow; **crāstinus diēs,** tomorrow

īnstō (in- + stō), īnstāre, īnstitī, īnstātūrus press (hostilely); loom, threaten
irrītō (1-tr.) annoy, vex, irritate; arouse
posterus, -a, -um next, following
redūcō (re- + dūcō) lead back
reor, rērī, ratus sum believe, think, imagine

58. The historian reports that after the Romans retook certain towns in southern Italy from the Carthaginians, they distinguished themselves in a disgraceful way.

. . . tantum Pleminius Hamilcarem praesidiī praefectum,* tantum praesidiāriī mī-

litēs Rōmānī Poenōs scelere atque avāritiā superāvērunt ut nōn armīs sed vitiīs

vidērētur certārī. (Livy, *Ab Urbe Conditā* XXIX.8.7)

*praefectus, praefectī *m.* commander, officer
avāritia, avāritiae *f.* greed, avarice
certō (1-intr.) struggle, contend, strive
Hamilcar, Hamilcaris *m.* Hamilcar, Carthaginian commander
Pleminius, Pleminiī *m.* (Q.) Pleminius, Roman military officer

Poenī, Poenōrum *m. pl.* (the) Phoenicians, (the) Carthaginians
praesidiārius, -a, -um forming a guard or garrison
praesidium, praesidiī *n.* guard, garrison
vitium, vitiī *n.* vice, fault

59. Seneca quotes the second-century B.C.E. philosopher Posidonius, who explains why he objects to the inclusion of explanations and introductions in Plato's *Laws*.

lēgem enim brevem esse oportet, quō facilius ab inperītīs teneātur.

(Seneca the Younger, *Epistulae Mōrālēs* XCIV.38)

imperītus, -a, -um inexperienced, unacquainted

60. Seneca quotes a line that is said to have made the audience look at Caesar. It was uttered by the writer and actor Decimus Laberius at the time of the civil war.

necesse est multōs timeat quem multī timent. (Seneca the Younger, *Dialogī* IV.11.3)

61. Seneca reports how the Stoic philosopher Diogenes responded to being spit upon by one of his students during class.

tulit hoc ille lēniter et sapienter: "nōn quidem" inquit "īrāscor, sed dubitō* tamen an

oporteat īrāscī." (Seneca the Younger, *Dialogī* V.38.1)

*dubitō, *here,* wonder
inquam (defective verb) say; **inquit** = *3rd sing. pres. act. indic.*
īrāscor, īrāscī, ——, become angry
lēniter (adv.) gently, mildly
sapienter (adv.) wisely

62. A definition and contemplation of death

mors dolōrum omnium exsolūtiō est et fīnis ultrā quem mala nostra nōn exeunt,
quae nōs in illam tranquillitātem in quā antequam nāscerēmur iacuimus repōnit. sī
mortuōrum aliquis miserētur, et nōn nātōrum misereātur. mors nec bonum nec
malum est; id enim potest aut bonum aut malum esse quod aliquid est; quod vērō
ipsum nihil est et omnia in nihilum redigit, nūllī nōs fortūnae trādit.

(SENECA THE YOUNGER, *DIALOGĪ* VI.19.5)

dolor, dolōris *m.* grief, sorrow, pain
exeō (ex- + eō), exīre, exiī or **exīvī, exitum** go out,
    exit
exsolūtiō, exsolūtiōnis *f.* dissolution
iaceō, iacēre, iacuī, —— lie, rest; lie dead
misereor, miserērī, miseritus sum pity, take pity
    on (+ gen.)

redigō (red- + agō), redigere, redēgī, redāctus
    drive back; restore, convert
repōnō (re- + pōnō) put *or* place back
tranquillitās, tranquillitātis *f.* calm, tranquility
ultrā (prep. + acc.) beyond

63. A character in a Senecan dialogue expresses his opinion on the nature of human life.

nihil est tam fallāx quam vīta hūmāna, nihil tam īnsidiōsum: nōn meherculēs
quisquam illam accēpisset nisi darētur ignōrantibus.

(SENECA THE YOUNGER, *DIALOGĪ* VI.22.3)

fallāx, fallācis deceptive, treacherous
hūmānus, -a, -um human
ignōrō (1-tr.) be unaware (of), be ignorant (of)
īnsidiōsus, -a, -um treacherous, deceitful

64. The poet vividly characterizes Julius Caesar.

. . . sed Caesar in omnia praeceps,

nīl āctum crēdēns cum quid superesset agendum, . . .

(LUCAN, *BELLUM CĪVĪLE* II.656–57)

praeceps, praecipitis rushing forward, headlong
supersum (super- + sum), superesse, superfuī, superfutūrus remain, be left

65. The poet makes a concession.

Sexte, nihil dēbēs, nīl dēbēs, Sexte, fatēmur.

dēbet enim, sī quis solvere, Sexte, potest. (MARTIAL II.3)

solvō, solvere, solvī, solūtus loosen; free; pay

66. Pliny describes to Trajan the effect of his having made two well-respected senators consuls.

praecipuē tamen ex hōrum* cōnsulātū nōn ad partem aliquam senātūs sed ad tōtum
senātum tanta laetitia pervēnit ut eundem honōrem omnēs sibi et dedisse et accē-
pisse videantur. (PLINY THE YOUNGER, *PANĒGYRICUS* 62.1)

***hōrum** refers to the two new consuls.
laetitia, laetitiae *f.* happiness
perveniō (per- + veniō) arrive (at), reach, extend
praecipuē (adv.) especially; more than anything else

67. Pliny reassures the senators about the emperor Trajan's concern for them.

   vōs ille* praesentēs, vōs etiam absentēs in cōnsiliō habet. (PLINY, *PANĒGYRICUS* 62.5)

*ille refers to Trajan.
praesēns, praesentis present

68. A battle between Roman troops and Batavians revolting in Germany

   pugnātum longō agmine et incertō Marte dōnec praelium nox dīrimeret.*

   (TACITUS, *HISTORIAE* IV.35)

*The subjunctive in a subordinate clause in later Latin often does not express anticipation.
dīrimō, dīrimere, dīrēmī, dīrēmptus break up, dissolve
praelium = proelium

69. The historian reports an eclipse that stops a nascent mutiny of Roman troops prone to superstition.

   noctem minācem et in scelus ēruptūram fors lēnīvit: nam lūna clārō repente caelō

   vīsa languēscere. (TACITUS, *ANNĀLĒS* I.28)

ērumpō, ērumpere, ērūpī, ēruptus break out, burst forth
**languēscō, languēscere, languī, —— ** grow weak; fail; wane
lēniō, lēnīre, lēnīvī or **lēniī, lēnītus** moderate, calm, mitigate
mināx, minācis menacing, threatening
repente (adv.) suddenly, without warning

70. A group of Roman soldiers battling the Britons meets with a reversal.

   ubi ventum ad aggerem, dum missilibus certābātur, plūs vulnerum in nōs et

   plēraeque caedēs oriēbantur. (TACITUS, *ANNĀLĒS* XII.35)

agger, aggeris *m.* earthwork; fortification, rampart
caedēs, caedis, -ium *f.* slaughter
certō (1-intr.) struggle, contend, strive
missile, missilis, -ium *n.* projectile
plērīque, plēraeque, plēraque very many, most

71. The biographer describes the changes made by Augustus to Rome.

   urbem neque prō* maiestāte imperiī ornātam et inundātiōnibus incendiīsque ob-

   noxiam excoluit adeō ut iūre sit glōriātus marmoream sē relinquere quam latericiam

   accēpisset. (SUETONIUS, *VĪTA AUGUSTĪ* 28)

*prō, *here*, in accordance with
excolō, excolere, excoluī, excultus cultivate, improve, develop, decorate
glōrior (1-tr.) boast
incendium, incendiī *n.* fire
inundātiō, inundātiōnis *f.* flood

latericius, -a, -um made of brick
maiestās, maiestātis *f.* dignity, majesty
marmoreus, -a, -um made of marble, marble
obnoxius, -a, -um exposed, vulnerable
ornō (1-tr.) dress, adorn, decorate

72. Macrobius comments on an aspect of Vergilian style.

vīs audīre illum tantā brevitāte dīcentem ut artārī magis et contrahī brevitās ipsa nōn possit? "Et campōs, ubi Troia fuit." ecce paucissimīs verbīs maximam cīvitātem hausit et absorpsit, nōn relīquit illī nec* ruīnam. (Macrobius, *Saturnālia* V.1.8)

*The redundant negative strengthens the
  negative idea.
absorbeō, absorbēre, absorpsī, absorptus engulf,
  devour
artō (1-tr.) tighten, restrict, make narrow; reduce,
  compress

brevitās, brevitātis *f.* brevity
contrahō, contrahere, contrāxī, contractus
  contract, reduce
hauriō, haurīre, hausī, haustus drain, empty out,
  consume
ruīna, ruīnae *f.* ruin(s)

Longer Readings

1. Cicero, *In Verrem II* 2.162

Cicero attacks Verres directly for his barbarous treatment of a Roman citizen.

cum ignēs ardentēsque lāminae cēterīque cruciātūs admovēbantur, sī tē illīus*
acerba implōrātiō et vōx miserābilis nōn inhibēbat, nē cīvium quidem Rōmānōrum
quī tum aderant flētū et gemitū maximō commovēbāre? in crucem tū agere ausus es
quemquam quī sē cīvem Rōmānum esse dīceret?

*illīus refers to one of Verres's victims.

admoveō (ad- + moveō) move toward; apply, inflict
ardeō, ardēre, arsī, arsūrus burn, be on fire
commoveō (con- + moveō) disturb, trouble
cruciātus, cruciātūs *m.* (instrument of) torture
crux, crucis *f.* wooden frame, cross

flētus, flētūs *m.* weeping, tears
gemitus, gemitūs *m.* groan(ing), moan(ing)
implōrātiō, implōrātiōnis *f.* appeal, entreaty
inhibeō (in- + habeō), inhibēre, inhibuī, inhibitus hold back, restrain, check
lāmina, lāminae *f.* thin sheet of metal, blade
miserābilis, miserābile miserable, wretched

2. Cicero, *In Catilīnam I* 1–2

Cicero opens his first speech against Catiline with a barrage of hostile questions directed at Catiline himself, who was present in the senate for the speech.

Quō ūsque tandem abūtēre, Catilīna, patientiā nostrā? quam diū etiam furor iste tuus
nōs ēlūdet? quem ad fīnem sēsē effrēnāta iactābit audācia? nihilne tē nocturnum
praesidium Palātī, nihil urbis vigiliae, nihil timor populī, nihil concursus bonōrum
omnium, nihil hic mūnītissimus habendī senātūs locus, nihil hōrum ōra voltūsque
mōvērunt? patēre tua cōnsilia nōn sentīs, cōnstrictam iam hōrum omnium scientiā
tenērī coniūrātiōnem tuam nōn vidēs? quid proximā, quid superiōre nocte ēgeris, ubi
fuerīs, quōs convocāverīs, quid cōnsilī cēperīs quem nostrum ignōrāre arbitrāris? ō
tempora, ō mōrēs! senātus haec intellegit, cōnsul videt; hic tamen vīvit. vīvit? immō
vērō etiam in senātum venit, fit pūblicī cōnsilī particeps, notat et dēsignat oculīs ad
caedem unum quemque nostrum.

abūtor (ab- + ūtor) abuse (+ abl.)
caedēs, caedis, -ium *f.* slaughter
concursus, concursūs *m.* gathering
coniūrātiō, coniūrātiōnis *f.* conspiracy
cōnstringō, cōnstringere, cōnstrīnxī, cōnstrictus restrain
convocō (con- + vocō) (1-tr.) summon *or* call together
dēsignō (1-tr.) point out
effrēnātus, -a, -um unbridled, unrestrained
ēlūdō, ēlūdere, ēlūsī, ēlūsus mock
furor, furōris *m.* madness
iactō (1-tr.) throw, hurl
ignōrō (1-tr.) be unaware of, fail to recognize
immō vērō (adv.) no, even
mūnītus, -a, -um well fortified, well defended

nocturnus, -a, -um at night, nocturnal
notō (1-tr.) mark
Palātium, Palātiī *n.* (the) Palatine (hill)
particeps, participis *m.* participant, sharer
pateō, patēre, patuī, —— lie open
patientia, patientiae *f.* endurance, patience
praesidium, praesidiī *n.* guard, garrison
proximus, -a, -um nearest; most recent, last
scientia, scientiae *f.* knowledge
superior, superius (comparative adj.) upper; previous, earlier
ūsque (adv.) continuously, all the way (to);
    quō ūsque, (up) to what point, how far
vigilia, vigiliae *f.* watch (divided into four segments to cover a night)
vultus, vultūs *m.* expression; face

3.　Cicero, *Prō Lēge Mānīliā* 14–16

Cicero explains how even the threat of war affects the provinces, particularly Asia, one of the wealthiest.

itaque haec vōbīs prōvincia, Quirītēs, sī et bellī ūtilitātem et pācis dignitātem retinēre voltis, nōn modo ā calamitāte sed etiam ā metū calamitātis est dēfendenda. nam in cēterīs rēbus cum vēnit calamitās, tum dētrīmentum accipitur; at in vectīgālibus nōn sōlum adventus malī sed etiam metus ipse adfert calamitātem. nam cum hostium cōpiae nōn longē absunt, etiam sī inruptiō nūlla facta est, tamen pecua relinquuntur, agrī cultūra dēseritur, mercātōrum nāvigātiō conquiēscit. ita neque ex portū neque ex decumīs* neque ex scrīptūrā vectīgal cōnservārī potest; quārē saepe tōtīus annī frūctus ūnō rūmōre perīculī atque ūnō bellī terrōre āmittitur.

*decumus, *here, as subst.,* tenth, (a type of) tax

afferō (ad- + ferō), afferre, attulī, allātus bring toward, bring forth

adventus, adventūs *m.* arrival

āmittō (ā- + mittō) send away; lose

at (conj.) but

calamitās, calamitātis *f.* disaster, misfortune, injury

conquiēscō, conquiēscere, conquiēvī, —— rest; cease

cōnservō (con- + servō) (1-tr.) preserve thoroughly, maintain

cultūra, cultūrae *f.* cultivation

dēfendō, dēfendere, dēfendī, dēfēnsus protect, defend

dēserō, dēserere, dēseruī, dēsertus abandon, desert, forsake

dētrīmentum, dētrīmentī *n.* harm

dignitās, dignitātis *f.* rank, status, dignity

frūctus, frūctūs *m.* profit, benefit; revenue

irruptiō, irruptiōnis *f.* assault, incursion

itaque (conj.) and so, and therefore

mercātor, mercātōris *m.* merchant, trader

nāvigātiō, nāvigātiōnis *f.* sailing, voyaging

pecua, pecuum *n. pl.* farm animals

portus, portūs *m.* harbor, port

Quirītēs, Quirītium *m. pl.* Quirites, the name for Roman citizens in their public capacity

retineō (re- + teneō), retinēre, retinuī, retentus keep hold of, retain

scrīptūra, scrīptūrae *f.* writing; tax

terror, terrōris *m.* fear, terror

ūtilitās, ūtilitātis *f.* usefulness, advantage

vectīgal, vectīgālis, -ium *n.* (tax) revenue

In 66 B.C.E. Cicero delivered the *Dē Lēge Mānīliā* endorsing a bill that was meant to strengthen Pompey's hand in dealing with Rome's enemies in the East.

4. Cicero, *Ad Familiārēs* VII.1.3

Cicero writes to his friend Marius about the barbarity of the **vēnātiōnēs**, the hunting portion of Roman games.

sed quae potest hominī esse polītō dēlectātiō cum aut homō imbecillus ā valentissimā bestiā laniātur aut praeclāra bestia vēnābulō trānsverberātur? quae tamen, sī videnda sunt, saepe vīdistī, neque nōs quī haec spectāvimus quicquam novī vīdimus. extrē- mus elephantōrum diēs fuit. in quō admīrātiō magna vulgī atque turbae, dēlectātiō nūlla exstitit; quīn etiam* misericordia quaedam cōnsecūta est atque opīniō eius modī: esse quandam illī bēluae cum genere hūmānō societātem.

*****quīn etiam**, *introduces a correction of something just said*, no, even

admīrātiō, admīrātiōnis *f.* wonder, astonishment

bēlua, bēluae *f.* beast

bestia, bestiae *f.* beast, animal, creature

cōnsequor (con- + sequor) follow (as a consequence)

dēlectātiō, dēlectātiōnis *f.* (source of) delight, amusement

elephantus, elephantī *m.* elephant

ex(s)istō, ex(s)istere, ex(s)titī, —— stand out, appear, emerge

extrēmus, -a, -um last

hūmānus, -a, -um human

imbecillus, -a, -um weak, feeble

laniō (1-tr.) tear savagely, mutilate

misericordia, misericordiae *f.* pity

opīniō, opīniōnis *f.* opinion, belief

polītus, -a, -um polished; refined

praeclārus, -a, -um very famous; splendid, magnificent

societās, societātis *f.* fellowship, society; (close) relationship, connection

trānsverberō (1-tr.) strike so as to pierce through, transfix

turba, turbae *f.* crowd

vēnābulum, vēnābulī *n.* hunting spear

vulgus, vulgī *n.* common people, (the) multitude

Cicero's letters *Ad Familiārēs* in sixteen books are addressed to a wide variety of friends and acquaintances and treat of many subjects. Also included in the collection are replies from many of the addressees. The *Ad Familiārēs* may have been edited for publication by Cicero's freedman and secretary, Tiro.

5. Catullus XII (hendecasyllable)

The poet addresses an acquaintance with an annoying habit.

Marrūcīne Asinī, manū sinistrā
nōn bellē ūteris: in iocō atque vīnō
tollis lintea neglegentiōrum.
hoc salsum esse putās? fugit tē,* inepte:
quamvīs sordida rēs et invenustast.   5
nōn crēdis mihi? crēde Polliōnī
frātrī, quī tua furta vel talentō
mūtārī velit: est enim lepōrum
differtus puer ac facētiārum.
quārē aut hendecasyllabōs trecentōs   10
exspectā, aut mihi linteum remitte;
quod mē nōn movet aestimātiōne,
vērumst mnēmosynum meī sodālis.
nam sūdāria Saetaba ex Hibērīs
mīsērunt mihi mūnerī Fabullus   15
et Vērānius: haec amem necessest
ut Vērāniolum meum et Fabullum.

*__fugit tē__, *sc.,* __ratiō, ratiōnis__ *f.* reason
__aestimātiō, aestimātiōnis__ *f.* value, (monetary) worth
__bellē__ (adv.) prettily, neatly, becomingly
__differtus, -a, -um__ stuffed, filled full (+ gen.)
__Fabullus, Fabullī__ *m.* Fabullus
__facētiae, facētiārum__ *f. pl.* wit, drollery, humor
__furtum, furtī__ *n.* theft, robbery
__hendecasyllabī, hendecasyllabōrum__ *m. pl.* hendecasyllables
__Hibērī, Hibērōrum__ *m. pl.* Iberians, Spaniards
__ineptus, -a, -um__ silly, inept, foolish
__invenustus, -a, -um__ ungraceful, inelegant
__iocus, iocī__ *m.* jest, joke
__lepor, lepōris__ *m.* pleasantness, charm
__linteum, linteī__ *n.* linen cloth, napkin
__Marrūcīnus Asinius, Marrūcīnī Asiniī__ *m.* Marrucinus Asinius
__mnēmosynum, mnēmosynī__ *n.* remembrance, token

__mūnus, mūneris__ *n.* present, gift
__neglegēns, neglegentis__ careless, heedless
__Polliō, Polliōnis__ *m.* Pollio
__quamvīs__ (adv.) as you will, ever so
__remittō (re- + mittō)__ send back, return
__Saetabus, -a, -um__ of Saetabis, a town in Spain; Spanish
__salsus, -a, -um__ salty; witty
__sinister, sinistra, sinistrum__ left
__sodālis, sodālis, -ium__ *m.* comrade, companion
__sordidus, -a, -um__ dirty; mean, vulgar
__sūdārium, sūdāriī__ *n.* cloth, napkin
__talentum, talentī__ *n.* talent, a sum of money
__tollō, tollere, sustulī, sublātus__ lift, raise; take away, carry off
__Vērāniolus, Vērāniolī__ *m.* (dear) little Veranius
__Vērānius, Vērāniī__ *m.* Veranius
__vīnum, vīnī__ *n.* wine

6. Lucretius, *Dē Rērum Nātūrā* I.199–207

The poet summarizes one of the most important principles of nature.

> dēnique cūr hominēs tantōs nātūra parāre
> nōn potuit, pedibus quī pontum per vada possent   200
> trānsīre et magnōs manibus dīvellere montīs
> multaque vīvendō vītālia vincere saecla,
> sī nōn māteriēs quia rēbus reddita certast
> gignundīs, ē quā cōnstat quid possit orīrī?
> nīl igitur fierī dē nīlō posse fatendumst,   205
> sēmine quandō opus est rēbus, quō quaeque creātae
> āeris in tenerās possint prōferrier aurās.

āēr, āeris *m.* air
aura, aurae *f.* breeze
cōnstō (con- + stō), cōnstāre, cōnstitī, ——
  stand still; be composed (of), consist (in);
  be fixed
creō (1-tr.) create, conceive
dēnique (adv.) finally
dīvellō, dīvellere, dīvellī, dīvulsus tear apart,
  tear up
gignō, gignere, genuī, genitus beget, produce;
  gignundīs = archaic form of **gignendīs**
māteriēs, māteriēī *f.* matter, material, primal
  substance
parō (1-tr.) prepare; furnish, produce
pēs, pedis *m.* foot

pontus, pontī *m.* sea
prōferō (prō- + ferō), prōferre, prōtulī, prōlātus
  bring forth; *in passive,* come forth, emerge;
  prōferrier = archaic form of **prōferrī**
quandō (conj.) since
reddō (red- + dō) give back; render
saec(u)lum, saec(u)lī *n.* age, generation
sēmen, sēminis *n.* seed
tener, tenera, tenerum tender, soft, delicate
trānseō (trāns- + eō), trānsīre, trānsiī or trānsīvī,
  trānsitus go across, cross
vadum, vadī *n.* shallow, shoal; *in pl.,* waters
  (of the sea)
vītālis, vītāle living, vital; life-giving

7. Caesar, *Dē Bellō Gallicō* I.39

The effect on Caesar's men of rumors about the Germans

dum paucōs diēs ad* Vesontiōnem reī frūmentāriae commeātūsque causā morātur,[†]
ex percontātiōne nostrōrum vōcibusque Gallōrum ac mercātōrum, quī ingentī magnitūdine corporum Germānōs, incrēdibilī virtūte atque exercitātiōne in armīs esse
praedicābant—saepe numerō sēsē cum hīs congressōs nē vultum quidem atque
aciem oculōrum dīcēbant ferre potuisse—tantus subitō timor omnem exercitum oc-
cupāvit ut nōn mediocriter omnium mentēs animōsque perturbāret. hic prīmum
ortus est ā tribūnīs mīlitum, praefectīs[‡] reliquīsque, quī ex urbe amīcitiae causā Caesarem secūtī nōn magnum in rē mīlitārī ūsum habēbant. quōrum alius aliā causā in-
lātā, quam sibi ad proficīscendum necessāriam esse dīceret, petēbat ut eius voluntāte
discēdere licēret; nōnnūllī pudōre adductī ut timōris suspīciōnem vītārent remanē-
bant. hī neque vultum fingere neque interdum lacrimās tenēre[§] poterant; abditī in
tabernāculīs aut suum fātum querēbantur aut cum familiāribus suīs commūne perīculum miserābantur. vulgō tōtīs castrīs testāmenta obsignābantur. hōrum vōcibus ac
timōre paulātim etiam iī quī magnum in castrīs ūsum habēbant, mīlitēs centuriō-
nēsque quīque equitātuī praeerant, perturbābantur.

*ad, *here,* at, near
[†]morātur, subject is Caesar
[‡]praefectus, praefectī *m.* commander, officer
[§]teneō, *here,* hold back
abditus, -a, -um hidden
addūcō (ad- + dūcō) lead (toward); induce,
    influence
centuriō, centuriōnis *m.* centurion, an officer
    commanding a century
commeātus, commeātūs *m.* cargo; provisions
commūnis, commūne common, shared
congredior (con- + gradior) approach; join battle
equitātus, equitātūs *m.* cavalry
exercitātiō, exercitātiōnis *f.* training, exercise;
    skill, proficiency
familiāris, familiāre belonging to one's house-
    hold; well known, familiar; *as subst.,* friend,
    intimate
fingō, fingere, fīnxī, fictus form, fashion; make
    (up), simulate; compose
frūmentārius, -a, -um of grain;
    rēs frūmentāria, grain supply, supplies
Gallī, Gallōrum *m. pl.* (the) Gauls
Germānī, Germānōrum *m. pl.* (the) Germans
incrēdibilis, incrēdibile unbelievable
interdum (adv.) from time to time, occasionally
lacrima, lacrimae *f.* tear
magnitūdō, magnitūdinis *f.* magnitude, size
mediocriter (adv.) to a moderate degree
mercātor, mercātōris *m.* merchant, trader

mīlitāris, mīlitāre military; rēs mīlitāris, military
    affairs, military practice
miseror (1-tr.) pity
necessārius, -a, -um necessary
nōnnūllī, -ae, -a a number, not a few, some
numerus, numerī *m.* number; saepe numerō,
    often (in respect to number)
obsignō (1-tr.) affix a seal to, seal
occupō (1-tr.) seize
paulātim (adv.) little by little
percontātiō, percontātiōnis *f.* interrogation
perturbō (1-tr.) upset, disturb, agitate
praedicō (1-tr.) proclaim, declare
pudor, pudōris *m.* shame, decency, modesty
queror, querī, questus sum complain, protest;
    lament
remaneō (re- + maneō) remain
subitō (adv.) suddenly
suspīciō, suspīciōnis *f.* suspicion; trace
tabernāculum, tabernāculī *n.* tent
testāmentum, testāmentī *n.* will
tribūnus, tribūnī *m.* tribune, military
    commander
ūsus, ūsūs *m.* use, experience
Vesontiō, Vesontiōnis *f.* Vesontio, the chief town
    of the Sequani, a Gallic tribe
vītō (1-tr.) avoid
voluntās, voluntātis *f.* will; willingness, approval
vulgō (adv.) commonly; all together, en masse
vultus, vultūs *m.* expression, countenance; face

8. Caesar, *Dē Bellō Gallicō* IV.1

A profile of the Suebi, a German tribe

Suēbōrum gēns est longē maxima et bellicōsissima Germānōrum omnium. hī centum pāgōs habēre dīcuntur, ex quibus quotannīs singula mīlia armātōrum bellandī causā suīs ex fīnibus ēdūcunt. reliquī, quī domī mānsērunt, sē atque illōs alunt. hī rursus invicem annō post in armīs sunt, illī domī remanent. sīc neque agrī cultūra nec ratiō atque ūsus bellī intermittitur. sed prīvātī ac sēparātī agrī apud eōs nihil est, neque longius annō remanēre ūnō in locō colendī causā licet. neque multum frūmentō, sed maximam partem lacte atque pecore vīvunt multumque sunt in vēnātiōnibus. quae rēs et cibī genere et cōtīdiānā exercitātiōne et lībertāte vītae, quod ā puerīs* nūllō officiō aut disciplīnā adsuēfactī nihil omnīnō contrā voluntātem faciunt, et vīrēs alit et immānī corporum magnitūdine hominēs efficit. atque in eam sē cōnsuētūdinem addūxērunt ut locīs frīgidissimīs neque vestītūs praeter pellēs habeant quicquam, quārum propter exiguitātem magna est corporis pars aperta, et laventur in flūminibus.

*ā puerīs, *here,* from boyhood
addūcō (ad- + dūcō) lead (toward)
assuēfaciō, assuēfacere, assuēfēcī, assuēfactus make accustomed, accustom
alō, alere, aluī, al(i)tus feed, nourish
apertus, -a, -um open; exposed, uncovered
armātus, armātī *m.* armed man, soldier
bellicōsus, -a, -um warlike, fond of war
bellō (1-intr.) wage war
cibus, cibī *m.* food
colō, colere, coluī, cultus cultivate, tend; farm
cōnsuētūdō, cōnsuētūdinis *f.* practice, custom, habit
cōtīdiānus, -a, -um daily
cultūra, cultūrae *f.* cultivation
disciplīna, disciplīnae *f.* training
ēdūcō (ē- + dūcō) lead out
exercitātiō, exercitātiōnis *f.* physical exercise, practice
exiguitās, exiguitātis *f.* smallness, scantiness
flūmen, flūminis *n.* river, stream
frīgidus, -a, -um cold, icy
frūmentum, frūmentī *n.* grain
Germānī, Germānōrum *m. pl.* (the) Germans
immānis, immāne enormous, tremendous

intermittō (inter- + mittō) interrupt
——, **vicis** *f.* turn; succession; **invicem**, in turn; against one another
lac, lactis *n.* milk
lavō, lavāre or **lavere, lāvī, lautus** or **lōtus** wash; *in passive,* wash oneself
magnitūdō, magnitūdinis *f.* size, magnitude
officium, officiī *n.* obligation; duty, task
pāgus, pāgī *m.* district
pecus, pecoris *n.* (herd) animal, livestock
pellis, pellis, -ium *f.* (animal) skin, hide
prīvātus, -a, -um private
quotannīs (adv.) yearly, every year
ratiō, ratiōnis *f.* account, reason; method, way
remaneō (re- + maneō) remain
rursus (adv.) again
sēparātus, -a, -um separate
singulī, -ae, -a individual
Suēbī, Suēbōrum *m. pl.* (the) Suebi, a German tribe
ūsus, ūsūs *m.* use, experience, practice
vēnātiō, vēnātiōnis *f.* hunting (activity)
vestītus, vestītūs *m.* clothes, clothing
voluntās, voluntātis *f.* will, intention; choice

9. Caesar, *Dē Bellō Gallicō* V.44

Caesar reports on a rivalry between two of his centurions.

erant in eā legiōne fortissimī virī centuriōnēs quī iam prīmīs ordinibus adpropin-
quārent, Tītus Pullō et Lūcius Vorēnus. hī perpetuās inter sē contrōversiās habēbant
uter alterī anteferrētur, omnibusque annīs dē locō summīs simultātibus contendē-
bant. ex hīs Pullō, cum ācerrimē ad* mūnītiōnēs pugnārētur, "quid dubitās," inquit,†
"Vorēne? aut quem locum tuae probandae virtūtis exspectās? hic diēs dē nostrīs con-
trōversiīs iūdicābit." haec cum dīxisset, prōcēdit† extrā mūnītiōnēs quāque‡ hostium
pars cōnfertissima est vīsa, inrumpit. nē Vorēnus quidem sēsē tum vallō continet,
sed omnium veritus exīstimātiōnem subsequitur. mediocrī spatiō relictō Pullō pīlum
in hostēs inmittit atque ūnum ex multitūdine prōcurrentem trāicit. quō percussō ex-
animātōque hunc scūtīs prōtegunt hostēs, in illum ūniversī tēla coniciunt neque dant
prōgrediendī facultātem. trānsfīgitur scūtum Pullōnī et verūtum in balteō dēfīgitur.
āvertit hic cāsus vāgīnam et gladium ēdūcere cōnantī dextram morātur manum
impedītumque hostēs circumsistunt. succurrit inimīcus illī Vorēnus et labōrantī

*ad, *here*, at, near

†inquit, prōcēdit, historical present tense, used
   here and in several subsequent verbs to add
   vividness; may be translated as present or past

‡quā, *here* (adv.), where

anteferō (ante- + ferō), anteferre, antetulī,
   antelātus place *or* rank above, prefer

appropinquō (1-intr.) approach; be close (to) (+dat)

āvertō, āvertere, āvertī, āversus turn (something)
   away

balteus, balteī *m.* shoulder band, sword belt

centuriō, centuriōnis *m.* centurion

circumsistō, circumsistere, ——, —— surround

cōnfertus, -a, -um crowded, dense, packed close
   together

coniciō (con- + iaciō) throw (together), cast

contendō, contendere, contendī, contentus
   struggle

contineō (con- + teneō), continēre, continuī,
   contentus hold in, contain

contrōversia, contrōversiae *f.* dispute

dēfīgō, dēfīgere, dēfīxī, dēfīxus embed, bury, stick

dexter, dextra, dextrum right

ēdūcō (ē- + dūcō) lead forth; draw

exanimō (1-tr.) deprive of life, kill

exīstimātiō, exīstimātiōnis *f.* opinion, judgment

extrā (prep. + acc.) outside

facultās, facultātis *f.* ability, power; opportunity,
   possibility

immittō (in- + mittō) send in, send against

impediō, impedīre, impedīvī or impediī,
   impedītus obstruct, hinder, impede

inquam (defective verb) say; inquit = *3rd sing.*
   pres. act. indic.

irrumpō, irrumpere, irrūpī, irruptus break in,
   burst into

iūdicō (1-tr.) judge, determine

mediocris, mediocre moderate, fairly small

multitūdō, multitūdinis *f.* multitude

mūnītiō, mūnītiōnis *f.* fortification

ordō, ordinis *m.* order, rank

percutiō, percutere, percussī, percussus strike

perpetuus, -a, -um continual

pīlum, pīlī *n.* spear, javelin

probō (1-tr.) prove, demonstrate

prōcēdō (prō- + cēdō) proceed, advance

prōcurrō, prōcurrere, prō(cu)currī, prōcursum
   run forward, run out in front

prōgredior (prō- + gradior) go forward, advance

prōtegō, prōtegere, prōtēxī, prōtēctus protect,
   defend

Tītus Pullō, Tītī Pullōnis *m.* Titus Pullo

scūtum, scūtī *n.* shield

simultās, simultātis *f.* quarrel, feud

spatium, spatiī *n.* space, interval

subsequor (sub- + sequor) follow close behind

succurrō, succurrere, succurrī, succursum run to
   aid, assist, help

trāiciō (trāns- + iaciō) pierce, transfix

trānsfīgō, trānsfīgere, trānsfīxī, trānsfīxus pierce
   through

ūniversus, -a, -um all together

vāgīna, vāgīnae *f.* sheath

vallum, vallī *n.* palisade (of stakes), fortification

vereor, verērī, veritus sum be in awe of, show
   respect to; dread, fear

verūtum, verūtī *n.* (short) throwing spear

Lūcius Vorēnus, Lūciī Vorēnī *m.* Lucius Vorenus

subvenit. ad hunc sē cōnfestim ā Pullōne omnis multitūdō convertit; illum verūtō trānsfīxum arbitrantur. Vorēnus gladiō rem comminus gerit atque ūnō interfectō reliquōs paulum prōpellit; dum cupidius īnstat, in locum īnferiōrem dēiectus concidit. huic rursus circumventō subsidium fert Pullō, atque ambō incolumēs complūribus interfectīs summā cum laude intrā mūnītiōnēs sē recipiunt. sīc fortūna in contentiōne et certāmine utrumque versāvit, ut alter alterī inimīcus auxiliō salūtīque esset neque dīiūdicārī posset uter utrī virtūte anteferendus vidērētur.

ambō, ambae, ambō (*pl. adj. and pron.*) both; ambō = *masc. pl. nom.*

anteferō (ante- + ferō), anteferre, antetulī, antelātus place *or* rank above, prefer

certāmen, certāminis *n.* contest; fight, battle

circumveniō (circum- + veniō) (tr.) surround

comminus (adv.) in close contact, at close quarters, hand to hand

complūrēs, complūra or complūria several, very many

concidō (con- + cadō), concidere, concidī, —— fall down, collapse

cōnfestim (adv.) immediately

contentiō, contentiōnis *f.* effort; rivalry; conflict

convertō, convertere, convertī, conversus reverse; change; sē convertere, to direct oneself

dēiciō (dē- + iaciō) throw *or* push down

dīiūdicō (1-tr.) settle, decide

incolumis, incolume unharmed; safe

īnferior, īnferius lower

īnstō (in- + stō), īnstāre, īnstitī, īnstātūrus press (hostilely), press on, pursue

intrā (prep. + acc.) within

laus, laudis *f.* praise

multitūdō, multitūdinis *f.* multitude

mūnītiō, mūnītiōnis *f.* fortification

prōpellō (prō- + pellō), prōpellere, prōpulī, prōpulsus push forward, repel

Pullō, Pullōnis *m.* Titus Pullo

recipiō (re- + capiō) take back; sē recipere, to withdraw

rursus (adv.) again

subsidium, subsidiī *n.* aid, help

subveniō (sub- + veniō) come to the aid (of), assist

trānsfīgō, trānsfīgere, trānsfīxī, trānsfīxus pierce through

uterque, utraque, utrumque (indef. pron.) each (of two)

versō (1-tr.) twist, keep turning round

verūtum, verūtī *n.* (short) throwing spear

Vorēnus, Vorēnī *m.* Vorenus

10. Sallust, *Bellum Catilīnae* 8

The historian identifies an important difference between the Athenians and the Romans.

sed profectō fortūna in omnī rē dominātur; ea rēs cūnctās ex lubīdine magis quam
ex vērō celebrat obscūratque. Athēniēnsium rēs gestae, sīcutī ego aestumō, satis
amplae magnificaeque fuēre, vērum aliquantō minōrēs tamen quam fāmā feruntur.
sed quia prōvēnēre ibi scrīptōrum magna ingenia, per terrārum orbem Athēniēnsium facta prō maxumīs celebrantur. ita eōrum quī fēcēre virtūs tanta habētur quantum eam verbīs potuēre extollere praeclāra ingenia. at populō Rōmānō numquam ea
cōpia fuit, quia prūdentissumus quisque maxumē negōtiōsus erat, ingenium nēmō
sine corpore exercēbat, optumus quisque facere quam dīcere, sua ab aliīs bene facta
laudārī quam ipse aliōrum nārrāre mālēbat.

aliquantō (adv.) somewhat, not a little
amplus, -a, -um great, distinguished
at (conj.) but
Athēniēnsēs, Athēniēnsium *m. pl.* Athenians
celebrō (1-tr.) make famous
dominor (1-intr.) be master, hold sway, rule
exerceō, exercēre, exercuī, exercitus keep busy,
    occupy; train, exercise
extollō, extollere, ——, —— raise up, elevate;
    praise
libīdō, libīdinis *f.* desire, pleasure, passion, lust
magnificus, -a, -um magnificent, splendid

nārrō (1-tr.) narrate, tell (of)
negōtiōsus, -a, -um busy, occupied, devoted to
    business
obscūrō (1-tr.) make obscure, cover up
orbis, orbis, -ium *m.* ring, circle; **orbis terrārum,**
    circle of lands, world
praeclārus, -a, -um very famous
profectō (adv.) in fact, actually; indeed, assuredly
prōveniō (prō- + veniō) come forth, appear
prūdēns, prūdentis wise, sensible, clever
scrīptor, scrīptōris *m.* writer
sīcutī (conj.) just as

11. Sallust, *Bellum Catilīnae* 25

The historian describes a fascinating woman from a noble family who was involved in the Catilinarian conspiracy.

sed in iīs* erat Semprōnia, quae multa saepe virīlis audāciae facinora conmīserat. haec mulier genere atque formā, praetereā virō, līberīs† satis fortūnāta fuit; litterīs Graecīs, Latīnīs docta, psallere, saltāre ēlegantius quam necesse est probae, multa alia,‡ quae īnstrūmenta luxuriae sunt. sed eī cāriōra semper omnia quam decus atque pudīcitia fuit; pecūniae an fāmae minus parceret haud facile discernerēs; lubīdō sīc adcēnsa ut saepius peteret virōs quam peterētur. sed ea saepe antehāc fidem prōdiderat, crēditum§ abiūrāverat, caedis cōnscia fuerat: luxuriā atque inopiā praeceps abierat. vērum ingenium eius haud absurdum: posse¶ versūs facere, iocum movēre, sermōne ūtī vel modestō vel mollī vel procācī; prōrsus multae facē-tiae multusque lepōs inerat.

*iīs refers to a number of women who were under Catiline's sway

†līberī, *here*, children

‡multa alia, Accusative of Respect; see §143, p. 479

§crēditum, crēditī *n*. that which has been entrusted (for safekeeping); loan

¶posse, Historical Infinitive; see §145, p. 480

abiūrō (1-tr.) falsely deny knowledge of under oath

absurdus, -a, -um discordant; inappropriate

accendō, accendere, accendī, accēnsus set on fire, kindle; stir up, arouse

antehāc (adv.) before this time, previously

caedēs, caedis, -ium *f*. slaughter; murder

committō (con- + mittō) join, engage in, commit

cōnscius, -a, -um sharing knowledge, privy (to) (+ gen.)

decus, decoris *n*. esteem, honor, glory; decorum

discernō, discernere, discrēvī, discrētus separate; distinguish, determine

doctus, -a, -um learned, educated, erudite

ēleganter (adv.) gracefully, in a refined manner

facētiae, facētiārum *f. pl.* wit, drollery, humor

facinus, facinoris *n*. deed; crime

forma, formae *f*. shape, form; beauty

fortūnātus, -a, -um fortunate

Graecus, -a, -um Greek

inopia, inopiae *f*. poverty, destitution

īnstrūmentum, īnstrūmentī *n*. equipment; instrument

īnsum (in- + sum), inesse, īnfuī, —— be in

iocus, iocī *m*. joke

Latīnus, -a, -um Latin

lepōs, lepōris *m*. pleasantness, charm

libīdō, libīdinis *f*. desire, pleasure, passion, lust

luxuria, luxuriae *f*. extravagance, excess, luxury

modestus, -a, -um restrained, temperate, mild

mollis, molle gentle, mild, soft

mulier, mulieris *f*. woman

parcō, parcere, pepercī, parsūrus be merciful, be sparing (+ dat.)

praeceps, praecipitis rushing forward, headlong

praetereā (adv.) besides, furthermore, in addition

probus, -a, -um excellent, upright, virtuous

procāx, procācis undisciplined, licentious; lively; frivolous

prōdō (prō- + dō) abandon, betray, forsake

prōrsus (adv.) in fact, all in all, in sum

psallō, psallere, ——, —— play on the cithara (or lyre)

pudīcitia, pudīcitiae *f*. chastity, virtue

saltō (1-intr.) dance

Semprōnia, Semprōniae *f*. Sempronia

sermō, sermōnis *m*. speech, (style of) conversation

versus, versūs *m*. verse, line (of poetry)

virīlis, virīle of *or* belonging to a man, masculine, virile

12. Vergil, *Eclogues* II.63–68

The lovesick shepherd Corydon speaks to his unattainable beloved, Alexis.

torva leaena lupum sequitur, lupus ipse capellam,

flōrentem cytisum sequitur lascīva capella,

tē Corydōn, ō Alexi: trahit sua quemque voluptās.   65

aspice, arātra iugō referunt suspēnsa iuvencī,

et sōl crēscentīs dēcēdēns duplicat umbrās:

mē tamen ūrit amor; quis* enim modus adsit amōrī?

*quis, interrog. pron. used adjectivally
Alexis, Alexis *m.* Alexis; **Alexi** = *voc. sing.*
arātrum, arātrī *n.* plough
aspiciō, aspicere, aspexī, aspectus look (toward), behold
capella, capellae *f.* she-goat
Corydōn, Corydōnis *m.* Corydon
crēscō, crēscere, crēvī, crētus grow, increase
cytisus, cytisī *m.* or *f.* clover
dēcēdō (dē- + cēdō) go down
duplicō (1-tr.) double
flōreō, flōrēre, flōruī, —— bloom, blossom

iugum, iugī *n.* yoke
iuvencus, iuvencī *m.* bull; ox
lascīvus, -a, -um playful, naughty, free from restraint
leaena, leaenae *f.* lioness
lupus, lupī *m.* wolf
suspendō, suspendere, suspendī, suspēnsus hang up, suspend
torvus, -a, -um fierce
trahō, trahere, trāxī, tractus draw, drag; attract
ūrō, ūrere, ussī, ustus burn; inflame; consume
voluptās, voluptātis *f.* pleasure, joy

13. Vergil, *Eclogues* IV.18–25

The poet addresses a child whose birth will initiate a new golden age on earth.

at tibi prīma, puer, nūllō mūnuscula cultū

errantīs hederās passim cum baccare tellūs

mixtaque rīdentī colocāsia fundet acanthō.   20

ipsae lacte domum referent distenta capellae

ūbera, nec magnōs metuent armenta leōnēs;

ipsa tibi blandōs fundent cūnābula flōrēs.

occidet et serpēns, et fallāx herba venēnī

occidet; Assyrium vulgō nāscētur amōmum.   25

acanthus, acanthī *m.* bear's foot, acanthus
amōmum, amōmī *n.* balsam
armentum, armentī *n.* herd (of cattle)
Assyrius, -a, -um Assyrian
at (conj.) but
baccar, baccaris *n. baccar,* the plant cyclamen
blandus, -a, -um charming, seductive, soothing
capella, capellae *f.* she-goat
colocāsium, colocāsiī *n.* Egyptian bean
cultus, cultūs *m.* cultivation
cūnābula, cūnābulōrum *n. pl.* cradle
distentus, -a, -um swollen, distended
fallāx, fallācis deceitful, treacherous
flōs, flōris *m.* flower

fundō, fundere, fūdī, fūsus pour out, pour forth
hedera, hederae *f.* ivy
herba, herbae *f.* grass; plant; herb
lac, lactis *n.* milk
leō, leōnis *m.* lion
misceō, miscēre, miscuī, mixtus mix
mūnusculum, mūnusculī *n.* small gift
passim (adv.) everywhere
rīdeō, rīdēre, rīsī, rīsus smile
serpēns, serpentis, -ium *m.* or *f.* serpent, snake
tellūs, tellūris *f.* earth, land
ūber, ūberis *n.* udder
venēnum, venēnī *n.* poison
vulgō (adv.) commonly

14. Vergil, *Aeneid* II.657–63

Aeneas reports what he said in response to his father's refusal to join the family in fleeing from Troy.

mēne efferre pedem, genitor, tē posse relictō

spērāstī tantumque nefās patriō excidit ōre?

sī nihil ex tantā superīs placet urbe relinquī,

et sedet hoc* animō peritūraeque addere Troiae 660

tēque tuōsque iuvat, patet istī iānua lētō,

iamque aderit multō Priamī dē sanguine Pyrrhus,

nātum ante ōra patris, patrem quī obtruncat ad† ārās.

*hoc, *here,* scans as if it were spelled **hocc**
†ad, *here,* at, near
addō (ad- + dō) add
efferō (ex- + ferō), **efferre, extulī, ēlātus** bear forth
excidō (ex- + cadō), **excidere, excidī,** —— fall (from)
genitor, genitōris *m.* father
iānua, iānuae *f.* door; doorway, entrance
iuvō, iuvāre, iūvī, iūtus help, assist; please

lētum, lētī *n.* death, destruction
obtruncō (1-tr.) slay, slaughter, butcher
pateō, patēre, patuī, —— lie open
patrius, -a, -um of a father, paternal
pēs, pedis *m.* foot
Pyrrhus, Pyrrhī *m.* Pyrrhus, son of Achilles
sanguis, sanguinis *m.* blood
sedeō, sedēre, sēdī, sessūrus sit, be seated; be fixed
superī, superōrum *m. pl.* (the) gods above

15. Vergil, *Aeneid* IV.382–87

Enraged Dido concludes her speech to Aeneas after he has claimed that the gods have ordered him to leave her realm.

spērō equidem mediīs, sī quid pia nūmina possunt,

supplicia hausūrum scopulīs et nōmine Dīdō

saepe vocātūrum. sequar ātrīs ignibus absēns

et, cum frīgida mors animā sēdūxerit artūs, 385

omnibus umbra locīs aderō. dabis, improbe, poenās.

audiam et haec Mānīs veniet mihi fāma sub īmōs.

artus, artūs *m.* joint (of the body), limb
āter, ātra, ātrum black, dark
frīgidus, -a, -um cold, icy
hauriō, haurīre, hausī, haustus (rarely, **hausus**) drink (in), absorb; **hausūrum,** *sc.* **tē**
improbus, -a, -um wicked; shameless
īmus, -a, -um lowest, deepest
Mānēs, Mānium *m. pl.* Manes, spirits of the dead; the underworld

nūmen, nūminis *n.* divine power, divinity, divine spirit, numen
scopulus, scopulī *m.* projecting rock, boulder, crag
sēdūcō (sē- + dūcō) lead away, separate
supplicium, suppliciī *n.* punishment

16. Horace, *Carmina* III.9 (Asclepiadean)

A dialogue between former lovers

Dōnec grātus eram tibi
　　nec quisquam* potior bracchia candidae
cervīcī iuvenis dabat,
　　Persārum viguī rēge beātior.

"dōnec nōn aliā magis 5
　　arsistī neque erat Lȳdia post Chloēn,
multī Lȳdia nōminis
　　Rōmānā viguī clārior Īliā."

mē nunc Thrēssa Chloē regit,
　　dulcīs docta modōs† et citharae sciēns, 10
prō quā nōn metuam morī,
　　sī parcent animae fāta superstitī.

"mē torret face mūtuā
　　Thūrīnī Calais fīlius Ornytī,
prō quō bis patiar morī, 15
　　sī parcent puerō fāta superstitī."

---

*quisquam, indef. pron. used adjectivally
†modōs, *here, Accusative of Respect,* in (respect to)
　　measures *or* verses
ardeō, ardēre, arsī, arsūrus burn, be on fire
beātus, -a, -um happy, blessed, fortunate
bis (adv.) two times, twice
bracchium, bracchiī *n.* (lower) arm
Calais, Calais *m.* Calais
candidus, -a, -um white, clear, bright, radiant
cervīx, cervīcis *f.* neck
Chloē, Chloēs *f.* Chloe; Chloēn = *acc. sing.*
cithara, citharae *f.* cithara; lute
doctus, -a, -um learned, skilled, clever
fax, facis *f.* firebrand, torch
Īlia, Īliae *f.* Ilia, mother of Romulus and Remus
iuvenis, iuvenis *m.* or *f.* young man, young
　　woman

Lȳdia, Lȳdiae *f.* Lydia
mūtuus, -a, -um shared, reciprocal, mutual
Ornytus, Ornytī *m.* Ornytus
parcō, parcere, pepercī, parsūrus be merciful,
　　be sparing (+ dat.)
Persae, Persārum *f. pl.* (the) Persians
potior, potius more powerful; preferable
superstes, superstitis standing by, present;
　　surviving
Thrēssa, Thrēssae *f.* (a) Thracian woman
Thūrīnus, -a, -um of Thurii, a city in southern
　　Italy
torreō, torrēre, torruī, tostus parch, roast, scorch,
　　burn
vigeō, vigēre, viguī, —— be vigorous, thrive,
　　flourish, live

quid sī prīsca redit Venus
    dīductōsque iugō cōgit aēneō,
sī flāva excutitur Chloē
    reiectaeque patet iānua Lȳdiae?   20

"quamquam sīdere pulchrior
    ille est, tū levior cortice et inprobō
īrācundior Hadriā,
    tēcum vīvere amem, tēcum obeam lubēns."

aēneus, -a, -um of bronze, bronze
Chloē, Chloēs *f.* Chloe
cōgō (cō- + agō), cōgere, coēgī, coāctus drive together, force, compel
cortex, corticis *m.* or *f.* cork
dīdūcō (dis- + dūcō) draw apart, separate
excutiō, excutere, excussī, excussus shake off, cast out
flāvus, -a, -um golden-yellow, flaxen, blond
Hadria, Hadriae *m.* or *f.* Adriatic sea
iānua, iānuae *f.* door

improbus, -a, -um wicked; shameless; relentless
īrācundus, -a, -um irascible, angry, moody
iugum, iugī *n.* yoke
libēns, libentis willing, glad
Lȳdia, Lȳdiae *f.* Lydia
obeō (ob- + eō), obīre, obiī or **obīvī, obitus** go to meet; fall, perish, die
pateō, patēre, patuī, —— lie open
prīscus, -a, -um of former times, old, ancient
reiciō (re- + iaciō) throw back, reject
sīdus, sīderis *n.* star

17. Propertius II.19.1–8

The poet imagines that a stay in the country will keep Cynthia safe from romantic entanglements.

Etsī mē invītō discēdis, Cynthia, Rōmā,
    laetor quod sine mē dēvia rūra colēs.
nūllus erit castīs iuvenis corruptor in agrīs,
    quī tē blanditiīs nōn sinat esse probam;
nūlla neque* ante tuās oriētur rixa fenestrās,   5
    nec* tibi clāmātae somnus amārus erit.
sōla eris et sōlōs spectābis, Cynthia, montēs
    et pecus et fīnēs pauperis agricolae.

*The redundant negatives strengthen the negative idea.
amārus, -a, -um bitter, harsh
blanditia, blanditiae *f.* ingratiating speech, blandishment; *in pl.,* sweet nothings
castus, -a, -um free from vice, moral, chaste
clāmō (1-tr.) shout for, call by name
colō, colere, coluī, cultus cultivate, tend; inhabit
corruptor, corruptōris *m.* corrupter, seducer
Cynthia, Cynthiae *f.* Cynthia
dēvius, -a, -um out of the way, remote, secluded

fenestra, fenestrae *f.* window
invītus, -a, -um unwilling
iuvenis, iuvenis young
laetor (1-intr.) rejoice, be glad, be delighted
pauper, pauperis poor
pecus, pecoris *n.* herd animal; livestock
probus, -a, -um excellent, upright, virtuous
rixa, rixae *f.* altercation, brawl
sinō, sinere, siī or **sīvī, situs** allow, permit
somnus, somnī *m.* sleep

18. Livy, *Ab Urbe Conditā* II.46.3–7

The historian describes a battle between the Romans and the Etruscans, particularly those from the city of Veii. Three members of the Fabii give evidence of Roman bravery.

vix explicandī ordinis spatium Etruscīs fuit cum, pīlīs inter prīmam trepidātiōnem abiectīs temere magis quam ēmissīs, pugna iam in manūs, iam ad gladiōs, ubi Mars est atrōcissimus, vēnerat. inter prīmōrēs genus Fabium īnsigne spectāculō exemplōque cīvibus erat. ex hīs Q. Fabium—tertiō hic annō ante cōnsul fuerat—prīncipem in cōnfertōs Veientēs euntem ferōx vīribus et armōrum arte Tuscus, incautum inter multās versantem hostium manūs, gladiō per pectus trānsfīgit; tēlō extractō praeceps Fabius in volnus abiit.* sēnsit utraque aciēs ūnīus virī cāsum, cēdēbatque inde Rōmānus† cum M. Fabius cōnsul trānsiluit iacentis corpus obiectāque parmā, "hoc iūrāstis" inquit, "mīlitēs, fugientēs vōs in castra reditūrōs? adeō ignāvissimōs hostēs magis timētis quam Iovem Martemque per‡ quōs iūrāstis? at ego iniūrātus aut victor revertar aut prope tē hīc, Q. Fabī, dīmicāns cadam." cōnsulī tum Caesō Fabius, priōris annī cōnsul: "verbīsne istīs, frāter, ut pugnent, tē

---

*abeō, *here*, fall over
†Rōmānus, *here, collective singular,* the Romans
‡per, *here* (in oaths), by
abiciō (ab- + iaciō) cast away, throw away, cast down
at (conj.) but
atrōx, atrōcis dark, gloomy; cruel, fierce
cōnfertus, -a, -um crowded, dense, packed close together
dīmicō (1-intr.) contend, fight
ēmittō (ē- + mittō) send forth, hurl, cast
Etruscī, Etruscōrum *m. pl.* (the) Etruscans
exemplum, exemplī *n.* example
explicō (1-tr.) unfold, unfurl; spread out, extend
extrahō, extrahere, extrāxī, extractus draw out, extract
Fabius, -a, -um of the Fabii, Fabian
Caesō Fabius, Caesōnis Fabiī *m.* Caeso Fabius
M. Fabius, M. Fabiī *m.* M. Fabius
Q. Fabius, Q. Fabiī *m.* Q. Fabius
ferōx, ferōcis fierce, savage; high-spirited, defiant
iaceō, iacēre, iacuī, —— lie; lie dead
ignāvus, -a, -um lazy; cowardly, spiritless; ignoble
incautus, -a, -um heedless, unaware
iniūrātus, -a, -um not having taken an oath, unsworn
inquam (defective verb) say; **inquit** = *3rd sing. pres. act. indic.*
īnsignis, īnsigne prominent, eminent, distinguished

iūrō (1-intr.) take an oath, swear
obiciō (ob- + iaciō) put in the way, interpose
ordō, ordinis *m.* order; row, line, arrangement; (battle) order
parma, parmae *f.* (small, round) shield (carried by infantry)
pīlum, pīlī *n.* (heavy) javelin
praeceps, praecipitis headlong, head first
prīmōrēs, prīmōrum *m. pl.* leading men, front ranks
prīnceps, prīncipis first, in front
prope (prep. + acc.) near
pugna, pugnae *f.* battle
revertor, revertī, reversus sum turn back; return
spatium, spatiī *n.* space; (space of) time, interval
spectāculum, spectāculī *n.* sight, spectacle
temere (adv.) by chance, at random; rashly
trānsfīgō, trānsfīgere, trānsfīxī, trānsfīxus pierce
trānsiliō, trānsilīre, trānsiluī, —— leap across, jump over
trepidātiō, trepidātiōnis *f.* alarm, agitation, confusion, consternation
Tuscus, -a, -um Tuscan, Etruscan
uterque, utraque, utrumque (indef. adj.) each (of two)
Veientēs, Veientium *m. pl.* the people of Veii, Veiians
versō (1-intr.) turn, twist, whirl about
victor, victōris *m.* victor, conqueror

impetrātūrum crēdis? dī impetrābunt per* quōs iūrāvēre; et nōs, ut decet procerēs, ut Fabiō nōmine est dignum, pugnandō potius quam adhortandō accendāmus mīlitum animōs." sīc in prīmum† īnfēnsīs hastīs prōvolant duo Fabiī, tōtamque mōvērunt sēcum aciem.

***per**, *here* (in oaths), by
†**prīmum, prīmī** *n.* front line
accendō, accendere, accendī, accēnsus set on fire, kindle; stir up, arouse
adhortor (1-tr.) encourage, urge on
decet, decēre, decuit (impersonal verb) it becomes, it befits
Fabius, -a, -um of the Fabiī, Fabian

hasta, hastae *f.* spear
impetrō (1-tr.) obtain by entreaty; persuade
īnfēnsus, -a, -um hostile, threatening
iūrō (1-intr.) take an oath, swear
potius (comparative adv.) rather
procerēs, procerum *m. pl.* leading men, leaders
prōvolō (1-intr.) fly out, fly forth; rush forward

19. Lucan, *Bellum Cīvīle* IX.961–69

The poet describes Caesar visiting the ruins of Troy.

Sīgēāsque petit* fāmae mīrātor harēnās

et Simoëntis aquās et Graiō nōbile bustō

Rhoetion et multum dēbentīs vātibus umbrās.

circumit exustae nōmen memorābile Troiae

magnaque Phoebēī quaerit vestīgia mūrī.   965

iam silvae sterilēs et putrēs rōbore truncī

Assaracī pressēre domōs et templa deōrum

iam lassā rādīce tenent, ac tōta teguntur

Pergama dūmētīs: etiam periēre ruīnae.

*petit, subject is Caesar
aqua, aquae *f.* water
Assaracus, Assaracī *m.* Assaracus, king of Troy
bustum, bustī *n.* funeral pyre; grave mound,
    tomb
circumeō (circum- + eō), circumīre, circumiī,
    circumitus go around, encircle
dūmēta, dūmētōrum *n. pl.* thorns, thickets,
    bushes
exūrō, exūrere, exussī, exustus destroy by fire,
    burn completely
Graius, -a, -um Greek
harēna, harēnae *f.* sand
lassus, -a, -um exhausted, weary, tired
memorābilis, memorābile memorable
mīrātor, mīrātōris *m.* admirer
nōbilis, nōbile noble; renowned, famous
Pergama, Pergamōrum *n. pl.* Pergama, citadel
    of Troy

Phoebēus, -a, -um of *or* associated with Phoebus
    (Apollo)
putris, putre decomposed, rotten, putrid
rādīx, rādīcis, -ium *f.* root
Rhoetion, Rhoetiī *n.* Rhoetion, a town near Troy
rōbur, rōboris *n.* oak tree; timber; strength,
    firmness
ruīna, ruīnae *f.* ruin
Sīgēus, -a, -um of *or* belonging to Sigeum,
    a town near Troy; Trojan
silva, silvae *f.* forest
Simoīs, Simoëntis *m.* (the river) Simois near
    Troy
sterilis, sterile barren, sterile
tegō, tegere, tēxī, tēctus cover
truncus, truncī *m.* (tree) trunk
vātēs, vātis, -ium *m.* or *f.* prophet; bard, poet
vestīgium, vestīgiī *n.* trace, remnant, vestige

Marcus Annaeus Lucānus (39–65 C.E.) was the nephew of Seneca the Younger and served as a quaestor under Nero. Discovered in a plot to kill the emperor, he was forced to take his own life. Lucan's epic style is marked by vivid and rapid narration, elegant and sometimes artificial language, and a pessimistic tone strongly in contrast to Vergil's *Aeneid*.

The *Pharsālia* or *Bellum Cīvīle* is an epic poem in ten books, which begins with Caesar's crossing of the Rubicon and recounts the closing episodes of Rome's civil wars. Many books are devoted to the exploits of Caesar and Pompey, their final rift, and Pompey's murder in Egypt.

20. Petronius, *Satyricon* 37

A first-time guest at a wealthy man's dinner party has asked the identity of a woman scurrying about the dining room. A veteran guest offers a description of the host's wife and of the host, Trimalchio.

"uxor," inquit, "Trimalchiōnis, Fortūnāta appellātur, quae nummōs modiō mētītur. et modo modo quid fuit? ignōscet mihi genius tuus, nōluissēs* dē manū illīus pānem accipere. nunc, nec quid nec quāre, in caelum abiit et Trimalchiōnis topanta est. ad summam,† merō merīdiē sī dīxerit illī tenebrās esse, crēdet. ipse nescit quid habeat, adeō saplūtus est; sed haec lupātria prōvidet omnia, est ubi nōn putēs. est sicca, sōbria, bonōrum cōnsiliōrum—tantum aurī vidēs—est tamen malae linguae, pīca pulvīnāris. quem amat, amat; quem nōn amat, nōn amat. ipse‡ fundōs habet, quā§ mīlvī volant, nummōrum nummōs. argentum in ostiāriī illīus cellā plūs iacet quam quisquam in fortūnīs habet. familia vērō babae babae, nōn mehercules putō decumam partem esse quae dominum suum nōverit.

*nōluissēs, verb in apodosis of Past Contrary-to-Fact conditional sentence (protasis is omitted)
†ad summam, *here,* in short, to sum up
‡ipse refers to Trimalchio.
§quā, *here* (adv.), where
appellō (1-tr.) name, call
argentum, argentī *n.* silver; silver plate
babae babae (interj.) *exclamation indicating surprise and admiration* babae! babae!
(< Greek *babai! babai!* transliterated into Latin)
cella, cellae *f.* small room; storeroom
Fortūnāta, Fortūnātae *f.* Fortunata
familia, familiae *f.* household; family slaves
fundus, fundī *m.* (piece of) land; farm, estate
genius, geniī *m. genius,* tutelary deity of a person or place; divine nature; spiritual part
iaceō, iacēre, iacuī, —— lie (open); be at hand
ignōscō (in- + nōscō), ignōscere, ignōvī, ignōtus forgive, pardon (+ dat.)
inquam (defective verb) say; **inquit** = *3rd sing. pres. act. indic.*
lingua, linguae *f.* tongue; language
lupātria, lupātriae *f. lupatria,* abusive term for a woman, whore

merō merīdiē (adv.) right at noon, at noon exactly
mētior, mētīrī, mēnsus sum measure; mete (out)
mīlvus, mīlvī *m.* kite (bird of prey)
modius, modiī *m. modius,* a Roman grain measure; peck
nummus, nummī *m. nummus,* a Roman coin
ostiārius, ostiāriī *m.* doorkeeper, porter
pānis, pānis, -ium *m.* bread
pīca, pīcae *f.* magpie
prōvideō (prō- + videō) see to, attend to
pulvīnāris, pulvīnāre of *or* pertaining to a cushion *or* pillow; resting on a couch; pīca pulvīnāris, *apparently* a gossipy bird
saplūtus, -a, -um very rich (< Greek *zaploutos* transliterated into Latin)
siccus, -a, -um dry
sōbrius, -a, -um sensible, sober; cautious
tenebrae, tenebrārum *f. pl.* darkness, shadows
topanta (indeclinable noun) everything
(< Greek *ta panta* transliterated into Latin)
Trimalchiō, Trimalchiōnis *m.* Trimalchio
uxor, uxōris *f.* wife
volō (1-intr.) fly

As identified by the historian Tacitus in his *Annālēs,* **Petronius** lived during the reign of Nero in the first century C.E. In the course of describing Petronius's protracted suicide—compelled by his loss of favor with Nero—the historian gives to Petronius the title **arbiter ēlegantiae** (minister of culture) and thereby suggests what role Petronius may have played in Neronian society. It is likely that this Petronius was the author of the work entitled the *Satyricon.*

From the surviving fragments the *Satyricon* appears to have been a long work of prose fiction recounting the Odyssean and surreal adventures of three young men. The fragments are written in a mixed literary style that includes many allusions to and parodies of other works of Latin and Greek literature. Since many of the characters are drawn from the common life of the Greek settlements in southern Italy, the *Satyricon*'s fragments are a valuable source of information about colloquial Latin, the **sermō cottīdiānus** (daily speech), of the first century C.E. The largest fragment, usually referred to as the *Cēna Trimalchiōnis* (Banquet of Trimalchio), contains vivid speeches in character by many of the dinner guests, for the most part successful businessmen of the upper middle class.

Continuous Readings

1. Cicero, *In Catilīnam I* 15–16

potestne tibi haec lūx, Catilīna, aut huius caelī spīritus esse iūcundus, cum sciās esse hōrum nēminem quī nesciat tē prīdiē Kalendās Iānuāriās Lepidō et Tullō cōnsulibus stetisse in Comitiō cum tēlō, manum cōnsulum et prīncipum cīvitātis interficiendōrum causā parāvisse, scelerī ac furōrī tuō nōn mentem aliquam aut timōrem tuum sed fortūnam populī Rōmānī obstitisse? ac iam illa omittō—neque enim* sunt aut obscūra aut nōn multa commissa posteā—quotiēns tū mē dēsignātum,† quotiēns vērō cōnsulem interficere cōnātus es! quot ego tuās petītiōnēs ita coniectās ut vītārī posse nōn vidērentur parvā quādam dēclīnātiōne et, ut aiunt, corpore effūgī! nihil agis, nihil adsequeris, neque tamen‡ cōnārī ac velle dēsistis. quotiēns iam tibi extorta est ista sīca dē manibus, quotiēns excidit cāsū aliquō et ēlāpsa est! quae quidem quibus abs tē initiāta sacrīs ac dēvōta sit nesciō, quod eam necesse putās esse in cōnsulis corpore dēfīgere.

*neque enim for . . . not . . .
†dēsignātum, *sc.* cōnsulem
‡neque tamen and yet . . . not . . .
abs = ab
assequor (ad- + sequor) gain, reach, attain
aiō (defective verb) say; aiunt = *3rd pl. pres. act. indic.*
Comitium, Comitiī *n.* (the) Comitium, place where the assembly met
commissum, commissī *n.* offense, crime
coniciō (con- + iaciō) throw (together), cast, bring
dēclīnātiō, dēclīnātiōnis *f.* swerving, swerve
dēfīgō, dēfīgere, dēfīxī, dēfīxus fix, plant
dēsignātus, -a, -um elect, appointed (but not yet installed)
dēsistō, dēsistere, dēstitī, —— cease, leave off
dēvoveō, dēvovēre, dēvōvī, dēvōtus dedicate
effugiō (ex- + fugiō) flee from, escape
ēlābor, ēlābī, ēlāpsus sum slip out
excidō (ex- + cadō), excidere, excidī, —— fall *or* slip from
extorqueō, extorquēre, extorsī, extortus twist out
furor, furōris *m.* madness

Iānuārius, -a, -um of January
initiō (1-tr.) consecrate
iūcundus, -a, -um pleasing, delightful, agreeable
Kalendae, Kalendārum *f. pl.* (the) Kalends, the first day of a month
Lepidus, Lepidī *m.* Lepidus
obscūrus, -a, -um dark, dim, obscure; uncertain
obstō (ob- + stō), obstāre, obstitī, obstātum stand in the way; hinder, block
omittō (ob- + mittō) disregard, pass over
parō (1-tr.) prepare; get
petītiō, petītiōnis *f.* attack, thrust
posteā (adv.) after, afterward
prīdiē (prep. + acc.) on the day before
prīnceps, prīncipis first, foremost, chief; *as subst.*, leading man
quotiēns (adv.) how many times
sacer, sacra, sacrum sacred
sīca, sīcae *f.* dagger
spīritus, spīritūs *m.* breath, breeze
Tullus, Tullī *m.* Tullus
vītō (1-tr.) avoid

2. Sallust, *Bellum Catilīnae* 4

igitur ubi animus ex multīs miseriīs atque perīculīs requiēvit et mihi relicuam aetātem ā rē pūblicā procul habendam dēcrēvī, nōn fuit cōnsilium socordiā atque dēsidiā
bonum ōtium conterere, neque vērō agrum colundō aut vēnandō, servīlibus officiīs,
intentum aetātem agere; sed ā quō inceptō studiōque mē ambitiō mala dētinuerat,
eōdem regressus statuī rēs gestās populī Rōmānī carptim, ut quaeque memoriā
digna vidēbantur, perscrībere, eō magis quod mihi ā spē, metū, partibus reī pūblicae
animus līber erat. igitur dē Catilīnae coniūrātiōne quam vērissumē poterō* paucīs†
absolvam; nam id facinus in prīmīs‡ ego memorābile exīstumō sceleris atque perīculī
novitāte. dē quoius hominis mōribus pauca prius explānanda sunt quam initium nār-
randī faciam.

*quam vērissumē poterō = quam vērissumē
†paucīs, *sc.* **verbīs**
‡in prīmīs, *here,* especially, above all; first
absolvō, absolvere, absolvī, absolūtus finish,
    complete; sum up, describe briefly
ambitiō, ambitiōnis *f.* flattery, adulation; desire
    for power, ambition
carptim (adv.) in parts, separately
colō, colere, coluī, cultus cultivate, tend; **colundō**
    = archaic form of **colendō**
coniūrātiō, coniūrātiōnis *f.* conspiracy
conterō, conterere, contrīvī, contrītus grind, wear
    out; consume, spend
dēcernō, dēcernere, dēcrēvī, dēcrētus determine,
    decide, decree
dēsidia, dēsidiae *f.* idleness, inactivity, sloth
dētineō (dē- + teneō), dētinēre, dētinuī, dētentus
    hold back, detain; hinder, prevent
exīstimō (ex- + aestimō) (1-tr.) reckon, suppose,
    estimate
explānō (1-tr.) make plain, make clear, explain
facinus, facinoris *n.* deed; crime

initium, initiī *n.* beginning
intentus, -a, -um stretched, attentive, intent
memorābilis, memorābile worthy of being
    remembered, remarkable
miseria, miseriae *f.* misery
nārrō (1-tr.) narrate, tell (of); describe
novitās, novitātis *f.* newness, strangeness
officium, officiī *n.* obligation; duty, task
ōtium, ōtiī *n.* leisure, idleness
perscrībō (per- + scrībō) write a detailed *or* full
    account of
procul (adv.) at a distance, far
regredior (re- + gradior) go back, return
relicuam = archaic form of **reliquam**
requiēscō, requiēscere, requiēvī, requiētum
    (take a) rest; desist
servīlis, servīle of *or* belonging to a slave, servile
socordia, socordiae *f.* laziness, indolence,
    inactivity
statuō, statuere, statuī, statūtus cause to stand,
    set up, establish; decide
vēnor (1-intr.) hunt

3. Vergil, *Aeneid* II.533–46

hīc Priamus, quamquam in mediā iam morte tenētur,

nōn tamen abstinuit nec vōcī īraeque pepercit:

"at tibi prō scelere," exclāmat, "prō tālibus ausīs* 535

dī, sī qua est caelō pietās quae tālia cūret,

persolvant grātēs dignās et praemia reddant

dēbita, quī nātī cōram mē cernere lētum

fēcistī et patriōs foedāstī fūnere vultūs.

at nōn ille, satum quō tē mentīris, Achillēs 540

tālis in† hoste fuit Priamō; sed iūra fidemque

supplicis ērubuit corpusque exsangue sepulcrō

reddidit Hectoreum mēque in mea rēgna remīsit."

sīc fātus senior tēlumque imbelle sine ictū

coniēcit, raucō quod prōtinus aere repulsum, 545

et summō clipeī nēquīquam umbōne pependit.

*ausum, ausī *n.* bold deed, exploit; crime, outrage
†in, *here,* in the case of
Achillēs, Achillis *m.* Achilles
abstineō (abs- + teneō), abstinēre, abstinuī, abstentus hold back, restrain, refrain
aes, aeris *n.* copper, bronze
at (conj.) but
cernō, cernere, crēvī, crētus distinguish, determine, perceive; see
clipeus, clipeī *m.* shield
coniciō (con- + iaciō) throw (together), cast
cōram (adv.) face to face, in person
cūrō (1-tr.) watch over, look after
ērubēscō, ērubēscere, ērubuī, —— blush (for shame); feel shame in the presence of
exclāmō (1-intr.) cry out
exsanguis, exsangue bloodless
foedō (1-tr.) befoul, defile
for (1-tr.) speak, utter
fūnus, fūneris *n.* in sing. or pl. funeral (procession); death
grātēs, grātium *f. pl.* thanks
Hectoreus, -a, -um of Hector, Hector's
ictus, ictūs *m.* thrust, blow
imbellis, imbelle not suited to warfare, unwarlike
lētum, lētī *n.* death, destruction

mentior, mentīrī, mentītus sum lie, tell a lie
nēquīquam (adv.) to no avail, in vain
parcō, parcere, pepercī, parsūrus be merciful, be sparing (+ dat.)
patrius, -a, -um of or belonging to a father, paternal
pendeō, pendēre, pependī, —— hang, be suspended
persolvō, persolvere, persolvī, persolūtus pay in full; render
pietās, pietātis *f.* sense of duty, dutifulness, piety
praemium, praemiī *n.* reward, prize
prōtinus (adv.) immediately, straightway
raucus, -a, -um harsh-sounding, noisy, raucous
reddō (red- + dō) give back, return; hand over, deliver
rēgnum, rēgnī *n.* kingdom, realm
remittō (re- + mittō) send back
repellō (re- + pellō), repellere, reppulī, repulsus push back, repel
serō, serere, sēvī, satus sow; engender, beget
senex, senis old
sepulcrum, sepulcrī *n.* tomb, grave
supplex, supplicis suppliant
umbō, umbōnis *m.* boss (of a shield)
vultus, vultūs *m.* expression, countenance; in pl., face

4. Ovid, *Metamorphōsēs* I.504–39

"nympha, precor, Pēnēi, manē! nōn īnsequor hostis;

nympha, manē! sīc agna lupum, sīc cerva leōnem,   505

sīc aquilam pennā fugiunt trepidante columbae,

hostēs quaeque suōs: amor est mihi causa sequendī!

mē miserum! nē prōna cadās indignave laedī

crūra notent sentēs et sim tibi causa dolōris!

aspera, quā* properās, loca sunt: moderātius, ōrō,   510

curre fugamque inhibē, moderātius īnsequar ipse.

cui placeās inquīre tamen: nōn incola montis,

nōn ego sum pāstor, nōn hīc armenta gregēsque

horridus observō. nescīs, temerāria, nescīs

quem fugiās, ideōque fugis: mihi Delphica tellūs   515

*quā, *here* (adv.) where

agna, agnae *f.* lamb

aquila, aquilae *f.* eagle

armentum, armentī *n.* herd

asper, aspera, asperum harsh, fierce; pitiless

cerva, cervae *f.* deer; doe

columba, columbae *f.* dove

crūs, crūris *n.* leg

currō, currere, cucurrī, cursum run, rush

Delphicus, -a, -um Delphic, of Delphi, a Greek town and seat of Apollo's oracle

dolor, dolōris *m.* grief, sorrow, pain

grex, gregis *m.* or *f.* flock

horridus, -a, -um rough, wild; horrible

ideō (adv.) for this reason; therefore

inhibeō (in- + habeō), inhibēre, inhibuī, inhibitus hold back, check, restrain

inquīrō (in- + quaerō), inquīrere, inquīsiī or **inquīsīvī, inquīsītus** inquire into, investigate

īnsequor (in- + sequor) follow closely, pursue

laedō, laedere, laesī, laesus injure, harm

leō, leōnis *m.* lion

lupus, lupī *m.* wolf

moderātē (adv.) moderately, temperately

notō (1-tr.) mark; scar

nympha, nymphae *f.* nymph, a semidivine spirit

observō (ob- + servō) (1-tr.) watch over, guard, observe

pāstor, pāstōris *m.* shepherd

Pēnēis, Pēnēidos descended from the river god Peneus; **Pēnēi** = *fem. sing. voc.*

penna, pennae *f.* wing

precor (1-tr.) pray

prōnus, -a, -um (leaning) forward, headlong

properō (1-intr.) hasten, rush

sentis, sentis, -ium *m.* briar, bramble

tellūs, tellūris *f.* earth, land

temerārius, -a, -um rash

trepidō (1-intr.) tremble

-ve (enclitic conj.) or

et Claros et Tenedos Patarēaque rēgia servit;

Iuppiter est genitor; per mē quod eritque fuitque

estque patet; per mē concordant carmina nervīs.

certa quidem nostra est, nostrā tamen ūna sagitta

certior, in vacuō quae vulnera pectore fēcit!   520

inventum* medicīna meum est, opiferque per orbem

dīcor,† et herbārum subiecta potentia nōbīs.

ei mihi, quod nūllīs amor est sānābilis herbīs

nec prōsunt dominō, quae prōsunt omnibus, artēs!"

plūra locūtūrum timidō Pēnēia cursū   525

fūgit cumque ipsō verba inperfecta relīquit,

tum quoque vīsa decēns; nūdābant corpora‡ ventī,

***inventum, inventī** *n.* discovery, invention

†**dīcō**, *here*, call

‡**corpora**, *here*, limbs

Claros, Clarī *f.* Claros, a town in Ionia

concordō (1-intr.) be in harmony

cursus, cursūs *m.* running, run

decēns, decentis becoming, graceful

ei (interj.) *expression of anguish,* o! alas!; **ei mihi,** woe is me!

genitor, genitōris *m.* father

herba, herbae *f.* grass; plant; herb

imperfectus, -a, -um unfinished, incomplete

medicīna, medicīnae *f.* medicine

nervus, nervī *m.* sinew; (bow-)string; string (of an instrument)

nūdō (1-tr.) make naked, bare, lay bare

obvius, -a, -um in the way, face to face; moving against, opposed in direction

opifer, opifera, opiferum aid-bringing

orbis, orbis, -ium *m.* ring, circle; world

Patarēus, -a, -um of Patara, a city in Asia Minor

pateō, patēre, patuī, —— lie open; be revealed

Pēnēius, -a, -um of Peneus (a river god)

potentia, potentiae *f.* power, influence

properō (1-intr.) hasten, rush

prōsum (prō- + sum), prōdesse, prōfuī, prōfutūrus be an aid, benefit

rēgia, rēgiae *f.* palace; royal seat, capital

sagitta, sagittae *f.* arrow

sānābilis, sānābile able to be healed, curable

serviō, servīre, servīvī or **serviī, servītum** be a slave, serve (+ dat.)

subiciō (sub- + iaciō) place below; make subject

Tenedos, Tenedī *f.* Tenedos, an island off Troy

timidus, -a, -um fearful, afraid, timid

vacuus, -a, -um empty; idle; free, available; carefree, disengaged

ventus, ventī *m.* wind

obviaque adversās vibrābant flāmina vestēs,

et levis inpulsōs retrō dabat aura capillōs,

auctaque forma fugā est. sed enim nōn sustinet ultrā   530

perdere blanditiās iuvenis deus, utque monēbat

ipse Amor, admissō sequitur vestīgia passū.

ut canis in vacuō leporem cum* Gallicus arvō

vīdit,* et hic praedam pedibus petit, ille salūtem;

alter inhaesūrō similis iam iamque† tenēre   535

spērat et extentō stringit vestīgia rostrō,

alter in ambiguō est an sit conprēnsus, et ipsīs

morsibus ēripitur tangentiaque ōra relinquit:

sīc deus et virgō est, hic spē celer, illa timōre.

---

*cum . . . vīdit whenever . . . sees

†iam iamque at any time now

admittō (ad- + mittō) admit; let go, release

adversus, -a, -um opposite, opposing

ambiguum, ambiguī *n.* ambiguity; **in ambiguō,** in an ambiguous state, in doubt

arvum, arvī *n.* (ploughed) field

augeō, augēre, auxī, auctus grow, increase

aura, aurae *f.* breeze

blanditia, blanditiae *f.* ingratiating speech, blandishment; *in pl.,* sweet nothings

canis, canis *m. or f.* dog

celer, celeris, celere swift, fast

capillus, capillī *m. in sing. or pl.* hair

comprendō, comprendere, comprendī, comprēnsus take hold of, seize, catch

ēripiō, ēripere, ēripuī, ēreptus tear away, snatch away

extendō, extendere, extendī, extentus or **extēnsus** make taut, stretch out

flāmen, flāminis *n.* blast, gust (of wind); breeze

forma, formae *f.* shape, form; beauty

Gallicus, -a, -um of Gaul, Gallic

impellō (in + pellō), impellere, impulī, impulsus push against; press upon

inhaereō, inhaerēre, inhaesī, inhaesūrus hold on tightly, stick, cling

iuvenis, iuvene young

lepus, leporis *m.* hare

morsus, morsūs *m.* bite; *in pl.,* teeth, jaws

obvius, -a, -um in the way, face to face; moving against, opposed in direction

passus, passūs *m.* pace, step, stride

pēs, pedis *m.* foot

praeda, praedae *f.* booty, plunder; prey

retrō (adv.) toward the rear, backward

rostrum, rostrī *n.* snout, muzzle

stringō, stringere, strīnxī, strīnctus graze, skim, touch lightly

sustineō (sub- + teneō), sustinēre, sustinuī, —— withstand, endure

tangō, tangere, tetigī, tāctus touch; reach

ultrā (adv.) beyond; further, more; *in negative clauses,* any more, any longer

vacuus, -a, -um empty

ventus, ventī *m.* wind

vestīgium, vestīgiī *n.* footprint, track, trace

vestis, vestis, -ium *f.* clothing, garment

vibrō (1-tr.) (cause to) move to and fro *or* flap

virgō, virginis *f.* maiden, virgin

CHAPTER XV

Vocabulary

➤ **caput, capitis** *n.* head
➤ **nūmen, nūminis** *n.* divine power, divinity, divine spirit, numen
➤ **orbis, orbis, -ium** *m.* ring, circle
  ➤ **orbis terrārum**, world

➤ **vultus, vultūs** *m. in sing. or pl.* expression; face

➤ **circumdō, circumdare, circumdedī, circumdatus** place round; surround
➤ **for** (1-tr.) speak, say
➤ **obstō, obstāre, obstitī, obstātum** stand in the way; hinder, block (§138)
➤ **vetō, vetāre, vetuī, vetitus** forbid (§138)

➤ **dēterreō, dēterrēre, dēterruī, dēterritus** deter, prevent (§138)
➤ **prohibeō, prohibēre, prohibuī, prohibitus** prevent; prohibit, forbid (§138)
➤ **vereor, verērī, veritus sum** be in awe of, show respect to; dread, fear (§137)

➤ **cingō, cingere, cīnxī, cīnctus** surround; gird (on oneself)
➤ **cōnstituō, cōnstituere, cōnstituī, cōnstitūtus** set up, establish; decide
➤ **rapiō, rapere, rapuī, raptus** seize, tear away, carry (off)
  ➤ **ēripiō, ēripere, ēripuī, ēreptus** tear away, snatch away
➤ **solvō, solvere, solvī, solūtus** loosen; free, release; dissolve

impediō, impedīre, impedīvī or **impediī, impedītus** hinder, impede (§138)

interest, interesse, interfuit it is important, it concerns (§139)
➤ **miseret, miserēre, miseruit** or **miseritum est** it moves (one) to pity (§139)
paenitet, paenitēre, paenituit it causes (one) to repent *or* regret (§139)
piget, pigēre, piguit it disgusts (one), it irks (one) (§139)
➤ **pudet, pudēre, puduit** or **puditum est** it makes (one) ashamed (§139)
rēfert, rēferre, rētulit it is important, it concerns (§139)
➤ **taedet, taedēre, taesum est** it makes (one) tired *or* sick (§139)

celer, celeris, celere swift
dulcis, dulce sweet, pleasant
turpis, turpe foul, ugly; base, shameful

nē (conj.) *introduces positive Fear clause,* that (§137)
quīn (conj.) *introduces Prevention clause,* that . . . not, from (§138)
➤ **quod** (conj.) the fact that
➤ **quōminus** (conj.) *introduces Prevention clause,* by which the less, from (§138)
ut (conj.) *introduces negative Fear clause,* that . . . not (§137)

Vocabulary Notes

In addition to meaning "head," **caput, capitis** *n.* may mean the "life" of a man, particularly in oaths and when representing the price paid for an offense. **Caput** is also used, with affection or contempt, to refer to the entire "person."

    nūmen, nūminis *n.* is a noun formed by the addition of the suffix **-men** to a stem of the verb *nuō, *nuere, *nuī, *nūtus, "nod."[1] **Nūmen** may mean the "divine will" that approves of or lies behind events or actions, or it may mean more generally the "divine power," "divinity," or "(divine) spirit" that each god possesses.

    orbis, orbis, -ium *m.* may indicate many circular shapes (ring, circle, sphere, ball, disk). The idiom **orbis terrārum** (occasionally **orbis terrae**) is so common that sometimes **orbis** unmodified by a genitive form of **terra** may also mean "world."

    vultus, vultūs *m.* may refer to a particular facial "expression" or more generally to a person's "countenance" or "appearance" (with an emphasis on the appearance of the face). In both the singular and the plural it may indicate a person's "face." When **vultus** is used in combination with **ōs**, **vultus** refers to the upper portion of the face, and **ōs** to the lower.

    circumdō, circumdare, circumdedī, circumdatus is a compound verb formed by the addition of the prefix **circum-** to **dō**. (For the prefix **circum-** see Appendix P.) It may appear with an Accusative, Direct Object of a Middle Voice Verb (see §144). **Circumdō** may also mean "place" something (Accusative, Direct Object) "around" something (Dative with a Compound Verb).

    for, fārī, fātus sum is cognate with **fāma**. **For** is far more common in poetry than in prose. It may take an Accusative, Direct Object or introduce a direct quotation. It does *not* introduce Indirect Statement. **For** is often used of the utterances of gods and occasionally of humans when they are speaking prophetically. The noun **fātum** is in origin a substantive of the neuter perfect passive participle of this verb (a having been spoken thing). COMPOUND VERBS FORMED FROM **FOR** DO *NOT* EXHIBIT VOWEL WEAKENING. WHEN A COMPOUND OF **FOR** APPEARS IN READINGS, ITS PRINCIPAL PARTS ARE NOT SUPPLIED, BUT THE PREFIX AND SIMPLE VERB ARE GIVEN.

    obstō, obstāre, obstitī, obstātum is a compound verb formed by the addition of the prefix **ob-** to **stō**. (For the prefix **ob-** see Appendix P.) It exhibits regular vowel weakening in the third principal part. **Obstō** may take a Dative with a Compound Verb and may introduce a Prevention clause (see §138).

    vetō, vetāre, vetuī, vetitus is an irregular first-conjugation verb. For constructions with **vetō** see §138.

    dēterreō, dēterrēre, dēterruī, dēterritus is a compound verb formed by the addition of the prefix **dē-** to **terreō**. (For the prefix **dē-** see Appendix P.) **Dēterreō** may introduce a Prevention clause (see §138).

    prohibeō, prohibēre, prohibuī, prohibitus is a compound verb formed by the addition of the prefix **prō-** to **habeō**. (For the prefix **prō-** see Appendix P.) It exhibits regular vowel weakening in all four principal parts. For constructions with **prohibeō** see §138.

    vereor, verērī, veritus sum may introduce a Fear clause (see §137), and while it may mean "fear" or "dread," it often means "show respect for" or "be in awe of" those who are greater in rank or being (gods, parents, kings). It has a broader meaning than **timeō**, a verb that reports fear but not awe or reverence. COMPOUND VERBS FORMED FROM **VEREOR** DO *NOT* EXHIBIT VOWEL WEAKENING.

    cingō, cingere, cīnxī, cīnctus often appears with an Accusative, Direct Object of a Middle Voice Verb (see §144). It may also be used to mean "surround" or "encircle" something (Accusative, Direct Object) with something (Ablative of Means). COMPOUND VERBS FORMED FROM **CINGŌ** DO *NOT* EXHIBIT VOWEL WEAKENING.

    cōnstituō, cōnstituere, cōnstituī, cōnstitūtus has a broad range of meanings, which include "station" or "draw up" (soldiers, troops); "establish" or "build" (towers, altars); "make" or "create" (the human race, laws, peace); and "fix," "appoint," or "agree upon" (a price, a specific day, boundaries). When **constituō** means "decide," it is followed by an Object Infinitive.

    rapiō, rapere, rapuī, raptus describes the violent action of seizing and carrying off things or people. It is also used to mean "(sexually) violate" or "rape."

    ēripiō, ēripere, ēripuī, ēreptus is a compound verb formed by the addition of the prefix **ē-** to **rapiō**. (For the prefix **ē-** see Appendix P.) It exhibits regular vowel weakening in all four principal parts. Although **ēripiō** is a synonym of **rapiō**, it is also used to mean "snatch" or "rescue" (from danger, death). THE PRINCIPAL PARTS OF *ALL* COMPOUNDS OF **RAPIŌ** FOLLOW THE PATTERN OF THE PRINCIPAL PARTS OF **ĒRIPIŌ**. WHEN A COMPOUND OF **RAPIŌ** APPEARS IN READINGS, ITS PRINCIPAL PARTS ARE NOT SUPPLIED, BUT THE PREFIX AND SIMPLE VERB ARE GIVEN.

---

    1. While the simple verb *nuō does not occur in the Latin that survives, several compounds (e.g., **abnuō, adnuō, innuō,** and **renuō**) are common.

The basic meaning of **solvō**, **solvere**, **solvī**, **solūtus** is "loosen" or "untie" (bonds, ropes). Its extended meanings include "free," "release," or "relax" (persons, souls, limbs). Finally, **solvō** is used to mean "resolve," "acquit," or "discharge" (problems, debts, vows, legal charges). COMPOUND VERBS FORMED FROM **SOLVŌ** DO *NOT* EXHIBIT VOWEL WEAKENING. WHEN A COMPOUND OF **SOLVŌ** APPEARS IN READINGS, ITS PRINCIPAL PARTS ARE NOT SUPPLIED, BUT THE PREFIX AND SIMPLE VERB ARE GIVEN.

miseret, **miserēre**, **miseruit** or **miseritum est** has *two* third principal parts, which are equivalent in meaning. Both are extremely rare in the Latin that survives.

pudet, **pudēre**, **puduit** or **puditum est** has *two* third principal parts, which are equivalent in meaning. **Puditum est** is extremely rare.

The third principal part of **taedet**, **taedēre**, **taesum est** appears only once in the Latin that survives. Slightly more frequent is the compound form **pertaesum est**.

When **quod** means "the fact that," it introduces a noun clause with a verb in the indicative mood. Such a clause may be used with the impersonal verbs **paenitet**, **piget**, and **pudet** (see §139), but **quod**-the-fact-that clauses also appear frequently with other verbs or in apposition to a variety of nouns or pronouns.

> **Eius factum fortissimum meminerimus, quod vulnere acceptō vītam cōnsulis servāvit.**
> We shall remember his very brave deed: the fact that, with a wound received, he saved the consul's life.

quōminus is a compound conjunction made up of the relative pronoun **quō** (by which degree) and the comparative adverb **minus** (less). It is often written as two separate words (**quō minus**). The use of **quōminus** to introduce Prevention clauses (see §138) reflects their origins as Purpose clauses.

	Derivatives	Cognates
cingō	cinch; suc*cinct*	
caput	*cap*ital; *cap*itulate; *cap*tain; *chap*ter; head; chief; de*cap*itate	
orbis	orb; *orb*it	
paenitet	penitent	
rapiō	rape; rapt; *rav*ish; *rav*en; *rap*id	
solvō	dis*solve*; solute	for*lorn*; -*less*; *loose*; *lose*; ana*lysis*
taedet	*ted*ium	
vereor	re*vere*	*wary*; a*ware*; ste*ward*; *guard*

§137. Fear Clauses

A verb or other expression of fearing may introduce a subordinate clause that expresses the thing feared. Such a clause, called a **Fear clause**, is introduced by the conjunction **ut** (that . . . not) or **nē** (that) and has its verb in the subjunctive mood according to the rules of sequence. For example:

Magnopere metuit *nē* filius in bellō *moriātur*.
Greatly he fears *that* (his) son in war *will die*.
He greatly fears *that* his son *will die* in war.
Pater timēbat *ut* filius ē bellō *redīsset*.
The father was fearing *that* (his) son (out) from the war *had not returned*.
The father was fearing *that* his son *had not returned* from the war.
Ūna cūra sociōs movēbat: *nē* Rōmānī auxilium *nōn mitterent*.
One concern the allies (d.o.) was stirring up: *that* the Romans aid (d.o.) *were not sending/would not send*.
One concern was stirring up the allies: *that* the Romans *were not sending/would not send* aid.

OBSERVATIONS

1. A Fear clause was originally an independent sentence whose verb was an Optative subjunctive expressing a wish in relation to a feeling of fear:

Magnopere metuit. *Nē* filius in bellō *moriātur*.
He greatly fears. *If only* his son *would not die* in war.

Such a paratactic arrangement easily became one sentence:

Magnopere metuit *nē* filius in bellō *moriātur*.
He greatly fears *that* his son *will die* in war.

The apparent reversal of the English translations of **ut** and **nē** can be accounted for in this way:

What one *wishes would* happen one *fears will not* happen (**ut**).
What one *wishes would not* happen one *fears will* happen (**nē**).

2. In the third sentence above **nē . . . nōn** (that . . . not) is used to introduce a negative Fear clause. In early Latin the conjunction **ut** introducing such a clause is much more common than **nē . . . nōn**. By the classical period **nē . . . nōn** is much more common than the simple **ut**, and it is regularly used when the expression of fearing is *negated*. For example:

***Nōn metuō nē* domum post bellum filius *nōn redeat*.**
I do not fear that my son *will not return* home after the war.

3. The subjunctive verbs in Fear clauses follow the rules of sequence. Thus the syntax of, for example, **moriātur** is **present subjunctive, Fear clause, primary sequence**. In this sentence the present tense of the subjunctive indicates an action that is *subsequent* to the action of the main verb.[2] Such a fear for the future may be expressed more emphatically with an active periphrastic:

Magnopere metuit *nē* filius in bellō *moritūrus sit*.
He greatly fears *that* his son *is going to/will die* in war.

---

2. Although the present subjunctive may also indicate an action that is simultaneous with the main verb, sense makes this less likely in this sentence.

4. In the second sentence above the subjunctive **redīsset** is *pluperfect* to indicate an action that is *prior to* the action of the main verb. In the third sentence **mitterent** is *imperfect* to indicate an action that is either *simultaneous with* or *subsequent to* the action of the main verb. The tense of the English translation is determined by the relative time of the subjunctive to the main verb.

☛ DRILL 137 MAY NOW BE DONE.

§138. Prevention Clauses

A verb of hindering or preventing may introduce a subordinate clause that expresses the action hindered or prevented. Such a clause, called a **Prevention clause**, is introduced by the conjunction **quōminus**, **nē**, or **quīn** and has its verb in the subjunctive mood according to the rules of sequence. For example:

> **Quid tibi obstat *nē* Rōmā *discēdās*? (obstō, obstāre, obstitī, obstātum** stand in the way; hinder, block)
> What hinders you *in order that* from Rome *you may not depart?*
> What hinders you *from departing* from Rome?
> **Timor mē dēterruit *quōminus* in senātū bene *dīcerem*.**
> Fear deterred me *by which the less* in the senate I *might speak* well. (**dēterreō, dēterrēre, dēterruī, dēterritus** deter, prevent)
> Fear deterred me *from speaking* well in the senate.
> **Bellum nōn dēterrēbit *quīn agricolae* in agrīs *labōrent*.**
> War will not prevent *that the farmers* in the fields *not work.*
> War will not prevent *the farmers from working* in the fields.

OBSERVATIONS

1. Prevention clauses closely resemble Purpose clauses. (Cf. the use of **nē** to introduce negative Purpose clauses and of **quō** to introduce Purpose clauses containing a comparative adjective or adverb.)

2. When the *main clause* is *negated,* or when negation is implied, the Prevention clause is introduced by the conjunction **quīn** (as in the third sentence) or, less frequently, by **quōminus.** When the main clause is *not* negated, the Prevention clause is introduced by **quōminus** or **nē.**

3. The English words "from _____ing" (employing the English gerund) are used in translating Prevention clauses. Sometimes the *subject of a Prevention clause* is better translated as the *direct object of the verb of preventing,* as in the third sentence.

Certain verbs of prohibiting or forbidding are *not* followed by a Prevention clause but regularly take an Object Infinitive with a Subject Accusative. For example:

> **Caesar *suōs* prohibuit castra *relinquere*. (prohibeō, prohibēre, prohibuī, prohibitus** prevent; prohibit, forbid)
> Caesar prohibited *his own men to abandon* the camp.
> Caesar prohibited *his own men from abandoning* the camp.
> **Tē** vetō dē hīs *loquī*. (**vetō, vetāre, vetuī, vetitus** forbid)
> I forbid *you to speak* about these things.

Object Infinitives that follow verbs such as **prohibeō** and **vetō** may be translated with the English words "from _____ing" or "to _____" according to correct English usage.

☛ DRILL 138 MAY NOW BE DONE.

§139. Impersonal Constructions II: *miseret, paenitet, piget, pudet, taedet, rēfert, interest*

Two groups of impersonal verbs, those expressing emotions and those expressing concern or interest, have a variety of words and constructions that may function as their *subjects*.

Verbs Expressing Emotion

miseret, miserēre, miseruit or **miseritum est** it moves (one) to pity
paenitet, paenitēre, paenituit it causes (one) to repent or regret
piget, pigēre, piguit it disgusts (one), it irks (one)
pudet, pudēre, puduit or **puditum est** it makes (one) ashamed
taedet, taedēre, taesum est it makes (one) tired *or* sick

The first and third principal parts of these verbs are given in the *third person singular* because impersonal verbs appear in that person and number *only*. **Miseret** and **pudet** have alternate third principal parts formed as impersonal passives. The third principal part of **taedet** is also an impersonal passive.

The *person affected* by an emotion is expressed by an Accusative, Direct Object, and the *cause* or *object* of the emotion is regularly expressed in the *genitive* case. For example:

Illārum mē **miseret.**	*Those women* move *me* to pity.
	I pity *those women*.
Num *Catilīnam scelerum* **paenituit?**	*(His) crimes* did not cause *Catiline* to repent, did they?
	Catiline did not repent *his crimes*, did he?

Because the syntax of Latin sentences using these verbs is so different from the way English would express similar ideas, literal translations should be avoided. Translations such as the second ones given above are to be preferred.

With the verbs **paenitet, piget, pudet,** and **taedet** the genitive that expresses the cause or object of the emotion may be replaced by a Subject Infinitive (with or without a Subject Accusative). In addition, with the verbs **paenitet, piget,** and **pudet** the genitive may be replaced by a Subject clause introduced by the conjunction **quod,** "the fact that".

For example:

> **Tē pudeat *haec dīcere.*** (Subject Infinitive)
> Let *saying these things* make you ashamed.
> Let it shame you *to say these things.*
> **Eum paenitēbat *quod nōs relīquerat.*** (subject clause introduced by **quod**)
> *The fact that he had abandoned us* was causing him to regret.
> He was regretting *the fact that he had abandoned us.*

Verbs Expressing Concern or Interest

> **rēfert, rēferre, rētulit** it is important, it concerns
> **interest, interesse, interfuit** it is important, it concerns

The *person to whom* something is important or of concern is regularly expressed by the *feminine singular ablative of a possessive adjective*: **meā**, **nostrā**, **tuā**, or **vestrā**.[3] The person concerned may also be expressed in the *genitive* case. The *cause* or *object* of concern may be expressed by any of these:

1. Neuter pronoun in the nominative case
2. Subject Infinitive (with or without a Subject Accusative)
3. Substantive **Ut** clause (subject clause); negative = **nē**
4. Indirect Question

For example:

> ***Tuāne hoc* rēfert?** (neuter pronoun)
> Is *this thing* important *to you?*
> ***Meā* rēfert *audīre* tuam sententiam.** (Subject Infinitive)
> *To hear* your opinion is important *to me.*
> ***Meā* maximē interest *ut* quam prīmum *discēdās.*** (Substantive **Ut** clause)
> It concerns *me* very greatly *that you depart* as soon as possible.
> ***Omnium* intererat *quid cōnsilī cōnsulēs caperent.*** (Indirect Question)
> It was important *to all people what (of) plan the consuls were forming.*
> *What plan the consuls were forming* was important *to all people.*

OBSERVATIONS

1. **Rēfert** is a compound verb formed by the addition of **rē** (feminine singular ablative of **rēs**) to the verb **ferō**. The feminine singular ablative of the possessive adjective in each of the first two sentences agrees with this prefixed **rē**: "it bears in respect to my situation (your situation)."

2. In the third sentence the feminine singular ablative of the possessive adjective (**meā**) is used with **interest** by analogy with the usage with **rēfert**. The genitive of the person concerned was originally used with **interest** only, but also by analogy occasionally appears with **rēfert**.

3. Literal English translations of sentences with **rēfert** and **interest** should be avoided. Translations such as those given above are to be preferred.

☛ DRILL 139 MAY NOW BE DONE.

---

3. The reflexive-possessive adjective **sua** is used rarely with **rēfert** or **interest** in Indirect Statement. In such situations, **sua** refers to the subject of the verb that introduces the Indirect Statement.

§140. Direct and Indirect Reflexives

Reflexive pronouns and reflexive-possessive adjectives have been said to *refer to the subjects of the clauses or sentences in which they appear* (see §44). A reflexive so used may be called a **direct reflexive**. When a reflexive word in a subordinate clause points *outside* its own clause to the *subject of the main verb*, it is called an **indirect reflexive**.

When the subject of an infinitive in Indirect Statement is different from the subject of the main verb, a reflexive pronoun or reflexive-possessive adjective appearing within the Indirect Statement may be either a direct or an indirect reflexive. For example:

> **Rēx sēnsit cīvēs *suam* urbem regere nōn posse.** (direct reflexive)
> The king perceived that the citizens were not able to rule *their own* city.
> **Rēx sēnsit cīvēs *sē* ōdisse.** (indirect reflexive)
> The king perceived that the citizens hated *him*.

OBSERVATIONS

1. In the first sentence **suam** is a direct reflexive because it refers to **cīvēs**, the subject of the clause in which **suam** appears. In the second sentence **sē** is an indirect reflexive because it refers to **rēx**, the subject of the main clause.

2. Context helps to determine whether a reflexive is direct or indirect. Sometimes the intensive adjective **ipse** modifies a reflexive pronoun and identifies it as direct or indirect. For example:

> **Rēx sēnsit cīvēs *sē ipsōs* ōdisse.** (direct reflexive)
> The king perceived that the citizens hated *themselves*.

In subordinate clauses such as Purpose clauses, Indirect Commands, and Indirect Questions, reflexive pronouns and reflexive-possessive adjectives are often *indirect* reflexives. That is, they refer to the *subjects of the main clauses* rather than to the subjects of the subordinate clauses in which they appear. For example:

> **Imperātor mīlitēs hortātus est ut glōriam *sibi* caperent.**
> The commander urged the soldiers that they win glory *for him*.
> **Caesar nescit cūr sociī *suīs* verbīs pārēre nōlint.**
> Caesar does not know why the allies are unwilling to obey *his* words.

Sometimes reflexives are freely used to refer to grammatical elements that are *not the subject* of any clause, and in certain authors, direct *and* indirect reflexives are found within the same clause. For example:

Ariovistus respondit . . . nēminem *sē*cum sine *suā* perniciē contendisse. (Caesar, *Dē Bellō Gallicō* I.36)

contendō, contendere, contendī, contentus struggle   **perniciēs, perniciēī** *f.* destruction, ruin

Ariovistus answered . . . that no one had contended with *him* without *his own* ruin.

OBSERVATION

In this sentence **sē** is an indirect reflexive referring to Ariovistus, the subject of the main verb. **Suā** is a direct reflexive referring to **nēminem**, the subject of the Indirect Statement.

☛ DRILL 140 MAY NOW BE DONE.

§141. Subjunctive by Attraction

It has been observed that subordinate clauses in Indirect Statement regularly have their verbs in the subjunctive to indicate that the clause is part of the original direct statement (see §108). Sometimes the subjunctive mood is also used in clauses that are subordinate to infinitives *not* in Indirect Statement or to other clauses with verbs in the subjunctive. A subjunctive verb so used is called the **Subjunctive by Attraction** and follows the rules of sequence. For example:

> **Sapientis est fugere ubi perīculum *sentiat.***
> It is characteristic of a wise man to flee when *he perceives* danger.
> **Scīsne quid pater, priusquam *mortuus sit,* dīxerit?**
> Do you know what the father said before *he died?*
> **Hortābātur ut eadem quae *dīxisset* dīcerem.**
> She was urging that I say the same things that *she had said.*

OBSERVATIONS

1. The information in a subordinate clause with a Subjunctive by Attraction is *essential* to the thought of the clause or infinitive on which it depends. For example, the clause **ubi perīculum sentiat** in the first sentence indicates the *essential circumstance* under which a wise man would flee. An indicative verb in such a clause would indicate *nonessential* information.

2. The syntax of, for example, **dīxisset** is **pluperfect subjunctive, Subjunctive by Attraction, secondary sequence (prior time).**

§142. Supine

In addition to the infinitive and the gerund, there is a third *verbal noun* in Latin called the **supine**, which appears in *only two forms,* the *accusative singular* and the *ablative singular.* The stem for the supine of *all verbs* may be obtained by dropping the ending from the fourth principal part. To this stem the endings **-um** (accusative) and **-ū** (ablative) are added. For example:

4th Principal Part	Stem	Accusative Supine	Ablative Supine
lēctus	lēct-	lēctum	lēctū
vīsus	vīs-	vīsum	vīsū

OBSERVATION

The endings of the supine have been borrowed from the fourth declension masculine/feminine endings.

Each case of the supine has only *one syntactic function.* The accusative supine *expresses purpose with a verb of motion* (or a verb implying motion). The ablative supine is an *Ablative of Respect.* For example:

> **Hostēs *oppugnātum* patriam nostram *veniunt.***
> The enemies *are coming for the purpose of attacking/to attack* our country.
> **Deōs superat—sī hoc fās est *dictū.***
> He surpasses the gods—if this thing is right *in respect to saying/to say.*

1. The accusative supine in the first sentence appears with a verb that expresses motion, **veniunt**. It takes a direct object, **patriam**. The accusative supine is translated "for the purpose of _____ing" or "to _____."[4]

2. The ablative supine may be translated literally, "in respect to _____ing," but an adverbial use of the English infinitive, "to _____," will often be more idiomatic.

§143. Accusative of Respect

Many Roman poets (and a few prose writers as well) chose to imitate Greek syntax in Latin for two distinct uses of the accusative case, *each* of which is sometimes called the **Greek Accusative**.

When a noun in the accusative case is used to qualify or limit an adjective (often a perfect passive participle), it is called the **Accusative of Respect**.[5] For example:

> **Aenēās . . . *ōs umerōs*que deō similis . . . (umerus, umerī** *m.* shoulder)
> Aeneas . . . similar to a god *in (respect to) (his) face* and *shoulders* . . . (Vergil, *Aeneid* I.589)
> **hōc concussa metū *mentem* . . . (concutiō, concutere, concussī, concussus** strike)
> (She) having been struck *in respect to (her) mind* by this fear . . . (Vergil, *Aeneid* XII.468)

The syntax of each italicized word (**ōs**, **umerōs**, **mentem**) is **Accusative of Respect**.

1. The Accusative of Respect developed from the idea of *extent* inherent in the accusative case. Thus, for example, **ōs umerōsque deō similis** means "similar to a god to the extent of (his) face and shoulders," "similar to a god as far as his face and shoulders."

2. The Accusative of Respect is similar in sense to the more common Ablative of Respect (see §39).

3. Sometimes the noun in the Accusative of Respect is an adjective used as a substantive. For example: **omnia sapiēns**, "wise in (respect to) all things."

§144. Accusative, Direct Object of a Middle Voice Verb

In addition to the active and passive voices, ancient Greek has a *middle* voice, whose forms are most often identical to those of the passive. The middle voice in Greek, which frequently takes a direct object, is often used for actions that benefit or physically affect the subject.[6] Certain *passive* verb forms in Latin are used to represent Greek *middle* voice verbs and so may take an Accusative, Direct Object. For example:

---

4. The rare future passive infinitive (see §104) is made with the accusative supine and the impersonal passive infinitive of **eō**. For example: **Putō eum captum īrī** (I think that there is a going to capture him, I think that he is going to be captured).

5. The Accusative of Respect is also known as the Accusative of the Part Affected.

6. The existence of the middle voice in Greek is a remnant of the system of voice in IE, which had active and middle voices *only*. Many deponent verbs in Latin—verbs with passive forms that take direct objects—were in origin middle voice verbs.

> *Ferrum* cingitur. (cingō, cingere, cīnxī, cīnctus surround; gird [oneself])
> He girds *a sword* on himself. (Vergil, *Aeneid* II.511)
> . . . cīnctus [est] honōre *caput*. (caput, capitis *n.* head)
> (He) surrounded (his) *head* with honor. (Ovid, *Ars Amātōria* III.392)

The syntax of each italicized word (**ferrum, caput**) is **Accusative, Direct Object of a Middle Voice Verb**.

OBSERVATION

Although **cingitur** and **cīnctus (est)** are *passive* in form, they should be considered *middle:* the subject of each *performs* the action of the verb, and each verb takes an Accusative, Direct Object of a Middle Voice Verb. Verbs that mean "put on" or "take off" (clothing, armor) may take such an accusative.

§145. Historical Infinitive

In vivid narration the present infinitive may appear in place of a finite verb in the imperfect or perfect tense (simple past). An infinitive so used, usually with a *subject* in the *nominative* case, is called a **Historical Infinitive**.[7] For example:

> *Rōmānī* ex omnibus partibus, signō datō, *oppugnāre.*
> The *Romans* from all parts, with the signal having been given, *attacked.*
> *Catilīna* in prīmā aciē *stāre*, sociōs *hortārī.*
> *Catiline was standing* in the first battle line; *he was encouraging* his allies.
> **Augustō mortuō, in urbe *timēre*, in prōvinciīs bellum *exspectāre.***
> With Augustus having died, in the city *people were afraid,* in the provinces *people were expecting* war.

OBSERVATIONS

1. In the first sentence the present active infinitive **oppugnāre** stands for a perfect active indicative verb, *past* time, *simple* aspect. In the second sentence **stāre** and **hortārī** stand for imperfect active indicative verbs, *past* time, *progressive* aspect. Context helps to determine which past tense a historical infinitive represents.

2. The *subjects* of the Historical Infinitives in the first two sentences are *nominative*. The nominative subject of a Historical Infinitive is an *exception* to the general rule that subjects of infinitives are in the accusative case (see §107).

3. In the third sentence the Historical Infinitives **timēre** and **exspectāre** appear without subjects. Such a usage emphasizes the verbal action *alone*. However, when a Historical Infinitive appears without a subject, a subject must be supplied (e.g., people, men, soldiers, they).

4. Several Historical Infinitives often appear together when a scene of intense activity is reported. Historical Infinitives may also appear in combination with finite verbs.

☛ DRILL 141–145 MAY NOW BE DONE.

---

7. The Historical Infinitive may look back to the earliest stage of the verb's development, in which a verbal noun (the infinitive) with no endings to indicate person and number was placed with a noun subject simply to name the action being performed.

Short Readings

1. Sosia, Amphitruo's slave, remains firm in the face of his master's threats to cut out his tongue.

   tamen quīn loquar haec utī facta sunt hīc,

   numquam ūllō modō mē potes dēterrēre. (PLAUTUS, *AMPHITRUŌ* 559–60)

   utī = ut

2. Megadorus describes his uncomfortable relationship with his would-be father-in-law, Euclio.

   . . . fastīdit meī

   quia videt mē suam amīcitiam velle: mōre hominum facit;

   nam sī opulentus it petītum pauperiōris grātiam,

   pauper metuit congredīrī, per metum male rem gerit.

   īdem, quandō occāsiō illaec periit, post sērō cupit. (PLAUTUS, *AULULĀRIA* 245–49)

   congredior (con- + gradior) go near, approach;
      congredīrī = archaic form of **congredī**
   fastīdiō, fastīdīre, fastīdīvī or **fastīdiī, fastīdītus**
      be scornful (of), disdain (+ gen.); *subject*
      is Euclio
   illaec = archaic form of **illa**

   occāsiō, occāsiōnis *f.* opportunity, chance
   opulentus, -a, -um rich
   pauper, pauperis poor
   quandō (conj.) when
   sērō (adv.) late; **post sērō**, too late

3. After doing all the talking, the slave Olympio won't let Chalinus answer.

   abeō intrō. taedet tuī sermōnis. (PLAUTUS, *CASĪNA* 142)

   intrō (adv.) within, inside
   sermō, sermōnis *m.* speech, talk, conversation

4. After explaining his plan of having one girl pretend to be two, Palaestrio lists possible excuses to avoid any request to see both girls at the same time.

   facilest: trēcentae possunt causae conligī:

   "nōn domīst, abiit ambulātum, dormit, ornātur, lavat,

   prandet, potat: . . . " (PLAUTUS, *MĪLES GLŌRIŌSUS* 250–52)

   colligō (con- + legō), colligere, collēgī, collēctus
      collect, amass
   dormiō, dormīre, dormīvī or **dormiī, dormītum**
      sleep, be asleep
   lavō, lavāre or **lavere, lāvī, lautus** or **lōtus** wash
      (oneself)

   ornō (1-tr.) prepare, arrange; dress, beautify
   potō (1-tr.) drink
   prandeō, prandēre, prandī, prānsus eat breakfast;
      eat lunch

5. Antipho's daughter Panegyris explains to her father why neither she nor her two sisters are willing to be remarried. (The three sisters are waiting for their long-lost husbands.)

> Pan. Stultitiast, pater, vēnātum dūcere invītās canēs.
>
> hostis est uxor, invīta quae virō nuptum datur.
>
> Ant. Certumne est neutram vostrārum* persequī imperium patris?
>
> Pan. Persequimur, nam quō† dedistī‡ nuptum, abīre nōlumus.

(PLAUTUS, STICHUS 139–42)

*vostrārum, sc. sorōrum
†quō = ab eō cui
‡dedistī, sc. nōs as direct object
canis, canis m. or f. dog
invītus, -a, -um unwilling
nūbō, nūbere, nūpsī, nuptus marry (of a woman)

persequor (per- + sequor) follow earnestly, conform to
stultitia, stultitiae f. foolishness, stupidity
uxor, uxōris f. wife
vēnor (1-intr.) go hunting, hunt

6. A despairing Cassandra addresses her mother, Hecuba.

> māter, optumārum multō mulier melior mulierum,
>
> missa sum* superstitiōsīs hariolātiōnibus;
>
> mē Apollō fātīs fandīs dēmentem invītam ciet.
>
> virginēs vereor aequālīs, patris meī meum factum pudet,
>
> optumī virī. mea māter, tuī mē miseret, meī piget.
>
> optumam prōgeniem Priamō peperistī extrā mē. hoc dolet.

(ENNIUS, TRAGOEDIAE FRAG. 34–39)

*mittō, here, drive
aequālis, aequāle equal, of the same age
cieō, ciēre, cīvī, citus rouse, stir up
dēmēns, dēmentis insane, (raving) mad
doleō, dolēre, doluī, —— cause pain, be painful
extrā (prep. + acc.) outside, except
hariolātiō, hariolātiōnis f. prophecy

invītus, -a, -um unwilling
mulier, mulieris f. woman
pariō, parere, peperī, partus give birth to, bear
prōgeniēs, *prōgeniēī f. offspring, progeny
superstitiōsus, -a, -um ecstatic, exalted
virgō, virginis f. maiden, virgin

7. A fragment from a lost Ennian tragedy, Erechtheus

> lapideō sunt corde multī quōs nōn miseret nēminis.*

(ENNIUS, TRAGOEDIAE FRAG. 140)

*The redundant negative strengthens the negative idea.
cor, cordis n. heart
lapideus, -a, -um (made of) stone

8. The poet employs alliteration to describe a gory death in battle.

> ōscitat in campīs caput ā cervīce revolsum
>
> sēmianimēsque micant oculī lūcemque requīrunt. (ENNIUS, SĒD. INC. FRAG. 483–84)

cervīx, cervīcis f. neck
micō, micāre, micuī, —— quiver, dart, flicker
ōscitō (1-intr.) gape
requīrō (re- + quaerō), requīrere, requīsiī or requīsīvī, requīsītus try to find, look for

revellō, revellere, revellī, revulsus tear, tear away
sēmianimis, sēmianime half-alive; the first -i- of sēmianimēs is consonantal

9. Micio discusses with his brother Demea the delinquent behavior of Demea's son Aeschinus.

> *Micio.* quid fēcit? *Demea.* quid ille fēcerit?* quem neque pudet
>
> quicquam neque metuit quemquam neque lēgem putat
>
> tenēre sē ūllam . . . (TERENCE, *ADELPHOE* 84–86)

*fēcerit, perfect subj. in implied Indirect Question, *sc.* **Rogāsne**

10. Parmenio describes Philumena's behavior toward her mother-in-law, Sostrata, since being forced to move into her mother-in-law's house.

> *Parmenio.* sī quandō ad eam* accesserat†
>
> cōnfābulātum, fugere ē cōnspectū īlicō,
>
> vidēre nōlle . . . (TERENCE, *HECYRA* 181–83)

*eam refers to Philumena.
†sī quandō . . . accesserat = cum . . . accesserat subject is Sostrata
cōnspectus, cōnspectūs *m.* (range of) sight, view
cōnfābulor (1-intr.) converse, have a talk
īlicō (adv) at once, immediately

11. In love with a prostitute, the young and poor Phaedria tries to get the pimp Dorio to listen to his excuses one more time.

> *Phaedria.* audī quod dīcam. *Dorio.* at enim taedet iam audīre eadem mīliēns.
>
> *Ph.* at nunc dīcam quod lubenter audiās. *Do.* loquere, audiō.
>
> (TERENCE, *PHORMIŌ* 487–88)

at (conj.) but
libenter (adv.) gladly
mīliēns (adv.) a thousand times

12. While advocating that Pompey be given command in the east, Cicero explains and decries the attitude of many nations toward Rome.

> difficile est dictū, Quirītēs, quantō in odiō sīmus apud exterās nātiōnēs propter
>
> eōrum quōs ad eās per hōs annōs cum imperiō mīsimus libīdinēs et iniūriās.
>
> (CICERO, *PRŌ LĒGE MĀNĪLIĀ* 65)

exter, extera, exterum external, foreign
iniūria, iniūriae *f.* injury, injustice
libīdō, libīdinis *f.* desire, pleasure, passion, lust
nātiō, nātiōnis *f.* nation
Quirītēs, Quirītium *m. pl.* Quirites, the name for Roman citizens in their public capacity

13. Cicero imagines what the populace would say to the prosecutor M. Juventus Laterensis if it were able to speak with one voice. Juventus was quaestor in Cyrene in 63 B.C.E., the year of the Catilinarian conspiracy.

"Dēsīderārunt tē," inquit, "oculī meī, cum tū essēs Cyrēnīs; mē enim quam sociōs

tuā fruī virtūte mālēbam, et quō plūs intererat, eō plūs aberat ā mē, cum tē nōn vidē-

bam." (CICERO, *PRŌ PLANCIŌ* 13)

Cyrēnae, Cyrēnārum *f. pl.* Cyrene, a town in northwest Libya
dēsīderō (1-tr.) long for, desire
fruor, fruī, frūctus sum enjoy, delight in (+ abl.)
inquam (defective verb) say; **inquit** = *3rd sing. pres. act. indic.*

14. Cicero pauses in a speech to comment on the value of his own friendship.

etenim ego dē mē tantum audeō dīcere amīcitiam meam voluptātī plūribus quam

praesidiō fuisse, mēque vehementer vītae meae paenitēret sī in meā familiāritāte

locus esset nēminī nisi lītigiōsō aut nocentī. (CICERO, *PRŌ PLANCIŌ* 82)

familiāritās, familiāritātis *f.* close friendship   **vehementer** (adv.) violently, strongly
lītigiōsus, -a, -um fond of going to law, litigious   **voluptās, voluptātis** *f.* pleasure, joy
nocēns, nocentis harmful, guilty
praesidium, praesidiī *n.* guard; defense,
    protection

15. After he speaks about appropriate embellishment in oratory, Crassus notes that much depends on the makeup of the audience and other factors.

rēfert etiam quī audiant, senātus an populus an iūdicēs: frequentēs an paucī an sin-

gulī, et quālēs: ipsīque ōrātōrēs quā sint aetāte, honōre, auctōritāte, dēbet vidērī;

tempus, pācis an bellī, festīnātiōnis an ōtī. (CICERO, *DĒ ŌRĀTŌRE* III.211)

festīnātiō, festīnātiōnis *f.* haste, hurry
frequēns, frequentis crowded; present in crowds
iūdex, iūdicis *m.* juror, judge
ōtium, ōtiī *n.* leisure
singulī, -ae, -a individual, single, one at a time

16. Scipio, a character in Cicero's dialogue, recalls a story about the newborns, Romulus and Remus.

is* igitur, ut nātus sit, cum Remō frātre dīcitur ab Amūliō, rēge Albānō, ob labefac-

tandī rēgnī timōrem ad† Tiberim expōnī iussus esse . . . (CICERO, *DĒ RĒ PŪBLICĀ* II.4)

*is refers to Romulus.   **expōnō (ex- + pōnō)** place out; expose, abandon
†ad, *here,* at, near   **labefactō** (1-tr.) weaken, undermine
Albānus, -a, -um of *or* belonging to Alba Longa,   **rēgnum, rēgnī** *n.* kingdom, realm; kingship, rule
    a Latin city predating Rome; Alban   **Tiberis, Tiberis** *m.* (the) Tiber, a river that flows
Amūlius, Amūliī *m.* Amulius, legendary king of   through Rome; **Tiberim** = *acc. sing.*
    Alba Longa

17. Cicero recalls an outstanding trait of the orator Hortensius.

prīmum memoria* tanta—quantam in nūllō cognōvisse mē arbitror—ut quae sēcum commentātus esset, ea sine scrīptō† verbīs eīsdem redderet quibus cōgi-tāvisset. (CICERO, BRŪTUS 301)

*memoria, *sc.* of Hortensius
†scrīptum, scrīptī *n.* writing; script
commentor (1-tr.) prepare beforehand, practice
reddō (red- + dō) give back; reproduce, repeat

18. Cicero explains why an orator must have a thorough knowledge of history.

nescīre autem quid antequam nātus sīs acciderit, id est semper esse puerum. quid enim est aetās hominis nisi ea memoriā rērum veterum cum superiōrum aetāte contexitur? (CICERO, ORĀTOR 120)

contexō, contexere, contexuī, contextus weave together, connect, link
superior, superius upper; previous, earlier

19. Referring to the long, fortunate life of the Persian king Cyrus, Cato speaks about the pursuits of old age.

hāc igitur fortūnā fruī licet senibus nec aetās impedit quō minus et cēterārum rērum et in prīmīs* agrī colendī studia teneāmus ūsque ad ultimum tempus senectūtis. (CICERO, DĒ SENECTŪTE 60)

*in prīmīs, *here,* especially, above all
colō, colere, coluī, cultus cultivate, tend
fruor, fruī, frūctus sum enjoy, delight in (+ abl.)
senectūs, senectūtis *f.* old age

senex, senis old; *as masc. subst.,* old man
ultimus, -a, -um farthest; last, final
ūsque (adv.) continuously, all the way

20. One of the most important laws of friendship

haec igitur lēx in amīcitiā sanciātur, ut neque rogēmus* rēs turpēs nec faciāmus* rogātī. turpis enim excūsātiō est et minimē accipienda cum in cēterīs peccātīs, tum sī quis contrā rem pūblicam sē amīcī causā fēcisse fateātur.† (CICERO, DĒ AMĪCITIĀ 40)

*ut . . . rogēmus . . . faciāmus, Substantive Ut clause in apposition to lēx
†fateor, *here,* claim
excūsātiō, excūsātiōnis *f.* excuse, justification
peccātum, peccātī *n.* error, mistake; offense
sanciō, sancīre, sānxī, sānctus ratify, confirm

21. The speaker stresses the importance of polished writing.

> fierī autem potest ut rēctē quis sentiat et id quod sentit polītē ēloquī nōn possit; sed mandāre quemquam litterīs cōgitātiōnēs suās, quī eās nec dispōnere nec inlūstrāre possit nec dēlectātiōne aliquā allicere lēctōrem, hominis est intemperanter abūtentis et ōtiō et litterīs. (CICERO, *TUSCULĀNAE DISPUTĀTIŌNĒS* I.6)

abūtor (ab- + ūtor) abuse (+ abl.)
alliciō, allicere, allēxī, allēctus entice, attract, lure
cōgitātiō, cōgitātiōnis *f.* thought
dēlectātiō, dēlectātiōnis *f.* delight
dispōnō (dis- + pōnō) arrange
ēloquor (ē- + loquor) speak
illūstrō (1-tr.) illuminate, make clear

intemperanter (adv.) immoderately
lēctor, lēctōris *m.* reader
mandō (1-tr.) entrust, commit
ōtium, ōtiī *n.* leisure
polītē (adv.) in a polished way
rēctē (adv.) rightly, correctly

22. With a series of rhetorical questions Cicero expresses his exasperation at Antony's actions.

> omniane bonīs virīs quae facere possunt facienda sunt, etiamne* sī turpia, sī perniciōsa erunt, sī facere omnīnō nōn licēbit? quid autem turpius aut foedius aut quod minus deceat quam contrā senātum, contrā cīvīs, contrā patriam exercitum dūcere? quid vērō magis vituperandum quam id facere quod nōn liceat? licet autem nēminī contrā patriam dūcere exercitum . . . (CICERO, *PHILIPPICS XIII* 14)

*-**ne** implies that the preceding question must be repeated.
decet, decēre, decuit, it is becoming, it is proper
foedus, -a, -um foul, loathsome, atrocious
perniciōsus, -a, -um destructive
vituperō (1-tr.) find fault with, criticize

23. A paragraph from a letter to Atticus on the unsavory state of affairs in the Roman Republic

> dē rē pūblicā nihil habeō ad tē scrībere* nisi summum odium omnium hominum in eōs quī tenent omnia. mūtātiōnis tamen spēs nūlla. sed, quod facile sentiās, taedet ipsum Pompeium eumque vehementer paenitet. nōn prōvideō satis quem exitum futūrum putem; sed certē videntur haec aliquō† ēruptūra. (CICERO, *AD ATTICUM* II.22.6)

*scrībere, *here,* infin. expressing purpose
†aliquō (adv.) in some direction
ērumpō, ērumpere, ērūpī, ēruptus break out, burst forth

exitus, exitūs *m.* outcome
mūtātiō, mūtātiōnis *f.* change
prōvideō (prō- + videō) foresee
vehementer (adv.) violently, strongly

24. A passage from a letter of Caesar to Cicero quoted in a letter of Cicero to his friend Atticus

> neque illud mē movet: quod iī quī ā mē dīmissī sunt discessisse dīcuntur ut mihi rursus bellum īnferrent; nihil enim mālō quam et mē meī similem esse et illōs suī. (CICERO, *AD ATTICUM* IX.16.2)

dīmittō (dis- + mittō) send away, let go
rursus (adv.) again

25. In a letter to Atticus, Cicero admits implicitly to sharing in a common conceit.

nēmō umquam neque* poēta neque* ōrātor fuit quī quemquam meliōrem quam

sē arbitrārētur. (CICERO, AD ATTICUM XIV.20.3)

*The redundant negatives strengthen the negative idea.

26. After admonishing Cicero not to let his grief over the death of his daughter keep him from
actively participating in political life at a time of crisis, Sulpicius finally shows a little
restraint.

plūra mē ad tē dē hāc rē scrībere pudet, nē videar prūdentiae tuae diffīdere.

(CICERO, AD FAMILIĀRĒS IV.5.6)

diffīdō, diffīdere, ——, diffīsum lack confidence in, have no faith in (+ dat.)
prūdentia, prūdentiae *f.* good sense, judgment, prudence

27. Cicero writes to Tiro, his freedman, secretary, and friend.

sīc habētō,* mī Tīrō, nēminem esse quī mē amet quīn īdem tē amet; et cum tuā et

meā maximē interest tē valēre, tum multīs est cūrae. (CICERO, AD FAMILIĀRĒS XVI.4.4)

***habētō**, *2nd sing. fut. act. imper.,* (ye shall) consider
Tīrō, Tīrōnis *m.* Tiro

28. Caesar reports an early contact between himself and the Aedui, a Gallic tribe.

Aeduī, cum sē suaque ab iīs* dēfendere nōn possent, lēgātōs ad Caesarem mittunt†

rogātum auxilium . . . (CAESAR, DĒ BELLŌ GALLICŌ I.11)

***iīs**, refers to the Helvetians, a Gallic tribe
†**mittunt**, historical use of present tense; translate as perfect
Aeduī, Aeduōrum *m. pl.* (the) Aedui, a Gallic tribe
dēfendō, dēfendere, dēfendī, dēfēnsus protect, defend

29. When explaining his reasons for crossing the Rhine and pursuing war against certain German tribes, Caesar mentions a plea of one tribe allied to him.

Ubiī autem, quī ūnī ex Trānsrhēnānīs ad Caesarem lēgātōs mīserant, amīcitiam

fēcerant, obsidēs dederant, magnopere ōrābant ut sibi auxilium ferret quod graviter

ab Suēbīs premerentur. (CAESAR, DĒ BELLŌ GALLICŌ IV.16)

obses, obsidis *m.* or *f.* hostage
Suēbī, Suēbōrum *m. pl.* (the) Suebi, a group of German tribes
Trānsrhēnānī, Trānsrhēnānōrum *m. pl.* those living across the Rhine
Ubiī, Ubiōrum *m. pl.* (the) Ubii, a German tribe

30. While on the march, the legions of Q. Titurius Sabinus and L. Aurunculeius Cotta are ambushed by the Eburones, a Belgic tribe led by Ambiorix. Several lieutenants are seriously injured.

hīs rēbus permōtus Q. Titurius cum procul Ambiorigem suōs cohortantem cōnspexisset, interpretem suum Cn. Pompeium ad eum mittit* rogātum ut sibi mīlitibusque parcat. (Caesar, *Dē Bellō Gallicō* V.36)

*mittit, historical use of present tense; here introduces both secondary (**cōnspexisset**) and primary (**parcat**) sequence, the latter to emphasize the Indirect Command

Ambiorix, Ambiorigis *m.* Ambiorix
cohortor (co- + hortor) (1-tr.) exhort, encourage
cōnspiciō, cōnspicere, cōnspexī, conspectus perceive, observe

interpres, interpretis *m.* or *f.* go-between, agent; interpreter
parcō, parcere, pepercī, parsūrus be merciful, be sparing (+ dat.)
permoveō (per- + moveō) thoroughly move, disturb
Cn. Pompeius, Cn. Pompeiī *m.* Gn. Pompey
procul (adv.) at a distance, from a distance
Q. Titurius, Q. Titurii *m.* Q. Titurius

31. Caesar summarizes the military situation after he has pursued and hemmed in the troops led by Afranius and Petreius, two of Pompey's generals.

sī proelium committerētur, propinquitās castrōrum celerem superātīs ex fugā receptum dabat.* hāc dē causā cōnstituerat signa īnferentibus resistere, prior proeliō nōn lacessere. (Caesar, *Dē Bellō Cīvīlī* I.82)

*dabat, imperf. indic. used for vividness in apodosis of Present Contrary-to-Fact conditional sentence

committō (con- + mittō) join, engage in
lacessō, lacessere, lacessiī or **lacessīvī, lacessītus** challenge; provoke, rouse

propinquitās, propinquitātis *f.* nearness, proximity
receptus, receptūs *m.* withdrawal, retreat
resistō, resistere, restitī, — halt; make a stand against, resist (+ dat.)

32. Varro discusses the precise meaning of the verb **for**.

fātur is quī prīmum homō significābilem ōre mittit vōcem. ab eō, antequam ita faciant, puerī dīcuntur īnfantēs; cum id faciunt, iam fārī.

(Varro, *Dē Linguā Latīnā* VI.52)

īnfāns, īnfantis not speaking; *as subst.,* infant
significābilis, significābile capable of conveying meaning, meaningful

33. The historian describes the scene after Marius and the Roman forces win a bloody battle against Jugurtha, a Numidian king.

> tum spectāculum horribile in campīs patentibus: sequī, fugere, occīdī, capī; equī atque virī adflictī, ac multī volneribus acceptīs neque fugere posse neque quiētem patī, nītī modo ac statim concidere . . . (SALLUST, BELLUM IUGURTHAE 101)

afflīgō, afflīgere, afflīxī, afflictus dash, strike, cast down; injure, shatter
concidō (con- + cadō) fall down, collapse; fall dead
equus, equī m. horse
horribilis, horribile terrifying, dreadful
nītor, nītī, nīxus or nīsus sum rest upon, rely upon; make an effort, strive

occīdō, occīdere, occīdī, occīsus kill, slaughter
pateō, patēre, patuī, —— lie open
quiēs, quiētis f. rest, repose; inaction
spectāculum, spectāculī n. sight, spectacle
statim (adv.) immediately

34. The historian describes the surprising fusion of the fugitive Trojans and the native people of Italy.

> hī* postquam in ūna moenia convēnēre, disparī genere, dissimilī linguā, alius aliō mōre vīventēs, incrēdibile memorātū est quam facile coaluerint: ita brevī† multitūdō dīvorsa atque vaga concordiā cīvitās facta erat. (SALLUST, BELLUM CATILĪNAE 6)

*hī refers to the Trojans and the native Italians
†brevī, sc. tempore
coalēscō, coalēscere, coaluī, coalitum grow together, combine, coalesce
concordia, concordiae f. harmony
conveniō (con- + veniō) come together
dispār, disparis unequal; different

dīversus, -a, -um different
incrēdibilis, incrēdibile unbelievable, incredible
lingua, linguae f. tongue; language
memorō (1-tr.) recount, recall, tell
multitūdō, multitūdinis f. multitude, mob
vagus, -a, -um roaming, wandering

35. The historian describes the virtue of the citizen of the early Roman Republic.

> sē quisque hostem ferīre, mūrum ascendere, cōnspicī dum tāle facinus faceret, properābat. (SALLUST, BELLUM CATILĪNAE 7)

ascendō, ascendere, ascendī, ascēnsus climb up, ascend, scale
cōnspiciō, cōnspicere, cōnspexī, cōnspectus perceive, observe
facinus, facinoris n. deed
feriō, ferīre, ——, —— strike, hit
properō (1-tr.) hasten, rush; be eager; hurry to bring it about that

36. After the historian describes the moral decline in Roman society, he comments on how Catiline made use of the situation.

> in tantā tamque conruptā cīvitāte Catilīna, id quod factū facillumum erat, omnium flāgitiōrum atque facinorum circum sē tamquam stīpātōrum catervās habēbat.
> (SALLUST, BELLUM CATILĪNAE 14)

caterva, catervae f. throng, crowd, troop
circum (prep. + acc.) around
corruptus, -a, -um corrupt
facinus, facinoris n. deed; crime

flāgitium, flāgitiī n. shame, outrage, disgrace
stīpātor, stīpātōris m. bodyguard, attendant
tamquam (conj.) as it were, as if

37. Speaking in the senate in the debate about punishment for the Catilinarian conspirators, a
young Julius Caesar credits the ancestors with good judgment.

maiōrēs nostrī, patrēs cōnscrīptī, neque cōnsilī neque audāciae umquam eguēre;

neque illīs superbia obstābat quō minus aliēna īnstitūta, sī modo proba erant, imi-

tārentur. (SALLUST, *BELLUM CATILĪNAE* 51)

aliēnus, -a, -um belonging to another; alien,
   foreign
egeō, egēre, eguī, —— lack, want, need (+ gen.)
imitor (1-tr.) copy, follow, imitate
īnstitūtum, īnstitūtī *n.* practice, custom, usage

probus, -a, -um excellent, well-developed; upright,
   virtuous
superbia, superbiae *f.* pride; arrogance,
   haughtiness

38. Queen Dido graciously welcomes a band of surviving Trojans.

tum breviter Dīdō vultum dēmissa profātur:

"solvite corde metum, Teucrī, sēclūdite cūrās." (VERGIL, *AENEID* I.561–62)

cor, cordis *n.* heart; mind
dēmittō (dē- + mittō) let down, drop
profor (prō- + for) speak out
sēclūdō, sēclūdere, sēclūsī, sēclūsus separate; put away
Teucrī, Teucrōrum *m. pl.* descendants of Teucer, Teucrians, Trojans

39. Aeneas describes the dreadful appearance of Hector's ghost.

ei mihi, quālis erat, quantum mūtātus ab illō

Hectore quī redit exuviās indūtus Achillī

vel Danaum Phrygiōs iaculātus puppibus ignīs! (VERGIL, *AENEID* II.274–76)

Achillēs, Achillī *m.* Achilles
Danaī, Danaōrum *m. pl.* Danaans, Greeks;
   Danaum = *gen. pl.*
ei (interj.) *expression of anguish*, o! alas!; **ei mihi**,
   woe is me!
exuviae, exuviārum *f. pl.* (stripped) armor
Hectōr, Hectoris *m.* Hector, son of Priam

iaculor (1-tr.) strike, throw, hurl
induō, induere, induī, indūtus put on, clothe,
   dress
Phrygius, -a, -um of *or* belonging to Phrygia (the
   region around Troy), Phrygian, Trojan
puppis, puppis, -ium *f.* stern (of a boat); ship

40. Aeneas describes the effects of hearing the ghostly voice of a former Trojan comrade,
Polydorus.

tum vērō ancipitī mentem formīdine pressus

obstipuī steteruntque* comae et vōx faucibus haesit. (VERGIL, *AENEID* III.47–48)

*****steterunt** = archaic form of **stetērunt**
anceps, ancipitis two-headed, double; wavering,
   doubtful
coma, comae *f. in sing. or pl.* hair
faucēs, faucium *f. pl.* jaws, gullet, throat

formīdō, formīdinis *f.* fear, terror
haereō, haerēre, haesī, haesūrus stick, cling, hold
   fast (+ dat.)
obstipēscō, obstipēscere, obstipuī, —— be
   stupefied, be dumbstruck

41. The poet describes Aeneas's perplexity after he has been commanded by Mercury to leave Carthage.

> heu quid agat? quō nunc rēgīnam ambīre furentem
>
> audeat adfātū? quae prīma exordia sūmat?
>
> atque animum nunc hūc celerem nunc dīvidit illūc
>
> in partīsque rapit variās perque omnia versat. (VERGIL, AENEID IV.283–86)

affātus, affātūs *m.* address, utterance
ambiō (ambi- + eō), ambīre, ambiī or **ambīvī, ambitus** go around
dīvidō, dīvidere, dīvīsī, dīvīsus separate, divide
exordium, exordiī *n.* starting point, beginning

furō, furere, ——, —— rage, rave
sūmō, sūmere, sūmpsī, sūmptus take up, seize
varius, -a, -um varied; changeable; conflicting
versō (1-tr.) twist, keep turning

42. The poet describes Mercury as he appears to Aeneas in a dream.

> huic sē forma deī vultū redeuntis eōdem
>
> obtulit in somnīs rursusque ita vīsa monēre est,
>
> omnia Mercuriō similis, vōcemque colōremque*
>
> et crīnīs flāvōs et membra decōra iuventā: . . . (VERGIL, AENEID IV.556–59)

*****colōremque** elides into next line.
color, colōris *m.* color
crīnis, crīnis, -ium *m. in sing. or pl.* hair
decōrus, -a, -um becoming; honorable, seemly
flāvus, -a, -um golden-yellow, flaxen, blond
forma, formae *f.* shape, form

iuventa, iuventae *f.* youth(fulness)
membrum, membrī *n.* limb
offerō (ob- + ferō), offerre, obtulī, oblātus put in (one's) path; offer, present, reveal
rursus (adv.) again
somnus, somnī *m.* sleep; dream

43. Pallas, son of King Evander, greets Aeneas and his companions, who have come to Evander's pastoral kingdom seeking aid for the war in Italy.

> . . . "iuvenēs, quae causa subēgit
>
> ignōtās temptāre viās? quō tenditis?" inquit.
>
> "quī genus? unde domō? pācemne hūc fertis an arma?" (VERGIL, AENEID VIII.112–14)

ignōtus, -a, -um unknown
inquam (defective verb) say; **inquit** = *3rd sing. pres. act. indic.*
iuvenis, iuvenis *m.* young man
subigō (sub- + agō), subigere, subēgī, subāctus incite, impel

temptō (1-tr.) try, test, attempt
tendō, tendere, tetendī, tentus or **tēnsus** stretch out, extend; aim, head

44. Abandoned by Theseus on the island of Naxos, Ariadne ponders her situation.

> quid faciam? quō sōla ferar? vacat īnsula cultū.
>
> nōn hominum videō, nōn ego facta boum.
>
> omne latus terrae cingit mare; nāvita nusquam,
>
> nūlla per ambiguās puppis itūra viās. (OVID, HĒRŌIDES X.59–62)

ambiguus, -a, -um wavering, doubtful;
  untrustworthy, treacherous
bōs, bovis *m.* or *f.* bull; cow; *in pl.*, cattle;
  boum = *gen. pl.*
cultus, cultūs *m.* cultivation; civilization

latus, lateris *n.* side
nāvita = **nauta**
nusquam (adv.) nowhere
puppis, puppis, -ium *f.* stern (of a boat); ship
vacō (1-intr.) be empty, be without (+ abl.)

45. The poet reveals why women go to public games and why men may wish to go there, too.

> spectātum veniunt, veniunt spectentur ut ipsae. (OVID, ARS AMĀTŌRIA I.99)

46. The poet describes the moment when the water nymph Salmacis fell in love with Hermaphroditus.

> nunc perlūcentī circumdata corpus amictū
>
> mollibus aut foliīs aut mollibus incubat herbīs,
>
> saepe legit flōrēs. et tum quoque forte legēbat,
>
> cum puerum vīdit vīsumque optāvit habēre. (OVID, METAMORPHŌSĒS IV.313–16)

amictus, amictūs *m.* mantle, cloak
flōs, flōris *m.* flower
folium, foliī *n.* leaf
herba, herbae *f.* small plant, herb, grass
incubō, incubāre, ——, incubitum lie on, recline
  on (+ dat.)

mollis, molle gentle, mild, soft
perlūceō, perlūcēre, ——, —— be transparent,
  be translucent; shine

47. Could the poet write prose?

> saepe pater dīxit, "studium quid inūtile temptās?
>
> > Maeonidēs nūllās ipse relīquit opēs."
>
> mōtus eram dictīs, tōtōque Helicōne relictō
>
> > scrībere temptābam verba solūta modīs.
>
> sponte suā carmen numerōs veniēbat ad aptōs,
>
> > et quod temptābam scrībere versus erat. (OVID, TRĪSTIA IV.10.21–26)

aptus, -a, -um composed, fitted together; ready,
  fitting
Helicōn, Helicōnis *m.* Mount Helicon (in
  Boeotia), sacred to Apollo and the Muses
inūtilis, inūtile useless
Maeonidēs, Maeonidae *m.* (a) Maeonian *or*
  Lydian man; Homer

numerus, numerī *m.* number; rhythm, meter
ops, opis *f.* power; *in pl.* resources, wealth
*spōns, *spontis* *f.* will, volition
temptō (1-tr.) test; try, attempt
versus, versūs *m.* verse, line (of poetry)

48. The exiled poet addresses his wife.

> barbara mē tellūs orbisque novissima* magnī
>
>> sustinet et saevō cīnctus ab hoste locus.
>
> hinc ego trāicerer—neque enim mea culpa cruenta est—
>
>> esset, quae dēbet, sī tibi cūra meī. (OVID, TRĪSTIA V.2.31–34)

*novissima, *here*, most remote, extreme
barbarus, -a, -um foreign, strange; barbarous, uncivilized
cruentus, -a, -um bloody
culpa, culpae *f.* guilt, blame; fault, offense

sustineō (sub- + teneō), sustinēre, sustinuī, —— support, sustain
tellūs, tellūris *f.* earth, land
trāiciō (trāns- + iaciō) transport, transfer

49. The exiled poet resorts to prayer.

> adloquor ēn absēns absentia nūmina supplex,
>
>> sī fās est hominī cum Iove posse loquī. (OVID, TRĪSTIA V.2.45–46)

alloquor (ad- + loquor) address
ēn (interj.) behold! look!
supplex, supplicis suppliant, humble

50. The poem informs a friend in Rome how the poet in exile feels about him.

> nec patriam magis ille* suam dēsīderat et quae
>
>> plūrima cum patriā sentit abesse sibi,
>
> quam vultūs oculōsque tuōs, ō dulcior illō
>
>> melle, quod in cērīs Attica pōnit apis. (OVID, TRĪSTIA V.4.27–30)

*ille refers to the poet.
apis, apis, -ium *f.* bee
Atticus, -a, -um Attic, Athenian

cēra, cērae *f.* beeswax; wax cell; *in pl.*, honeycomb
dēsīderō (1-tr.) long for, desire
mel, mellis *n.* honey

51. The exiled poet makes a confession.

> ille ego Rōmānus vātēs—ignōscite, Mūsae!—
>
>> Sarmaticō cōgor plūrima mōre loquī.
>
> ēn pudet et fateor, iam dēsuētūdine longā
>
>> vix subeunt ipsī verba Latīna mihi.
>
> nec dubitō quīn sint et in hōc nōn pauca libellō
>
>> barbara: nōn hominis culpa, sed ista locī. (OVID, TRĪSTIA V.7.55–60)

barbarus, -a, -um foreign, strange; barbarous, uncivilized
cōgō (cō- + agō), cōgere, coēgī, coāctus drive together, force, compel
culpa, culpae *f.* guilt, blame; fault
dēsuētūdō, dēsuētūdinis *f.* disuse, want of practice
ēn (interj.) lo! behold! see!
ignōscō (in- + nōscō), ignōscere, ignōvī, ignōtus forgive, pardon

Latīnus, -a, -um Latin
libellus, libellī *m.* (little) book
Mūsa, Mūsae *f.* Muse
Sarmaticus, -a, -um Sarmatian, of Sarmatia, a region between the Vistula and Don rivers
subeō (sub- + eō), subīre, subiī or subīvī, subitūrus go under; come up to; occur
vātēs, vātis, -ium *m. or f.* prophet, bard, poet

52. A plan of Tarquinius Priscus, fifth of the legendary kings of Rome, and an event that disrupted it

> mūrō quoque lapideō circumdāre urbem parābat cum Sabīnum bellum coeptīs* in-
> tervēnit. adeōque ea subita rēs fuit ut prius Aniēnem trānsīrent hostēs quam obviam
> īre ac prohibēre exercitus Rōmānus posset. (Livy, *Ab Urbe Conditā* I.36.1)

coeptum, coeptī n. undertaking, enterprise, scheme
Aniēn, Aniēnis m. (the) Anio, a river in northern Latium
interveniō (inter- + veniō) interrupt
lapideus, -a, -um (made of) stone
obviam (adv.) in the way of, so as to meet;
  obviam īre, to go to meet

parō (1-tr.) prepare, make ready
Sabīnus, -a, -um Sabine (of a territory and people northeast of Rome)
subitus, -a, -um sudden
trānseō (trāns- + eō), **trānsīre, trānsiī** or **trānsīvī, trānsitus** go across

53. The historian describes the consul Volumnius's experience in fighting the Sallentini, a Samnian people living in the heel of Italy.

> Volumnium prōvinciae* haud paenituit. multa secunda proelia fēcit; aliquot urbēs
> hostium vī cēpit. praedae erat largītor et benignitātem per sē grātam comitāte adiu-
> vābat mīlitemque† hīs artibus fēcerat et perīculī et labōris avidum. (Livy, *Ab Urbe*
> *Conditā* IX.42.5)

*prōvincia, *here*, task, assignment
†**mīles**, *here, collective singular,* soldiery, soldiers
adiuvō, adiuvāre, adiūvī, adiūtus help, assist;
  augment, enhance
aliquot (indecl. adj.) several
avidus, -a, -um greedy; eager, hungry (for)
  (+ gen.)

benignitās, benignitātis f. kindness, benevolence, generosity
comitās, comitātis f. friendliness, charm
largītor, largītōris m. bestower, giver
praeda, praedae f. booty, plunder
secundus, -a, -um favorable
Volumnius, Volumniī m. Volumnius

54. After describing a tremendous Roman victory over the Carthaginians in 207 b.c.e., the historian recounts a horrific moment in the Roman camp.

> C. Claudius cōnsul cum in castra redīsset, caput Hasdrubalis quod servātum cum
> cūrā attulerat prōicī ante hostium statiōnēs, captīvōsque Āfrōs vīnctōs ut erant os-
> tendī, duōs etiam ex iīs solūtōs īre ad Hannibalem et exprōmere quae ācta essent
> iussit. (Livy, *Ab Urbe Conditā* XXVII.51.11)

Āfer, Āfra, Āfrum African
afferō (ad- + ferō), **afferre, attulī, allātus** bring with one
C. Claudius, C. Claudiī m. C. Claudius (consul 207 b.c.e.)
captīvus, captīvī m. prisoner of war, captive
exprōmō, exprōmere, exprōmpsī, exprōmptus bring forth, disclose, reveal

Hasdrubal, Hasdrubalis m. Hasdrubal, Carthaginian general and brother of Hannibal
ostendō, ostendere, ostendī, ostentus or **ostēnsus** present, show
prōiciō (prō- + iaciō) throw forward, fling
statiō, statiōnis f. guard post
vinciō, vincīre, vīnxī, vīnctus bind, join, fetter

55. When Hannibal is crossing the Appenines near the end of winter, he and his troops are overwhelmed by a violent storm.

> tum vērō ingentī sonō caelum strepere et inter horrendōs fragōrēs micāre ignēs; captī auribus et oculīs metū omnēs torpēre; tandem effūsō imbre, cum eō magis accēnsa vīs ventī esset, ipsō illō quō dēprēnsī erant locō castra pōnere necessārium vīsum est. (Livy, *Ab Urbe Conditā* XXI.58.5)

accendō, accendere, accendī, accēnsus set on fire, kindle; stir up, arouse
auris, auris, -ium *f.* ear
dēprendō, dēprendere, dēprendī, dēprēnsus seize (suddenly); overtake, catch
effundō, effundere, effūdī, effūsus pour out; send forth
fragor, fragōris *m.* crash, roar
horrendus, -a, -um terrible, tremendous
imber, imbris, -ium *m.* rain, shower; (rain-)water
micō, micāre, micuī, —— dart, flicker, flash
necessārius, -a, -um necessary
sonus, sonī *m.* sound, noise
strepō, strepere, strepuī, strepitum make a loud noise, crash
torpeō, torpēre, ——, —— be struck numb, be paralyzed
ventus, ventī *m.* wind

56. The historian describes a particularly narrow pass through a mountain range.

> haec ūna mīlitāris via est, quā trādūcī exercitūs, sī nōn prohibeantur, possint.
>
> (Livy, *Ab Urbe Conditā* XXXVI.15.11)

mīlitāris, mīlitāre military, for soldiers
trādūcō (trāns- + dūcō) lead across

57. The leader of the Achaeans, allies of Rome involved in a dispute with the Spartans, concludes an appeal.

> verēmur quidem vōs, Rōmānī, et sī ita vultis, etiam timēmus: sed plūs et verēmur et timēmus deōs immortālēs. (Livy, *Ab Urbe Conditā* XXXIX.37.17)

immortālis, immortāle immortal

58. About to assume the governorship of Nearer Spain, Ti. Sempronius describes the nature of the people in that province and the challenges that lie ahead for him.

> dictū quam rē facilius est prōvinciam ingeniō ferōcem, rebellātrīcem cōnfēcisse.* paucae cīvitātēs, ut quidem ego audiō, quās vīcīna maximē hiberna premēbant, in iūs diciōnemque vēnērunt; ulteriōrēs in armīs sunt. (Livy, *Ab Urbe Conditā* XL.35.13)

*cōnficiō, *here,* subdue, pacify
diciō, diciōnis *f.* sovereignty, sway, power
ferōx, ferōcis fierce, savage; high-spirited, defiant
hiberna, hibernōrum *n. pl.* winter quarters, winter (military) camp
rebellātrīx, rebellātrīcis rebellious
ulterior, ulterius farther, more distant
vīcīnus, -a, -um neighboring

59. M. Servilius addresses the soldiers who are preventing the triumph of their general, L. Aemilius Paulus, after his victory in Macedonia. A jealous rival had roused the soldiers' resentment against Paulus, who had refused to let his troops indiscriminately seize booty after the victory.

aliquis est Rōmae, praeter Perseā, quī triumphārī dē Macedonibus nōlit: et eum nōn

īsdem manibus discerpitis quibus Macedonas vīcistis? vincere vōs prohibuisset sī

potuisset, quī triumphantīs urbem inīre prohibet. (LIVY, *AB URBE CONDITĀ* XLV.38.2)

discerpō, discerpere, discerpsī, discerptus tear to
  pieces
ineō (in + eō), inīre, iniī or **inīvī, initus** enter
Macedones, Macedonum *m. pl.* Macedonians, a
  people of northern Greece; **Macedonas** = *acc. pl.*

Perseus, Perseos *m.* Perseus, last king of
  Macedonia; **Perseā** = *acc. sing.*
triumphō (1-intr.) celebrate a triumph, triumph

60. Seneca concludes a letter to Lucilius, in which he has argued about the advantage of what many fear most.

negā nunc magnum beneficium esse nātūrae quod necesse est morī.

(SENECA THE YOUNGER, *EPISTULAE MŌRĀLĒS* CI.14)

beneficium, beneficiī *n.* service, kindness; favor, benefit
negō (1-tr.) deny

61. Clytaemnestra urges herself to action.

accingere, anime: bella nōn levia apparās.

scelus occupandum est; pigra, quem expectās diem?

(SENECA THE YOUNGER, *AGAMEMNŌN* 192–93)

accingō (ad + cingō) gird
apparō (1-tr.) prepare for; plan
occupō (1-tr.) seize; occupy; take up
piger, pigra, pigrum sluggish, slow; idle, lazy

62. While consoling his friend Polybius, whose brother has recently died, Seneca reminds him of a parallel from history.

quid tibi referam Scīpiōnem Āfricānum, cui mors frātris in exiliō nuntiāta est?

is frāter, quī ēripuit frātrem carcerī, nōn potuit ēripere fātō.

(SENECA THE YOUNGER, *DIALOGĪ* XI.14.4)

carcer, carceris *m.* prison
nuntiō (1-tr.) announce, report
Scīpiō Āfricānus, Scīpiōnis Āfricānī *m.* (P. Cornelius) Scipio Africanus (consul 205 B.C.E.)

63. Quintilian recalls an opinion of Socrates.

... Sōcratēs inhonestam sibi crēdidit ōrātiōnem quam eī Lysiās reō composuerat ...

(QUINTILIAN, *ĪNSTITŪTIŌ ŌRĀTŌRIA* II.15.30)

compōnō (com- + pōnō) put together; compose
inhonestus, -a, -um dishonorable, disgraceful
Lysiās, Lysiae *m.* Lysias, an Athenian orator and contemporary of Socrates
reus, reī *m.* defendant
Sōcratēs, Sōcratis *m.* Socrates

64. The satirist urges more care in the raising of a son than in preparing for a guest.

grātum est quod patriae cīvem populōque dedistī,

sī facis ut patriae sit idōneus, ūtilis agrīs,

ūtilis et bellōrum et pācis rēbus agendīs.

plūrimum enim intererit quibus artibus et quibus hunc tū

mōribus īnstituās ... (JUVENAL, *SATURAE* XIV.70–74)

idōneus, -a, -um suitable, apt, capable
īnstituō, īnstituere, īnstituī, īnstitūtus instruct, train, educate
ūtilis, ūtile useful

65. The beginning of a speech by Agricola to his troops before battle

septimus annus est, commīlitōnēs, ex quō virtūte et auspiciīs imperiī Rōmānī,
fidē atque operā vestrā Britanniam vīcistis. tot expedītiōnibus, tot proeliīs, seu fortitūdine adversus hostīs seu patientiā ac labōre paene adversus ipsam rērum nātūram opus fuit, neque mē mīlitum neque vōs ducis paenituit.
(TACITUS, *DĒ VĪTĀ AGRICOLAE* 33)

adversus (*prep.* + *acc.*) in opposition to, against, in the face of
auspicium, auspiciī *n.* augury, omen
Britannia, Britanniae *f.* Britain
commīlitō, commīlitōnis *m.* fellow soldier
expedītiō, expedītiōnis *f.* military operation, expedition

fortitūdō, fortitūdinis *f.* bravery, fortitude
opera, operae *f.* effort, work
paene (*adv.*) nearly, almost
patientia, patientiae *f.* endurance, hardiness
seu (*conj.*) or if, whether; **seu ... seu ...** whether ... or (if) ...

66. After recording the differing traditions about the emperor Galba's last words, the historian appends a tart remark.

nōn interfuit occīdentium quid dīceret.* (TACITUS, *HISTORIAE* I.41)

*dīceret, subject is Galba
occīdō, occīdere, occīdī, occīsus kill, slaughter

67. The historian describes a battle between Roman forces and the Cherusci, a German tribe led by the fierce Arminius, whose first attempt to break through the line of Roman archers had been rebuffed.

> nīsū tamen corporis et impetū equī pervāsit, oblitus faciem suō cruōre nē nōscerē-
>
> tur. quīdam adgnitum ā Chaucīs inter auxilia Rōmāna agentibus* ēmissumque trā-
>
> didērunt. (TACITUS, ANNĀLĒS II.17)

*ago, *here*, do service

adgnōscō (ad- + nōscō), adgnōscere, adgnōvī, adgnitus recognize, identify

Chaucī, Chaucōrum *m. pl.* (the) Chauci, a German tribe

cruor, cruōris *m.* blood, gore

ēmittō (ē- + mittō) set free, release

equus, equī *m.* horse

faciēs, faciēī *f.* face; appearance

impetus, impetūs *m.* attack; onset, rush; vigor, force

nīsus, *nīsūs *m.* exertion, effort

oblinō, oblinere, oblēvī, oblitus smear, coat, cover

pervādō, pervādere, pervāsī, pervāsus pass through, penetrate, prevail; **pervāsit**, *subject is Arminius*

68. The historian recounts an old story indicating the extent of the emperor Tiberius's frustration with the senate.

> memoriae prōditur Tiberium, quotiēs cūriā ēgrederētur, Graecīs verbīs in hunc
>
> modum ēloquī solitum "ō hominēs ad servitūtem parātōs!" scīlicet etiam illum quī
>
> lībertātem pūblicam nōllet tam prōiectae servientium patientiae taedēbat. (TACITUS,
>
> ANNĀLĒS III.65)

cūria, cūriae *f.* the Curia, the senate house

ēloquor (ē- + loquor) utter, say

Graecus, -a, -um Greek

parō (1-tr.) prepare

patientia, patientiae *f.* endurance, patience; submissiveness

prōdō (prō- + dō) hand down, transmit

prōiectus, -a, -um prominent; abject, groveling

quotiē(n)s (rel. adv.) as often as, whenever

scīlicet (particle) to be sure, no doubt, of course

serviō, servīre, servīvī or serviī, servītum be a slave, be enslaved

Tiberius, Tiberiī *m.* Tiberius, adopted son of and successor to Augustus

Longer Readings

1. Cicero, *Prō S. Rosciō Amerīnō* 56–57

Cicero likens prosecutors to the geese and dogs maintained at public expense in order to guard the Capitoline hill.

ānseribus cibāria pūblicē locantur et canēs aluntur in Capitōliō ut significent sī* fūrēs vēnerint. at fūrēs internōscere nōn possunt, significant tamen sī* quī noctū in Capitōlium vēnerint et, quia id est suspīciōsum, tametsī bestiae sunt, tamen in eam partem† potius peccant quae est cautior. quod sī lūce quoque canēs latrent cum deōs salūtātum aliquī vēnerint, opīnor, eīs crūra suffringantur quod ācrēs sint etiam tum cum suspīciō nūlla sit. simillima est accūsātōrum ratiō. aliī vestrum ānserēs sunt quī tantum modo‡ clāmant, nocēre nōn possunt, aliī canēs quī et latrāre et mordēre possunt. cibāria vōbīs praebērī vidēmus; vōs autem maximē dēbētis in eōs impetum facere quī merentur. hoc populō grātissimum est. deinde, sī volētis, etiam tum cum vērī simile erit aliquem commīsisse, in suspīciōne latrātōte; id quoque concēdī potest. sīn autem sīc agētis ut arguātis aliquem patrem occīdisse neque dīcere

---

***sī**, *here,* introduces Indirect Question
†**in eam partem . . . quae . . .** to that side that . . .
‡**tantum modo** only, merely
accūsātor, accūsātōris *m.* prosecutor
alō, alere, aluī, al(i)tus feed, nourish
ānser, ānseris *m.* or *f.* goose
arguō, arguere, arguī, argūtus charge, allege
at (conj.) but
bestia, bestiae *f.* beast, animal
canis, canis *m.* or *f.* dog
Capitōlium, Capitōliī *n.* (the) Capitoline hill
cautus, -a, -um cautious
cibāria, cibāriōrum *n. pl.* ration *or* allowance of food provided to animals; provisions
clāmō (1-intr.) shout, make a noise
committō (con- + mittō) commit (an offense); break a law, offend
concēdō (con- + cēdō) (tr.) concede, grant
crūs, crūris *n.* leg
deinde (adv.) then, thereupon; next
fūr, fūris, -ium *m.* thief, robber
impetus, impetūs *m.* attack, assault
internōscō (inter- + nōscō), internōscere, internōvī, internōtus distinguish; pick out (from others)
latrō (1-intr.) bark; make a noise; **latrātōte** = *2nd. pl. fut. act. imper.,* (ye shall) bark

locō (1-tr.) place
mereor, merērī, meritus sum deserve
mordeō, mordēre, momordī, morsus bite, wound (with the teeth)
noceō, nocēre, nocuī, nocitūrus be harmful, harm, do harm
noctū = nocte
occīdō, occīdere, occīdī, occīsus kill
opīnor (1-tr.) suppose, imagine, think
peccō (1-intr.) make a mistake, err
potius (adv.) rather
praebeō, praebēre, praebuī, praebitus furnish, provide
ratiō, ratiōnis *f.* account, reason; reasoning; way, method
salūtō (1-tr.) say hello; call upon, pay one's respects (to)
significō (1-tr.) indicate, signify
sīn (conj.) but if
suffringō, suffringere, ——, —— break the lower part of
suspīciō, suspīciōnis *f.* suspicion; reason for suspicion
suspīciōsus, -a, -um suspicious
tametsī (conj.) even though

possītis aut quā rē aut quō modō, ac tantum modo* sine suspīciōne latrābitis, crūra quidem vōbīs nēmō suffringet, sed, sī ego hōs† bene nōvī, litteram illam‡ cui vos ūsque eō inimīcī estis ut etiam Kal. omnīs ōderitis ita vehementer ad caput adfīgent ut posteā nēminem alium nisi fortūnās vestrās accūsāre possītis.

*tantum modo only, merely

†hōs refers to the judges

‡litteram illam that infamous letter, K, for kalumniātor, false accuser; *a prosecutor could be so branded if he was found guilty of bringing false charges*

accūsō (1-tr.) blame, find fault with; charge, accuse

affīgō, affīgere, affīxī, affīxus fix, fasten, attach

crūs, crūris *n.* leg

Kalendae, Kalendārum *f. pl.* the Kalends, the first day of a month; Kal. = Kalendās

latrō (1-intr.) bark; make a noise

posteā (adv.) after, afterward

suffringō, suffringere, ——, —— break the lower part of

suspīciō, suspīciōnis *f.* suspicion; reason for suspicion

ūsque (adv.) continuously; all the way (to); ūsque eō, to such an extent, so

vehementer (adv.) violently, strongly

While Sulla ruled Rome as a dictator in 80 B.C.E., young Cicero defended S. Roscius Amerinus against charges of murdering his own father. Roscius had been framed by those who had arranged the murder, two of his father's relatives conspiring with a freedman of Sulla to acquire the property of the dead man. The *Prō S. Rosciō Amerīnō* shows Cicero's rhetorical style in the making amid a complex political situation.

2. Cicero, *Tusculānae Disputātiōnēs* I.9

In the hope that a discussion about death may be presented more suitably, Cicero offers an imitation of a Socratic dialogue.

Audītor. Malum mihi vidētur esse mors.

Magister. Iīsne, quī mortuī sunt, an iīs, quibus moriendum est?

A. Utrīsque.

M. Est miserum, igitur, quoniam malum.

A. Certē.

M. Ergō et iī quibus ēvēnit iam ut morerentur et iī quibus ēventūrum est miserī.

A. Mihi ita vidētur.

M. Nēmō ergō nōn miser.

A. Prorsus nēmō.

M. Et quidem, sī tibi cōnstāre vīs, omnēs, quīcumque nātī sunt eruntve, nōn sōlum miserī, sed etiam semper miserī. nam sī sōlōs eōs dīcerēs miserōs quibus moriendum esset, nēminem tū quidem eōrum quī vīverent exciperēs (moriendum est enim omnibus), esset tamen miseriae fīnis in morte. quoniam autem etiam mortuī miserī sunt, in miseriam nāscimur sempiternam. necesse est enim miserōs esse eōs quī centum mīlibus annōrum ante occidērunt, vel potius omnīs, quīcumque nātī sunt.

auditor, audītōris *m.* listener

cōnstō (con- + stō), cōnstāre, cōnstitī, ——
stand still; be consistent with (+ dat.)

ergō (adv.) therefore

ēveniō (ē- + veniō) come out, turn out; *here,* introduces Subst. Ut clause

excipiō (ex- + capiō) take out, exclude

magister, magistrī *m.* teacher

miseria, miseriae *f.* misery

potius (adv.) rather

prorsus (adv.) thoroughly, in every respect, altogether

quīcumque, quaecumque, quodcumque (indef. pron.) whoever, whatever

sempiternus, -a, -um everlasting, perpetual

uterque, utraque, utrumque (indef. pron.) each (of two), both

-ve (enclitic adv.) or

3. Cicero, *Ad Familiārēs* V.15

Cicero responds to a letter from his friend L. Lucceius (praetor 67 B.C.E.), politician, lawyer, historian, and an ally of Cicero during the Catilinarian conspiracy. Beset by ill health, Lucceius wrote to Cicero in order both to console him in his grief over the recent death of his daughter Tullia and to encourage him to attend to the business of the crumbling Roman Republic.

M. CICERO S. D. L. LUCCEIO Q. F.*

Omnis amor tuus ex omnibus partibus sē ostendit in iīs litterīs quās ā tē proximē accēpī, nōn ille quidem mihi ignōtus sed tamen grātus et optātus; dīcerem "iūcundus" nisi id verbum in† omne tempus perdidissem, neque ob eam ūnam causam quam tū suspicāris et in quā mē lēnissimīs et amantissimīs verbīs ūtēns rē graviter accūsās, sed quod illīus tantī vulneris quae remedia esse dēbēbant ea nūlla sunt. quid enim? ad amīcōsne cōnfugiam? quam multī sunt? habuimus enim ferē commūnīs; quōrum aliī occidērunt, aliī nescio quō‡ pactō obdūruērunt. tēcum vīvere possem equidem et maximē vellem. vetustās, amor, cōnsuētūdō, studia paria—quod vinclum, quaesō, dēest nostrae coniūnctiōnī? possumusne igitur esse ūnā?§ nec mehercule intellegō quid impediat; sed certē adhūc nōn fuimus cum essēmus vīcīnī in Tusculānō, in Puteolānō. nam quid dīcam in urbe, in quā, cum forum commūne sit, vīcīnitās nōn requīritur?

*Q. F. = Quintī fīliō

†in, *here, expressing expected duration,* for

‡nescioquī, nescioquae, nescioquod (indef. adj.) *sometimes written as two words,* I-don't-know-who, I-don't-know-which, some . . . or other

§ūnā (adv.) together

accūsō (1-tr.) find fault with, censure

adhūc (adv.) up to the present time; still

commūnis, commūne common, shared; held in common

cōnfugiō (con- + fugiō) flee for refuge *or* safety

coniūnctiō, coniūnctiōnis *f.* union, bond

cōnsuētūdō, cōnsuētūdinis *f.* custom, usage

dēsum (dē- + sum), dēesse, dēfuī, —— be absent, be lacking, be missing

ferē (adv.) almost, nearly

ignōtus, -a, -um unknown

iūcundus, -a, -um pleasing, delightful, agreeable

lēnis, lēne mild, gentle

L. Lucceius, L. Lucceiī *m.* L. Lucceius

obdūrēscō, obdūrēscere, obdūruī, —— become hard(ened), become callous

ostendō, ostendere, ostendī, ostentus *or* ostēnsus present, show; offer

pactum, pactī *n.* means, manner, method, way

pār, paris equal; similar

proximē (adv.) most recently

Puteolānum, Puteolānī *n.* Puteolanum, an estate at or near Puteoli, a town near Naples

quaesō, *quaesere, ——, —— seek, pray for; *1st sing. pres. act. indic.,* I ask you, please

remedium, remediī *n.* remedy, cure

requīrō (re- + quaerō), requīrere, requīsiī *or* requīsīvī, requīsītus seek again; call for, need

suspicor (1-tr.) imagine; suspect

Tusculānum, Tusculānī *n.* Tusculanum, an estate (particularly Cicero's estate) at or near Tusculum, a town in Latium

vetustās, vetustātis *f.* (old) age, antiquity

vīcīnitās, vīcīnitātis *f.* proximity, nearness

vīcīnus, -a, -um neighboring; *as subst.,* neighbor

vinc(u)lum, vinc(u)lī *n.* bond, chain, link

sed cāsū nescio quō* in ea tempora nostra aetās incidit ut, cum maximē flōrēre
nōs oportēret, tum vīvere etiam pudēret. quod enim esse poterat mihi perfugium
spoliātō et domesticīs et forēnsibus ornāmentīs atque sōlāciīs? litterae, crēdō, quibus
ūtor adsiduē; quid enim aliud facere possum? sed nescio quō* modō ipsae illae exclūdere mē ā portū et perfugiō videntur et quasi exprobrāre quod in eā vītā maneam
in quā nihil īnsit nisi propāgātiō miserrimī temporis.

Hīc tū mē abesse urbe mīrāris, in quā domus nihil dēlectāre possit, summum
sit odium temporum, hominum, forī, cūriae? itaque sīc litterīs ūtor, in quibus cōnsūmō omne tempus, nōn ut ab iīs medicīnam perpetuam sed ut exiguam oblīviōnem
dolōris petam. quod sī id ēgissēmus ego atque tū quod nē in mentem quidem nōbīs
veniēbat propter cottīdiānōs metūs et omne tempus ūnā† fuissēmus, neque mē
valētūdō tua offenderet neque tē maeror meus. quod, quantum fierī poterit, cōnse-
quāmur. quid enim est utrīque nostrum aptius? propediem tē igitur vidēbō.

*nescioquī, nescioquae, nescioquod (indef. adj.)
  sometimes written as two words, I-don't-know-
  who, I-don't-know-which, some . . .
  or other
†ūnā (adv.) together
aptus, -a, -um suitable, fit(ting), appropriate
assiduē (adv.) continually, constantly
cōnsequor (con- + sequor) follow after, pursue
cōnsūmō, cōnsūmere, cōnsūmpsī, cōnsūmptus
  wear away, consume; spend, pass
cottīdiānus, -a, -um daily
cūria, cūriae *f.* the Curia, the senate house
dēlectō (1-tr.) delight, please, charm
dolor, dolōris *m.* grief, sorrow, pain
domesticus, -a, -um personal, domestic
exclūdō, exclūdere, exclūsī, exclūsus keep out,
  exclude, debar
exiguus, -a, -um small, slight, brief
exprobrō (1-tr.) bring up as a reproach
flōreō, flōrēre, flōruī, —— blossom; prosper;
  be at the height of one's power
forēnsis, forēnse of *or* belonging to the forum,
  forensic; public
incidō (in- + cadō), incidere, incidī, incāsūrus
  fall into, pass; slip
īnsum (in- + sum), inesse, īnfuī, —— be in;
  be present, be contained

itaque (conj.) and so, accordingly
maeror, maerōris *m.* grief, sorrow, mourning
medicīna, medicīnae *f.* medicine; treatment, cure
mīror (1-tr.) admire, marvel at, be astonished
oblīviō, oblīviōnis *f.* (state of) forgetfulness,
  oblivion
offendō, offendere, offendī, offēnsus trouble,
  upset, give offense to, annoy
ornāmentum, ornāmentī *n.* adornment, embellishment; distinction, honor
perfugium, perfugiī *n.* place of refuge, shelter,
  sanctuary
perpetuus, -a, -um continuous, without interruption; perpetual, everlasting
portus, portūs *m.* harbor; refuge, haven
propāgātiō, propāgātiōnis *f.* continuation, prolongation
propediem (adv.) before long, any day now, very
  soon
quasi (adv.) as (if), as (it were)
sōlācium, sōlāciī *n.* comfort, solace, relief
spoliō (1-tr.) strip, rob
uterque, utraque, utrumque (indef. pron.) each
  (of two)
valētūdō, valētūdinis *f.* health; illness, indispo-
  sition

4. Catullus III (hendecasyllable)

A mock-tragic dirge

Lūgēte, ō Venerēs Cupīdinēsque,
et quantumst hominum venustiōrum:
passer mortuus est meae puellae,
passer, dēliciae meae puellae,
quem plūs illa oculīs suīs amābat: 5
nam mellītus erat suamque nōrat
ipsam* tam bene quam puella mātrem,
nec sēsē ā gremiō illius† movēbat,
sed circumsiliēns modo hūc modo illūc
ad sōlam dominam ūsque pīpiābat.   10
quī nunc it per iter tenebricōsum
illūc, unde negant redīre quemquam.
at vōbīs male sit, malae tenebrae
Orcī, quae omnia bella‡ dēvorātis:
tam bellum‡ mihi passerem abstulistis.   15
ō factum male, ō miselle passer!
tuā nunc operā meae puellae
flendō turgidulī rubent ocellī.

*ipsa, *here*, mistress
†The second **-i-** of **illīus** here scans *short*.
‡**bellus, -a, -um** pretty, charming, lovely
at (conj.) but
circumsiliō, circumsilīre, ——, —— leap about,
    hop
dēliciae, dēliciārum *f. pl.* delight, darling, beloved
dēvorō (1-tr.) swallow up, gulp down, devour
domina, dominae *f.* mistress
fleō, flēre, flēvī, flētus weep (for)
gremium, gremiī *n.* bosom; lap
iter, itineris *n.* passage; road, route
lūgeō, lūgēre, lūxī, lūctus mourn (for); grieve,
    lament
mellītus, -a, -um honey-sweet

misellus, -a, -um wretched (little), pitiable
negō (1-tr.) deny, say . . . not
ocellus, ocellī *m.* (little) eye
opera, operae *f.* effort, work; *in abl.*, fault
Orcus, Orcī *m.* Orcus, god of the underworld
    (= Dis)
passer, passeris *m.* sparrow
pīpiō (1-intr.) chirp, cheep, peep
rubeō, rubēre, ——, —— be red
tenebrae, tenebrārum *f. pl.* darkness, shadows
tenebricōsus, -a, -um full of shadows, gloomy
turgidulus, -a, -um swollen (little)
ūsque (adv.) continuously
venustus, -a, -um charming, pleasing

5. Caesar, *Dē Bellō Gallicō* I.44

Caesar reports the German king Ariovistus's response to a series of Caesar's demands.

Ariovistus ad postulāta Caesaris pauca respondit, dē suīs virtūtibus multa praedicāvit: trānsīsse Rhēnum sēsē nōn suā sponte, sed rogātum et arcessītum ā Gallīs; nōn sine magnā spē magnīsque praemiīs domum propinquōsque relīquisse; sēdēs habēre in Galliā ab ipsīs concessās, obsidēs ipsōrum voluntāte datōs; stīpendium capere iūre bellī, quod victōrēs victīs impōnere cōnsuērint. nōn sēsē Gallīs, sed Gallōs sibi bellum intulisse; omnēs Galliae cīvitātēs ad sē oppugnandum vēnisse ac contrā sē castra habuisse; eās omnēs cōpiās ūnō ā sē proeliō pulsās ac superātās esse.

arcessō, arcessere, arcessiī or **arcessīvī, arcessītus** send for, summon; invite

Ariovistus, Ariovistī *m.* Ariovistus, a German king

concēdō (con- + cēdō) (tr.) concede, grant

cōnsuēscō, cōnsuēscere, cōnsuēvī, cōnsuētus accustom, habituate; *in perfect active and passive,* be accustomed; **cōnsuērint,** *perf. subj. as if in primary sequence*

Gallia, Galliae *f.* Gaul

Gallī, Gallōrum *m. pl.* (the) Gauls

impōnō (in- + pōnō) place on, impose on

obses, obsidis *m.* or *f.* hostage

postulātum, postulātī *n.* demand

praedicō (1-tr.) proclaim, declare

praemium, praemiī *n.* reward, prize

propinquus, -a, -um near, close; *as subst.,* relative

Rhēnus, Rhēnī *m.* (the) Rhine, a river in northeastern Gaul

sēdēs, sēdis, -ium *f.* seat; home, abode

*spōns, *spontis *f.* (one's own) will

stīpendium, stīpendiī *n.* tax, tribute

trānseō (trāns- + eō), trānsīre, trānsiī or **trānsīvī, trānsitus** go across, cross

victor, victōris *m.* conqueror, victor

voluntās, voluntātis *f.* will, intention; choice

6. Caesar, *Dē Bellō Gallicō* V.14

Caesar reports on practices of the Celtic tribes that he observed in Britain.

ex hīs* omnibus longē sunt hūmānissimī quī Cantium incolunt, quae regiō est mari-
tima omnis, neque multum ā Gallicā differunt cōnsuētūdine. interiōrēs plērīque frū-
menta nōn serunt, sed lacte et carne vīvunt pellibusque sunt vestītī. omnēs vērō sē
Britannī vitrō īnficiunt, quod caeruleum efficit colōrem, atque hōc horribiliōrēs sunt
in pugnā adspectū; capillōque sunt prōmissō atque omnī parte corporis rāsā praeter
caput et labrum superius. uxōrēs habent dēnī duodēnīque inter sē commūnēs et maximē frātrēs cum frātribus parentēsque cum līberīs.† sed sī quī sunt ex iīs nātī, eōrum
habentur līberī,† quō prīmum virgō quaeque dēducta est.

*hīs refers to the tribes of Britain.

†līberī, *here,* children

aspiciō, aspicere, aspexī, aspectus look at, look
    upon; behold

Britannī, Britannōrum *m. pl.* (the) Britons
    (inhabitants of Britain)

caeruleus, -a, -um (sky) blue

Cantium, Cantiī *n.* Cantium, a town in Britain

capillus, capillī *m.* hair

carō, carnis *f.* flesh, meat

color, colōris *m.* color

commūnis, commūne common, shared; held in
    common

cōnsuētūdō, cōnsuētūdinis *f.* custom, usage

dēdūcō (dē- + dūcō) lead away; bring home
    (as one's bride)

dēnī, dēnae, dēna ten together

duodēnī, duodēnae, duodēna twelve together

frūmentum, frūmentī *n.* grain

Gallicus, -a, -um of Gaul, Gallic

horribilis, horribile terrifying, dreadful

hūmānus, -a, -um human; humane, civilized

incolō, incolere, incoluī, —— inhabit

īnficiō (in- + faciō) dye

interior, interius situated farther from the coast,
    more remote

labrum, labrī *n.* lip

lac, lactis *n.* milk

maritimus, -a, -um of *or* belonging to the sea;
    situated near the sea, coastal

parēns, parentis, -ium *m. or f.* parent

pellis, pellis, -ium *f.* (animal) skin, hide

plērīque, plēraeque, plēraque very many, most

prōmittō (prō- + mittō) send forth; (let) grow
    long

pugna, pugnae *f.* fight, battle

rādō, rādere, rāsī, rāsus scrape; shave

regiō, regiōnis *f.* region, locality

serō, serere, sēvī, satus plant, sow

superior, superius upper

uxor, uxōris *f.* wife

vestiō, vestīre, vestīvī or **vestiī, vestītus** clothe,
    dress

virgō, virginis *f.* maiden, virgin

vitrum, vitrī *n.* woad, a plant from which a blue
    dye is made; blue dye

7. Sallust, *Bellum Iugurthae* 12

The historian describes how Jugurtha's soldiers murdered King Hiempsal in his house.

quī* postquam in aedīs inrūpēre, dīvorsī rēgem quaerere, dormientīs aliōs, aliōs occursantīs interficere, scrūtārī loca abdita, clausa effringere, strepitū et tumultū omnia miscēre, quom interim Hiempsal reperītur† occultāns sē tuguriō mulieris ancillae, quō initiō pavidus et ignārus locī perfūgerat. Numidae caput eius, utī iussī erant, ad Iugurtham referunt.†

***quī**, connective relative referring to Jugurtha's soldiers

†**reperītur, referunt**, historical use of present tense; translate as perfect

abdō (ab- + dō) hide, conceal, keep secret

aedēs, aedis, -ium *f.* sanctuary, shrine; *in pl.,* house, abode

ancilla, ancillae *f.* maidservant

claudō, claudere, clausī, clausus close, shut, close up

dīversus, -a, -um different, separate

dormiō, dormīre, dormīvī or **dormiī, dormītum** sleep, be asleep

effringō, effringere, effrēgī, effrāctus break off, break open

Hiempsal, Hiempsalis *m.* Hiempsal, an African king and cousin of Jugurtha

ignārus, -a, -um not knowing, unacquainted (with) (+ gen.)

initium, initiī *n.* beginning

interim (adv.) meanwhile

irrumpō, irrumpere, irrūpī, irruptus break (in), burst (into)

Iugurtha, Iugurthae *m.* Jugurtha, a Numidian king

misceō, miscēre, miscuī, mixtus mix; throw into confusion

mulier, mulieris *f.* woman

Numidae, Numidārum *m. pl.* (the) Numidians

occultō (1-tr.) hide, conceal

occursō (1-tr.) run to meet, rush against, oppose

pavidus, -a, -um fearful

perfugiō (per- + fugiō) flee (for refuge)

reperiō, reperīre, repperī, repertus find, discover

scrūtor (1-tr.) ransack, search, investigate

strepitus, strepitūs *m.* noise

tugurium, tuguriī *n.* hut, cottage, small dwelling

tumultus, tumultūs *m.* commotion, tumult, panic

utī = ut

8. Sallust, *Bellum Catilīnae* 36

The historian reflects on the terrible power of the Catilinarian conspiracy.

eā tempestāte mihi imperium populī Rōmānī multō maxumē miserābile visum est.
quoi quom ad occāsum ab ortū sōlis omnia domita armīs pārērent, domī ōtium atque
dīvitiae, quae prīma mortālēs putant, adfluerent, fuēre tamen cīvēs quī sēque remque
pūblicam obstinātīs animīs perditum īrent. namque duōbus senātī dēcrētīs ex tantā
multitūdine neque praemiō inductus coniūrātiōnem patefēcerat neque ex castrīs
Catilīnae quisquam omnium discesserat: tanta vīs morbī atque utī tābēs plērōsque
cīvium animōs invāserat.

affluō, affluere, affluxī, affluxus flow toward,
   flow in; abound
coniūrātiō, coniūrātiōnis *f.* conspiracy
dēcrētum, dēcrētī *n.* decree
dīvitiae, dīvitiārum *f. pl.* wealth, riches
domō, domāre, domuī, domitus tame, subdue,
   conquer
indūcō (in- + dūcō) lead in; persuade, induce
invādō, invādere, invāsī, invāsus enter (hostilely);
   invade, attack
miserābilis, miserābile pitiable, wretched
morbus, morbī *m.* sickness, disease
mortālis, mortāle mortal

multitūdō, multitūdinis *f.* multitude
obstinātus, -a, -um determined, resolute,
   inflexible
occāsus, occāsūs *m.* falling, setting
ortus, ortūs *m.* rising
ōtium, ōtiī *n.* leisure; peace
patefaciō, patefacere, patefēcī, patefactus lay
   open, disclose, expose
plērīque, plēraeque, plēraque very many, most
praemium, praemiī *n.* reward
tābēs, tābis *f.* wasting away, decay; plague
tempestās, tempestātis *f.* storm; time
utī = ut, as if, as it were

9. Sallust, *Bellum Catilīnae* 60–61

With frequent use of the historical present, the historian vividly describes the final battle between Catiline's forces and those loyal to Rome. He then concludes his monograph with a description of the battle's aftermath.

sed ubi omnibus rēbus explōrātīs Petreius tubā signum dat, cohortīs paulātim incēdere iubet; idem facit hostium exercitus. postquam eō ventum est unde ā ferentāriīs proelium conmittī posset, maxumō clāmōre cum īnfestīs signīs concurrunt; pīla omittunt, gladiīs rēs geritur. veterānī, pristinae virtūtis memorēs, comminus ācriter īnstāre, illī haud timidī resistunt: maxumā vī certātur. intereā Catilīna cum expedītīs in prīmā aciē vorsārī, labōrantibus succurrere, integrōs prō sauciīs arcessere, omnia prōvidēre, multum ipse pugnāre, saepe hostem ferīre: strēnuī mīlitis et bonī imperātōris officia simul exequēbātur. Petreius, ubi videt Catilīnam contrā ac* ratus

*contrā ac different from, otherwise than

arcessō, arcessere, arcessiī or arcessīvī, arcessītus send for, summon

certō (1-intr.) struggle, contend, strive

clāmor, clāmōris *m.* shout, shouting; noise

cohors, cohortis, -ium *f.* company of soldiers, division of an army, cohort

comminus (adv.) in close contact, at close quarters, hand to hand

committō (con- + mittō) join, engage in; enter upon, commence

concurrō, concurrere, concurrī, concursum rush together, charge

ex(s)equor (ex- + sequor) perform, execute, accomplish

expedītus, expedītī *m.* light-armed soldier

explōrō (1-tr.) examine, investigate

ferentārius, ferentāriī *m.* light-armed troop

feriō, ferīre, ——, —— strike, hit

incēdō (in- + cēdō) go in, enter; advance

īnfestus, -a, -um hostile, harmful

īnstō (in- + stō), īnstāre, īnstitī, īnstātūrus press (hostilely), press on, pursue

integer, integra, integrum untouched; unhurt; fresh, vigorous

intereā (adv.) meanwhile

memor, memoris mindful, remembering (+ gen.)

officium, officiī *n.* obligation; duty, task; function

omittō (ob- + mittō) let loose, let go, let fall

paulātim (adv.) little by little, gradually

Petreius, Petreiī *m.* (M.) Petreius, leader of the Roman troops who defeated Catiline at Pistoria

pīlum, pīlī *n.* heavy javelin (of the Roman infantry)

pristinus, -a, -um ancient; former; original

prōvideō (prō- + videō) foresee; provide for, see to

reor, rērī, ratus sum believe, think, imagine

resistō, resistere, restitī, —— oppose, resist

saucius, -a, -um wounded

simul (adv.) at the same time

strēnuus, -a, -um active, vigorous, energetic

succurrō, succurrere, succurrī, succursum run to aid, assist, help (+ dat.)

timidus, -a, -um fearful, afraid, timid

tuba, tubae *f.* horn, (war) trumpet

versor (1-intr.) remain, stay

veterānus, -a, -um old, veteran; *as subst.,* veteran (soldier)

erat, magnā vī tendere, cohortem praetōriam in mediōs hostīs indūcit eōsque perturbātōs atque aliōs alibī resistentīs interficit. deinde utrimque ex lateribus cēterōs adgreditur. Manlius et Faesulānus in prīmīs pugnantēs cadunt. Catilīna postquam fūsās cōpiās sēque cum paucīs relicuom videt, memor generis atque pristinae suae dignitātis in cōnfertissumōs hostīs incurrit ibique pugnāns cōnfoditur.

sed cōnfectō proeliō, tum vērō cernerēs quanta audācia quantaque animī vīs fuisset in exercitū Catilīnae. nam ferē quem quisque vīvos pugnandō locum cēperat, eum āmissā animā corpore tegēbat. paucī autem, quōs mediōs cohors praetōria disiēcerat, paulō dīvorsius,* sed omnēs tamen advorsīs volneribus conciderant. Catilīna vērō

*****paulō dīvorsius**, *sc.* **conciderant**, had fallen a little more spread out

adversus, -a, -um turned toward; received in front

aggredior (ad- + gradior) assault, attack

alibī (adv.) elsewhere, in another place

āmittō (ā- + mittō) send away; lose

cernō, cernere, crēvī, crētus distinguish, determine, perceive, see

cohors, cohortis, -ium *f.* company of soldiers, division of an army, cohort

concidō (con- + cadō), concidere, concidī, —— fall down, collapse; fall lifeless, die

cōnfertus, -a, -um crowded, dense, packed close together

cōnfodiō, cōnfodīre, cōnfōdī, cōnfossus dig thoroughly; pierce, transfix

deinde (adv.) then, thereupon; next

dignitās, dignitātis *f.* dignity, rank, status

disiciō (dis- + iaciō) break, rout, disperse

dīversē (adv.) scattered, in different directions

Faesulānus, -a, -um of *or* belonging to Faesulae, a city in Etruria; *as subst.*, the Faesulan, referring to a commander of part of Catiline's troops

ferē (adv.) almost, nearly; for the most part

fundō, fundere, fūdī, fūsus pour out, pour forth; rout, disperse; slay

incurrō (in- + currō), incurrere, incucurrī, incursum rush (into), attack

indūcō (in- + dūcō) bring (in), lead (in)

ingenuus, -a, -um natural, freeborn

latus, lateris *n.* side, flank

Manlius, Manliī *m.* (C.) Manlius, centurion under Sulla, leader of Catiline's army

memor, memoris mindful, remembering (+ gen.)

perturbō (1-tr.) throw into disorder, confuse, disturb

praetōrius, -a, -um of *or* belonging to the praetor, praetorian

pristinus, -a, -um ancient; former; original

relicuom = archaic form of **reliquum**

resistō, resistere, restitī, —— oppose, resist

tegō, tegere, tēxī, tēctus cover

tendō, tendere, tetendī, tentus or **tēnsus** stretch out, extend; strain, exert oneself, contend

timidus, -a, -um fearful, afraid, timid

utrimque (adv.) from both sides, on both sides

vīvus, -a, -um living, alive

longē ā suīs inter hostium cadāvera repertus est, paululum etiam spīrāns ferō-
ciamque animī, quam habuerat vīvos, in voltū retinēns. postrēmō ex omnī cōpiā*
neque in proeliō neque in fugā quisquam† cīvis ingenuos captus est: ita cūnctī suae
hostiumque vītae iuxtā pepercerant. neque tamen exercitus populī Rōmānī laetam
aut incruentam victōriam adeptus erat. nam strēnuissumus quisque aut occiderat in
proeliō aut graviter volnerātus discesserat. multī autem, quī ē castrīs vīsundī aut spo-
liandī grātiā prōcesserant, volventēs hostīlia cadāvera amīcum aliī, pars hospitem aut
cognātum reperiēbant; fuēre item quī inimīcōs suōs cognōscerent. ita variē per
omnem exercitum laetitia, maeror, lūctus, atque gaudia agitābantur.

***cōpia**, *here,* number; body of men
†**quisquam**, *indef. pron. used adjectivally*
adipīscor, adipīscī, adeptus sum reach, obtain,
   get
agitō (1-tr.) stir up, set in motion, arouse
cadāver, cadāveris *n.* corpse
cognātus, cognātī *m.* kinsman, relative
dīversē (adv.) scattered, in different directions
ferōcia, ferōciae *f.* fierceness, savagery
gaudium, gaudiī *n.* joy
hospes, hospitis *m.* guest, visitor, stranger; host
hostīlis, hostīle of *or* belonging to an enemy,
   hostile
incruentus, -a, -um bloodless
ingenuus, -a, -um natural, freeborn
item (adv.) similarly, in turn, likewise
iuxtā (adv.) near, nearby; in like manner, equally
laetitia, laetitiae *f.* happiness
lūctus, lūctūs *m.* mourning
maeror, maerōris *m.* grief, sorrow, mourning

parcō, parcere, pepercī, parsūrus be merciful,
   be sparing (+ dat.)
paululum (adv.) a little
postrēmō (adv.) finally
prōcēdō (prō- + cēdō) go forward, advance
reperiō, reperīre, repperī, repertus find, discover
retineō (re- + teneō), retinēre, retinuī, retentus
   keep hold of, retain, grasp
spīrō (1-tr.) breathe
spoliō (1-tr.) strip; plunder, pillage
strēnuus, -a, -um active, vigorous, energetic
variē (adv.) variously, differently, in different
   ways
victōria, victōriae *f.* victory
vīsō, vīsere, vīsī, vīsus go to see, visit; view;
   vīsundī = archaic form of **vīsendī**
vīvus, -a, -um living, alive
volvō, volvere, volvī, volūtus turn, turn over
vulnerō (1-tr.) wound

10. Vergil, *Aeneid* XI.816–31

The poet describes the death of Camilla, leader of a band of Volscian warrior-maidens fighting on the side of Turnus. The Trojan Arruns has wounded her with his spear.

illa manū moriēns tēlum trahit, ossa sed inter*

ferreus ad† costās altō stat vulnere mucrō.

lābitur exsanguis, lābuntur frīgida lētō

lūmina, purpureus quondam color ōra relīquit.

tum sīc exspīrāns Accam ex aequālibus ūnam   820

adloquitur, fīda ante aliās quae sōla Camillae

quīcum partīrī cūrās, atque haec ita fātur:

"hāctenus, Acca soror, potuī: nunc vulnus acerbum

cōnficit, et tenebrīs nigrēscunt omnia circum.

effuge et haec Turnō mandāta novissima‡ perfer: 825

succēdat pugnae Troiānōsque arceat urbe.

iamque valē." simul hīs dictīs linquēbat habēnās

ad terram nōn sponte fluēns. tum frīgida tōtō

paulātim exsolvit sē corpore, lentaque colla

et captum lētō posuit caput, arma relinquēns,   830

vītaque cum gemitū fugit indignāta sub umbrās.

***ossa . . . inter = inter ossa** by anastrophe, the reversal in order of a preposition and its object
†**ad**, *here*, at, near
‡**novissima**, *here*, last
Acca, Accae *f.* Acca, sister of Camilla
aequālis, aequāle equal, like; *as subst.,* contemporary, fellow
alloquor (ad- + loquor) address
arceō, arcēre, arcuī, —— keep away, hold out
Camilla, Camillae *f.* Camilla
circum (adv.) all round, round about
collum, collī *n. in sing. or pl.,* neck
color, colōris *m.* color
costa, costae *f.* rib
effugiō (ex- + fugiō) flee away
exsanguis, exsangue bloodless; lifeless
exsolvō (ex- + solvō) set loose, release
exspīrō (1-intr.) breathe out, exhale, expire
ferreus, -a, -um (made of) iron
fīdus, -a, -um trustworthy, faithful
fluō, fluere, fluxī, fluxus flow, stream; fall
frīgidus, -a, -um cold
gemitus, gemitūs *m.* groan(ing), moan(ing)
habēna, habēnae *f.* rein
hāctenus (adv.) as far as this, thus far

indignātus, -a, -um angered, reluctant
labor, lābī, lāpsus sum slip; slide, glide, fall
lentus, -a, -um pliant, supple, yielding
lētum, lētī *n.* death
linquō, linquere, līquī, —— forsake, give up, relinquish
mandātum, mandātī *n.* charge, command, order
mucrō, mucrōnis *m.* sharp point
nigrēscō, nigrēscere, ——, —— become black, grow dark
os, ossis *n.* bone
partior, partīrī, partītus sum divide, distribute, share; **partīrī**, Historical Infinitive
paulātim (adv.) little by little, gradually
pugna, pugnae *f.* battle, fight
purpureus, -a, -um dark red, rosy, ruddy
quīcum = quācum
quondam (adv.) once, formerly
simul (adv.) at the same time
***spōns, *spontis** *f.* (one's own) will
succēdō (sub- + cēdō) draw near
tenebrae, tenebrārum *f. pl.* darkness, shadows
trahō, trahere, trāxī, tractus draw, drag; draw out, pull out
Troiānī, Troiānōrum *m. pl.* Trojans

11. Vergil, *Aeneid* XII.938–52

The end of the *Aeneid*: after Turnus begs for his life, Aeneas hesitates.

. . . stetit ācer in armīs

Aenēās volvēns oculōs dextramque repressit;

et iam iamque* magis cūnctantem flectere sermō   940

coeperat, īnfēlīx umerō cum appāruit altō

balteus et nōtīs† fulsērunt cingula bullīs

Pallantis puerī, victum quem vulnere Turnus

strāverat atque umerīs inimīcum īnsigne gerēbat.

ille, oculīs postquam saevī monimenta dolōris   945

exuviāsque hausit, furiīs accēnsus et īrā

terribilis: "tūne hinc spoliīs indūte meōrum

ēripiāre mihī?‡ Pallās tē hōc vulnere, Pallās

immolat et poenam scelerātō ex sanguine sūmit."

hoc dīcēns ferrum adversō sub pectore condit   950

fervidus; ast illī solvuntur frīgore membra

vītaque cum gemitū fugit indignāta sub umbrās.

*iam iamque, at any time now, now almost
†nōtus, *here,* well-known
‡The final -i of mihi here scans *long.*

accendō, accendere, accendī, accēnsus inflame, burn

adversus, -a -um turned toward, opposite; hostile

appāreō, appārēre, appāruī, appāritum be visible, be clear; appear, become evident

ast (conj.) but

balteus, balteī *m.* shoulder band, sword belt

bulla, bullae *f.* boss *or* raised ornament, knob, stud

cingulum, cingulī *n.* band

condō, condere, condidī, conditus found, build; bury

cūnctor, cūnctārī, cūnctātus sum hesitate, delay; cūnctantem, *sc.* Aenēān

dexter, dextra, dextrum right; *as fem. subst.* (*sc.* manus) right hand

dolor, dolōris *m.* grief, sorrow, pain

exuviae, exuviārum *f. pl.* (stripped) armor, spoils

fervidus, -a, -um seething, burning; passionate, furious

flectō, flectere, flexī, flexus bend; soften, influence

frīgus, frīgoris *n.* cold, chill

fulgeō, fulgēre, fulsī, —— shine, gleam

furiae, furiārum *f. pl.* madness, mad desire, frenzy

gemitus, gemitūs *m.* groan(ing), moan(ing)

hauriō, haurīre, hausī, haustus drink (in), absorb

immolō (1-tr.) offer (someone) in sacrifice, kill (someone) in the manner of a sacrifice

indignātus, -a, -um angered, reluctant

induō, induere, induī, indūtus put on, clothe, dress

īnsigne, īnsignis, -ium *n.* emblem, decoration

membrum, membrī *n.* limb

monimentum, monimentī *n.* token, reminder

Pallās, Pallantis *m.* Pallas, son of Evander and comrade of Aeneas

reprimō (re- + premō) push back, repress; check, hold back

sanguis, sanguinis *m.* blood

scelerātus, -a, -um wicked, criminal

sermō, sermōnis *m.* speech

spolium, spoliī *n.* booty, spoil

sternō, sternere, strāvī, strātus strew; lay low, slay, kill

sūmō, sūmere, sūmpsī, sūmptus take up, seize; exact

terribilis, terribile terrifying, frightening

umerus, umerī *m.* shoulder

volvō, volvere, volvī, volūtus turn, turn over, roll

12. Horace, *Carmina* I.37 (Alcaic strophe)

On the death of Cleopatra

Nunc est bibendum, nunc pede līberō

pulsanda tellūs, nunc Saliāribus

    ornāre pulvīnar deōrum

        tempus erat dapibus, sodālēs.

antehāc[8] nefās dēprōmere Caecubum   5

cellīs avītīs, dum Capitōliō

    rēgīna dēmentīs ruīnās

        fūnus et* imperiō parābat

contāminātō cum grege turpium

morbō virōrum, quidlibet inpotēns   10

    spērāre fortūnāque dulcī

        ēbria. sed minuit furōrem

*et in poetry is frequently placed in the position of -que.

antehāc (adv.) before this time, previously

avītus, -a, -um of a grandfather, ancestral

bibō, bibere, bibī, —— drink

Caecubum, Caecubī *n.* Caecuban wine (from the plain of Caecubum in Latium)

Capitōlium, Capitōliī *n.* (the) Capitoline hill

cella, cellae *f.* storeroom

contāminō (1-tr.) defile, pollute

daps, dapis *f.* feast, banquet

dēmēns, dēmentis insane, (raving) mad

dēprōmō, dēprōmere, dēprōmpsī, dēprōmptus bring out, draw forth

ēbrius, -a, -um drunk, intoxicated

fūnus, fūneris *n. in sing. or pl.* funeral (procession); ruin, destruction; death

furor, furōris *m.* madness

grex, gregis *m.* flock, herd; swarm, crowd

impotēns, impotentis powerless, helpless; unrestrained, unbridled

minuō, minuere, minuī, minūtus reduce, diminish

morbus, morbī *m.* sickness, disease

ornō (1-tr.) dress, adorn, decorate

parō (1-tr.) prepare

pēs, pedis *m.* foot

pulsō (1-tr.) strike, beat

pulvīnar, pulvīnāris *n.* couch (for a statue of a god)

quīlibet, quaelibet, quidlibet (indef. pron.) anyone *or* anything it pleases; anyone, anything

ruīna, ruīnae *f.* downfall, ruin, destruction

Saliāris, Saliāre Salian, of the Saliī, a college of priests of Mars noted for their sumptuous processions through the city every March

sodālis, sodālis, -ium *m.* comrade, companion

tellūs, tellūris *f.* earth, land

8. The vowels -e- and -ā- of antehāc here elide into a single sound -ā-. This internal elision is called synizesis (< Greek *synizesis,* collapse).

vix ūna sospes nāvis ab ignibus

mentemque lymphātam Mareōticō

    redēgit in vērōs timōrēs   15

        Caesar ab Italiā volantem

rēmīs adurgēns, accipiter velut

mollīs columbās aut leporem citus

    vēnātor in campīs nīvālis

        Haemoniae, daret ut catēnīs   20

fātāle mōnstrum: quae generōsius

perīre quaerēns nec muliebriter

    expāvit ēnsem nec latentīs

        classe citā reparāvit ōrās,

accipiter, accipitris *m.* bird of prey, hawk
adurgeō, adurgēre, ——, —— press on, pursue closely
catēna, catēnae *f.* chain
citus, -a, -um swift, fast
classis, classis, -ium *f.* fleet
columba, columbae *f.* dove
ēnsis, ēnsis *m.* sword
expavēscō, expavēscere, expāvī, —— become frightened of, take fright at
fātālis, fātāle destined, fated; deadly, dangerous
generōsē (adv.) nobly
Haemonia, Haemoniae *f.* Haemonia, old name of Thessaly
lateō, latēre, latuī, —— hide, lie hidden, be concealed
lepus, leporis *m.* hare
lymphātus, -a, -um frenzied, deranged

Mareōticum, Mareōticī *n.* Mareotic wine (from Mareotis in Egypt)
mollis, molle gentle, mild, soft
mōnstrum, mōnstrī *n.* omen, portent; monster
muliebriter (adv.) like a woman
nāvis, nāvis, -ium *f.* ship
nīvālis, nīvāle snowy
ōra, ōrae *f.* shore, coast
redigō (red- + agō), redigere, redēgī, redāctus bring back (down), force, subdue
rēmus, rēmī *m.* oar
reparō (1-tr.) recover; take in exchange
sospes, sospitis safe, unharmed, spared
triumphus, triumphī *m.* (a) triumph, the procession through Rome of a victorious general
velut (conj.) even as, just as
vēnātor, vēnātōris *m.* hunter
volō (1-intr.) fly

ausa et iacentem vīsere rēgiam   25

voltū serēnō, fortis et asperās

     tractāre serpentēs, ut ātrum

         corpore conbiberet venēnum,

dēlīberātā morte ferōcior:

saevīs Liburnīs scīlicet invidēns   30

     prīvāta dēdūcī superbō

         nōn humilis mulier triumphō.

asper, aspera, asperum harsh, fierce, pitiless

āter, ātra, ātrum black, dark

**combibō, combibere, combibī, —— ** drink (deeply)

dēdūcō (dē- + dūcō) lead down; bring back (to Rome)

dēlīberō (1-tr.) weigh, consider; resolve, determine

ferōx, ferōcis fierce, savage; high-spirited, defiant

**iaceō, iacēre, iacuī, —— ** lie, rest; lie in ruins

invideō (in- + videō) envy, be jealous; begrudge, refuse

Liburna, Liburnae *f.* (a) Liburnian galley

mulier, mulieris *f.* woman

prīvātus, -a, -um private; *as subst.*, ordinary citizen

rēgia, rēgiae *f.* royal residence, palace

scīlicet (particle) to be sure, no doubt, of course

serēnus, -a, -um calm, serene

serpēns, serpentis, -ium *m.* or *f.* serpent

superbus, -a, -um proud; haughty

tractō (1-tr.) keep on dragging; touch, handle

triumphus, triumphī *m.* (a) triumph, the procession through Rome of a victorious general

venēnum, venēnī *n.* poison

vīsō, vīsere, vīsī, vīsus go to see, visit; view

13. Horace, *Carmina* III.30 (Asclepiadean)

The poet reflects on his achievements.

> Exēgī monumentum aere perennius
> rēgālīque sitū pȳramidum altius,
> quod nōn imber edāx, nōn Aquilō impotēns
> possit dīruere aut innumerābilis
> annōrum seriēs et fuga temporum.   5
> nōn omnis moriar multaque pars meī
> vītābit Libitīnam: ūsque ego posterā
> crēscam laude recēns, dum Capitōlium
> scandet cum tacitā virgine pontifex:

aes, aeris *n.* copper, bronze; money
Aquilō, Aquilōnis *m.* Aquilo, the north wind
Capitōlium, Capitōliī *n.* (the) Capitoline hill
crēscō, crēscere, crēvī, crētus grow, increase
dīruō, dīruere, dīruī, dīrutus demolish, destroy
edāx, edācis corrosive
exigō (ex- + agō), exigere, exēgī, exāctus drive
  out; finish, complete
imber, imbris *m.* rain; water
impotēns, impotentis powerless, helpless;
  unrestrained, unbridled
innumerābilis, innumerābile innumerable
laus, laudis *f.* praise
Libitīna, Libitīnae *f.* Libitina, goddess of corpses,
  at whose temple the registers of deaths were
  kept

monumentum, monumentī *n.* monument
perennis, perenne everlasting, perpetual,
  perennial
pontifex, pontificis *m.* priest; pontifex
posterus, -a, -um later, following, future
pȳramis, pȳramidis *f.* pyramid
recēns, recentis recent, fresh, new
rēgālis, rēgāle royal, kingly
scandō, scandere, ——, —— climb, mount,
  ascend
seriēs, seriēī *f.* series, chain
situs, sitūs *m.* position, structure; neglect, decay
tacitus, -a, -um silent
ūsque (adv.) continuously
virgō, virginis *f.* maiden, virgin
vītō (1-tr.) avoid

dīcar, quā* violēns obstrepit Aufidus   10
et quā* pauper aquae Daunus agrestium
rēgnāvit populōrum, ex humilī potēns
prīnceps Aeolium carmen ad Ītalōs
dēdūxisse modōs. sūme superbiam
quaesītam meritīs et mihi Delphicā
laurō cinge volēns, Melpomenē, comam.   15

***quā**, *here* (adv.), where

Aeolius, -a, -um Aeolic, Aeolian, of Aeolia,
    a region in northwest Asia Minor, supposed
    birthplace of Greek lyric poetry

agrestis, agreste rustic

Aufidus, Aufidī *m.* (the) Aufidus (river)
    (in Apulia)

coma, comae *f.* hair

Daunus, Daunī *m.* Daunus, legendary king of
    Apulia (Horace's home district)

dēdūcō (dē- + dūcō) lead down; introduce;
    convert, adapt

Delphicus, -a, -um Delphic, of Delphi

impotēns, impotentis powerless, helpless;
    unrestrained, unbridled

Ītalus, -a, -um Italian

laurus, laurī *f.* laurel

Melpomenē, Melpomenēs *f.* Melpomene, a Muse

meritum, meritī *n.* merit; service

obstrepō, obstrepere, obstrepuī, obstrepitus roar

pauper, pauperis poor

potēns, potentis powerful

prīnceps, prīncipis first

rēgnō (1-tr.) rule, rule over (+ gen.)

situs, sitūs *m.* position, structure; neglect, decay

sūmō, sūmere, sūmpsī, sūmptus take (up), adopt
    as suitable

superbia, superbiae *f.* pride; haughtiness, arro-
    gance

violēns, violentis violent, forceful

14. Propertius II.29a

The poet receives an unusual escort back to his beloved.

Hesternā, mea lūx, cum pōtus nocte vagārer,

    nec mē servōrum dūceret ūlla manus,

obvia, nescio quot* puerī, mihi turba, minūtī,

    vēnerat† (hōs vetuit mē numerāre timor);

quōrum aliī faculās, aliī retinēre sagittās,   5

    pars etiam vīsast vincla parāre mihi.

sed nūdī fuerant.† quōrum lascīvior ūnus

    "arripite hunc," inquit, "nam bene nōstis eum.

hic‡ erat, hunc mulier nōbīs īrāta locāvit."

    dīxit, et in collō iam mihi nōdus erat.   10

hīc alter iubet in medium prōpellere, at alter

    "intereat, quī nōs nōn putat esse deōs!

***nescio quot**, I-don't-know-how-many, some

†**vēnerat, fuerant**, pluperfects used to express a sudden action; translate as perfects

‡**hic**, *here*, scans as if it were spelled **hicc**

arripiō, arripere, arripuī, arreptus grasp, take hold of, seize; arrest

at (conj.) but

collum, collī *n.* neck

facula, faculae *f.* (little) torch

hesternus, -a, -um of *or* belonging to yesterday; **hesterna nox**, last night

inquam (defective verb) say; **inquit** = *3rd sing. pres. act. indic.*

intereō (inter- + eō), interīre, interiī, interitūrus perish, die

īrātus, -a, -um angry, irate

lascīvus, -a, -um playful, naughty, free from restraint

locō (1-tr.) place; assign

minūtus, -a, -um small, tiny, minute

mulier, mulieris *f.* woman

nōdus, nōdī *m.* knot; (knotted) rope

nūdus, -a, -um naked, nude

numerō (1-tr.) number, count

obvius, -a, -um in the way, face to face; moving against, opposed in direction

parō (1-tr.) prepare, make ready

pōtō, pōtāre, pōtāvī, pōtātus or **pōtus** drink intoxicating drinks; *perf. pass. part. with active meaning,* having drunk, being drunk

prōpellō (prō- + pellō), prōpellere, prōpulī, prōpulsus push forward, propel; compel to go

retineō (re- + teneō), retinēre, retinuī, retentus keep hold of, retain, grasp

sagitta, sagittae *f.* arrow

turba, turbae *f.* crowd

vagor (1-intr.) wander

vinc(u)lum, vinc(u)lī *n.* bond, chain

haec tē nōn meritum tōtās exspectat in* hōrās:

 at tū nescio quam† quaeris, inepte, forīs.

quae cum Sīdoniae nocturna ligāmina mitrae   15

 solverit atque oculōs mōverit illa gravīs,

afflābunt tibi nōn Arabum dē grāmine odōrēs,

 sed quōs ipse suīs fēcit Amor manibus.

parcite iam, frātrēs, iam certōs spondet amōrēs;

 et iam ad mandātam vēnimus ecce domum."   20

atque ita mī iniectō dīxērunt rursus amictū:

 "ī nunc et noctēs disce manēre domī."

---

*in, *here, expressing duration,* for

†**nescioquī, nescioquae, nescioquod** (indef. adj.),
sometimes written as two words, I-don't-know-
who, I-don't-know-which, some . . . or other

afflō (1-intr.) blow, breathe (upon) (+ dat.)

amictus, amictūs *m.* mantle, cloak

Arabēs, Arabum *m. pl.* Arabians, Arabs

discō, discere, didicī, —— learn (how) (+ inf.)

forīs (adv.) out of doors, outside; abroad

grāmen, grāminis *n.* grass; herb

hōra, hōrae *f.* hour

ineptus, -a, -um having no sense of what is fitting, foolish

iniciō (in- + iaciō) throw upon

ligāmen, ligāminis *n.* fastening, string

mandō (1-tr.) entrust, commit; assign, order

mereor, merērī, meritus sum deserve, earn

mī = mihi

mitra, mitrae *f.* (eastern) headdress

nocturnus, -a, -um at night, nocturnal

odor, odōris *m.* odor, scent

parcō, parcere, pepercī, parsūrus be merciful, be
sparing (+ dat.)

rursus (adv.) again

Sīdonius, -a, -um of Sidon, a Phoenician city
famed for its export of purple dye

spondeō, spondēre, spopondī, spōnsus pledge

15. Ovid, *Metamorphōsēs* I.253–73

When mortal men reached the Iron Age of greed and crime, Jupiter decided to destroy the human race and begin again.

iamque erat in tōtās sparsūrus fulmina terrās;

sed timuit nē forte sacer tot ab ignibus aethēr

conciperet flammās longusque ardēsceret axis: 255

esse quoque in fātīs reminīscitur adfore tempus

quō mare, quō tellūs correptaque rēgia caelī

ardeat et mundī mōlēs obsessa labōret.

tēla repōnuntur manibus fabricāta Cyclōpum;

poena placet dīversa, genus mortāle sub undīs   260

perdere et ex omnī nimbōs dēmittere caelō.

prōtinus Aeoliīs Aquilōnem claudit in antrīs

Aeolius, -a, -um of Aeolus, ruler of the winds; Aeolian

aethēr, aetheris *m. aether* or ether, the upper region of the sky; heaven

antrum, antrī *n.* cave, cavern

Aquilō, Aquilōnis *m.* Aquilo, the north wind

ardeō, ardēre, arsī, arsūrus burn, be on fire

ardēscō, ardēscere, ——, —— become inflamed, begin to burn

axis, axis, -ium *m.* (celestial) axis, pole

claudō, claudere, clausī, clausus close, shut; confine, enclose

concipiō (con- + capiō) take on, absorb, catch

corripiō (con- + rapiō) snatch up, seize; ignite

Cyclōps, Cyclōpos *m.* one of the Cyclopes, the fabulous giants of Sicily

dēmittō (dē- + mittō) send down

dīversus, -a, -um different

fabricō (1-tr.) fashion, forge

flamma, flammae *f.* flame

fulmen, fulminis *n.* lightning; thunderbolt

mōlēs, mōlis, -ium *f.* (huge) mass

mortālis, mortāle mortal

mundus, mundī *m.* universe, world

nimbus, nimbī *m.* rain cloud

obsideō, obsidēre, obsēdī, obsessus besiege, beset, assail

prōtinus (adv.) immediately, straightway

rēgia, rēgiae *f.* royal house, palace

reminīscor, reminīscī, —— recall, recollect

repōnō (re- + pōnō) put back, put down, put away

sacer, sacra, sacrum sacred

spargō, spargere, sparsī, sparsus scatter, sprinkle; shower; cast

tellūs, tellūris *f.* earth, land

unda, undae *f.* wave

et quaecumque fugant inductās flāmina nūbēs

ēmittitque Notum. madidīs Notus ēvolat ālīs,

terribilem piceā tēctus cālīgine vultum;   265

barba gravis nimbīs, cānīs fluit unda capillīs;

fronte sedent nebulae, rōrant pennaeque sinūsque.

utque manū lātē pendentia nūbila pressit,

fit fragor: hinc dēnsī funduntur ab aethere nimbī.

nuntia Iūnōnis, variōs indūta colōrēs,   270

concipit Īris aquās alimentaque nūbibus adfert.

sternuntur segetēs et dēplōrāta colōnī

vōta iacent, longīque perit labor inritus annī.

afferō (ad- + ferō), afferre, attulī, allātus bring,
    add

aethēr, aetheris *m. aether* or ether, the upper
    region of the sky, heaven

āla, ālae *f.* wing

alimentum, alimentī *n.* nourishment

aqua, aquae *f.* water

barba, barbae *f.* beard

cālīgō, cālīginis *f.* darkness; mist, fog

cānus, -a, -um white; gray

capillus, capillī *m. in sing. or pl.* hair

colōnus, colōnī *m.* settler; farmer

color, colōris *m.* color

concipiō (con- + capiō) catch, take up

dēnsus, -a, -um thick, dense

dēplōrō (1-tr.) weep, lament, cry over

ēmittō (ē- + mittō) send out, release

ēvolō (1-intr.) fly out

flāmen, flāminis *n.* blast, gust (of wind)

fluō, fluere, flūxī, fluxus flow, run

fragor, fragōris *m.* crash, roar, din

frōns, frontis, -ium *f.* forehead, brow

fugō (1-tr.) put to flight, rout

fundō, fundere, fūdī, fūsus pour out, pour forth

iaceō, iacēre, iacuī, —— lie, rest; lie in ruins

indūcō (in- + dūcō) bring in; draw over, spread
    over

induō, induere, induī, indūtus put on, clothe,
    dress

Īris, Īridis *f.* Iris, female messenger goddess
    (of the rainbow)

irritus, -a, -um useless, vain

lātē (adv.) widely, far and wide

madidus, -a, -um wet, drenched, dripping

nebula, nebulae *f.* mist, fog; cloud

nimbus, nimbī *m.* rain cloud

Notus, Notī *m.* Notus, the south wind

nūbēs, nūbis, -ium *f.* cloud

nūbila, nūbilōrum *n. pl.* (rain) clouds

nuntia, nuntiae *f.* (female) messenger

pendeō, pendēre, pependī, —— hang, be sus-
    pended

penna, pennae *f.* feather; wing

piceus, -a, -um pitch black

quīcumque, quaecumque, quodcumque (indef.
    rel. adj.) whatever

rōrō (1-intr.) shed moisture, drip

sedeō, sedēre, sēdī, sessūrus sit

segēs, segitis *f.* field; crop

sinus, sinūs *m.* curve; fold

sternō, sternere, strāvī, strātus strew, spread out,
    scatter

tegō, tegere, tēxī, tēctus cover

terribilis, terribile terrifying, frightening

unda, undae *f.* wave

varius, -a, -um various, different

vōtum, vōtī *n.* vow, prayer; desire, hope; pledge

16. Livy, *Ab Urbe Conditā* I.13.1–5

In need of wives for his male citizens, Romulus had arranged for the capture and forced marriage of many women from the nearby Sabines. When the Sabines later attacked Rome, these women became the peacemakers.

tum Sabīnae mulieres, quārum ex iniūriā bellum ortum erat, crīnibus passīs* scis-sāque veste, victō malīs muliebrī pavōre, ausae sē inter tēla volantia īnferre, ex trāns-versō impetū factō dīrimere īnfestās aciēs, dīrimere īrās, hinc patrēs, hinc virōs ōrantēs nē sanguine sē nefandō socerī generīque respergerent, nē parricīdiō macu-lārent partūs suōs, nepōtum illī, hī līberum† prōgeniem. "Sī adfīnitātis inter vōs, sī cōnūbiī piget, in nōs vertite īrās; nōs causa bellī, nōs volnerum ac caedium virīs ac parentibus sumus; melius perībimus quam sine alterīs vestrum viduae aut orbae vīvēmus." movet rēs cum multitūdinem tum ducēs; silentium et repentīna fit quiēs; inde ad foedus faciendum ducēs prōdeunt. nec pācem modo sed cīvitātem ūnam ex duābus faciunt. rēgnum cōnsociant: imperium omne cōnferunt Rōmam. ita gemi-nātā urbe, ut Sabīnīs tamen aliquid darētur Quirītēs ā Curibus appellātī.

*passīs, *here,* **pandō, pandere, pandī, passus** spread, extend; dishevel

†līberī, *here,* children; **līberum = līberōrum**

affīnitās, affīnitātis *f.* relationship by marriage

appellō (1-tr.) name, call

caedēs, caedis, -ium *f.* slaughter, killing

cōnsociō (1-tr.) unite

cōnūbium, cōnūbiī *n.* marriage

crīnis, crīnis, -ium *m. in sing. or pl.* hair

Curēs, Curium *m. pl.* Cures, a Sabine town

dīrimō, dīrimere, dīrēmī, dīrēmptus break apart, separate, divide

foedus, foederis *n.* pact, treaty

geminō (1-tr.) double

gener, generī *m.* son-in-law

impetus, impetūs *m.* attack, assault, onrush

īnfestus, -a, -um hostile; dangerous

iniūria, iniūriae *f.* injury, injustice

maculō (1-tr.) stain, defile, pollute

muliebris, muliebre of a woman, womanly

mulier, mulieris *f.* woman

multitūdō, multitūdinis *f.* multitude; populace

nefandus, -a, -um unspeakable; abominable

nepōs, nepōtis *m.* grandson

orbus, -a, -um bereft, bereaved; childless, orphaned

parēns, parentis, -ium *m. or f.* parent

parricīdium, parricīdiī *n.* murder (of parents or kinsmen), parricide

partus, partūs *m.* birth; offspring

pavor, pavōris *m.* trembling; fear, dread

prōdeō (prō- + eō), **prōdīre, prōdiī, prōditūrus** go or come forward

prōgeniēs, *prōgeniēī *f.* offspring, progeny

quiēs, quiētis *f.* quiet

Quirītēs, Quirītium *m. pl.* Quirites, the name for Roman citizens in their public capacity

rēgnum, rēgnī *n.* realm, kingdom; rule, kingship

repentīnus, -a, -um sudden

respergō, respergere, respersī, respersus besprinkle; defile

Sabīnus, -a, -um Sabine; *as subst. pl.,* (the) Sabines

sanguis, sanguinis *m.* blood

scindō, scindere, scīdī, scissus rend, tear

silentium, silentiī *n.* silence

socer, socerī *m.* father-in-law

trānsversus, -a, -um crosswise, transverse; **ex trānsversō,** from the flank

vertō, vertere, vertī, versus turn

vestis, vestis, -ium *f.* clothing, garment

viduus, -a, -um bereft, bereaved; spouseless, widowed

volō (1-intr.) fly

17. Petronius, *Satyricon* 45

A dinner guest tires of hearing the complaints of another guest and decides to interrupt.

"ōrō tē," inquit Echīōn centōnārius, "melius loquere. 'modo sīc, modo sīc,' inquit rūsticus; varium porcum perdiderat. quod hodiē nōn est, crās erit: sīc vīta trūditur. nōn meherculēs patria melior dīcī potest* sī hominēs habēret. sed labōrat hōc tempore, nec haec sōla. nōn dēbēmus dēlicātī esse, ubique† medius caelus‡ est. tū sī aliubi fueris, dīcēs hīc porcōs coctōs ambulāre. et ecce habitūrī sumus mūnus excellente in trīduō diē fēstā; familia nōn lanistīcia, sed plūrimī lībertī. et Tītus noster magnum animum habet et est caldicerebrius: aut hoc aut illud, erit quid§ utique. nam illī domesticus sum, nōn est mixcix. ferrum optimum datūrus est, sine fugā, carnārium in mediō, ut amphitheāter videat.

*potest, pres. indic. used for vividness in
  apodosis of Present Contrary-to-Fact
  conditional sentence
†ubique (adv.) everywhere
‡caelus = caelum
§quid = aliquid
aliubi (adv.) in another place, in other places,
  elsewhere
amphitheāter (= amphitheātrum), amphitheātrī
  m. oval theater, amphitheater
caldicerebrius, -a, -um hot headed, impetuous
carnārium, carnāriī *n.* meat rack; slaughter-
  house; carnage, butchery
centōnārius, centōnāriī *m.* maker of patchwork,
  rag seller; man who uses mats to extinguish
  fires
coquō, coquere, coxī, coctus cook, bake, boil,
  roast
crās (adv.) tomorrow
dēlicātus, -a, -um self-indulgent; hard to please;
  fastidious
domesticus, -a, -um belonging to the family;
  familiar

Echīōn, Echīonis *m.* Echion
excellēns, excellentis superior, excellent;
  excellente = *neut. sing. acc.*
familia, familiae *f.* household; troop, group
fēstus, -a, -um festal; **fēsta** or **fēstus diēs** festival
  day, holiday
hodiē (adv.) today
inquam (defective verb) say; **inquit** = *3rd sing.*
  pres. act. indic.
lanistīcius, -a, -um belonging to a **lanista**, a
  trainer of gladiators; gladiatorial
lībertus, lībertī *m.* freedman
mixcix (unknown) given to half-measures (?)
mūnus, mūneris *n.* present, gift; public show,
  spectacle, entertainment
porcus, porcī *m.* pig
rūsticus, rūsticī *m.* country man, peasant, rustic
trīduum, trīduī *n.* period of three days
trūdō, trūdere, trūsī, trūsus shove, push; drive on
utique (adv.) in any case, at any rate, at least,
  certainly
varius, -a, -um varied; multicolored, mottled;
  spotted

18. Tacitus, *Dē Vītā Agricolae* 46

The reverent conclusion of the biography of the historian's father-in-law

sī quis* piōrum mānibus locus, sī, ut sapientibus placet, nōn cum corpore extin-
guuntur magnae animae, placidē quiēscās,† nōsque domum tuam ab īnfirmō dēsī-
deriō et muliebribus lamentīs ad contemplātiōnem virtūtum tuārum vocēs, quās
neque lūgērī neque plangī fās est. admīrātiōne tē potius et immortālibus laudibus
et, sī nātūra suppeditet, similitūdine colāmus: is vērus honōs, ea coniūnctissimī
cuiusque pietās. id fīliae quoque uxōrīque praecēperim, sīc patris, sīc marītī memoriam venerārī, ut omnia facta dictaque eius sēcum revolvant, formamque ac figūram animī magis quam corporis complectantur, nōn quia intercēdendum putem‡
imāginibus quae marmore aut aere finguntur, sed, ut vultūs hominum, ita simu-
lācra vultūs imbecilla ac mortālia sunt, forma mentis aeterna, quam tenēre et exprimere nōn per aliēnam māteriam et artem, sed tuīs ipse mōribus possīs. quidquid

*quis, indef. pron. used adjectivally

†quiēscās, addressee is the deceased Agricola

‡putem, subjunctive in a clause of rejected reason; translate as indicative

admīrātiō, admīrātiōnis *f.* wonder; admiration, veneration

aes, aeris *n.* bronze

aeternus, -a, -um eternal, everlasting

aliēnus, -a, -um belonging to another; foreign

colō, colere, coluī, cultus inhabit; cultivate; adorn; cherish

complector, complectī, complexus sum embrace, cling to; comprehend; remember

coniūnctus, -a, -um linked together; closely associated, related

contemplātiō, contemplātiōnis *f.* contemplation, consideration

dēsīderium, dēsīderiī *n.* desire; regret; longing

extinguō, extinguere, extīnxī, extīnctus extinguish; annihilate

exprimō (ex- + premō) express

figūra, figūrae *f.* form, composition; appearance

fingō, fingere, fīnxī, fictus form, fashion, make

forma, formae *f.* form, appearance; state, kind

imāgō, imāginis *f.* image, likeness; bust

imbecillus, -a, -um weak, feeble; fragile

immortālis, immortāle immortal

īnfirmus, -a, -um weak, feeble; ineffectual

intercēdō (inter- + cēdō) intervene, interfere; obstruct, oppose

lamenta, lamentōrum *n. pl.* wailing, weeping

laus, laudis *f.* praise

lūgeō, lūgēre, lūxī, lūctus mourn (for); grieve, lament

mānēs, mānium *m. pl. Manes,* spirits of the dead; shade (of a particular person)

marītus, marītī *m.* husband

marmor, marmoris *n.* marble

māteria, māteriae *f.* material, matter

mortālis, mortāle mortal

muliebris, muliebre of a woman, womanly

pietās, pietātis *f.* dutifulness; loyalty

placidē (adv.) calmly, quietly

plangō, plangere, plānxī, plānctus beat (the breast), mourn (for), bewail

potius (comparative adv.) rather

praecipiō (prae- + capiō) advise, instruct

quiēscō, quiēscere, quiēvī, quiētum be asleep; rest

quisquis, quidquid/quicquid (indef. rel. pron.) whoever, whatever

revolvō, revolvere, revolvī, revolūtus go back over; review, recall

similitūdō, similitūdinis *f.* similarity, resemblance, likeness

simulācrum, simulācrī *n.* likeness, image; statue

suppeditō (1-tr.) support; supply; be available, be adequate

uxor, uxōris *f.* wife

veneror (1-tr.) revere, venerate

ex Agricolā amāvimus, quidquid mīrātī sumus, manet mānsūrumque est in animīs
hominum in aeternitāte temporum, fāmā rērum; nam multōs veterum velut inglō-
riōs et ignōbilīs oblīviō obruit: Agricola posteritātī nārrātus et trāditus superstes erit.

aeternitās, aeternitātis *f.* eternity
Agricola, Agricolae *m.* Agricola
ignōbilis, ignōbile unknown, undistinguished
inglōrius, -a, -um lacking renown, obscure
mīror (1-tr.) admire, marvel at
nārrō (1-tr.) narrate, tell (of); describe
oblīviō, oblīviōnis *f.* act *or* state of forgetting *or* being forgotten, oblivion

obruō, obruere, obruī, obrutus cover up, bury
posteritās, posteritātis *f.* later generations, posterity
quisquis, quidquid/quicquid (indef. rel. pron.) whoever, whatever
superstes, superstitis surviving, lasting
velut (conj.) even as, just as; as if

19. Tacitus, *Dialogus dē Ōrātōribus* 25

In a discussion of contemporary oratory's enormous debt to the great speakers of past ages, one participant grants the vigor and variety of the old orators but insists that for both the Greeks and the Romans one greatest period can be identified.

sed quō modō* inter Atticōs ōrātōrēs prīmae† Dēmosthenī tribuuntur, proximum
locum Aeschinēs et Hyperidēs et Lysiās et Lycurgus obtinent, omnium autem con-
cessū haec ōrātōrum aetās maximē probātur, sīc apud nōs Cicerō quidem cēterōs
eōrundem temporum disertōs antecessit, Calvus autem et Asinius et Caesar et
Caelius et Brūtus iūre et priōribus et sequentibus antepōnuntur. nec rēfert quod inter
sē speciē differunt, cum genere cōnsentiant. adstrictior Calvus, numerōsior Asinius, splendidior Caesar, amārior Caelius, gravior Brūtus, vehementior et plēnior et

*__quō modō__, *here, correlative with* **sīc**, in the way in which
†__prīmae__, *sc.* **partēs**, first place
adstrictus, -a, -um constricted; restrained, terse
Aeschinēs, Aeschinis *m.* Aeschines, Athenian orator of the fourth century B.C.E.
amārus, -a, -um bitter; acrimonious; biting, caustic
antecēdō (ante- + cēdō) (tr.) go before, precede; surpass, excel
antepōnō (ante- + pōnō) place before, rank ahead of
Asinius, Asiniī *m.* (C.) Asinius (Pollio), Roman writer and orator of the first century B.C.E.
Atticus, -a, -um Attic, Athenian
Brūtus, Brūtī *m.* (M. Junius) Brutus, Roman orator and politician of the first century B.C.E.
Caelius, Caeliī *m.* (M.) Caelius (Rufus), Roman orator and advocate of the first century B.C.E.
Calvus, Calvī *m.* (M. Licinius) Calvus, Roman orator and poet of the first century B.C.E.
concessus, concessūs *m.* permission, leave; agreement, concession
cōnsentiō (con- + sentiō) be in agreement; be similar

Dēmosthenēs, Dēmosthenis *m.* Demosthenes, Athenian orator of the fourth century B.C.E.
disertus, -a, -um skilled in speaking, eloquent
Hyperidēs, Hyperidis *m.* Hyperides, Athenian orator of the fourth century B.C.E.
Lycurgus, Lycurgī *m.* Lycurgus, Athenian orator of the fourth century B.C.E.
Lysiās, Lysiae *m.* Lysias, Athenian orator of the fifth and fourth centuries B.C.E.
numerōsus, -a, -um plentiful, abundant; harmonious, rhythmical
obtineō (ob- + teneō), obtinēre, obtinuī, obtentus have a hold on
plēnus, -a, -um full, abundant; sonorous; covering the whole range
probō (1-tr.) approve of, commend, esteem
proximus, -a, -um nearest, next
splendidus, -a, -um bright, shining, vivid
tribuō, tribuere, tribuī, tribūtus grant, bestow, assign
vehemēns, vehementis energetic, vigorous, forceful

valentior Cicerō: omnēs tamen eandem sānitātem ēloquentiae prae sē ferunt, ut, sī omnium pariter librōs in manum sūmpseris, sciās, quamvīs in dīversīs ingeniīs, esse quandam iūdiciī ac voluntātis similitūdinem et cognātiōnem. nam quod invicem sē* obtrectāvērunt et sunt aliqua epistulīs eōrum īnserta, ex quibus mūtua malignitās dētegitur, nōn est ōrātōrum vitium, sed hominum. nam et Calvum et Asinium et ipsum Cicerōnem crēdō solitōs et invidēre et līvēre et cēterīs hūmānae īnfirmitātis vitiīs adficī: sōlum inter hōs arbitror Brūtum nōn malignitāte nec invidiā, sed simpliciter et ingenuē iūdicium animī suī dētēxisse. an† ille Cicerōnī invidēret, quī mihi vidētur nē Caesarī quidem invīdisse?

*sē, *here, with reciprocal force,* each other
†an, *here, introduces an indignant or surprised question expecting a negative answer,* can it really be that . . .
afficiō (ad- + faciō) affect, influence
Asinius, Asiniī *m.* (C.) Asinius (Pollio)
Brūtus, Brūtī *m.* (M. Junius) Brutus
Calvus, Calvī *m.* (M. Licinius) Calvus
cognātiō, cognātiōnis *f.* kinship, affinity
dētegō, dētegere, dētēxī, dētēctus uncover, disclose, reveal
dīversus, -a, -um different
ēloquentia, ēloquentiae *f.* eloquence; rhetoric
epistula, epistulae *f.* letter
hūmānus, -a, -um human
īnfirmitās, īnfirmitātis *f.* weakness, sickness
ingenuē (adv.) in a manner befitting a freeborn person; honorably, generously
īnserō, īnserere, īnseruī, īnsertus put in, insert, include

——, vicis *f.* turn; succession; invicem in turn; against one another
invideō (in- + videō) envy, be jealous (of)
iūdicium, iūdiciī *n.* judgment, opinion
līveō, līvēre, ——, —— be livid, be envious *or* jealous
malignitās, malignitātis *f.* ill-will, spite, malice
mūtuus, -a, -um shared, reciprocal, mutual
obtrectō (1-tr.) criticize maliciously, disparage, belittle
pariter (adv.) equally; together, side by side
prae (prep. + abl.) in front of, before; prae sē ferre, exhibit, display
quamvīs (conj.) although
sānitās, sānitātis *f.* healthiness, soundness
similitūdō, similitūdinis *f.* similarity
simpliciter (adv.) simply
sūmō, sūmere, sūmpsī, sūmptus take (up), seize
vitium, vitiī *n.* vice, fault
voluntās, voluntātis *f.* will, intention; choice

The *Dialogus dē Ōrātōribus* (Dialogue About Orators), which may date from around 100 C.E., is modeled on Ciceronian philosophical dialogues and is written in a Ciceronian style that contrasts dramatically with the elliptical, unbalanced style of Tacitus's other surviving works. The interlocutors in the *Dialogus* discuss rhetoric generally and treat in particular the interesting question of the relation between flourishing oratory and political turmoil.

Chapter XV

Continuous Readings

1. Cicero, *In Catilīnam I* 16–17

nunc vērō quae tua est ista vīta? sīc enim iam tēcum loquar, nōn ut odiō permōtus

esse videar, quō dēbeō, sed ut misericordiā, quae tibi nūlla dēbētur. vēnistī paulō ante

in senātum. quis tē ex hāc tantā frequentiā, tot ex tuīs amīcīs ac necessāriīs salūtāvit?

sī hoc post* hominum memoriam contigit nēminī, vōcis exspectās contumēliam,

cum sīs gravissimō iūdiciō taciturnitātis oppressus? quid, quod† adventū tuō ista sub-

sellia vacuēfacta sunt, quod omnēs cōnsulārēs quī tibi‡ persaepe ad caedem cōnstitūtī

fuērunt,§ simul atque adsēdistī, partem istam subselliōrum nūdam atque inānem

relīquērunt, quō tandem animō tibi ferendum putās? servī mehercule meī sī mē istō

pactō metuerent ut tē metuunt omnēs cīvēs tuī, domum meam relinquendam

*post, *here,* since
†quid, quod, what about the fact that
‡tibi, *here,* Dative of Agent
§cōnstitūtī fuērunt = cōnstitūtī sunt
adventus, adventūs *m.* arrival
assīdō, assīdere, assēdī, —— sit down
caedēs, caedis, -ium *f.* slaughter
cōnsulāris, cōnsulāris, -ium *m.* ex-consul
contingō, contingere, contigī, contāctus happen,
   befall (+ dat.)
contumēlia, contumēliae *f.* abuse, insult
frequentia, frequentiae *f.* crowd
inānis, ināne empty
iūdicium, iūdiciī *n.* judgment, opinion

misericordia, misericordiae *f.* pity
necessārius, -a, -um necessary; *as subst.,* relative;
   friend, client, patron
nūdus, -a, -um naked, nude; bare, deserted
pactum, pactī *n.* stipulation; way, manner
permoveō (per- + moveō) thoroughly move
persaepe (adv.) very often
salūtō (1-tr.) greet, hail, salute
simul atque (conj.) as soon as
subsellium, subselliī *n.* bench, seat
taciturnitās, taciturnitātis *f.* silence
vacuēfaciō, vacuēfacere, vacuēfēcī, vacuēfactus
   (make) empty

putārem: tū tibi urbem nōn arbitrāris? et sī mē meīs cīvibus iniūriā suspectum tam
graviter atque offēnsum vidērem, carēre mē aspectū cīvium quam īnfestīs omnium
oculīs cōnspicī māllem: tū, cum cōnscientiā scelerum tuōrum agnōscās odium omnium iūstum et iam diū tibi dēbitum, dubitās quōrum mentīs sēnsūsque volnerās,
eōrum aspectum praesentiamque vītāre? sī tē parentēs timērent atque ōdissent tuī
neque eōs ratiōne ūllā plācāre possēs, ut opīnor, ab eōrum oculīs aliquō* concēderēs.
nunc tē patria, quae commūnis est parēns omnium nostrum, ōdit ac metuit et iam
diū nihil tē iūdicat nisi dē parricīdiō suō cōgitāre: huius tū neque auctōritātem
verēbere nec iūdicium sequēre nec vim pertimēscēs?

*aliquō, *here* (adv.), to some place
agnōscō (ad- + nōscō), agnōscere, agnōvī, agnitus
  recognize
aspectus, aspectūs *m.* sight
commūnis, commūne common, shared
concēdō (con- + cēdō) concede; go away
cōnscientia, cōnscientiae *f.* awareness
cōnspiciō, cōnspicere, cōnspexī, cōnspectus
  catch sight of, perceive, observe
īnfestus, -a, -um hostile
iniūria, iniūriae *f.* injury, injustice; **iniūriā,** *abl.*
  sing. as adv., unjustifiably, unjustly
iūdicium, iūdiciī *n.* judgment, opinion
iūdicō (1-tr.) form an opinion, judge
iūstus, -a, -um just, fair, right

offēnsus, -a, -um offensive
opīnor (1-tr.) suppose, imagine, think
parēns, parentis, -ium *m.* or *f.* parent
parricīdium, parricīdiī *n.* murder
pertimēscō, pertimēscere, pertimuī, ——
  become very afraid, take fright; thoroughly
  fear
plācō (1-tr.) appease, calm
praesentia, praesentiae *f.* presence
ratiō, ratiōnis *f.* account, reason; way, method
suspectus, -a, -um viewed with suspicion,
  suspect
vītō (1-tr.) avoid
vulnerō (1-tr.) wound

2. Sallust, *Bellum Catilīnae* 5

L. Catilīna, nōbilī genere nātus, fuit magnā vī et animī et corporis, sed ingeniō malō prāvōque. huic ab adulēscentiā bella intestīna, caedēs, rapīnae, discordia cīvīlis grāta fuēre, ibique iuventūtem suam exercuit. corpus patiēns inediae, algōris, vigiliae, suprā quam quoiquam crēdibile est. animus audāx, subdolus, varius, quoius reī lubet* simulātor ac dissimulātor, aliēnī adpetēns, suī profūsus, ardēns in cupidi-tātibus; satis ēloquentiae, sapientiae parum. vāstus animus inmoderāta, incrēdi-bilia, nimis alta semper cupiēbat. hunc post dominātiōnem L. Sullae lubīdō max-uma invāserat reī pūblicae capiundae;† neque id quibus modīs adsequerētur, dum sibi rēgnum parāret, quicquam pēnsī habēbat. agitābātur magis magisque in diēs‡ animus ferōx inopiā reī familiāris et cōnscientiā scelerum, quae utraque iīs

*quī . . . libet, quae . . . libet, quod . . . libet
    (indef. adj.) any . . . it pleases
†capiundae = archaic form of capiendae
‡in diēs day by day
adulēscentia, adulēscentiae *f.* youth, adolescence
agitō (1-tr.) stir up, set in motion; vex, harass
algor, algōris *m.* cold
aliēnus, -a, -um belonging to another
appetēns, appetentis desirous (of), greedy (for)
    (+ gen.)
ardeō, ardēre, arsī, arsūrus burn, be on fire; rage
assequor (ad- + sequor) gain, reach, attain
audāx, audācis bold, daring, confident; auda-cious, presumptuous, rash
caedēs, caedis, -ium *f.* slaughter
cīvīlis, cīvīle of *or* connected with citizens, civil
cōnscientia, cōnscientiae *f.* consciousness, awareness
crēdibilis, crēdibile believable, credible
cupiditās, cupiditātis *f.* desire
discordia, discordiae *f.* discord, dissension, con-flict
dissimulātor, dissimulātōris *m.* dissembler, con-cealer
dominātiō, dominātiōnis *f.* absolute rule, tyranny
ēloquentia, ēloquentiae *f.* eloquence
exerceō, exercēre, exercuī, exercitus keep busy, occupy; exercise, train
familiāris, familiāre of *or* belonging to the house-hold; rēs familiāris, (one's) private property, estate, patrimony

ferōx, ferōcis fierce, savage; high-spirited, defiant
immoderātus, -a, -um without measure, unre-strained, excessive
incrēdibilis, incrēdibile unbelievable
inedia, inediae *f.* lack of food
inopia, inopiae *f.* lack of resources, poverty; lack
intestīnus, -a, -um internal
invādō, invādere, invāsī, invāsus enter (hostilely); take hold of
iuventūs, iuventūtis *f.* youth, early manhood
libīdō, libīdinis *f.* desire, pleasure, passion, lust
nimis (adv.) excessively, too
nōbilis, nōbile noble
parō (1-tr.) prepare; get
pēnsum, pēnsī *n.* weight; importance
prāvus, -a, -um twisted, corrupt, perverse
profūsus, -a, -um generous, lavish
rapīna, rapīnae *f.* plundering, pillaging
rēgnum, rēgnī *n.* kingdom, realm; kingship, rule
simulātor, simulātōris *m.* feigner, pretender
subdolus, -a, -um somewhat crafty, cunning
suprā (adv.) above, beyond; further, more
uterque, utraque, utrumque (indef. pron.) each (of two)
varius, -a, -um varying, changeable
vāstus, -a, -um desolate; vast, immense; ravaged
vigilia, vigiliae *f.* wakefulness

artibus auxerat, quās suprā memorāvī. incitābant praetereā conruptī cīvitātis mōrēs, quōs pessuma ac dīvorsa, inter sē mala, luxuria atque avāritia, vexābant. rēs ipsa hortārī vidētur, quoniam dē mōribus cīvitātis tempus admonuit, suprā repetere ac paucīs* īnstitūta maiōrum domī mīlitiaeque, quō modō rem pūblicam habuerint quantamque relīquerint, ut† paulātim inmūtāta ex pulcherrumā <atque optumā> pessuma ac flāgitiōsissuma facta sit, disserere.

*paucīs, *sc.* verbīs
†ut, *here* (interrog. adv.), how
admoneō (ad- + moneō) bring to mind, remind, suggest
augeō, augēre, auxī, auctus grow, increase
avāritia, avāritiae *f.* greed, avarice
corrumpō, corrumpere, corrūpī, corruptus corrupt
disserō, disserere, disseruī, dissertus examine, discuss, treat
dīversus, -a, -um opposite, separate, different
flāgitiōsus, -a, -um shameful, disgraceful, infamous

immūtō (in- + mūtō) (1-tr.) change, alter, transform
incitō (1-tr.) rouse, excite, urge forward
īnstitūtum, īnstitūtī *n.* custom, institution
luxuria, luxuriae *f.* extravagance, excess, luxury
memorō (1-tr.) mention, recount, tell
mīlitia, mīlitiae *f.* military service; mīlitiae = *loc.*
paulātim (adv.) little by little, gradually
praetereā (adv.) besides, furthermore, in addition
repetō (re- + petō) seek again, seek back
suprā (adv.) above, beyond; further, more
vexō (1-tr.) trouble, disturb, harass

3. Vergil, *Aeneid* II.547–58

cui Pyrrhus: "referēs ergō haec et nuntius ībis

Pēlīdae genitōrī. illī mea trīstia facta

dēgeneremque Neoptolemum nārrāre mementō.

nunc morere." hoc dīcēns altāria ad* ipsa trementem　　　　　550

trāxit et in multō lāpsantem sanguine nātī,

implicuitque comam laevā, dextrāque coruscum

extulit ac laterī capulō tenus abdidit ēnsem.

haec fīnis Priamī fātōrum, hic exitus illum

sorte tulit† Troiam incēnsam et prōlāpsa videntem　　　　　555

Pergama, tot quondam populīs terrīsque superbum

rēgnātōrem Asiae. iacet ingēns lītore truncus,

āvulsumque umerīs caput et sine nōmine corpus.

***ad**, *here*, at, near

†**ferō**, *here*, carry away

abdō (ab- + **dō**) hide, put away; plunge, bury

altāria, altārium *n. pl.* (high) altar (for sacrifice)

Asia, Asiae *f.* Asia, a Roman province (Asia Minor)

āvellō, āvellere, āvellī or **āvolsī, āvulsus** tear away

capulus, capulī *m.* sword handle, hilt

coma, comae *f.* hair

coruscus, -a, -um quivering; glittering, gleaming, flashing

dēgener, dēgeneris low-born; degenerate

dexter, dextra, dextrum right; *as fem. subst.* (*sc.* **manus**), right hand

ēnsis, ēnsis *m.* sword

ergō (adv.) therefore

exitus, exitūs *m.* departure; end, conclusion

efferō (ex- + **ferō**), **efferre, extulī, ēlātus** carry out; raise

genitor, genitōris *m.* father

iaceō, iacēre, iacuī, —— lie, rest; lie dead

implicō, implicāre, implicāvī or **implicuī, implicātus** or **implicitus** entwine, enfold; take hold of

incendō, incendere, incendī, incēnsus set on fire, (cause to) burn

laevus, -a, -um left; *as fem. subst.* (*sc.* **manus**), left hand

lāpsō (1-intr.) lose one's footing, slip

latus, lateris *n.* side, flank

lītus, lītoris *n.* shore, beach

nārrō (1-tr.) tell, say; describe

Neoptolemus, Neoptolemī *m.* Neoptolemus, son of Achilles (= Pyrrhus)

nuntius, nuntiī *m.* messenger

Pēlīdēs, Pēlīdae *m.* son of Peleus, Achilles

Pergama, Pergamōrum *n. pl.* Pergama, citadel of Troy

prōlābor, prōlābī, prōlāpsus sum slip forward; give way, collapse

Pyrrhus, Pyrrhī *m.* Pyrrhus, son of Achilles (= Neoptolemus)

quondam (adv.) at one time, once, formerly

rēgnātor, rēgnātōris *m.* ruler, king, lord

sanguis, sanguinis *m.* blood

sors, sortis, -ium *f.* lot, portion; destiny

superbus, -a, -um proud; haughty

tenus (prep. + *preceding* abl.) (right) up to, as far as

trahō, trahere, trāxī, tractus draw, drag

tremō, tremere, tremuī, —— tremble, quiver, quake

trīstis, trīste sad, gloomy, melancholy, grim

truncus, truncī *m.* trunk, torso

umerus, umerī *m.* shoulder

4. Ovid, *Metamorphōsēs* I.540–67

qui tamen īnsequitur pennīs adiūtus amōris,   540

ōcior est requiemque negat tergōque fugācis

inminet et crīnem sparsum cervīcibus adflat.

vīribus absūmptīs expalluit illa citaeque

victa labōre fugae spectāns Pēnēidas undās

"fer, pater," inquit "opem! sī flūmina nūmen habētis,   545

quā nimium placuī, mūtandō perde figūram!"   547

vix prece fīnītā torpor gravis occupat artūs,

mollia cinguntur tenuī praecordia librō,†

in frondem crīnēs, in rāmōs bracchia crēscunt,   550

pēs modo tam vēlōx pigrīs rādīcibus haeret,

ōra cacūmen habet: remanet nitor ūnus in illā.

hanc quoque Phoebus amat positāque in stīpite dextrā

sentit adhūc trepidāre novō sub cortice pectus

*A line is missing because of textual corruption.

†liber, *here,* (inner) bark (of a tree)

absūmō, absūmere, absūmpsī, absūmptus
use up, spend; exhaust

adhūc (adv.) up to the present time; still

adiuvō, adiuvāre, adiūvī, adiūtus aid, assist;
strengthen, nourish

afflō (1-tr.) breathe upon

artus, artūs *m.* joint (of the body), limb

bracchium, bracchiī *n.* (lower) arm

cacūmen, cacūminis *n.* peak, top (of a tree)

cervīx, cervīcis *f.* in sing. or pl. neck

citus, -a, -um swift

cortex, corticis *m.* or *f.* outer covering of a tree,
bark

crēscō, crēscere, crēvī, crētus grow, increase

crīnis, crīnis, -ium *m.* in sing. or pl. hair

dexter, dextra, dextrum right; *as fem. subst.*
(*sc.* **manus**), right hand

expallēscō, expallēscere, expalluī, —— turn pale

figūra, figūrae *f.* form, shape, appearance

fīniō, fīnīre, fīnīvī or **fīniī, fīnītus** end, complete,
conclude

flūmen, flūminis *n.* river, stream

frōns, frondis *f.* foliage, leafy bough

fugāx, fugācis fugitive, fleeing, running away

haereō, haerēre, haesī, haesūrus cling, stick
(+ dat.)

immineō, imminēre, ——, —— hang over,
threaten (+ dat.)

inquam (defective verb) say; **inquit** = *3rd sing.*
pres. act. indic.

īnsequor (**in-** + **sequor**) follow closely, pursue,
chase

mollis, molle gentle, mild, soft

negō (1-tr.) deny, refuse

nimium (adv.) too much, excessively

nitor, nitōris *m.* brightness, splendor

occupō (1-tr.) seize; occupy

ōcior, ōcius swifter

ops, opis *f.* aid, help

Pēnēis, Pēnēidos of *or* belonging to the river god
Peneus; **Pēnēidas** = *fem. pl. acc.*

penna, pennae *f.* wing

pēs, pedis *m.* foot

Phoebus, Phoebī *m.* Phoebus (Apollo)

piger, pigra, pigrum sluggish, inactive, slow

praecordia, praecordiōrum *n. pl.* (lower) chest,
breast

***prex, *precis** *f.* prayer

rādīx, rādīcis *f.* root

rāmus, rāmī *m.* branch

remaneō (**re-** + **maneō**) remain

requiēs, requiētis *f.* rest, respite; **requiem** = *acc.*
sing.

spargō, spargere, sparsī, sparsus scatter,
distribute

stīpes, stīpitis *m.* trunk (of a tree)

tenuis, tenue thin, slight, slender

tergum, tergī *n.* back

torpor, torpōris *m.* loss of power, numbness

trepidō (1-intr.) tremble

unda, undae *f.* wave

vēlōx, vēlōcis rapid, swift, speedy

conplexusque suīs rāmōs ut membra lacertīs   555

ōscula dat lignō; refugit tamen ōscula lignum.

cui deus "at, quoniam coniūnx mea nōn potes esse,

arbor eris certē" dīxit "mea! semper habēbunt

tē coma, tē citharae, tē nostrae, laure, pharetrae;

tū ducibus Latiīs aderis, cum laeta triumphum   560

vōx canet et vīsent longās Capitōlia pompās;

postibus augustīs eadem fīdissima custōs

ante forēs stābis mediamque* tuēbere quercum,

utque meum intōnsīs caput est iuvenāle capillīs,

tū quoque perpetuōs semper gere frondis honōrēs!"   565

fīnierat Paeān: factīs modo laurea rāmīs

adnuit utque caput vīsa est agitāsse cacūmen.

---

*medius, *here,* in the middle

adnuō, adnuere, adnuī, adnūtum nod (in agreement), assent

agitō (1-tr.) stir up, set in motion, shake

arbor, arboris *f.* tree

at (conj.) but

augustus, -a, -um solemn, venerable; majestic, august

cacūmen, cacūminis *n.* peak, top (of a tree)

capillus, capillī *m. in sing. or pl.* hair

Capitōlia, Capitōliōrum *n. pl.* (the) Capitoline hill, site of the Temple of Jupiter Optimus Maximus and the end point of a triumph

cithara, citharae *f.* cithara; lute

coma, comae *f.* hair

coniūnx, coniugis *m. or f.* spouse; husband; wife

complector, complectī, complexus sum embrace

custōs, custōdis *m. or f.* guardian, protector, sentry

fīdus, -a, -um trustworthy

fīniō, fīnīre, fīnīvī or **fīniī, fīnītus** end, complete, conclude

foris, foris, -ium *f.* door; *in pl.,* double doors

frōns, frondis *f.* foliage, leafy bough

intōnsus, -a, -um uncut, unshorn

iuvenālis, iuvenāle of or belonging to a young man, youthful, young

lacertus, lacertī *m.* (upper) arm

Latius, -a, -um of Latium, Latin, Roman

laurea, laureae *f.* laurel tree

laurus, laurī *f.* laurel tree; sprig *or* branch of laurel

lignum, lignī *n.* wood

membrum, membrī *n.* limb

ōsculum, ōsculī *n.* kiss

Paeān, Paeānis *m.* Paean, a Greek god (= Apollo)

perpetuus, -a, -um continuous, without interruption; perpetual, everlasting

pharetra, pharetrae *f.* quiver

pompa, pompae *f.* (ceremonial) procession, parade

postis, postis, -ium *m.* doorpost, jamb

quercus, quercūs *f.* oak tree; oak wreath

rāmus, rāmī *m.* branch

refugiō (re- + fugiō) flee, shun

triumphus, triumphī *m.* (a) triumph, the procession through Rome of a victorious general; a ritual cry that accompanies a triumph

tueor, tuērī, tuitus or **tūtus sum** look at; protect

vīsō, vīsere, vīsī, vīsus go to see; view, behold

LATIN TO ENGLISH VOCABULARY

Note: This Latin to English Vocabulary includes all words from vocabulary lists in both Parts I and II of *Learn to Read Latin*. Numbers in parentheses refer to chapter (6, e.g.) or section (§16, e.g.) in which the vocabulary word is introduced. If a chapter number is listed, the word appears in the chapter-opening vocabulary list.

ā, ab (prep. + abl.) (away) from (1); (prep. + abl.) by (3)

A. = Aulus, Aulī *m.* Aulus (§16)

abeō, abīre, abiī, abitum go away (5)

absēns, absentis absent (14)

absum, abesse, āfuī, āfutūrus be absent, be distant (14)

ac or **atque** (conj.) and (what's more) (3)

accēdō, accēdere, accessī, accessum go *or* come to, approach (5)

accidō, accidere, accidī, —— happen (14)

accipiō, accipere, accēpī, acceptus receive; accept; hear (of), learn (of) (5)

ācer, ācris, ācre sharp, keen; fierce (8)

acerbus, -a, -um bitter; harsh (7)

aciēs, aciēī *f.* sharp edge; keenness; battle line (8)

ad (prep. + acc.) toward, to (1); (prep. + acc.) for the purpose of (13)

adeō (adv.) to such *or* so great an extent, (so) very (14)

adsum, adesse, adfuī, adfutūrus be present, be near (14)

Aenēās, Aenēae *m.* Aeneas; **Aenēān** = *acc. sing.;* **Aenēā** = *voc. sing.* (§16)

aequus, -a, -um level, even; equitable, just; calm, tranquil (10)

aestimō (1-tr.) estimate, value (13)

aetās, aetātis *f.* age; lifetime; time (14)

ager, agrī *m.* field (1)

agmen, agminis *n.* line (of march), column; army; multitude, throng (14)

agō, agere, ēgī, āctus drive; do; spend, conduct (4)
    causam agere (idiom) to conduct *or* plead a case (4)
    grātiās agere (idiom) to give thanks (12)

age, agite, *used to strengthen other commands,* come on! (4)

agricola, agricolae *m.* farmer (1)

aliquī, aliqua, aliquod (indef. adj.) some, any (14)

aliquis, aliquid (indef. pron.) someone, something; anyone, anything (14)

alius, alia, aliud other, another (9)

alter, altera, alterum the other (of two) (9)

altum, altī *n.* deep sea; height (4)

altus, -a, -um tall, high; deep (4)

ambulō (1-intr.) walk (2)

amīcitia, amīcitiae *f.* friendship (5)

amīcus, -a, -um friendly (+ dat.) (3)

amīcus, amīcī *m.* friend (3)

amō (1-tr.) love (2)

amor, amōris *m.* love (6)

Amor, Amōris *m.* Love, Amor (§60)

an (conj.) *introduces an alternative question,* or; *introduces an indirect question,* whether (12)
    —— . . . an . . . whether . . . or . . . (12)

anima, animae *f.* breath; life force; soul (1)

animal, animālis, -ium *n.* animal (6)

animus, animī *m.* (rational) soul, mind; spirit; *in pl.,* strong feelings (2)

annus, annī *m.* year (8)

ante (adv.) before, earlier, previously; (prep. + acc.) before; in front of (7)

antequam (conj.) before (13)

antīquus, -a, -um old, ancient (6)

M. Antōnius, M. Antōniī *m.* Marcus Antonius, Marc Antony (§16)

Apollō, Apollinis *m.* Apollo (§60)

App. = Appius, Appiī *m.* Appius (§16)

Appius, Appiī *m.* Appius (§16)

apud (prep. + acc.) at, near; at the house of, in the presence of, among (10)

āra, ārae *f.* altar (7)

arbitror (1-tr.) judge, consider, think (11)

arma, armōrum *n. pl.* arms, weapons (2)

ars, artis, -ium *f.* skill, art; guile; trick (7)

Athēnae, Athēnārum *f. pl.* Athens (6)

atque or **ac** (conj.) and (what's more) (3)

auctōritās, auctōritātis *f.* authority; influence (14)

audācia, audāciae *f.* boldness; recklessness, audacity (11)

audeō, audēre, ausus sum dare (8)

audiō, audīre, audīvī, audītus hear, listen (to) (4)

auferō, auferre, abstulī, ablātus carry away, take away, remove (7)

Aulus, Aulī *m.* Aulus (§16)

aurum, aurī *n.* gold (1)

aut (conj.) or; **aut . . . aut . . .** either . . . or . . . (7)

autem (postpositive conj.) however; moreover (6)

auxilia, auxiliōrum *n. pl.* auxiliary troops (4)

auxilium, auxiliī *n.* aid, help (4)

Bacchus, Bacchī *m.* Bacchus (§60)

bellum, bellī *n.* war (1)

    bellum gerere (idiom) to wage war (4)

bene (adv.) well (5)

    bene velle (idiom) to wish well (12)

bonus, -a, -um good (3)

brevis, breve short, brief (11)

C. = Gaius, Gaiī *m.* Gaius (§16)

cadō, cadere, cecidī, cāsum fall, sink; die (10)

caecus, -a, -um blind; hidden, secret, dark (9)

caelum, caelī *n.* sky, heaven (4)

Caesar, Caesaris *m.* Caesar

campus, campī *m.* (flat) plain (11)

canō, canere, cecinī, cantus sing (of) (4)

capiō, capere, cēpī, captus take (up), capture; win (4)

    cōnsilium capere (idiom) to form a plan (4)

caput, capitis *n.* head (15)

careō, carēre, caruī, caritūrus lack, be without, be free from (+ abl.) (6)

carmen, carminis *n.* song, poem (6)

Carthāgō, Carthāginis *f.* Carthage (6)

cārus, -a, -um precious; dear (to) (+ dat.) (7)

castra, castrōrum *n. pl.* (military) camp (11)

    castra movēre (idiom) to break camp (11)

    castra pōnere (idiom) to pitch *or* make camp (11)

cāsus, cāsūs *m.* fall; occurrence, chance, misfortune (10)

Catilīna, Catilīnae *m.* Catiline (§16)

Catō, Catōnis *m.* Cato (§60)

Catullus, Catullī *m.* Catullus (§16)

causā (+ *preceding* gen.) for the purpose of, for the sake of (13)

causa, causae *f.* reason, cause; case (4)

    causam agere (idiom) to conduct *or* plead a case (4)

cēdō, cēdere, cessī, cessum go, move; yield; withdraw (5)

celer, celeris, celere swift (15)

centēsimus, -a, -um hundredth (§91)

centum (indeclinable adj.) hundred (§91)

Cerēs, Cereris *f.* Ceres (§60)

certē (adv.) surely, certainly; at least (7)

certō (adv.) surely, certainly (7)

certus, -a, -um sure, certain, reliable (7)

cēterus, -a, -um rest (of), remaining part (of), (the) other (13)

Cicerō, Cicerōnis *m.* Cicero (§60)

cingō, cingere, cīnxī, cīnctus surround; gird (on oneself) (15)

circumdō, circumdare, circumdedī, circumdatus place round; surround (15)

cīvis, cīvis, -ium *m.* or *f.* citizen (6)

cīvitās, cīvitātis *f.* state, citizenry; citizenship (7)

clārus, -a, -um bright, clear; famous (4)

Cn. = Gnaeus, Gnaeī *m.* Gnaeus (§16)

——, ——, coepī, coeptus (defective verb) began, have begun (13)

cōgitō (1-tr.) think; ponder (2)

cognōscō, cognōscere, cognōvī, cognitus come to know, learn; *in perfect,* know (10)

cōnferō, cōnferre, contulī, collātus bring together; collect, compare; direct; confer (on) (14)

    sē cōnferre (idiom) to betake oneself, to go (14)

cōnficiō, cōnficere, cōnfēcī, cōnfectus accomplish, complete (12)

cōnor (1-tr.) try, attempt (8)

cōnsilium, cōnsiliī *n.* deliberation; plan, advice; judgment (1)

    cōnsilium capere (idiom) to form a plan (4)

cōnstituō, cōnstituere, cōnstituī, cōnstitūtus set up, establish; decide (15)

cōnsul, cōnsulis *m.* consul (8)

cōnsulātus, cōnsulātūs *m.* consulship (8)

contrā (adv.) face to face; in opposition, in turn; (prep. + acc.) facing; against, contrary to (10)

cōpia, cōpiae *f.* wealth, abundance; *in pl.,* troops, forces (7)

Corinna, Corinnae *f.* Corinna (§60)

L. Cornēlius Sulla, L. Cornēliī Sullae *m.* Lucius Cornelius Sulla (§16)

Cornēlius Tacitus, Cornēliī Tacitī *m.* Cornelius Tacitus (§16)

corpus, corporis *n.* body (6)

Crassus, Crassī *m.* Crassus (§16)

crēdō, crēdere, crēdidī, crēditus trust, believe (+ dat.) (11)

cum (prep. + abl.) with (1); (conj.) when; since; although (12)

cūnctus, -a, -um all (14)

Cupīdō, Cupīdinis *m.* Cupid, Amor (§60)

cupidus, -a, -um desirous (+ gen.) (4)

cupiō, cupere, cupiī or **cupīvī, cupītus** desire, long for, want (7)

cūr (interrog. adv.) why (2)

cūra, cūrae *f.* care, concern; anxiety (2)

Cynthia, Cynthiae *f.* Cynthia (§60)

D. = Decimus, Decimī *m.* Decimus (§16)

dē (prep. + abl.) (down) from; about, concerning (1)

dea, deae *f.* goddess (1)

dēbeō, dēbēre, dēbuī, dēbitus owe; ought (2)

decem (indeclinable adj.) ten (4)

decimus, -a, -um tenth (§91)

Decimus, Decimī *m.* Decimus (§16)

dēleō, dēlēre, dēlēvī, dēlētus destroy (10)

dēterreō, dēterrēre, dēterruī, dēterritus deter, prevent (15)

deus, deī *m.* god (1)

Diāna, Diānae *f.* Diana (§60)

dīcō, dīcere, dīxī, dictus say, speak, tell (4)

dictum, dictī *n.* word; saying (6)

Dīdō, Dīdōnis *f.* Dido (§60)

diēs, diēī *m.* or *f.* day (8)

differō, differre, distulī, dīlātus carry in different directions, scatter; postpone, defer; *(intr.)* differ, be different (7)

difficilis, difficile difficult (8)

difficiliter or **difficulter** (adv.) with difficulty (8)

dignus, -a, -um worthy (of) (+ abl.) (12)

dīligentia, dīligentiae *f.* diligence, attentiveness (3)

Dīs, Dītis *m.* Dis, Pluto (§60)

discēdō, discēdere, discessī, discessum go away, depart (5)

dissimilis, dissimile dissimilar, unlike, different (+ gen. or dat.) (11)

diū (adv.) for a long time (11)

  diūtius (adv.) longer (11)

  diūtissimē (adv.) longest (11)

dīvīnus, -a, -um belonging to the gods, divine (§60)

dīvus, -a, -um deified, divine (§60)

dō, dare, dedī, datus give, grant (2)

  poenās dare (idiom) to pay the penalty (2)

  vēla dare (idiom) to set sail

dominus, dominī *m.* master, lord (1)

domus, domī *f.* house, home (6);

domus, domūs *f.* house, home (8)

dōnec (conj.) while, as long as; until (13)

dōnō (1-tr.) give; present, reward (2)

dōnum, dōnī *n.* gift (1)

dubitō (1-tr.) hesitate; doubt (12)

dubium, dubiī *n.* doubt, hesitation (12)

dubius, -a, -um doubtful (12)

dūcō, dūcere, dūxī, ductus lead; consider (4)

dulcis, dulce sweet, pleasant (15)

dum (conj.) while, as long as; until; provided that (13)

dummodo (conj.) provided that (13)

duo, duae, duo two (§91)

dūrus, -a, -um hard; harsh (5)

dux, ducis *m.* or *f.* leader (10)

ē, ex (prep. + abl.) (out) from (1)

ecce (interj.) lo! behold! look!

efficiō, efficere, effēcī, effectus make; bring about (14)

ego, meī (personal pron.) I; me (4)

—, meī (reflexive pron.) myself (5)

ēgredior, ēgredī, ēgressus sum go *or* come out (13)

ēiciō, ēicere, ēiēcī, ēiectus throw out, expel

  sē ēicere (idiom) to rush forth (11)

emō, emere, ēmī, ēmptus buy (13)

enim (postpositive conj.) in fact, indeed; for (2)

eō (adv.) to that place, thither (§130)

eō, īre, iī or **īvī, itum** go (3)

eōdem (adv.) to the same place (§130)

equidem (adv.) indeed, certainly; for my part (4)

ēripiō, ēripere, ēripuī, ēreptus tear away, snatch away (15)

errō (1-intr.) wander; err, make a mistake (2)

et (conj.) and; **et . . . et . . .** both . . . and . . .; (adv.) even, also (1)

etenim (conj.) and indeed; for in fact (2)

etiam (adv.) also, even; still (7)

etsī (conj.) although (5)

exercitus, exercitūs *m.* army (8)

experior, experīrī, expertus sum test; try; experience (8)

ex(s)ilium, ex(s)iliī *n.* exile, banishment (9)

ex(s)pectō (1-tr.) wait for, await, expect (13)

facile (adv.) easily, readily (8)

facilis, facile easy (8)

faciō, facere, fēcī, factus make; do (4); reckon (13)

factum, factī *n.* deed (1)

falsō (adv.) falsely (7)

falsus, -a, -um deceptive, false (7)

fāma, fāmae *f.* report, rumor; reputation, fame (1)

fās (indeclinable noun) *n.* (what is divinely) right; (what is) permitted (12)

fateor, fatērī, fassus sum confess, admit (8)

fātum, fātī *n.* destiny, fate; *in pl. (often),* death (5)

fēlīx, fēlīcis lucky, fortunate, happy (8)

fēmina, fēminae *f.* woman; wife (1)

ferō, ferre, tulī, lātus bring, bear, carry; endure (5)
    lēgem ferre (idiom) to pass a law (9)
    sē ferre (idiom) to proceed (quickly), to go (5)

ferrum, ferrī *n.* iron; sword (1)

fidēs, fideī *f.* faith, trust; trustworthiness; confidence (8)

fīlia, fīliae *f.* daughter (1)

fīlius, fīliī *m.* son (1)

fīnis, fīnis, -ium *m. or f.* end, limit, boundary; *in pl.,* territory (10)

fīō, fierī, factus sum become, happen; be made, be done (13)

for (1-tr.) speak, say (15)

fore = futūrus, -a, -um esse (11)

fors, fortis, -ium *f.* chance, luck (12)

fortis, forte brave; strong (8)

fortūna, fortūnae *f.* fortune, chance (7)

forum, forī *n.* public square, marketplace, forum (3)

frāter, frātris *m.* brother (6)

fuga, fugae *f.* flight (8)

fugiō, fugere, fūgī, fugitūrus flee (7)

Gaius, Gaiī *m.* Gaius (§16)

gēns, gentis, -ium *f.* nation, people; clan, family (12)

genus, generis *n.* descent, origin; race, stock; kind, sort (10)

gerō, gerere, gessī, gestus bear; manage, conduct; perform (4)
    bellum gerere (idiom) to wage war (4)

gladius, gladiī *m.* sword (1)

glōria, glōriae *f.* renown, glory (4)

Gnaeus, Gnaeī *m.* Gnaeus (§16)

Gracchus, Gracchī *m.* Gracchus (either of the Gracchi brothers) (§16)

gradior, gradī, gressus sum walk, step, proceed (13)

Graecia, Graeciae *f.* Greece (§16)

grātiā (+ *preceding* gen.) for the purpose of, for the sake of (13)

grātia, grātiae *f.* favor, kindness; gratitude, thanks (12)
    grātiās agere (idiom) to give thanks (12)
    grātiam or **grātiās habēre** (idiom) to feel grateful (12)
    grātiam or **grātiās referre** (idiom) to render thanks, to return a favor (12)

grātus, -a, -um charming, pleasing; grateful, pleased (13)

gravis, grave heavy, deep; important, serious; severe (9)

habeō, habēre, habuī, habitus have, hold; consider (2)
    grātiam or **grātiās habēre** (idiom) to feel grateful (12)
    ōrātiōnem habēre (idiom) to make a speech (10)

Hannibal, Hannibalis *m.* Hannibal (§60)

haud (adv.) not at all, by no means (14)

herc(u)le (interj.) by Hercules! (§71)

heu (interj.) alas! O!

hīc (adv.) here, in this place; at this time (§130)

hic, haec, hoc (demonstr. adj./pron.) this; these (8)

hinc (adv.) from here, hence; henceforth; **hinc . . . hinc . . .** on this side . . . on that side . . .; **hinc . . . illinc . . .** on this side . . . on that side . . . (§130)

homō, hominis *m.* human being, man; *in pl.,* people (6)

honestus, -a, -um honorable, respectable (10)

honor or **honōs, honōris** *m.* honor, respect; (political) office (13)

Q. Horātius Flaccus, Q. Horātiī Flaccī *m.* Quintus Horatius Flaccus, Horace (§16)

hortor (1-tr.) urge, encourage, exhort (9)

hostis, hostis, -ium *m.* (public) enemy (6)

hūc (adv.) to here, hither (§130)

humilis, humile humble (11)

iaciō, iacere, iēcī, iactus throw; utter; lay, establish (11)

iam (adv.) now; by now, by then, already (9)

ibi (adv.) in that place, there; then, thereupon (§130)

īdem, eadem, idem same (9)

igitur (postpositive conj.) therefore (11)

ignis, ignis, -ium *m.* fire (11)

Īlium, Īliī *n.* Ilium, Troy (§16)

ille, illa, illud (demonstr. adj./pron.) that; those (8)

illīc (adv.) there, in that place (§130)

illinc (adv.) from there, thence; **hinc . . . illinc . . .** on this side . . . on that side . . . (§130)

illūc (adv.) to there, thither (§130)

impediō, impedīre, impedīvī or **impediī, impedītus** hinder, impede (15)

imperātor, imperātōris *m.* commander, general (11)

imperium, imperiī *n.* power, authority, command; empire (3)

imperō (1-intr.) give an order, order, command (+ dat.) (9)

impius, -a, -um disloyal, wicked (5)

in (prep. + acc.) into, onto; against; (prep. + abl.) in, on (1)

inceptum, inceptī *n.* beginning, undertaking (13)

incertō (adv.) uncertainly (7)

incertus, -a, -um unsure, uncertain, unreliable (7)

incipiō, incipere, incēpī, inceptus take on, begin (13)

incola, incolae *m. or f.* inhabitant (3)

inde (adv.) from that place, from there, thence; from that time, thereupon (§130)

indignus, -a, -um unworthy (of) (+ abl.) (12)

īnfēlīx, īnfēlīcis unlucky, unfortunate, unhappy (8)

īnferō, īnferre, intulī, illātus carry (into); inflict (on) (12)

ingenium, ingeniī n. ability, talent; disposition (7)

ingēns, ingentis huge (8)

ingrātus, -a, -um unpleasant, displeasing; ungrateful, displeased (13)

inimīcitia, inimīcitiae f. enmity, hostility; in pl., unfriendly relations, enmity (5)

inimīcus, -a, -um unfriendly, hostile (+ dat.) (3)

inimīcus, inimīcī m. (personal) enemy (3)

inīquus, -a, -um uneven; inequitable, unjust (10)

īnsidiae, īnsidiārum f. pl. ambush, plot, treachery (7)

īnsula, īnsulae f. island (1)

intellegō, intellegere, intellēxī, intellēctus understand (6)

inter (prep. + acc.) between, among; during (6)

interest, interesse, interfuit it is important, it concerns (15)

interficiō, interficere, interfēcī, interfectus kill (5)

inveniō, invenīre, invēnī, inventus find, discover (11)

invidia, invidiae f. envy, jealousy; ill-will, resentment (4)

ipse, ipsa, ipsum (intensive adj.) -self, -selves; very (5)

īra, īrae f. anger, wrath (2)

is, ea, id (demonstr. adj.) this, that; these, those; (personal pron.) he, she, it; they; him, her, it; them (4)

iste, ista, istud (demonstr. adj./pron.) that (of yours); those (of yours) (8)

ita (adv.) in this manner, thus, so (7)

Italia, Italiae f. Italy (1)

iubeō, iubēre, iussī, iussus order (2)

Iūlia, Iūliae f. Julia (§16)

C. Iūlius Caesar, C. Iūliī Caesaris m. Gaius Julius Caesar (§60)

Iūnō, Iūnōnis f. Juno (§60)

Iuppiter, Iovis m. Jupiter (§60)

iūre (adv.) rightly, justly (6)

iūs, iūris n. right, law; judgment; court (6)

L. = Lūcius, Lūciī m. Lucius (§16)

labor, labōris m. work; effort, hardship (10)

labōrō (1-intr.) work; suffer, be distressed (2)

laetus, -a, -um happy (3)

Latīnus, Latīnī m. Latinus (§60)

laudō (1-tr.) praise (3)

lēgātus, lēgātī m. legate, envoy; lieutenant (10)

legiō, legiōnis f. legion (11)

legō, legere, lēgī, lēctus gather; choose; read (6)

Lesbia, Lesbiae f. Lesbia (§60)

levis, leve light; trivial; fickle (9)

lēx, lēgis f. law
    lēgem ferre (idiom) to pass a law (9)

līber, lībera, līberum free (3)

Līber, Līberī m. Liber, Bacchus (§60)

liber, librī m. book (1)

līberō (1-tr.) free, liberate (6)

lībertās, lībertātis f. freedom (9)

licet, licēre, licuit or licitum est it is permitted (14)

M. Licinius Crassus, M. Liciniī Crassī m. Marcus Licinius Crassus (§16)

littera, litterae f. letter (of the alphabet); in pl., letter, epistle; literature (12)

Līvia, Līviae f. Livia (§16)

locus, locī m. place; loca, locōrum n. pl. places (8)

longē (adv.) a long way, far; by far (11)

longus, -a, -um long; far; long-standing; far-reaching (11)

loquor, loquī, locūtus sum speak (11)

Lūcius, Lūciī m. Lucius (§16)

lūmen, lūminis n. light, radiance; in pl., eyes (13)

lūna, lūnae f. moon (14)

lūx, lūcis f. light, daylight (11)
    prīmā lūce (idiom) at daybreak

M. = Marcus, Marcī m. Marcus (§16)

M' = Manius, Maniī, m. Manius (§16)

magis (adv.) more greatly (11)

magnopere (adv.) greatly (10)

magnus, -a, -um large, big; great (3)

maior, maius (adj.) greater (11)

maiōrēs, maiōrum m. pl. ancestors (11)

male (adv.) badly (5)
    male velle (idiom) to wish ill (12)

mālō, mālle, māluī, —— want more, prefer (12)

malus, -a, -um bad, evil (3)

maneō, manēre, mānsī, mānsūrus remain, stay; await (7)

Manius, Maniī, m. Manius (§16)

manus, manūs f. hand; band, troop (8)

Marcus, Marcī m. Marcus (§16)

mare, maris, *-ium n. sea (6)

Mars, Martis m. Mars (§60)

māter, mātris f. mother (6)

maximē (adv.) most greatly; especially (11)

maximus, -a, -um greatest (11)

medius, -a, -um middle (of); as subst., midst (10)

mehercule or meherculēs (interj.) by Hercules! (§71)

——, meī (reflexive pron.) myself (5)

melior, melius (adj.) better (11)

melius (adv.) better (11)

meminī, meminisse (defective verb) remember, be mindful (of) (5)

memoria, memoriae f. memory (12)

mēns, mentis, -ium f. mind; intention, purpose; attitude (6)

Mercurius, Mercuriī m. Mercury (§60)

metuō, metuere, metuī, —— fear, dread (14)

metus, metūs *m.* fear, dread, anxiety (9)

meus, -a, -um my, mine (4); my (own) (5)

mī, *masc. sing. voc. of* **meus, -a, -um** (4)

mīles, mīlitis *m.* soldier (6)

mīlle; mīlia, mīlium thousand (§91)

mīllēsimus, -a, -um thousandth (§91)

Minerva, Minervae *f.* Minerva (§60)

minimē (adv.) least; not at all (11)

minimus, -a, -um smallest (11)

minor, minus (adj.) smaller (11)

minus (adv.) less (11)

miser, misera, miserum wretched, pitiable, miserable (3)

miseret, miserēre, miseruit or **miseritum est** it moves (one) to pity (15)

mittō, mittere, mīsī, missus send (4)

modo (adv.) only, just; now, just now (12); (conj.) provided that (13)

modus, modī *m.* measure; limit; rhythm, meter; manner, way (9)

   quō modō, in what manner, how (9)

moenia, moenium *n. pl.* (city) walls (6)

moneō, monēre, monuī, monitus warn; remind; advise (9)

mōns, montis, -ium *m.* mountain (12)

mōnstrō (1-tr.) show, point out (2)

mora, morae *f.* delay (3)

morior, morī, mortuus sum die (8)

moror (1-tr.) hinder, delay, wait (13)

mors, mortis, -ium *f.* death (7)

mōs, mōris *m.* custom, practice; *in pl. (sometimes),* character (10)

mōtus, mōtūs *m.* motion, movement; disturbance (8)

moveō, movēre, mōvī, mōtus set in motion, stir (up), move (2)

mox (adv.) soon; then (3)

multum (adv.) much, a lot (5)

multus, -a, -um much, many (3)

mūrus, mūrī *m.* wall (11)

mūtō (1-tr.) change; take in exchange, give in exchange (13)

nam (conj.) for (2)

namque (conj.) for in fact (2)

nāscor, nāscī, nātus sum be born (10)

nātūra, nātūrae *f.* nature (6)

nātus, nātī *m.* son (10)

nauta, nautae *m.* sailor (1)

-ne (interrog. enclitic particle) *added to the first word of a question* (2)

-ne . . . an . . . whether . . . or . . . (12)

nē (adv.) not (7); (conj.) *introduces negative Purpose clause,* in order that . . . not (9); *introduces negative Indirect Command,* that . . . not (9); (conj.) *introduces positive Fear clause,* that (15)

nē . . . quidem not . . . even (4)

nec or **neque** (conj.-adv.) and not; **neque/nec . . . neque/nec . . .** neither . . . nor . . . (2)

necesse (indeclinable adj.) necessary (14)

necne (conj.) *in Indirect Question,* or not (12)

nefās (indeclinable noun) *n.* (what is divinely) forbidden, sacrilege (12)

nēmō, nēminis *m.* or *f.* no one (10)

Neptūnus, Neptūnī *m.* Neptune (§60)

neque or **nec** (conj./adv.) and not; **neque/nec . . . neque/nec . . .** neither . . . nor . . . (2)

Nerō Claudius Caesar, Nerōnis Claudiī Caesaris *m.* Nero Claudius Caesar, Nero (§60)

nesciō, nescīre, nescīvī or **nesciī, nescītus** not know (11)

neuter, neutra, neutrum neither (of two) (9)

nihil or **nīl** (indeclinable noun) *n.* nothing (3)

nihilum, nihilī or **nīlum, nīlī** *n.* nothing (13)

nisi (conj.) if . . . not, unless (5)

nōlō, nōlle, nōluī, —— be unwilling, not want, not wish (12)

   nōlī, nōlīte (+ inf.) do not (12)

nōmen, nōminis *n.* name (14)

nōn (adv.) not (2)

nōn sōlum . . . sed/vērum etiam . . . not only . . . but also . . . (7)

nōnne (interrog. particle) *introduces a direct question expecting the answer "yes"* (12)

nōnus, -a, -um ninth (§91)

nōs, nostrum/nostrī (personal pron.) we; us (4)

nōscō, nōscere, nōvī, nōtus come to know, learn; *in perfect,* know (10)

noster, nostra, nostrum our, ours (4); our (own) (5)

——, nostrum/nostrī (reflexive pron.) ourselves (5)

novem (indeclinable adj.) nine (§91)

novus, -a, -um new; strange (6)

nox, noctis, -ium *f.* night (8)

nūllus, -a, -um not any, no (9)

num (interrogative particle) *introduces a direct question expecting the answer "no"; introduces an Indirect Question,* whether (12)

nūmen, nūminis *n.* divine power, divinity, divine spirit, numen (15)

numquam (adv.) never (6)

nunc (adv.) now (3)

ō (interj.) O (1)

ob (prep. + acc.) on account of, because of (9)

oblīvīscor, oblīvīscī, oblītus sum forget (+ gen.) (12)

obstō, obstāre, obstitī, obstātum stand in the way; hinder, block (15) occidēns, occidentis *m.* west (14)

occidō, occidere, occidī, occāsūrus fall, set; die (14)

octāvus, -a, -um eighth (§91)

octō (indeclinable adj.) eight (§91)

oculus, oculī *m.* eye (9)

ōdī, ōdisse (defective verb) hate (5)

odium, odiī *n.* hatred (3)

omnīnō (adv.) entirely; *in negative or virtual negative statements or questions,* at all (8)

omnis, omne every; all (8)

oportet, oportēre, oportuit it is proper, it is right (14)

oppidum, oppidī *n.* town (1)

opprimō, opprimere, oppressī, oppressus press on; close; overwhelm, oppress (14)

oppugnō (1-tr.) attack (10)

optimē (adv.) best (11)

optimus, -a, -um best (11)

optō (1-tr.) desire; choose (2)

opus, operis *n.* work, need (10)
    opus est there is need of (+ abl. *or* nom.) (10)

ōrātiō, ōrātiōnis *f.* oration, speech (10)
    ōrātiōnem habēre (idiom) to make a speech (10)

ōrātor, ōrātōris *m.* speaker (10)

orbis, orbis, -ium *m.* ring, circle (15)
    orbis terrārum world (15)

oriēns, orientis *m.* east (14)

orior, orīrī, ortus sum rise, arise (14)

ōrō (1-tr.) pray (for), beg (for) (12)

ōs, ōris *n. in sing. or pl.* mouth; face (14)

P. Ovidius Nāsō, P. Ovidiī Nāsōnis *m.* Publius Ovidius Naso, Ovid (§60)

P. = Publius, Publiī *m.* Publius (§16)

paenitet, paenitēre, paenituit it causes (one) to repent *or* regret (15)

pāreō, pārēre, pāruī, pāritūrus be obedient, obey (+ dat.) (9)

pars, partis, -ium *f.* part; *in sing. or pl.,* (political) faction (7)

parum (indeclinable subst.) too little, not enough; (adv.) too little, inadequately (11)

parvus, -a, -um small, little (3)

pater, patris *m.* father (6)

patior, patī, passus sum experience, suffer, endure; permit, allow (9)

patrēs cōnscrīptī *voc. pl.* enrolled fathers, senators (6)

patria, patriae *f.* country, homeland (1)

paucī, paucae, pauca few (6)

paulum, *paulī *n.* small amount, a little (11)

pāx, pācis *f.* peace; favor (9)

pectus, pectoris *n.* chest, breast; heart (10)

pecūnia, pecūniae *f.* money (1)

peior, peius (comparative adj.) worse (11)

peius (comparative adv.) worse (11)

pellō, pellere, pepulī, pulsus push, drive (off) (9)

per (prep. + acc.) through (4)

perditē (adv.) recklessly, desperately, ruinously (13)

perditus, -a, -um (morally) lost, ruined, depraved (13)

perdō, perdere, perdidī, perditus destroy; lose (13)

pereō, perīre, periī, peritūrus pass away, be destroyed; perish, die (11)

perferō, perferre, pertulī, perlātus suffer, endure; report (10)

perficiō, perficere, perfēcī, perfectus complete, accomplish (5)

perīculum, perīculī *n.* danger (1)

pessimē (adv.) worst (11)

pessimus, -a, -um worst (11)

petō, petere, petiī *or* petīvī, petītus ask (for), seek; attack (7)

piget, pigēre, piguit it disgusts (one), it irks (one) (15)

pius, -a, -um dutiful, loyal (5)

placeō, placēre, placuī, placitum be pleasing, please (+ dat.) (9)

plūrimē (adv.) most (11)

plūrimus, -a, -um most (11)

plūs (adv.) more (11)

plūs; plūrēs, plūra (adj.) more (11)

poena, poenae *f.* punishment, penalty (2)
    poenās dare (idiom) to pay the penalty (2)

poēta, poētae *m.* poet (1)

Cn. Pompeius Magnus, Cn. Pompeiī Magnī *m.* Gnaeus Pompeius Magnus, Pompey the Great (§16)

pōnō, pōnere, posuī, positus put, place; set aside (4)

populus, populī *m.* (the) people; populace (3)

M. Porcius Catō, M. Porciī Catōnis *m.* Marcus Porcius Cato, Cato the Elder *or* Cato the Censor (§60)

possum, posse, potuī, —— be able, can (2)

post (adv.) after(ward), later; behind; (prep. + acc.) after; behind (7)

postquam (conj.) after (5)

praeferō, praeferre, praetulī, praelātus prefer (to) (12)

praeficiō, praeficere, praefēcī, praefectus put in charge (of) (12)

praesum, praeesse, praefuī, praefutūrus be in charge (of) (12)

praeter (prep. + acc.) beyond; except (12)

premō, premere, pressī, pressus press (hard); overpower; check (14)

pretium, pretiī *n.* price, value (13)

Priamus, Priamī *m.* Priam (§60)

prīmum (adv.) first; for the first time (11)
    quam prīmum as soon as possible (11)

prīmus, -a, -um first (§91)

    prīmā lūce (idiom) at daybreak (11)

prior, prius (adj.) earlier (11)

prius (adv.) before, sooner (11)

priusquam (conj.) before (13)

prō (prep. + abl.) in front of; on behalf of, for; in return for, instead of (3)

proelium, proeliī *n.* battle (5)

proficīscor, proficīscī, profectus sum set out, set forth (10)

prohibeō, prohibēre, prohibuī, prohibitus prevent; prohibit, forbid (15)

Sex. Propertius, Sex. Propertiī *m.* Sextus Propertius (§60)

propter (prep. + acc.) on account of, because of (3)

prōvincia, prōvinciae *f.* province (3)

pūblicus, -a, -um public (8)

Publius, Publiī *m.* Publius (§16)

pudet, pudēre, puduit or **puditum est** it makes (one) ashamed (15)

puella, puellae *f.* girl (1)

puer, puerī *m.* boy (1)

pugnō (1-intr.) fight (3)

pulcher, pulchra, pulchrum beautiful, handsome (3)

putō (1-tr.) think, suppose (11)

Q. = Quintus, Quintī *m.* Quintus (§16)

quaerō, quaerere, quaesiī or **quaesīvī, quaesītus** search for, seek, ask (9)

quālis, quāle what sort of; of which sort, as (13)

quam (adv.) as, how; (conj.) than (11)

quam ob rem (adv.) on account of which thing, why; therefore (9)

quam prīmum as soon as possible (11)

quamquam (conj.) although (5)

quantus, -a, -um how much, how great; as much, as great (13)

quārē (adv.) because of which thing, why; therefore (9)

quartus, -a, -um fourth (§91)

quattuor (indeclinable adj.) four (§91)

-que (enclitic conj.) and (1)

quī, qua, quod (indef. adj.) some, any (14)

quī, quae, quod (interrog. adj.) what . . ., which . . . (9)

quī, quae, quod (rel. pron.) who, which, that (9)

quia (conj.) because (13)

quīdam, quaedam, quiddam (indef. pron.) (a) certain person, (a) certain thing (10)

quīdam, quaedam, quoddam (indef. adj.) (a) certain (10)

quidem (adv.) indeed, certainly; at least (4)

    nē . . . quidem not even (4)

quīn (rel. adv.) *introduces Relative Clause of Characteristic,* who, that . . . not (10); (conj.)

introduces Doubting clause, that (12); (conj.) *introduces Prevention clause,* that . . . not, from (15)

quīnque (indeclinable adj.) five (§91)

quintus, -a, -um fifth (§91)

Quintus, Quintī *m.* Quintus (§16)

quīque, quaeque, quodque (indef. adj.) each, every (14)

quis, quid (interrog. pron.) who, what (9); (indef. pron.) someone, something; anyone, anything (14)

quisquam, quicquam (indef. pron.) someone, something; anyone, anything (14)

quisque, quidque (quicque) (indef. pron.) each/every man/woman, each/every thing (14)

quō (rel. adv.) to where, whither (10); (interrog. adv.) to where, whither (12)

quod (conj.) because (13); (conj.) the fact that (15)

quodsī (conj.) but if (14)

quōminus (conj.) *introduces Prevention clause,* by which the less, from (15)

quō modō in what manner, how (9)

quoniam (conj.) since, because (5)

quoque (adv.) also, too (8)

quot (indeclinable adj.) how many; as many (13)

rapiō, rapere, rapuī, raptus seize, tear away, carry (off) (15)

redeō, redīre, rediī, reditum go back, return (5)

referō, referre, rettulī, relātus bring back; report (10)

    grātiam or **grātiās referre** (idiom) to render thanks, to return a favor (12)

rēfert, rēferre, rētulit it is important, it concerns (15)

rēgīna, rēgīnae *f.* queen (1)

regō, regere, rēxī, rēctus rule, control (4)

relinquō, relinquere, relīquī, relictus leave (behind), abandon (8)

reliquus, -a, -um remaining, rest (of) (14)

Remus, Remī *m.* Remus (§16)

rēs, reī *f.* thing; property; matter, affair; activity; situation (8)

    rēs gestae, rērum gestārum *f. pl.* accomplishments; history (8)

    rēs novae, rērum novārum *f. pl.* revolution (8)

    rēs pūblica, reī pūblicae *f.* republic (8)

respondeō, respondēre, respondī, respōnsus answer (2)

rēx, rēgis *m.* king (6)

rogō (1-tr.) ask (for) (12)

Rōma, Rōmae *f.* Rome (6)

Rōmānī, Rōmānōrum *m. pl.* (the) Romans (3)

Rōmānus, -a, -um Roman (3)

Rōmulus, Rōmulī *m.* Romulus (§16)
rūmor, rūmōris *m.* rumor (12)
rūs, rūris *n. in sing. or pl.* country(side) (6)

saepe (adv.) often (8)
   saepius (adv.) more often (11)
   saepissimē (adv.) most often (11)
saevus, -a, -um cruel, savage (13)
C. Sallustius Crispus, C. Sallustiī Crispī *m.* Gaius
   Sallustius Crispus, Sallust (§16)
salūs, salūtis *f.* safety; health (§71)
   salūtem dīcere to say "greetings," to say hello (§71)
salvē/salvēte hello! good day! (§71)
sapiēns, sapientis wise (11)
sapientia, sapientiae *f.* wisdom (2)
satis or sat (indeclinable subst.) enough; (adv.)
   enough, sufficiently (10)
scelus, sceleris *n.* wicked deed, crime; villainy (13)
sciō, scīre, scīvī or sciī, scītus know (11)
scrībō, scrībere, scrīpsī, scrīptus write (4)
secundus, -a, -um second (§91)
sed (conj.) but (2)
semper (adv.) always (3)
Semprōnia, Semprōniae *f.* Sempronia (§16)
C. Semprōnius Gracchus, C. Semprōniī Gracchī *m.*
   Gaius Sempronius Gracchus (§16)
Ti. Semprōnius Gracchus, Ti. Semprōniī Gracchī *m.*
   Tiberius Sempronius Gracchus (§16)
senātus, senātūs *m.* senate (8)
sēnsus, sēnsūs *m.* perception, feeling; sense (11)
sententia, sententiae *f.* thought, feeling; opinion (4)
sentiō, sentīre, sēnsī, sēnsus perceive; feel (4)
septem (indeclinable adj.) seven (§91)
septimus, -a, -um seventh (§91)
sequor, sequī, secūtus sum follow (8)
Ser. = Servius, Serviī *m.* Servius (§16)
L. Sergius Catilīna, L. Sergiī Catilīnae *m.* Lucius
   Sergius Catilina, Catiline (§16)
servitūs, servitūtis *f.* slavery (6)
Servius, Serviī *m.* Servius (§16)
servō (1-tr.) save, preserve (10)
servus, servī *m.* slave (1)
sex (indeclinable adj.) six (§91)
Sex. = Sextus, Sextī *m.* Sextus (§16)
sextus, -a, -um sixth (§91)
Sextus, Sextī *m.* Sextus (§16)
sī (conj.) if (5)
sīc (adv.) thus, so, in this way, in such a way (5)
signum, signī *n.* sign, signal; standard (11)
similis, simile similar (+ gen. or dat.) (11)
sine (prep. + abl.) without (3)
socius, -a, -um allied (4)
socius, sociī *m.* ally, comrade (4)

sōl, sōlis *m.* sun (14)
soleō, solēre, solitus sum be accustomed (11)
sōlum (adv.) only (7)
sōlus, -a, -um alone, only (9)
solvō, solvere, solvī, solūtus loosen; free, release;
   dissolve (15)
soror, sorōris *f.* sister (6)
Sp. = Spurius, Spuriī *m.* Spurius (§16)
speciēs, *speciēī *f.* appearance, aspect (8)
spectō (1-tr.) look (at), observe (14)
spērō (1-tr.) hope (for) (12)
spēs, speī *f.* hope (9)
Spurius, Spuriī *m.* Spurius (§16)
stō, stāre, stetī, statum stand; stand fast, endure (10)
studium, studiī *n.* zeal, enthusiasm; pursuit, study (2)
sub (prep. + acc.) under; up to; (prep. + abl.) under;
   at the foot of; near (6)
—, suī (reflexive pron.) himself, herself, itself;
   themselves (5)
Sulla, Sullae *m.* Sulla
sum, esse, fuī, futūrus be; exist (2)
summus, -a, -um highest; top (of); last, final (11)
superō (1-tr.) overcome, conquer; surpass (3)
suus, -a, -um his (own), her (own), its (own); their
   (own) (5)

T. = Tītus, Tītī *m.* Titus (§16)
Tacitus, Tacitī *m.* Tacitus (§16)
taedet, taedēre, taesum est it makes (one) tired *or*
   sick (15)
tālis, tāle such, of such a sort (13)
tam (adv.) so (13)
tamen (adv.) nevertheless (5)
tandem (adv.) finally, at last; *in questions and*
   commands, pray, I ask you, then (9)
tantus, -a, -um so much, so great (13)
tēlum, tēlī *n.* spear; weapon (11)
templum, templī *n.* temple (7)
tempus, temporis *n.* time (8)
teneō, tenēre, tenuī, tentus hold, grasp; keep,
   possess; occupy (3)
terra, terrae *f.* land, earth (3)
terreō, terrēre, terruī, territus terrify, frighten (7)
tertius, -a, -um third (§91)
Ti. = Tiberius, Tiberiī *m.* Tiberius (§16)
Tiberius, Tiberiī *m.* Tiberius (§16)
timeō, timēre, timuī, —— fear, be afraid (of) (2)
timor, timōris *m.* fear (6)
Tītus, Tītī *m.* Titus (§16)
tot (indeclinable adj.) so many (13)
tōtus, -a, -um whole (9)
trādō, trādere, trādidī, trāditus hand over, surrender;
   hand down (7)

trēs, tria three (§91)

Troia, Troiae *f.* Troy (§16)

tū, tuī (personal pron.) you (4)

—, tuī (reflexive pron.) yourself (5)

Tullia, Tulliae *f.* Tullia (§16)

M. Tullius Cicerō, M. Tulliī Cicerōnis *m.* Marcus
    Tullius Cicero (§60)

tum or **tunc** (adv.) then, at that time (12)

Turnus, Turnī *m.* Turnus (§60)

turpis, turpe foul, ugly; base, shameful (15)

tuus, -a, -um your, yours (4); your (own) (5)

ubi (conj.) when (5); (interrog. adv.) where, when (5);
    (rel. adv.) where (10)

ūllus, -a, -um any (9)

umbra, umbrae *f.* shadow, shade (7)

umquam (adv.) ever (6)

unde (rel. adv.) from where, whence (10); (interrog.
    adv.) from where, whence (12)

ūnus, -a, -um one; only (9)

urbs, urbis, -ium *f.* city (6)

ut (conj.) as; when (5); (conj.) *introduces Purpose
    clause,* in order that (9); *introduces Indirect
    Command,* that (9); (conj.) *introduces negative
    Fear clause,* that . . . not (15)

uter, utra, utrum (interrog. adj.) which (of two) (9)

utinam (particle) *introduces an Optative subjunctive* (7)

ūtor, ūtī, ūsus sum use; experience, enjoy (+ abl.) (10)

utrum (interrog. particle) *introduces the first question
    of a double direct or Indirect Question* (12)

utrum . . . an . . . whether . . . or . . . (12)

valdē (adv.) strongly

valē/valēte greetings! farewell! (§71)

valeō, valēre, valuī, valitūrus be strong, be able; be
    well, fare well (§71)

C. Valerius Catullus, C. Valeriī Catullī *m.* Gaius
    Valerius Catullus (§16)

validus, -a, -um strong; healthy (4)

vel (conj.) or; **vel . . . vel . . .** either . . . or . . .; (adv.)
    even (14)

vēlum, vēlī *n.* sail (2)

vēla dare (idiom) to set sail (2)

vendō, vendere, vendidī, venditus sell (13)

veniō, venīre, vēnī, ventum come (4)

Venus, Veneris *f.* Venus (§60)

verbum, verbī *n.* word (1)

vereor, verērī, veritus sum be in awe of, show respect
    to; dread, fear (15)

P. Vergilius Marō, P. Vergiliī Marōnis *m.* Publius
    Vergilius Maro, Vergil (§60)

vērō (adv.) certainly, indeed; but (in fact) (7)

vērum (conj.) but (7)

vērus, -a, -um real, true (7)

Vesta, Vestae *f.* Vesta (§60)

vester, vestra, vestrum your (pl.), yours (pl.) (4); your
    (pl.) (own) (5)

——, vestrum/vestrī (reflexive pron.) yourselves (5)

vetō, vetāre, vetuī, vetitus forbid (15)

vetus, veteris old (14)

via, viae *f.* way, road, path, street (1)

videō, vidēre, vīdī, vīsus see (2); *in passive,* be seen;
    seem (3)

vincō, vincere, vīcī, victus conquer, overcome; win (7)

vir, virī *m.* man; husband (1)

virtūs, virtūtis *f.* manliness, courage; excellence,
    virtue (7)

vīs, ——, -ium *f.* force, power; violence; *in pl.,*
    (physical) strength (6)

vīta, vītae *f.* life (2)

vīvō, vīvere, vīxī, vīctūrus live, be alive (6)

vix (adv.) scarcely, hardly (14)

vocō (1-tr.) call; summon; name (2)

volō, velle, voluī, —— be willing, want, wish (12)

bene velle (idiom) to wish well (12)

male velle (idiom) to wish ill (12)

vōs, vestrum/vestrī (personal pron.) you (pl.) (4)

——, vestrum/vestrī (reflexive pron.) yourselves (5)

vōx, vōcis *f.* voice; word (7)

Vulcānus, Vulcānī *m.* Vulcan (§60)

vulnus, vulneris *n.* wound (13)

vultus, vultūs *m. in sing. or pl.* expression; face (15)

ENGLISH TO LATIN VOCABULARY

Note: This English to Latin Vocabulary includes all words from vocabulary lists in both Parts I and II of *Learn to Read Latin*. Numbers in parentheses refer to chapter (6, e.g.) or section (§16, e.g.) in which the vocabulary word is introduced. If a chapter number is listed, the word appears in the chapter-opening vocabulary list. For distinctions between different Latin words for the same English word, consult the appropriate vocabulary notes.

? -ne (enclitic) *added to the first word of a question* (2)
? *expecting the answer "no"* num (12)
? *expecting the answer "yes"* nōnne (12)
abandon relinquō, relinquere, relīquī, relictus (8)
ability ingenium, ingeniī *n.* (7)
about dē (prep. + abl.) (1)
absent absēns, absentis (14)
abundance cōpia, cōpiae *f.* (7)
accept accipiō, accipere, accēpī, acceptus (5)
accomplish perficiō, perficere, perfēcī, perfectus (5); cōnficiō, cōnficere, cōnfēcī, cōnfectus (12)
accomplishments rēs gestae, rērum gestārum *f. pl.* (8)
activity rēs, reī *f.* (8)
admit fateor, fatērī, fassus sum (8)
advice cōnsilium, cōnsiliī *n.* (1)
advise moneō, monēre, monuī, monitus (9)
Aeneas Aenēās, Aenēae *m.*; Aenēān = *acc. sing.*; Aenēā = *voc. sing.* (§16)
affair rēs, reī *f.* (8)
after postquam (conj.) (5); post (adv.) (7); post (prep. + acc.) (7)
afterward post (adv.) (7)
against in (prep. + acc.) (1); contrā (prep. + acc.) (10)
age aetās, aetātis *f.* (14)
aid auxilium, auxiliī *n.* (4)
alas heu (interj.) (§71)
all omnis, omne (8); cūnctus, -a, -um (14)
allied socius, -a, -um (4)
allow patior, patī, passus sum (9)
ally socius, sociī *m.* (4)

alone sōlus, -a, -um (9); ūnus, -a, -um (9)
already iam (adv.) (9)
also et (adv.) (1); etiam (adv.) (7); quoque (adv.) (8)
altar āra, ārae *f.* (7)
although etsī (conj.) (5); quamquam (conj.) (5); cum (conj.) (12)
always semper (adv.) (3)
ambush īnsidiae, īnsidiārum *f. pl.* (7)
among inter (prep. + acc.) (6); apud (prep. + acc.) (10)
Amor Amor, Amōris *m.* (§60); Cupīdō, Cupīdinis *m.* (§60)
ancestors maiōrēs, maiōrum *m. pl.* (11)
ancient antīquus, -a, -um (6)
and et (conj.) (1); -que (enclitic conj.) (1)
and (what's more) atque (conj.) (3); ac (conj.) (3)
and indeed etenim (conj.) (2)
and not neque, nec (conj. *and* adv.) (2)
anger īra, īrae *f.* (2)
animal animal, animālis, -ium *n.* (6)
another alius, -a, -um (9)
answer respondeō, respondēre, respondī, respōnsus (2)
Antony Antōnius, Antōniī *m.* (§16)
anxiety cūra, cūrae *f.* (2); metus, metūs *m.* (9)
any ūllus, -a, -um (9); aliquī, aliqua, aliquod (indef. adj.) (14); quī, qua, quod (indef. adj.) (14)
anyone aliquis, aliquid (indef. pron.) (14); quis, quid (indef. pron.) (14); quisquam, quicquam (indef. pron.) (14)

anything aliquis, aliquid (indef. pron.) (14); quis, quid (indef. pron.) (14); quisquam, quicquam (indef. pron.) (14)

Apollo Apollō, Apollinis *m.* (§60)

appearance speciēs, *speciēī *f.* (8)

Appius Appius, Appiī *m.* (abbreviation: App.) (§16)

approach accēdō, accēdere, accessī, accessum (5)

arise orior, orīrī, ortus sum (14)

arms arma, armōrum *n. pl.* (2)

army exercitus, exercitūs *m.* (8); agmen, agminis *n.* (14)

art ars, artis, -ium *f.* (7)

as ut (conj.) (5); quam (adv.) (11); quālis, quāle (13)

as great quantus, -a, -um (13)

as long as dōnec (conj.) (13); dum (conj.) (13)

as many quot (indeclinable adj.) (13)

as much quantus, -a, -um (13)

as soon as possible quam prīmum (11)

it makes (one) ashamed pudet, pudēre, puduit *or* puditum est (15)

ask quaerō, quaerere, quaesiī *or* quaesīvī, quaesītus (9)

ask (for) petō, petere, petiī *or* petīvī, petītus (7); rogō (1-tr.) (12)

aspect speciēs, *speciēī *f.* (8)

at apud (prep. + acc.) (10)

at all omnīnō (adv.) *in negative or virtual negative statements or questions* (8)

at daybreak prīmā lūce (11)

at last tandem (adv.) (9)

at least quidem (adv.) (4); certē (adv.) (7)

at that time tum *or* tunc (adv.) (12)

at the foot of sub (prep. + abl.) (6)

at the house of apud (prep. + acc.) (10)

at this time hīc (adv.) (§130)

Athens Athēnae, Athēnārum *f. pl.* (6)

attack petō, petere, petiī *or* petīvī, petītus (7); oppugnō (1-tr.) (10)

attempt cōnor (1-tr.) (8)

attentiveness dīligentia, dīligentiae *f.* (3)

attitude mēns, mentis, -ium *f.* (6)

audacity audācia, audāciae *f.* (11)

Aulus Aulus, Aulī *m.* (abbreviation: A.) (§16)

authority imperium, imperiī *n.* (3); auctōritās, auctōritātis *f.* (14)

auxiliary troops auxilia, auxiliōrum *n. pl.* (4)

await maneō, manēre, mānsī, mānsūrus (7); ex(s)pectō (1-tr.) (13)

away from ā, ab (prep. + abl.) (1)

Bacchus Bacchus, Bacchī *m.* (§60)

bad malus, -a, -um (3)

badly male (adv.) (5)

band manus, manūs *f.* (8)

banishment ex(s)ilium, ex(s)iliī *n.* (9)

base turpis, turpe (15)

battle proelium, proeliī *n.* (5)

battle line aciēs, aciēī *f.* (8)

be sum, esse, fuī, futūrus (2)

be able possum, posse, potuī, —— (2); valeō, valēre, valuī, valitūrus (§71)

be absent absum, abesse, āfuī, āfutūrus (14)

be accustomed soleō, solēre, solitus sum (11)

be afraid (of) timeō, timēre, timuī, —— (2)

be alive vīvō, vīvere, vīxī, vīctūrus (6)

be born nāscor, nāscī, nātus sum (10)

be destroyed pereō, perīre, periī, peritūrus (11)

be different differō, differre, distulī, dīlātus (8)

be distant absum, abesse, āfuī, āfutūrus (14)

be distressed labōrō (1-intr.) (2)

be done fīō, fierī, factus sum (13)

be free from careō, carēre, caruī, caritūrus (+ abl.) (6)

be in awe of vereor, verērī, veritus sum (15)

be in charge (of) praesum, praeesse, praefuī, praefutūrus (12)

be made fīō, fierī, factus sum (13)

be mindful (of) meminī, meminisse (defective verb) (5)

be near adsum, adesse, adfuī, adfutūrus (14)

be obedient pāreō, pārēre, pāruī, pāritūrus (+ dat.) (9)

be pleasing placeō, placēre, placuī, placitum (+ dat.) (9)

be present adsum, adesse, adfuī, adfutūrus (14)

be strong valeō, valēre, valuī, valitūrus (§71)

be unwilling nōlō, nōlle, nōluī, —— (12)

be well valeō, valēre, valuī, valitūrus (§71)

be willing volō, velle, voluī, —— (12)

be without careō, carēre, caruī, caritūrus (+ abl.) (6)

bear gerō, gerere, gessī, gestus (4); ferō, ferre, tulī, lātus (5)

beautiful pulcher, pulchra, pulchrum (3)

because quoniam (conj.) (5); quia (conj.) (13); quod (conj.) (13)

because of propter (prep. + acc.) (3); ob (prep. + acc.) (9)

because of which thing quārē (adv.) (9)

become fīō, fierī, factus sum (13)

before ante (adv.) (7); ante (prep. + acc.) (7); antequam (conj.) (13); priusquam (conj.) (13)

beg ōrō (1-tr.) (12)

began ——, ——, coepī, coeptus (13)

begin incipiō, incipere, incēpī, inceptus (13)

beginning inceptum, inceptī *n.* (13)

behind post (adv.) (7); post (prep. + acc.) (7)

behold! ecce (interj.) (§71)

believe crēdō, crēdere, crēdidī, crēditus (+ dat.) (11)

belonging to the gods dīvīnus, -a, -um (§60)

best optimus, -a, -um (11); optimē (adv.) (11)
to betake oneself sē cōnferre (14)
better melior, melius (11); melius (11)
between inter (prep. + acc.) (6)
beyond praeter (prep. + acc.) (12)
big magnus, -a, -um (3)
bitter acerbus, -a, -um (7)
blind caecus, -a, -um (9)
block obstō, obstāre, obstitī, obstātum (15)
body corpus, corporis n. (6)
boldness audācia, audāciae f. (11)
book liber, librī m. (1)
both . . . and . . . et . . . et . . . (1)
boundary fīnis, fīnis, -ium m. or f. (10)
boy puer, puerī m. (1)
brave fortis, forte (8)
to break camp castra movēre (11)
breast pectus, pectoris n. (10)
breath anima, animae f. (1)
brief brevis, breve (11)
bright clārus, -a, -um (4)
bring ferō, ferre, tulī, lātus (5)
bring about efficiō, efficere, effēcī, effectus (14)
bring back referō, referre, rettulī, relātus (10)
bring together cōnferō, cōnferre, contulī, collātus (14)
brother frāter, frātris m. (6)
but sed (conj.) (2); vērum (conj.) (7)
but (in fact) vērō (adv.) (7)
but if quodsī (conj.) (14)
buy emō, emere, ēmī, ēmptus (13)
by ā, ab (prep. + abl.) (3)
by far longē (adv.) (11)
by Hercules! herc(u)le (interj.) (§71); mehercule
    (interj.) (§71); meherculēs (interj.) (§71)
by no means haud (adv.) (14)
by now iam (adv.) (9)
by then iam (adv.) (9)
by which the less quōminus (conj.) *introduces
    Prevention clause* (15)

Caesar Caesar, Caesaris m. (§60)
call vocō (1-tr.) (2)
calm aequus, -a, -um (10)
(military) camp castra, castrōrum n. pl. (11)
can possum, posse, potuī, ⸺ (2)
capture capiō, capere, cēpī, captus (4)
care cūra, cūrae f. (2)
carry ferō, ferre, tulī, lātus (5)
carry (into) īnferō, īnferre, intulī, illātus (12)
carry (off) rapiō, rapere, rapuī, raptus (15)
carry away auferō, auferre, abstulī, ablātus (7)
carry in different directions differō, differre, distulī,
    dīlātus (8)
Carthage Carthāgō, Carthāginis f. (6)

case causa, causae f. (4)
Catiline Catilīna, Catilīnae m. (§16)
Cato Catō, Catōnis m. (§60)
Catullus Catullus, Catullī m. (§16)
cause causa, causae f. (4)
Ceres Cerēs, Cereris f. (§60)
certain certus, -a, -um (7)
(a) certain quīdam, quaedam, quoddam (indef. adj.)
    (10)
(a) certain person, (a) certain thing quīdam,
    quaedam, quiddam (indef. pron.) (10)
certainly equidem (adv.) (4); quidem (adv.) (4); certō
    (adv.) (7); vērō (adv.) (7)
chance fortūna, fortūnae f. (7); cāsus, cāsūs m. (10);
    fors, fortis, -ium f. (12)
change mūtō (1-tr.) (13)
character mōrēs, mōrum m. pl. (10)
charming grātus, -a, -um (13)
check premō, premere, pressī, pressus (14)
chest pectus, pectoris n. (10)
choose optō (1-tr.) (2); legō, legere, lēgī, lēctus (6)
Cicero Cicerō, Cicerōnis m. (§60)
circle orbis, orbis, -ium m. (15)
citizen cīvis, cīvis, -ium m. or f. (6)
citizenry cīvitās, cīvitātis f. (7)
citizenship cīvitās, cīvitātis f. (7)
city urbs, urbis, -ium f. (6)
city walls moenia, moenium n. pl. (6)
clan gēns, gentis, -ium f. (12)
clear clārus, -a, -um (4)
close opprimō, opprimere, oppressī, oppressus (14)
collect cōnferō, cōnferre, contulī, collātus (14)
column agmen, agminis n. (14)
come veniō, venīre, vēnī, ventus (4)
come on! age, agite (4)
come out ēgredior, ēgredī, ēgressus sum (13)
come to accēdō, accēdere, accessī, accessum (5)
come to know nōscō, nōscere, nōvī, nōtus (10);
    cognōscō, cognōscere, cognōvī, cognitus (10)
command imperium, imperiī n. (3); imperō (1-intr.)
    (9)
commander imperātor, imperātōris m. (11)
compare cōnferō, cōnferre, contulī, collātus (14)
complete perficiō, perficere, perfēcī, perfectus (5);
    cōnficiō, cōnficere, cōnfēcī, cōnfectus (12)
comrade socius, sociī m. (4)
concern cūra, cūrae f. (2)
concerning dē (prep. + abl.) (1)
it concerns interest, interesse, interfuit (15); rēfert,
    rēferre, rētulit (15)
conduct agō, agere, ēgī, āctus (4); gerō, gerere, gessī,
    gestus (4)
to conduct a case causam agere (4)
confer (on) cōnferō, cōnferre, contulī, collātus (14)

confess fateor, fatērī, fassus sum (8)
confidence fidēs, fideī *f.* (8)
conquer superō (1-tr.) (3); vincō, vincere, vīcī, victus (7)
consider habeō, habēre, habuī, habitus (2); dūcō, dūcere, dūxī, ductus (4); arbitror (1-tr.) (11)
consul cōnsul, cōnsulis *m.* (8)
consulship cōnsulātus, cōnsulātūs *m.* (8)
contrary to contrā (prep. + acc.) (10)
control regō, regere, rēxī, rēctus (4)
Corinna Corinna, Corinnae *f.* (§60)
Cornelius Sulla (L.) Cornēlius Sulla, (L.) Cornēliī Sullae *m.* (§16)
Cornelius Tacitus Cornēlius Tacitus, (P.) Cornēliī Tacitī *m.* (§16)
country patria, patriae *f.* (1)
country(side) *in sing. or plur.* rūs, rūris *n.* (6)
courage virtūs, virtūtis *f.* (7)
court iūs, iūris *n.* (6)
Crassus Crassus, Crassī *m.* (§16)
crime scelus, sceleris *n.* (13)
cruel saevus, -a, -um (13)
Cupid Cupīdō, Cupīdinis *m.* (§60)
custom mōs, mōris *m.* (10)
Cynthia Cynthia, Cynthiae *f.* (§60)

danger perīculum, perīculī *n.* (1)
dare audeō, audēre, ausus sum (8)
dark caecus, -a, -um (9)
daughter fīlia, fīliae *f.* (1)
day diēs, diēī *m. or f.* (8)
at daybreak prīmā lūce (11)
daylight lūx, lūcis *f.* (11)
dear (to) cārus, -a, -um (+ dat.) (7)
death fāta, fātōrum *n. pl.* (5); mors, mortis, -ium *f.* (7)
deceptive falsus, -a, -um (7)
decide cōnstituō, cōnstituere, cōnstituī, cōnstitūtus (15)
Decimus Decimus, Decimī *m.* (abbreviation: D.) (§16)
deed factum, factī *n.* (1)
deep altus, -a, -um (4); gravis, grave (9)
deep sea altum, altī *n.* (4)
defer differō, differre, distulī, dīlātus (8)
deified dīvus, -a, -um (§60)
delay mora, morae *f.* (3); moror (1-tr.) (13)
deliberation cōnsilium, cōnsiliī *n.* (1)
depart discēdō, discēdere, discessī, discessum (5)
depraved perditus, -a, -um (13)
descent genus, generis *n.* (10)
desire optō (1-tr.) (2); cupiō, cupere, cupiī *or* cupīvī, cupītus (7)
desirous cupidus, -a, -um (+ gen.) (4)
desperately perditē (adv.) (13)

destiny fātum, fātī *n.* (5)
destroy dēleō, dēlēre, dēlēvī, dēlētus (10); perdō, perdere, perdidī, perditus (13)
deter dēterreō, dēterrēre, dēterruī, dēterritus (15)
Diana Diāna, Diānae *f.* (§60)
Dido Dīdō, Dīdōnis *f.* (§60)
die morior, morī, mortuus sum (8); cadō, cadere, cecidī, cāsum (10); pereō, perīre, periī, peritūrus (11); occidō, occidere, occidī, occāsūrus (14)
differ differō, differre, distulī, dīlātus (8)
different dissimilis, dissimile (+ gen. *or* dat.) (11)
difficult difficilis, difficile (8)
with difficulty difficiliter *or* difficulter (adv.) (8)
diligence dīligentia, dīligentiae *f.* (3)
direct cōnferō, cōnferre, contulī, collātus (14)
Dis Dīs, Dītis *m.* (§60)
discover inveniō, invenīre, invēnī, inventus (11)
it disgusts (one) piget, pigēre, piguit (15)
disloyal impius, -a, -um (5)
displeased ingrātus, -a, -um (13)
displeasing ingrātus, -a, -um (13)
disposition ingenium, ingeniī *n.* (7)
dissimilar dissimilis, dissimile (+ gen. *or* dat.) (11)
dissolve solvō, solvere, solvī, solūtus (15)
disturbance mōtus, mōtūs *m.* (8)
divine dīvīnus, -a, -um (§60); dīvus, -a, -um (§60)
divine power nūmen, nūminis *n.* (15)
divine spirit nūmen, nūminis *n.* (15)
divinity nūmen, nūminis *n.* (15)
do agō, agere, ēgī, āctus (4); faciō, facere, fēcī, factus (4)
doubt dubium, dubiī *n.* (12); dubitō (1-tr.) (12)
doubtful dubius, -a, -um (12)
down from dē (prep. + abl.) (1)
dread metus, metūs *m.* (9); metuō, metuere, metuī, —— (14); vereor, verērī, veritus sum (15)
drive agō, agere, ēgī, āctus (4)
drive (off) pellō, pellere, pepulī, pulsus (9)
during inter (prep. + acc.) (6)
dutiful pius, -a, -um (5)

each quīque, quaque, quodque (indef. adj.) (14)
each man, each woman, each thing quisque, quidque (quicque) (indef. pron.) (14)
earlier ante (adv.) (7)
earth terra, terrae *f.* (3)
easily facile (adv.) (8)
east oriēns, orientis *m.* (14)
easy facilis, facile (8)
effort labor, labōris *m.* (10)
eight octō (indeclinable adj.) (§91)
eighth octāvus, -a, -um (§91)
either . . . or . . . aut . . . aut . . . (7); vel . . . vel . . . (14)

empire imperium, imperiī *n.* (3)

encourage hortor (1-tr.) (9)

end fīnis, fīnis, -ium *m.* or *f.* (10)

endure ferō, ferre, tulī, lātus (5); patior, patī, passus sum (9); perferō, perferre, pertulī, perlātus (10); stō, stāre, stetī, statum (10)

(personal) enemy inimīcus, inimīcī *m.* (3)

(public) enemy hostis, hostis, -ium *m.* (6)

enjoy ūtor, ūtī, ūsus sum (+ abl.) (10)

enmity inimīcitia, inimīcitiae *f.* (5)

enough satis *or* sat (adv.) (10); satis *or* sat (indeclinable subst.) (10)

enrolled fathers patrēs cōnscrīptī (voc. pl.) (6)

enthusiasm studium, studiī *n.* (2)

entirely omnīnō (adv.) (8)

envoy lēgātus, lēgātī *m.* (10)

envy invidia, invidiae *f.* (4)

epistle litterae, litterārum *f. pl.* (12)

equitable aequus, -a, -um (10)

err errō (1-intr.) (2)

especially maximē (adv.) (11)

establish iaciō, iacere, iēcī, iactus (11); cōnstituō, cōnstituere, cōnstituī, cōnstitūtus (15)

estimate aestimō (1-tr.) (13)

even et (adv.) (1); etiam (adv.) (7); aequus, -a, -um (10); vel (adv.) (14)

  not even nē . . . quidem (4)

ever umquam (adv.) (6)

every omnis, omne (8); quīque, quaque, quodque (indef. adj.) (14)

every man, every woman, every thing quisque, quidque (quicque) (indef. pron.) (14)

evil malus, -a, -um (3)

excellence virtūs, virtūtis *f.* (7)

except praeter (prep. + acc.) (12)

exchange mūtō (1-tr.) (13)

exhort hortor (1-tr.) (9)

exile ex(s)ilium, ex(s)iliī *n.* (9)

exist sum, esse, fuī, futūrus (2)

expect ex(s)pectō (1-tr.) (13)

it is expedient interest, interesse, interfuit (15)

expel ēiciō, ēicere, ēiēcī, ēiectus (11)

experience experior, experīrī, expertus sum (8); patior, patī, passus sum (9); ūtor, ūtī, ūsus sum (+ abl.) (10)

expression *in sing. or pl.,* vultus, vultūs *m.* (15)

eye oculus, oculī *m.* (9)

eyes lūmina, lūminum *n. pl.* (13)

face *in sing. or pl.,* ōs, ōris *n.* (14); *in sing. or pl.,* vultus, vultūs *m.* (15)

face to face contrā (adv.) (10)

facing contrā (prep. + acc.) (10)

the fact that quod (conj.) (15)

(political) faction *in sing. or pl.,* pars, partis, -ium *f.* (7)

faith fidēs, fideī *f.* (8)

fall cāsus, cāsūs *m.* (10); cadō, cadere, cecidī, cāsum (10); occidō, occidere, occidī, occāsūrus (14)

false falsus, -a, -um (7)

falsely falsō (7)

fame fāma, fāmae *f.* (1)

family gēns, gentis, -ium *f.* (12)

famous clārus, -a, -um (4)

far longus, -a, -um (11); longē (adv.) (11)

fare well valeō, valēre, valuī, valitūrus (§71)

farewell! valē/valēte (§71)

farmer agricola, agricolae *m.* (1)

far-reaching longus, -a, -um (11)

fate fātum, fātī *n.* (5)

father pater, patris *m.* (6)

favor pāx, pācis *f.* (9); grātia, grātiae *f.* (12)

fear timeō, timēre, timuī, —— (2); timor, timōris *m.* (6); metus, metūs *m.* (9); metuō, metuere, metuī, —— (14); vereor, verērī, veritus sum (15)

feel sentiō, sentīre, sēnsī, sēnsus (4)

to feel grateful grātiam *or* grātiās habēre (12)

feeling sententia, sententiae *f.* (4); sēnsus, sēnsūs *m.* (11)

few paucī, paucae, pauca (6)

fickle levis, leve (9)

field ager, agrī *m.* (1)

fierce ācer, ācris, ācre (8)

fifth quintus, -a, -um (§91)

fight pugnō (1-intr.) (3)

final summus, -a, -um (11)

finally tandem (adv.) (9)

find inveniō, invenīre, invēnī, inventus (11)

fire ignis, ignis, -ium *m.* (11)

first prīmus, -a, -um (§91); prīmum (adv.) (11)

five quīnque (indeclinable adj.) (§91)

flat plain campus, campī *m.* (11)

flee fugiō, fugere, fūgī, fugitūrus (7)

flight fuga, fugae *f.* (8)

follow sequor, sequī, secūtus sum (8)

for enim (postpositive conj.) (2); nam (conj.) (2); prō (prep. + abl.) (3)

for a long time diū (adv.) (11)

for in fact etenim (conj.) (2); namque (conj.) (2)

for my part equidem (adv.) (4)

for the first time prīmum (adv.) (11)

for the purpose of ad (prep. + acc.) (13); causā (+ *preceding* gen.) (13); grātiā (+ *preceding* gen.) (13)

for the sake of causā (+ *preceding* gen.) (13); grātiā (+ *preceding* gen.) (13)

forbid prohibeō, prohibēre, prohibuī, prohibitus (15); vetō, vetāre, vetuī, vetitus (15)

(what is divinely) forbidden nefās (indeclinable noun) *n.* (12)

force vīs, ——, -ium *f.* (6)

forces cōpiae, cōpiārum *f. pl.* (7)

forget oblīvīscor, oblīvīscī, oblītus sum (+ gen.) (12)

to form a plan cōnsilium capere (4)

fortunate fēlīx, fēlīcis (8)

fortune fortūna, fortūnae *f.* (7); cāsus, cāsūs *m.* (10)

forum forum, forī *n.* (3)

foul turpis, turpe (15)

four quattuor (indeclinable adj.) (§91)

fourth quartus, -a, -um (§91)

free līber, lībera, līberum (3)

free līberō (1-tr.) (6); solvō, solvere, solvī, solūtus (15)

freedom lībertās, lībertātis *f.* (9)

friend amīcus, amīcī *m.* (3)

friendly amīcus, -a, -um (+ dat.) (3)

friendship amīcitia, amīcitiae *f.* (5)

frighten terreō, terrēre, terruī, territus (7)

from quīn (conj.) *introduces Prevention clause* (15); quōminus (conj.) *introduces Prevention clause* (15)

(away) from ā, ab (prep. + abl.) (1)

(down) from dē (prep. + abl.) (1)

(out) from ē, ex (prep. + abl.) (1)

from here hinc (adv.) (§130)

from that place inde (adv.) (§130)

from that time inde (adv.) (§130)

from there illinc (adv.) (§130); inde (adv.) (§130)

from where unde (rel. adv.) (10); unde (interrog. adv. (12)

Gaius Gaius, Gaiī *m.* (abbreviation: C.) (§16)

gather legō, legere, lēgī, lēctus (6)

general imperātor, imperātōris *m.* (11)

gift dōnum, dōnī *n.* (1)

gird (on oneself) cingō, cingere, cīnxī, cīnctus (15)

girl puella, puellae *f.* (1)

give dō, dare, dedī, datus (2); dōnō (1-tr.) (2)

give an order imperō (1-intr.) (+ dat.) (9)

give in exchange mūtō (1-tr.) (13)

glory glōria, glōriae *f.* (4)

Gnaeus Gnaeus, Gnaeī *m.* (abbreviation: Gn.) (§16)

go eō, īre, iī *or* īvī, itum (3); cēdō, cēdere, cessī, cessum (5)

to go sē ferre (5); sē cōnferre (14)

go away abeō, abīre, abiī, abitum (5); discēdō, discēdere, discessī, discessum (5)

go back redeō, redīre, rediī, reditum (5)

go out ēgredior, ēgredī, ēgressus sum (13)

go to accēdō, accēdere, accessī, accessum (5)

god deus, deī *m.* (1)

goddess dea, deae *f.* (1)

gold aurum, aurī *n.* (1)

good bonus, -a, -um (3)

good day! salvē/salvēte (§71)

Gracchus Gracchus, Gracchī *m.* (§16)

grant dō, dare, dedī, datus (2)

grasp teneō, tenēre, tenuī, tentus (3)

grateful grātus, -a, -um (13)

gratitude grātia, grātiae *f.* (12)

great magnus, -a, -um (3)

greater maior, maius (11)

greatest maximus, -a, -um (11)

greatly magnopere (adv.) (10)

Greece Graecia, Graeciae *f.* (§16)

greetings! valē/valēte (§71)

guile ars, artis, -ium *f.* (7)

hand manus, manūs *f.* (8)

hand down trādō, trādere, trādidī, trāditus (7)

hand over trādō, trādere, trādidī, trāditus (7)

handsome pulcher, pulchra, pulchrum (3)

Hannibal Hannibal, Hannibalis *m.* (§60)

happen fīō, fierī, factus sum (13); accidō, accidere, accidī, —— (14)

happy laetus, -a, -um (3); fēlīx, fēlīcis (8)

hard dūrus, -a, -um (5)

hardly vix (adv.) (14)

hardship labor, labōris *m.* (10)

harsh dūrus, -a, -um (5); acerbus, -a, -um (7)

hate ōdī, ōdisse (defective verb) (5)

hatred odium, odiī *n.* (3)

have habeō, habēre, habuī, habitus (2)

have begun ——, ——, coepī, coeptus (13)

he is, ea, id (demonstr. adj. *as third-person pron.*) (4)

head caput, capitis *n.* (15)

health salūs, salūtis *f.* (§71)

healthy validus, -a, -um (4)

hear audiō, audīre, audīvī, audītus (4)

hear (of) accipiō, accipere, accēpī, acceptus (5)

heart pectus, pectoris *n.* (10)

heaven caelum, caelī *n.* (4)

heavy gravis, grave (9)

height altum, altī *n.* (4)

hello! salvē/salvēte (§71)

help auxilium, auxiliī *n.* (4)

hence hinc (adv.) (§130)

henceforth hinc (adv.) (§130)

her is, ea, id (demonstr. adj. *as third-person pron.*) (4)

her (own) suus, -a, -um (5)

here hīc (adv.) (§130)

herself ——, suī (reflexive pron.) (5)

hesitate dubitō (1-tr.) (12)

hesitation dubium, dubiī *n.* (12)

hidden caecus, -a, -um (9)

high altus, -a, -um (4)

highest summus, -a, -um (11)

him is, ea, id (demonstr. adj. *as third-person pron.*) (4)

himself —, suī (reflexive pron.) (5)

hinder moror (1-tr.) (13); impediō, impedīre, impedīvī *or* impediī, impedītus (15); obstō, obstāre, obstitī, obstātum (15)

his (own) suus, -a, -um (5)

history rēs gestae, rērum gestārum *f. pl.* (8)

hither hūc (adv.) (§130)

hold habeō, habēre, habuī, habitus (2); teneō, tenēre, tenuī, tentus (3)

home domus, domī *f.* (6); domus, domūs (8)

homeland patria, patriae *f.* (1)

honor honor *or* honōs, honōris *m.* (13)

honorable honestus, -a, -um (10)

hope spēs, speī *f.* (9)

hope (for) spērō (1-tr.) (12)

Horace (Q.) Horātius Flaccus, (Q.) Horātiī Flaccī *m.* (§16)

hostile inimīcus, -a, -um (+ dat.) (3)

hostility inimīcitia, inimīcitiae *f.* (5)

house domus, domī *f.* (6); domus, domūs *f.* (8)

how ut (interrog. adv.) (§71); quō modō (9); quam (adv.) (11)

how great quantus, -a, -um (13)

how many quot (indeclinable adj.) (13)

how much quantus, -a, -um (13)

however autem (postpositive conj.) (6)

huge ingēns, ingentis (8)

human being homō, hominis *m.* (6)

humble humilis, humile (11)

hundred centum (indeclinable adj.) (§91)

hundredth centēsimus, -a, -um (§91)

husband vir, virī *m.* (1)

I ego, meī (personal pron.) (4)

I ask you tandem *(in questions and commands)* (adv.) (9)

if sī (conj.) (5)

if . . . not nisi (conj.) (5)

Ilium Īlium, Īliī *n.* (§16)

ill-will invidia, invidiae *f.* (4)

impede impediō, impedīre, impedīvī *or* impediī, impedītus (15)

important gravis, grave (9)

it is important interest, interesse, interfuit (15); rēfert, rēferre, rētulit (15)

in in (prep. + abl.) (1)

in fact enim (postpositive conj.) (2)

in front of prō (prep. + abl.) (3); ante (prep. + acc.) (7)

in opposition contrā (adv.) (10)

in order that ut (conj.) *introduces Purpose clause* (9)

in order that . . . not nē (adv.) *introduces negative Purpose clause* (9)

in return for prō (prep. + abl.) (3)

in such a way sīc (adv.) (5)

in that place ibi (adv.) (§130); illīc (adv.) (§130)

in the presence of apud (prep. + acc.) (10)

in this manner ita (adv.) (7)

in this place hīc (adv.) (§130)

in this way sīc (adv.) (5)

in turn contrā (adv.) (10)

in what manner quō modō (9)

inadequately parum (adv.) (11)

indeed enim (postpositive conj.) (2); equidem (adv.) (4); quidem (adv.) (4); vērō (adv.) (7)

inequitable inīquus, -a, -um (10)

inflict (on) īnferō, īnferre, intulī, illātus (12)

influence auctōritās, auctōritātis *f.* (14)

inhabitant incola, incolae *m. or f.* (3)

instead of prō (prep. + abl.) (3)

intention mēns, mentis, -ium *f.* (6)

into in (prep. + acc.) (1)

it irks (one) piget, pigēre, piguit (15)

iron ferrum, ferrī *n.* (1)

island īnsula, īnsulae *f.* (1)

it is, ea, id (demonstr. adj. *as third-person pron.*) (4)

it causes (one) to repent *or* **regret** paenitet, paenitēre, paenituit (15)

it concerns interest, interesse, interfuit (15); rēfert, rēferre, rētulit (15)

it disgusts (one) piget, pigēre, piguit (15)

it irks (one) piget, pigēre, piguit (15)

it is important interest, interesse, interfuit (15); rēfert, rēferre, rētulit (15)

it is permitted licet, licēre, licuit *or* licitum est (14)

it is proper oportet, oportēre, oportuit (14)

it is right oportet, oportēre, oportuit (14)

it makes (one) ashamed pudet, pudēre, puduit *or* puditum est (15)

it makes (one) sick taedet, taedēre, taesum est (15)

it makes (one) tired taedet, taedēre, taesum est (15)

it moves (one) to pity miseret, miserēre, miseruit *or* miseritum est (15)

Italy Italia, Italiae *f.* (1)

its (own) suus, -a, -um (5)

itself —, suī (reflexive pron.) (5)

jealousy invidia, invidiae *f.* (4)

judge arbitror (1-tr.) (11)

judgment cōnsilium, cōnsiliī *n.* (1); iūs, iūris *n.* (6)

Julia Iūlia, Iūliae *f.* (§16)

Julius Caesar (C.) Iūlius Caesar, (C.) Iūliī Caesaris *m.* (§60)

Juno Iūnō, Iūnōnis *f.* (§60)

Jupiter Iuppiter, Iovis *m.* (§60)

just aequus, -a, -um (10)

just modo (adv.) (12)

just now modo (adv.) (12)
justly iūre (adv.) (6)

keen ācer, ācris, ācre (8)
keenness aciēs, aciēī *f.* (8)
keep teneō, tenēre, tenuī, tentus (3)
kill interficiō, interficere, interfēcī, interfectus (5)
kind genus, generis *n.* (10)
kindness grātia, grātiae *f.* (12)
king rēx, rēgis *m.* (6)
know *in perfect,* nōscō, nōscere, nōvī, nōtus (10); *in perfect,* cognōscō, cognōscere, cognōvī, cognitus (10); sciō, scīre, scīvī *or* sciī, scītus (11)

lack careō, carēre, caruī, caritūrus (+ abl.) (6)
land terra, terrae *f.* (3)
large magnus, -a, -um (3)
last summus, -a, -um (11)
later post (adv.) (7)
Latinus Latīnus, Latīnī *m.* (§60)
law iūs, iūris *n.* (6); lēx, lēgis *f.* (9)
lay iaciō, iacere, iēcī, iactus (11)
lead dūcō, dūcere, dūxī, ductus (4)
leader dux, ducis *m.* or *f.* (10)
learn nōscō, nōscere, nōvī, nōtus (10); cognōscō, cognōscere, cognōvī, cognitus (10)
learn (of) accipiō, accipere, accēpī, acceptus (5)
leave (behind) relinquō, relinquere, relīquī, relictus (8)
legate lēgātus, lēgātī *m.* (10)
legion legiō, legiōnis *f.* (11)
Lesbia Lesbia, Lesbiae *f.* (§60)
letter litterae, litterārum *f. pl.* (12)
letter (of the alphabet) littera, litterae *f.* (12)
level aequus, -a, -um (10)
Liber Līber, Līberī *m.* (§60)
liberate līberō (1-tr.) (6)
Licinius Crassus (M.) Licinius Crassus, (M.) Liciniī Crassī *m.* (§16)
lieutenant lēgātus, lēgātī *m.* (10)
life vīta, vītae *f.* (2)
life force anima, animae *f.* (1)
lifetime aetās, aetātis *f.* (14)
light levis, leve (9)
light lūx, lūcis *f.* (11); lūmen, lūminis *n.* (13)
limit modus, modī *m.* (9); fīnis, fīnis, -ium *m.* or *f.* (10)
line (of march) agmen, agminis *n.* (14)
listen (to) audiō, audīre, audīvī, audītus (4)
literature litterae, litterārum *f. pl.* (12)
little parvus, -a, -um (3)
a little paulum, *paulī *n.* (11)
live vīvō, vīvere, vīxī, vīctūrus (6)
Livia Līvia, Līviae *f.* (§16)

lo ecce (interj.) (§71)
long longus, -a, -um (11)
long for cupiō, cupere, cupiī *or* cupīvī, cupītus (7)
long-standing longus, -a, -um (11)
a long way longē (adv.) (11)
look ecce (interj.) (§71)
look (at) spectō (1-tr.) (14)
loosen solvō, solvere, solvī, solūtus (15)
lord dominus, dominī *m.* (1)
lose perdō, perdere, perdidī, perditus (13)
(morally) lost perditus, -a, -um (13)
a lot multum (adv.) (5)
love amō (1-tr.) (2); amor, amōris *m.* (6)
Love Amor, Amōris *m.* (§60)
loyal pius, -a, -um (5)
Lucius Lūcius, Lūciī *m.* (abbreviation: L.) (§16)
luck fors, fortis, -ium *f.* (12)
lucky fēlīx, fēlīcis (8)

make faciō, facere, fēcī, factus (4); efficiō, efficere, effēcī, effectus (14)
to make camp castra pōnere (11)
make a mistake errō (1-intr.) (2)
to make a speech ōrātiōnem habēre (10)
man vir, virī *m.* (1); homō, hominis *m.* (6)
manage gerō, gerere, gessī, gestus (4)
Manius Manius, Maniī *m.* (abbreviation: M'.) (§16)
manliness virtūs, virtūtis *f.* (7)
manner modus, modī *m.* (9)
many multus, -a, -um (3)
Marcus Marcus, Marcī *m.* (abbreviation: M.) (§16)
Marcus Antonius (Marc Antony) Marcus Antōnius, Marcī Antōniī *m.* (§16)
marketplace forum, forī *n.* (3)
Mars Mars, Martis *m.* (§60)
master dominus, dominī *m.* (1)
matter rēs, reī *f.* (8)
me ego, meī (personal pron.) (4)
measure modus, modī *m.* (9)
memory memoria, memoriae *f.* (12)
Mercury Mercurius, Mercuriī *m.* (§60)
meter modus, modī *m.* (9)
middle (of) medius, -a, -um (10)
midst medium, mediī *n.* (10)
military camp castra, castrōrum *n. pl.* (11)
mind animus, animī *m.* (2); mēns, mentis, -ium *f.* (6)
mine meus, -a, -um (4)
Minerva Minerva, Minervae *f.* (§91)
miserable miser, misera, miserum (3)
misfortune cāsus, cāsūs *m.* (10)
money pecūnia, pecūniae *f.* (1)
moon lūna, lūnae *f.* (14)
morally lost perditus, -a, -um (13)

more plūs/plūrēs, plūra (11); plūs (11)
more greatly magis (comparative adv.) (11)
moreover autem (postpositive conj.) (6)
most plūrimus, -a, -um (11); plūrimē (adv.) (11)
most greatly maximē (adv.) (11)
mother māter, mātris *f.* (6)
motion mōtus, mōtūs *m.* (8)
mountain mōns, montis, -ium *m.* (12)
mouth *in sing. or pl.,* ōs, ōris *n.* (14)
move moveō, movēre, mōvī, mōtus (2); cēdō, cēdere, cessī, cessum (5)
movement mōtus, mōtūs *m.* (8)
much multus, -a, -um (3)
much multum (adv.) (5)
multitude agmen, agminis *n.* (14)
my meus, -a, -um (4)
my (own) meus, -a, -um (5)
myself —, meī (reflexive pron.) (5)

name nōmen, nōminis *n.* (14)
name vocō (1-tr.) (2)
nation gēns, gentis, -ium *f.* (12)
nature nātūra, nātūrae *f.* (6)
near sub (prep. + abl.) (6); apud (prep. + acc.) (10)
necessary necesse (indeclinable adj.) (14)
need opus, operis *n.* (10)
neither (of two) neuter, neutra, neutrum (9)
neither . . . nor . . . neque/nec . . . neque/nec . . . (2)
Neptune Neptūnus, Neptūnī *m.* (§60)
Nero Nerō, Nerōnis *m.* (§60)
Nero Claudius Caesar Nerō Claudius Caesar, Nerōnis Claudiī Caesaris *m.* (§60)
never numquam (adv.) (6)
nevertheless tamen (adv.) (5)
new novus, -a, -um (6)
night nox, noctis, -ium *f.* (8)
nine novem (indeclinable adj.) (§91)
ninth nōnus, -a, -um (§91)
no nūllus, -a, -um (9)
no one nēmō, nēminis *m. or f.* (10)
not nōn (adv.) (2); nē (adv.) (7)
not any nūllus, -a, -um (9)
not at all haud (adv.) (14)
not enough parum (indeclinable subst. *and* adv.) (11)
not even nē . . . quidem (4)
not know nesciō, nescīre, nescīvī *or* nesciī, nescītus (11)
not only . . . but also . . . nōn sōlum . . . sed/vērum etiam (7)
not want nōlō, nōlle, nōluī, —— (12)
not wish nōlō, nōlle, nōluī, —— (12)
nothing nihil, nīl (indeclinable noun) (3); nihilum, nihilī *n. or* nīl, nīlī *n.* (13)

now nunc (adv.) (3); iam (adv.) (9); modo (adv.) (12)
numen nūmen, nūminis *n.* (15)

O ō (interj.) *used with vocatives* (1); (interj.) heu (interj.) (§71)
obey pāreō, pārēre, pāruī, pāritūrus (+ dat.) (9)
observe spectō (1-tr.) (14)
occupy teneō, tenēre, tenuī, tentus (3)
occurrence cāsus, cāsūs *m.* (10)
of such a sort tālis, tāle (13)
of which sort quālis, quāle (13)
(political) office honor *or* honōs, honōris *m.* (13)
often saepe (adv.) (8)
old antīquus, -a, -um (6); vetus, veteris (14)
on in (prep. + abl.) (1)
on account of propter (prep. + acc.) (3); ob (prep. + acc.) (9)
on account of which thing quam ob rem (adv.) (9)
on behalf of prō (prep. + abl.) (3)
on this side . . . on that side . . . hinc . . . hinc . . . (§130); hinc . . . illinc . . . (§130)
one ūnus, -a, -um (9)
only sōlum (adv.) (7); sōlus, -a, -um (9); ūnus, -a, -um (9); modo (adv.) (12)
onto in (prep. + acc.) (1)
opinion sententia, sententiae *f.* (4)
oppress opprimō, opprimere, oppressī, oppressus (14)
or aut (conj.) (7); an (conj.) *introduces an alternative question* (12); vel (conj.) (14)
or not an nōn *(in direct question)* (12); necne *(in Indirect Question)* (12)
oration ōrātiō, ōrātiōnis *f.* (10)
order iubeō, iubēre, iussī, iussus (2); imperō (1-intr.) (+ dat.) (9)
origin genus, generis *n.* (10)
other alius, -a, -um (9)
(the) other cēterus, -a, -um (13)
(the) other (of two) alter, altera, alterum (9)
ought dēbeō, dēbēre, dēbuī, dēbitus (2)
our noster, nostra, nostrum (4)
our (own) noster, nostra, nostrum (5)
ours noster, nostra, nostrum (4)
ourselves ——, nostrum/nostrī (reflexive pron.) (5)
out from ē, ex (prep. + abl.) (1)
overcome superō (1-tr.) (3); vincō, vincere, vīcī, victus (7)
overpower premō, premere, pressī, pressus (14)
overwhelm opprimō, opprimere, oppressī, oppressus (14)
Ovidius Naso (Ovid) (P.) Ovidius Nasō, (P.) Ovidius Nasōnis *m.* (§60)
owe dēbeō, dēbēre, dēbuī, dēbitus (2)

part pars, partis, -ium *f.* (7)

pass away pereō, perīre, periī, peritūrus (11)

to pass a law lēgem ferre (9)

path via, viae *f.* (1)

to pay the penalty poenās dare (2)

peace pāx, pācis *f.* (9)

penalty poena, poenae *f.* (2)

people hominēs, hominum *m. pl.* (6)

(a) people gēns, gentis, -ium *f.* (12)

(the) people populus, populī *m.* (3)

perceive sentiō, sentīre, sēnsī, sēnsus (4)

perception sēnsus, sēnsūs *m.* (11)

perform gerō, gerere, gessī, gestus (4)

perish pereō, perīre, periī, peritūrus (11)

permit patior, patī, passus sum (9)

it is permitted licet, licēre, licuit *or* licitum est (14)

(what is) permitted fās (indeclinable noun) *n.* (12)

personal enemy inimīcus, inimīcī *m.* (3)

physical strength vīrēs, vīrium *f. pl.* (6)

to pitch camp castra pōnere (11)

pitiable miser, misera, miserum (3)

it moves (one) to pity miseret, miserēre, miseruit *or* miseritum est (15)

place pōnō, pōnere, posuī, positus (4)

place locus, locī *m.; in pl.,* loca, locōrum *n. pl. or sometimes* locī, locōrum *m. pl.* (8)

place around circumdō, circumdare, circumdedī, circumdatus (15)

(flat) plain campus, campī *m.* (11)

plan cōnsilium, cōnsiliī *n.* (1)

to plead a case causam agere (4)

pleasant dulcis, dulce (15)

please placeō, placēre, placuī, placitum (+ dat.) (9)

pleased grātus, -a, -um (13)

pleasing grātus, -a, -um (13)

plot īnsidiae, īnsidiārum *f. pl.* (7)

Pluto Dīs, Dītis *m.* (§60)

poem carmen, carminis *n.* (6)

poet poēta, poētae *m.* (1)

point out mōnstrō (1-tr.) (2)

political faction *in sing. or pl.,* pars, partis, -ium *f.* (7)

political office honor *or* honōs, honōris *m.* (13)

Pompeius Magnus (Pompey the Great) (Cn.) Pompeius Magnus, (Cn.) Pompeiī Magnī *m.* (§16)

ponder cōgitō (1-tr.) (2)

populace populus, populī *m.* (3)

Porcius Cato (M.) Porcius Catō, (M.) Porciī Catōnis *m.* (§60)

possess teneō, tenēre, tenuī, tentus (3)

postpone differō, differre, distulī, dīlātus (8)

power imperium, imperiī *n.* (3); vīs, ——, -ium *f.* (6)

practice mōs, mōris *m.* (10)

praise laudō (1-tr.) (3)

pray tandem *in questions and commands* (adv.) (9); ōrō (1-tr.) (12)

precious cārus, -a, -um (+ dat.) (7)

prefer mālō, mālle, māluī, —— (12); praeferō, praeferre, praetulī, praelātus (12)

present dōnō (1-tr.) (2)

preserve servō (1-tr.) (10)

press (hard) premō, premere, pressī, pressus (14)

press on opprimō, opprimere, oppressī, oppressus (14)

prevent dēterreō, dēterrēre, dēterruī, dēterritus (15); prohibeō, prohibēre, prohibuī, prohibitus (15)

previously ante (adv.) (7)

Priam Priamus, Priamī *m.* (§60)

price pretium, pretiī *n.* (13)

proceed gradior, gradī, gressus sum (13)

to proceed (quickly) sē ferre (5)

prohibit prohibeō, prohibēre, prohibuī, prohibitus (15)

it is proper oportet, oportēre, oportuit (14)

Propertius (Sex.) Propertius, (Sex.) Propertiī *m.* (§60)

property rēs, reī *f.* (8)

provided that dum (conj.) (13); dummodo (conj.) (13); modo (conj.) (13)

province prōvincia, prōvinciae *f.* (3)

public pūblicus, -a, -um (8)

public enemy hostis, hostis, -ium *m.* (6)

public square forum, forī *n.* (3)

Publius Publius, Publiī *m.* (abbreviation: P.) (§16)

punishment poena, poenae *f.* (2)

purpose mēns, mentis, -ium *f.* (6)

pursuit studium, studiī *n.* (2)

push pellō, pellere, pepulī, pulsus (9)

put pōnō, pōnere, posuī, positus (4)

put in charge (of) praeficiō, praeficere, praefēcī, praefectus (12)

queen rēgīna, rēgīnae *f.* (1)

Quintus Quintus, Quintī *m.* (abbreviation: Q.) (§16)

race genus, generis *n.* (10)

radiance lūmen, lūminis *n.* (13)

rational soul animus, animī *m.* (2)

read legō, legere, lēgī, lēctus (6)

readily facile (adv.) (8)

real vērus, -a, -um (7)

reason causa, causae *f.* (4)

receive accipiō, accipere, accēpī, acceptus (5)

recklessly perditē (adv.) (13)

recklessness audācia, audāciae *f.* (11)

reckon faciō, facere, fēcī, factus (13)

it causes (one) to regret paenitet, paenitēre, paenituit (15)

release solvō, solvere, solvī, solūtus (15)
reliable certus, -a, -um (7)
remain maneō, manēre, mānsī, mānsūrus (7)
remaining reliquus, -a, -um (14)
remaining part (of) cēterus, -a, -um (13)
remember meminī, meminisse (defective verb) (5)
remind moneō, monēre, monuī, monitus (9)
remove auferō, auferre, abstulī, ablātus (7)
Remus Remus, Remī *m.* (§16)
to render thanks grātiam *or* grātiās referre (12)
renown glōria, glōriae *f.* (4)
it causes (one) to repent paenitet, paenitēre, paenituit (15)
report fāma, fāmae *f.* (1)
report perferō, perferre, pertulī, perlātus (10); referō, referre, rettulī, relātus (10)
republic rēs pūblica, reī pūblicae *f.* (8)
reputation fāma, fāmae *f.* (1)
resentment invidia, invidiae *f.* (4)
respect honor *or* honōs, honōris *m.* (13)
respectable honestus, -a, -um (10)
rest (of) cēterus, -a, -um (13); reliquus, -a, -um (14)
return redeō, redīre, rediī, reditum (5)
to return a favor grātiam *or* grātiās referre (12)
revolution rēs novae, rērum novārum *f. pl.* (8)
reward dōnō (1-tr.) (2)
rhythm modus, modī *m.* (9)
right iūs, iūris *n.* (6)
(what is divinely) right fās (indeclinable noun) *n.* (12)
it is right oportet, oportēre, oportuit (14)
rightly iūre (adv.) (6)
ring orbis, orbis, -ium *m.* (15)
rise orior, orīrī, ortus sum (14)
road via, viae *f.* (1)
Roman Rōmānus, -a, -um (3)
(the) Romans Rōmānī, Rōmānōrum *m. pl.* (3)
Rome Rōma, Rōmae *f.* (6)
Romulus Rōmulus, Rōmulī *m.* (§16)
ruined perditus, -a, -um (13)
ruinously perditē (adv.) (13)
rule regō, regere, rēxī, rēctus (4)
rumor fāma, fāmae *f.* (1); rūmor, rūmōris *m.* (12)
to rush forth sē ēicere (11)

sacrilege nefās (indeclinable noun) *n.* (12)
safety salūs, salūtis *f.* (§71)
sail vēlum, vēlī *n.* (2)
sailor nauta, nautae *m.* (1)
Sallust (C.) Sallustius Crispus, (C.) Sallustiī Crispī *m.* (§16)
same īdem, eadem, idem (9)
savage saevus, -a, -um (13)

save servō (1-tr.) (10)
say dīcō, dīcere, dīxī, dictus (4); for (1-tr.) (15)
to say "greetings" or **hello** salūtem dīcere (§71)
saying dictum, dictī *n.* (6)
scarcely vix (adv.) (14)
scatter differō, differre, distulī, dīlātus (8)
sea mare, maris, *-ium *n.* (6)
search for quaerō, quaerere, quaesiī *or* quaesīvī, quaesītus (9)
second secundus, -a, -um (§91)
secret caecus, -a, -um (9)
see videō, vidēre, vīdī, vīsus (2)
seek petō, petere, petiī *or* petīvī, petītus (7); quaerō, quaerere, quaesiī *or* quaesīvī, quaesītus (9)
seem *in passive,* videō, vidēre, vīdī, vīsus (3)
seize rapiō, rapere, rapuī, raptus (15)
-self, -selves ipse, ipsa, ipsum (5)
sell vendō, vendere, vendidī, venditus (13)
Sempronius Gracchus (C. or Ti.) Semprōnius, (C. or Ti.) Semprōniī Gracchī *m* (§16)
senate senātus, senātūs *m.* (8)
senators patrēs cōnscrīptī *(voc. pl.)* (6)
send mittō, mittere, mīsī, missus (4)
sense sēnsus, sēnsūs *m.* (11)
Sergius Catilina (Catiline) (L.) Sergius Catilīna, (L.) Sergiī Catilīnae *m.* (§16)
serious gravis, grave (9)
Servius Servius, Serviī *m.* (abbreviation: Ser.) (§16)
set occidō, occidere, occidī, occāsūrus (14)
set aside pōnō, pōnere, posuī, positus (4)
set forth proficīscor, proficīscī, profectus sum (10)
set in motion moveō, movēre, mōvī, mōtus (2)
set out proficīscor, proficīscī, profectus sum (10)
to set sail vēla dare (2)
set up cōnstituō, cōnstituere, cōnstituī, cōnstitūtus (15)
seven septem (indeclinable adj.) (§91)
seventh septimus, -a, -um (§91)
severe gravis, grave (9)
Sextus Sextus, Sextī *m.* (abbreviation: Sex.) (§16)
shade umbra, umbrae *f.* (7)
shadow umbra, umbrae *f.* (7)
shameful turpis, turpe (15)
sharp ācer, ācris, ācre (8)
sharp edge aciēs, aciēī *f.* (8)
she is, ea, id (demonstr. adj. *as third-person pron.*) (4)
short brevis, breve (11)
show mōnstrō (1-tr.) (2)
show respect to vereor, verērī, veritus sum (15)
it makes (one) sick taedet, taedēre, taesum est (15)
sign signum, signī *n.* (11)
signal signum, signī *n.* (11)
similar similis, simile (+ gen. *or* dat.) (11)

since quoniam (conj.) (5); cum (conj.) (12)

sing (of) canō, canere, cecinī, cantus (4)

sink cadō, cadere, cecidī, cāsum (10)

sister soror, sorōris *f.* (6)

situation rēs, reī *f.* (8)

six sex (indeclinable adj.) (§91)

sixth sextus, -a, -um (§91)

skill ars, artis, -ium *f.* (7)

sky caelum, caelī *n.* (4)

slave servus, servī *m.* (1)

slavery servitūs, servitūtis *f.* (6)

small parvus, -a, -um (3)

small amount paulum, *paulī *n.* (11)

snatch away ēripiō, ēripere, ēripuī, ēreptus (15)

so sīc (adv.) (5); ita (adv.) (7); tam (adv.) (13)

so great tantus, -a, -um (13)

so many tot (indeclinable adj.) (13)

so much tantus, -a, -um (13)

so very adeō (adv.) (14)

soldier mīles, mīlitis *m.* (6)

some aliquī, aliqua, aliquod (indef. adj.) (14); quī, qua, quod (indef. adj.) (14)

someone, something aliquis, aliquid (indef. pron.) (14); quis, quid (indef. pron.) (14); quisquam, quicquam (indef. pron.) (14)

son fīlius, fīliī *m.* (1); nātus, nātī *m.* (10)

song carmen, carminis *n.* (6)

soon mox (adv.) (3)

sort genus, generis *n.* (10)

soul anima, animae *f.* (1)

(rational) soul animus, animī *m.* (2)

speak dīcō, dīcere, dīxī, dictus (4); loquor, loquī, locūtus sum (11); for (1-tr.) (15)

speaker ōrātor, ōrātōris *m.* (10)

spear tēlum, tēlī *n.* (11)

speech ōrātiō, ōrātiōnis *f.* (10)

spend agō, agere, ēgī, āctus (4)

spirit animus, animī *m.* (2)

Spurius Spurius, Spuriī *m.* (abbreviation: Sp.) (§16)

stand stō, stāre, stetī, statum (10)

stand fast stō, stāre, stetī, statum (10)

stand in the way obstō, obstāre, obstitī, obstātum (15)

standard signum, signī *n.* (11)

state cīvitās, cīvitātis *f.* (7)

stay maneō, manēre, mānsī, mānsūrus (7)

step gradior, gradī, gressus sum (13)

still etiam (adv.) (7)

stir (up) moveō, movēre, mōvī, mōtus (2)

stock genus, generis *n.* (10)

strange novus, -a, -um (6)

street via, viae *f.* (1)

(physical) strength vīrēs, vīrium *f. pl.* (6)

strong validus, -a, -um (4); fortis, forte (8)

strong feelings animī, animōrum *m. pl.* (2)

strongly valdē (adv.) (5)

study studium, studiī *n.* (2)

such tālis, tāle (13)

suffer labōrō (1-intr.) (2); patior, patī, passus sum (9); perferō, perferre, pertulī, perlātus (10)

sufficiently satis *or* sat (adv.) (10)

Sulla Sulla, Sullae *m.* (§16)

summon vocō (1-tr.) (2)

sun sōl, sōlis *m.* (14)

suppose putō (1-tr.) (11)

sure certus, -a, -um (7)

surely certō (adv.) (7)

surpass superō (1-tr.) (3)

surrender trādō, trādere, trādidī, trāditus (7)

surround cingō, cingere, cīnxī, cīnctus (15); circumdō, circumdare, circumdedī, circumdatus (15)

sweet dulcis, dulce (15)

swift celer, celeris, celere (15)

sword ferrum, ferrī *n.* (1); gladius, gladiī *m.* (1)

Tacitus Tacitus, Tacitī *m.* (§16)

take (up) capiō, capere, cēpī, captus (4)

take away auferō, auferre, abstulī, ablātus (7)

take in exchange mūtō (1-tr.) (13)

take on incipiō, incipere, incēpī, inceptus (13)

talent ingenium, ingeniī *n.* (7)

tall altus, -a, -um (4)

tear away rapiō, rapere, rapuī, raptus (15); ēripiō, ēripere, ēripuī, ēreptus (15)

tell dīcō, dīcere, dīxī, dictus (4)

temple templum, templī *n.* (7)

ten decem (indeclinable adj.) (4)

tenth decimus, -a, -um (§91)

terrify terreō, terrēre, terruī, territus (7)

territory fīnēs, fīnium *m. or f.* (10)

test experior, experīrī, expertus sum (8)

than quam (conj.) (11)

thanks grātia, grātiae *f.* (12)

that is, ea, id (demonstr. adj.) (4); ille, illa, illud (demonstr. adj./pron.) (8); quī, quae, quod (rel. pron.) (9); ut (conj.) *introduces Indirect Command* (9); quīn (conj.) *introduces Doubting clause* (12); nē (conj.) *introduces positive Fear clause* (15)

that (of yours) iste, ista, istud (8)

that . . . not nē (adv.) *introduces negative Indirect Command* (9); quīn (rel. adv.) *introduces negative Relative Clause of Characteristic* (10); quīn (rel. adv.) *introduces negative Relative Clause of Result* (14); quīn (conj.) *introduces Prevention clause* (15); ut (conj.) *introduces negative Fear clause* (15)

the fact that quod (conj.) (15)

their (own) suus, -a, -um (5)

them is, ea, id (demonstr. adj. *as third-person pron.*) (4)

themselves —, suī (reflexive pron.) (5)

then mox (adv.) (3); tandem (adv.) *in questions and commands* (9); tum *or* tunc (adv.) (12); ibi (adv.) (§130)

thence illinc (adv.) (§130); inde (adv.) (§130)

there ibi (adv.) (§130); illīc (adv.) (§130)

there is need of opus est (+ abl. *or* nom.) (10)

therefore quam ob rem (adv.) (9); quārē (adv.) (9); igitur (postpositive conj.) (11)

thereupon ibi (adv.) (§130); inde (adv.) (§130)

these is, ea, id (demonstr. adj.) (4); hic, haec, hoc (demonstr. adj./pron.) (8)

they is, ea, id (demonstr. adj. *as third-person pron.*) (4)

thing rēs, reī *f.* (8)

think cōgitō (1-tr.) (2); arbitror (1-tr.) (11); putō (1-tr.) (11)

third tertius, -a, -um (§91)

this is, ea, id (demonstr. adj.) (4); hic, haec, hoc (demonstr. adj./pron.) (8)

thither eō (adv.) (§130); illūc (adv.) (§130)

those is, ea, id (demonstr. adj.) (4); ille, illa, illud (demonstr. adj./pron.) (8)

those (of yours) iste, ista, istud (8)

thought sententia, sententiae *f.* (4)

thousand mīlle; mīlia, mīlium (§91)

thousandth mīllēsimus, -a, -um (§91)

three trēs, tria (§91)

throng agmen, agminis *n.* (14)

through per (prep. + acc.) (4)

throw iaciō, iacere, iēcī, iactus (11)

throw out ēiciō, ēicere, ēiēcī, ēiectus (11)

thus sīc (adv.) (5); ita (adv.) (7)

Tiberius Tiberius, Tiberiī *m.* (abbreviation: Ti.) (§16)

time tempus, temporis *n.* (8); aetās, aetātis *f.* (14)

it makes (one) tired taedet, taedēre, taesum est (15)

Titus Tītus, Tītī *m.* (abbreviation: T.) (§16)

to ad (prep. + acc.) (1)

to be going to be fore (11); futūrus, -a, -um esse (11)

to here hūc (adv.) (§130)

to such *or* **so great an extent** adeō (adv.) (14)

to that place eō (adv.) (§130)

to the same place eōdem (adv.) (§130)

to there illūc (adv.) (§130)

to where quō (rel. adv.) (10); quō (interrog. adv.) (12)

too quoque (adv.) (8)

too little parum (indeclinable subst.) (11); parum (adv.) (11)

top (of) summus, -a, -um (11)

toward ad (prep. + acc.) (1)

town oppidum, oppidī *n.* (1)

tranquil aequus, -a, -um (10)

treachery īnsidiae, īnsidiārum *f. pl.* (7)

trick ars, artis, -ium *f.* (7)

trivial levis, leve (9)

troop manus, manūs *f.* (8)

troops cōpiae, cōpiārum *f. pl.* (7)

Troy Īlium, Īliī *n.* (§16); Troia, Troiae *f.* (§16)

true vērus, -a, -um (7)

trust crēdō, crēdere, crēdidī, crēditus (+ dat.) (11)

trust fidēs, fideī *f.* (8)

trustworthiness fidēs, fideī *f.* (8)

try cōnor (1-tr.) (8); experior, experīrī, expertus sum (8)

Tullia Tullia, Tulliae *f.* (§16)

Tullius Cicero (M.) Tullius Cicerō, (M.) Tulliī Cicerōnis *m.* (§60)

Turnus Turnus, Turnī *m.* (§60)

two duo, duae, duo (§91)

ugly turpis, turpe (15)

uncertain incertus, -a, -um (7)

uncertainly incertō (7)

under sub (prep. + abl.) (6); sub (prep. + acc.) (6)

understand intellegō, intellegere, intellēxī, intellēctus (6)

undertaking inceptum, inceptī *n.* (13)

uneven inīquus, -a, -um (10)

unfortunate īnfēlīx, īnfēlīcis (8)

unfriendly inimīcus, -a, -um (+ dat.) (3)

ungrateful ingrātus, -a, -um (13)

unhappy īnfēlīx, īnfēlīcis (8)

unjust inīquus, -a, -um (10)

unless nisi (conj.) (5)

unlike dissimilis, dissimile (+ gen. or dat.) (11)

unlucky īnfēlīx, īnfēlīcis (8)

unpleasant ingrātus, -a, -um (13)

unreliable incertus, -a, -um (7)

unsure incertus, -a, -um (7)

until dōnec (conj.) (13); dum (conj.) (13)

unworthy (of) indignus, -a, -um (+ abl.) (12)

up to sub (prep. + acc.) (6)

urge hortor (1-tr.) (9)

us nōs, nostrum/nostrī (personal pron.) (4)

use ūtor, ūtī, ūsus sum (+ abl.) (10)

utter iaciō, iacere, iēcī, iactus (11)

Valerius Catullus (C.) Valerius Catullus, (C.) Valeriī Catullī *m.* (§16)

value aestimō (1-tr.) (13)

value pretium, pretiī *n.* (13)

Venus Venus, Veneris *f.* (§60)

Vergilius Maro (Vergil) P. Vergilius Marō, P. Vergiliī Marōnis *m.* (§60)

very ipse, ipsa, ipsum (5)

(so) very adeō (adv.) (14)

Vesta Vesta, Vestae *f.* (§60)
villainy scelus, sceleris *n.* (13)
violence vīs, ——, -ium *f.* (6)
virtue virtūs, virtūtis *f.* (7)
voice vōx, vōcis *f.* (7)
Vulcan Vulcānus, Vulcānī *m.* (§60)

to wage war bellum gerere (4)
wait moror (1-tr.) (13)
wait for ex(s)pectō (1-tr.) (13)
walk ambulō (1-intr.) (2); gradior, gradī, gressus sum (13)
wall mūrus, mūrī *m.* (11)
(city) walls moenia, moenium *n. pl.* (6)
wander errō (1-intr.) (2)
want cupiō, cupere, cupiī *or* cupīvī, cupītus (7); volō, velle, voluī, —— (12)
want more mālō, mālle, māluī, —— (12)
war bellum, bellī *n.* (1)
warn moneō, monēre, monuī, monitus (9)
way via, viae *f.* (1); modus, modī *m.* (9)
we nōs, nostrum/nostrī (personal pron.) (4)
weapon tēlum, tēlī *n.* (11)
weapons arma, armōrum *n. pl.* (2)
well bene (adv.) (5)
west occidēns, occidentis *m.* (14)
what quis, quid (interrog. pron. (9); quī, quae, quod (interrog. adj.) (9) **what sort of** quālis, quāle (13)
when ubi (conj.) (5); ubi (interrog. adv.) (5); ut (conj.) (5); cum (conj.) (12)
whence unde (rel. adv.) (10); unde (interrog. adv.) (12)
where ubi (interrog. adv.) (5); ubi (rel. adv.) (10)
whether an (conj.) *introduces an Indirect Question* (12); num (adv.) *introduces an Indirect Question* (12); utrum (interrog. particle) *introduces an Indirect Question* (12)
whether . . . or . . . utrum . . . an . . . (12); -ne . . . an . . . (12); —— . . . an . . . (12)
which quī, quae, quod (rel. pron.) (9); quī, quae, quod (interrog. adj.) (9)
which (of two) uter, utra, utrum (9)
while dōnec (conj.) (13); dum (conj.) (13)
whither quō (rel. adv.) (10); quō (interrog. adv.) (12)
who quī, quae, quod (rel. pron.) (9); quis, quid (interrog. pron.) (9)

who . . . not quīn (rel. adv.) *introduces negative Relative Clause of Characteristic or Result* (10) (14)
whole tōtus, -a, -um (9)
why cūr (interrog. adv.) (2); quam ob rem (interrog. adv.) (9); quārē (interrog. adv.) (9)
wicked impius, -a, -um (5)
wicked deed scelus, sceleris *n.* (13)
wife fēmina, fēminae *f.* (1)
win capiō, capere, cēpī, captus (4); vincō, vincere, vīcī, victus (7)
wisdom sapientia, sapientiae *f.* (2)
wise sapiēns, sapientis (11)
wish volō, velle, voluī, —— (12)
to wish ill male velle (12)
to wish well bene velle (12)
with cum (prep. + abl.) (1)
with difficulty difficulter (adv.) (8)
withdraw cēdō, cēdere, cessī, cessum (5)
without sine (prep. + abl.) (3)
woman fēmina, fēminae *f.* (1)
word verbum, verbī *n.* (1); dictum, dictī *n.* (6); vōx, vōcis *f.* (7)
work labōrō (1-intr.) (2); labor, labōris *m.* (10); opus, operis *n.* (10)
world orbis terrārum (15)
worse peior, peius (11); peius (11)
worst pessimus, -a, -um (11); pessimē (adv.) (11)
worthy (of) dignus, -a, -um (+ abl.) (12)
wound vulnus, vulneris *n.* (13)
wrath īra, īrae *f.* (2)
wretched miser, misera, miserum (3)
write scrībō, scrībere, scrīpsī, scrīptus (4)

year annus, annī *m.* (8)
yield cēdō, cēdere, cessī, cessum (5)
you tū, tuī (personal pron.) (4)
you (pl.) vōs, vestrum/vestrī (personal pron.) (4)
your tuus, -a, -um (4)
your (pl.) vester, vestra, vestrum (4)
your (own) tuus, -a, -um (5)
your (pl.) own vester, vestra, vestrum (5)
yours tuus, -a, -um (4)
yours (pl.) vester, vestra, vestrum (4)
yourself ——, tuī (reflexive pron.) (5)
yourselves ——, vestrum/vestrī (reflexive pron.) (5)

zeal studium, studiī *n.* (2)

MORPHOLOGY APPENDIX

Note: Forms in brackets are not introduced in this book.

Verbs

First Conjugation

Principal Parts: **vocō, vocāre, vocāvī, vocātus**

INDICATIVE			SUBJUNCTIVE	
Present				
Active	Passive		Active	Passive
		Singular		
1 **vocō**	**vocor**		1 **vocem**	**vocer**
2 **vocās**	**vocāris/vocāre**		2 **vocēs**	**vocēris/vocēre**
3 **vocat**	**vocātur**		3 **vocet**	**vocētur**
		Plural		
1 **vocāmus**	**vocāmur**		1 **vocēmus**	**vocēmur**
2 **vocātis**	**vocāminī**		2 **vocētis**	**vocēminī**
3 **vocant**	**vocantur**		3 **vocent**	**vocentur**
Imperfect				
Active	Passive		Active	Passive
		Singular		
1 **vocābam**	**vocābar**		1 **vocārem**	**vocārer**
2 **vocābās**	**vocābāris/vocābāre**		2 **vocārēs**	**vocārēris/vocārēre**
3 **vocābat**	**vocābātur**		3 **vocāret**	**vocārētur**
		Plural		
1 **vocābāmus**	**vocābāmur**		1 **vocārēmus**	**vocārēmur**
2 **vocābātis**	**vocābāminī**		2 **vocārētis**	**vocārēminī**
3 **vocābant**	**vocābantur**		3 **vocārent**	**vocārentur**

	INDICATIVE			SUBJUNCTIVE

Future

	Active	Passive
	Singular	
1	vocābō	vocābor
2	vocābis	vocāberis/vocābere
3	vocābit	vocābitur
	Plural	
1	vocābimus	vocābimur
2	vocābitis	vocābiminī
3	vocābunt	vocābuntur

Perfect

	Active	Passive		Active	Passive
		Singular			
1	vocāvī	vocātus, -a, -um sum	1	vocāverim	vocātus, -a, -um sim
2	vocāvistī	vocātus, -a, -um es	2	vocāveris	vocātus, -a, -um sīs
3	vocāvit	vocātus, -a, -um est	3	vocāverit	vocātus, -a, -um sit
		Plural			
1	vocāvimus	vocātī, -ae, -a sumus	1	vocāverimus	vocātī, -ae, -a sīmus
2	vocāvistis	vocātī, -ae, -a estis	2	vocāveritis	vocātī, -ae, -a sītis
3	vocāvērunt/ vocāvēre	vocātī, -ae, -a sunt	3	vocāverint	vocātī, -ae, -a sint

Pluperfect

	Active	Passive		Active	Passive
		Singular			
1	vocāveram	vocātus, -a, -um eram	1	vocāvissem	vocātus, -a, -um essem
2	vocāverās	vocātus, -a, -um erās	2	vocāvissēs	vocātus, -a, -um essēs
3	vocāverat	vocātus, -a, -um erat	3	vocāvisset	vocātus, -a, -um esset
		Plural			
1	vocāverāmus	vocātī, -ae, -a erāmus	1	vocāvissēmus	vocātī, -ae, -a essēmus
2	vocāverātis	vocātī, -ae, -a erātis	2	vocāvissētis	vocātī, -ae, -a essētis
3	vocāverant	vocātī, -ae, -a erant	3	vocāvissent	vocātī, -ae, -a essent

Future Perfect

	Active	Passive
	Singular	
1	vocāverō	vocātus, -a, -um erō
2	vocāveris	vocātus, -a, -um eris
3	vocāverit	vocātus, -a, -um erit
	Plural	
1	vocāverimus	vocātī, -ae, -a erimus
2	vocāveritis	vocātī, -ae, -a eritis
3	vocāverint	vocātī, -ae, -a erunt

Participle

	Active	Passive
Present	**vocāns, vocantis**	
Perfect		**vocātus, -a, -um**
Future	**vocātūrus, -a, -um**	**vocandus, -a, -um**

Infinitive

	Active	Passive
Present	**vocāre**	**vocārī**
Perfect	**vocāvisse**	**vocātus, -a, -um esse**
Future	**vocātūrus, -a, -um esse**	**[vocātum īrī]**

Imperative

Present	Active		Passive
Singular	2	**vocā**	**vocāre**
Plural	2	**vocāte**	**vocāminī**

[Future	Active		Passive
Singular	2	**vocātō**	**vocātor**
	3	**vocātō**	**vocātor**
Plural	2	**vocātōte**	
	3	**vocantō**	**vocantor]**

Second Conjugation

Principal Parts: **moveō, movēre, mōvī, mōtus**

INDICATIVE		SUBJUNCTIVE	

Present

Active	Passive		Active	Passive
Singular				
1 moveō	moveor	1	moveam	movear
2 movēs	movēris/movēre	2	moveās	moveāris/moveāre
3 movet	movētur	3	moveat	moveātur
Plural				
1 movēmus	movēmur	1	moveāmus	moveāmur
2 movētis	movēminī	2	moveātis	moveāminī
3 movent	moventur	3	moveant	moveantur

Imperfect

Active	Passive		Active	Passive
Singular				
1 movēbam	movēbar	1	movērem	movērer
2 movēbās	movēbāris/movēbāre	2	movērēs	movērēris/movērēre
3 movēbat	movēbātur	3	movēret	movērētur
Plural				
1 movēbāmus	movēbāmur	1	movērēmus	movērēmur
2 movēbātis	movēbāminī	2	movērētis	movērēminī
3 movēbant	movēbantur	3	movērent	movērentur

INDICATIVE   **SUBJUNCTIVE**

Future

	Active	Passive
		Singular
1	movēbō	movēbor
2	movēbis	movēberis/movēbere
3	movēbit	movēbitur
		Plural
1	movēbimus	movēbimur
2	movēbitis	movēbiminī
3	movēbunt	movēbuntur

Perfect

	Active	Passive		Active	Passive
			Singular		
1	mōvī	mōtus, -a, -um sum	1	mōverim	mōtus, -a, -um sim
2	mōvistī	mōtus, -a, -um es	2	mōveris	mōtus, -a, -um sīs
3	mōvit	mōtus, -a, -um est	3	mōverit	mōtus, -a, -um sit
			Plural		
1	mōvimus	mōtī, -ae, -a sumus	1	mōverimus	mōtī, -ae, -a sīmus
2	mōvistis	mōtī, -ae, -a estis	2	mōveritis	mōtī, -ae, -a sītis
3	mōvērunt/mōvēre	mōtī, -ae, -a sunt	3	mōverint	mōtī, -ae, -a sint

---

Pluperfect

	Active	Passive		Active	Passive
			Singular		
1	mōveram	mōtus, -a, -um eram	1	mōvissem	mōtus, -a, -um essem
2	mōverās	mōtus, -a, -um erās	2	mōvissēs	mōtus, -a, -um essēs
3	mōverat	mōtus, -a, -um erat	3	mōvisset	mōtus, -a, -um esset
			Plural		
1	mōverāmus	mōtī, -ae, -a erāmus	1	mōvissēmus	mōtī, -ae, -a essēmus
2	mōverātis	mōtī, -ae, -a erātis	2	mōvissētis	mōtī, -ae, -a essētis
3	mōverant	mōtī, -ae, -a erant	3	mōvissent	mōtī, -ae, -a essent

---

Future Perfect

	Active	Passive
		Singular
1	mōverō	mōtus, -a, -um erō
2	mōveris	mōtus, -a, -um eris
3	mōverit	mōtus, -a, -um erit
		Plural
1	mōverimus	mōtī, -ae, -a erimus
2	mōveritis	mōtī, -ae, -a eritis
3	mōverint	mōtī, -ae, -a erunt

Participle

	Active	Passive
Present	**movēns, moventis**	
Perfect		**mōtus, -a, -um**
Future	**mōtūrus, -a, -um**	**movendus, -a, -um**

Infinitive

	Active	Passive
Present	**movēre**	**movērī**
Perfect	**mōvisse**	**mōtus, -a, -um esse**
Future	**mōtūrus, -a, -um esse**	**[mōtum īrī]**

Imperative

Present	Active	Passive
Singular	2 **movē**	**movēre**
Plural	2 **movēte**	**movēminī**

[Future	Active	Passive
Singular	2 **movētō**	**movētor**
	3 **movētō**	**movētor**
Plural	2 **movētōte**	
	3 **moventō**	**moventor**]

Third Conjugation

Principal Parts: **regō, regere, rēxī, rēctus**

	INDICATIVE		SUBJUNCTIVE	
Present				
	Active	Passive	Active	Passive
		Singular		
1	**regō**	**regor**	1 **regam**	**regar**
2	**regis**	**regeris/regere**	2 **regās**	**regāris/regāre**
3	**regit**	**regitur**	3 **regat**	**regātur**
		Plural		
1	**regimus**	**regimur**	1 **regāmus**	**regāmur**
2	**regitis**	**regiminī**	2 **regātis**	**regāminī**
3	**regunt**	**reguntur**	3 **regant**	**regantur**
Imperfect				
	Active	Passive	Active	Passive
		Singular		
1	**regēbam**	**regēbar**	1 **regerem**	**regerer**
2	**regēbās**	**regēbāris/regēbāre**	2 **regerēs**	**regerēris/regerēre**
3	**regēbat**	**regēbātur**	3 **regeret**	**regerētur**
		Plural		
1	**regēbāmus**	**regēbāmur**	1 **regerēmus**	**regerēmur**
2	**regēbātis**	**regēbāminī**	2 **regerētis**	**regerēminī**
3	**regēbant**	**regēbantur**	3 **regerent**	**regerentur**

INDICATIVE		SUBJUNCTIVE

Future

	Active	Passive
		Singular
1	regam	regar
2	regēs	regēris/regēre
3	reget	regētur
		Plural
1	regēmus	regēmur
2	regētis	regēminī
3	regent	regentur

Perfect

	Active	Passive		Active	Passive
			Singular		
1	rēxī	rēctus, -a, -um sum	1	rēxerim	rēctus, -a, -um sim
2	rēxistī	rēctus, -a, -um es	2	rēxeris	rēctus, -a, -um sīs
3	rēxit	rēctus, -a, -um est	3	rēxerit	rēctus, -a, -um sit
			Plural		
1	rēximus	rēctī, -ae, -a sumus	1	rēxerimus	rēctī, -ae, -a sīmus
2	rēxistis	rēctī, -ae, -a estis	2	rēxeritis	rēctī, -ae, -a sītis
3	rēxērunt/rēxēre	rēctī, -ae, -a sunt	3	rēxerint	rēctī, -ae, -a sint

Pluperfect

	Active	Passive		Active	Passive
			Singular		
1	rēxeram	rēctus, -a, -um eram	1	rēxissem	rēctus, -a, -um essem
2	rēxerās	rēctus, -a, -um erās	2	rēxissēs	rēctus, -a, -um essēs
3	rēxerat	rēctus, -a, -um erat	3	rēxisset	rēctus, -a, -um esset
			Plural		
1	rēxerāmus	rēctī, -ae, -a erāmus	1	rēxissēmus	rēctī, -ae, -a essēmus
2	rēxerātis	rēctī, -ae, -a erātis	2	rēxissētis	rēctī, -ae, -a essētis
3	rēxerant	rēctī, -ae, -a erant	3	rēxissent	rēctī, -ae, -a essent

Future Perfect

	Active	Passive
		Singular
1	rēxerō	rēctus, -a, -um erō
2	rēxeris	rēctus, -a, -um eris
3	rēxerit	rēctus, -a, -um erit
		Plural
1	rēxerimus	rēctī, -ae, -a erimus
2	rēxeritis	rēctī, -ae, -a eritis
3	rēxerint	rēctī, -ae, -a erunt

Participle

	Active	Passive
Present	**regēns, regentis**	
Perfect		**rēctus, -a, -um**
Future	**rēctūrus, -a, -um**	**regendus, -a, -um**

Infinitive

	Active	Passive
Present	**regere**	**regī**
Perfect	**rēxisse**	**rēctus, -a, -um esse**
Future	**rēctūrus, -a, -um esse**	**[rēctum īrī]**

Imperative

		Active	Passive
Present		Active	Passive
Singular	2	**rege**	**regere**
Plural	2	**regite**	**regiminī**

[Future		Active	Passive
Singular	2	**regitō**	**regitor**
	3	**regitō**	**regitor**
Plural	2	**regitōte**	
	3	**reguntō**	**reguntor]**

Third I-stem Conjugation

Principal Parts: **capiō, capere, cēpī, captus**

INDICATIVE		**SUBJUNCTIVE**	

Present

	Active	Passive		Active	Passive
			Singular		
1	**capiō**	**capior**	1	**capiam**	**capiar**
2	**capis**	**caperis/capere**	2	**capiās**	**capiāris/capiāre**
3	**capit**	**capitur**	3	**capiat**	**capiātur**
			Plural		
1	**capimus**	**capimur**	1	**capiāmus**	**capiāmur**
2	**capitis**	**capiminī**	2	**capiātis**	**capiāminī**
3	**capiunt**	**capiuntur**	3	**capiant**	**capiantur**

Imperfect

	Active	Passive		Active	Passive
			Singular		
1	**capiēbam**	**capiēbar**	1	**caperem**	**caperer**
2	**capiēbās**	**capiēbāris/capiēbāre**	2	**caperēs**	**caperēris/caperēre**
3	**capiēbat**	**capiēbātur**	3	**caperet**	**caperētur**
			Plural		
1	**capiēbāmus**	**capiēbāmur**	1	**caperēmus**	**caperēmur**
2	**capiēbātis**	**capiēbāminī**	2	**caperētis**	**caperēminī**
3	**capiēbant**	**capiēbantur**	3	**caperent**	**caperentur**

INDICATIVE   SUBJUNCTIVE

Future

	Active	Passive
		Singular
1	capiam	capiar
2	capiēs	capiēris/capiēre
3	capiet	capiētur
		Plural
1	capiēmus	capiēmur
2	capiētis	capiēminī
3	capient	capientur

Perfect

	Active	Passive		Active	Passive
				Singular	
1	cēpī	captus, -a, -um sum	1	cēperim	captus, -a, -um sim
2	cēpistī	captus, -a, -um es	2	cēperis	captus, -a, -um sīs
3	cēpit	captus, -a, -um est	3	cēperit	captus, -a, -um sit
				Plural	
1	cēpimus	captī, -ae, -a sumus	1	cēperimus	captī, -ae, -a sīmus
2	cēpistis	captī, -ae, -a estis	2	cēperitis	captī, -ae, -a sītis
3	cēpērunt/cēpēre	captī, -ae, -a sunt	3	cēperint	captī, -ae, -a sint

Pluperfect

	Active	Passive		Active	Passive
				Singular	
1	cēperam	captus, -a, -um eram	1	cēpissem	captus, -a, -um essem
2	cēperās	captus, -a, -um erās	2	cēpissēs	captus, -a, -um essēs
3	cēperat	captus, -a, -um erat	3	cēpisset	captus, -a, -um esset
				Plural	
1	cēperāmus	captī, -ae, -a erāmus	1	cēpissēmus	captī, -ae, -a essēmus
2	cēperātis	captī, -ae, -a erātis	2	cēpissētis	captī, -ae, -a essētis
3	cēperant	captī, -ae, -a erant	3	cēpissent	captī, -ae, -a essent

Future Perfect

	Active	Passive
		Singular
1	cēperō	captus, -a, -um erō
2	cēperis	captus, -a, -um eris
3	cēperit	captus, -a, -um erit
		Plural
1	cēperimus	captī, -ae, -a erimus
2	cēperitis	captī, -ae, -a eritis
3	cēperint	captī, -ae, -a erunt

Participle

	Active	Passive
Present	capiēns, capientis	
Perfect		captus, -a, -um
Future	captūrus, -a, -um	capiendus, -a, -um

Infinitive

	Active	Passive
Present	capere	capī
Perfect	cēpisse	captus, -a, -um esse
Future	captūrus, -a, -um esse	[captum īrī]

Imperative

Present	Active	Passive
Singular	2 cape	capere
Plural	2 capite	capiminī

[Future	Active	Passive
Singular	2 capitō	capitor
	3 capitō	capitor
Plural	2 capitōte	
	3 capiuntō	capiuntor]

Fourth Conjugation

Principal Parts: **audiō, audīre, audīvī, audītus**

	INDICATIVE		SUBJUNCTIVE	
Present	Active	Passive	Active	Passive
Singular				
1	audiō	audior	1 audiam	audiar
2	audīs	audīris/audīre	2 audiās	audiāris/audiāre
3	audit	audītur	3 audiat	audiātur
Plural				
1	audīmus	audīmur	1 audiāmus	audiāmur
2	audītis	audīminī	2 audiātis	audiāminī
3	audiunt	audiuntur	3 audiant	audiantur
Imperfect	Active	Passive	Active	Passive
Singular				
1	audiēbam	audiēbar	1 audīrem	audīrer
2	audiēbās	audiēbāris/audiēbāre	2 audīrēs	audīrēris/audīrēre
3	audiēbat	audiēbātur	3 audīret	audīrētur
Plural				
1	audiēbāmus	audiēbāmur	1 audīrēmus	audīrēmur
2	audiēbātis	audiēbāminī	2 audīrētis	audīrēminī
3	audiēbant	audiēbantur	3 audīrent	audīrentur

INDICATIVE   **SUBJUNCTIVE**

Future

	Active	Passive
		Singular
1	audiam	audiar
2	audiēs	audiēris/audiēre
3	audiet	audiētur
		Plural
1	audiēmus	audiēmur
2	audiētis	audiēminī
3	audient	audientur

Perfect

	Active	Passive		Active	Passive
			Singular		
1	audīvī	audītus, -a, -um sum	1	audīverim	audītus, -a, -um sim
2	audīvistī	audītus, -a, -um es	2	audīveris	audītus, -a, -um sīs
3	audīvit	audītus, -a, -um est	3	audīverit	audītus, -a, -um sit
			Plural		
1	audīvimus	audītī, -ae, -a sumus	1	audīverimus	audītī, -ae, -a sīmus
2	audīvistis	audītī, -ae, -a estis	2	audīveritis	audītī, -ae, -a sītis
3	audīvērunt/audīvēre	audītī, -ae, -a sunt	3	audīverint	audītī, -ae, -a sint

Pluperfect

	Active	Passive		Active	Passive
			Singular		
1	audīveram	audītus, -a, -um eram	1	audīvissem	audītus, -a, -um essem
2	audīverās	audītus, -a, -um erās	2	audīvissēs	audītus, -a, -um essēs
3	audīverat	audītus, -a, -um erat	3	audīvisset	audītus, -a, -um esset
			Plural		
1	audīverāmus	audītī, -ae, -a erāmus	1	audīvissēmus	audītī, -ae, -a essēmus
2	audīverātis	audītī, -ae, -a erātis	2	audīvissētis	audītī, -ae, -a essētis
3	audīverant	audītī, -ae, -a erant	3	audīvissent	audītī, -ae, -a essent

Future Perfect

	Active	Passive
		Singular
1	audīverō	audītus, -a, -um erō
2	audīveris	audītus, -a, -um eris
3	audīverit	audītus, -a, -um erit
		Plural
1	audīverimus	audītī, -ae, -a erimus
2	audīveritis	audītī, -ae, -a eritis
3	audīverint	audītī, -ae, -a erunt

Participle

	Active	Passive
Present	audiēns, audientis	
Perfect		audītus, -a, -um
Future	audītūrus, -a, -um	audiendus, -a, -um

Infinitive

	Active	Passive
Present	**audīre**	**audīrī**
Perfect	**audīvisse**	**audītus, -a, -um esse**
Future	**audītūrus, -a, -um esse**	**[audītum īrī]**

Imperative

Present	Active	Passive
Singular	2 **audī**	**audīre**
Plural	2 **audīte**	**audīminī**

[Future	Active	Passive
Singular	2 **audītō**	**audītor**
	3 **audītō**	**audītor**
Plural	2 **audītōte**	
	3 **audiuntō**	**audiuntor]**

Irregular Verbs

Principal Parts: **sum, esse, fuī, futūrus**

	INDICATIVE			SUBJUNCTIVE
Present	*Imperfect*	*Future*	*Present*	*Imperfect*
		Singular		
1 sum	eram	erō	sim	essem
2 es	erās	eris	sīs	essēs
3 est	erat	erit	sit	esset
		Plural		
1 sumus	erāmus	erimus	sīmus	essēmus
2 estis	erātis	eritis	sītis	essētis
3 sunt	erant	erunt	sint	essent
Perfect	*Pluperfect*	*Future Perfect*	*Perfect*	*Pluperfect*
		Singular		
1 fuī	fueram	fuerō	fuerim	fuissem
2 fuistī	fuerās	fueris	fueris	fuissēs
3 fuit	fuerat	fuerit	fuerit	fuisset
		Plural		
1 fuimus	fuerāmus	fuerimus	fuerimus	fuissēmus
2 fuistis	fuerātis	fueritis	fueritis	fuissētis
3 fuērunt/fuēre	fuerant	fuerint	fuerint	fuissent

Participle:	Future Active: **futūrus, -a, -um**

Infinitive:	Present Active: **esse**
	Perfect Active: **fuisse**
	Future Active: **futūrus, -a, -um esse** or **fore**

[Imperative	*Present Active*	*Future Active*	
Singular	2 **es**	2 **estō**	3 **estō**
Plural	2 **este**	2 **estōte**	3 **suntō]**

Principal Parts: **possum, posse, potuī, ——**

	INDICATIVE			SUBJUNCTIVE	
Present	*Imperfect*	*Future*	*Present*	*Imperfect*	
		Singular			
1 possum	poteram	poterō	possim	possem	
2 potes	poterās	poteris	possīs	possēs	
3 potest	poterat	poterit	possit	posset	
		Plural			
1 possumus	poterāmus	poterimus	possīmus	possēmus	
2 potestis	poterātis	poteritis	possītis	possētis	
3 possunt	poterant	poterunt	possint	possent	
Perfect	*Pluperfect*	*Future Perfect*	*Perfect*	*Pluperfect*	
		Singular			
1 potuī	potueram	potuerō	potuerim	potuissem	
2 potuistī	potuerās	potueris	potueris	potuissēs	
3 potuit	potuerat	potuerit	potuerit	potuisset	
		Plural			
1 potuimus	potuerāmus	potuerimus	potuerimus	potuissēmus	
2 potuistis	potuerātis	potueritis	potueritis	potuissētis	
3 potuērunt/ potuēre	potuerant	potuerint	potuerint	potuissent	

Infinitive:	Present Active: **posse**	Perfect Active: **potuisse**

Principal Parts: **eō, īre, iī** or **īvī, itum**

	INDICATIVE			SUBJUNCTIVE	
Present	*Imperfect*	*Future*	*Present*	*Imperfect*	
		Singular			
1 eō	ībam	ībō	eam	īrem	
2 īs	ībās	ībis	eās	īrēs	
3 it	ībat	ībit	eat	īret	
		Plural			
1 īmus	ībāmus	ībimus	eāmus	īrēmus	
2 ītis	ībātis	ībitis	eātis	īrētis	
3 eunt	ībant	ībunt	eant	īrent	

INDICATIVE   SUBJUNCTIVE

	Perfect	*Pluperfect*	*Future Perfect*	*Perfect*	*Pluperfect*
			Singular		
1	iī/īvī	ieram/īveram	ierō/īverō	ierim/īverim	īssem/īvissem
2	īstī/īvistī	ierās/īverās	ieris/īveris	ieris/īveris	īssēs/īvissēs
3	iit/īt/īvit	ierat/īverat	ierit/īverit	ierit/īverit	īsset/īvisset
			Plural		
1	iimus/īmus/	ierāmus/	ierimus/	ierimus/	īssēmus/
	īvimus	īverāmus	īverimus	īverimus	īvissēmus
2	īstis/īvistis	ierātis/īverātis	ieritis/īveritis	ieritis/īveritis	īssētis/īvissētis
3	iērunt/iēre	ierant/īverant	ierint/īverint	ierint/īverint	īssent/īvissent
	īvērunt/īvēre				

Participle

	Active	Passive
Present	iēns, euntis	
Perfect		itum
Future	itūrus, -a, -um	eundum

Infinitive

	Active	Passive
Present	īre	[īrī]
Perfect	īsse/īvisse	itum esse
Future	itūrus, -a, -um esse	

Imperative	*Present Active*	[*Future Active*	
Singular	2 ī	2 ītō	3 ītō
Plural	2 īte	2 ītōte	3 euntō]

Principal Parts: **ferō, ferre, tulī, lātus**

INDICATIVE   SUBJUNCTIVE

Present

	Active	Passive			Active	Passive
			Singular			
1	ferō	feror		1	feram	ferar
2	fers	ferris/ferre		2	ferās	ferāris/ferāre
3	fert	fertur		3	ferat	ferātur
			Plural			
1	ferimus	ferimur		1	ferāmus	ferāmur
2	fertis	feriminī		2	ferātis	ferāminī
3	ferunt	feruntur		3	ferant	ferantur

INDICATIVE		SUBJUNCTIVE	

Imperfect

Active	Passive		Active	Passive
		Singular		
1 ferēbam	ferēbar	1	ferrem	ferrer
2 ferēbās	ferēbāris/ferēbāre	2	ferrēs	ferrēris/ferrēre
3 ferēbat	ferēbātur	3	ferret	ferrētur
		Plural		
1 ferēbāmus	ferēbāmur	1	ferrēmus	ferrēmur
2 ferēbātis	ferēbāminī	2	ferrētis	ferrēminī
3 ferēbant	ferēbantur	3	ferrent	ferrentur

Future

Active		Passive
	Singular	
1 feram		ferar
2 ferēs		ferēris/ferēre
3 feret		ferētur
	Plural	
1 ferēmus		ferēmur
2 ferētis		ferēminī
3 ferent		ferentur

Perfect

Active	Passive		Active	Passive
		Singular		
1 tulī	lātus, -a, -um sum	1	tulerim	lātus, -a, -um sim
2 tulistī	lātus, -a, -um es	2	tuleris	lātus, -a, -um sīs
3 tulit	lātus, -a, -um est	3	tulerit	lātus, -a, -um sit
		Plural		
1 tulimus	lātī, -ae, -a sumus	1	tulerimus	lātī, -ae, -a sīmus
2 tulistis	lātī, -ae, -a estis	2	tuleritis	lātī, -ae, -a sītis
3 tulērunt/tulēre	lātī, -ae, -a sunt	3	tulerint	lātī, -ae, -a sint

Pluperfect

Active	Passive		Active	Passive
		Singular		
1 tuleram	lātus, -a, -um eram	1	tulissem	lātus, -a, -um essem
2 tulerās	lātus, -a, -um erās	2	tulissēs	lātus, -a, -um essēs
3 tulerat	lātus, -a, -um erat	3	tulisset	lātus, -a, -um esset
		Plural		
1 tulerāmus	lātī, -ae, -a erāmus	1	tulissēmus	lātī, -ae, -a essēmus
2 tulerātis	lātī, -ae, -a erātis	2	tulissētis	lātī, -ae, -a essētis
3 tulerant	lātī, -ae, -a erant	3	tulissent	lātī, -ae, -a essent

	INDICATIVE		SUBJUNCTIVE

Future Perfect

	Active	Passive
	Singular	
1	tulerō	lātus, -a, -um erō
2	tuleris	lātus, -a, -um eris
3	tulerit	lātus, -a, -um erit
	Plural	
1	tulerimus	lātī, -ae, -a erimus
2	tuleritis	lātī, -ae, -a eritis
3	tulerint	lātī, -ae, -a erunt

Participle

	Active	Passive
Present	ferēns, ferentis	
Perfect		lātus, -a, -um
Future	lātūrus, -a, -um	ferendus, -a, -um

Infinitive

	Active	Passive
Present	ferre	ferrī
Perfect	tulisse	lātus, -a, -um esse
Future	lātūrus, -a, -um esse	[lātum īrī]

Imperative

Present	Active	Passive
Singular	2 fer	ferre
Plural	2 ferte	feriminī

[Future	Active	
Singular	2 fertō	fertor
	3 fertō	fertor
Plural	2 fertōte	——
	3 feruntō	feruntur]

Principal Parts: **volō, velle, voluī, ——**
nōlō, nōlle, nōluī, ——
mālō, mālle, māluī, ——

	INDICATIVE ACTIVE			SUBJUNCTIVE ACTIVE		

Present

			Singular			
1	volō	nōlō	mālō	velim	nōlim	mālim
2	vīs	nōn vīs	māvīs	velīs	nōlīs	mālīs
3	vult	nōn vult	māvult	velit	nōlit	mālit
			Plural			
1	volumus	nōlumus	mālumus	velīmus	nōlīmus	mālīmus
2	vultis	nōn vultis	māvultis	velītis	nōlītis	mālītis
3	volunt	nōlunt	mālunt	velint	nōlint	mālint

INDICATIVE ACTIVE			SUBJUNCTIVE ACTIVE		

Imperfect

Singular

1 volēbam	nōlēbam	mālēbam	vellem	nōllem	mallem
2 volēbās	nōlēbās	mālēbās	vellēs	nōllēs	mallēs
3 volēbat	nōlēbat	mālēbat	vellet	nōlit	mallet

Plural

1 volēbāmus	nōlēbāmus	mālēbāmus	vellēmus	nōllēmus	mallēmus
2 volēbātis	nōlēbātis	mālēbātis	vellētis	nōllētis	mallētis
3 volēbant	nōlēbant	mālēbant	vellent	nōllent	mallent

Future

Singular

1 volam	*nōlam	*mālam
2 volēs	nōlēs	mālēs
3 volet	nōlet	mālet

Plural

1 volēmus	nōlēmus	mālēmus
2 volētis	nōlētis	mālētis
3 volent	nōlent	mālent

Perfect

Singular

1 voluī	nōluī	māluī	voluerim	nōluerim	māluerim
2 voluistī	nōluistī	mālistī	volueris	nōlueris	mālueris
3 voluit	nōluit	māluit	voluerit	nōluerit	māluerit

Plural

1 voluimus	nōluimus	māluimus	voluerimus	nōluerimus	māluerimus
2 voluistis	nōluistis	māluistis	volueritis	nōlueritis	mālueritis
3 voluērunt/	nōluērunt/	māluērunt/	voluerint	nōluerint	māluerint
voluēre	nōluēre	māluēre			

Pluperfect

Singular

1 volueram	nōlueram	mālueram	voluissem	nōluissem	māluissem
2 voluerās	nōluerās	māluerās	voluissēs	nōluissēs	māluissēs
3 voluerat	nōluerat	māluerat	voluisset	nōluisset	māluisset

Plural

1 voluerāmus	nōluerāmus	māluerāmus	voluissēmus	nōluissēmus	māluissēmus
2 voluerātis	nōluerātis	māluerātis	voluissētis	nōluissētis	māluissētis
3 voluerant	nōluerant	māluerant	voluissent	nōluissent	māluissent

INDICATIVE ACTIVE

Future Perfect

		Singular	
1	voluerō	nōluerō	māluerō
2	volueris	nōlueris	mālueris
3	voluerit	nōluerit	māluerit
		Plural	
1	voluerimus	nōluerimus	māluerimus
2	volueritis	nōlueritis	mālueritis
3	voluerint	nōluerint	māluerint

Participle:	Present Active: **volēns, volentis; nōlēns, nōlentis**
Infinitive:	Present Active: **velle, nōlle, mālle**
	Perfect Active: **voluisse, nōluisse, māluisse**
Imperative	Present Active: **nōlī** (2nd sing.), **nōlīte** (2nd pl.)

fīō, fierī, factus sum

INDICATIVE ACTIVE			**SUBJUNCTIVE ACTIVE**	
Present	*Imperfect*	*Future*	*Present*	*Imperfect*
		Singular		
1 fīō	fīēbam	fīam	fīam	fierem
2 fīs	fīēbās	fīēs	fīās	fierēs
3 fit	fīēbat	fīēt	fīat	fieret
		Plural		
1 fīmus	fīēbāmus	fīēmus	fīāmus	fierēmus
2 fītis	fīēbātis	fīētis	fīātis	fierētis
3 fīunt	fīēbant	fīent	fīant	fierent

Infinitive:	Present Active: **fierī**
Imperative	Present Active: **fī** (2nd sing.), **fīte** (2nd pl.)

Nouns

First Declension

puella, puellae *f.*

Second Declension

servus, servī *m.*
puer, puerī *m.*
perīculum, perīculī *n.*

		M./F.		N.
Singular				
Nom.	puella	servus	puer	perīculum
Gen.	puellae	servī	puerī	perīculī
Dat.	puellae	servō	puerō	perīculō
Acc.	puellam	servum	puerum	perīculum
Abl.	puellā	servō	puerō	perīculō
Voc.	puella	serve	puer	perīculum
Plural				
Nom./Voc.	puellae	servī	puerī	perīcula
Gen.	puellārum	servōrum	puerōrum	perīculōrum
Dat.	puellīs	servīs	puerīs	perīculīs
Acc.	puellās	servōs	puerōs	perīcula
Abl.	puellīs	servīs	puerīs	perīculīs

Third Declension

mīles, mīlitis *m.*
urbs, urbis, -ium *f.*

corpus, corporis *n.*
animal, animālis, -ium *n.*

	M./F.	M./F. I-stem	N.	N. I-stem
Singular				
Nom./Voc.	mīles	urbs	corpus	animal
Gen.	mīlitis	urbis	corporis	animālis
Dat.	mīlitī	urbī	corporī	animālī
Acc.	mīlitem	urbem	corpus	animal
Abl.	mīlite	urbe	corpore	animālī
Plural				
Nom./Voc.	mīlitēs	urbēs	corpora	animālia
Gen.	mīlitum	urbium	corporum	animālium
Dat.	mīlitibus	urbibus	corporibus	animālibus
Acc.	mīlitēs	urbēs/urbīs	corpora	animālia
Abl.	mīlitibus	urbibus	corporibus	animālibus

Fourth Declension

mōtus, mōtūs *m.*
cornū, cornūs *n.*

	M./F.	[N.
Singular		
Nom./Voc.	mōtus	cornū
Gen.	mōtūs	cornūs
Dat.	mōtuī/mōtū	cornū
Acc.	mōtum	cornū
Abl.	mōtū	cornū
Plural		
Nom./Voc.	mōtūs	cornua
Gen.	mōtuum	cornuum
Dat.	mōtibus	cornibus
Acc.	mōtūs	cornua
Abl.	mōtibus	cornibus]

Fifth Declension

rēs, reī *f.*
aciēs, aciēī *f.*

	Stem ends in *consonant*	Stem ends in *vowel*
Singular		
Nom./Voc.	rēs	aciēs
Gen.	reī	aciēī
Dat.	reī	aciēī
Acc.	rem	aciem
Abl.	rē	aciē
Plural		
Nom./Voc.	rēs	aciēs
Gen.	rērum	aciērum
Dat.	rēbus	aciēbus
Acc.	rēs	aciēs
Abl.	rēbus	aciēbus

Adjectives and Pronouns

First-Second-Declension Adjectives

bonus, bona, bonum
pulcher, pulchra, pulchrum

Singular	M.	F.	N.	M.	F.	N.
Nom.	bonus	bona	bonum	pulcher	pulchra	pulchrum
Gen.	bonī	bonae	bonī	pulchrī	pulchrae	pulchrī
Dat.	bonō	bonae	bonō	pulchrō	pulchrae	pulchrō
Acc.	bonum	bonam	bonum	pulchrum	pulchram	pulchrum
Abl.	bonō	bonā	bonō	pulchrō	pulchrā	pulchrō
Voc.	bone	bona	bonum	pulcher	pulchra	pulchrum
Plural						
Nom./Voc.	bonī	bonae	bona	pulchrī	pulchrae	pulchra
Gen.	bonōrum	bonārum	bonōrum	pulchrōrum	pulchrārum	pulchrōrum
Dat.	bonīs	bonīs	bonīs	pulchrīs	pulchrīs	pulchrīs
Acc.	bonōs	bonās	bonōs	pulchrōs	pulchrās	pulchra
Abl.	bonīs	bonīs	bonīs	pulchrīs	pulchrīs	pulchrīs

Third-Declension Adjectives

With three nominative singular forms: ācer, ācris, ācre
With two nominative singular forms: **fortis, forte**

Singular	M.	F.	N.	M.	F.	N.
Nom./Voc.	ācer	ācris	ācre	fortis	fortis	forte
Gen.	ācris	ācris	ācris	fortis	fortis	fortis
Dat.	ācrī	ācrī	ācrī	fortī	fortī	fortī
Acc.	ācrem	ācrem	ācre	fortem	fortem	forte
Abl.	ācrī	ācrī	ācrī	fortī	fortī	fortī
Plural						
Nom./Voc.	ācrēs	ācrēs	ācria	fortēs	fortēs	fortia
Gen.	ācrium	ācrium	ācrium	fortium	fortium	fortium
Dat.	ācribus	ācribus	ācribus	fortibus	fortibus	fortibus
Acc.	ācrēs/ācrīs	ācrēs/ācrīs	ācria	fortēs/ fortīs	fortēs/ fortīs	fortia
Abl.	ācribus	ācribus	ācribus	fortibus	fortibus	fortibus

With one nominative singular form: **ingēns, ingentis; vocāns, vocantis**

Singular	M.	F.	N.	M.	F.	N.
Nom./Voc.	ingēns	ingēns	ingēns	vocāns	vocāns	vocāns
Gen.	ingentis	ingentis	ingentis	vocantis	vocantis	vocantis
Dat.	ingentī	ingentī	ingentī	vocantī	vocantī	vocantī
Acc.	ingentem	ingentem	ingēns	vocantem	vocantem	vocāns
Abl.	ingentī	ingentī	ingentī	vocantī/ vocante	vocantī/ vocante	vocantī/ vocante
Plural						
Nom./Voc.	ingentēs	ingentēs	ingentia	vocantēs	vocantēs	vocantia
Gen.	ingentium	ingentium	ingentium	vocantium	vocantium	vocantium
Dat.	ingentibus	ingentibus	ingentibus	vocantibus	vocantibus	vocantibus
Acc.	ingentēs/ ingentīs	ingentēs/ ingentīs	ingentia	vocantēs/ vocantīs	vocantēs/ vocantīs	vocantia
Abl.	ingentibus	ingentibus	ingentibus	vocantibus	vocantibus	vocantibus

Comparative Adjectives

	Singular			Plural		
	M.	F.	N.	M.	F.	N.
Nom./Voc.	pulchrior	pulchrior	pulchrius	pulchriōrēs	pulchriōrēs	pulchriōra
Gen.	pulchriōris	pulchriōris	pulchriōris	pulchriōrum	pulchriōrum	pulchriōrum
Dat.	pulchriōrī	pulchriōrī	pulchriōrī	pulchriōribus	pulchriōribus	pulchriōribus
Acc.	pulchriōrem	pulchriōrem	pulchrius	pulchriōrēs/ pulchriōrīs	pulchriōrēs/ pulchriōrīs	pulchriōra
Abl.	pulchriōre/ pulchriōrī	pulchriōre/ pulchriōrī	pulchriōre/ pulchriōrī	pulchriōribus	pulchriōribus	pulchriōribus

Demonstrative Adjectives and Pronouns

hic, haec, hoc

	Singular			Plural		
	M.	F.	N.	M.	F.	N.
Nom.	hic	haec	hoc	hī	hae	haec
Gen.	huius	huius	huius	hōrum	hārum	hōrum
Dat.	huic	huic	huic	hīs	hīs	hīs
Acc.	hunc	hanc	hoc	hōs	hās	haec
Abl.	hōc	hāc	hōc	hīs	hīs	hīs

ille, illa, illud

	Singular			Plural		
	M.	F.	N.	M.	F.	N.
Nom.	ille	illa	illud	illī	illae	illa
Gen.	illīus	illīus	illīus	illōrum	illārum	illōrum
Dat.	illī	illī	illī	illīs	illīs	illīs
Acc.	illum	illam	illud	illōs	illās	illa
Abl.	illō	illā	illō	illīs	illīs	illīs

is, ea, id

	Singular			Plural		
	M.	F.	N.	M.	F.	N.
Nom.	is	ea	id	eī/iī	eae	ea
Gen.	eius	eius	eius	eōrum	eārum	eōrum
Dat.	eī	eī	eī	eīs/iīs	eīs/iīs	eīs/iīs
Acc.	eum	eam	id	eōs	eās	ea
Abl.	eō	eā	eō	eīs/iīs	eīs/iīs	eīs/iīs

iste, ista, istud

	Singular			Plural		
	M.	F.	N.	M.	F.	N.
Nom.	iste	ista	istud	istī	istae	ista
Gen.	istīus	istīus	istīus	istōrum	istārum	istōrum
Dat.	istī	istī	istī	istīs	istīs	istīs
Acc.	istum	istam	istud	istōs	istās	ista
Abl.	istō	istā	istō	istīs	istīs	istīs

Personal Pronouns

First Person   **ego, meī**
                        nōs, nostrum/nostrī
Second Person   **tū, tuī**
                        vōs, vestrum/vestrī

	Singular	Plural	Singular	Plural
Nom.	ego	nōs	tū	vōs
Gen.	meī	nostrum/nostrī	tuī	vestrum/vestrī
Dat.	mihi	nōbīs	tibi	vōbīs
Acc.	mē	nōs	tē	vōs
Abl.	mē	nōbīs	tē	vōbīs

Third Person   **is, ea, id**

	Singular			Plural		
	M.	F.	N.	M.	F.	N.
Nom.	is	ea	id	eī/iī	eae	ea
Gen.	eius	eius	eius	eōrum	eārum	eōrum
Dat.	eī	eī	eī	eīs/iīs	eīs/iīs	eīs/iīs
Acc.	eum	eam	id	eōs	eās	ea
Abl.	eō	eā	eō	eīs/iīs	eīs/iīs	eīs/iīs

Reflexive Pronouns

First Person   ——, **meī**
                        ——, **nostrum/nostrī**
Second Person   ——, **tuī**
                        ——, **vestrum/vestrī**
Third Person   ——, **suī**

	Singular	Plural	Singular	Plural	Sing./Pl.
Nom.	——	——	——	——	——
Gen.	meī	nostrum/nostrī	tuī	vestrum/vestrī	suī
Dat.	mihi	nōbīs	tibi	vōbīs	sibi
Acc.	mē	nōs	tē	vōs	sē/sēsē
Abl.	mē	nōbīs	tē	vōbīs	sē/sēsē

Intensive Adjective

ipse, ipsa, ipsum

	Singular			Plural		
	M.	F.	N.	M.	F.	N.
Nom.	ipse	ipsa	ipsum	ipsī	ipsae	ipsa
Gen.	ipsīus	ipsīus	ipsīus	ipsōrum	ipsārum	ipsōrum
Dat.	ipsī	ipsī	ipsī	ipsīs	ipsīs	ipsīs
Acc.	ipsum	ipsam	ipsum	ipsōs	ipsās	ipsa
Abl.	ipsō	ipsā	ipsō	ipsīs	ipsīs	ipsīs

Relative Pronoun

quī, quae, quod

	Singular			Plural		
	M.	F.	N.	M.	F.	N.
Nom.	quī	quae	quod	quī	quae	quae
Gen.	cuius	cuius	cuius	quōrum	quārum	quōrum
Dat.	cui	cui	cui	quibus	quibus	quibus
Acc.	quem	quam	quod	quōs	quās	quae
Abl.	quō	quā	quō	quibus	quibus	quibus

Interrogative Pronoun and Adjective

quis, quid

	Singular		Plural		
	M./F.	N.	M.	F.	N.
Nom.	quis	quid	quī	quae	quae
Gen.	cuius	cuius	quōrum	quārum	quōrum
Dat.	cui	cui	quibus	quibus	quibus
Acc.	quem	quid	quōs	quās	quae
Abl.	quō	quō	quibus	quibus	quibus

quī, quae, quod

	Singular			Plural		
	M.	F.	N.	M.	F.	N.
Nom.	quī	quae	quod	quī	quae	quae
Gen.	cuius	cuius	cuius	quōrum	quārum	quōrum
Dat.	cui	cui	cui	quibus	quibus	quibus
Acc.	quem	quam	quod	quōs	quās	quae
Abl.	quō	quā	quō	quibus	quibus	quibus

Indefinite Pronouns and Adjectives

aliquis, aliquid (pron.)

Singular

	M./F.	N.
Nom.	aliquis	aliquid
Gen.	alicuius	alicuius
Dat.	alicui	alicui
Acc.	aliquem	aliquid
Abl.	aliquō	aliquā

Does not occur in the plural

aliquī, aliqua, aliquod (adj.)

Singular

	M.	F.	N.
Nom.	aliquī	aliqua	aliquod
Gen.	alicuius	alicuius	alicuius
Dat.	alicui	alicui	alicui
Acc.	aliquem	aliquam	aliquod
Abl.	aliquō	aliquā	aliquō

Does not occur in the plural

quis, quid (pron.)

	Singular			*Plural*		
	M./F.	N.		M.	F.	N.
Nom.	quis	quid		quī	quae	quae
Gen.	cuius	cuius		quōrum	quārum	quōrum
Dat.	cui	cui		quibus	quibus	quibus
Acc.	quem	quid		quōs	quās	quae
Abl.	quō	quō		quibus	quibus	quibus

quī, qua, quod (adj.)

	Singular			*Plural*		
	M.	F.	N.	M.	F.	N.
Nom.	quī	qua	quod	quī	quae	qua
Gen.	cuius	cuius	cuius	quōrum	quārum	quōrum
Dat.	cui	cui	cui	quibus	quibus	quibus
Acc.	quem	quam	quod	quōs	quās	qua
Abl.	quō	quā	quō	quibus	quibus	quibus

quisquam, quicquam (pron.)

Singular

	M./F.	N.
Nom.	quisquam	quicquam (quidquam)
Gen.	cuiusquam	cuiusquam
Dat.	cuiquam	cuiquam
Acc.	quemquam	quicquam (quidquam)
Abl.	quōquam	quōquam

Does not occur in the plural

quisque, quidque (pron.)

	Singular		Plural		
	M./F.	N.	M.	F.	N.
Nom.	quisque	quidque (quicque)	quīque	quaeque	quaeque
Gen.	cuiusque	cuiusque	quōrumque	quārumque	quōrumque
Dat.	cuique	cuique	quibusque	quibusque	quibusque
Acc.	quemque	quidque (quicque)	quōsque	quāsque	quaeque
Abl.	quōque	quāque	quibusque	quibusque	quibusque

quīque, quaeque, quodque (adj.)

	Singular			Plural		
	M.	F.	N.	M.	F.	N.
Nom.	quīque	quaeque	quodque	quīque	quaeque	quaeque
Gen.	cuiusque	cuiusque	cuiusque	quōrumque	quārumque	quōrumque
Dat.	cuique	cuique	cuique	quibusque	quibusque	quibusque
Acc.	quemque	quamque	quodque	quōsque	quāsque	quaeque
Abl.	quōque	quāque	quōque	quibusque	quibusque	quibusque

quīdam, quaedam, quiddam (pron.)

	Singular			Plural		
	M.	F.	N.	M.	F.	N.
Nom.	quīdam	quaedam	quiddam	quīdam	quaedam	quaedam
Gen.	cuiusdam	cuiusdam	cuiusdam	quōrundam	quārundam	quōrundam
Dat.	cuidam	cuidam	cuidam	quibusdam	quibusdam	quibusdam
Acc.	quendam	quandam	quiddam	quōsdam	quāsdam	quaedam
Abl.	quōdam	quādam	quōdam	quibusdam	quibusdam	quibusdam

quīdam, quaedam, quoddam (adj.)

	Singular			Plural		
	M.	F.	N.	M.	F.	N.
Nom.	quīdam	quaedam	quoddam	quīdam	quaedam	quaedam
Gen.	cuiusdam	cuiusdam	cuiusdam	quōrundam	quārundam	quōrundam
Dat.	cuidam	cuidam	cuidam	quibusdam	quibusdam	quibusdam
Acc.	quendam	quandam	quoddam	quōsdam	quāsdam	quaedam
Abl.	quōdam	quādam	quōdam	quibusdam	quibusdam	quibusdam

Irregular Adjectives

First-Second-Declension Adjectives Irregular in the Singular Only

alius, alia, aliud
alter, altera, alterum
neuter, neutra, neutrum
nūllus, -a, -um
sōlus, -a, -um
tōtus, -a, -um
ūllus, -a, -um
ūnus, -a, -um
uter, utra, utrum

Singular	M.	F.	N.
Nom.	tōtus	tōta	tōtum
Gen.	tōtīus	tōtius	tōtīus
Dat.	tōtī	tōtī	tōtī
Acc.	tōtum	tōtam	tōtum
Abl.	tōtō	tōtā	tōtō

īdem, eadem, idem

	Singular			*Plural*		
	M.	F.	N.	M.	F.	N.
Nom.	īdem	eadem	idem	īdem/eīdem	eaedem	eadem
Gen.	eiusdem	eiusdem	eiusdem	eōrundem	eārundem	eōrundem
Dat.	eīdem	eīdem	eīdem	īsdem/eīsdem	īsdem/eīsdem	īsdem/eīsdem
Acc.	eundem	eandem	idem	eōsdem	eāsdem	eadem
Abl.	eōdem	eādem	eōdem	īsdem/eīsdem	īsdem/eīsdem	īsdem/eīsdem

Adverbs

Adverbs in the Positive Degree Formed from First-Second-Declension Adjectives

acerbē < acerbus, -a, -um
pulchrē < pulcher, pulchra, pulchrum

Adverbs in the Positive Degree Formed from Third-Declension Adjectives

fortiter < fortis, forte

Adverbs in the Comparative Degree

acerbius < acerbus, -a, -um
pulchrius < pulcher, pulchra, pulchrum
fortius < fortis, forte

Adverbs in the Superlative Degree

acerbissimē < acerbus, -a, -um
pulcherrimē < pulcher, pulchra, pulchrum
fortissimē < fortis, forte

APPENDIX P

Prefixes may be used to form compound verbs, nouns, adjectives, or adverbs. In the list of prefixes below the first form given is the *unassimilated* form. It is followed, where applicable, by forms of the prefix that may occur according to fixed rules of assimilation and compensatory lengthening. The meanings given are the general meanings associated with these prefixes, and often one may guess the meanings of compound words with a knowledge of these meanings and the meanings of the simple word to which a prefix has been joined.

In this list prefixes that may be used separately as adverbs, prepositions, or both are *italicized*.

ā-, ***ab-***, ***abs-***, **au-** from, away from; at a distance; completely, thoroughly; *indicates absence*

ad-, **ac-**, **af-**, **ag-**, **al-**, **ar-**, **as-**, **at-** to, toward; against; upon; near; *intensifier*

ante- before; in front

circum- around; round about

com-, **co-**, **col-**, **con-**, **cor-** (< *cum-*) together (with); completely

dē- down from; utterly

dis-, **dī-**, **dif-** apart; in different directions

ē-, ***ex-***, **ef-** out, away; thoroughly

in-[1] in, on; against

in-[2], **il-**, **im-**, **ir-** not

inter- between; at intervals; to the bottom

ob-, **oc-**, **of-**, **op-** to meet; toward; against

per- through; thoroughly

post- after

prae- in front; ahead; *with adjectives, indicates preeminence in the quality*, very

praeter- past; by; beyond

prō-, **pro-**, **prōd-** forward, forth; in front of

re-, **red-** back; again

sē- apart

sub-, **suc-**, **suf-**, **sum-**, **sup-**, **sur-**, **sus-** under; up from under; somewhat

super- over; above

trāns- across

INDEX OF
AUTHORS AND PASSAGES

This index includes authors and passages from both Parts I and II of *Learn to Read Latin*. A **boldfaced** citation indicates a Longer Reading or a Continuous Reading. An asterisk next to a page number indicates that a biography of an author or a description of a work appears with the passage.

GENERAL INDEX

This index includes entries from both Parts I and II of *Learn to Read Latin*. *Note:* Subentries for Morphology and Syntax appear at the end of entries for parts of speech.